RESTORATION AND
EIGHTEENTH-CENTURY COMEDY

AUTHORITATIVE TEXTS OF THE PLAYS

BACKGROUNDS

CRITICISM

A NORTON CRITICAL EDITION

RESTORATION AND EIGHTEENTH-CENTURY COMEDY

Authoritative Texts of

THE COUNTRY WIFE · THE MAN OF MODE
THE WAY OF THE WORLD
THE CONSCIOUS LOVERS
THE SCHOOL FOR SCANDAL

Backgrounds
Criticism

Edited by

SCOTT McMILLIN

CORNELL UNIVERSITY

W · W · NORTON & COMPANY

New York · London

W. W. Norton & Company, Inc., 500 Fifth Avenue, New York, N.Y. 10110
W. W. Norton & Company Ltd., 37 Great Russell Street, London WC1B 3NU
Library of Congress Cataloging in Publication Data
McMillin, Scott, comp.
    Restoration and eighteenth-century comedy.

    (A Norton critical edition)
    Bibliography: p.
    1. English drama (Comedy). 2. English drama—
Restoration. 3. English drama—18th century.
I. Title.
PR1248.M3   822'.052   71-152309

        Printed in the United States of America

                        0

    ISBN 0-393-04352-5 CL
    ISBN 0-393-09997-0 PBK

Contents

Criticism: From Lamb to the Present

Preface

The five plays in this volume are comedies about men and women who live in London, care for sex and money, and make fools of one another if not of themselves. There is nothing strange about that combination of activities, as anyone who has lived in London or cared for sex and money will know; and since more than a thousand comedies in English concern the same matters, the reader may wonder why these five should be drawn together for special attention. The answer is not that these five are classics which anyone interested in drama should read; and the obvious point that they belong, more or less, to one period in the chronology of English literature, while a better answer, is only a beginning. The reason for drawing together plays from one period is that in reading them, in attending to their relationships to one another and to the age from which they come, we can learn to imagine the theater at the same time as we learn to imagine history.

Take the theater first. Readers of a play are in a difficult position, because they are reading something that was not primarily meant to be read. Plays are performances, and they need actors, a stage, an audience before they fully exist. Hence, reading plays ought to make one feel a bit silly—like wearing sunglasses to see how the flower grows—until one develops an imagination to witness a printed drama as a performed event, an enactment occurring within a particular set of theatrical circumstances. The London theater from 1660 through most of the eighteenth century was a place of unusual excitement and innovation, and it deserves to be imagined. It was not a "transitional" stage, standing a bit uncertainly (as some have thought) between the Shakespearean playhouse and the theater of realism, but a coherent stage where established traditions were enlivened with new intentions, and where a sense of risk and venture could be based upon trusted conventions. Modern scholarship, particularly in the magnificent eleven-volume *The London Stage*, has finally brought this theater into focus, an achievement I have tried to represent under the heading "Stages, Actors, and Audiences." The reader will find the basic theatrical information there.

The historical imagination reaches beyond the playhouse to the city, and to the range of social and intellectual attitudes from which comedy was observed in London between 1660 and 1800. This period presents the first example in England of a transaction between the theater and an articulate body of social criticism. The drama has always been *related* to society, of course, and in earlier periods the theater was often interrupted or sustained by specific social influences. But by "transaction," I mean a continuing relationship between the theater and its observers, both sides giving a literary statement of their interests and making a record of social and dramatic change as it occurred. The first time this transaction can be witnessed in England is the period of Dryden, John Dennis, Congreve, Jeremy Collier, Addison, anonymous writers for the weekly papers, unknown essayists from the coffeehouses, and gentlemanly letter-writers from country homes. Comedy held a special position in the transaction, not only because the plays usually represented phases of contemporary London life and thus touched upon immediate social interests, but also because performances depending upon laughter, wit, and mockery pose a social criticism which some perceive as a benefit and others as a threat. Much of the background material in this volume is intended to represent the prevalent attitudes of the age about comedy, beginning with general statements about the nature of comic experience and narrowing down to the specific cases of the plays included here.

The general discussions of comedy are grouped under "Wit, Humour, and Laughter." The selections begin with Hobbes's statement about laughter as an expression of personal superiority, continue through Dryden's and Congreve's more formal approach to literary wit and humour, and pass on to various reactions of eighteenth-century writers, who tended to speak for the gentler and more benevolent qualities of comedy. The change of attitude reflected here corresponds to the emergence in drama of "sentimental" or "weeping" comedy near the turn of the century, in reaction to the raillery and licentiousness of the Restoration mode. In the final selection, Goldsmith denigrates the drama of sentiment and appeals for a return to something like the Restoration style—although his own "laughing comedies," and those of his contemporary Sheridan, surely retain some elements of sentimentality themselves.

Then follow two sections on specific critical quarrels of the age. The first concerns Jeremy Collier's notorious attack on the theater, *A Short View of the Immorality and Profaneness of the English Stage* (1698). This is an extraordinary book, for its long-winded complaining against the immorality of plays serves as the rhetorical surface of a deeply conservative reaction against what Collier regarded as the licentiousness of English social life after the abdication of James II and the political settlement of 1689. This reactionary intention, always implied but never declared, made the book both provocative and elusive—provocative because it touched political nerves, elusive because it refrained from political statement. The resulting controversy lasted for thirty years and, whatever its impact on English politics, changed the course of English comedy. I have tried to represent the first stage of the argument ("The Collier Controversy: 1698") by including a portion of the *Short View* along with the early replies of a dramatist (Congreve), a professional critic (Dennis), and one of the anonymous essayists who got into the fray (*A Vindication of the Stage*). Then, to show how the controversy later came to bear upon the theory and practice of comedy, I have reprinted selections from the prominent literary feud between Sir Richard Steele and John Dennis, which occurred early in the eighteenth century and centered on two of the plays in this volume, Etherege's *The Man of Mode* and Steele's own *The Conscious Lovers*.

Finally—and this should always be the goal of the theatrical and historical imagination—matters come home to our own time and our own language. Modern criticism of Restoration and eighteenth-century drama remains an uncertain and interesting enterprise, for the best work has not yet formed into broadly shared opinions about the meanings of these plays. Some of the possibilities of meaning, however, have been shrewdly set forth, with the result that the examples collected under "Criticism: From Lamb to the Present" are notable more for their diversity of opinion than for their consolidation of dogma. I have tried to suggest some of the earlier shifts of opinion by beginning with Charles Lamb's famous essay from 1822 (still a focal point for critics) and then supplying, in the selections from Palmer, Dobree, and Knights, three influential and divergent views from the first half of the twentieth century. The rest of the selections represent criticism since 1950 and are not meant to fall into any pattern at all. I have chosen them because they are serious efforts to discuss plays that are too often treated casually, and because they have been found helpful by some of the students I have known.

I am grateful to Professors M. H. Abrams, Cecil Price, and Robert D. Hume for their advice on the arrangement and contents of this volume. In preparing the manuscript, I am glad to have had the assistance of Michael Nash and Nancy Wallack. And on all matters, large and small, John Benedict and his staff at Norton have been expert and kind.

SCOTT McMILLIN

A Note on the Texts

In editing the Restoration and eighteenth-century texts, I have modernized spelling and punctuation throughout, although "humour" has been retained in order to distinguish its original meaning from our casual use of the word today. The text of *The School for Scandal* calls for special comment. I have followed the text of the Crewe manuscript, now located in the Georgetown University Library, which has been accepted as authoritative since George H. Nettleton published it in *British Dramatists from Dryden to Sheridan* (1939). Recently, however, another manuscript has been found (the Hodgson Ms.) which, like the Crewe, contains corrections in Sheridan's hand.[1] Although there is no reason at present for preferring the Hodgson text of the dialogue, it does include several stage directions which the Crewe Ms. lacks, and these I have included in the present edition. The other plays present no major textual difficulties, and with only the most obvious emendations I have followed the text of the first edition in each case, expanding contracted forms of characters' names in speech prefixes and stage directions, and making a few necessary additions to the stage directions.

The Country Wife: quarto of 1675.

The Man of Mode: quarto of 1676. (Sir Fopling's attempts at French have not been corrected when he is obviously mispronouncing, but otherwise I have regularized these forms.)

The Way of the World: quarto of 1700.

The Conscious Lovers: quarto of 1722 (dated 1723).

---

1. See Cecil Price, "The Second Crewe Ms. of *The School for Scandal*," *Papers of the Bibliographical Society of America*, 61 (1967), 351–356.

The Texts of the Plays

WILLIAM WYCHERLEY

The Country Wife†

*Indignor quicquam reprehendi, non quia crasse
Compositum illepideve putetur, sed quia nuper:
Nec veniam antiquis, sed honorem et praemia posci.[1]*

Prologue

Spoken by Mr. Hart[2]

Poets, like cudgel'd bullies, never do
At first or second blow submit to you;
But will provoke you still, and ne'er have done,
Till you are weary first with laying on.
The late so baffled scribbler of this day,
Though he stands trembling, bids me boldly say,
What we before most plays are us'd to do,
For poets out of fear first draw on you;
In a fierce prologue the still pit defy,
And ere you speak, like Castril give the lie.[3]
But though our Bayes's[4] battles oft I've fought,
And with bruis'd knuckles their dear conquests bought;
Nay, never yet fear'd odds upon the stage,
In prologue dare not hector with the age,
But would take quarter from your saving hands,
Though Bayes within all yielding countermands,
Says you confed'rate wits no quarter give,
Therefore his play shan't ask your leave to live.
Well, let the vain rash fop, by huffing so,
Think to obtain the better terms of you;
But we, the actors, humbly will submit,
Now, and at any time, to a full pit;
Nay, often we anticipate your rage,
And murder poets for you on our stage.

† First performed in 1675 and published in the same year.
1. Horace, *Epistles*, II.i.76–78: "I hate to see something censured not because it is deemed coarse or inelegant in style, but because it is modern; when for the ancients not only indulgence but honor and rewards are demanded."
2. Who acted Horner's role.
3. A quarreler in Ben Johnson's *The Alchemist*.
4. Poet's. Bayes is the poet in the Duke of Buckingham's *The Rehearsal*; the role lampoons John Dryden.

We set no guards upon our tiring-room,[5]
But when with flying colors there you come,
We patiently, you see, give up to you
Our poets, virgins, nay, our matrons too.

The Persons

MR. HORNER	*Mr. Hart*
MR. HARCOURT	*Mr. Kynaston*
MR. DORILANT	*Mr. Lydal*
MR. PINCHWIFE	*Mr. Mohun*
MR. SPARKISH	*Mr. Haines*
SIR JASPER FIDGET	*Mr. Cartwright*
MRS. MARGERY PINCHWIFE	*Mrs. Boutell*
MRS. ALITHEA	*Mrs. James*
MY LADY FIDGET	*Mrs. Knep*
MRS. DAINTY FIDGET	*Mrs. Corbet*
MRS. SQUEAMISH	*Mrs. Wyatt*
OLD LADY SQUEAMISH	*Mrs. Rutter*
WAITERS, SERVANTS, AND ATTENDANTS	
A BOY	
A QUACK	*Mr. Shatterel*
LUCY, ALITHEA'S MAID	*Mrs. Cory*

The Scene: *London*

The Country Wife

Act I. Scene i. Horner's *lodging*
Enter Horner, *and* Quack *following him at a distance.*

HORNER [*aside*] A quack is as fit for a pimp as a midwife for a
  bawd; they are still but in their way both helpers of nature. —
  Well, my dear doctor, hast thou done what I desired?
QUACK I have undone you forever with the women, and reported
  you throughout the whole town as bad as a eunuch, with as
  much trouble as if I had made you one in earnest.
HORNER But have you told all the midwives you know, the orange-
  wenches at the playhouses, the city husbands, and old fumbling
  keepers of this end of the town? for they'll be the readiest to
  report it.
QUACK I have told all the chambermaids, waiting-women, tire-
  women, and old women of my acquaintance; nay, and whispered
  it as a secret to 'em, and to the whisperers of Whitehall; so that
  you need not doubt 'twill spread, and you will be as odious to the
  handsome young women as—

5. Dressing-room in the theater.

HORNER As the smallpox. Well—

QUACK And to the married women of this end of the town as—

HORNER As the great ones; nay, as their own husbands.

QUACK And to the city dames as aniseed Robin[6] of filthy and contemptible memory; and they will frighten their children with your name, especially their females.

HORNER And cry, "Horner's coming to carry you away." I am only afraid 'twill not be believed. You told 'em 'twas by an English-French disaster,[7] and an English-French surgeon, who has given me at once not only a cure but an antidote for the future against that damned malady, and that worse distemper, love, and all other women's evils?

QUACK Your late journey into France has made it the more credible, and your being here a fortnight before you appeared in public looks as if you apprehended the shame, which I wonder you do not. Well, I have been hired by young gallants to belie 'em t'other way; but you are the first would be thought a man unfit for women.

HORNER Dear Mr. Doctor, let vain rogues be contented only to be thought abler men than they are, generally 'tis all the pleasure they have; but mine lies another way.

QUACK You take, methinks, a very preposterous way to it, and as ridiculous as if we operators in physic should put forth bills to disparage our medicaments, with hopes to gain customers.

HORNER Doctor, there are quacks in love as well as physic, who get but the fewer and worse patients for their boasting; a good name is seldom got by giving it oneself, and women no more than honor are compassed by bragging. Come, come, doctor, the wisest lawyer never discovers[8] the merits of his cause till the trial; the wealthiest man conceals his riches, and the cunning gamester his play. Shy husbands and keepers, like old rooks,[9] are not to be cheated but by a new unpracticed trick; false friendship will pass now no more than false dice upon 'em; no, not in the city.

Enter Boy.

BOY There are two ladies and a gentleman coming up.

Exit.

HORNER A pox! some unbelieving sisters of my former acquaintance, who, I am afraid, expect their sense should be satisfied of the falsity of the report. No—this formal fool and women!

Enter Sir Jasper Fidget, Lady Fidget, *and* Mrs. Dainty Fidget.

QUACK His wife and sister.

SIR JASPER FIDGET My coach breaking just now before your door, sir, I look upon as an occasional[1] reprimand to me, sir, for not kissing your hands, sir, since your coming out of France, sir; and so my disaster, sir, has been my good fortune, sir; and this is my wife and sister, sir.

6. A notorious hermaphrodite.
7. Venereal disease.
8. Reveals.

9. Swindlers, cheats.
1. Timely.

HORNER What then, sir?

SIR JASPER FIDGET My lady, and sister, sir.—Wife, this is Master Horner.

LADY FIDGET Master Horner, husband!

SIR JASPER FIDGET My lady, my Lady Fidget, sir.

HORNER So, sir.

SIR JASPER FIDGET Won't you be acquainted with her sir? — [*Aside.*] So, the report is true, I find, by his coldness or aversion to the sex; but I'll play the wag with him. —Pray salute my wife, my lady, sir.

HORNER I will kiss no man's wife, sir, for him, sir; I have taken my eternal leave, sir, of the sex already, sir.

SIR JASPER FIDGET [*aside*] Ha, ha, ha! I'll plague him yet. —Not know my wife, sir?

HORNER I do know your wife, sir; she's a woman, sir, and consequently a monster, sir, a greater monster than a husband, sir.

SIR JASPER FIDGET A husband! how, sir?

HORNER So, sir; but I make no more cuckolds, sir.
  Makes horns.[2]

SIR JASPER FIDGET Ha, ha, ha! Mercury, Mercury![3]

LADY FIDGET Pray, Sir Jasper, let us be gone from this rude fellow.

MRS. DAINTY FIDGET Who, by his breeding, would think he had ever been in France?

LADY FIDGET Foh! he's but too much a French fellow, such as hate women of quality and virtue for their love to their husbands, Sir Jasper; a woman is hated by 'em as much for loving her husband as for loving their money. But pray let's be gone.

HORNER You do well, madam, for I have nothing that you came for. I have brought over not so much as a bawdy picture, new postures, nor the second part of the *École des Filles*, nor—[4]

QUACK [*apart to* Horner] Hold, for shame, sir! What d'ye mean? You'll ruin yourself forever with the sex—

SIR JASPER FIDGET Ha, ha, ha! He hates women perfectly, I find.

MRS. DAINTY FIDGET What pity 'tis he should.

LADY FIDGET Ay, he's a base, rude fellow for't; but affectation makes not a woman more odious to them than virtue.

HORNER Because your virtue is your greatest affectation, madam.

LADY FIDGET How, you saucy fellow! Would you wrong my honor?

HORNER If I could.

LADY FIDGET How d'ye mean, sir?

SIR JASPER FIDGET Ha, ha, ha! No, he can't wrong your ladyship's honor, upon my honor; he, poor man—hark you in your ear—a mere eunuch.

LADY FIDGET O filthy French beast! foh, foh! Why do we stay? Let's be gone; I can't endure the sight of him.

SIR JASPER FIDGET Stay but till the chairs come; they'll be here presently.

2. Sign of the cuckold.
3. Used in treating venereal disease.
4. Horner refers to pornographic items: "postures" (obscene engravings) had long been associated with the *Sonetti lussuriosi* of Aretino (c. 1524); *École des filles*, by one Mililot, was available in London at least by 1668.

LADY FIDGET No, no.

SIR JASPER FIDGET Nor can I stay longer. 'Tis—let me see, a quarter and a half quarter of a minute past eleven; the council will be sat, I must away. Business must be preferred always before love and ceremony with the wise, Mr. Horner.

HORNER And the impotent, Sir Jasper.

SIR JASPER FIDGET Ay, ay, the impotent, Master Horner, ha, ha, ha!

LADY FIDGET What, leave us with a filthy man alone in his lodgings?

SIR JASPER FIDGET He's an innocent man now, you know. Pray stay, I'll hasten the chairs to you. —Mr. Horner, your servant; I should be glad to see you at my house. Pray come and dine with me, and play at cards with my wife after dinner; you are fit for women at that game yet, ha, ha! —[*Aside.*] 'Tis as much a husband's prudence to provide innocent diversion for a wife as to hinder her unlawful pleasures, and he had better employ her than let her employ herself. —Farewell.

HORNER Your servant, Sir Jasper.

Exit Sir Jasper.

LADY FIDGET I will not stay with him, foh!

HORNER Nay, madam, I beseech you stay, if it be but to see I can be as civil to ladies yet as they would desire.

LADY FIDGET No, no, foh! You cannot be civil to ladies.

MRS. DAINTY FIDGET You as civil as ladies would desire?

LADY FIDGET No, no, no! foh, foh, foh!

Exeunt Lady Fidget *and* Mrs. Dainty.

QUACK Now, I think, I, or you yourself rather, have done your business with the women.

HORNER Thou art an ass. Don't you see already, upon the report and my carriage, this grave man of business leaves his wife in my lodgings, invites me to his house and wife, who before would not be acquainted with me out of jealousy?

QUACK Nay, by this means you may be the more acquainted with the husbands, but the less with the wives.

HORNER Let me alone; if I can but abuse the husbands, I'll soon disabuse the wives. Stay—I'll reckon you up the advantages I am like to have by my stratagem: First, I shall be rid of all my old acquaintances, the most insatiable sorts of duns, that invade our lodgings in a morning. And next to the pleasure of making a new mistress is that of being rid of an old one, and of all old debts; love, when it comes to be so, is paid the most unwillingly.

QUACK Well, you may be so rid of your old acquaintances; but now will you get any new ones?

HORNER Doctor, thou wilt never make a good chemist, thou art so incredulous and impatient. Ask but all the young fellows of the town if they do not lose more time, like huntsmen, in starting the game than in running it down; one knows not where to find 'em, who will or will not. Women of quality are so civil you can hardly distinguish love from good breeding, and a man is often mistaken; but now I can be sure she that shows an aversion to me loves the sport, as those women that are gone, whom I warrant to be right.[5] And then the next thing is, your women of honor, as you call 'em, are only chary of their reputations, not their persons, and 'tis scandal they would avoid, not men. Now may I have, by the reputation of a eunuch, the privileges of one; and be seen in a lady's chamber in a morning as early as her husband; kiss virgins before their parents or lovers; and may be, in short, the *passe partout*[6] of the town. Now, doctor.

QUACK Nay, now you shall be the doctor; and your process is so new that we do not know but it may succeed.

HORNER Not so new neither; *probatum est*,[7] doctor.

QUACK Well, I wish you luck and many patients whilst I go to mine.

Exit Quack.

Enter Harcourt *and* Dorilant *to* Horner.

HARCOURT Come, your appearance at the play yesterday has, I hope, hardened you for the future against the women's contempt and the men's raillery; and now you'll abroad as you were wont.

HORNER Did I not bear it bravely?

DORILANT With a most theatrical impudence; nay, more than the orange-wenches show there, or a drunken vizard-mask,[8] or a great-bellied actress; nay, or the most impudent of creatures, an ill poet; or what is yet more impudent, a secondhand critic.

HORNER But what say the ladies? Have they no pity?

HARCOURT What ladies? The vizard-masks, you know, never pity a man when all's gone, though in their service.

DORILANT And for the women in the boxes, you'd never pity them when 'twas in your power.

HARCOURT They say, 'tis pity but all that deal with common women should be served so.

DORILANT Nay, I dare swear, they won't admit you to play at cards with them, go to plays with 'em, or do the little duties which other shadows of men are wont to do for 'em.

HORNER Who do you call shadows of men?

DORILANT Half-men.

HORNER What, boys?

DORILANT Ay, your old boys, old *beaux garçons*,[9] who, like superannuated stallions, are suffered to run, feed, and whinny with the mares as long as they live, though they can do nothing else.

HORNER Well, a pox on love and wenching! Women serve but to keep a man from better company; though I can't enjoy them, I shall you the more. Good fellowship and friendship are lasting, rational, and manly pleasures.

HARCOURT For all that, give me some of those pleasures you call effeminate too; they help to relish one another.

HORNER They disturb one another.

HARCOURT No, mistresses are like books. If you pore upon them too much, they doze you and make you unfit for company; but if used discreetly, you are the fitter for conversation by 'em.

DORILANT A mistress should be like a little country retreat near the

---

5. Morally loose.
6. Pass-key.
7. It has been proved.

8. Whore.
9. Harmless or sexless escorts.

town, not to dwell in constantly, but only for a night and away, to taste the town the better when a man returns.

HORNER I tell you, 'tis as hard to be a good fellow, a good friend, and a lover of women, as 'tis to be a good fellow, a good friend, and a lover of money. You cannot follow both, then choose your side. Wine gives you liberty, love takes it away.

DORILANT Gad, he's in the right on't.

HORNER Wine gives you joy; love, grief and tortures, besides the surgeon's. Wine makes us witty; love, only sots. Wine makes us sleep; love breaks it.

DORILANT By the world, he has reason, Harcourt.

HORNER Wine makes—

DORILANT Ay, wine makes us—makes us princes; love makes us beggars, poor rogues, egad—and wine—

HORNER So, there's one converted. —No, no, love and wine, oil and vinegar.

HARCOURT I grant it; love will still be uppermost.

HORNER Come, for my part I will have only those glorious, manly pleasures of being very drunk and very slovenly.

Enter Boy.

BOY Mr. Sparkish is below, sir.

Exit.

HARCOURT What, my dear friend! a rogue that is fond of me only, I think, for abusing him.

DORILANT No, he can no more think the men laugh at him than that women jilt him, his opinion of himself is so good.

HORNER Well, there's another pleasure by drinking I thought not of; I shall 'lose his acquaintance, because he cannot drink; and you know 'tis a very hard thing to be rid of him, for he's one of those nauseous offerers at wit, who, like the worst fiddlers, run themselves into all companies.

HARCOURT One that, by being in the company of men of sense, would pass for one.

HORNER And may so to the shortsighted world, as a false jewel amongst true ones is not discerned at a distance. His company is as troublesome to us as a cuckold's when you have a mind to his wife's.

HARCOURT No, the rogue will not let us enjoy one another, but ravishes our conversation, though he signifies no more to't than Sir Martin Mar-all's gaping, and awkward thrumming upon the lute, does to his man's voice and music.[1]

DORILANT And to pass for a wit in town shows himself a fool every night to us, that are guilty of the plot.

HORNER Such wits as he are, to a company of reasonable men, like rooks to the gamesters, who only fill a room at the table, but are so far from contributing to the play that they only serve to spoil the fancy of those that do.

DORILANT Nay, they are used like rooks too, snubbed, checked, and abused; yet the rogues will hang on.

---

1. In Dryden's *Sir Martin Mar-all* (1667), the title character pretends to serenade his mistress while his concealed servant sings and plays the lute.

HORNER A pox on 'em, and all that force nature, and would be still what she forbids 'em! Affectation is her greatest monster.

HARCOURT Most men are the contraries to that they would seem. Your bully, you see, is a coward with a long sword; the little, humbly fawning physician, with his ebony cane, is he that destroys men.

DORILANT The usurer, a poor rogue possessed of moldy bonds and mortgages; and we they call spendthrifts are only wealthy who lay out his money upon daily new purchases of pleasure.

HORNER Ay, your arrantest cheat is your trustee, or executor; your jealous man, the greatest cuckold; your churchman, the greatest atheist; and your noisy, pert rogue of a wit, the greatest fop, dullest ass, and worst company, as you shall see. For here he comes.

Enter Sparkish *to them.*

SPARKISH How is't, sparks, how is't? Well, faith, Harry, I must rally thee a little, ha, ha, ha! upon the report in town of thee, ha, ha, ha! I can't hold i' faith; shall I speak?

HORNER Yes, but you'll be so bitter then.

SPARKISH Honest Dick and Frank here shall answer for me, I will not be extreme bitter, by the universe.

HARCOURT We will be bound in ten thousand pound bond, he shall not be bitter at all.

DORILANT Nor sharp, nor sweet.

HORNER What, not downright insipid?

SPARKISH Nay then, since you are so brisk and provoke me, take what follows. You must know, I was discoursing and rallying with some ladies yesterday, and they happened to talk of the fine new signs in town.

HORNER Very fine ladies, I believe.

SPARKISH Said I, "I know where the best new sign is." "Where?" says one of the ladies. "In Covent Garden," I replied. Said another, "In what street?" "In Russell Street," answered I."[2] "Lord," says another, "I'm sure there was ne'er a fine new sign there yesterday." "Yes, but there was," said I again, "and it came out of France, and has been there a fortnight."

DORILANT A pox! I can hear no more, prithee.

HORNER No, hear him out; let him tune his crowd[3] a while.

HARCOURT The worst music, the greatest preparation.

SPARKISH Nay, faith, I'll make you laugh. "It cannot be," says a third lady. "Yes, yes," quoth I again. Says a fourth lady—

HORNER Look to't, we'll have no more ladies.

SPARKISH No—then mark, mark, now. Said I to the fourth, "Did you never see Mr. Horner? He lodges in Russell Street, and he's a sign of a man, you know, since he came out of France." He, ha, he!

HORNER But the devil take me, if thine be the sign of a jest.

SPARKISH With that they all fell a-laughing, till they bepissed themselves! What, but it does not move you, methinks? Well, I see one had as good go to law without a witness, as break a jest with-

<hr />

2. Covent Garden and Russell Street were   3. Fiddle.
fashionable areas.

out a laugher on one's side. Come, come, sparks, but where do
we dine? I have left at Whitehall an earl to dine with you.

DORILANT Why, I thought thou hadst loved a man with a title
better than a suit with a French trimming to't.

HARCOURT Go to him again.

SPARKISH No, sir, a wit to me is the greatest title in the world.

HORNER But go dine with your earl, sir; he may be exceptious. We
are your friends, and will not take it ill to be left, I do assure you.

HARCOURT Nay, faith, he shall go to him.

SPARKISH Nay, pray, gentlemen.

DORILANT We'll thrust you out, if you wo'not. What, disappoint
anybody for us?

SPARKISH Nay, dear gentlemen, hear me.

HORNER No, no, sir, by no means; pray go, sir.

SPARKISH Why, dear rogues—

DORILANT No, no.

They all thrust him out of the room.

ALL Ha, ha, ha!

Sparkish *returns.*

SPARKISH But, sparks, pray hear me. What, d'ye think I'll eat then
with gay, shallow fops and silent coxcombs? I think wit as necessary at dinner as a glass of good wine, and that's the reason I
never have any stomach when I eat alone.—Come, but where do
we dine?

HORNER Even where you will.

SPARKISH At Chateline's?

DORILANT Yes, if you will.

SPARKISH Or at the Cock?

DORILANT Yes, if you please.

SPARKISH Or at the Dog and Partridge?[4]

HORNER Ay, if you have mind to't, for we shall dine at neither.

SPARKISH Pshaw! with your fooling we shall lose the new play; and
I would no more miss seeing a new play the first day than I
would miss sitting in the wits' row. Therefore I'll go fetch my
mistress and away.

Exit Sparkish.

Manent Horner, Harcourt, Dorilant. *Enter to them* Mr.
Pinchwife.

HORNER Who have we here? Pinchwife?

PINCHWIFE Gentlemen, your humble servant.

HORNER Well, Jack, by thy long absence from the town, the grum-
ness of thy countenance, and the slovenliness of thy habit, I
should give thee joy, should I not, of marriage?

PINCHWIFE [*aside*] Death! does he know I'm married too? I
thought to have concealed it from him at least. —My long stay
in the country will excuse my dress, and I have a suit of law, that
brings me up to town, that puts me out of humour; besides, I
must give Sparkish tomorrow five thousand pound to lie with my
sister.

HORNER Nay, you country gentlemen, rather than not purchase,

4. Sparkish, keen on fashion, names well-known restaurants near Covent Garden.

will buy anything; and he is a cracked title, if we may quibble. Well, but am I to give thee joy? I heard thou wert married.

PINCHWIFE What then?

HORNER Why, the next thing that is to be heard is, thou'rt a cuckold.

PINCHWIFE [*aside*] Insupportable name!

HORNER But I did not expect marriage from such a whoremaster as you, one that knew the town so much, and women so well.

PINCHWIFE Why, I have married no London wife.

HORNER Pshaw! that's all one; that grave circumspection in marrying a country wife is like refusing a deceitful, pampered Smithfield jade[5] to go and be cheated by a friend in the country.

PINCHWIFE [*aside*] A pox on him and his simile! —At least we are a little surer of the breed there, know what her keeping has been, whether foiled[6] or unsound.

HORNER Come, come, I have known a clap gotten in Wales; and there are cousins, justices' clerks, and chaplains in the country, I won't say coachmen. But she's handsome and young?

PINCHWIFE [*aside*] I'll answer as I should do. —No, no, she has no beauty but her youth; no attraction but her modesty; wholesome, homely, and housewifely; that's all.

DORILANT He talks as like a grazier[7] as he looks.

PINCHWIFE She's too awkward, ill-favored, and silly to bring to town.

HARCOURT Then methinks you should bring her, to be taught breeding.

PINCHWIFE To be taught! no, sir, I thank you. Good wives and private soldiers should be ignorant. —[*Aside*.] I'll keep her from your instructions, I warrant you.

HARCOURT [*aside*] The rogue is as jealous as if his wife were not ignorant.

HORNER Why, if she be ill-favored, there will be less danger here for you than by leaving her in the country; we have such variety of danties that we are seldom hungry.

DORILANT But they have always coarse, constant, swingeing[8] stomachs in the country.

HARCOURT Foul feeders indeed.

DORILANT And your hospitality is great there.

HARCOURT Open house, every man's welcome.

PINCHWIFE So, so, gentlemen.

HORNER But, prithee, why wouldst thou marry her? If she be ugly, ill-bred, and silly, she must be rich then.

PINCHWIFE As rich as if she brought me twenty thousand pound out of this town; for she'll be as sure not to spend her moderate portion as a London baggage would be to spend hers, let it be what it would; so 'tis all one. Then, because she's ugly, she's the

5. Worn-out horse; also, a loose woman.
6. Injured—i.e., a deflowered or diseased woman.
7. Cattle-breeder.
8. Huge.

likelier to be my own; and being ill-bred, she'll hate conversation; and since silly and innocent, will not know the difference betwixt a man of one-and-twenty and one of forty.

HORNER Nine—to my knowledge; but if she be silly, she'll expect as much from a man of forty-nine as from him of one-and-twenty. But methinks wit is more necessary than beauty, and I think no young woman ugly that has it, and no handsome woman agreeable without it.

PINCHWIFE 'Tis my maxim, he's a fool that marries, but he's a greater that does not marry a fool. What is wit in a wife good for, but to make a man cuckold?

HORNER Yes, to keep it from his knowledge.

PINCHWIFE A fool cannot contrive to make her husband a cuckold.

HORNER No, but she'll club with a man that can; and what is worse, if she cannot make her husband a cuckold, she'll make him jealous, and pass for one, and then 'tis all one.

PINCHWIFE Well, well, I'll take care for one, my wife shall make me no cuckold, though she had your help, Mr. Horner; I understand the town, sir.

DORILANT [*aside*] His help!

HARCOURT [*aside*] He's come newly to town, it seems, and has not heard how things are with him.

HORNER But tell me, has marriage cured thee of whoring, which it seldom does?

HARCOURT 'Tis more than age can do.

HORNER No, the word is, I'll marry and live honest[9]; but a marriage vow is like a penitent gamester's oath, and entering into bonds and penalties to stint himself to such a particular small sum at play for the future, which makes him but the more eager, and not being able to hold out, loses his money again, and his forfeit to boot.

DORILANT Ay, ay, a gamester will be a gamester whilst his money lasts, and a whoremaster whilst his vigor.

HARCOURT Nay, I have known 'em, when they are broke and can lose no more, keep a-fumbling with the box[1] in their hands to fool with only, and hinder other gamesters.

DORILANT That had wherewithal to make lusty stakes.

PINCHWIFE Well, gentlemen, you may laugh at me, but you shall never lie with my wife; I know the town.

HORNER But prithee, was not the way you were in better? Is not keeping better than marriage?

PINCHWIFE A pox on't! The jades would jilt me; I could never keep a whore to myself.

HORNER So, then you only married to keep a whore to yourself. Well, but let me tell you, women, as you say, are like soldiers, made constant and loyal by good pay rather than by oaths and covenants. Therefore I'd advise my friends to keep rather than

---

9. Chaste.   1. Dice-box, obscenely intended.

marry, since too I find, by your example, it does not serve one's turn; for I saw you yesterday in the eighteen-penny place[2] with a pretty country wench.

PINCHWIFE [*aside*] How the devil! Did he see my wife then? I sat there that she might not be seen. But she shall never go to a play again.

HORNER What, dost thou blush at nine-and-forty, for having been seen with a wench?

DORILANT No, faith, I warrant 'twas his wife, which he seated there out of sight, for he's a cunning rogue and understands the town.

HARCOURT He blushes. Then 'twas his wife, for men are now more ashamed to be seen with them in public than with a wench.

PINCHWIFE [*aside*] Hell and damnation! I'm undone, since Horner has seen her, and they know 'twas she.

HORNER But prithee, was it thy wife? She was exceedingly pretty; I was in love with her at that distance.

PINCHWIFE You are like never to be nearer to her. Your servant, gentlemen.

> *Offers to go.*

HORNER Nay, prithee stay.

PINCHWIFE I cannot, I will not.

HORNER Come, you shall dine with us.

PINCHWIFE I have dined already.

HORNER Come, I know thou hast not. I'll treat thee, dear rogue; thou shalt spend none of thy Hampshire[3] money today.

PINCHWIFE [*aside*] Treat me! So, he uses me already like his cuckold.

HORNER Nay, you shall not go.

PINCHWIFE I must, I have business at home.

> *Exit* Pinchwife.

HARCOURT To beat his wife; he's as jealous of her as a Cheapside husband of a Covent Garden wife.[4]

HORNER Why, 'tis as hard to find an old whoremaster without jealousy and the gout, as a young one without fear or the pox.

> As gout in age from pox in youth proceeds,
> So wenching past, then jealousy succeeds,
> The worst disease that love and wenching breeds.

> [*Exeunt.*]

Act II. Scene i. Pinchwife's *house*
Mrs. Margery Pinchwife *and* Alithea.
Mr. Pinchwife *peeping behind at the door.*

MRS. PINCHWIFE Pray, sister, where are the best fields and woods to walk in, in London?

ALITHEA A pretty question! Why, sister, Mulberry Garden and St. James's Park; and for close walks, the New Exchange.[5]

---

2. Seat in the middle gallery of the theater, notorious for whores.
3. Common term for the country.
4. As a merchant husband of a fashiona-

ble (or pretentious) wife.
5. Popular gathering places. The New Exchange, a fashionable shoppng arcade, is the setting for III.ii.

MRS. PINCHWIFE Pray, sister, tell me why my husband looks so grum here in town, and keeps me up so close, and will not let me go a-walking, nor let me wear my best gown yesterday.

ALITHEA Oh, he's jealous, sister.

MRS. PINCHWIFE Jealous? What's that?

ALITHEA He's afraid you should love another man.

MRS. PINCHWIFE How should he be afraid of my loving another man, when he will not let me see any but himself?

ALITHEA Did he not carry you yesterday to a play?

MRS. PINCHWIFE Ay, but we sat amongst ugly people; he would not let me come near the gentry, who sat under us, so that I could not see 'em. He told me none but naughty women sat there, whom they toused and moused.[6] But I would have ventured for all that.

ALITHEA But how did you like the play?

MRS. PINCHWIFE Indeed, I was a-weary of the play, but I liked hugeously the actors; they are the goodliest, properest men, sister!

ALITHEA Oh, but you must not like the actors, sister.

MRS. PINCHWIFE Ay, how should I help it, sister? Pray, sister, when my husband comes in, will you ask leave for me to go a-walking?

ALITHEA [*aside*] A-walking! Ha, ha! Lord, a country gentlewoman's leisure is the drudgery of a foot-post; and she requires as much airing as her husband's horses.

   Enter Mr. Pinchwife *to them.*

But here comes your husband; I'll ask, though I'm sure he'll not grant it.

MRS. PINCHWIFE He says he won't let me go abroad for fear of catching the pox.

ALITHEA Fie! the smallpox you should say.

MRS. PINCHWIFE O my dear, dear bud, welcome home! Why dost thou look so fropish? Who has nangered thee?

PINCHWIFE You're a fool.

   Mrs. Pinchwife *goes aside and cries.*

ALITHEA Faith, so she is, for crying for no fault, poor tender creature!

PINCHWIFE What, you would have her as impudent as yourself, as arrant a jill-flirt, a gadder, a magpie, and to say all, a mere, notorious town-woman?

ALITHEA Brother, you are my only censurer; and the honor of your family shall sooner suffer in your wife there than in me, though I take the innocent liberty of the town.

PINCHWIFE Hark you, mistress, do not talk so before my wife. The innocent liberty of the town!

ALITHEA Why, pray, who boasts of any intrigue with me? What lampoon has made my name notorious? What ill women frequent my lodgings? I keep no company with any women of scandalous reputations.

PINCHWIFE No, you keep the men of scandalous reputations company.

6. Handled and fondled.

ALITHEA Where? Would you not have me civil? answer 'em in a box at the plays, in the drawing room at Whitehall, in St. James's Park, Mulberry Garden, or—

PINCHWIFE Hold, hold! Do not teach my wife where the men are to be found! I believe she's the worse for your town documents already. I bid you keep her in ignorance, as I do.

MRS. PINCHWIFE Indeed, be not angry with her, bud; she will tell me nothing of the town, though I ask her a thousand times a day.

PINCHWIFE Then you are very inquisitive to know, I find!

MRS. PINCHWIFE Not I, indeed, dear; I hate London. Our place-house in the country is worth a thousand of't; would I were there again!

PINCHWIFE So you shall, I warrant. But were you not talking of plays and players when I came in? —[*To* Alithea.] You are her encourager in such discourses.

MRS. PINCHWIFE No, indeed, dear; she chid me just now for liking the playermen.

PINCHWIFE [*aside*] Nay, if she be so innocent as to own to me her liking them, there is no hurt in't. —Come, my poor rogue, but thou lik'st none better than me?

MRS. PINCHWIFE Yes, indeed, but I do; the playermen are finer folks.

PINCHWIFE But you love none better than me?

MRS. PINCHWIFE You are mine own dear bud, and I know you; I hate a stranger.

PINCHWIFE Ay, my dear, you must love me only, and not be like the naughty town-women, who only hate their husbands and love every man else, love plays, visits, fine coaches, fine clothes, fiddles, balls, treats, and so lead a wicked town-life.

MRS. PINCHWIFE Nay, if to enjoy all these things be a town-life, London is not so bad a place, dear.

PINCHWIFE How! If you love me, you must hate London.

ALITHEA [*aside*] The fool has forbid me discovering to her the pleasures of the town, and he is now setting her agog upon them himself.

MRS. PINCHWIFE But, husband, do the town-women love the playermen too?

PINCHWIFE Yes, I warrant you.

MRS. PINCHWIFE Ay, I warrant you.

PINCHWIFE Why, you do not, I hope?

MRS. PINCHWIFE No, no, bud; but why have we no playermen in the country?

PINCHWIFE Ha! —Mrs. Minx, ask me no more to go to a play.

MRS. PINCHWIFE Nay, why, love? I did not care for going; but when you forbid me, you make me, as 'twere, desire it.

ALITHEA [*aside*] So t'will be in other things, I warrant.

MRS. PINCHWIFE Pray let me go to a play, dear.

PINCHWIFE Hold your peace, I wo'not.

MRS. PINCHWIFE Why, love?

PINCHWIFE Why, I'll tell you.

ALITHEA [*aside*] Nay, if he tell her, she'll give him more cause to forbid her that place.

MRS. PINCHWIFE Pray, why, dear?

PINCHWIFE First, you like the actors, and the gallants may like you.

MRS. PINCHWIFE What, a homely country girl? No, bud, nobody will like me.

PINCHWIFE I tell you, yes, they may.

MRS. PINCHWIFE No, no, you jest—I won't believe you, I will go.

PINCHWIFE I tell you then that one of the lewdest fellows in town, who saw you there, told me he was in love with you.

MRS. PINCHWIFE Indeed! Who, who, pray who was't?

PINCHWIFE [*aside*] I've gone too far, and slipped before I was aware. How overjoyed she is!

MRS. PINCHWIFE Was it any Hampshire gallant, any of our neighbors? I promise you, I am beholding to him.

PINCHWIFE I promise you, you lie; for he would but ruin you, as he has done hundreds. He has no other love for women but that; such as he look upon women, like basilisks,[7] but to destroy 'em.

MRS. PINCHWIFE Ay, but if he loves me, why should he ruin me? Answer me to that. Methinks he should not; I would do him no harm.

ALITHEA Ha, ha, ha!

PINCHWIFE 'Tis very well; but I'll keep him from doing you any harm, or me either.

Enter Sparkish *and* Harcourt.

But here comes company; get you in, get you in.

MRS. PINCHWIFE But pray, husband, is he a pretty gentleman that loves me?

PINCHWIFE In, baggage, in. [*Thrusts her in; shuts the door.*] — [*Aside.*] What, all the lewd libertines of the town brought to my lodging by this easy coxcomb! 'Sdeath, I'll not suffer it.

SPARKISH Here, Harcourt, do you approve my choice? —[*To* Alithea.] Dear little rogue, I told you I'd bring you acquainted with all my friends, the wits, and—

Harcourt *salutes her.*

PINCHWIFE [*aside*] Ay, they shall know her, as well as you yourself will, I warrant you.

SPARKISH This is one of those, my pretty rogue, that are to dance at your wedding tomorrow; and him you must bid welcome ever to what you and I have.

PINCHWIFE [*aside*] Monstrous!

SPARKISH Harcourt, how dost thou like her, faith? —Nay, dear, do not look down; I should hate to have a wife of mine out of countenance at anything.

PINCHWIFE [*aside*] Wonderful!

SPARKISH Tell me, I say, Harcourt, how dost thou like her? Thou hast stared upon her enough to resolve me.

7. Fabled serpents whose glance meant death.

HARCOURT So infinitely well that I could wish I had a mistress too, that might differ from her in nothing but her love and engagement to you.

ALITHEA Sir, Master Sparkish has often told me that his acquaintance were all wits and railleurs, and now I find it.

SPARKISH No, by the universe, madam, he does not rally now; you may believe him. I do assure you, he is the honestest, worthiest, true-hearted gentleman—a man of such perfect honor, he would say nothing to a lady he does not mean.

PINCHWIFE [aside] Praising another man to his mistress!

HARCOURT Sir, you are so beyond expectation obliging that—

SPARKISH Nay, egad, I am sure you do admire her extremely; I see't in your eyes. —He does admire you, madam. —By the world, don't you?

HARCOURT Yes, above the world, or the most glorious part of it, her whole sex; and till now I never thought I should have envied you, or any man about to marry, but you have the best excuse for marriage I ever knew.

ALITHEA Nay, now, sir, I'm satisfied you are of the society of the wits and railleurs, since you cannot spare your friend, even when he is but too civil to you; but the surest sign is, since you are an enemy to marriage, for that, I hear, you hate as much as business or bad wine.

HARCOURT Truly, madam, I never was an enemy to marriage till now, because marriage was never an enemy to me before.

ALITHEA But why, sir, is marriage an enemy to you now? Because it robs you of your friend here? For you look upon a friend married as one gone into a monastery, that is, dead to the world.

HARCOURT 'Tis indeed because you marry him; I see, madam, you can guess my meaning. I do confess heartily and openly, I wish it were in my power to break the match; by heavens I would.

SPARKISH Poor Frank!

ALITHEA Would you be so unkind to me?

HARCOURT No, no, 'tis not because I would be unkind to you.

SPARKISH Poor Frank! No, gad, 'tis only his kindness to me.

PINCHWIFE [aside] Great kindness to you indeed! Insensible fop, let a man make love to his wife to his face!

SPARKISH Come, dear Frank, for all my wife there that shall be, thou shalt enjoy me sometimes, dear rogue. By my honor, we men of wit condole for our deceased brother in marriage as much as for one dead in earnest. I think that was prettily said of me, ha, Harcourt? But come, Frank, be not melancholy for me.

HARCOURT No, I assure you I am not melancholy for you.

SPARKISH Prithee, Frank, dost think my wife that shall be there a fine person?

HARCOURT I could gaze upon her till I became as blind as you are.

SPARKISH How, as I am? How?

HARCOURT Because you are a lover, and true lovers are blind, stock blind.

SPARKISH True, true; but by the world, she has wit too, as well as beauty. Go, go with her into a corner, and try if she has wit; talk to her anything; she's bashful before me.

HARCOURT Indeed, if a woman wants wit in a corner, she has it nowhere.

ALITHEA [*aside to* Sparkish] Sir, you dispose of me a little before your time—

SPARKISH Nay, nay, madam, let me have an earnest of your obedience, or—go, go, madam—

Harcourt *courts* Alithea *aside.*

PINCHWIFE How, sir! If you are not concerned for the honor of a wife, I am for that of a sister; he shall not debauch her. Be a pander to your own wife, bring men to her, let 'em make love before your face, thrust 'em into a corner together, then leave 'em in private! Is this your own town wit and conduct?

SPARKISH Ha, ha, ha! A silly wise rogue would make one laugh more than a stark fool, ha, ha! I shall burst. Nay, you shall not disturb 'em; I'll vex thee, by the world.

Struggles with Pinchwife *to keep him from* Harcourt *and* Alithea.

ALITHEA The writings are drawn, sir, settlements made; 'tis too late, sir, and past all revocation.

HARCOURT Then so is my death.

ALITHEA I would not be unjust to him.

HARCOURT Then why to me so?

ALITHEA I have no obligation to you.

HARCOURT My love.

ALITHEA I had his before.

HARCOURT You never had it; he wants, you see, jealousy, the only infallible sign of it.

ALITHEA Love proceeds from esteem; he cannot distrust my virtue; besides, he loves me, or he would not marry me.

HARCOURT Marrying you is no more sign of his love than bribing your woman, that he may marry you, is a sign of his generosity. Marriage is rather a sign of interest than love; and he that marries a fortune covets a mistress, not loves her. But if you take marriage for a sign of love, take it from me immediately.

ALITHEA No, now you have put a scruple in my head; but, in short, sir, to end our dispute, I must marry him, my reputation would suffer in the world else.

HARCOURT No, if you do marry him, with your pardon, madam, your reputation suffers in the world, and you would be thought in necessity for a cloak.[8]

ALITHEA Nay, now you are rude, sir. —Mr. Sparkish, pray come hither, your friend here is very troublesome, and very loving.

HARCOURT [*aside to* Alithea] Hold, hold!—

PINCHWIFE D'ye hear that?

SPARKISH Why, d'ye think I'll seem to be jealous, like a country bumpkin?

8. In need of a disguise.

PINCHWIFE No, rather be a cuckold, like a credulous cit.[9]

HARCOURT Madam, you would not have been so little generous as to have told him.

ALITHEA Yes, since you could be so little generous as to wrong him.

HARCOURT Wrong him! No man can do't, he's beneath an injury; a bubble, a coward, a senseless idiot, a wretch so contemptible to all the world but you that—

ALITHEA Hold, do not rail at him, for since he is like to be my husband, I am resolved to like him. Nay, I think I am obliged to tell him you are not his friend. —Master Sparkish, Master Sparkish!

SPARKISH What, what? —Now, dear rogue, has not she wit?

HARCOURT [*speaks surlily*] Not so much as I thought, and hoped she had.

ALITHEA Mr. Sparkish, do you bring people to rail at you?

HARCOURT Madam—

SPARKISH How! No, but if he does rail at me, 'tis but in jest, I warrant; what we wits do for one another, and never take any notice of it.

ALITHEA He spoke so scurrilously of you, I had no patience to hear him; besides, he has been making love to me.

HARCOURT [*aside*] True, damned, telltale woman!

SPARKISH Pshaw! to show his parts—we wits rail and make love often but to show our parts; as we have no affections, so we have no malice; we—

ALITHEA He said you were a wretch, below an injury.

SPARKISH Pshaw!

HARCOURT [*aside*] Damned, senseless, impudent, virtuous jade! well, since she won't let me have her, she'll do as good, she'll make me hate her.

ALITHEA A common bubble.

SPARKISH Pshaw!

ALITHEA A coward.

SPARKISH Pshaw, pshaw!

ALITHEA A senseless, driveling idiot.

SPARKISH How! Did he disparage my parts? Nay, then my honor's concerned; I can't put up that, sir, by the world. Brother, help me to kill him. —[*Aside.*] I may draw now, since we have the odds of him. 'Tis a good occasion, too, before my mistress—
     Offers to draw.

ALITHEA Hold, hold!

SPARKISH What, what?

ALITHEA [*aside*] I must not let 'em kill the gentleman neither, for his kindness to me; I am so far from hating him that I wish my gallant had his person and understanding. Nay, if my honor—

SPARKISH I'll be thy death.

ALITHEA Hold, hold! Indeed, to tell the truth, the gentleman said after all that what he spoke was but out of friendship to you.

SPARKISH How! say I am—I am a fool, that is, no wit, out of friendship to me?

ALITHEA Yes, to try whether I was concerned enough for you, and

9. Contemptuous term for citizen.

made love to me only to be satisfied of my virtue, for your sake.

HARCOURT [*aside*] Kind, however—

SPARKISH Nay, if it were so, my dear rogue, I ask thee pardon; but why would not you tell me so, faith?

HARCOURT Because I did not think on't, faith.

SPARKISH Come, Horner does not come; Harcourt, let's be gone to the new play. —Come, madam.

ALITHEA I will not go if you intend to leave me alone in the box and run into the pit, as you use to do.

SPARKISH Pshaw! I'll leave Harcourt with you in the box to entertain you, and that's as good; if I sat in the box, I should be thought no judge, but of trimmings. —Come, away, Harcourt, lead her down.

> *Exeunt* Sparkish, Harcourt, *and* Alithea.

PINCHWIFE Well, go thy ways, for the flower of the true town fops, such as spend their estates before they come to 'em, and are cuckolds before they're married. But let me go look to my own freehold. —How!—

> *Enter* My Lady Fidget, Mrs. Dainty Fidget, *and* Mrs. Squeamish.

LADY FIDGET Your servant, sir; where is your lady? We are come to wait upon her to the new play.

PINCHWIFE New play!

LADY FIDGET And my husband will wait upon you presently.

PINCHWIFE [*aside*] Damn your civility. —Madam, by no means; I will not see Sir Jasper here till I have waited upon him at home; nor shall my wife see you till she has waited upon your ladyship at your lodgings.

LADY FIDGET Now we are here, sir—

PINCHWIFE No, madam.

MRS. DAINTY FIDGET Pray, let us see her.

MRS. SQUEAMISH We will not stir till we see her.

PINCHWIFE [*aside*] A pox on you all! [*Goes to the door, and returns.*] —She has locked the door, and is gone abroad.

LADY FIDGET No, you have locked the door, and she's within.

MRS. DAINTY FIDGET They told us below she was here.

PINCHWIFE [*aside*] Will nothing do? —Well, it must out then. To tell you the truth, ladies, which I was afraid to let you know before, lest it might endanger your lives, my wife has just now the smallpox come out upon her. Do not be frightened; but pray, be gone, ladies; you shall not stay here in danger of your lives; pray get you gone, ladies.

LADY FIDGET No, no, we have all had 'em.

MRS. SQUEAMISH Alack, alack!

MRS. DAINTY FIDGET Come, come, we must see how it goes with her; I understand the disease.

LADY FIDGET Come.

PINCHWIFE [*aside*] Well, there is no being too hard for women at their own weapon, lying; therefore I'll quit the field.

> *Exit* Pinchwife.

MRS. SQUEAMISH Here's an example of jealousy.

LADY FIDGET Indeed, as the world goes, I wonder there are no more jealous, since wives are so neglected.

MRS. DAINTY FIDGET Pshaw! as the world goes, to what end should they be jealous?

LADY FIDGET Foh! 'tis a nasty world.

MRS. SQUEAMISH That men of parts, great acquaintance, and quality should take up with and spend themselves and fortunes in keeping little playhouse creatures, foh!

LADY FIDGET Nay, that women of understanding, great aquaintance, and good quality should fall a-keeping too of little creatures, foh!

MRS. SQUEAMISH Why, 'tis the men of quality's fault; they never visit women of honor and reputation, as they used to do; and have not so much as common civility for ladies of our rank, but use us with the same indifferency and ill-breeding as if we were all married to 'em.

LADY FIDGET She says true; 'tis an arrant shame women of quality should be so slighted. Methinks birth—birth should go for something; I have known men admired, courted, and followed for their titles only.

MRS. SQUEAMISH Ay, one would think men of honor should not love, no more than marry, out of their own rank.

MRS. DAINTY FIDGET Fie, fie upon 'em! They are come to think crossbreeding for themselves best, as well as for their dogs and horses.

LADY FIDGET They are dogs and horses for't.

MRS. SQUEAMISH One would think, if not for love, for vanity a little.

MRS. DAINTY FIDGET Nay, they do satisfy their vanity upon us sometimes; and are kind to us in their report, tell all the world they lie with us.

LADY FIDGET Damned rascals! That we should be only wronged by 'em; to report a man has had a person, when he has not had a person, is the greatest wrong in the whole world that can be done to a person.

MRS. SQUEAMISH Well, 'tis an arrant shame noble persons should be so wronged and neglected.

LADY FIDGET But still 'tis an arranter shame for a noble person to neglect her own honor, and defame her own noble person with little inconsiderable fellows, foh!

MRS. DAINTY FIDGET I suppose the crime against our honor is the same with a man of quality as with another.

LADY FIDGET How! No, sure, the man of quality is likest one's husband, and therefore the fault should be the less.

MRS. DAINTY FIDGET But then the pleasure should be the less.

LADY FIDGET Fie, fie, fie, for shame, sister! Whither shall we ramble? Be continent in your discourse, or I shall hate you.

MRS. DAINTY FIDGET Besides, an intrigue is so much the more notorious for the man's quality.

MRS. SQUEAMISH 'Tis true, nobody takes notice of a private man, and therefore with him 'tis more secret, and the crime's the less when 'tis not known.

LADY FIDGET You say true; i'faith, I think you are in the right on't. 'Tis not an injury to a husband till it be an injury to our honors; so that a woman of honor loses no honor with a private person; and to say truth—

MRS. DAINTY FIDGET [*apart to* Mrs. Squeamish] So, the little fellow is grown a private person—with her—

LADY FIDGET But still my dear, dear honor.

Enter Sir Jasper, Horner, Dorilant.

SIR JASPER FIDGET Ay, my dear, dear of honor, thou hast still so much honor in thy mouth—

HORNER [*aside*] That she has none elsewhere.

LADY FIDGET Oh, what d'ye mean to bring in these upon us?

MRS. DAINTY FIDGET Foh! these are as bad as wits.

MRS. SQUEAMISH Foh!

LADY FIDGET Let us leave the room.

SIR JASPER FIDGET Stay, stay; faith, to tell you the naked truth—

LADY FIDGET Fie, Sir Jasper! Do not use that word "naked."

SIR JASPER FIDGET Well, well, in short, I have business at Whitehall, and cannot go to the play with you, therefore would have you go—

LADY FIDGET With those two to a play?

SIR JASPER FIDGET No, not with t'other, but with Mr. Horner; there can be no more scandal to go with him than with Mr. Tattle, or Master Limberham.[1]

LADY FIDGET With that nasty fellow! No—no!

SIR JASPER FIDGET Nay, prithee, dear, hear me.

Whispers to Lady Fidget.

HORNER Ladies—

Horner, Dorilant *drawing near* Mrs. Squeamish *and* Mrs. Dainty.

MRS. DAINTY FIDGET Stand off.

MRS. SQUEAMISH Do not approach us.

MRS. DAINTY FIDGET You herd with the wits, you are obscenity all over.

MRS. SQUEAMISH And I would as soon look upon a picture of Adam and Eve, without fig leaves, as any of you, if I could help it; therefore keep off, and do not make us sick.

DORILANT What a devil are these?

HORNER Why, these are pretenders to honor, as critics to wit, only by censuring others; and as every raw, peevish, out-of-humored, affected, dull, tea-drinking, arithmetical fop sets up for a wit by railing at men of sense, so these for honor by railing at the Court, and ladies of as great honor as quality.

SIR JASPER FIDGET Come, Mr. Horner, I must desire you to go with these ladies to the play, sir.

HORNER I, sir!

SIR JASPER FIDGET Ay, ay, come, sir.

HORNER I must beg your pardon, sir, and theirs; I will not be seen in women's company in public again for the world.

1. Common names for fops. Limberham would later appear in Dryden's *The Kind Keeper* (1678), and Tattle in Congreve's *Love for Love* (1695).

SIR JASPER FIDGET Ha, ha! strange aversion!

MRS. SQUEAMISH No, he's for women's company in private.

SIR JASPER FIDGET He—poor man—he! Ha, ha, ha!

MRS. DAINTY FIDGET 'Tis a greater shame amongst lewd fellows to be seen in virtuous women's company than for the women to be seen with them.

HORNER Indeed, madam, the time was I only hated virtuous women, but now I hate the other too; I beg your pardon, ladies.

LADY FIDGET You are very obliging, sir, because we would not be troubled with you.

SIR JASPER FIDGET In sober sadness, he shall go.

DORILANT Nay, if he wo'not, I am ready to wait upon the ladies; and I think I am the fitter man.

SIR JASPER FIDGET You, sir, no, I thank you for that—Master Horner is a privileged man amongst the virtuous ladies; 'twill be a great while before you are so, he, he, he! He's my wife's gallant, he, he, he! No, pray withdraw, sir, for as I take it, the virtuous ladies have no business with you.

DORILANT And I am sure he can have none with them. 'Tis strange a man can't come amongst virtuous women now but upon the same terms as men are admitted into the Great Turk's seraglio; but heavens keep me from being an ombre[2] player with 'em! But where is Pinchwife?

Exit Dorilant.

SIR JASPER FIDGET Come, come, man; what, avoid the sweet society of womankind? that sweet, soft, gentle, tame, noble creature, woman, made for man's companion—

HORNER So is that soft, gentle, tame and more noble creature a spaniel, and has all their tricks—can fawn, lie down, suffer beating, and fawn the more; barks at your friends when they come to see you; makes your bed hard; gives you fleas, and the mange sometimes. And all the difference is, the spaniel's the more faithful animal, and fawns but upon one master.

SIR JASPER FIDGET He, he, he!

MRS. SQUEAMISH Oh, the rude beast!

MRS. DAINTY FIDGET Insolent brute!

LADY FIDGET Brute! Stinking, mortified, rotten French wether,[3] to dare—

SIR JASPER FIDGET Hold, an't please your ladyship. —For shame, Master Horner, your mother was a woman. —[*Aside.*] Now shall I never reconcile 'em. —[*Aside to* Lady Fidget.] Hark you, madam, take my advice in your anger. You know you often want one to make up your drolling pack of ombre players; and you may cheat him easily, for he's an ill gamester, and consequently loves play. Besides, you know, you have but two old civil gentlemen, with stinking breaths too, to wait upon you abroad; take in the third into your service. The other are but crazy[4]; and a lady should have a supernumerary gentleman-usher, as a super-

2. Fashionable card game, with a pun on *hombre* (Spanish for *man*).
3. Castrated ram.
4. Infirm.

numerary coach-horse, lest sometimes you should be forced to
stay at home.

LADY FIDGET But are you sure he loves play, and has money?

SIR JASPER FIDGET He loves play as much as you, and has money as
much as I.

LADY FIDGET Then I am contented to make him pay for his scurrility; money makes up in a measure all other wants in men.
—[*Aside.*] Those whom we cannot make hold for gallants, we make
fine.[5]

SIR JASPER FIDGET [*aside*] So, so; now to mollify, to wheedle him.
—Master Horner, will you never keep civil company? Methinks
'tis time now, since you are only fit for them. Come, come, man,
you must e'en fall to visiting our wives, eating at our tables,
drinking tea with our virtuous relations after dinner, dealing
cards to 'em, reading plays and gazettes to 'em, picking fleas out
of their shocks[6] for 'em, collecting receipts, new songs, women,
pages and footmen for 'em.

HORNER I hope they'll afford me better employment, sir.

SIR JASPER FIDGET He, he he! 'Tis fit you know your work before
you come into your place; and since you are unprovided of a lady
to flatter and a good house to eat at, pray frequent mine, and call
my wife mistress, and she shall call you gallant, according to the
custom.

HORNER Who, I?

SIR JASPER FIDGET Faith, thou shalt for my sake; come, for my sake
only.

HORNER For your sake—

SIR JASPER FIDGET [*to Lady Fidget*] Come, come here's a gamester for you; let him be a little familiar sometimes; nay, what if a
little rude? Gamesters may be rude with ladies, you know.

LADY FIDGET Yes, losing gamesters have a privilege with women.

HORNER I always thought the contrary, that the winning gamester
had most privilege with women; for when you have lost your
money to a man, you'll lose anything you have, all you have, they
say, and he may use you as he pleases.

SIR JASPER FIDGET He, he, he! Well, win or lose, you shall have
your liberty with her.

LADY FIDGET As he behaves himself; and for your sake I'll give him
admittance and freedom.

HORNER All sorts of freedom, madam?

SIR JASPER FIDGET Ay, ay, ay, all sorts of freedom thou canst take
and so go to her, begin thy new employment; wheedle her, jest
with her, and be better acquainted one with another.

HORNER [*aside*] I think I know her already, therefore may venture
with her, my secret for hers.

    Horner *and* Lady Fidget *whisper.*

SIR JASPER FIDGET Sister, cuz, I have provided an innocent playfellow for you there.

MRS. DAINTY FIDGET Who, he!

5. Pay the penalty.   6. Poodles.

MRS. SQUEAMISH There's a playfellow indeed!

SIR JASPER FIDGET Yes, sure; what, he is good enough to play at cards, blindman's buff, or the fool with sometimes.

MRS. SQUEAMISH Foh! we'll have no such playfellows.

MRS. DAINTY FIDGET No, sir, you shan't choose playfellows for us, we thank you.

SIR JASPER FIDGET Nay, pray hear me.
        Whispering to them.

LADY FIDGET [*aside to* Horner] But, poor gentleman, could you be so generous, so truly a man of honor, as for the sakes of us women of honor, to cause yourself to be reported no man? No man! And to suffer yourself the greatest shame that could fall upon a man, that none might fall upon us women by your conversation? But indeed, sir, as perfectly, perfectly, the same man as before your going into France, sir? as perfectly, perfectly, sir?

HORNER As perfectly, perfectly, madam. Nay, I scorn you should take my word; I desire to be tried only, madam.

LADY FIDGET Well, that's spoken again like a man of honor; all men of honor desire to come to the test. But, indeed, generally you men report such things of yourselves, one does not know how or whom to believe; and it is come to that pass we dare not take your words, no more than your tailor's, without some staid servant of yours be bound with you. But I have so strong a faith in your honor, dear, dear, noble sir, that I'd forfeit mine for yours at any time, dear sir.

HORNER No, madam, you should not need to forfeit it for me; I have given you security already to save you harmless, my late reputation being so well known in the world, madam.

LADY FIDGET But if upon any future falling out, or upon a suspicion of my taking the trust out of your hands, to employ some other, you yourself should betray your trust, dear sir? I mean, if you'll give me leave to speak obscenely, you might tell, dear sir.

HORNER If I did, nobody would believe me; the reputation of impotency is as hardly recovered again in the world as that of cowardice, dear madam.

LADY FIDGET Nay then, as one may say, you may do your worst, dear, dear sir.

SIR JASPER FIDGET Come, is your ladyship reconciled to him yet? Have you agreed on matters? For I must be gone to Whitehall.

LADY FIDGET Why, indeed, Sir Jasper, Master Horner is a thousand, thousand times a better man than I thought him. Cousin Squeamish, Sister Dainty, I can name him now; truly, not long ago, you know, I thought his very name obscenity, and I would as soon have lain with him as have named him.

SIR JASPER FIDGET Very likely, poor madam.

MRS. DAINTY FIDGET I believe it.

MRS. SQUEAMISH No doubt on't.

SIR JASPER FIDGET Well, well—that your ladyship is as virtuous as any she, I know, and him all the town knows—he, he, he! Therefore, now you like him, get you gone to your business together;

go, go to your business, I say, pleasure, whilst I go to my pleasure, business.

LADY FIDGET Come, then, dear gallant.

HORNER Come away, my dearest mistress.

SIR JASPER FIDGET So, so; why, 'tis as I'd have it.

Exit Sir Jasper.

HORNER And as I'd have it.

LADY FIDGET

> Who for his business from his wife will run,
> Takes the best care to have her business done.

Exeunt omnes.

Act III. Scene i. Pinchwife's *house.*

Alithea *and* Mrs. Pinchwife.

ALITHEA Sister, what ails you? You are grown melancholy.

MRS. PINCHWIFE Would it not make anyone melancholy, to see you go every day fluttering about abroad, whilst I must stay at home like a poor, lonely, sullen bird in a cage?

ALITHEA Ay, sister, but you came young and just from the nest to your cage, so that I thought you liked it, and could be as cheerful in't as others that took their flight themselves early, and are hopping abroad in the open air.

MRS. PINCHWIFE Nay, I confess I was quiet enough till my husband told me what pure[7] lives the London ladies live abroad, with their dancing, meetings, and junketings, and dressed every day in their best gowns; and I warrant you, play at ninepins every day of the week, so they do.

Enter Mr. Pinchwife.

PINCHWIFE Come, what's here to do? You are putting the town pleasures in her head, and setting her a-longing.

ALITHEA Yes, after ninepins; you suffer none to give her those longings, you mean, but yourself.

PINCHWIFE I tell her of the vanities of the town like a confessor.

ALITHEA A confessor! Just such a confessor as he that, by forbidding a silly ostler to grease the horse's teeth,[8] taught him to do't.

PINCHWIFE Come, Mistress Flippant, good precepts are lost when bad examples are still before us; the liberty you take abroad makes her hanker after it, and out of humour at home. Poor wretch! she desired not to come to London; I would bring her.

ALITHEA Very well.

PINCHWIFE She has been this week in town, and never desired, till this afternoon, to go abroad.

ALITHEA Was she not at a play yesterday?

PINCHWIFE Yes, but she ne'er asked me; I was myself the cause of her going.

ALITHEA Then, if she ask you again, you are the cause of her asking, and not my example.

PINCHWIFE Well, tomorrow night I shall be rid of you; and the

7. Fine.   from eating.
8. A trick of innkeepers to prevent horses

next day, before 'tis light, she and I'll be rid of the town, and my dreadful apprehensions. —[*To* Mrs. Pinchwife.] Come, be not melancholy, for thou shalt go into the country after tomorrow, dearest.

ALITHEA Great comfort!

MRS. PINCHWIFE Pish! what d'ye tell me of the country for?

PINCHWIFE How's this! What, pish at the country?

MRS. PINCHWIFE Let me alone, I am not well.

PINCHWIFE Oh, if that be all—what ails my dearest?

MRS. PINCHWIFE Truly I don't know; but I have not been well since you told me there was a gallant at the play in love with me.

PINCHWIFE Ha!—

ALITHEA That's by my example too!

PINCHWIFE Nay, if you are not well, but are so concerned because a lewd fellow chanced to lie, and say he liked you, you'll make me sick too.

MRS. PINCHWIFE Of what sickness?

PINCHWIFE Oh, of that which is worse than the plague, jealousy.

MRS. PINCHWIFE Pish, you jeer! I'm sure there's no such disease in our receipt-book at home.

PINCHWIFE No, thou never met'st with it, poor innocent. — [*Aside.*] Well, if thou cuckold me, 'twill be my own fault—for cuckolds and bastards are generally makers of their own fortune.

MRS. PINCHWIFE Well, but pray, bud, let's go to a play tonight.

PINCHWIFE 'Tis just done, she comes from it. But why are you so eager to see a play?

MRS. PINCHWIFE Faith, dear, not that I care one pin for their talk there; but I like to look upon the playermen, and would see, if I could, the gallant you say loves me; that's all, dear bud.

PINCHWIFE Is that all, dear bud?

ALITHEA This proceeds from my example.

MRS. PINCHWIFE But if the play be done, let's go abroad, however, dear bud.

PINCHWIFE Come, have a little patience, and thou shalt go into the country on Friday.

MRS. PINCHWIFE Therefore I would see first some sights, to tell my neighbors of. Nay, I will go abroad, that's once.

ALITHEA I'm the cause of this desire too.

PINCHWIFE But now I think on't, who was the cause of Horner's coming to my lodging today? That was you.

ALITHEA No, you, because you would not let him see your handsome wife out of your lodging.

MRS. PINCHWIFE Why, O Lord! did the gentleman come hither to see me indeed?

PINCHWIFE No, no. —You are not cause of that damned question too, Mistress Alithea? —[*Aside.*] Well, she's in the right of it. He is in love with my wife—and comes after her—'tis so—but I'll nip his love in the bud; lest he should follow us into the country, and break his chariot-wheel near our house on purpose for an excuse to come to't. But I think I know the town.

MRS. PINCHWIFE Come, pray, bud, let's go abroad before 'tis late; for I will go, that's flat and plain.

PINCHWIFE [aside] So! the obstinacy already of a town-wife, and I must, whilst she's here, humour her like one. —Sister, how shall we do, that she may not be seen or known?

ALITHEA Let her put on her mask.

PINCHWIFE Pshaw! A mask makes people but the more inquisitive, and is as ridiculous a disguise as a stage-beard; her shape, stature, habit will be known. And if we should meet with Horner, he would be sure to take acquaintance with us, must wish her joy, kiss her, talk to her, leer upon her, and the devil and all. No, I'll not use her to a mask, 'tis dangerous; for masks have made more cuckolds than the best faces that ever were known.

ALITHEA How will you do then?

MRS. PINCHWIFE Nay, shall we go? The Exchange will be shut, and I have a mind to see that.

PINCHWIFE So—I have it—I'll dress her up in the suit we are to carry down to her brother, little sir James; nay, I understand the town tricks. Come, let's go dress her. A mask! No—a woman masked, like a covered dish, gives a man curiosity and appetite, when, it may be, uncovered, 'twould turn his stomach; no, no.

ALITHEA Indeed your comparison is something a greasy one. But I had a gentle gallant used to say, "A beauty masked, like the sun in eclipse, gathers together more gazers than if it shined out."

Exeunt.

Act III. Scene ii. The scene changes to the New Exchange. Enter Horner, Harcourt, Dorilant.

DORILANT Engaged to women, and not sup with us?

HORNER Ay, a pox on 'em all!

HARCOURT You were much a more reasonable man in the morning, and had as noble resolutions against 'em as a widower of a week's liberty.

DORILANT Did I ever think to see you keep company with women in vain?

HORNER In vain! No—'tis, since I can't love 'em, to be revenged on 'em.

HARCOURT Now your sting is gone, you looked in the box, amongst all those women, like a drone in the hive, all upon you; shoved and ill-used by 'em all, and thrust from one side to t'other.

DORILANT Yet he must be buzzing amongst 'em still, like other old beetle-headed, liquorish drones. Avoid 'em, and hate 'em as they hate you.

HORNER Because I do hate 'em, and would hate 'em yet more, I'll frequent 'em; you may see by marriage, nothing makes a man hate a woman more than her constant conversation. In short, I converse with 'em, as you do with rich fools, to laugh at 'em and use 'em ill.

DORILANT But I would no more sup with women, unless I could lie with 'em, than sup with a rich coxcomb, unless I could cheat him.

HORNER Yes, I have known thee sup with a fool for his drinking; if
he could set out your hand that way only, you were satisfied, and
if he were a wine-swallowing mouth 'twas enough.

HARCOURT Yes, a man drinks often with a fool, as he tosses with a
marker, only to keep his hand in ure.[9] But do the ladies drink?

HORNER Yes, sir, and I shall have the pleasure at least of laying 'em
flat with a bottle, and bring as much scandal that way upon 'em
as formerly t'other.

HARCOURT Perhaps you may prove as weak a brother amongst 'em
that way as t'other.

DORILANT Foh! drinking with women is as unnatural as scolding
with 'em; but 'tis a pleasure of decayed fornicators, and the
basest way of quenching love.

HARCOURT Nay, 'tis drowning love instead of quenching it. But
leave us for civil women too!

DORILANT Ay, when he can't be the better for 'em. We hardly
pardon a man that leaves his friend for a wench, and that's a
pretty lawful call.

HORNER Faith, I would not leave you for 'em, if they would not
drink.

DORILANT Who would disappoint his company at Lewis's for a gos-
siping?

HARCOURT Foh! Wine and women, good apart, together as nauseous as sack and sugar. But hark you, sir, before you go, a little
of your advice; an old maimed general, when unfit for action, is
fittest for counsel. I have other designs upon women than eating
and drinking with them. I am in love with Sparkish's mistress,
whom he is to marry tomorrow. Now how shall I get her?

Enter Sparkish, *looking about.*

HORNER Why, here comes one will help you to her.

HARCOURT He! He, I tell you, is my rival, and will hinder my love.

HORNER No, a foolish rival and a jealous husband assist their rival's
designs; for they are sure to make their women hate them, which
is the first step to their love for another man.

HARCOURT But I cannot come near his mistress but in his company.

HORNER Still the better for you, for fools are most easily cheated
when they themselves are accessories; and he is to be bubbled[1] of
his mistress, as of his money, the common mistress, by keeping
him company:

SPARKISH Who is that, that is to be bubbled? Faith, let me snack,[2]
I han't met with a bubble since Christmas. Gad, I think bubbles
are like their brother woodcocks,[3] go out with cold weather.

HARCOURT [*apart to* Horner] A pox! he did not hear all, I hope.

SPARKISH Come, you bubbling rogues you, where do we sup? —Oh,
Harcourt, my mistress tells me you have been making fierce love
to her all the play long, ha, ha! But I—

HARCOURT I make love to her?

9. Keeps in practice (*ure*) by playing
with the scorekeeper (*marker*).
1. Duped.

2. Share.
3. Simpletons.

SPARKISH Nay, I forgive thee; for I think I know thee, and I know her, but I am sure I know myself.

HARCOURT Did she tell you so? I see all women are like these of the Exchange, who, to enhance the price of their commodities, report to their fond customers offers which were never made 'em.

HORNER Ay, women are as apt to tell before the intrigue as men after it, and so show themselves the vainer sex. But hast thou a mistress, Sparkish? 'Tis as hard for me to believe it as that thou ever hadst a bubble, as you bragged just now.

SPARKISH Oh, your servant, sir; are you at your raillery, sir? But we were some of us beforehand with you today at the play. The wits were something bold with you, sir; did you not hear us laugh?

HORNER Yes, but I thought you had gone to plays to laugh at the poet's wit, not at your own.

SPARKISH Your servant, sir; no, I thank you. Gad, I go to a play as to a country treat; I carry my own wine to one, and my own wit to t'other, or else I'm sure I should not be merry at either. And the reason why we are so often louder than the players is because we think we speak more wit, and so become the poet's rivals in his audience. For to tell you the truth, we hate the silly rogues; nay, so much that we find fault even with their bawdy upon the stage, whilst we talk nothing else in the pit as loud.

HORNER But why shouldst thou hate the silly poets? Thou hast too much wit to be one, and they, like whores, are only hated by each other; and thou dost scorn writing, I'm sure.

SPARKISH Yes, I'd have you to know I scorn writing; but women, women, that make men do all foolish things, make 'em write songs too; everybody does it. 'Tis even as common with lovers as playing with fans; and you can no more help rhyming to your Phyllis than drinking to your Phyllis.

HARCOURT Nay, poetry in love is no more to be avoided than jealousy.

DORILANT But the poets damned your songs, did they?

SPARKISH Damn the poets! They turned 'em into burlesque, as they call it. That burlesque is a hocus-pocus trick they have got, which, by the virtue of *hictius doctius, topsy-turvy*, they make a wise and witty man in the world a fool upon the stage, you know not how; and 'tis therefore I hate 'em too, for I know not but it may be my own case; for they'll put a man into a play for looking asquint. Their predecessors were contented to make serving-men only their stage-fools, but these rogues must have gentlemen, with a pox to 'em, nay, knights. And, indeed, you shall hardly see a fool upon the stage but he's a knight; and to tell you the truth, they have kept me these six years from being a knight in earnest, for fear of being knighted in a play, and dubbed a fool.

DORILANT Blame 'em not; they must follow their copy, the age.

HARCOURT But why shouldst thou be afraid of being in a play, who expose yourself every day in the playhouses, and at public places?

HORNER 'Tis but being on the stage, instead of standing on a bench in the pit.

DORILANT Don't you give money to painters to draw you like? And are you afraid of your pictures at length in a playhouse, where all your mistresses may see you?

SPARKISH A pox! Painters don't draw the smallpox or pimples in one's face. Come, damn all your silly authors whatever, all books and booksellers, by the world, and all readers, courteous or uncourteous.

HARCOURT But who comes here, Sparkish?

Enter Mr. Pinchwife, *and his wife in man's clothes,* Alithea, Lucy *her maid.*

SPARKISH Oh, hide me! There's my mistress too.

Sparkish *hides himself behind* Harcourt.

HARCOURT She sees you.

SPARKISH But I will not see her. 'Tis time to go to Whitehall, and I must not fail the drawing room.

HARCOURT Pray, first carry me, and reconcile me to her.

SPARKISH Another time; faith, the King will have supped.

HARCOURT Not with the worse stomach for thy absence; thou art one of those fools that think their attendance at the King's meals as necessary as his physicians', when you are more troublesome to him than his doctors, or his dogs.

SPARKISH Pshaw! I know my interest, sir; prithee, hide me.

HORNER Your servant, Pinchwife. —What, he knows us not!

PINCHWIFE [*to his wife aside*] Come along.

MRS. PINCHWIFE Pray, have you any ballads? Give me sixpenny worth.

CLASP[3a] We have no ballads.

MRS. PINCHWIFE Then give me *Covent Garden Drollery,* and a play or two—Oh, here's *Tarugo's Wiles,* and *The Slighted Maiden,*[4] I'll have them.

PINCHWIFE [*apart to her*] No, plays are not for your reading. Come along; will you discover yourself?

HORNER Who is that pretty youth with him, Sparkish?

SPARKISH I believe his wife's brother, because he's something like her; but I never saw her but once.

HORNER Extremely handsome; I have seen a face like it too. Let us follow 'em.

Exeunt Pinchwife, Mrs. Pinchwife, Alithea, Lucy, Horner, Dorilant *following them.*

HARCOURT Come, Sparkish, your mistress saw you, and will be angry you go not to her. Besides, I would fain be reconciled to her, which none but you can do, dear friend.

SPARKISH Well, that's a better reason, dear friend. I would not go near her now, for hers or my own sake, but I can deny you nothing; for though I have known thee a great while, never go, if I do not love thee as well as a new acquaintance.

HARCOURT I am obliged to you indeed, dear friend. I would be well

3a. A bookseller. His stall is part of the scenery.
4. The *Drollery* (1672) contained songs and other selections from plays. The other titles are comedies by (respectively) Thomas St. Serfe and Robert Stapylton, performed during the 1660s.

with her, only to be well with thee still; for these ties to wives usually dissolve all ties to friends. I would be contented she should enjoy you a-night, but I would have you to myself a-days, as I have had, dear friend.

SPARKISH And thou shalt enjoy me a-days, dear, dear friend, never stir; and I'll be divorced from her sooner than from thee. Come along.

HARCOURT [*aside*] So, we are hard put to't when we make our rival our procurer; but neither she nor her brother would let me come near her now. When all's done, a rival is the best cloak to steal to a mistress under, without suspicion; and when we have once got to her as we desire, we throw him off like other cloaks.

Exit Sparkish, *and* Harcourt *following him.*
Re-enter Mr. Pinchwife, Mrs. Pinchwife *in man's clothes.*

PINCHWIFE [*to* Alithea][5] Sister, if you will not go, we must leave you. —[*Aside.*] The fool her gallant and she will muster up all the young saunterers of this place, and they will leave their dear seamstress to follow us. What a swarm of cuckolds, and cuckold-makers, are here! —Come, let's be gone, Mistress Margery.

MRS. PINCHWIFE Don't you believe that, I han't half my bellyfull of sights yet.

PINCHWIFE Then walk this way.

MRS. PINCHWIFE Lord, what a power of brave signs are here! Stay —the Bull's-Head, the Ram's Head, and the Stag's-Head, dear—

PINCHWIFE Nay, if every husband's proper sign[6] here were visible, they would be all alike.

MRS. PINCHWIFE What d'ye mean by that, bud?

PINCHWIFE 'Tis no matter—no matter, bud.

MRS. PINCHWIFE Pray tell me; nay, I will know.

PINCHWIFE They would be all bulls', stags', and rams' heads.

Exeunt Mr. Pinchwife, Mrs. Pinchwife.
Re-enter Sparkish, Harcourt, Alithea, Lucy, *at t'other door.*

SPARKISH Come, dear madam, for my sake you shall be reconciled to him.

ALITHEA For your sake I hate him.

HARCOURT That's something too cruel, madam, to hate me for his sake.

SPARKISH Ay indeed, madam, too, too cruel to me, to hate my friend for my sake.

ALITHEA I hate him because he is your enemy; and you ought to hate him too, for making love to me, if you love me.

SPARKISH That's a good one; I hate a man for loving you! If he did love you, 'tis but what he can't help; and 'tis your fault, not his, if he admires you. I hate a man for being of my opinion! I'll ne'er do't, by the world.

ALITHEA Is it for your honor or mine, to suffer a man to make love to me, who am to marry you tomorrow?

SPARKISH It is for your honor or mine, to have me jealous? That he makes love to you is a sign you are handsome; and that I am not

---

5. She is off-stage.   6. Cuckold's horns.

jealous is a sign you are virtuous. That, I think, is for your honor.

ALITHEA But 'tis your honor too I am concerned for.

HARCOURT But why, dearest madam, will you be more concerned for his honor than he is himself? Let his honor alone, for my sake and his. He, he has no honor—

SPARKISH How's that?

HARCOURT But what my dear friend can guard himself.

SPARKISH O ho—that's right again.

HARCOURT Your care of his honor argues his neglect of it, which is no honor to my dear friend here; therefore once more, let his honor go which way it will, dear madam.

SPARKISH Ay, ay, were it for my honor to marry a woman whose virtue I suspected, and could not trust her in a friend's hands?

ALITHEA Are you not afraid to lose me?

HARCOURT He afraid to lose you, madam! No, no—you may see how the most estimable and most glorious creature in the world is valued by him. Will you not see it?

SPARKISH Right, honest Frank, I have that noble value for her that I cannot be jealous of her.

ALITHEA You mistake him, he means you care not for me, nor who has me.

SPARKISH Lord, madam, I see you are jealous.[7] Will you wrest a poor man's meaning from his words?

ALITHEA You astonish me, sir, with your want of jealousy.

SPARKISH And you make me giddy, madam, with your jealousy and fears, and virtue and honor. Gad, I see virtue makes a woman as troublesome as a little reading or learning.

ALITHEA Monstrous!

LUCY [*behind*] Well, to see what easy husbands these women of quality can meet with; a poor chambermaid can never have such lady-like luck. Besides, he's thrown away upon her; she'll make no use of her fortune, her blessing; none to a gentleman for a pure cuckold, for it requires good breeding to be a cuckold.

ALITHEA I tell you then plainly, he pursues me to marry me.

SPARKISH Pshaw!

HARCOURT Come, madam, you see you strive in vain to make him jealous of me; my dear friend is the kindest creature in the world to me.

SPARKISH Poor fellow.

HARCOURT But his kindness only is not enough for me, without your favor; your good opinion, dear madam, 'tis that must perfect my happiness. Good gentleman, he believes all I say; would you would do so. Jealous of me! I would not wrong him nor you for the world.

SPARKISH Look you there; hear him, hear him, and do not walk away so.

    Alithea *walks carelessly to and fro.*

HARCOURT I love you, madam, so—

SPARKISH How's that! Nay—now you begin to go too far indeed.

7. Vehement in feeling.

HARCOURT So much, I confess, I say I love you, that I would not have you miserable, and cast yourself away upon so unworthy and inconsiderable a thing as what you see here.

Clapping his hand on his breast, points at Sparkish.

SPARKISH No, faith, I believe thou wouldst not; now his meaning is plain. But I knew before thou wouldst not wrong me nor her.

HARCOURT No, no, heavens forbid the glory of her sex should fall so low as into the embraces of such a contemptible wretch, the last of mankind—my dear friend here—I injure him!

Embracing Sparkish.

ALITHEA Very well.

SPARKISH No, no, dear friend, I knew it. —Madam, you see he will rather wrong himself than me, in giving himself such names.

ALITHEA Do not you understand him yet?

SPARKISH Yes, how modestly he speaks of himself, poor fellow.

ALITHEA Methinks he speaks imprudently of yourself, since—before yourself too; insomuch that I can no longer suffer his scurrilous abusiveness to you, no more than his love to me.

Offers to go.

SPARKISH Nay, nay, madam, pray stay—his love to you! Lord, madam, has he not spoke yet plain enough?

ALITHEA Yes, indeed, I should think so.

SPARKISH Well then, by the world, a man can't speak civilly to a woman now but presently[8] she says he makes love to her. Nay, madam, you shall stay, with your pardon, since you have not yet understood him, till he has made an *éclaircissement* of his love to you, that is, what kind of love it is. —[*To* Harcourt.] Answer to thy catechism. Friend, do you love my mistress here?

HARCOURT Yes, I wish she would not doubt it.

SPARKISH But how do you love her?

HARCOURT With all my soul.

ALITHEA I thank him; methinks he speaks plain enough now.

SPARKISH [*to* Alithea] You are out still. —But with what kind of love, Harcourt?

HARCOURT With the best and truest love in the world.

SPARKISH Look you there then, that is with no matrimonial love, I'm sure.

ALITHEA How's that? Do you say matrimonial love is not best?

SPARKISH Gad, I went too far ere I was aware. But speak for thyself, Harcourt; you said you would not wrong me nor her.

HARCOURT No, no, madam, e'en take him for heaven's sake—

SPARKISH Look you there, madam.

HARCOURT Who should in all justice be yours, he that loves you most.

Claps his hand on his breast.

ALITHEA Look you there, Mr. Sparkish, who's that?

SPARKISH Who should it be? —Go on, Harcourt.

HARCOURT Who loves you more than women titles, or fortune fools.

Points at Sparkish.

8. Immediately.

SPARKISH Look you there, he means me still, for he points at me.

ALITHEA Ridiculous!

HARCOURT Who can only match your faith and constancy in love.

SPARKISH Ay.

HARCOURT Who knows, if it be possible, how to value so much beauty and virtue.

SPARKISH Ay.

HARCOURT Whose love can no more be equaled in the world than that heavenly form of yours.

SPARKISH No.

HARCOURT Who could no more suffer a rival than your absence, and yet could no more suspect your virtue than his own constancy in his love to you.

SPARKISH No.

HARCOURT Who, in fine, loves you better than his eyes, that first made him love you.

SPARKISH Ay—nay, madam, faith, you shan't go till—

ALITHEA Have a care, lest you make me stay too long—

SPARKISH But till he has saluted you; that I may be assured you are friends, after his honest advice and declaration. Come, pray, madam, be friends with him.

> *Enter* Mr. Pinchwife, Mrs. Pinchwife.

ALITHEA You must pardon me, sir, that I am not yet so obedient to you.

PINCHWIFE What, invite your wife to kiss men? Monstrous! Are you not ashamed? I will never forgive you.

SPARKISH Are you not ashamed that I should have more confidence in the chastity of your family than you have? You must not teach me; I am a man of honor, sir, though I am frank[9] and free; I am frank, sir—

PINCHWIFE Very frank, sir, to share your wife with your friends.

SPARKISH He is an humble, menial friend, such as reconciles the differences of the marriage bed. You know man and wife do not always agree; I design him for that use, therefore would have him well with my wife.

PINCHWIFE A menial friend! you will get a great many menial friends by showing your wife as you do.

SPARKISH What then? It may be I have a pleasure in't, as I have to show fine clothes at a playhouse the first day, and count money before poor rogues.

PINCHWIFE He that shows his wife or money will be in danger of having them borrowed sometimes.

SPARKISH I love to be envied, and would not marry a wife that I alone could love; loving alone is as dull as eating alone. Is it not a frank age? and I am a frank person. And to tell you the truth, it may be I love to have rivals in a wife, they make her seem to a man still but as a kept mistress; and so good night, for I must to Whitehall. —Madam, I hope you are now reconciled to my friend; and so I wish you a good night, madam, and sleep if you

---

9. Generous.

can, for tomorrow you know I must visit you early with a canonical gentleman. Good night, dear Harcourt.

Exit Sparkish.

HARCOURT Madam, I hope you will not refuse my visit tomorrow, if it should be earlier, with a canonical gentleman, than Mr. Sparkish's.

PINCHWIFE This gentlewoman is yet under my care; therefore you must yet forbear your freedom with her, sir.

Coming between Alithea *and* Harcourt.

HARCOURT Must, sir!—

PINCHWIFE Yes, sir, she is my sister.

HARCOURT 'Tis well she is, sir—for I must be her servant, sir.— Madam—

PINCHWIFE Come away, sister; we had been gone, if it had not been for you, and so avoided these lewd rakehells, who seem to haunt us.

Enter Horner, Dorilant *to them.*

HORNER How now, Pinchwife!

PINCHWIFE Your servant.

HORNER What! I see a little time in the country makes a man turn wild and unsociable, and only fit to converse with his horses, dogs, and his herds.

PINCHWIFE I have business, sir, and must mind it; your business is pleasure; therefore you and I must go different ways.

HORNER Well, you may go on, but this pretty young gentleman—

Takes hold of Mrs. Pinchwife.

HARCOURT The lady—

DORILANT And the maid—

HORNER Shall stay with us, for I suppose their business is the same with ours, pleasure.

PINCHWIFE [*aside*] 'Sdeath, he know her, she carries it so sillily! Yet if he does not, I should be more silly to discover it first.

ALITHEA Pray, let us go, sir.

PINCHWIFE Come, come—

HORNER [*to* Mrs. Pinchwife] Had you not rather stay with us? —Prithee, Pinchwife, who is this pretty young gentleman?

PINCHWIFE One to whom I'm a guardian. —[*Aside.*] I wish I could keep her out of your hands.

HORNER Who is he? I never saw anything so pretty in all my life.

PINCHWIFE. Pshaw! do not look upon him so much; he's a poor bashful youth, you'll put him out of countenance. —Come away, brother.

Offers to take her away.

HORNER Oh, your brother.

PINCHWIFE Yes, my wife's brother. —Come, come, she'll stay supper for us.

HORNER I thought so, for he is very like her I saw you at the play with, whom I told you I was in love with.

MRS. PINCHWIFE [*aside*] O jeminy! Is this he that was in love with me? I am glad on it, I vow, for he's a curious[1] fine gentleman,

1. Exquisite.

and I love him already too. —[*To* Mr. Pinchwife.] Is this he, bud?

PINCHWIFE [*to his wife*] Come away, come away.

HORNER Why, what haste are you in? Why won't you let me talk with him?

PINCHWIFE Because you'll debauch him; he's yet young and inno-cent, and I would not have him debauched for anything in the world. —[*Aside.*] How she gazes on him! the devil!

HORNER Harcourt, Dorilant, look you here; this is the likeness of that dowdy he told us of, his wife. Did you ever see a lovelier creature? The rogue has reason to be jealous of his wife, since she is like him, for she would make all that see her in love with her.

HARCOURT And as I remember now, she is as like him here as can be.

DORILANT She is indeed very pretty, if she be like him.

HORNER Very pretty? A very pretty commendation! —She is a glo-rious creature, beautiful beyond all things I ever beheld.

PINCHWIFE So, so.

HARCOURT More beautiful than a poet's first mistress of imagina-tion.

HORNER Or another man's last mistress of flesh and blood.

MRS. PINCHWIFE Nay, now you jeer, sir; pray don't jeer me.

PINCHWIFE Come, come. —[*Aside.*] By heavens, she'll discover herself!

HORNER I speak of your sister, sir.

PINCHWIFE Ay, but saying she was handsome, if like him, made him blush. —[*Aside.*] I am upon a rack!

HORNER Methinks he is so handsome he should not be a man.

PINCHWIFE [*aside*] Oh, there 'tis out! He has discovered her! I am not able to suffer any longer. —[*To his wife.*] Come, come away, I say.

HORNER Nay, by your leave, sir, he shall not go yet. —[*To them.*] Harcourt, Dorilant, let us torment this jealous rogue a little.

HARCOURT, DORILANT How?

HORNER I'll show you.

PINCHWIFE Come, pray let him go, I cannot stay fooling any longer; I tell you his sister stays supper for us.

HORNER Does she? Come then, we'll all go sup with her and thee.

PINCHWIFE No, now I think on't, having stayed so long for us, I warrant she's gone to bed. —[*Aside.*] I wish she and I were well out of their hands. —Come, I must rise early tomorrow, come.

HORNER Well, then, if she be gone to bed, I wish her and you a good night. But pray, young gentlemen, present my humble serv-ice to her.

MRS. PINCHWIFE Thank you heartily, sir.

PINCHWIFE [*aside*] 'Sdeath! she will discover herself yet in spite of me. —He is something more civil to you, for your kindness to his sister, than I am, it seems.

HORNER Tell her, dear sweet little gentleman, for all your brother there, that you revived the love I had for her at first sight in the playhouse.

MRS. PINCHWIFE But did you love her indeed, and indeed?

PINCHWIFE [*aside*] So, so. —Away, I say.

HORNER Nay, stay. Yes, indeed, and indeed, pray do you tell her so, and give her this kiss from me.

> *Kisses her.*

PINCHWIFE [*aside*] O heavens! what do I suffer! Now 'tis too plain he knows her, and yet—

HORNER And this, and this—

> *Kisses her again.*

MRS. PINCHWIFE What do you kiss me for? I am no woman.

PINCHWIFE [*aside*] So—there, 'tis out. —Come, I cannot, nor will stay any longer.

HORNER Nay, they shall send your lady a kiss too. Here, Harcourt, Dorilant, will you not?

> *They kiss her.*

PINCHWIFE [*aside*] How! do I suffer this? Was I not accusing another just now for this rascally patience, in permitting his wife to be kissed before his face? Ten thousand ulcers gnaw away their lips! —Come, come.

HORNER Good night, dear little gentleman; madam, good night; farewell, Pinchwife. —[*Apart to* Harcourt *and* Dorilant.] Did not I tell you I would raise his jealous gall?

> *Exeunt* Horner, Harcourt, *and* Dorilant.

PINCHWIFE So, they are gone at last; stay, let me see first if the coach be at this door.

> *Exit.*

> Horner, Harcourt, Dorilant *return.*

HORNER What, not gone yet? Will you be sure to do as I desired you, sweet sir?

MRS. PINCHWIFE Sweet sir, but what will you give me then?

HORNER Anything. Come away into the next walk.

> *Exit* Horner, *haling away* Mrs. Pinchwife.

ALITHEA Hold, hold! What d'ye do?

LUCY Stay, stay, hold—

HARCOURT Hold, madam, hold! let him present him, he'll come presently; nay, I will never let you go till you answer my question.

LUCY For God's sake, sir, I must follow 'em.

DORILANT No, I have something to present you with too; you shan't follow them.

> Alithea, Lucy *struggling with* Harcourt *and* Dorilant.
> Pinchwife *returns.*

PINCHWIFE Where?—how?—what's become of—gone!—whither?

LUCY He's only gone with the gentleman, who will give him something, an't please your worship.

PINCHWIFE Something!—give him something, with a pox!—where are they?

ALITHEA In the next walk only, brother.

PINCHWIFE Only, only! Where, where?

> *Exit* Pinchwife, *and returns presently, then goes out again.*

HARCOURT What's the matter with him? Why so much concerned? But dearest madam—

ALITHEA Pray let me go, sir; I have said and suffered enough already.

HARCOURT Then you will not look upon, nor pity, my sufferings?

ALITHEA To look upon 'em, when I cannot help 'em, were cruelty, not pity; therefore I will never see you more.

HARCOURT Let me then, madam, have my privilege of a banished lover, complaining or railing, and giving you but·a farewell reason why, if you cannot condescend to marry me, you should not take that wretch, my rival.

ALITHEA He only, not you, since my honor is engaged so far to him, can give me a reason why I should not marry him; but if he be true, and what I think him to me, I must be so to him. Your servant, sir.

HARCOURT Have women only constancy when 'tis a vice, and, like fortune, only true to fools?

DORILANT [*to* Lucy, *who struggles to get from him*] Thou shalt not stir, thou robust creature; you see I can deal with you, therefore you should stay the rather, and be kind.

> *Enter* Pinchwife.

PINCHWIFE Gone, gone, not to be found! quite gone! Ten thousand plagues go with 'em! Which way went they?

ALITHEA But into t'other walk, brother.

LUCY Their business will be done presently sure, an't please your worship; it can't be long in doing, I'm sure on't.

ALITHEA Are they not there?

PINCHWIFE No; you know where they are, you infamous wretch, eternal shame of your family, which you do not dishonor enough yourself, you think, but you must help her to do it too, thou legion of bawds!

ALITHEA Good brother—

PINCHWIFE Damned, damned sister!

ALITHEA Look you here, she's coming.

> *Enter Mrs. Pinchwife* in man's clothes, running, with her hat under her arm, full of oranges and dried fruit; Horner following.

MRS. PINCHWIFE O dear bud, look you here what I have got, see!

PINCHWIFE [*aside, rubbing his forehead*] And what I have got here too, which you can't see.

MRS. PINCHWIFE The fine gentleman has given me better things yet.

PINCHWIFE Has he so? —[*Aside.*] Out of breath and colored! I must hold yet.

HORNER I have only given your little brother an orange, sir.

PINCHWIFE [*to* Horner] Thank you, sir. —[*Aside.*] You have only squeezed my orange, I suppose, and given it me again; yet I must have a city patience.[2] —[*To his wife.*] Come, come away.

2. Patience of an outclassed cuckold.

MRS. PINCHWIFE Stay, till I have put up my fine things, bud.

Enter Sir Jasper Fidget.

SIR JASPER FIDGET Master Horner, come, come, the ladies stay for you; your mistress, my wife, wonders you make not more haste to her.

HORNER I have stayed this half hour for you here, and 'tis your fault I am not now with your wife.

SIR JASPER FIDGET But pray, don't let her know so much; the truth on't is, I was advancing a certain project to his Majesty about— I'll tell you.

HORNER No, let's go, and hear it at your house. —Good night, sweet little gentleman. One kiss more; you'll remember me now, I hope.

Kisses her.

DORILANT What, Sir Jasper, will you separate friends? He promised to sup with us; and if you take him to your house, you'll be in danger of our company too.

SIR JASPER FIDGET Alas, gentlemen, my house is not fit for you; there are none but civil women there, which are not for your turn. He, you know, can bear with the society of civil women now, ha, ha, ha! Besides, he's one of my family—he's—he, he, he!

DORILANT What is he?

SIR JASPER FIDGET Faith, my eunuch, since you'll have it, he, he, he!

Exeunt Sir Jasper Fidget, *and* Horner.

DORILANT I rather wish thou wert his, or my cuckold. Harcourt, what a good cuckold is lost there for want of a man to make him one! Thee and I cannot have Horner's privilege, who can make use of it.

HARCOURT Ay, to poor Horner 'tis like coming to an estate at three-score, when a man can't be the better for't.

PINCHWIFE Come.

MRS. PINCHWIFE Presently, bud.

DORILANT Come, let us go too. —[*To* Alithea.] Madam, your servant. —[*To* Lucy.] Good night, strapper.

HARCOURT Madam, though you will not let me have a good day or night, I wish you one; but dare not name the other half of my wish.

ALITHEA Good night, sir, forever.

MRS. PINCHWIFE I don't know where to put this here, dear bud, you shall eat it; nay, you shall have part of the fine gentleman's good things, or treat as you call it, when we come home.

PINCHWIFE Indeed, I deserve it, since I furnished the best part of it.

Strikes away the orange.

The gallant treats, presents, and gives the ball;
But 'tis the absent cuckold pays for all.

[*Exeunt.*]

Act IV. Scene i.

In Pinchwife's *house in the morning.*

Lucy, Alithea *dressed in new clothes.*

LUCY Well—madam, now have I dressed you, and set you out with so many ornaments, and spent upon you ounces of essence and pulvilio[3]; and all this for no other purpose but as people adorn and perfume a corpse for a stinking secondhand grave; such or as bad I think Master Sparkish's bed.

ALITHEA Hold your peace.

LUCY Nay, madam, I will ask you the reason why you would banish poor Master Harcourt forever from your sight. How could you be so hardhearted?

ALITHEA 'Twas because I was not hardhearted.

LUCY No, no; 'twas stark love and kindness, I warrant.

ALITHEA It was so; I would see him no more because I love him.

LUCY Hey-day, a very pretty reason!

ALITHEA You do not understand me.

LUCY I wish you may yourself.

ALITHEA I was engaged to marry, you see, another man, whom my justice will not suffer me to deceive or injure.

LUCY Can there be a greater cheat or wrong done to a man than to give him your person without your heart? I should make a conscience of it.

ALITHEA I'll retrieve it for him after I am married a while.

LUCY The woman that marries to love better will be as much mistaken as the wencher that marries to live better. No, madam, marrying to increase love is like gaming to become rich; alas, you only lose what little stock you had before.

ALITHEA I find by your rhetoric you have been bribed to betray me.

LUCY Only by his merit, that has bribed your heart, you see, against your word and rigid honor. But what a devil is this honor! 'Tis sure a disease in the head, like the megrim, or falling sickness, that always hurries people away to do themselves mischief. Men lose their lives by it; women what's dearer to 'em, their love, the life of life.

ALITHEA Come, pray talk you no more of honor, nor Master Harcourt. I wish the other would come to secure my fidelity to him and his right in me.

LUCY You will marry him then?

ALITHEA Certainly; I have given him already my word, and will my hand too, to make it good when he comes.

LUCY Well, I wish I may never stick pin more if he be not an arrant natural[4] to t'other fine gentleman.

ALITHEA I own he wants the wit of Harcourt, which I will dispense withal for another want he has, which is want of jealousy, which men of wit seldom want.

LUCY Lord, madam, what should you do with a fool to your husband? You intend to be honest, don't you? Then that husbandly virtue, credulity, is thrown away upon you.

3. Perfumed powder.   4. Simpleton.

ALITHEA He only that could suspect my virtue should have cause to do it; 'tis Sparkish's confidence in my truth that obliges me to be so faithful to him.

LUCY You are not sure his opinion may last.

ALITHEA I am satisfied 'tis impossible for him to be jealous after the proofs I have had of him. Jealousy in a husband—Heaven defend me from it! It begets a thousand plagues to a poor woman, the loss of her honor, her quiet, and her—

LUCY And her pleasure.

ALITHEA What d'ye mean, impertinent?

LUCY Liberty is a great pleasure, madam.

ALITHEA I say, loss of her honor, her quiet, nay, her life sometimes; and what's as bad almost, the loss of this town; that is, she is sent into the country, which is the last ill usage of a husband to a wife, I think.

LUCY [*aside*] Oh, does the wind lie there? —Then, of necessity, madam, you think a man must carry his wife into the country, if he be wise. The country is as terrible, I find, to our young English ladies as a monastery to those abroad; and on my virginity, I think they would rather marry a London jailer than a high sheriff of a county, since neither can stir from his employment. Formerly women of wit married fools for a great estate, a fine seat, or the like; but now 'tis for a pretty seat only in Lincoln's Inn Fields, St. James's Fields, or the Pall Mall.[5]

Enter to them Sparkish, *and* Harcourt *dressed like a parson.*

SPARKISH Madam, your humble servant, a happy day to you, and to us all.

HARCOURT Amen.

ALITHEA Who have we here?

SPARKISH My chaplain, faith. O madam, poor Harcourt remembers his humble service to you; and in obedience to your last commands, refrains coming into your sight.

ALITHEA Is not that he?

SPARKISH No, fie, no; but to show that he ne'er intended to hinder our match, has sent his brother here to join our hands. When I get me a wife, I must get her a chaplain, according to the custom; this is his brother, and my chaplain.

ALITHEA His brother?

LUCY [*aside*] And your chaplain, to preach in your pulpit then.

ALITHEA His brother!

SPARKISH Nay, I knew you would not believe it. —I told you, sir, she would take you for your brother Frank.

ALITHEA Believe it!

LUCY [*aside*] His brother! ha, ha, he! He has a trick left still, it seems.

SPARKISH Come, my dearest, pray let us go to church before the canonical hour[6] is past.

ALITHEA For shame, you are abused still.

SPARKISH By the world, 'tis strange now you are so incredulous.

5. Fashionable districts in London.   6. Time proper for marriage ceremonies.

ALITHEA 'Tis strange you are so credulous.

SPARKISH Dearest of my life, hear me. I tell you this is Ned Harcourt of Cambridge, by the world; you see he has a sneaking college look. 'Tis true he's something like his brother Frank, and they differ from each other no more than in their age, for they were twins.

LUCY Ha, ha, he!

ALITHEA Your servant, sir; I cannot be so deceived, though you are. But come, let's hear, how do you know what you affirm so confidently?

SPARKISH Why, I'll tell you all. Frank Harcourt coming to me this morning, to wish me joy and present his service to you, I asked him if he could help me to a parson; whereupon he told me he had a brother in town who was in orders, and he went straight away and sent him you see there to me.

ALITHEA Yes, Frank goes and puts on a black coat, then tells you he is Ned; that's all you have for't.

SPARKISH Pshaw, pshaw! I tell you by the same token, the midwife put her garter about Frank's neck to know 'em asunder, they were so like.

ALITHEA Frank tells you this too.

SPARKISH Ay, and Ned there too; nay, they are both in a story.

ALITHEA So, so; very foolish!

SPARKISH Lord, if you won't believe one, you had best try him by your chambermaid there; for chambermaids must needs know chaplains from other men, they are so used to 'em.

LUCY Let's see; nay, I'll be sworn he has the canonical smirk, and the filthy, clammy palm of a chaplain.

ALITHEA Well, most reverend doctor, pray let us make an end of this fooling.

HARCOURT With all my soul, divine, heavenly creature, when you please.

ALITHEA He speaks like a chaplain indeed.

SPARKISH Why, was there not "soul," "divine," "heavenly," in what he said?

ALITHEA Once more, most impertinent black coat, cease your persecution, and let us have a conclusion of this ridiculous love.

HARCOURT [*aside*] I had forgot; I must suit my style to my coat, or I wear it in vain.

ALITHEA I have no more patience left; let us make once an end of this troublesome love, I say.

HARCOURT So be it, seraphic lady, when your honor shall think it meet and convenient so to do.

SPARKISH Gad, I'm sure none but a chaplain could speak so, I think.

ALITHEA Let me tell you, sir, this dull trick will not serve your turn; though you delay our marriage, you shall not hinder it.

HARCOURT Far be it from me, munificent patroness, to delay your marriage. I desire nothing more than to marry you presently, which I might do, if you yourself would; for my noble, good-natured, and thrice generous patron here would not hinder it.

SPARKISH No, poor man, not I, faith.

HARCOURT And now, madam, let me tell you plainly, nobody else shall marry you; by heavens, I'll die first, for I'm sure I should die after it.[7]

LUCY [*aside*] How his love has made him forget his function, as I have seen it in real parsons!

ALITHEA That was spoken like a chaplain too! Now you understand him, I hope.

SPARKISH Poor man, he takes it heinously to be refused; I can't blame him, 'tis putting an indignity upon him not to be suffered. But you'll pardon me, madam, it shan't be, he shall marry us; come away, pray, madam.

LUCY Ha, ha, he! More ado! 'Tis late.

ALITHEA Invincible stupidity! I tell you he would marry me as your rival, not as your chaplain.

SPARKISH Come, come, madam.
    Pulling her away.

LUCY I pray, madam, do not refuse this reverend divine the honor and satisfaction of marrying you; for I dare say he has set his heart upon't, good doctor.

ALITHEA What can you hope, or design by this?

HARCOURT [*aside*] I could answer her, a reprieve for a day only often revokes a hasty doom; at worst, if she will not take mercy on me and let me marry her, I have at least the lover's second pleasure, hindering my rival's enjoyment, though but for a time.

SPARKISH Come, madam, 'tis e'en twelve o'clock, and my mother charged me never to be married out of the canonical hours. Come, come; Lord, here's such a deal of modesty, I warrant, the first day.

LUCY Yes, an't please your worship, married women show all their modesty the first day, because married men show all their love the first day.

            Exeunt Sparkish, Alithea, Harcourt, *and* Lucy.
    Act IV. *Scene ii.*
    The scene changes to a bedchamber, where appear Pinch-wife, Mrs. Pinchwife.

PINCHWIFE Come, tell me, I say.

MRS. PINCHWIFE Lord! han't I told it an hundred times over?

PINCHWIFE [*aside*] I would try if, in the repetition of the ungrateful tale, I could find her altering it in the least circumstance; for if her story be false, she is so too. —Come, how was't, baggage?

MRS. PINCHWIFE Lord, what pleasure you take to hear it, sure!

PINCHWIFE No, you take more in telling it, I find; but speak, how was't?

MRS. PINCHWIFE He carried me up into the house next to the Exchange.

7. A pun. "To die" refers to sexual intercourse.

PINCHWIFE So; and you two were only in the room.

MRS. PINCHWIFE Yes, for he sent away a youth that was there, for some dried fruit and China oranges.

PINCHWIFE Did he so? Damn him for it—and for—

MRS. PINCHWIFE But presently came up the gentlewoman of the house.

PINCHWIFE Oh, 'twas well she did; but what did he do whilst the fruit came?

MRS. PINCHWIFE He kissed me an hundred times, and told me he fancied he kissed my fine sister, meaning me, you know, whom he said he loved with all his soul, and bid me be sure to tell her so, and to desire her to be at her window by eleven of the clock this morning, and he would walk under it at that time.

PINCHWIFE [*aside*] And he was as good as his word, very punctual; a pox reward him for't.

MRS. PINCHWIFE Well, and he said if you were not within, he would come up to her, meaning me, you know, bud, still.

PINCHWIFE [*aside*] So—he knew her certainly; but for this confession, I am obliged to her simplicity. —But what, you stood very still when he kissed you?

MRS. PINCHWIFE Yes, I warrant you; would you have had me discovered myself?

PINCHWIFE But you told me he did some beastliness to you, as you called it; what was't?

MRS. PINCHWIFE Why, he put—

PINCHWIFE What?

MRS. PINCHWIFE Why, he put the tip of his tongue between my lips, and so mousled me—and I said, I'd bite it.

PINCHWIFE An eternal canker seize it, for a dog!

MRS. PINCHWIFE Nay, you need not be so angry with him neither, for to say truth, he has the sweetest breath I ever knew.

PINCHWIFE The devil!—you were satisfied with it then, and would do it again.

MRS. PINCHWIFE Not unless he should force me.

PINCHWIFE Force you, changeling! I tell you no woman can be forced.

MRS. PINCHWIFE Yes, but she may sure by such as he, for he's a proper, goodly strong man; 'tis hard, let me tell you, to resist him.

PINCHWIFE [*aside*] So, 'tis plain she loves him, yet she has not love enough to make her conceal it from me; but the sight of him will increase her aversion for me and love for him, and that love instruct her how to deceive me and satisfy him, all idiot as she is. Love! 'Twas he gave women first their craft, their art of deluding; out of nature's hands they came plain, open, silly, and fit for slaves, as she and Heaven intended 'em; but damned love —well—I must strangle that little monster whilst I can deal with him. —Go fetch pen, ink, and paper out of the next room.

MRS. PINCHWIFE Yes, bud.

Exit Mrs. Pinchwife.

PINCHWIFE [*aside.*] Why should women have more invention in love than men? It can only be because they have more desires, more soliciting passions, more lust, and more of the devil.

    Mrs. Pinchwife *returns.*

Come, minx, sit down and write.

MRS. PINCHWIFE Ay, dear bud, but I can't do't very well.

PINCHWIFE I wish you could not at all.

MRS. PINCHWIFE But what should I write for?

PINCHWIFE I'll have you write a letter to your lover.

MRS. PINCHWIFE O Lord, to the fine gentleman a letter!

PINCHWIFE Yes, to the fine gentleman.

MRS. PINCHWIFE Lord, you do but jeer; sure you jest.

PINCHWIFE I am not so merry; come, write as I bid you.

MRS. PINCHWIFE What, do you think I am a fool?

PINCHWIFE [*aside*] She's afraid I would not dictate any love to him, therefore she's unwilling. —But you had best begin.

MRS. PINCHWIFE Indeed, and indeed, but I won't, so I won't!

PINCHWIFE Why?

MRS. PINCHWIFE Because he's in town; you may send for him if you will.

PINCHWIFE Very well, you would have him brought to you; is it come to this? I say, take the pen and write, or you'll provoke me.

MRS. PINCHWIFE Lord, what d'ye make a fool of me for? Don't I know that letters are never writ but from the country to London, and from London into the country? Now he's in town, and I am in town too; therefore I can't write to him, you know.

PINCHWIFE [*aside*] So, I am glad it is no worse; she is innocent enough yet. —Yes, you may, when your husband bids you, write letters to people that are in town.

MRS. PINCHWIFE Oh, may I so? Then I'm satisfied.

PINCHWIFE Come, begin. —[*Dictates.*] "Sir"—

MRS. PINCHWIFE Shan't I say, "Dear Sir"? You know one says always something more than bare "Sir."

PINCHWIFE Write as I bid you, or I will write "whore" with this penknife in your face.

MRS. PINCHWIFE Nay, good bud—[*She writes.*] "Sir"—

PINCHWIFE "Though I suffered last night your nauseous, loathed kisses and embraces"—Write.

MRS. PINCHWIFE Nay, why should I say so? You know I told you he had a sweet breath.

PINCHWIFE Write!

MRS. PINCHWIFE Let me but put out "loathed."

PINCHWIFE Write, I say!

MRS. PINCHWIFE Well then.

    Writes.

PINCHWIFE Let's see, what have you writ? —[*Takes the paper, and reads.*] "Though I suffered last night your kisses and embraces" —Thou impudent creature! Where is "nauseous" and "loathed"?

MRS. PINCHWIFE I can't abide to write such filthy words.

PINCHWIFE Once more write as I'd have you, and question it not, or I will spoil thy writing with this. [*Holds up the penknife.*] I will stab out those eyes that cause my mischief.

MRS. PINCHWIFE O Lord, I will!

PINCHWIFE So—so—let's see now! —[*Reads.*] "Though I suffered last night your nauseous, loathed kisses and embraces" —go on —"Yet I would not have you presume that you shall ever repeat them." —So.
She writes.

MRS. PINCHWIFE I have writ it.

PINCHWIFE On then. —"I then concealed myself from your knowledge, to avoid your insolencies"—
She writes.

MRS. PINCHWIFE So—

PINCHWIFE "The same reason, now I am out of your hands"—
She writes.

MRS. PINCHWIFE So—

PINCHWIFE "Makes me own to you my unfortunate, though innocent frolic, of being in man's clothes"—
She writes.

MRS. PINCHWIFE So—

PINCHWIFE "That you may forevermore cease to pursue her, who hates and detests you"—
She writes on.

MRS. PINCHWIFE So-h—
Sighs.

PINCHWIFE What, do you sigh? —"detests you—as much as she loves her husband and her honor."

MRS. PINCHWIFE I vow, husband, he'll ne'er believe I should write such a letter.

PINCHWIFE What, he'd expect a kinder from you? Come, now your name only.

MRS. PINCHWIFE What, shan't I say, "Your most faithful, humble servant till death"?

PINCHWIFE No, tormenting fiend! —[*Aside.*] Her style, I find, would be very soft. —Come, wrap it up now, whilst I go fetch wax and a candle; and write on the backside, "For Mr. Horner."
Exit Pinchwife.

MRS. PINCHWIFE "For Mr. Horner." —So, I am glad he has told me his name. Dear Mr. Horner! But why should I send thee such a letter that will vex thee, and make thee angry with me? —Well, I will not send it—Ay, but then my husband will kill me —for I see plainly he won't let me love Mr. Horner—but what care I for my husband? —I won't, so I won't send poor Mr. Horner such a letter—But then my husband—But oh, what if I writ at bottom, my husband made me write it?—Ay, but then my husband would see't—Can one have no shift? Ah, a London woman would have had a hundred presently. Stay—what if I should write a letter, and wrap it up like this, and write upon't too? Ay, but then my husband would see't—I don't know what

to do—But yet y'vads[8] I'll try, so I will—for I will not send this
letter to poor Mr. Horner, come what will on't.

She writes, and repeats what she hath writ.

"Dear, sweet Mr. Horner"—so—"my husband would have me
send you a base, rude, unmannerly letter—but I won't"—so—
"and would have me forbid you loving me—but I won't"—so—
"and would have me say to you, I hate you, poor Mr. Horner—
but I won't tell a lie for him"—there—"for I'm sure if you and I
were in the country at cards together"—so—"I could not help
treading on your toe under the table"—so—"or rubbing knees
with you, and staring in your face till you saw me"—very well—
"and then looking down, and blushing for an hour together"—so
—"but I must make haste before my husband come; and now he
has taught me to write letters, you shall have longer ones from
me, who am, dear, dear, poor, dear Mr. Horner, your most
humble friend, and servant to command till death, Margery
Pinchwife."

Stay, I must give him a hint at bottom—so—now wrap it up
just like t'other—so—now write, "For Mr. Horner"—But, oh
now, what shall I do with it? for here comes my husband.

Enter Pinchwife.

PINCHWIFE [*aside*] I have been detained by a sparkish coxcomb,
who pretended a visit to me; but I fear 'twas to my wife.—
What, have you done?

MRS. PINCHWIFE Ay, ay, bud, just now.

PINCHWIFE Let's see't; what d'ye tremble for? What, you would
not have it go?

MRS. PINCHWIFE Here. —[*Aside.*] No, I must not give him that;
so I had been served if I had given him this.

PINCHWIFE [*he opens, and reads the first letter*] Come, where's
the wax and seal?

MRS. PINCHWIFE [*aside*] Lord, what shall I do now? Nay, then, I
have it. —Pray let me see't. Lord, you think me so arrant a fool
I cannot seal a letter; I will do't, so I will.

*Snatches the letter from him, changes it for the other, seals
it, and delivers it to him.*

PINCHWIFE Nay, I believe you will learn that, and other things too,
which I would not have you.

MRS. PINCHWIFE So, han't I done it curiously?[9] —[*Aside.*] I think
I have; there's my letter going to Mr. Horner, since he'll needs
have me send letters to folks.

PINCHWIFE 'Tis very well; but I warrant you would not have it go
now?

MRS. PINCHWIFE Yes, indeed, but I would, bud, now.

PINCHWIFE Well, you are a good girl then. Come, let me lock you
up in your chamber till I come back; and be sure you come not
within three strides of the window when I am gone, for I have
a spy in the street.

Exit Mrs. Pinchwife.

8. In faith.   9. Cleverly.

[Pinchwife *locks the door.*] At least, 'tis fit she think so. If we do not cheat women, they'll cheat us; and fraud may be justly used with secret enemies, of which a wife is the most dangerous; and he that has a handsome one to keep, and a frontier town, must provide against treachery rather than open force. Now I have secured all within, I'll deal with the foe without with false intelligence.

Holds up the letter.

Exit Pinchwife.

Act IV. Scene iii.

The scene changes to Horner's *lodging.* Quack *and* Horner.

QUACK Well, sir, how fadges[1] the new design? Have you not the luck of all your brother projectors, to deceive only yourself at last?

HORNER No, good domine[2] doctor, I deceive you, it seems, and others too; for the grave matrons and old, rigid husbands think me as unfit for love as they are; but their wives, sisters, and daughters know some of 'em better things already.

QUACK Already!

HORNER Already, I say. Last night I was drunk with half a dozen of your civil persons, as you call 'em, and people of honor, and so was made free of their society and dressing rooms forever hereafter; and am already come to the privileges of sleeping upon their pallets, warming smocks, tying shoes and garters, and the like, doctor, already, already, doctor.

QUACK You have made use of your time, sir.

HORNER I tell thee, I am now no more interruption to 'em when they sing, or talk, bawdy than a little squab[3] French page who speaks no English.

QUACK But do civil persons and women of honor drink, and sing bawdy songs?

HORNER Oh, amongst friends, amongst friends. For your bigots in honor are just like those in religion; they fear the eye of the world more than the eye of Heaven, and think there is no virtue but railing at vice, and no sin but giving scandal. They rail at a poor, little, kept player, and keep themselves some young, modest pulpit comedian to be privy to their sins in their closets,[4] not to tell 'em of them in their chapels.

QUACK Nay, the truth on't is, priests amongst the women now have quite got the better of us lay confessors, physicians.

HORNER And they are rather their patients, but—

Enter My Lady Fidget, *looking about her.*

Now we talk of women of honor, here comes one. Step behind the screen there, and but observe if I have not particular privileges with the women of reputation already, doctor, already.

Quack steps behind screen.

LADY FIDGET Well, Horner, am not I a woman of honor? You see I'm as good as my word.

1. Succeeds.
2. Master.
3. Dumpy.
4. Private rooms.

HORNER And you shall see, madam, I'll not be behindhand with you in honor; and I'll be as good as my word too, if you please but to withdraw into the next room.

LADY FIDGET But first, my dear sir, you must promise to have a care of my dear honor.

HORNER If you talk a word of your honor, you'll make me incapable to wrong it. To talk of honor in the mysteries of love is like talking of Heaven or the Deity in an operation of witchcraft, just when you are employing the devil; it makes the charm impotent.

LADY FIDGET Nay, fie! let us not be smutty. But you talk of mysteries and bewitching to me; I don't understand you.

HORNER I tell you, madam, the word "money" in a mistress's mouth, at such a nick of time, is not a more disheartening sound to a younger brother than that of "honor" to an eager lover like myself.

LADY FIDGET But you can't blame a lady of my reputation to be chary.

HORNER Chary! I have been chary of it already, by the report I have caused of myself.

LADY FIDGET Ay, but if you should ever let other women know that dear secret, it would come out. Nay, you must have a great care of your conduct; for my acquaintance are so censorious (oh, 'tis a wicked, censorious world, Mr. Horner!), I say, are so censorious and detracting that perhaps they'll talk, to the prejudice of my honor, though you should not let them know the dear secret.

HORNER Nay, madam, rather than they shall prejudice your honor, I'll prejudice theirs; and to serve you, I'll lie with 'em all, make the secret their own, and then they'll keep it. I am a Machiavel[5] in love, madam.

LADY FIDGET Oh, no, sir, not that way.

HORNER Nay, the devil take me if censorious women are to be silenced any other way.

LADY FIDGET A secret is better kept, I hope, by a single person than a multitude; therefore pray do not trust anybody else with it, dear, dear Mr. Horner.

Embracing him.

Enter Sir Jasper Fidget.

SIR JASPER FIDGET How now!

LADY FIDGET [*aside*] Oh, my husband!—prevented—and what's almost as bad, found with my arms about another man—that will appear too much—what shall I say?

Sir Jasper, come hither. I am trying if Mr. Horner were ticklish, and he's as ticklish as can be; I love to torment the confounded toad; let you and I tickle him.

SIR JASPER FIDGET No, your ladyship will tickle him better without me, I suppose. But is this your buying china? I thought you had been at the china house.

HORNER [*aside*] China house! That's my cue, I must take it.—A pox! can't you keep your impertinent wives at home? Some men

5. Shrewd plotter.

are troubled with the husbands, but I with the wives. But I'd have you to know, since I cannot be your journeyman by night, I will not be your drudge by day, to squire your wife about and be your man of straw, or scarecrow, only to pies and jays, that would be nibbling at your forbidden fruit; I shall be shortly the hackney⁶ gentleman-usher of the town.

SIR JASPER FIDGET [*aside*] He, he, he! Poor fellow, he's in the right on't, faith; to squire women about for other folks is as ungrateful an employment as to tell money for other folks.—He, he, he! Ben't angry, Horner.

LADY FIDGET No, 'tis I have more reason to be angry, who am left by you to go abroad indecently alone; or, what is more indecent to pin myself upon such ill-bred people of your acquaintance as this is.

SIR JASPER FIDGET Nay, prithee what has he done?

LADY FIDGET Nay, he has done nothing.

SIR JASPER FIDGET But what d'ye take ill, if he has done nothing?

LADY FIDGET Ha, ha, ha! Faith, I can't but laugh, however; why, d'ye think the unmannerly toad would come down to me to the coach? I was fain to come up to fetch him, or go without him, which I was resolved not to do; for he knows china very well, and has himself very good, but will not let me see it lest I should beg some. But I will find it out, and have what I came for yet.

Exit Lady Fidget, *and locks the door, followed by* Horner *to the door.*

HORNER [*apart to* Lady Fidget] Lock the door, madam.—So, she has got into my chamber, and locked me out. Oh, the impertinency of womankind! Well, Sir Jasper, plain dealing is a jewel; if ever you suffer your wife to trouble me again here, she shall carry you home a pair of horns, by my Lord Mayor she shall; though I cannot furnish you myself, you are sure, yet I'll find a way.

SIR JASPER FIDGET [*aside*] Ha, ha, he! At my first coming in and finding her arms about him, tickling him it seems, I was half jealous, but now I see my folly. —He, he, he! Poor Horner.

HORNER Nay, though you laugh now, 'twill be my turn ere long. Oh, women, more impertinent, more cunning, and more mischievous than their monkeys, and to me almost as ugly! Now is she throwing my things about and rifling all I have, but I'll get in to her the back way, and so rifle her for it.

SIR JASPER FIDGET Ha, ha, ha! Poor angry Horner.

HORNER Stay here a little; I'll ferret her out to you presently, I warrant.

Exit Horner *at t'other door.*

SIR JASPER FIDGET Wife! My Lady Fidget! Wife! He is coming in to you the back way.

Sir Jasper *calls through the door to his wife; she answers from within.*

LADY FIDGET Let him come, and welcome, which way he will.

6. Hired.

SIR JASPER FIDGET He'll catch you, and use you roughly, and be too strong for you.

LADY FIDGET Don't you trouble yourself, let him if he can.

QUACK [*behind*] This indeed I could not have believed from him, nor any but my own eyes.

Enter Mrs. Squeamish.

MRS. SQUEAMISH Where's this woman-hater, this toad, this ugly, greasy, dirty sloven?

SIR JASPER FIDGET [*aside*] So, the women all will have him ugly; methinks he is a comely person, but his wants make his form contemptible to 'em; and 'tis e'en as my wife said yesterday, talking of him, that a proper handsome eunuch was as ridiculous a thing as a gigantic coward.

MRS. SQUEAMISH Sir Jasper, your servant. Where is the odious beast?

SIR JASPER FIDGET He's within in his chamber, with my wife; she's playing the wag with him.

MRS. SQUEAMISH Is she so? And he's a clownish beast, he'll give her no quarter, he'll play the wag with her again, let me tell you. Come, let's go help her. —What, the door's locked?

SIR JASPER FIDGET Ay, my wife locked it.

MRS. SQUEAMISH Did she so? Let us break it open then.

SIR JASPER FIDGET No, no, he'll do her no hurt.

MRS. SQUEAMISH No. —[*Aside.*] But is there no other way to get in to 'em? Whither goes this? I will disturb 'em.

Exit Mrs. Squeamish *at another door.*

Enter Old Lady Squeamish.

OLD LADY SQUEAMISH Where is this harlotry, this impudent baggage, this rambling tomrig?[7] O Sir Jasper, I'm glad to see you here, did you not see my vile grandchild come in hither just now?

SIR JASPER FIDGET Yes.

OLD LADY SQUEAMISH Ay, but where is she then? where is she? Lord, Sir Jasper, I have e'en rattled myself to pieces in pursuit of her. But can you tell what she makes here? They say below, no woman lodges here.

SIR JASPER FIDGET No.

OLD LADY SQUEAMISH No! What does she here then? Say, if it be not a woman's lodging, what makes she here? But are you sure no woman lodges here?

SIR JASPER FIDGET No, nor no man neither; this is Mr. Horner's lodging.

OLD LADY SQUEAMISH Is it so, are you sure?

SIR JASPER FIDGET Yes, yes.

OLD LADY SQUEAMISH So; then there's no hurt in't, I hope. But where is he?

SIR JASPER FIDGET He's in the next room with my wife.

OLD LADY SQUEAMISH Nay, if you trust him with your wife, I may with my Biddy. They say he's a merry harmless man now, e'en as

7. Tomboy or strumpet.

harmless a man as ever came out of Italy with a good voice,[8] and as pretty harmless company for a lady as a snake without his teeth.

SIR JASPER FIDGET Ay, ay, poor man.

Enter Mrs. Squeamish.

MRS. SQUEAMISH I can't find 'em. —Oh, are you here, Grandmother? I followed, you must know, my Lady Fidget hither; 'tis the prettiest lodging, and I have been staring on the prettiest pictures.

Enter Lady Fidget *with a piece of china in her hand, and* Horner *following.*

LADY FIDGET And I have been toiling and moiling for the prettiest piece of china, my dear.

HORNER Nay, she has been too hard for me, do what I could.

MRS. SQUEAMISH O Lord, I'll have some china too. Good Mr. Horner, don't think to give other people china, and me none; come in with me too.

HORNER Upon my honor, I have none left now.

MRS. SQUEAMISH Nay, Nay, I have known you deny your china before now, but you shan't put me off so. Come.

HORNER This lady had the last there.

LADY FIDGET Yes, indeed, madam, to my certain knowledge he has no more left.

MRS. SQUEAMISH Oh, but it may be he may have some you could not find.

LADY FIDGET What, d'ye think if he had had any left, I would not have had it too? For we women of quality never think we have china enough.

HORNER Do not take it ill, I cannot make china for you all, but I will have a rol-waggon[9] for you too, another time.

MRS. SQUEAMISH Thank you, dear toad.

LADY FIDGET [*to* Horner, *aside*] What do you mean by that promise?

HORNER [*apart to* Lady Fidget] Alas, she has an innocent, literal understanding.

OLD LADY SQUEAMISH Poor Mr. Horner! He has enough to do to please you all, I see.

HORNER Ay, madam, you see how they use me.

OLD LADY SQUEAMISH Poor gentleman, I pity you.

HORNER I thank you, madam. I could never find pity but from such reverend ladies as you are; the young ones will never spare a man.

MRS. SQUEAMISH Come, come, beast, and go dine with us, for we shall want a man at ombre after dinner.

HORNER That's all their use of me, madam, you see.

MRS. SQUEAMISH Come, sloven, I'll lead you, to be sure of you.

Pulls him by the cravat.

OLD LADY SQUEAMISH Alas, poor man, how she tugs him! Kiss, kiss her; that's the way to make such nice women quiet.

8. A castrated singer. Italian male sopranos and altos were popular in the period.

9. China vase, cylindrically shaped.

HORNER No, madam, that remedy is worse than the torment; they know I dare suffer anything rather than do it.

OLD LADY FIDGET Prithee kiss her, and I'll give you her picture in little, that you admired so last night; prithee do.

HORNER Well, nothing but that could bribe me; I love a woman only in effigy and good painting, as much as I hate them. I'll do't, for I could adore the devil well painted.

Kisses Mrs. Squeamish.

MRS. SQUEAMISH Foh, you filthy toad! Nay, now I've done jesting.

OLD LADY SQUEAMISH Ha, ha, ha! I told you so.

MRS. SQUEAMISH Foh! a kiss of his—

SIR JASPER FIDGET Has no more hurt in't than one of my spaniel's.

MRS. SQUEAMISH Nor no more good neither.

QUACK [*behind*] I will now believe anything he tells me.

Enter Mr. Pinchwife.

LADY FIDGET O Lord, here's a man! Sir Jasper, my mask, my mask! I would·not be seen here for the world.

SIR JASPER FIDGET What, not when I am with you?

LADY FIDGET No, no, my honor—let's be gone.

MRS. SQUEAMISH Oh, grandmother, let us be gone; make haste, make haste, I know not how he may censure us.

LADY FIDGET Be found in the lodging of anything like a man! Away!

Exeunt Sir Jasper, Lady Fidget, Old Lady Squeamish, Mrs. Squeamish.

QUACK [*behind*] What's here? another cuckold? He looks like one, and none else sure have any business with him.

HORNER Well, what brings my dear friend hither?

PINCHWIFE Your impertinency.

HORNER My impertinency! —Why, you gentlemen that have got handsome wives think you have a privilege of saying anything to your friends, and are as brutish as if you were our creditors.

PINCHWIFE No, sir, I'll ne'er trust you any way.

HORNER But why not, dear Jack? Why diffide[1] in me thou know'st so well?

PINCHWIFE Because I do know you so well.

HORNER Han't I been always thy friend, honest Jack, always ready to serve thee, in love or battle, before thou wert married, and am so still?

PINCHWIFE I believe so; you would be my second now indeed.

HORNER Well then, dear Jack, why so unkind, so grum, so strange to me? Come, prithee kiss me, dear rogue. Gad, I was always, I say, and am still as much thy servant as—

PINCHWIFE As I am yours, sir. What, you send a kiss to my wife, is that it?

HORNER So, there 'tis—a man can't show his friendship to a married man, but presently he talks of his wife to you. Prithee, let thy wife alone, and let thee and I be all one, as we were wont. What,

1. Distrust.

thou art as shy of my kindness as a Lombard Street alderman of a courtier's civility at Locket's.[2]

PINCHWIFE But you are overkind to me, as kind as if I were your cuckold already; yet I must confess you ought to be kind and civil to me, since I am so kind, so civil to you, as to bring you this. Look you there sir.

    Delivers him a letter.

HORNER What is't?

PINCHWIFE Only a love letter, sir.

HORNER From whom?—how! this is from your wife!—hum—and hum—

PINCHWIFE Even from my wife, sir. Am I not wondrous kind and civil to you now too? —[*Aside.*] But you'll not think her so.

HORNER [*aside*] Ha! Is this a trick of his or hers?

PINCHWIFE The gentleman's surprised, I find. What, you expected a kinder letter?

HORNER No, faith, not I, how could I?

PINCHWIFE Yes, yes, I'm sure you did; a man so well made as you are must needs be disappointed if the women declare not their passion at first sight or opportunity.

HORNER [*aside*] But what should this mean? Stay, the postscript. —[*Reads aside.*] "Be sure you love me whatsoever my husband says to the contrary, and let him not see this, lest he should come home and pinch me, or kill my squirrel." —[*Aside.*] It seems he knows not what the letter contains.

PINCHWIFE Come, ne'er wonder at it so much.

HORNER Faith, I can't help it.

PINCHWIFE Now, I think, I have deserved your infinite friendship and kindness, and have showed myself sufficiently an obliging kind friend and husband; am I not so, to bring a letter from my wife to her gallant?

HORNER Ay, the devil take me, art thou the most obliging, kind friend and husband in the world, ha, ha!

PINCHWIFE Well, you may be merry, sir; but in short I must tell you, sir, my honor will suffer no jesting.

HORNER What dost thou mean?

PINCHWIFE Does the letter want a comment? Then know, sir, though I have been so civil a husband as to bring you a letter from my wife, to let you kiss and court her to my face, I will not be a cuckold, sir, I will not.

HORNER Thou art mad with jealousy. I never saw thy wife in my life but at the play yesterday, and I know not if it were she or no. I court her, kiss her!

PINCHWIFE I will not be a cuckold, I say; there will be danger in making me a cuckold.

HORNER Why, wert thou not well cured of thy last clap?

PINCHWIFE I wear a sword.

2. Lombard Street was in the financial district; Locket's was a fashionable tavern. The sense is that Pinchwife suspects Horner's friendliness as a financier would suspect a courtier's politeness in seeking a loan.

HORNER It should be taken from thee lest thou shouldst do thyself a mischief with it; thou art mad, man.

PINCHWIFE As mad as I am, and as merry as you are, I must have more reason from you ere we part. I say again, though you kissed and courted last night my wife in man's clothes, as she confesses in her letter—

HORNER [*aside*] Ha!

PINCHWIFE Both she and I say, you must not design it again, for you have mistaken your woman, as you have done your man.

HORNER [*aside*] Oh—I understand something now. —Was that thy wife? Why wouldst thou not tell me 'twas she? Faith, my freedom with her was your fault, not mine.

PINCHWIFE [*aside*] Faith, so 'twas.

HORNER Fie! I'd never do't to a woman before her husband's face, sure.

PINCHWIFE But I had rather you should do't to my wife before my face than behind my back, and that you shall never do.

HORNER No—you will hinder me.

PINCHWIFE If I would not hinder you, you see by her letter, she would.

HORNER Well, I must e'en acquiesce then, and be contented with what she writes.

PINCHWIFE I'll assure you 'twas voluntarily writ; I had no hand in't, you may believe me.

HORNER I do believe thee, faith.

PINCHWIFE And believe her too, for she's an innocent creature, has no dissembling in her; and so fare you well, sir.

HORNER Pray, however, present my humble service to her, and tell her I will obey her letter to a tittle, and fulfill her desires, be what they will, or with what difficulty soever I do't, and you shall be no more jealous of me, I warrant her and you.

PINCHWIFE Well, then, fare you well, and play with any man's honor but mine, kiss any man's wife but mine, and welcome.

Exit Mr. Pinchwife.

HORNER Ha, ha, ha! doctor.

QUACK It seems he has not heard the report of you, or does not believe it.

HORNER Ha, ha! Now, doctor, what think you?

QUACK Pray let's see the letter—hum—[*Reads the letter.*] "for—dear—love you"—

HORNER I wonder how she could contrive it! What say's thou to't? 'Tis an original.

QUACK So are your cuckolds, too, originals, for they are like no other common cuckolds, and I will henceforth believe it not impossible for you to cuckold the Grand Signior amidst his guards of eunuchs, that I say.

HORNER And I say for the letter, 'tis the first love letter that ever was without flames, darts, fates, destinies, lying and dissembling in't.

Enter Sparkish, *pulling in* Mr. Pinchwife.

SPARKISH Come back, you are a pretty brother-in-law, neither go to church, nor to dinner with your sister bride!

PINCHWIFE My sister denies her marriage, and you see is gone away from you dissatisfied.

SPARKISH Pshaw! upon a foolish scruple, that our parson was not in lawful orders, and did not say all the Common Prayer; but 'tis her modesty only, I believe. But let women be never so modest the first day, they'll be sure to come to themselves by night, and I shall have enough of her then. In the meantime, Harry Horner, you must dine with me; I keep my wedding at my aunt's in the Piazza.³

HORNER Thy wedding! What stale maid has lived to despair of a husband, or what young one of a gallant?

SPARKISH Oh, your servant, sir—this gentleman's sister then—no stale maid.

HORNER I'm sorry for't.

PINCHWIFE [*aside*] How comes he so concerned for her?

SPARKISH You sorry for't? Why, do you know any ill by her?

HORNER No, I know none but by thee; 'tis for her sake, not yours, and another man's sake that might have hoped, I thought.

SPARKISH Another man! another man! What is his name?

HORNER Nay, since 'tis past he shall be nameless. —[*Aside.*] Poor Harcourt! I am sorry thou hast missed her.

PINCHWIFE [*aside*] He seems to be much troubled at the match.

SPARKISH Prithee tell me—nay, you shan't go, brother.

PINCHWIFE I must of necessity, but I'll come to you to dinner.

Exit Pinchwife.

SPARKISH But, Harry, what, have I a rival in my wife already? But with all my heart, for he may be of use to me hereafter; for though my hunger is now my sauce, and I can fall on heartily without, but the time will come when a rival will be as good sauce for a married man to a wife as an orange to veal.

HORNER O thou damned rogue! Thou has set my teeth on edge with thy orange.

SPARKISH Then let's to dinner—there I was with you again. Come.

HORNER But who dines with thee?

SPARKISH My friends and relations, my brother Pinchwife, you see, of your acquaintance.

HORNER And his wife?

SPARKISH No, gad, he'll ne'er let her come amongst us good fellows. Your stingy country coxcomb keeps his wife from his friends, as he does his little firkin⁴ of ale for his own drinking, and a gentleman can't get a smack⁵ on't; but his servants, when his back is turned, broach it at their pleasures, and dust it away, ha, ha, ha! Gad, I am witty, I think, considering I was married today, by the world; but come—

HORNER No, I will not dine with you, unless you can fetch her too.

3. An open arcade in Covent Garden. V.iii. occurs there.   4. Cask.
5. Taste.

sparkish Pshaw! what pleasure canst thou have with women now, Harry?

horner My eyes are not gone; I love a good prospect yet, and will not dine with you unless she does too. Go fetch her, therefore, but do not tell her husband 'tis for my sake.

sparkish Well, I'll go try what I can do; in the meantime come away to my aunt's lodging, 'tis in the way to Pinchwife's.

horner The poor woman has called for aid, and stretched forth her hand, doctor; I cannot but help her over the pale out of the briars.

Exeunt Sparkish, Horner, Quack.

Act IV. Scene iv. The scene changes to Pinchwife's *house.* Mrs. Pinchwife *alone, leaning on her elbow. A table, pen, ink, and paper.*

mrs. pinchwife Well, 'tis e'en so, I have got the London disease they call love; I am sick of my husband, and for my gallant. I have heard this distemper called a fever, but methinks 'tis liker an ague, for when I think of my husband, I tremble and am in a cold sweat and have inclinations to vomit; but when I think of my gallant, dear Mr. Horner, my hot fit comes and I am all in a fever, indeed, and as in other fevers my own chamber is tedious to me, and I would fain be removed to his, and then methinks I should be well. Ah, poor Mr. Horner! Well, I cannot, will not stay here; therefore I'll make an end of my letter to him, which shall be a finer letter than my last, because I have studied it like anything. Oh, sick, sick!

Takes the pen and writes.

Enter Mr. Pinchwife, *who seeing her writing steals softly behind her, and looking over her shoulder, snatches the paper from her.*

pinchwife What, writing more letters?

mrs. pinchwife O Lord, bud! why d'ye fright me so?

She offers to run out; he stops her, and reads.

pinchwife How's this! Nay, you shall not stir, madam. "Dear, dear, dear Mr. Horner"—very well—I have taught you to write letters to good purpose—but let's see't.

"First, I am to beg your pardon for my boldness in writing to you, which I'd have you to know I would not have done had not you said first you loved me so extremely, which if you do, you will never suffer me to lie in the arms of another man, whom I loathe, nauseate, and detest."—Now you can write these filthy words. But what follows? —"Therefore I hope you will speedily find some way to free me from this unfortunate match, which was never, I assure you, of my choice, but I'm afraid 'tis already too far gone. However, if you love me, as I do you, you will try what you can do, but you must help me away before tomorrow, or else, alas, I shall be forever out of your reach, for I can defer no longer our—our" [*The letter concludes.*]—What is to follow "our"?—Speak, what? Our journey into the country, I suppose—

Oh, woman, damned woman! and love, damned love, their old
tempter! for this is one of his miracles; in a moment he can make
those blind that could see, and those see that were blind, those
dumb that could speak, and those prattle who were dumb before;
nay, what is more than all, make these dough-baked, senseless,
indocile animals, women, too hard for us, their politic lords and
rulers, in a moment. But make an end of your letter, and then
I'll make an end of you thus, and all my plagues together.
        Draws his sword.
MRS. PINCHWIFE O Lord, O Lord, you are such a passionate man,
bud!
        Enter Sparkish.
SPARKISH How now, what's here to do?
PINCHWIFE This fool here now!
SPARKISH What, drawn upon your wife? You should never do that
but at night in the dark, when you can't hurt her. This is my sis-
ter-in-law, is it not? [*Pulls aside her handkerchief.*] Ay, faith,
e'en our country Margery; one may know her. Come, she and you
must go dine with me; dinner's ready, come. But where's my
wife? Is she not come home yet? Where is she?
PINCHWIFE Making you a cuckold; 'tis that they all do, as soon as
they can.
SPARKISH What, the wedding day? No, a wife that designs to make
a cully[6] of her husband will be sure to let him win the first stake
of love, by the world. But come, they stay dinner for us; come,
I'll lead down our Margery.
MRS. PINCHWIFE No—so, go, we'll follow you.
SPARKISH I will not wag without you.
PINCHWIFE [*aside*] This coxcomb is a sensible[7] torment to me
amidst the greatest in the world.
SPARKISH Come, come, Madam Margery.
PINCHWIFE No, I'll lead her my own way. What, would you treat
your friends with mine, for want of your own wife? [*Leads her to
t'other door, and locks her in, and returns.*] —[*Aside.*] I am con-
tented my rage should take breath.
SPARKISH [*aside*] I told Horner this.
PINCHWIFE Come now.
SPARKISH Lord, how shy you are of your wife! But let me tell you,
brother, we men of wit have amongst us a saying that cuckolding,
like the smallpox, comes with a fear, and you may keep your wife
as much as you will out of danger of infection, but if her constitution incline her to't, she'll have it sooner or later, by the world,
say they.
PINCHWIFE [*aside*] What a thing is a cuckold, that every fool can
make him ridiculous!—Well, sir—but let me advise you, now you
are come to be concerned, because you suspect the danger, not to
neglect the means to prevent it, especially when the greatest
share of the malady will light upon your own head, for

6. Fool.   7. Acutely felt.

Hows'e'er the kind wife's belly comes to swell,
The husband breeds[8] for her, and first is ill.

[*Exeunt* Pinchwife *and* Sparkish.]

Act V. Scene i. Mr. Pinchwife's *house.*

Enter Mr. Pinchwife *and* Mrs. Pinchwife. A *table and candle.*

PINCHWIFE Come, take the pen and make an end of the letter, just as you intended; if you are false in a tittle, I shall soon perceive it, and punish you with this as you deserve. [*Lays his hand on his sword.*] Write what was to follow—let's see—"You must make haste and help me away before tomorrow, or else I shall be forever out of your reach, for I can defer no longer our"—What follows "our"?

MRS. PINCHWIFE Must all out then, bud? [Mrs. Pinchwife *takes the pen and writes.*] Look you there then.

PINCHWIFE Let's see—"For I can defer no longer our—wedding—Your slighted Alithea."—What's the meaning of this? My sister's name to't. Speak, unriddle!

MRS. PINCHWIFE Yes, indeed, bud.

PINCHWIFE But why her name to't? Speak—speak, I say!

MRS. PINCHWIFE Ay, but you'll tell her then again; if you would not tell her again—

PINCHWIFE I will not—I am stunned, my head turns around. Speak.

MRS. PINCHWIFE Won't you tell her indeed, and indeed?

PINCHWIFE No, speak, I say.

MRS. PINCHWIFE She'll be angry with me, but I had rather she should be angry with me than you, bud; and to tell you the truth, 'twas she made me write the letter, and taught me what I should write.

PINCHWIFE [*aside*] Ha! I thought the style was somewhat better than her own.—But how could she come to you to teach you, since I had locked you up alone?

MRS. PINCHWIFE Oh, through the keyhole, bud.

PINCHWIFE But why should she make you write a letter for her to him, since she can write herself?

MRS. PINCHWIFE Why, she said because—for I was unwilling to do it.

PINCHWIFE Because what—because?

MRS. PINCHWIFE Because, lest Mr. Horner should be cruel, and refuse her; or vain afterwards, and show the letter, she might disown it, the hand not being hers.

PINCHWIFE [*aside*] How's this? Ha! —then I think I shall come to myself again. This changeling could not invent this lie; but if she could, why should she? She might think I should soon discover it —stay—now I think on't too, Horner said he was sorry she had married Sparkish, and her disowning her marriage to me makes

8. Sprouts horns.

me think she has evaded it for Horner's sake. Yet why should she take this course? But men in love are fools; women may well be so. —But hark you, madam, your sister went out in the morning, and I have not seen her within since.

MRS. PINCHWIFE Alackaday, she has been crying all day above, it seems, in a corner.

PINCHWIFE Where is she? Let me speak with her.

MRS. PINCHWIFE [*aside*] O Lord, then he'll discover all! —Pray hold, bud; what, d'ye mean to discover me? She'll know I have told you then. Pray, bud, let me talk with her first.

PINCHWIFE I must speak with her, to know whether Horner ever made her any promise, and whether she be married to Sparkish or no.

MRS. PINCHWIFE Pray, dear bud, don't, till I have spoken with her and told her that I have told you all, for she'll kill me else.

PINCHWIFE Go then, and bid her come out to me.

MRS. PINCHWIFE Yes, yes, bud.

PINCHWIFE Let me see—

MRS. PINCHWIFE [*aside*] I'll go, but she is not within to come to him. I have just got time to know of Lucy her maid, who first set me on work, what lie I shall tell next, for I am e'en at my wit's end.

Exit Mrs. Pinchwife.

PINCHWIFE Well, I resolve it; Horner shall have her. I'd rather give him my sister than lend him my wife, and such an alliance will prevent his pretensions to my wife, sure. I'll make him of kin to her, and then he won't care for her.

Mrs. Pinchwife *returns.*

MRS. PINCHWIFE O Lord, bud! I told you what anger you would make me with my sister.

PINCHWIFE Won't she come hither?

MRS. PINCHWIFE No, no, alackaday, she's ashamed to look you in the face, and she says, if you go in to her, she'll run away downstairs, and shamefully go herself to Mr. Horner, who has promised her marriage, she says, and she will have no other, so she won't.

PINCHWIFE Did he so—promise her marriage?—then she shall have no other. Go tell her so, and if she will come and discourse with me a little concerning the means, I will about it immediately. Go.

Exit Mrs. Pinchwife.

His estate is equal to Sparkish's, and his extraction as much better than his as his parts are; but my chief reason is, I'd rather be of kin to him by the name of brother-in-law than that of cuckold.

Enter Mrs. Pinchwife.

Well, what says she now?

MRS. PINCHWIFE Why, she says she would only have you lead her to Horner's lodging—with whom she first will discourse the matter before she talk with you, which yet she cannot do; for alack, poor creature, she says she can't so much as look you in the face, therefore she'll come to you in a mask; and you must excuse her if she make you no answer to any question of yours, till you have brought her to Mr. Horner; and if you will not chide her, nor question her, she'll come out to you immediately.

PINCHWIFE Let her come; I will not speak a word to her, nor require a word from her.

MRS. PINCHWIFE Oh, I forgot; besides, she says she cannot look you in the face though through a mask, therefore would desire you to put out the candle.

PINCHWIFE I agree to all; let her make haste—there, 'tis out.

Puts out the candle.

Exit Mrs. Pinchwife.

—My case is something better. I'd rather fight with Horner for not lying with my sister than for lying with my wife, and of the two I had rather find my sister too forward than my wife; I expected no other from her free education, as she calls it, and her passion for the town. Well—wife and sister are names which make us expect love and duty, pleasure and comfort, but we find 'em plagues and torments, and are equally, though differently, troublesome to their keeper; for we have as much ado to get people to lie with our sisters as to keep 'em from lying with our wives.

Enter Mrs. Pinchwife *masked, and in hoods and scarves and a nightgown*[9] *and petticoat of* Alithea's, *in the dark.*

What, are you come, sister? Let us go then—but first let me lock up my wife. —Mrs. Margery, where are you?

MRS. PINCHWIFE Here, bud.

PINCHWIFE Come hither, that I may lock you up; get you in. [*Locks the door.*]—Come, sister, where are you now?

Mrs. Pinchwife *gives him her hand, but when he lets her go, she steals softly on t'other side of him, and is led away by him for his sister* Alithea.

Act V. Scene ii. The scene changes to Horner's *lodging.*

Quack, Horner.

QUACK What, all alone? Not so much as one of your cuckolds here, nor one of their wives! They use to take their turns with you, as if they were to watch you.

HORNER Yes, it often happens that a cuckold is but his wife's spy, and is more upon family duty when he is with her gallant abroad, hindering his pleasure, than when he is at home with her, playing the gallant. But the hardest duty a married woman imposes upon a lover is keeping her husband company always.

QUACK And his fondness wearies you almost as soon as hers.

HORNER A pox! keeping a cuckold company, after you have had his

9. Dressing gown.

wife, is as tiresome as the company of a country squire to a witty fellow of the town, when he has got all his money.

QUACK And as at first a man makes a friend of the husband to get the wife, so at last you are fain to fall out with the wife to be rid of the husband.

HORNER Ay, most cuckold-makers are true courtiers; when once a poor man has cracked his credit for 'em, they can't abide to come near him.

QUACK But at first, to draw him in, are so sweet, so kind, so dear, just you are to Pinchwife. But what becomes of that intrigue with his wife?

HORNER A pox! he's as surly as an alderman that has been bit, and since he's so coy, his wife's kindness is in vain, for she's a silly innocent.

QUACK Did she not send you a letter by him?

HORNER Yes, but that's a riddle I have not yet solved. Allow the poor creature to be willing, she is silly too, and he keeps her up so close—

QUACK Yes, so close that he makes her but the more willing, and adds but revenge to her love, which two, when met, seldom fail of satisfying each other one way or other.

HORNER What! here's the man we are talking of, I think.

Enter Mr. Pinchwife, *leading in his wife masked, muffled, and in her sister's gown.*

Pshaw!

QUACK Bringing his wife to you is the next thing to bringing a love letter from her.

HORNER What means this?

PINCHWIFE The last time, you know, sir, I brought you a love letter; now, you see, a mistress. I think you'll say I am a civil man to you.

HORNER Ay, the devil take me, will I say thou art the civilest man I ever met with, and I have known some. I fancy I understand thee now better than I did the letter; but hark thee, in thy ear—

PINCHWIFE What?

HORNER Nothing but the usual question, man: is she sound, on thy word?

PINCHWIFE What, you take her for a wench, and me for a pimp?

HORNER Pshaw! wench and pimp, paw[1] words. I know thou art an honest fellow, and hast a great acquaintance among the ladies, and perhaps hast made love for me rather than let me make love to thy wife.

PINCHWIFE Come, sir, in short, I am for no fooling.

HORNER Nor I neither; therefore prithee let's see her face presently. Make her show, man; art thou sure I don't know her?

PINCHWIFE I am sure you do know her.

HORNER A pox! why dost thou bring her to me then?

1. Naughty.

PINCHWIFE Because she's a relation of mine—

HORNER Is she, faith, man? Then thou are still more civil and obliging, dear rogue.

PINCHWIFE Who desired me to bring her to you.

HORNER Then she is obliging, dear rogue.

PINCHWIFE You'll make her welcome for my sake, I hope.

HORNER I hope she is handsome enough to make herself welcome. Prithee, let her unmask.

PINCHWIFE Do you speak to her; she would never be ruled by me.

HORNER Madam—[Mrs. Pinchwife *whispers to* Horner.] —She says she must speak with me in private. Withdraw, prithee.

PINCHWIFE [*aside*] She's unwilling, it seems, I should know all her undecent conduct in this business. —Well then, I'll leave you together, and hope when I am gone you'll agree; if not, you and I shan't agree, sir.

HORNER [*aside*] What means the fool? —If she and I agree, 'tis no matter what you and I do.

   Whispers to Mrs. Pinchwife, *who makes signs with her hand for* Pinchwife *to be gone.*

PINCHWIFE In the meantime, I'll fetch a parson, and find out Sparkish and disabuse him. You would have me fetch a parson, would you not? Well then—now I think I am rid of her, and shall have no more trouble with her. Our sisters and daughters, like usurers' money, are safest when put out; but our wives, like their writings,[2] never safe but in our closets under lock and key.

                                            Exit Mr. Pinchwife.

   Enter Boy.

BOY Sir Jasper Fidget, sir, is coming up.

                                                            Exit.

HORNER Here's the trouble of a cuckold, now, we are talking of. A pox on him! Has he not enough to do to hinder his wife's sport, but he must other women's too? —Step in here, madam.

                                            Exit Mrs. Pinchwife.

   Enter Sir Jasper.

SIR JASPER FIDGET My best and dearest friend.

HORNER [*aside to* Quack] The old style, doctor. —Well, be short, for I am busy. What would your impertinent wife have now?

SIR JASPER FIDGET Well guessed, i'faith, for I do come from her.

HORNER To invite me to supper. Tell her I can't come; go.

SIR JASPER FIDGET Nay, now you are out, faith; for my lady and the whole knot of the virtuous gang, as they call themselves, are resolved upon a frolic of coming to you tonight in a masquerade, and are all dressed already.

HORNER I shan't be at home.

SIR JASPER FIDGET [*aside*] Lord, how churlish he is to women! —Nay, prithee don't disappoint 'em; they'll think 'tis my fault; prithee don't. I'll send in the banquet and the fiddles. But make

2. Legal documents.

no noise on't, for the poor virtuous rogues would not have it known for the world that they go a-masquerading, and they would come to no man's ball but yours.

HORNER Well, well—get you gone, and tell 'em, if they come, 'twill be at the peril of their honor and yours.

SIR JASPER FIDGET He, he, he!—we'll trust you for that; farewell.

Exit Sir Jasper.

HORNER

Doctor, anon you too shall be my guest,
But now I'm going to a private feast.

Exeunt.

Act V. Scene iii. The scene changes to the Piazza of Covent Garden.

Sparkish, Pinchwife.

SPARKISH [*with the letter in his hand*] But who would have thought a woman could have been false to me? By the world, I could not have thought it.

PINCHWIFE You were for giving and taking liberty; she has taken it only, sir, now you find in that letter. You are a frank person, and so is she, you see there.

SPARKISH Nay, if this be her hand—for I never saw it.

PINCHWIFE 'Tis no matter whether that be her hand or no; I am sure this hand, at her desire, led her to Mr. Horner, with whom I left her just now, to go fetch a parson to 'em, at their desire too, to deprive you of her forever, for it seems yours was but a mock marriage.

SPARKISH Indeed, she would needs have it that 'twas Harcourt himself in a parson's habit that married us, but I'm sure he told me 'twas his brother Ned.

PINCHWIFE Oh, there 'tis out, and you were deceived, not she, for you are such a frank person—but I must be gone. You'll find her at Mr. Horner's; go and believe your eyes.

Exit Mr. Pinchwife.

SPARKISH Nay, I'll to her, and call her as many crocodiles, sirens, harpies, and other heathenish names as a poet would do a mistress who had refused to hear his suit, nay more, his verses on her. —But stay, is not that she following a torch at t'other end of the Piazza? And from Horner's certainly—'tis so.

Enter Alithea, *following a torch, and* Lucy *behind.*

You are well met, madam, though you don't think so. What, you have made a short visit to Mr. Horner, but I suppose you'll return to him presently; by that time the parson can be with him.

ALITHEA Mr. Horner, and the parson, sir!

SPARKISH Come, madam, no more dissembling, no more jilting, for I am no more a frank person.

ALITHEA How's this?

LUCY [*aside*] So, 'twill work, I see.

SPARKISH Could you find out no easy country fool to abuse? none but me, a gentleman of wit and pleasure about the town? But it was your pride to be too hard for a man of parts, unworthy false woman! false as a friend that lends a man money to lose; false as dice, who undo those that trust all they have to 'em.

LUCY [*aside*] He has been a great bubble by his similes, as they say.

ALITHEA You have been too merry, sir, at your wedding dinner, sure.

SPARKISH What, d'ye mock me too?

ALITHEA Or you have been deluded.

SPARKISH By you.

ALITHEA Let me understand you.

SPARKISH Have you the confidence—I should call it something else, since you know your guilt—to stand my just reproaches? You did not write an impudent letter to Mr. Horner! who I find now has clubbed with you in deluding me with his aversion for women, that I might not, forsooth, suspect him for my rival.

LUCY [*aside*] D'ye think the gentleman can be jealous now, madam?

ALITHEA I write a letter to Mr. Horner!

SPARKISH Nay, madam, do not deny it; your brother showed it me just now, and told me likewise he left you at Horner's lodging to fetch a parson to marry you to him, and I wish you joy, madam, joy, joy! and to him, too, much joy, and to myself more joy for not marrying you.

ALITHEA [*aside*] So, I find my brother would break off the match, and I can consent to't, since I see this gentleman can be made jealous. —O Lucy, by his rude usage and jealousy, he makes me almost afraid I am married to him. Art thou sure 'twas Harcourt himself and no parson that married us?

SPARKISH No, madam, I thank you. I suppose that was a contrivance too of Mr. Horner's and yours, to make Harcourt play the parson; but I would as little as you have him one now, no, not for the world, for shall I tell you another truth? I never had any passion for you till now, for now I hate you. 'Tis true I might have married your portion, as other men of parts of the town do sometimes, and so your servant; and to show my unconcernedness, I'll come to your wedding, and resign you with as much joy as I would a stale wench to a new cully; nay, with as much joy as I would after the first night, if I had been married to you. There's for you, and so your servant, servant.

Exit Sparkish.

ALITHEA How was I deceived in a man!

LUCY You'll believe, then, a fool may be made jealous now? For that easiness in him that suffers him to be led by a wife will likewise permit him to be persuaded against her by others.

ALITHEA But marry Mr. Horner! My brother does not intend it, sure; if I thought he did, I would take thy advice, and Mr. Harcourt for my husband. And now I wish that if there be any overwise woman of the town, who, like me, would marry a fool for fortune, liberty, or title, first, that her husband may love play, and be a cully to all the town but her, and suffer none but fortune to be mistress of his purse; then, if for liberty, that he may send her into the country under the conduct of some housewifely mother-in-law; and if for title, may the world give 'em none but that of cuckold.

LUCY And for her greater curse, madam, may he not deserve it.

ALITHEA Away, impertinent! —Is not this my old Lady Lanterlu's?[3]

LUCY Yes, madam. —[*Aside.*] And here I hope we shall find Mr. Harcourt.

Exeunt Alithea, Lucy.

Act V. *Scene iv.*

The scene changes again to Horner's *lodging.* Horner, Lady Fidget, Mrs. Dainty Fidget, Mrs. Squeamish. A *table, banquet, and bottles.*

HORNER [*aside*] A pox! they are come too soon—before I have sent back my new mistress. All I have now to do is to lock her in, that they may not see her.

LADY FIDGET That we may be sure of our welcome, we have brought our entertainment with us, and are resolved to treat thee, dear toad.

MRS. DAINTY FIDGET And that we may be merry to purpose, have left Sir Jasper and my old Lady Squeamish quarreling at home at backgammon.

MRS. SQUEAMISH Therefore let us make use of our time, lest they should chance to interrupt us.

LADY FIDGET Let us sit then.

HORNER First, that you may be private, let me lock this door and that, and I'll wait upon you presently.

LADY FIDGET No, sir, shut 'em only and your lips forever, for we must trust you as much as our women.

HORNER You know all vanity's killed in me; I have no occasion for talking.

LADY FIDGET Now, ladies, supposing we had drank each of us our two bottles, let us speak the truth of our hearts.

MRS. DAINTY FIDGET AND MRS. SQUEAMISH Agreed.

LADY FIDGET By this brimmer, for truth is nowhere else to be found. —[Aside to Horner.] Not in thy heart, false man!

HORNER [*aside to* Lady Fidget] You have found me a true man, I'm sure.

LADY FIDGET [*aside to* Horner] Not every way. —But let us sit and be merry.

Lady Fidget *sings.*

1

Why should our damn'd tyrants oblige us to live
On the pittance of pleasure which they only give?
We must not rejoice,
With wine and with noise.

3. Lanterloo was a card game; also called "loo."

In vain we must wake in a dull bed alone,
Whilst to our warm rival, the bottle, they're gone.
    Then lay aside charms,
    And take up these arms.[4]

2

'Tis wine only gives 'em their courage and wit;
Because we live sober, to men we submit.
    If for beauties you'd pass,
    Take a lick of the glass,
'Twill mend your complexions, and when they are gone,
The best red we have is the red of the grape.
    Then, sisters, lay't on,
    And damn a good shape.

MRS. DAINTY FIDGET Dear brimmer![5] Well, in token of our openness and plain-dealing, let us throw our masks over our heads.

HORNER So, 'twill come to the glasses anon.

MRS. SQUEAMISH Lovely brimmer! Let me enjoy him first.

LADY FIDGET No, I never part with a gallant till I've tried him. Dear brimmer, that mak'st our husbands shortsighted.

MRS. DAINTY FIDGET And our bashfull gallants bold.

MRS. SQUEAMISH And for want of a gallant, the butler lovely in our eyes. —Drink, eunuch.

LADY FIDGET Drink, thou representative of a husband. Damn a husband!

MRS. DAINTY FIDGET And, as it were a husband, an old keeper.

MRS. SQUEAMISH And an old grandmother.

HORNER And an English bawd, and a French surgeon.[6]

LADY FIDGET Ay, we have all reason to curse 'em.

HORNER For my sake, ladies?

LADY FIDGET No, for our own, for the first spoils all young gallants' industry.

MRS. DAINTY FIDGET And the other's art makes 'em bold only with common women.

MRS. SQUEAMISH And rather run the hazard of the vile distemper amongst them than of a denial amongst us.

MRS. DAINTY FIDGET The filthy toads choose mistresses now as they do stuffs, for having been fancied and worn by others.

MRS. SQUEAMISH For being common and cheap.

LADY FIDGET Whilst women of quality, like the richest stuffs, lie untumbled and unasked for.

HORNER Ay, neat, and cheap, and new, often they think best.

MRS. DAINTY FIDGET No, sir, the beasts will be known by a mistress longer than by a suit.

MRS. SQUEAMISH And 'tis not for cheapness neither.

LADY FIDGET No, for the vain fops will take up druggets[7] and embroider 'em. But I wonder at the depraved appetites of witty

---

4. The glasses.
5. Full glass.
6. Doctor for the "French pox" (venereal

disease).
7. Cheap woolen material.

men; they use to be out of the common road, and hate imitation. Pray tell me, beast, when you were a man, why you rather chose to club with a multitude in a common house for an entertainment than to be the only guest at a good table.

HORNER Why, faith, ceremony and expectation are unsufferable to those that are sharp bent; people always eat with the best stomach at an ordinary, where every man is snatching for the best bit.

LADY FIDGET Though he get a cut over the fingers. —But I have heard people eat most heartily of another man's meat, that is, what they do not pay for.

HORNER When they are sure of their welcome and freedom, for ceremony in love and eating is as ridiculous as in fighting; falling on briskly is all should be done in those occasions.

LADY FIDGET Well, then, let me tell you, sir, there is nowhere more freedom than in our houses, and we take freedom from a young person as a sign of good breeding, and a person may be as free as he pleases with us, as frolic, as gamesome, as wild as he will.

HORNER Han't I heard you all declaim against wild men?

LADY FIDGET Yes, but for all that, we think wildness in a man as desirable a quality as in a duck or rabbit; a tame man, foh!

HORNER I know not, but your reputations frightened me, as much as your faces invited me.

LADY FIDGET Our reputation! Lord, why should you not think that we women make use of our reputation, as you men of yours, only to deceive the world with less suspicion? Our virtue is like the statesman's religion, the Quaker's word, the gamester's oath, and the great man's honor—but to cheat those that trust us.

MRS. SQUEAMISH And that demureness, coyness, and modesty that you see in our faces in the boxes at plays, is as much a sign of a kind woman as a vizard-mask in the pit.

MRS. DAINTY FIDGET For, I assure you, women are least masked when they have the velvet vizard on.

LADY FIDGET You would have found us modest women in our denials only.

MRS. SQUEAMISH Our bashfulness is only the reflection of the men's.

MRS. DAINTY FIDGET We blush when they are shamefaced.

HORNER I beg your pardon, ladies; I was deceived in you devilishly. But why that mighty pretense to honor?

LADY FIDGET We have told you. But sometimes 'twas for the same reason you men pretend business often, to avoid ill company, to enjoy the better and more privately those you love.

HORNER But why would you ne'er give a friend a wink then?

LADY FIDGET Faith, your reputation frightened us as much as ours did you, you were so notoriously lewd.

HORNER And you so seemingly honest.[8]

LADY FIDGET Was that all that deterred you?

HORNER And so expensive—you allow freedom, you say—

LADY FIDGET Ay, ay.

8. Chaste.

HORNER That I was afraid of losing my little money, as well as my little time, both which my other pleasures required.

LADY FIDGET Money, foh! You talk like a little fellow now; do such as we expect money?

HORNER I beg your pardon, madam; I must confess, I have heard that great ladies, like great merchants, set but the higher prices upon what they have, because they are not in necessity of taking the first offer.

MRS. DAINTY FIDGET Such as we make sale of our hearts?

MRS. SQUEAMISH We bribed for our love? Foh!

HORNER With your pardon, ladies, I know, like great men in offices, you seem to exact flattery and attendance only from your followers; but you have receivers about you, and such fees to pay, a man is afraid to pass your grants.[9] Besides, we must let you win at cards, or we lose your hearts; and if you make an assignation, 'tis at a goldsmith's, jeweler's, or china house, where, for your honor you deposit to him, he must pawn his to the punctual cit, and so paying for what you take up, pays for what he takes up.

MRS. DAINTY FIDGET Would you not have us assured of our gallant's love?

MRS. SQUEAMISH For love is better known by liberality than by jealousy.

LADY FIDGET For one may be dissembled, the other not. —[*Aside.*] But my jealously can be no longer dissembled, and they are telling ripe. —Come, here's to our gallants in waiting, whom we must name, and I'll begin. This is my false rogue.
     Claps him on the back.

MRS. SQUEAMISH How!

HORNER [*aside*] So, all will out now.

MRS. SQUEAMISH [*aside to* Horner] Did you not tell me, 'twas for my sake only you reported yourself no man?

MRS. DAINTY FIDGET [*aside to* Horner] Oh, wretch! Did you not swear to me, 'twas for my love and honor you passed for that thing you do?

HORNER So, so.

LADY FIDGET Come, speak, ladies; this is my false villain.

MRS. SQUEAMISH And mine too.

MRS. DAINTY FIDGET And mine.

HORNER Well then, you are all three my false rogues too, and there's an end on't.

LADY FIDGET Well then, there's no remedy; sister sharers, let us not fall out, but have a care of our honor. Though we get no presents, no jewels of him, we are savers of our honor, the jewel of most value and use, which shines yet to the world unsuspected, though it be counterfeit.

HORNER Nay, and is e'en as good as if it were true, provided the world think so; for honor, like beauty now, only depends on the opinion of others.

9. Accept your gifts.

LADY FIDGET Well, Harry Common, I hope you can be true to three. Swear—but 'tis no purpose to require your oath, for you are as often forsworn as you swear to new women.

HORNER Come, faith, madam, let us e'en pardon one another, for all the difference I find betwixt we men and you women, we forswear ourselves at the beginning of an amour, you as long as it lasts.

Enter Sir Jasper Fidget, *and* Old Lady Squeamish.

SIR JASPER FIDGET Oh, my Lady Fidget, was this your cunning, to come to Mr. Horner without me? But you have been nowhere else, I hope.

LADY FIDGET No, Sir Jasper.

OLD LADY SQUEAMISH And you came straight hither, Biddy?

MRS. SQUEAMISH Yes, indeed, Lady Grandmother.

SIR JASPER FIDGET 'Tis well, 'tis well; I knew when once they were thoroughly acquainted with poor Horner, they'd ne'er be from him. You may let her masquerade it with my wife and Horner, and I warrant her reputation safe.

Enter Boy.

BOY Oh, sir, here's the gentleman come whom you bid me not suffer to come up without giving you notice, with a lady too, and other gentlemen.

HORNER Do you all go in there, whilst I send 'em away, and, boy, do you desire 'em to stay below till I come, which shall be immediately.

Exeunt Sir Jasper, Lady Squeamish, Lady Fidget, Mrs. Dainty, Mrs. Squeamish.

BOY Yes, sir.

Exit.

Exit Horner *at t'other door, and returns with* Mrs. Pinchwife.

HORNER You would not take my advice to be gone home before your husband came back; he'll now discover all. Yet pray, my dearest, be persuaded to go home, and leave the rest to my management; I'll let you down the back way.

MRS. PINCHWIFE I don't know the way home, so I don't.

HORNER My man shall wait upon you.

MRS. PINCHWIFE No, don't you believe that I'll go at all; what, are you weary of me already?

HORNER No, my life, 'tis that I may love you long, 'tis to secure my love, and your reputation with your husband; he'll never receive you again else.

MRS. PINCHWIFE What care I? D'ye think to frighten me with that? I don't intend to go to him again; you shall be my husband now.

HORNER I cannot be your husband, dearest, since you are married to him.

MRS. PINCHWIFE Oh, would you make me believe that? Don't I see every day, at London here, women leave their first husbands, and go and live with other men as their wives? Pish, pshaw! you'd make me angry, but that I love you so mainly.

HORNER So, they are coming up—in again, in, I hear 'em.

Exit Mrs. Pinchwife.

Well, a silly mistress is like a weak place, soon got, soon lost, a man has scarce time for plunder; she betrays her husband first to her gallant, and then her gallant to her husband.

Enter Pinchwife, Alithea, Harcourt, Sparkish, Lucy, *and a* Parson.

PINCHWIFE Come, madam, 'tis not the sudden change of your dress, the confidence of your asseverations, and your false witness there, shall persuade me I did not bring you hither just now; here's my witness, who cannot deny it, since you must be confronted. —Mr. Horner, did not I bring this lady to you just now?

HORNER [*aside*] Now must I wrong one woman for another's sake, but that's no new thing with me; for in these cases I am still on the criminal's side, against the innocent.

ALITHEA Pray, speak, sir.

HORNER [*aside*] It must be so—I must be impudent, and try my luck; impudence uses to be too hard for truth.

PINCHWIFE What, you are studying an evasion or excuse for her. Speak, sir.

HORNER No, faith, I am something backward only to speak in women's affairs or disputes.

PINCHWIFE She bids you speak.

ALITHEA Ay, pray, sir, do; pray satisfy him.

HORNER Then truly, you did bring that lady to me just now.

PINCHWIFE O ho!

ALITHEA How, sir!

HARCOURT How, Horner!

ALITHEA What mean you, sir? I always took you for a man of honor.

HORNER [*aside*] Ay, so much a man of honor that I must save my mistress, I thank you, come what will on't.

SPARKISH So, if I had had her, she'd have made me believe the moon had been made of a Christmas pie.

LUCY [*aside*] Now could I speak, if I durst, and solve the riddle, who am the author of it.

ALITHEA O unfortunate woman! A combination against my honor, which most concerns me now, because you share in my disgrace, sir, and it is your censure, which I must now suffer, that troubles me, not theirs.

HARCOURT Madam, then have no trouble, you shall now see 'tis possible for me to love too, without being jealous; I will not only believe your innocence myself, but make all the world believe it. —[*Apart to* Horner]. Horner, I must now be concerned for this lady's honor.

HORNER And I must be concerned for a lady's honor too.

HARCOURT This lady has her honor, and I will protect it.

HORNER My lady has not her honor, but has given it me to keep, and I will preserve it.

HARCOURT I understand you not.

HORNER I would not have you.

MRS. PINCHWIFE [*peeping in behind*] What's the matter with 'em all?

PINCHWIFE Come, come, Mr. Horner, no more disputing; here's the parson. I brought him not in vain.

HARCOURT No, sir, I'll employ him, if this lady please.

PINCHWIFE How! what d'ye mean?

SPARKISH Ay, what does he mean?

HORNER Why, I have resigned your sister to him; he has my consent.

PINCHWIFE But he has not mine, sir; a woman's injured honor, no more than a man's, can be repaired or satisfied by any but him that first wronged it; and you shall marry her presently, or—
Lays his hand on his sword.
Enter to them Mrs. Pinchwife.

MRS. PINCHWIFE [*aside*] O Lord, they'll kill poor Mr. Horner! Besides, he shan't marry her whilst I stand by and look on; I'll not lose my second husband so.

PINCHWIFE What do I see?

ALITHEA My sister in my clothes!

SPARKISH Ha!

MRS. PINCHWIFE [*to* Mr. Pinchwife] Nay, pray now don't quarrel about finding work for the parson; he shall marry me to Mr. Horner; for now, I believe, you have enough of me.

HORNER [*aside*] Damned, damned, loving changeling!

MRS. PINCHWIFE Pray, sister, pardon me for telling so many lies of you.

HARCOURT I suppose the riddle is plain now.

LUCY No, that must be my work. Good sir, hear me.
Kneels to Mr. Pinchwife, *who stands doggedly, with his hat over his eyes.*

PINCHWIFE I will never hear woman again, but make 'em all silent, thus—
Offers to draw upon his wife.

HORNER No, that must not be.

PINCHWIFE You then shall go first, 'tis all one to me.
Offers to draw on Horner; *stopped by* Harcourt.

HARCOURT Hold!
Enter Sir Jasper Fidget, Lady Fidget, Lady Squeamish, Mrs. Dainty Fidget, Mrs. Squeamish.

SIR JASPER FIDGET What's the matter? what's the matter? pray, what's the matter, sir? I beseech you communicate, sir.

PINCHWIFE Why, my wife has communicated, sir, as your wife may have done too, sir, if she knows him, sir.

SIR JASPER FIDGET Pshaw! with him! Ha, ha, he!

PINCHWIFE D'ye mock me, sir? A cuckold is a kind of a wild beast; have a care, sir.

SIR JASPER FIDGET No, sure, you mock me, sir—he cuckold you! It can't be, ha, ha, he! Why, I'll tell you, sir—
Offers to whisper.

PINCHWIFE I tell you again, he has whored my wife, and yours too, if he knows her, and all the women he comes near; 'tis not his dissembling, his hypocrisy, can wheedle me.

SIR JASPER FIDGET How! does he dissemble? Is he a hypocrite? Nay, then— how—wife—sister, is he an hypocrite?

OLD LADY SQUEAMISH An hypocrite! a dissembler! Speak, young harlotry, speak, how?

SIR JASPER FIDGET Nay, then—oh, my head too!—O thou libidinous lady!

OLD LADY SQUEAMISH O thou harloting harlotry! Hast thou done't then?

SIR JASPER FIDGET Speak, good Horner, art thou a dissembler, a rogue? Hast thou—

HORNER Soh!

LUCY [*apart to* Horner] I'll fetch you off, and her too, if she will but hold her tongue.

HORNER [*apart to* Lucy] Canst thou? I'll give thee—

LUCY [*to* Mr. Pinchwife] Pray have but patience to hear me, sir, who am the unfortunate cause of all this confusion. Your wife is innocent, I only culpable; for I put her upon telling you all these lies concerning my mistress, in order to the breaking off the match between Mr. Sparkish and her, to make way for Mr. Harcourt.

SPARKISH Did you so, eternal rotten tooth? Then, it seems, my mistress was not false to me, I was only deceived by you.—Brother that should have been, now, man of conduct, who is a frank person now? to bring your wife to her lover—ha!

LUCY I assure you, sir, she came not to Mr. Horner out of love, for she loves him no more—

MRS. PINCHWIFE Hold, I told lies for you, but you shall tell none for me, for I do love Mr. Horner with all my soul, and nobody shall say me nay; pray, don't you go to make poor Mr. Horner believe to the contrary, 'tis spitefully done of you, I'm sure.

HORNER [*aside to* Mrs. Pinchwife] Peace, dear idiot.

MRS. PINCHWIFE Nay, I will not peace.

PINCHWIFE Not till I make you.

Enter Dorilant, Quack.

DORILANT Horner, your servant; I am the doctor's guest, he must excuse our intrusion.

QUACK But what's the matter, gentlemen? For heaven's sake, what's the matter?

HORNER Oh, 'tis well you are come. 'Tis a censorious world we live in; you may have brought me a reprieve, or else I had died for a crime I never committed, and these innocent ladies had suffered with me; therefore pray satisfy these worthy, honorable, jealous gentlemen—that—

Whispers.

QUACK Oh, I understand you; is that all? —[*Whispers to* Sir Jasper.] Sir Jasper, by heavens and upon the word of a physician, sir—

SIR JASPER FIDGET Nay, I do believe you truly. —Pardon me, my virtuous lady, and dear of honor.

OLD LADY SQUEAMISH What, then all's right again?

SIR JASPER FIDGET Ay, ay, and now let us satisfy him too.

They whisper with Mr. Pinchwife.

PINCHWIFE An eunuch! Pray, no fooling with me.

QUACK I'll bring half the surgeons in town to swear it.

PINCHWIFE They!—they'll swear a man bled to death through his wounds died of an apoplexy.

QUACK Pray hear me, sir—why, all the town has heard the report of him.

PINCHWIFE But does all the town believe it?

QUACK Pray inquire a little, and first of all these.

PINCHWIFE I'm sure when I left the town he was the lewdest fellow in't.

QUACK I tell you, sir, he has been in France since; pray ask but these ladies and gentlemen, your friend Mr. Dorilant. —Gentlemen and ladies han't you all heard the late sad report of poor Mr. Horner?

ALL THE LADIES Ay, ay, ay.

DORILANT Why, thou jealous fool, dost thou doubt it? He's an arrant French capon.[1]

MRS. PINCHWIFE 'Tis false, sir, you shall not disparage poor Mr. Horner, for to my certain knowledge—

LUCY Oh, hold!

MRS. SQUEAMISH [*aside to* Lucy] Stop her mouth!

LADY FIDGET [*to* Pinchwife] Upon my honor, sir, 'tis as true—

MRS. DAINTY FIDGET D'ye think we would have been seen in his company?

MRS. SQUEAMISH Trust our unspotted reputations with him!

LADY FIDGET [*aside to* Horner] This you get, and we too, by trusting your secret to a fool.

HORNER Peace, madam. —[*Aside to* Quack.] Well, doctor, is not this a good design, that carries a man on unsuspected, and brings him off safe?

PINCHWIFE [*aside*] Well, if this were true, but my wife—

Dorilant *whispers with* Mrs. Pinchwife.

ALITHEA Come, brother, your wife is yet innocent, you see; but have a care of too strong an imagination, lest like an overconcerned, timorous gamester, by fancying an unlucky cast, it should come. Women and fortune are truest still to those that trust 'em.

LUCY And any wild thing grows but the more fierce and hungry for being kept up, and more dangerous to the keeper.

ALITHEA There's doctrine for all husbands, Mr. Harcourt.

HARCOURT I edify, madam, so much that I am impatient till I am one.

DORILANT And I edify so much by example I will never be one.

SPARKISH And because I will not disparage my parts I'll ne'er be one.

1. Impotent man.

HORNER And I, alas, can't be one.

PINCHWIFE But I must be one—against my will, to a country wife, with a country murrain[2] to me.

MRS. PINCHWIFE [*aside*] And I must be a country wife still too, I find, for I can't, like a city one, be rid of my musty husband and do what I list.

HORNER Now, sir, I must pronounce your wife innocent, though I blush whilst I do it, and I am the only man by her now exposed to shame, which I will straight drown in wine, as you shall your suspicion, and the ladies' troubles we'll divert with a ballet. —Doctor, where are your maskers?

LUCY Indeed, she's innocent, sir, I am her witness; and her end of coming out was but to see her sister's wedding, and what she has said to your face of her love to Mr. Horner was but the usual innocent revenge on a husband's jealousy—was it not, madam? Speak.

MRS. PINCHWIFE [*aside to* Lucy *and* Horner] Since you'll have me tell more lies—Yes, indeed, bud.

PINCHWIFE

> For my own sake fain I would all believe;
> Cuckolds, like lovers, should themselves deceive.
> But—[*Sighs.*]
> His honor is least safe, too late I find,
> Who trusts it with a foolish wife or friend.

A dance of cuckolds.

HORNER

> Vain fops but court, and dress, and keep a pother,
> To pass for women's men with one another;
> But he who aims by women to be priz'd,
> First by the men, you see, must be despis'd.

FINIS

Epilogue

Spoken by Mrs. Knep.[3]

> Now, you the vigorous, who daily here
> O'er vizard-mask in public domineer,
> And what you'd do to her if in place where;
> Nay, have the confidence to cry, "Come out!"
> Yet when she says, "Lead on," you are not stout;
> But to your well-dress'd brother straight turn round
> And cry, "Pox on her, Ned, she can't be sound!"
> Then slink away, a fresh one to engage,
> With so much seeming heat and loving rage,
> You'd frighten listening actress on the stage;

2. Plague.　　　3. Who played Lady Fidget.

Till she at last has seen you huffing come,⎫
And talk of keeping in the tiring-room,⎬
Yet cannot be provok'd to lead her home.⎭
Next, you Falstaffs of fifty, who beset
Your buckram maidenheads,[4] which your friends get;
And whilst to them you of achievements boast,
They share the booty, and laugh at your cost.
In fine, you essenc'd boys, both old and young,⎫
Who would be thought so eager, brisk, and strong,⎬
Yet do the ladies, not their husbands, wrong;⎭
Whose purses for your manhood make excuse,
And keep your Flanders mares[5] for show, not use;
Encourag'd by our woman's man today,
A Horner's part may vainly think to play;
And may intrigues so bashfully disown
That they may doubted be by few or none;
May kiss the cards at picquet, ombre, loo,⎫
And so be thought to kiss the lady too;⎬
But, gallants, have a care, faith, what you do.⎭
The world, which to no man his due will give,
You by experience know you can deceive,
And men may still believe you vigorous,
But then we women—there's no coz'ning us.

FINIS.

---

4. Buckram is stiff, and hence troublesome to "Falstaffs of fifty." But the line
also alludes to Shakespeare's *1 Henry IV*
II.iv., in which Falstaff, having been
robbed (by his friends, as it turns out),
lies about the number of "rogues in buckram" he killed in the fray.
5. Mistresses.

GEORGE ETHEREGE

The Man of Mode
or
Sir Fopling Flutter†

To Her Royal Highness

The Duchess[1]

MADAM,

Poets, however they may be modest otherwise, have always too good an opinion of what they write. The world, when it sees this play dedicated to your Royal Highness, will conclude I have more than my share of that vanity. But I hope the honor I have of belonging to you will excuse my presumption. 'Tis the first thing I have produced in your service, and my duty obliges me to what my choice durst not else have aspired.

I am very sensible, madam, how much it is beholding to your indulgence for the success it had in the acting, and your protection will be no less fortunate to it in the printing; for all are so ambitious of making their court to you that none can be severe to what you are pleased to favor.

This universal submission and respect is due to the greatness of your rank and birth; but you have other illustrious qualities which are much more engaging. Those would but dazzle, did not these really charm the eyes and understandings of all who have the happiness to approach you.

Authors on these occasions are never wanting to publish a particular of their patron's virtues and perfections; but your Royal Highness's are so eminently known that, did I follow their examples, I should but paint those wonders here of which everyone already has the idea in his mind. Besides, I do not think it proper to aim at that in prose which is so glorious a subject for verse, in which hereafter if I show more zeal than skill, it will not grieve me much, since I less passionately desire to be esteemed a poet than to be thought,

Madam,
Your Royal Highness's
most humble, most obedient,
and most faithful servant,
GEORGE ETHEREGE

† First performed in 1676 and published   1. Mary of Modena, Duchess of York.
in the same year.

Prologue

By Sir Car Scroope, Baronet[2]

Like dancers on the ropes poor poets fare:
Most perish young, the rest in danger are.
This, one would think, should make our authors wary,
But, gamester-like, the giddy fools miscarry;
A lucky hand or two so tempts 'em on,
They cannot leave off play till they're undone.
With modest fears a muse does first begin,
Like a young wench newly enticed to sin;
But tickled once with praise, by her good will,
The wanton fool would never more lie still.
'Tis an old mistress you'll meet here tonight,
Whose charms you once have looked on with delight.
But now, of late, such dirty drabs have known ye,
A muse o'th' better sort's ashamed to own ye.
Nature well-drawn and wit must now give place
To gaudy nonsense and to dull grimace;
Nor is it strange that you should like so much
That kind of wit, for most of yours is such.
But I'm afraid that while to France we go, ⎫
To bring you home fine dresses, dance, and show, ⎬
The stage, like you, will but more foppish grow. ⎭
Of foreign wares why should we fetch the scum,
When we can be so richly served at home?
For, heav'n be thanked, 'tis not so wise an age
But your own follies may supply the stage.
Though often plowed, there's no great fear the soil
Should barren grow by the too-frequent toil,
While at your doors are to be daily found
Such loads of dunghill to manure the ground.
'Tis by your follies that we players thrive,
As the physicians by diseases live;
And as each year some new distemper reigns,
Whose friendly poison helps to increase their gains,
So, among you, there starts up every day
Some new, unheard-of fool for us to play.
Then, for your own sakes, be not too severe,
Nor what you all admire at home, damn here.
Since each is fond of his own ugly face,
Why should you, when we hold it, break the glass?

2. Poet and courtier.

Dramatis Personae[3]

MR. DORIMANT
MR. MEDLEY
OLD BELLAIR
YOUNG BELLAIR, [*in love with Emilia*] ⎬ *Gentlemen*
SIR FOPLING FLUTTER

LADY TOWNLEY, [*sister of Old Bellair*]
EMILIA
MRS. LOVEIT, [*in love with Dorimant*]
BELLINDA, [*in love with Dorimant*] ⎬ *Gentlewomen*
LADY WOODVILL, *and*
HARRIET, *her daughter*

PERT
and ⎬ *Waiting women*
BUSY

A SHOEMAKER
AN ORANGE-WOMAN
THREE SLOVENLY BULLIES
TWO CHAIRMEN
MR. SMIRK, *a parson*
HANDY, *a valet de chambre*
PAGES. FOOTMEN, *etc.*

3. No list of actors was published in the original edition, but other sources indicate that the great actor Thomas Betterton played Dorimant and that Elizabeth Barry, beginning a brilliant career, took over the role of Mrs. Loveit in an early revival.

82 · George Etherege

The Man of Mode

Act I. Scene i.
A dressing room. A table covered with a toilet; clothes
laid ready. Enter Dorimant in his gown and slippers, with a
note in his hand made up, repeating verses.

DORIMANT

"Now, for some ages, had the pride of Spain
Made the sun shine on half the world in vain."[4]

Then looking on the note.
"For Mrs. Loveit." What a dull, insipid thing is a billet-doux
written in cold blood, after the heat of the business is over! It is
a tax upon good nature which I have here been laboring to pay,
and have done it, but with as much regret as ever fanatic[5] paid
the Royal Aid or church duties. 'Twill have the same fate, I
know, that all my notes to her have had of late; 'twill not be
thought kind enough. Faith, women are i' the right when they
jealously examine our letters, for in them we always first discover
our decay of passion.—Hey! Who waits?
Enter Handy.

HANDY Sir—
DORIMANT Call a footman.
HANDY None of 'em are come yet.
DORIMANT Dogs! Will they ever lie snoring abed till noon?
HANDY 'Tis all one, sir: if they're up, you indulge 'em so, they're
ever poaching after whores all the morning.
DORIMANT Take notice henceforward who's wanting in his duty;
the next clap he gets, he shall rot for an example. What vermin
are those chattering without?
HANDY Foggy Nan, the orange-woman, and swearing Tom, the
shoemaker.
DORIMANT Go, call in that overgrown jade with the flasket of guts
before her. Fruit is refreshing in a morning.
Exit Handy.

"It is not that I love you less,
Than when before your feet I lay—"[6]

Enter Orange-Woman and Handy.
How now, double-tripe, what news do you bring?
ORANGE-WOMAN News! Here's the best fruit has come to town
t'year. Gad, I was up before four o'clock this morning and
bought all the choice i' the market.
DORIMANT The nasty refuse of your shop.
ORANGE-WOMAN You need not make mouths at it. I assure you, 'tis
all culled ware.

4. The opening lines of Edmund Waller's "Of a War with Spain, and a Fight at Sea."
5. Dissenter. The Royal Aid and church duties were taxes.
6. Waller again. The opening lines of "The Self Banished."

DORIMANT The citizens buy better on a holiday in their walk to Totnam.[7]

ORANGE-WOMAN Good or bad, 'tis all one; I never knew you commend anything. Lord, would the ladies had heard you talk of 'em as I have done.

> *Sets down the fruit.*

Here, bid your man give me an angel.[8]

DORIMANT [*to* Handy] Give the bawd her fruit again.

ORANGE-WOMAN Well, on my conscience, there never was the like of you.—God's my life, I had almost forgot to tell you, there is a young gentlewoman, lately come to town with her mother, that is so taken with you.

DORIMANT Is she handsome?

ORANGE-WOMAN Nay, gad, there are few finer women, I tell you but so, and a hugeous fortune, they say. Here, eat this peach, it comes from the stone; 'tis better than any Newington y' have tasted.

DORIMANT [*taking the peach*] This fine woman, I'll lay my life, is some awkward, ill-fashioned country toad, who, not having above four dozen of black hairs on her head, has adorned her baldness with a large white fruz,[9] that she may look sparkishly in the forefront of the King's box at an old play.

ORANGE-WOMAN Gad, you'd change your note quickly if you did but see her!

DORIMANT How came she to know me?

ORANGE-WOMAN She saw you yesterday at the Change.[1] She told me you came and fooled with the woman at the next shop.

DORIMANT I remember, there was a mask[2] observed me, indeed. Fooled, did she say?

ORANGE-WOMAN Ay; I vow she told me twenty things you said too, and acted with head and with her body so like you—

> *Enter* Medley.

MEDLEY Dorimant, my life, my joy, my darling sin! How dost thou?

> *Embraces him.*

ORANGE-WOMAN Lord, what a filthy trick these men have got of kissing one another!

> *She spits.*

MEDLEY Why do you suffer this cartload of scandal to come near you and make your neighbors think you so improvident to need a bawd?

ORANGE-WOMAN [*to* Dorimant] Good, now, we shall have it, you did but want him to help you. Come, pay me for my fruit.

MEDLEY Make us thankful for it, huswife, bawds are as much out of fashion as gentlemen-ushers: none but old formal ladies use the one, and none but foppish old stagers employ the other. Go, you are an insignificant brandy bottle.

---

7. Tottenham, a lower middle-class district.
8. Gold coin, worth about ten shillings.
9. Short, curled wig.

1. The New Exchange, a fashionable arcade of shops.
2. A masked woman.

DORIMANT Nay, there you wrong her. Three quarts of canary[3] is her business.

ORANGE-WOMAN What you please, gentlemen.

DORIMANT To him! Give him as good as he brings.

ORANGE-WOMAN Hang him, there is not such another heathen in the town again, except it be the shoemaker without.

MEDLEY I shall see you hold up your hand at the bar next sessions for murder, huswife. That shoemaker can take his oath you are in fee with the doctors to sell green fruit to the gentry, that the crudities may breed diseases.

ORANGE-WOMAN Pray give me my money.

DORIMANT Not a penny! When you bring the gentlewoman hither you spoke of, you shall be paid.

ORANGE-WOMAN The gentlewoman! The gentlewoman may be as honest[4] as your sisters, for aught as I know. Pray pay me, Mr. Dorimant, and do not abuse me so. I have an honester way of living; you know it.

MEDLEY Was there ever such a resty[5] bawd?

DORIMANT Some jade's tricks she has, but she makes amends when she's in good humour. —Come, tell me the lady's name, and Handy shall pay you.

ORANGE-WOMAN I must not; she forbid me.

DORIMANT That's a sure sign she would have you.

MEDLEY Where does she live?

ORANGE-WOMAN They lodge at my house.

MEDLEY Nay, then she's in a hopeful way.

ORANGE-WOMAN Good Mr. Medley, say your pleasure of me, but take heed how you affront my house. God's my life, in a hopeful way!

DORIMANT Prithee, peace. What kind of woman's the mother?

ORANGE-WOMAN A goodly, grave gentlewoman. Lord, how she talks against the wild young men o' the town! As for your part, she thinks you an arrant devil: should she see you, on my conscience she would look if you had not a cloven foot.

DORIMANT Does she know me?

ORANGE-WOMAN Only by hearsay. A thousand horrid stories have been told her of you, and she believes 'em all.

MEDLEY By the character, this should be the famous Lady Wood-vill and her daughter Harriet.

ORANGE-WOMAN [*aside*] The devil's in him for guessing, I think.

DORIMANT Do you know 'em?

MEDLEY Both very well. The mother's a great admirer of the forms and civility of the last age.

DORIMANT An antiquated beauty may be allowed to be out of humour at the freedoms of the present. This is a good account of the mother. Pray, what is the daughter?

MEDLEY Why, first, she's an heiress, vastly rich.

DORIMANT And handsome?

3. Wine from the Canary Islands; *canary-bird* was also slang for *whore*.

4. Chaste.

5. Restive.

MEDLEY What alteration a twelvemonth may have bred in her, I know not, but a year ago she was the beautifulest creature I ever saw: a fine, easy, clean shape; light brown hair in abundance; her features regular; her complexion clear and lively; large, wanton eyes; but above all, a mouth that has made me kiss it a thousand times in imagination—teeth white and even, and pretty, pouting lips, with a little moisture ever hanging on them, that look like the Provins rose fresh on the bush, ere the morning sun has quite drawn up the dew.

DORIMANT Rapture, mere[6] rapture!

ORANGE-WOMAN Nay, gad he tells you true. She's a delicate creature.

DORIMANT Has she wit?

MEDLEY More than is usual in her sex, and as much malice. Then, she's as wild as you would wish her, and has a demureness in her looks that makes it so surprising.

DORIMANT Flesh and blood cannot hear this and not long to know her.

MEDLEY I wonder what makes her mother bring her up to town? An old, doting keeper cannot be more jealous of his mistress.

ORANGE-WOMAN She made me laugh yesterday. There was a judge came to visit 'em, and the old man (she told me) did so stare upon her and, when he saluted her, smacked so heartily—who would think it of 'em?

MEDLEY God-a-mercy, Judge!

DORIMANT Do 'em right, the gentlemen of the long robe[7] have not been wanting by their good examples to countenance the crying sin o' the nation.

MEDLEY Come, on with your trappings; 'tis later than you imagine.

DORIMANT Call in the shoemaker, Handy!

ORANGE-WOMAN Good Mr. Dorimant, pay me. Gad, I had rather give you my fruit than stay to be abused by that foul-mouthed rogue. What you gentlemen say, it matters not much; but such a dirty fellow does one more disgrace.

DORIMANT [*to* Handy] Give her ten shillings. [*To* Orange-Woman.] And be sure you tell the young gentlewoman I must be acquainted with her.

ORANGE-WOMAN Now do you long to be tempting this pretty creature. Well, heavens mend you!

MEDLEY Farewell, bog!

Exeunt Orange-Woman *and* Handy.
Dorimant, when did you see your *pis aller*,[8] as you call her, Mrs. Loveit?

DORIMANT Not these two days.

MEDLEY And how stand affairs between you?

DORIMANT There has been great patching of late, much ado; we make a shift to hang together.

MEDLEY I wonder how her mighty spirit bears it?

6. Absolute.   8. Last resort.
7. Lawyers.

DORIMANT Ill enough, on all conscience. I never knew so violent a creature.

MEDLEY She's the most passionate in her love and the most extravagant in her jealousy of any women I ever heard of. What note is that?

DORIMANT An excuse I am going to send her for the neglect I am guilty of.

MEDLEY Prithee, read it.

DORIMANT No, but if you will take the pains, you may.

MEDLEY [*reads*] "I never was a lover of business, but now I have a just reason to hate it, since it has kept me these two days from seeing you. I intend to wait upon you in the afternoon, and in the pleasure of your conversation forget all I have suffered during this tedious absence." —This business of yours, Dorimant, has been with a vizard[9] at the playhouse; I have had an eye on you. If some malicious body should betray you, this kind note would hardly make your peace with her.

DORIMANT I desire no better.

MEDLEY Why, would her knowledge of it oblige you?

DORIMANT Most infinitely; next to the coming to a good understanding with a new mistress, I love a quarrel with an old one. But the devil's in't, there has been such a calm in my affairs of late, I have not had the pleasure of making a woman so much as break her fan, to be sullen, or forswear herself, these three days.

MEDLEY A very great misfortune! Let me see, I love mischief well enough to forward this business myself. I'll about it presently, and though I know the truth of what y'ave done will set her a-raving, I'll heighten it a little with invention, leave her in a fit o' the mother,[1] and be here again before y'are ready.

DORIMANT Pray, stay; you may spare yourself the labor. The business is undertaken already by one who will manage it with as much address and, I think, with a little more malice than you can.

MEDLEY Who i' the devil's name can this be?

DORIMANT Why, the vizard, that very vizard you saw me with.

MEDLEY Does she love mischief so well as to betray herself to spite another?

DORIMANT Not so neither, Medley; I will make you comprehend the mystery. This mask, for a farther confirmation of what I have been these two days swearing to her, made me yesterday at the playhouse make her a promise, before her face, utterly to break off with Loveit; and because she tenders my reputation and would not have me do a barbarous thing, has contrived a way to give me a handsome occasion.

MEDLEY Very good.

DORIMANT She intends, about an hour before me this afternoon, to make Loveit a visit; and (having the privilege by reason of a professed friendship between 'em to talk of her concerns)—

9. Masked woman, often a whore.   1. Hysteria.

MEDLEY Is she a friend?

DORIMANT Oh, an intimate friend!

MEDLEY Better and better! Pray proceed.

DORIMANT She means insensibly to insinuate a discourse of me and artificially raise her jealousy to such a height that, transported with the first motions of her passion, she shall fly upon me with all the fury imaginable as soon as ever I enter. The quarrel being thus happily begun, I am to play my part: confess and justify all my roguery, swear her impertinence and ill humor makes her intolerable, tax her with the next fop that comes into my head, and in a huff march away, slight her, and leave her to be taken by whosoever thinks it worth his time to lie down before her.

MEDLEY This vizard is a spark, and has a genius that makes her worthy of yourself, Dorimant.

Enter Handy, Shoemaker, *and* Footman.

DORIMANT [to Footman] You rogue there, who sneak like a dog that has flung down a dish! If you do not mend your waiting, I'll uncase[2] you and turn you loose to the wheel of fortune.—Handy, seal this and let him run with it presently.

Exit Footman.

MEDLEY Since y'are resolved on a quarrel, why do you send her this kind note?

DORIMANT To keep her at home in order to the business. [To the Shoemaker.] How now, you drunken sot?

SHOEMAKER 'Zbud, you have no reason to talk. I have not had a bottle of sack of yours in my belly this fortnight.

MEDLEY The orange-woman says your neighbors take notice what a heathen you are, and design to inform the bishop and have you burned for an atheist.

SHOEMAKER Damn her, dunghill! If her husband does not remove her, she stinks so, the parish intend to indict him for a nuisance.

MEDLEY I advise you like a friend, reform your life. You have brought the envy of the world upon you by living above yourself. Whoring and swearing are vices too genteel for a shoemaker.

SHOEMAKER 'Zbud, I think you men of quality will grow as unreasonable as the women: you would engross[3] the sins o' the nation. Poor folks can no sooner be wicked but th'are railed at by their betters.

DORIMANT Sirrah, I'll have you stand i' the pillory for this libel.

SHOEMAKER Some of you deserve it, I'm sure. There are so many of 'em that our journeymen nowadays, instead of harmless ballads, sing nothing but your damned lampoons.

DORIMANT Our lampoons, you rogue?

SHOEMAKER Nay, good master, why should not you write your own commentaries[4] as well as Caesar?

MEDLEY The rascal's read, I perceive.

SHOEMAKER You know the old proverb, ale and history.[5]

2. Strip you of your livery.
3. Monopolize.
4. A pun. *Commentary* could mean *trea-* *tise* or *satiric "comment."*
5. "Truth is in ale as in history."

DORIMANT Draw on my shoes, sirrah.

SHOEMAKER Here's a shoe—

DORIMANT Sits with more wrinkles than there are in an angry bully's forehead.

SHOEMAKER 'Zbud, as smooth as your mistress's skin does upon her. So, strike your foot in home. 'Zbud, if e'er a monsieur of 'em all make more fashionable ware, I'll be content to have my ears whipped off with my own paring knife.

MEDLEY And served up in a ragout, instead of coxcombs, to a company of French shoemakers for a collation.

SHOEMAKER Hold, hold! Damn 'em caterpillars, let 'em feed upon cabbage!—Come master, your health this morning next my heart now.[6]

DORIMANT Go, get you home, and govern your family better! Do not let your wife follow you to the alehouse, beat your whore, and lead you home in triumph.

SHOEMAKER 'Zbud, there's never a man i' the town lives more like a gentleman with his wife than I do. I never mind her motions; she never inquires into mine. We speak to one another civilly, hate one another heartily, and because 'tis vulgar to lie and soak[7] together, we have each of us our several settle-bed.

DORIMANT [*to* Handy] Give him half a crown.

MEDLEY Not without he will promise to be bloody drunk.

SHOEMAKER Tope's the word, i' the eye of the world. [*To* Handy.] For my master's honor, Robin![8]

DORIMANT Do not debauch my servants, sirrah.

SHOEMAKER I only tip him the wink; he knows an alehouse from a hovel.

Exit Shoemaker.

DORIMANT [*to* Handy] My clothes, quickly!

MEDLEY Where shall we dine today?

Enter Young Bellair.

DORIMANT Where you will. Here comes a good third man.

YOUNG BELLAIR Your servant, gentlemen.

MEDLEY Gentle sir, how will you answer this visit to your honorable mistress? 'Tis not her interest you should keep company with men of sense, who will be talking reason.

YOUNG BELLAIR I do not fear her pardon, do you but grant me yours for my neglect of late.

MEDLEY Though y'ave made us miserable by the want of your good company, to show you I am free from all resentment, may the beautiful cause of our misfortune give you all the joys happy lovers have shared ever since the world began.

YOUNG BELLAIR You wish me in heaven, but you believe me on my journey to hell.

MEDLEY You have a good strong faith, and that may contribute much towards your salvation. I confess I am but of an untoward

6. He is asking for money.
7. Drink.
8. "Tope" is a more polite version of

Medley's "bloody drunk." "Robin" is colloquial for *servant*—i.e., Handy.

constitution, apt to have doubts and scruples; and in love they are no less distracting than in religion. Were I so near marriage, I should cry out by fits as I ride in my coach, "Cuckold, cuckold!" with no less fury than the mad fanatic does "Glory!" in Bethlem.[9]

YOUNG BELLAIR Because religion makes some run mad, must I live an atheist?

MEDLEY Is it not great indiscretion for a man of credit, who may have money enough on his word, to go and deal with Jews, who for little sums make men enter into bonds and give judgments?[1]

YOUNG BELLAIR Preach no more on this text; I am determined, and there is no hope of my conversion.

DORIMANT [*to* Handy, *who is fiddling about him*] Leave your unnecessary fiddling. A wasp that's buzzing about a man's nose at dinner is not more troublesome than thou art.

HANDY You love to have your clothes hang just, sir.

DORIMANT I love to be well-dressed, sir, and think it no scandal to my understanding.

HANDY Will you use the essence, or orange-flower water?

DORIMANT I will smell as I do today, no offense to the ladies' noses.

HANDY Your pleasure, sir.

Exit Handy.

DORIMANT That a man's excellency should lie in neatly tying of a ribbon or a cravat! How careful's nature in furnishing the world with necessary coxcombs!

YOUNG BELLAIR That's a mighty pretty suit of yours, Dorimant.

DORIMANT I am glad 't has your approbation.

YOUNG BELLAIR No man in town has a better fancy in his clothes than you have.

DORIMANT You will make me have an opinion of my genius.

MEDLEY There is a great critic, I hear, in these matters lately arrived piping hot from Paris.

YOUNG BELLAIR Sir Fopling Flutter, you mean.

MEDLEY The same.

YOUNG BELLAIR He thinks himself the pattern of modern gallantry.

DORIMANT He is indeed the pattern of modern foppery.

MEDLEY He was yesterday at the play, with a pair of gloves up to his elbows and a periwig more exactly curled than a lady's head newly dressed for a ball.

YOUNG BELLAIR What a pretty lisp he has!

DORIMANT Ho, that he affects in imitation of the people of quality of France.

MEDLEY His head stands for the most part on one side, and his looks are more languishing than a lady's when she lolls at stretch in her coach or leans her head carelessly against the side of a box 'i the playhouse.

DORIMANT He is a person indeed of great acquired follies.

MEDLEY He is like many others, beholding to his education for making him so eminent a coxcomb. Many a fool had been lost to

9. Bethlehem Hospital, the insane asylum.   1. Securities.

the world, had their indulgent parents wisely bestowed neither learning nor good breeding on 'em.

YOUNG BELLAIR He has been, as the sparkish word is, brisk upon the ladies already. He was yesterday at my Aunt Townley's and gave Mrs. Loveit a catalogue of his good qualities, under the character of a complete gentleman, who (according to Sir Fopling) ought to dress well, dance well, fence well, have a genius for love letters, an agreeable voice for a chamber, be very amorous, something discreet, but not overconstant.

MEDLEY Pretty ingredients to make an accomplished person!

DORIMANT I am glad he pitched upon Loveit.

YOUNG BELLAIR How so?

DORIMANT I wanted a fop to lay to her charge; and this is as pat as may be.

YOUNG BELLAIR I am confident she loves no man but you.

DORIMANT The good fortune were enough to make me vain, but that I am in my nature modest.

YOUNG BELLAIR Hark you, Dorimant.—With your leave, Mr. Medley. 'Tis only a secret concerning a fair lady.

MEDLEY Your good breeding, sir, gives you too much trouble. You might have whispered without all this ceremony.

YOUNG BELLAIR [*to* Dorimant] How stand your affairs with Bellinda of late?

DORIMANT She's a little jilting baggage.

YOUNG BELLAIR Nay, I believe her false enough, but she's ne'er the worse for your purpose. She was with you yesterday in a disguise at the play.

DORIMANT There we fell out and resolved never to speak to one another more.

YOUNG BELLAIR The occasion?

DORIMANT Want of courage to meet me at the place appointed. These young women apprehend loving as much as the young men do fighting at first; but once entered, like them too, they all turn bullies straight.

Enter Handy.

HANDY [*to* Young Bellair] Sir, your man without desires to speak with you.

YOUNG BELLAIR Gentlemen, I'll return immediately.

Exit Young Bellair.

MEDLEY A very pretty fellow, this.

DORIMANT He's handsome, well-bred, and by much the most tolerable of all the young men that do not abound in wit.

MEDLEY Ever well-dressed, always complaisant, and seldom impertinent; you and he are grown very intimate, I see.

DORIMANT It is our mutual interest to be so. It makes the women think the better of his understanding and judge more favorably of my reputation; it makes him pass upon some for a man of very good sense, and I upon others for a very civil person.

MEDLEY What was that whisper?

DORIMANT A thing which he would fain have known, but I did not think it fit to tell him. It might have frighted him from his honorable intentions of marrying.

MEDLEY Emilia, give her her due, has the best reputation of any young woman about the town who has beauty enough to provoke detraction. Her carriage is unaffected, her discourse modest—not at all censorious nor pretending, like the counterfeits of the age.

DORIMANT She's a discreet maid, and I believe nothing can corrupt her but a husband.

MEDLEY A husband?

DORIMANT Yes, a husband. I have known many women make a difficulty of losing a maidenhead, who have afterwards made none of making a cuckold.

MEDLEY This prudent consideration, I am apt to think, has made you confirm poor Bellair in the desperate resolution he has taken.

DORIMANT Indeed, the little hope I found there was of her, in the state she was in, has made me by my advice contribute something towards the changing of her condition.

Enter Young Bellair.

Dear Bellair, by heavens I thought we had lost thee! Men in love are never to be reckoned on when we would form a company.

YOUNG BELLAIR Dorimant, I am undone. My man has brought the most surprising news i' the world.

DORIMANT Some strange misfortune is befall'n your love?

YOUNG BELLAIR My father came to town last night and lodges i' the very house where Emilia lies.

MEDLEY Does he know it is with her you are in love?

YOUNG BELLAIR He knows I love, but knows not whom, without some officious sot has betrayed me.

DORIMANT Your Aunt Townley is your confidante and favors the business.

YOUNG BELLAIR I do not apprehend any ill office from her. I have received a letter, in which I am commanded by my father to meet him at my aunt's this afternoon. He tells me farther he has made a match for me, and bids me resolve to be obedient to his will or expect to be disinherited.

MEDLEY Now's your time, Bellair. Never had lover such an opportunity of giving a generous proof of his passion.

YOUNG BELLAIR As how, I pray?

MEDLEY Why, hang an estate, marry Emilia out of hand, and provoke your father to do what he threatens. 'Tis but despising a coach, humbling yourself to a pair of galoshes, being out of countenance when you meet your friends, pointed at and pitied wherever you go by all the amorous fops that know you, and your fame will be immortal.

YOUNG BELLAIR I could find in my heart to resolve not to marry at all.

DORIMANT Fie, fie! That would spoil a good jest and disappoint the well-natured town of an occasion of laughing at you.

YOUNG BELLAIR The storm I have so long expected hangs o'er my head and begins to pour down upon me. I am on the rack and can have no rest till I'm satisfied in what I fear. Where do you dine?

DORIMANT At Long's or Locket's.[2]

MEDLEY At Long's let it be.

YOUNG BELLAIR I'll run and see Emilia and inform myself how matters stand. If my misfortunes are not so great as to make me unfit for company, I'll be with you.

Exit Young Bellair.

Enter a Footman, *with a letter.*

FOOTMAN [*to* Dorimant] Here's a letter, sir.

DORIMANT The superscripiton's right: "For Mr. Dorimant."

MEDLEY Let's see. The very scrawl and spelling of a true-bred whore.

DORIMANT I know the hand. The style is admirable, I assure you.

MEDLEY Prithee, read it.

DORIMANT [*reads*] "I told a you you dud not love me, if you dud, you would have seen me again ere now. I have no money and am very malicolly. Pray send me a guynie to see the operies. Your servant to command, Molly."

MEDLEY Pray let the whore have a favorable answer, that she may spark it in a box and do honor to her profession.

DORIMANT She shall, and perk up i' the face of quality. [*To* Handy.] Is the coach at door?

HANDY You did not bid me send for it.

DORIMANT Eternal blockhead!

Handy *offers to go out.*

Hey, sot!

HANDY Did you call me, sir?

DORIMANT I hope you have no just exception to the name, sir?

HANDY I have sense, sir.

DORIMANT Not so much as a fly in winter.—How did you come, Medley?

MEDLEY In a chair.

FOOTMAN You may have a hackney coach if you please, sir.

DORIMANT I may ride the elephant if I please, sir. Call another chair and let my coach follow to Long's.

Exeunt Footman *and* Handy.

"Be calm, ye great parents, etc."[3]

Exeunt, singing.

Act II. Scene i. Lady Townley's *house.*
Enter my Lady Townley *and* Emilia.

LADY TOWNLEY I was afraid, Emilia, all had been discovered.

EMILIA I tremble with the apprehension still.

LADY TOWNLEY That my brother should take lodgings i' the very house where you lie!

EMILIA 'Twas lucky we had timely notice to warn the people to be secret. He seems to be a mighty good-humoured old man.

2. Fashionable taverns.   3. Apparently a contemporary song.

LADY TOWNLEY He ever had a notable smirking way with him.

EMILIA He calls me rogue, tells me he can't abide me, and does so bepat me.

LADY TOWNLEY On my word, you are much in his favor then.

EMILIA He has been very inquisitive, I am told, about my family, my reputation, and my fortune.

LADY TOWNLEY I am confident he does not i' the least suspect you are the woman his son's in love with.

EMILIA What should make him then inform himself so particularly of me?

LADY TOWNLEY He was always of a very loving temper himself. It may be he has a doting fit upon him, who knows?

EMILIA It cannot be.

Enter Young Bellair.

LADY TOWNLEY Here comes my nephew.—Where did you leave your father?

YOUNG BELLAIR Writing a note within.—Emilia, this early visit looks as if some kind jealousy would not let you rest at home.

EMILIA The knowledge I have of my rival gives me a little cause to fear your constancy.

YOUNG BELLAIR My constancy! I vow—

EMILIA Do not vow. Our love is frail as is our life, and full as little in our power; and are you sure you shall outlive this day?

YOUNG BELLAIR I am not, but when we are in perfect health, 'twere an idle thing to fright ourselves with the thoughts of sudden death.

LADY TOWNLEY Pray, what has passed between you and your father i' the garden?

YOUNG BELLAIR He's firm in his resolution, tells me I must marry Mrs. Harriet, or swears he'll marry himself and disinherit me. When I saw I could not prevail with him to be more indulgent, I dissembled an obedience to his will, which has composed his passion and will give us time—and I hope opportunity—to deceive him.

Enter Old Bellair, *with a note in his hand.*

LADY TOWNLEY Peace, here he comes.

OLD BELLAIR Harry, take this and let your man carry it for me to Mr. Fourbe's[4] chamber—my lawyer, i' the Temple.[5]

Exit Young Bellair.

[*To* Emilia.] Neighbor, adod I am glad to see thee here.—Make much of her, sister. She's one of the best of your acquaintance. I like her countenance and behavior well; she has a modesty that is not common i' this age, adod she has.

LADY TOWNLEY I know her value, brother, and esteem her accordingly.

OLD BELLAIR Advise her to wear a little more mirth in her face. Adod, she's too serious.

4. From *fourbe* (French), a cheat.
5. Center of the legal profession in London.

LADY TOWNLEY The fault is very excusable in a young woman.

OLD BELLAIR Nay, adod, I like her ne'er the worse; a melancholy beauty has her charms. I love a pretty sadness in a face which varies now and then, like changeable colors, into a smile.

LADY TOWNLEY Methinks you speak very feelingly, brother.

OLD BELLAIR I am but five-and-fifty, sister, you know—an age not altogether insensible. [*To Emilia.*] Cheer up, sweetheart, I have a secret to tell thee may chance to make thee merry. We three will make collation together anon. I' the meantime, mum, I can't abide you; go, I can't abide you.

Enter Young Bellair.

Harry! Come, you must along with me to my Lady Woodvill's. —I am going to slip the boy at a mistress.

YOUNG BELLAIR At a wife, sir, you would say.

OLD BELLAIR You need not look so glum, sir. A wife is no curse when she brings the blessing of a good estate with her. But an idle town flirt, with a painted face, a rotten reputation, and a crazy fortune, adod, is the devil and all; and such a one I hear you are in league with.

YOUNG BELLAIR I cannot help detraction, sir.

OLD BELLAIR Out, a pize[6] o' their breeches, there are keeping fools enough for such flaunting baggages, and they are e'en too good for 'em. [*To Emilia.*] Remember night. [*Aloud.*] Go, y'are a rogue, y'are a rogue. Fare you well, fare you well. [*To Young Bellair.*] Come, come, come along, sir.

Exeunt Old *and* Young Bellair.

LADY TOWNLEY On my word, the old man comes on apace. I'll lay my life he's smitten.

EMILIA This is nothing but the pleasantness of his humour.

LADY TOWNLEY I know him better than you. Let it work; it may prove lucky.

Enter a Page.

PAGE Madam, Mr. Medley has sent to know whether a visit will not be troublesome this afternoon?

LADY TOWNLEY Send him word his visits never are so.

Exit Page.

EMILIA He's a very pleasant man.

LADY TOWNLEY He's a very necessary man among us women. He's not scandalous i' the least, perpetually contriving to bring good company together, and always ready to stop up a gap at ombre.[7] Then, he knows all the little news o' the town.

EMILIA I love to hear him talk o' the intrigues. Let 'em be never so dull in themselves, he'll make 'em pleasant i' the relation.

LADY TOWNLEY But he improves things so much one can take no measure of the truth from him. Mr. Dorimant swears a flea or a maggot is not made more monstrous by a magnifying glass than a story is by his telling it.

Enter Medley.

6. An imprecation, as in *a pox.*   7. Card game, often for three players.

EMILIA Hold, here he comes.

LADY TOWNLEY Mr. Medley.

MEDLEY Your servant, madam.

LADY TOWNLEY You have made yourself a stranger of late.

EMILIA I believe you took a surfeit of ombre last time you were here.

MEDLEY Indeed I had my bellyful of that termagant, Lady Dealer. There never was so insatiable a carder; an old gleeker[8] never loved to sit to 't like her. I have played with her, now at least a dozen times, till she 'as worn out all her fine complexion and her tour[9] would keep in curl no longer.

LADY TOWNLEY Blame her not, poor woman. She loves nothing so well as a black ace.

MEDLEY The pleasure I have seen her in when she has had hope in drawing for a matador![1]

EMILIA 'Tis as pretty sport to her as persuading masks off is to you, to make discoveries.

LADY TOWNLEY Pray, where's your friend Mr. Dorimant?

MEDLEY Soliciting his affairs. He's a man of great employment— has more mistresses now depending than the most eminent lawyer in England has causes.

EMILIA Here has been Mrs. Loveit so uneasy and out of humor these two days.

LADY TOWNLEY How strangely love and jealousy rage in that poor woman!

MEDLEY She could not have picked out a devil upon earth so proper to torment her. H'as made her break a dozen or two of fans already, tear half a score points in pieces, and destroy hoods and knots without number.

LADY TOWNLEY We heard of a pleasant serenade he gave her t'other night.

MEDLEY A Danish serenade, with kettledrums and trumpets.

EMILIA Oh, barbarous!

MEDLEY What, you are of the number of the ladies whose ears are grown so delicate since our operas, you can be charmed with nothing but *flûtes* douces and French hautboys?[2]

EMILIA Leave your raillery and tell us, is there any new wit come forth—songs, or novels?

MEDLEY A very pretty piece of gallantry, by an eminent author, called *The Diversions of Brussels*[3]—very necessary to be read by all old ladies who are desirous to improve themselves at questions and commands, blindman's buff, and the like fashionable recreations.

EMILIA Oh, ridiculous!

MEDLEY Then there is *The Art of Affectation*, written by a late beauty of quality, teaching you how to draw up your breasts, stretch up your neck, to thrust out your breech, to play with your

---

8. Gleek was a card game.
9. Front of false hair.
1. High trump—such as a black ace.

2. High-pitched flutes and French oboes.
3. Medley's book titles are imaginary.

head, to toss up your nose, to bite your lips, to turn up your eyes, to speak in a silly soft tone of a voice, and use all the foolish French words that will infallibly make your person and conversation charming; with a short apology at the latter end, in the behalf of young ladies who notoriously wash and paint, though they have naturally good complexions.

EMILIA What a deal of stuff you tell us!

MEDLEY Such as the town affords, madam. The Russians, hearing the great respect we have for foreign dancing, have lately sent over some of their best balladines, who are now practicing a famous ballet which will be suddenly danced at the Bear Garden.[4]

LADY TOWNLEY Pray forbear your idle stories, and give us an account of the state of love as it now stands.

MEDLEY Truly there has been some revolutions in those affairs: great chopping and changing among the old, and some new lovers, whom malice, indiscretion, and misfortune have luckily brought into play.

LADY TOWNLEY What think you of walking into the next rom and sitting down, before you engage in this business?

MEDLEY I wait upon you; and I hope (though women are commonly unreasonable) by the plenty of scandal I shall discover, to give you very good content, ladies.

Exeunt.

Act II. *Scene ii.* Mrs. Loveit's.
Enter Mrs. Loveit *and* Pert; Mrs. Loveit *putting up a letter, then pulling out her pocket glass and looking in it.*

MRS. LOVEIT Pert.

PERT Madam?

MRS. LOVEIT I hate myself, I look so ill today.

PERT Hate the wicked cause on't, that base man Mr. Dorimant, who makes you torment and vex yourself continually.

MRS. LOVEIT He is to blame, indeed.

PERT To blame to be two days without sending, writing, or coming near you, contrary to his oath and covenant! 'Twas to much purpose to make him swear! I'll lay my life there's not an article but he has broken: talked to the vizards i' the pit, waited upon the ladies from the boxes to their coaches, gone behind the scenes and fawned upon those little insignificant creatures, the players. 'Tis impossible for a man of his inconstant temper to forbear, I'm sure.

MRS. LOVEIT I know he is a devil, but he has something of the angel yet undefaced in him, which makes him so charming and agreeable that I must love him, be he never so wicked.

PERT I little thought, madam, to see your spirit tamed to this degree, who banished poor Mr. Lackwit but for taking up another lady's fan in your presence.

MRS. LOVEIT My knowing of such odious fools contributes to the making of me love Dorimant the better.

4. Theater for bear-baiting. Medley is still carrying on.

PERT Your knowing of Mr. Dorimant, in my mind, should rather make you hate all mankind.

MRS. LOVEIT So it does, besides himself.

PERT Pray, what excuse does he make in his letter?

MRS. LOVEIT He has had business.

PERT Business in general terms would not have been a current excuse for another. A modish man is always very busy when he is in pursuit of a new mistress.

MRS. LOVEIT Some fop has bribed you to rail at him. He had business; I will believe it and will forgive him.

PERT You may forgive him anything, but I shall never forgive him his turning me into ridicule, as I hear he does.

MRS. LOVEIT I perceive you are of the number of those fools his wit had made his enemies.

PERT I am of the number of those he's pleased to rally, madam; and if we may believe Mr. Wagfan and Mr. Caperwell, he sometimes makes merry with yourself, too, among his laughing companions.

MRS. LOVEIT Blockheads are as malicious to witty men as ugly women are to the handsome; 'tis their interest, and they make it their business to defame 'em.

PERT I wish Mr. Dorimant would not make it his business to defame you.

MRS. LOVEIT Should he, I had rather be made infamous by him than owe my reputation to the dull discretion of those fops you talk of.

Enter Bellinda.

Bellinda!

Running to her.

BELLINDA My dear!

MRS. LOVEIT You have been unkind of late.

BELLINDA Do not say unkind, say unhappy.

MRS. LOVEIT I could chide you. Where have you been these two days?

BELLINDA Pity me rather, my dear, where I have been so tired with two or three country gentlewomen, whose conversation has been more insufferable than a country fiddle.

MRS. LOVEIT Are they relations?

BELLINDA No, Welsh acquaintance I made when I was last year at St. Winifred's.[5] They have asked me a thousand questions of the modes and intrigues of the town, and I have told 'em almost as many things for news that hardly were so when their gowns were in fashion.

MRS. LOVEIT Provoking creatures, how could you endure 'em?

BELLINDA [*aside*] Now to carry on my plot; nothing but love could make me capable of so much falsehood. 'Tis time to begin, lest Dorimant should come before her jealousy has stung her.

Laughs and then speaks on.

5. In Wales. The town of Holywell takes its name from St. Winifred's well, which supposedly arose where St. Winifred was killed by a pagan.

I was yesterday at a play with 'em, where I was fain to show 'em the living, as the man at Westminster does the dead. That is Mrs. Such-a-one, admired for her beauty; this is Mr. Such-a-one, cried up for a wit; that is sparkish Mr. Such-a-one, who keeps reverend Mrs. Such-a-one; and there sits fine Mrs. Such-a-one, who was lately cast off by my Lord Such-a-one.

MRS. LOVEIT Did you see Dorimant there?

BELLINDA I did; and imagine you were there with him and have no mind to own it.

MRS. LOVEIT What should make you think so?

BELLINDA A lady masked, in a pretty *déshabillé*, whom Dorimant entertained with more respect than the gallants do a common vizard.

MRS. LOVEIT [*aside*] Dorimant at a play entertaining a mask! Oh, heavens!

BELLINDA [*aside*] Good!

MRS. LOVEIT Did he stay all the while?

BELLINDA Till the play was done, and then led her out; which confirms me it was you.

MRS. LOVEIT Traitor!

PERT Now you may believe he had business, and you may forgive him too.

MRS. LOVEIT Ungrateful, perjured man!

BELLINDA You seem so much concerned, my dear, I fear I have told you unawares what I had better have concealed for your quiet.

MRS. LOVEIT What manner of shape had she?

BELLINDA Tall and slender. Her motions were very genteel. Certainly she must be some person of condition.

MRS. LOVEIT Shame and confusion be ever in her face when she shows it!

BELLINDA I should blame your discretion for loving that wild man, my dear; but they say he has a way so bewitching that few can defend their hearts who know him.

MRS. LOVEIT I will tear him from mine, or die i' the attempt!

BELLINDA Be more moderate.

MRS. LOVEIT Would I had daggers, darts, or poisoned arrows in my breast, so I could but remove the thoughts of him from thence!

BELLINDA Fie, fie, your transports are too violent, my dear. This may be but an accidental gallantry, and 'tis likely ended at her coach.

PERT Should it proceed farther, let your comfort be, the conduct Mr. Dorimant affects will quickly make you know your rival, ten to one let you see her ruined, her reputation exposed to the town —a happiness none will envy her but yourself, madam.

MRS. LOVEIT Whoe'er she be, all the harm I wish her is, may she love him as well as I do, and may he give her as much cause to hate him!

PERT Never doubt the latter end of your curse, madam.

MRS. LOVEIT May all the passions that are raised by neglected love

—jealousy, indignation, spite, and thirst of revenge—eternally rage in her soul, as they do now in mine!

Walks up and down with a distracted air.

Enter a Page.

PAGE Madam, Mr. Dorimant—

MRS. LOVEIT I will not see him.

PAGE I told him you were within, madam.

MRS. LOVEIT Say you lied, say I'm busy—shut the door—say anything!

PAGE He's here, madam.

Enter Dorimant.

Exit Page.

DORIMANT

"They taste of death who do at heaven arrive;
   But we this paradise approach alive."[6]

[*To* Mrs. Loveit.] What, dancing the galloping nag[7] without a fiddle?

Offers to catch her by the hand; she flings away and walks on.

I fear this restlessness of the body, madam, [*pursuing her*] proceeds from an unquietness of the mind. What unlucky accident puts you out of humour—a point ill-washed, knots spoiled i' the making up, hair shaded awry, or some other little mistake in setting you in order?

PERT A trifle, in my opinion, sir, more inconsiderable than any you mention.

DORIMANT Oh, Mrs. Pert! I never knew you sullen enough to be silent. Come, let me know the business.

PERT The business, sir, the business that has taken you up these two days. How have I seen you laugh at men of business, and now to become a man of business yourself!

DORIMANT We are not masters of our own affections; our inclinations daily alter. Now we love pleasure, and anon we shall dote on business. Human frailty will have it so, and who can help it?

MRS. LOVEIT Faithless, inhuman, barbarous man—

DORIMANT [*aside*] Good. Now the alarm strikes.

MRS. LOVEIT —Without sense of love, of honor, or of gratitude! Tell me, for I will know, what devil masked she was, you were with at the play yesterday.

DORIMANT Faith, I resolved as much as you, but the devil was obstinate and would not tell me.

MRS. LOVEIT False in this as in your vows to me! You do know!

DORIMANT The truth is, I did all I could to know.

MRS. LOVEIT And dare you own it to my face? Hell and furies!

Tears her fan in pieces.

DORIMANT Spare your fan, madam. You are growing hot and will want it to cool you.

6. Opening lines of Waller's "Of Her Chamber."   7. Country dance.

MRS. LOVEIT Horror and distraction seize you! Sorrow and remorse gnaw your soul and punish all your perjuries to me!

Weeps.

DORIMANT [*turning to* Bellinda]

"So thunder breaks the cloud in twain.
And makes a passage for the rain."[8]

[*To* Bellinda.] Bellinda, you are the devil that have raised this storm. You were at the play yesterday and have been making discoveries to your dear.

BELLINDA Y'are the most mistaken man i' the world.

DORIMANT It must be so, and here I vow revenge—resolve to pursue and persecute you more impertinently than ever any loving fop did his mistress, hunt you i' the Park, trace you i' the Mall,[9] dog you in every visit you make, haunt you at the plays and i' the drawing room, hang my nose in your neck and talk to you whether you will or no, and ever look upon you with such dying eyes till your friends grow jealous of me, send you out of town, and the world suspect your reputation. [*In a lower voice.*] At my Lady Townley's when we go from hence.

He looks kindly on Bellinda.

BELLINDA I'll meet you there.

DORIMANT Enough.

MRS. LOVEIT [*pushing* Dorimant *away*] Stand off! You sha' not stare upon her so.

DORIMANT Good, there's one made jealous already.

MRS. LOVEIT Is this the constancy you vowed?

DORIMANT Constancy at my years? 'Tis not a virtue in season; you might as well expect the fruit the autumn ripens i' the spring.

MRS. LOVEIT Monstrous principle!

DORIMANT Youth has a long journey to go, madam. Should I have set up my rest at the first inn I lodged at, I should never have arrived at the happiness I now enjoy.

MRS. LOVEIT Dissembler, damned dissembler!

DORIMANT I am so, I confess. Good nature and good manners corrupt me. I am honest in my inclinations and would not, wer't not to avoid offense, make a lady a little in years believe I think her young, wilfully mistake art for nature, and seem as fond of a thing I am weary of as when I doted on't in earnest.

MRS. LOVEIT False man!

DORIMANT True woman.

MRS. LOVEIT Now you begin to show yourself.

DORIMANT Love gilds us over and makes us show fine things to one another for a time; but soon the gold wears off, and then again the native brass appears.

MRS. LOVEIT Think on your oaths, your vows, and protestations, perjured man!

DORIMANT I made 'em when I was in love.

---

8. Matthew Roydon, "An Elegy ... for his Astrophel" (i.e., Sir Philip Sidney), lines 59–60.
9. A fashionable walk in St. James's Park.

MRS. LOVEIT And therefore ought they not to bind? Oh, impious!

DORIMANT What we swear at such a time may be a certain proof of a present passion; but to say truth, in love there is no security to be given for the future.

MRS. LOVEIT Horrid and ungrateful, begone! And never see me more!

DORIMANT I am not one of those troublesome coxcombs who, because they were once well-received, take the privilege to plague a woman with their love ever after. I shall obey you, madam, though I do myself some violence.

He offers to go, and Mrs. Loveit *pulls him back.*

MRS. LOVEIT Come back, you sha' not go! Could you have the ill nature to offer it?

DORIMANT When love grows diseased, the best thing we can do is to put it to a violent death. I cannot endure the torture of a ling'ring and consumptive passion.

MRS. LOVEIT Can you think mine sickly?

DORIMANT Oh, 'tis desperately ill! What worse symptoms are there than your being always uneasy when I visit you, your picking quarrels with me on slight occasions, and in my absence kindly list'ning to the impertinences of every fashionable fool that talks to you?

MRS. LOVEIT What fashionable fool can you lay to my charge?

DORIMANT Why, the very cock-fool of all those fools, Sir Fopling Flutter.

MRS. LOVEIT I never saw him in my life but once.

DORIMANT The worse woman you, at first sight to put on all your charms, to entertain him with that softness in your voice and all that wanton kindness in your eyes you so notoriously affect when you design a conquest.

MRS. LOVEIT So damned a lie did never malice yet invent. Who told you this?

DORIMANT No matter. That ever I should love a woman that can dote on a senseless caper, a tawdry French ribbon, and a formal cravat!

MRS. LOVEIT You make me mad!

DORIMANT A guilty conscience may do much. Go on, be the game-mistress of the town and enter[1] all our young fops, as fast as they come from travel.

MRS. LOVEIT Base and scurrilous!

DORIMANT A fine mortifying reputation 'twill be for a woman of your pride, wit, and quality!

MRS. LOVEIT This jealousy's a mere pretense, a cursed trick of your own devising. I know you.

DORIMANT Believe it and all the ill of me you can. I would not have a woman have the least good thought of me that can think well of Fopling. Farewell. Fall to, and much good may do you with your coxcomb.

1. Train.

MRS. LOVEIT Stay! Oh stay, and I will tell you all.

DORIMANT I have been told too much already.

Exit Dorimant.

MRS. LOVEIT Call him again!

PERT E'en let him go. A fair riddance!

MRS. LOVEIT Run, I say, call him again. I will have him called!

PERT The devil should carry him away first, were it my concern.

Exit Pert.

BELLINDA H'as frighted me from the very thoughts of loving men. For heav'n's sake, my dear, do not discover what I told you. I dread his tongue as much as you ought to have done his friendship.

Enter Pert.

PERT He's gone, madam.

MRS. LOVEIT Lightning blast him!

PERT When I told him you desired him to come back, he smiled, made a mouth at me, flung into his coach and said—

MRS. LOVEIT What did he say?

PERT "Drive away"; and then repeated verses.

MRS. LOVEIT Would I had made a contract to be a witch when first I entertained this greater devil. Monster, barbarian! I could tear myself in pieces. Revenge, nothing but revenge can ease me. Plague, war, famine, fire, all that can bring universal ruin and misery on mankind—with joy I'd perish to have you in my power but this moment!

Exit Mrs. Loveit.

PERT Follow, madam. Leave her not in this outrageous passion.

Pert *gathers up the things.*

BELLINDA H'as given me the proof which I desired of his love; but 'tis a proof of his ill nature too. I wish I had not seen him use her so.

I sigh to think that Dorimant may be
One day as faithless and unkind to me.

Exeunt.

Act III. Scene i. Lady Woodvill's *lodgings.*
Enter Harriet *and* Busy, *her woman.*

BUSY Dear madam, let me set that curl in order.

HARRIET Let me alone, I will shake 'em all out of order!

BUSY Will you never leave this wildness?

HARRIET Torment me not.

BUSY Look, there's a knot falling off.

HARRIET Let it drop.

BUSY But one pin, dear madam.

HARRIET How do I daily suffer under thy officious fingers!

BUSY Ah, the difference that is between you and my Lady Dapper! How uneasy she is if the least thing be amiss about her!

HARRIET She is indeed most exact. Nothing is ever wanting to make her ugliness remarkable.

BUSY Jeering people say so.

HARRIET Her powdering, painting, and her patching never fail in public to draw the tongues and eyes of all the men upon her.

BUSY She is indeed a little too pretending.

HARRIET That women should set up for beauty as much in spite of nature as some men have done for wit!

BUSY I hope without offense one may endeavor to make one's self agreeable.

HARRIET Not when 'tis impossible. Women then ought to be no more fond of dressing than fools should be of talking. Hoods and modesty, masks and silence, things that shadow and conceal— they should think of nothing else.

BUSY Jesu, madam! What will your mother think is become of you? For heav'n's sake, go in again.

HARRIET I won't.

BUSY This is the extravagant'st thing that ever you did in your life, to leave her and a gentleman who is to be your husband.

HARRIET My husband! Hast thou so little wit to think I spoke what I meant when I overjoyed her in the country with a low curtsy and "What you please, madam; I shall ever be obedient"?

BUSY Nay, I know not, you have so many fetches.[2]

HARRIET And this was one, to get her up to London. Nothing else, I assure thee.

BUSY Well! The man, in my mind, is a fine man.

HARRIET The man indeed wears his clothes fashionably and has a pretty, negligent way with him, very courtly and much affected. He bows, and talks, and smiles so agreeably as he thinks.

BUSY I never saw anything so genteel.

HARRIET Varnished over with good breeding, many a blockhead makes a tolerable show.

BUSY I wonder you do not like him.

HARRIET I think I might be brought to endure him, and that is all a reasonable woman should expect in a husband; but there is duty i' the case, and like the haughty Merab, I

> "Find much aversion in my stubborn mind,"

which

> "Is bred by being promised and designed."[3]

BUSY I wish you do not design your own ruin. I partly guess your inclinations, madam. That Mr. Dorimant—

HARRIET Leave your prating and sing some foolish song or other.

BUSY I will—the song you love so well ever since you saw Mr. Dorimant.

SONG

When first Amintas charmed my heart,
My heedless sheep began to stray;
The wolves soon stole the greatest part,
and all will now be made a prey.

2. Tricks.
3. Merab (see 1 Samuel) was promised to David but then married to Adriel. The couplet is based upon Abraham Cowley's description of Merab in *Davideis*, Book III.

Ah, let not love your thoughts possess,
'Tis fatal to a shepherdess;
The dang'rous passion you must shun,
Or else like me be quite undone.

HARRIET Shall I be paid down by a covetous parent for a purchase?
I need no land. No, I'll lay myself out all in love. It is decreed.
Enter Young Bellair.

YOUNG BELLAIR What generous resolution are you making,
madam?

HARRIET Only to be disobedient, sir.

YOUNG BELLAIR Let me join hands with you in that.

HARRIET With all my heart. I never thought I should have given
you mine so willingly. Here.
They join hands.
I, Harriet—

YOUNG BELLAIR And I, Harry—

HARRIET Do solemnly protest—

YOUNG BELLAIR And vow—

HARRIET That I with you—

YOUNG BELLAIR And I with you—

HARRIET, YOUNG BELLAIR Will never marry.

HARRIET A match!

YOUNG BELLAIR And no match! How do you like this indifference
now?

HARRIET You expect I should take it ill, I see.

YOUNG BELLAIR 'Tis not unnatural for you women to be a little
angry, you miss a conquest—though you would slight the poor
man were he in your power.

HARRIET There are some, it may be, have an eye like Bart'lomew,
big enough for the whole fair;[4] but I am not of the number, and
you may keep your gingerbread.[5] 'Twill be more acceptable to
the lady whose dear image it wears.

YOUNG BELLAIR I must confess, madam, you came a day after the
fair.

HARRIET And own then you are in love?

YOUNG BELLAIR I do.

HARRIET The confidence is generous, and in return I could almost
find in my heart to let you know my inclinations.

YOUNG BELLAIR Are you in love?

HARRIET Yes—with this dear town, to that degree I can scarce
endure the country in landscapes and in hangings.

YOUNG BELLAIR What a dreadful thing 'twould be to be hurried
back to Hampshire!

HARRIET Ah, name it not.

YOUNG BELLAIR As for us, I find we shall agree well enough.
Would we could do something to deceive the grave people!

HARRIET Could we delay their quick proceeding, 'twere well. A

4. An allusion to Bartholomew Cokes in
Jonson's *Bartholomew Fair*, who wants to
buy everything in sight. The fair was held
annually in August.
5. A popular item at the fair.

reprieve is a good step towards the getting of a pardon.

YOUNG BELLAIR If we give over the game, we are undone. What think you of playing it on booty?[6]

HARRIET What do you mean?

YOUNG BELLAIR Pretend to be in love with one another. 'Twill make some dilatory excuses we may feign pass the better.

HARRIET Let us do't, if it be but for the dear pleasure of dissembling.

YOUNG BELLAIR Can you play your part?

HARRIET I know not what it is to love, but I have made pretty remarks by being now and then where lovers meet. Where did you leave their gravities?

YOUNG BELLAIR I' th' next room. Your mother was censuring our modern gallant.

Enter Old Bellair *and* Lady Woodvill.

HARRIET Peace, here they come. I will lean against this wall and look bashfully down upon my fan while you, like an amorous spark, modishly entertain me.

LADY WOODVILL [*to* Old Bellair] Never go about to excuse 'em. Come, come, it was not so when I was a young woman.

OLD BELLAIR Adod, they're something disrespectful—

LADY WOODVILL Quality was then considered and not rallied by every fleering fellow.

OLD BELLAIR Youth will have its jest, adod it will.

LADY WOODVILL 'Tis good breeding now to be civil to none but players and Exchange women.[7] They are treated by 'em as much above their condition as others are below theirs.

OLD BELLAIR Out, a pize on 'em! Talk no more: the rogues ha' got an ill habit of preferring beauty, no matter where they find it.

LADY WOODVILL See your son and my daughter. They have improved their acquaintance since they were within.

OLD BELLAIR Adod, methinks they have! Let's keep back and observe.

YOUNG BELLAIR [*to* Harriet] Now for a look and gestures that may persuade 'em I am saying all the passionate things imaginable.

HARRIET Your head a little more on one side. Ease yourself on your left leg and play with your right hand.

YOUNG BELLAIR Thus, is it not?

HARRIET Now set your right leg firm on the ground, adjust your belt, then look about you.

YOUNG BELLAIR A little exercising will make me perfect.

HARRIET Smile, and turn to me again very sparkish.

YOUNG BELLAIR Will you take your turn and be instructed?

HARRIET With all my heart.

YOUNG BELLAIR At one motion play your fan, roll your eyes, and then settle a kind look upon me.

HARRIET So.

YOUNG BELLAIR Now spread your fan, look down upon it, and tell the sticks with a finger.

HARRIET Very modish.

6. Conspiring against the others.   7. Shopkeepers at the New Exchange.

YOUNG BELLAIR Clap your hand upon your bosom, hold down your gown. Shrug a little, draw up your breasts and let 'em fall again, gently, with a sigh or two, *etc.*

HARRIET By the good instructions you give, I suspect you for one of those malicious observers who watch people's eyes, and from innocent looks make scandalous conclusions.

YOUNG BELLAIR I know some, indeed, who out of mere love to mischief are as vigilant as jealousy itself, and will give you an account of every glance that passes at a play and i' th' Circle.[8]

HARRIET 'Twill not be amiss now to seem a little pleasant.

YOUNG BELLAIR Clap your fan then in both your hands, snatch it to your mouth, smile, and with a lively motion fling your body a little forwards. So! Now spread it, fall back on the sudden, cover your face with it, and break out into a loud laughter. —Take up! Look grave and fall a-fanning to yourself. Admirably well acted!

HARRIET I think I am pretty apt at these matters.

OLD BELLAIR [*to* Lady Woodvill] Adod, I like this well.

LADY WOODVILL This promises something.

OLD BELLAIR Come, there is love i' th' case, adod there is, or will be. [*To* Harriet] —What say you, young lady?

HARRIET All in good time, sir. You expect we should fall to and love as gamecocks fight, as soon as we are set together. Adod, y'are unreasonable!

OLD BELLAIR Adod, sirrah, I like thy wit well.

   Enter a Servant.

SERVANT The coach is at the door, madam.

OLD BELLAIR Go, get you and take the air together.

LADY WOODVILL Will not you go with us?

OLD BELLAIR Out a pize! Adod, I ha' business and cannot. We shall meet at night at my sister Townley's.

YOUNG BELLAIR [*aside*] He's going to Emilia. I overheard him talk of a collation.

                                                    Exeunt.

   Act III. Scene ii. Lady Townley's.
   Enter Lady Townley, Emilia, *and* Medley.

LADY TOWNLEY I pity the young lovers we last talked of, though to say truth, their conduct has been so indiscreet they deserve to be unfortunate.

MEDLEY Y' have an exact account, from the great lady i' th' box down to the little orange-wench.

EMILIA Y'are a living libel, a breathing lampoon. I wonder you are not torn in pieces.

MEDLEY What think you of setting up an office of intelligence for these matters? The project may get money.

LADY TOWNLEY You would have great dealings with country ladies.

MEDLEY More than Muddiman[9] has with their husbands!

   Enter Bellinda.

8. Circular path in Hyde Park.   of "newsletters."
9. Henry Muddiman, contemporary writer

LADY TOWNLEY Bellinda, what has been become of you? We have
not seen you here of late with your friend Mrs. Loveit.

BELLINDA Dear creature, I left her but now so sadly afflicted.

LADY TOWNLEY With her old distemper, jealousy?

MEDLEY Dorimant has played her some new prank.

BELLINDA Well, that Dorimant is certainly the worst man breathing.

EMILIA I once thought so.

BELLINDA And do you not think so still?

EMILIA No, indeed.

BELLINDA Oh, Jesu!

EMILIA The town does him a great deal of injury, and I will never
believe what it says of a man I do not know, again, for his sake.

BELLINDA You make me wonder.

LADY TOWNLEY He's a very well-bred man.

BELLINDA But strangely ill-natured.

EMILIA Then he's a very witty man.

BELLINDA But a man of no principles.

MEDLEY Your man of principles is a very fine thing, indeed!

BELLINDA To be preferred to men of parts by women who have
regard to their reputation and quiet. Well, were I minded to play
the fool, he should be the last man I'd think of.

MEDLEY He has been the first in many ladies' favors, though you
are so severe, madam.

LADY TOWNLEY What he may be for a lover, I know not; but he's a
very pleasant acquaintance, I am sure.

BELLINDA Had you seen him use Mrs. Loveit as I have done, you
would never endure him more.

EMILIA What, he has quarreled with her again?

BELLINDA Upon the slightest occasion. He's jealous of Sir Fopling.

LADY TOWNLEY She never saw him in her life but yesterday; and
that was here.

EMILIA On my conscience, he's the only man in town that's her
aversion. How horribly out of humour she was all the while he
talked to her!

BELLINDA And somebody has wickedly told him—

Enter Dorimant.

EMILIA Here he comes.

MEDLEY Dorimant, you are luckily come to justify yourself. Here's
a lady—

BELLINDA —Has a word or two to say to you from a disconsolate
person.

DORIMANT You tender your reputation too much, I know, madam,
to whisper with me before this good company.

BELLINDA To serve Mrs. Loveit, I'll make a bold venture.

DORIMANT Here's Medley, the very spirit of scandal.

BELLINDA No matter.

EMILIA 'Tis something you are unwilling to hear, Mr. Dorimant.

LADY TOWNLEY Tell him, Bellinda, whether he will or no.

BELLINDA [*aloud*] Mrs. Loveit—

DORIMANT Softly, these are laughers; you do not know 'em.

BELLINDA [*to* Dorimant, *apart*] In a word, y'ave made me hate you, which I thought you never could have done.

DORIMANT In obeying your commands?

BELLINDA 'Twas a cruel part you played. How could you act it?

DORIMANT Nothing is cruel to a man who could kill himself to please you. Remember, five o'clock tomorrow morning.

BELLINDA I tremble when you name it.

DORIMANT Be sure you come.

BELLINDA I sha' not.

DORIMANT Swear you will.

BELLINDA I dare not.

DORIMANT Swear, I say!

BELLINDA By my life, by all the happiness I hope for—

DORIMANT You will.

BELLINDA I will.

DORIMANT Kind.

BELLINDA I am glad I've sworn. I vow I think I should have failed you else.

DORIMANT Surprisingly kind! In what temper did you leave Loveit?

BELLINDA Her raving was prettily over, and she began to be in a brave way of defying you and all your works. Where have you been since you went from thence?

DORIMANT I looked in at the play.

BELLINDA I have promised and must return to her again.

DORIMANT Persuade her to walk in the Mall this evening.

BELLINDA She hates the place and will not come.

DORIMANT Do all you can to prevail with her.

BELLINDA For what purpose?

DORIMANT Sir Fopling will be here anon. I'll prepare him to set upon her there before me.

BELLINDA You persecute her too much. But I'll do all you'll ha' me.

DORIMANT [*aloud*] Tell her plainly, 'tis grown so dull a business I can drudge on no longer.

EMILIA There are afflictions in love, Mr. Dorimant.

DORIMANT You women make 'em, who are commonly as unreasonable in that as you are at play: without the advantage be on your side, a man can never quietly give over when he's weary.

MEDLEY If you would play without being obliged to complaisance, Dorimant, you should play in public places.

DORIMANT Ordinaries[1] were a very good thing for that, but gentlemen do not of late frequent 'em. The deep play is now in private houses.

Bellinda *offering to steal away.*

LADY TOWNLEY Bellinda, are you leaving us so soon?

BELLINDA I am to go to the Park with Mrs. Loveit, madam.

Exit Bellinda.

1. Taverns.

LADY TOWNLEY This confidence[2] will go nigh to spoil this young creature.

MEDLEY 'Twill do her good, madam. Young men who are brought up under practicing lawyers prove the abler counsel when they come to be called to the bar themselves.

DORIMANT The town has been very favorable to you this afternoon, my Lady Townley. You use to have an *embarras*[3] of chairs and coaches at your door, an uproar of footmen in your hall, and a noise of fools above here.

LADY TOWNLEY Indeed, my house is the general rendezvous and, next to the playhouse, is the common refuge of all the young idle people.

EMILIA Company is a very good thing, madam, but I wonder you do not love it a little more chosen.

LADY TOWNLEY 'Tis good to have an universal taste. We should love wit, but for variety be able to divert ourselves with the extravagancies of those who want it.

MEDLEY Fools will make you laugh.

EMILIA For once or twice; but the repetition of their folly after a visit or two grows tedious and insufferable.

LADY TOWNLEY You are a little too delicate, Emilia.

Enter a Page.

PAGE Sir Fopling Flutter, madam, desires to know if you are to be seen.

LADY TOWNLEY Here's the freshest fool in town, and one who has not cloyed you yet.—Page!

PAGE Madam?

LADY TOWNLEY Desire him to walk up.

Exit Page.

DORIMANT Do not you fall on him, Medley, and snub him. Soothe him up in his extravagance. He will show the better.

MEDLEY You know I have a natural indulgence for fools and need not this caution, sir.

Enter Sir Fopling, *with his Page after him.*

SIR FOPLING Page, wait without.

Exit Page.

[*To* Lady Townley.] Madam, I kiss your hands. I see yesterday was nothing of chance; the *belles assemblées*[4] form themselves here every day. [*To* Emilia.] Lady, your servant.—Dorimant, let me embrace thee. Without lying, I have not met with any of my acquaintance who retain so much of Paris as thou dost—the very air thou hadst when the marquise mistook thee i' th' Tuileries[5] and cried "Hé, chevalier!" and then begged thy pardon.

DORIMANT I would fain wear in fashion as long as I can, sir. 'Tis a thing to be valued in men as well as baubles.

SIR FOPLING Thou art a man of wit and understands the town. Prithee let thee and I be intimate. There is no living without

2. Confiding.
3. Congestion.

4. Fashionable gatherings.
5. The famous gardens in Paris.

making some good man the confidant of our pleasures.

DORIMANT 'Tis true; but there is no man so improper for such a business as I am.

SIR FOPLING Prithee, why hast thou so modest an opinion of thyself?

DORIMANT Why, first, I could never keep a secret in my life; and then, there is no charm so infallibly makes me fall in love with a woman as my knowing a friend loves her. I deal honestly with you.

SIR FOPLING. Thy humour's very gallant, or let me perish. I knew a French count so like thee.

LADY TOWNLEY Wit, I perceive, has more power over you than beauty, Sir Fopling, else you would not have let this lady stand so long neglected.

SIR FOPLING [*to* Emilia] A thousand pardons, madam. Some civility's due of course upon the meeting a long absent friend. The *éclat*[6] of so much beauty, I confess, ought to have charmed me sooner.

EMILIA The *brillant*[7] of so much good language, sir, has much more power than the little beauty I can boast.

SIR FOPLING I never saw anything prettier than this high work on your *point d'Espaigne*.[8]

EMILIA 'Tis not so rich as *point de Venise*.

SIR FOPLING Not altogether, but looks cooler, and is more proper for the season. —Dorimant, is not that Medley?

DORIMANT The same, sir.

SIR FOPLING [*to* Medley] Forgive me, sir; in this *embarras* of civilities I could not come to have you in my arms sooner. You understand an equipage the best of any man in town, I hear.

MEDLEY By my own you would not guess it.

SIR FOPLING There are critics who do not write, sir.

MEDLEY Our peevish poets will scarce allow it.

SIR FOPLING Damn 'em, they'll allow no man wit who does not play the fool like themselves and show it! Have you taken notice of the gallesh[9] I brought over?

MEDLEY Oh, yes! 'T has quite another air than th' English makes.

SIR FOPLING 'Tis as easily known from an English tumbril[1] as an Inns of Court man is from one of us.

DORIMANT Truly there is a *bel air*[2] in galleshes as well as men.

MEDLEY But there are few so delicate to observe it.

SIR FOPLING The world is generally very *grossier*[3] here, indeed.

LADY TOWNLEY [*to* Emilia] He's very fine.

EMILIA Extreme proper!

SIR FOPLING A slight suit I made to appear in at my first arrival— not worthy your consideration, ladies.

DORIMANT The pantaloon is very well mounted.

6. Brilliance.
7. Glitter.
8. Spanish lace. In the next line, Venetian lace.

9. *Calèche* (French), a light carriage.
1. Cart, often for dung.
2. Fine style.
3. Crude.

SIR FOPLING The tassels are new and pretty.

MEDLEY I never saw a coat better cut.

SIR FOPLING It makes me show long-waisted, and I think slender.

DORIMANT That's the shape our ladies dote on.

MEDLEY Your breech, though, is a handful too high, in my eye, Sir Fopling.

SIR FOPLING Peace, Medley, I have wished it lower a thousand times; but a pox on't, 'twill not be!

LADY TOWNLEY His gloves are well fringed, large and graceful.

SIR FOPLING I was always eminent for being *bien ganté*.[4]

EMILIA He wears nothing but what are originals of the most famous hands in Paris.

SIR FOPLING You are in the right, madam.

LADY TOWNLEY The suit?

SIR FOPLING Barroy.[5]

EMILIA The garniture?

SIR FOPLING Le Gras.

MEDLEY The shoes?

SIR FOPLING Piccar.

DORIMANT The periwig?

SIR FOPLING Chedreux.

LADY TOWNLEY, EMILIA The gloves?

SIR FOPLING Orangerie.[6] You know the smell, ladies. —Dorimant, I could find in my heart for an amusement to have a gallantry with some of our English ladies.

DORIMANT 'Tis a thing no less necessary to confirm the reputation of your wit than a duel will be to satisfy the town of your courage.

SIR FOPLING Here was a woman yesterday—

DORIMANT Mistress Loveit.

SIR FOPLING You have named her!

DORIMANT You cannot pitch on a better for your purpose.

SIR FOPLING Prithee, what is she?

DORIMANT A person of quality, and one who has a rest of reputation enough to make the conquest considerable. Besides, I hear she likes you too.

SIR FOPLING Methoughts she seemed, though, very reserved and uneasy all the time I entertained her.

DORIMANT Grimace and affectation! You will see her i' th' Mall tonight.

SIR FOPLING Prithee, let thee and I take the air together.

DORIMANT I am engaged to Medley, but I'll meet you at Saint James's[7] and give you some information upon the which you may regulate your proceedings.

SIR FOPLING All the world will be in the Park tonight. —Ladies, 'twere pity to keep so much beauty longer within doors and rob the Ring of all those charms that should adorn it. —Hey, page!

4. Well gloved.
5. Sir Fopling names a series of fashionable Parisian merchants.
6. Scented with orange.
7. St. James's Park.

Enter Page.

See that all my people be ready.

Page goes out again.

Dorimant, *a revoir.*[8]

Exit Sir Fopling.

MEDLEY A fine-mettled coxcomb.

DORIMANT Brisk and insipid.

MEDLEY Pert and dull.

EMILIA However you despise him, gentlemen, I'll lay my life he passes for a wit with many.

DORIMANT That may very well be. Nature has her cheats, stums[9] a brain, and puts sophisticate dullness often on the tasteless multitude for true wit and good humour. —Medley, come.

MEDLEY I must go a little way; I will meet you i' the Mall.

DORIMANT I'll walk through the garden thither. [*To the women.*] We shall meet anon and bow.

LADY TOWNLEY Not tonight. We are engaged about a business, the knowledge of which may make you laugh hereafter.

MEDLEY Your servant, ladies.

DORIMANT A *revoir*, as Sir Fopling says.

Exeunt Medley and Dorimant.

LADY TOWNLEY The old man will be here immediately.

EMILIA Let's expect him i' th' garden.

LADY TOWNLEY Go, you are a rogue!

EMILIA I can't abide you!

Exeunt.

Act III. Scene iii. *The Mall.*
Enter Harriet *and* Young Bellair, *she pulling him.*

HARRIET Come along!

YOUNG BELLAIR And leave your mother?

HARRIET Busy will be sent with a hue and cry after us; but that's no matter.

YOUNG BELLAIR 'Twill look strangely in me.

HARRIET She'll believe it a freak of mine and never blame your manners.

YOUNG BELLAIR [*pointing*] What reverend acquaintance is that she has met?

HARRIET A fellow beauty of the last king's time, though by the ruins you would hardly guess it.

Exeunt.

Enter Dorimant *and crosses the stage.*
Enter Young Bellair *and* Harriet.

YOUNG BELLAIR By this time your mother is in a fine taking.

HARRIET If your friend Mr. Dorimant were but here now, that she might find me talking with him!

YOUNG BELLAIR She does not know him but dreads him, I hear, of all mankind.

8. Sir Fopling mispronounces *au revoir.* At the end of the scene, Dorimant mimics him.

9. Renews, as wine is fermented by the addition of stum.

HARRIET She concludes if he does but speak to a woman, she's undone—is on her knees every day to pray heav'n defend me from him.

YOUNG BELLAIR You do not apprehend him so much as she does?

HARRIET I never saw anything in him that was frightful.

YOUNG BELLAIR On the contrary, have you not observed something extreme delightful in his wit and person?

HARRIET He's agreeable and pleasant, I must own, but he does so much affect being so, he displeases me.

YOUNG BELLAIR Lord, madam, all he does and says is so easy and so natural.

HARRIET Some men's verses seem so to the unskilful; but labor i' the one and affectation in the other to the judicious plainly appear.

YOUNG BELLAIR I never heard him accused of affectation before.

Enter Dorimant *and stares upon her.*

HARRIET It passes on the easy town, who are favorably pleased in him to call it humour.

Exeunt Young Bellair *and* Harriet.

DORIMANT 'Tis she! It must be she—that lovely hair, that easy shape, those wanton eyes, and all those melting charms about her mouth which Medley spoke of. I'll follow the lottery and put in for a prize with my friend Bellair.

Exit Dorimant, *repeating*:

"In love the victors from the vanquished fly;
They fly that wound, and they pursue that die."[1]

Enter Young Bellair *and* Harriet; *and after them* Dorimant, *standing at a distance.*

YOUNG BELLAIR Most people prefer High Park to this place.

HARRIET It has the better reputation, I confess; but I abominate the dull diversions there—the formal bows, the affected smiles, the silly by-words and amorous tweers[2] in passing. Here one meets with a little conversation now and then.

YOUNG BELLAIR These conversations have been fatal to some of your sex, madam.

HARRIET It may be so. Because some who want temper have been undone by gaming, must others who have it wholly deny themselves the pleasure of play?

DORIMANT [*coming up gently and bowing to her*] Trust me, it were unreasonable, madam.

She starts and looks grave.

HARRIET Lord, who's this?

YOUNG BELLAIR Dorimant.

DORIMANT Is this the woman your father would have you marry?

YOUNG BELLAIR It is.

DORIMANT Her name?

1. From Waller's "To a Friend, of the Different Success of their Loves," lines 27–28.

2. Leers.

YOUNG BELLAIR Harriet.

DORIMANT [*aside*] I am not mistaken. —She's handsome.

YOUNG BELLAIR Talk to her; her wit is better than her face. We were wishing for you but now.

DORIMANT [*to* Harriet] Overcast with seriousness o' the sudden! A thousand smiles were shining in the face but now. I never saw so quick a change of weather.

HARRIET [*aside*] I feel as great a change within, but he shall never know it.

DORIMANT You were talking of play, madam. Pray, what may be your stint?[3]

HARRIET A little harmless discourse in public walks or at most an appointment in a box, barefaced, at the playhouse. You are for masks and private meetings, where women engage for all they are worth, I hear.

DORIMANT I have been used to deep play, but I can make one at small game when I like my gamester well.

HARRIET And be so unconcerned you'll ha' no pleasure in't.

DORIMANT Where there is a considerable sum to be won, the hope of drawing people in makes every trifle considerable.

HARRIET The sordidness of men's natures, I know, makes 'em willing to flatter and comply with the rich, though they are sure never to be the better for 'em.

DORIMANT 'Tis in their power to do us good, and we despair not but at some time or other they may be willing.

HARRIET To men who have fared in this town like you, 'twould be a great mortification to live on hope. Could you keep a Lent for a mistress?

DORIMANT In expectation of a happy Easter; and though time be very precious, think forty days well lost to gain your favor.

HARRIET Mr. Bellair! Let us walk, 'tis time to leave him. Men grow dull when they begin to be particular.

DORIMANT Y'are mistaken: flattery will not ensue, though I know y'are greedy of the praises of the whole Mall.

HARRIET You do me wrong.

DORIMANT I do not. As I followed you, I observed how you were pleased when the fops cried "She's handsome, very handsome, by God she is!" and whispered aloud your name—the thousand several forms you put your face into; then, to make yourself more agreeable, how wantonly you played with your head, flung back your locks, and looked smilingly over your shoulder at 'em.

HARRIET I do not go begging men's, as you do the ladies' good liking, with a sly softness in your looks and a gentle slowness in your bows as you pass by 'em. As thus, sir. [*Acts him.*] Is not this like you?

Enter Lady Woodvill *and* Busy.

YOUNG BELLAIR Your mother, madam!

Pulls Harriet. *She composes herself.*

3. Limit.

LADY WOODVILL Ah, my dear child Harriet!

BUSY [aside] Now is she so pleased with finding her again, she cannot chide her.

LADY WOODVILL Come away!

DORIMANT 'Tis now but high Mall,[4] madam—the most entertaining time of all the evening.

HARRIET I would fain see that Dorimant, mother, you so cry out of for a monster. He's in the Mall, I hear.

LADY WOODVILL Come away, then! The plague is here, and you should dread the infection.

YOUNG BELLAIR You may be misinformed of the gentleman.

LADY WOODVILL Oh, no! I hope you do not know him. He is the prince of all the devils in the town—delights in nothing but in rapes and riots.

DORIMANT If you did but hear him speak, madam—

LADY WOODVILL Oh, he has a tongue, they say, would tempt the angels to a second fall.

Enter Sir Fopling *with his equipage, six footmen and a page*.

SIR FOPLING Hey, Champagne, Norman, La Rose, La Fleur, La Tour, La Verdure!—Dorimant!—

LADY WOODVILL Here, here he is among this rout! He names him! Come away, Harriet, come away!

Exeunt Lady Woodvill, Harriet, Busy, *and* Young Bellair.

DORIMANT This fool's coming has spoiled all: she's gone. But she has left a pleasing image of herself behind that wanders in my soul. It must not settle there.

SIR FOPLING What reverie is this? Speak, man.

DORIMANT

"Snatched from myself, how far behind
Already I behold the shore!"[5]

Enter Medley.

MEDLEY Dorimant, a discovery! I met with Bellair—

DORIMANT You can tell me no news, sir. I know all.

MEDLEY How do you like the daughter?

DORIMANT You never came so near truth in your life as you did in her description.

MEDLEY What think you of the mother?

DORIMANT Whatever I think of her, she thinks very well of me, I find.

MEDLEY Did she know you?

DORIMANT She did not. Whether she does now or no, I know not. Here was a pleasant scene towards, when in came Sir Fopling, mustering up his equipage, and at the latter end named me and frighted her away.

MEDLEY Loveit and Bellinda are not far off. I saw 'em alight at St. James's.[6]

4. The fashionable hour on the Mall.
5. From Waller's "Of Loving at First Sight," lines 3–4.
6. The palace, opposite St. James's Park and to the west end of the Mall.

DORIMANT Sir Fopling, hark you, a word or two. [*Whispers.*] Look you do not want assurance.

SIR FOPLING I never do on these occasions.

DORIMANT Walk on; we must not be seen together. Make your advantage of what I have told you. The next turn you will meet the lady.

SIR FOPLING Hey! Follow me all.

Exeunt Sir Fopling *and his equipage.*

DORIMANT Medley, you shall see good sport anon between Loveit and this Fopling.

MEDLEY I thought there was something toward, by that whisper.

DORIMANT You know a worthy principle of hers?

MEDLEY Not to be so much as civil to a man who speaks to her in the presence of him she professes to love.

DORIMANT I have encouraged Fopling to talk to her tonight.

MEDLEY Now you are here, she will go nigh to beat him.

DORIMANT In the humour she's in, her love will make her do some very extravagant thing, doubtless.

MEDLEY What was Bellinda's business with you at my Lady Townley's?

DORIMANT To get me to meet Loveit here in order to an *éclaircisse-ment*[7]. I made some difficulty of it and have prepared this rencounter to make good my jealousy.

Enter Mrs. Loveit, Bellinda, *and* Pert.

MEDLEY Here they come.

DORIMANT I'll meet her and provoke her with a deal of dumb civility in passing by, then turn short and be behind her when Sir Fopling sets upon her.

Bows to Mrs. Loveit.

"See how unregarded now
That piece of beauty passes."[8]

Exeunt Dorimant *and* Medley.

BELLINDA How wonderful respectfully he bowed!

PERT He's always over-mannerly when he has done a mischief.

BELLINDA Methoughts, indeed, at the same time he had a strange, despising countenance.

PERT The unlucky look he thinks becomes him.

BELLINDA I was afraid you would have spoke to him, my dear.

MRS. LOVEIT I would have died first. He shall no more find me the loving fool he has done.

BELLINDA You love him still!

MRS. LOVEIT No.

PERT I wish you did not.

MRS. LOVEIT I do not, and I will have you think so!—What made you hale me to this odious place, Bellinda?

7. Clarification. "Sonnet I."
8. Opening lines of Sir John Suckling's

BELLINDA I hate to be hulched up in a coach. Walking is much better.

MRS. LOVEIT Would we could meet Sir Fopling now!

BELLINDA Lord, would you not avoid him?

MRS. LOVEIT I would make him all the advances that may be.

BELLINDA That would confirm Dorimant's suspicion, my dear.

MRS. LOVEIT He is not jealous; but I will make him so, and be revenged a way he little thinks on.

BELLINDA [*aside*] If she should make him jealous, that may make him fond of her again. I must dissuade her from it. —Lord, my dear, this will certainly make him hate you.

MRS. LOVEIT 'Twill make him uneasy, though he does not care for me. I know the effects of jealousy on men of his proud temper.

BELLINDA 'Tis a fantastic remedy: its operations are dangerous and uncertain.

MRS. LOVEIT 'Tis the strongest cordial we can give to dying love. It often brings it back when there's no sign of life remaining. But I design not so much the reviving his, as my revenge.

> *Enter* Sir Fopling *and his equipage.*

SIR FOPLING Hey! Bid the coachman send home four of his horses and bring the coach to Whitehall.[9] I'll walk over the Park. [*To* Mrs. Loveit.] Madam, the honor of kissing your fair hands is a happiness I missed this afternoon at my Lady Townley's.

MRS. LOVEIT You were very obliging, Sir Fopling, the last time I saw you there.

SIR FOPLING The preference was due to your wit and beauty. [*To* Bellinda.] Madam, your servant. There never was so sweet an evening.

BELLINDA 'T has drawn all the rabble of the town hither.

SIR FOPLING 'Tis pity there's not an order made that none but the *beau monde* should walk here.

MRS. LOVEIT 'Twould add much to the beauty of the place. See what a sort of nasty fellows are coming!

> *Enter four ill-fashioned fellows singing:*

> " 'Tis not for kisses alone, etc."[1]

MRS. LOVEIT Foh! Their periwigs are scented with tobacco so strong—

SIR FOPLING —It overcomes our pulvilio.[2] Methinks I smell the coffeehouse they come from.

FIRST MAN Dorimant's convenient, Madam Loveit.

SECOND MAN I like the oily buttock[3] with her.

THIRD MAN [*pointing to* Sir Fopling] What spruce prig is that?

FIRST MAN A caravan,[4] lately come from Paris.

9. Whitehall Palace, across the park from the Mall.
1. From a popular song, "Tell me no more you love," published in the same year as the play.
2. Scented powder.
3. Smooth wench.
4. Dupe, fit for plunder.

118 · George Etherege

SECOND MAN Peace, they smoke![5]

All of them coughing; exeunt singing:
"There's something else to be done, etc."

Enter Dorimant and Medley.

DORIMANT They're engaged.

MEDLEY She entertains him as if she liked him.

DORIMANT Let us go forward, seem earnest in discourse, and show ourselves. Then you shall see how she'll use him.

BELLINDA Yonder's Dorimant, my dear.

MRS. LOVEIT I see him. [*Aside.*] He comes insulting, but I will disappoint him in his expectation. [*To Sir Fopling.*] I like this pretty, nice humour of yours, Sir Fopling. [*To Bellinda.*] With what a loathing eye he looked upon those fellows!

SIR FOPLING I sat near one of 'em at a play today and was almost poisoned with a pair of cordovan gloves he wears.

MRS. LOVEIT Oh, filthy cordovan! How I hate the smell!

Laughs in a loud, affected way.

SIR FOPLING Did you observe, madam, how their cravats hung loose an inch from their neck, and what a frightful air it gave 'em?

MRS. LOVEIT Oh! I took particular notice of one that is always spruced up with a deal of dirty, sky-colored ribbon.

BELLINDA That's one of the walking flageolets[6] who haunt the Mall o' nights.

MRS. LOVEIT Oh, I remember him. H' has a hollow tooth, enough to spoil the sweetness of an evening.

SIR FOPLING I have seen the tallest walk the streets with a dainty pair of boxes,[7] neatly buckled on.

MRS. LOVEIT And a little footboy at his heels, pocket-high, with a flat cap, a dirty face—

SIR FOPLING —And a snotty nose.

MRS. LOVEIT Oh, odious! There's many of my own sex, with that Holborn equipage, trig[8] to Gray's Inn Walks, and now and then travel hither on a Sunday.

MEDLEY [*to Dorimant*] She takes no notice of you.

DORIMANT Damn her! I am jealous of a counterplot.

MRS. LOVEIT Your liveries are the finest, Sir Fopling. Oh, that page! That page is the prettily'st dressed. They are all Frenchmen?

SIR FOPLING There's one damned English blockhead among 'em. You may know him by his mien.

MRS. LOVEIT Oh, that's he, that's he! What do you call him?

SIR FOPLING [*calling* Footman] Hey!—I know not what to call him.

MRS. LOVEIT What's your name?

FOOTMAN John Trott, madam.

SIR FOPLING Oh, insufferable! Trott, Trott, Trott! There's nothing so barbarous as the names of our English servants. What country-man are you, sirrah?

5. Notice.
6. Flutes; or perhaps tall, thin persons.
7. Clogs or overshoes.
8. Walk briskly, trip along. *"Holborn*

equipage" means middle-class attendants; *Gray's Inn Walks* were gardens at one of the Inns of Court in Holborn.

FOOTMAN Hampshire, sir.

SIR FOPLING Then Hampshire be your name. Hey, Hampshire!

MRS. LOVEIT Oh, that sound! That sound becomes the mouth of a man of quality.

MEDLEY Dorimant, you look a little bashful on the matter.

DORIMANT She dissembles better than I thought she could have done.

MEDLEY You have tempted her with too luscious a bait. She bites at the coxcomb.

DORIMANT She cannot fall from loving me to that?

MEDLEY You begin to be jealous in earnest.

DORIMANT Of one I do not love?

MEDLEY You did love her.

DORIMANT The fit has long been over.

MEDLEY But I have known men fall into dangerous relapses when they have found a woman inclining to another.

DORIMANT [*to himself*] He guesses the secret of my heart. I am concerned but dare not show it, lest Bellinda should mistrust all I have done to gain her.

BELLINDA [*aside*] I have watched his look and find no alteration there. Did he love her, some signs of jealousy would have appeared.

DORIMANT [*to* Mrs. Loveit] I hope this happy evening, madam, has reconciled you to the scandalous Mall. We shall have you now hankering here again.

MRS. LOVEIT Sir Fopling, will you walk?

SIR FOPLING I am all obedience, madam.

MRS. LOVEIT Come along then, and let's agree to be malicious on all the ill-fashioned things we meet.

SIR FOPLING We'll make a critique on the whole Mall, madam.

MRS. LOVEIT Bellinda, you shall engage.

BELLINDA To the reserve of our friends, my dear.

MRS. LOVEIT No! No exceptions.

SIR FOPLING We'll sacrifice all to our diversion.

MRS. LOVEIT All, all.

SIR FOPLING All!

BELLINDA All? Then let it be.

Exeunt Sir Fopling, Mrs. Loveit, Bellinda, *and* Pert, *laughing.*

MEDLEY Would you had brought some more of your friends, Dorimant, to have been witnesses of Sir Fopling's disgrace and your triumph!

DORIMANT 'Twere unreasonable to desire you not to laugh at me; but pray do not expose me to the town this day or two.

MEDLEY By that time you hope to have regained your credit?

DORIMANT I know she hates Fopling and only makes use of him in hope to work me on again. Had it not been for some powerful considerations which will be removed tomorrow morning, I had made her pluck off this mask and show the passion that lies panting under.

Enter a Footman.

MEDLEY Here comes a man from Bellair, with news of your last adventure.

DORIMANT I am glad he sent him. I long to know the consequence of our parting.

FOOTMAN Sir, my master desires you to come to my Lady Townley's presently and bring Mr. Medley with you. My Lady Woodvill and her daughter are there.

MEDLEY Then all's well, Dorimant.

FOOTMAN They have sent for the fiddles and mean to dance. He bid me to tell you, sir, the old lady does not know you; and would have you own yourself to be Mr. Courtage. They are all prepared to receive you by that name.

DORIMANT That foppish admirer of quality, who flatters the very meat at honorable tables and never offers love to a woman below a lady-grandmother!

MEDLEY You know the character you are to act, I see.

DORIMANT This is Harriet's contrivance—wild, witty, lovesome, beautiful and young.[9] —Come along, Medley.

MEDLEY This new woman would well supply the loss of Loveit.

DORIMANT That business must not end so. Before tomorrow sun is set, I will revenge and clear it.

> And you and Loveit, to her cost, shall find
> I fathom all the depths of womankind.

Exeunt.

Act IV. Scene i. Lady Townley's.
The scene opens with the fiddlers playing a country dance. Enter Dorimant and Lady Woodville, Young Bellair and Mrs. Harriet, Old Bellair and Emilia, Mr. Medley and Lady Townley, as having just ended the dance.

OLD BELLAIR So, so, so! A smart bout, a very smart bout, adod!

LADY TOWNLEY How do you like Emilia's dancing, brother?

OLD BELLAIR Not at all, not at all!

LADY TOWNLEY You speak not what you think, I am sure.

OLD BELLAIR No matter for that; go, bid her dance no more. It don't become her, it don't become her. Tell her I say so. [*Aside.*] Adod, I love her.

DORIMANT [*to* Lady Woodville] All people mingle nowadays, madam. And in public places women of quality have the least respect showed 'em.

LADY WOODVILL I protest you say the truth, Mr. Courtage.

DORIMANT Forms and ceremonies, the only things that uphold quality and greatness, are now shamefully laid aside and neglected.

LADY WOODVILL Well, this is not the women's age, let 'em think what they will. Lewdness is the business now; love was the bus'ness in my time.

DORIMANT The women, indeed, are little beholding to the young men of this age. They're generally only dull admirers of them-

9. Loosely derived from Waller's "Of the Danger his Majesty (Being Prince) Es-   caped . . . ," lines 13–14.

selves and make their court to nothing but their periwigs and their cravats—and would be more concerned for the disordering of 'em, though on a good occasion, than a young maid would be for the tumbling of her head or handkercher.

LADY WOODVILL I protest you hit 'em.

DORIMANT They are very assiduous to show themselves at court, well-dressed, to the women of quality; but their bus'ness is with the stale mistresses of the town, who are prepared to receive their lazy addresses by industrious old lovers who have cast 'em off and made 'em easy.

HARRIET [to Medley] He fits my mother's humour so well, a little more and she'll dance a kissing dance with him anon.

MEDLEY Dutifully observed, madam.

DORIMANT They pretend to be great critics in beauty—by their talk you would think they liked no face—and yet can dote on an ill one if it belong to a laundress or a tailor's daughter. They cry a woman's past her prime at twenty, decayed at four-and-twenty, old and insufferable at thirty.

LADY WOODVILL Insufferable at thirty! That they are in the wrong, Mr. Courtage, at five-and-thirty there are living proofs enough to convince 'em.

DORIMANT Ay, madam; there's Mrs. Setlooks, Mrs. Droplip, and my Lady Loud. Show me among all our opening buds a face that promises so much beauty as the remains of theirs.

LADY WOODVILL The depraved appetite of this vicious age tastes nothing but green fruit and loathes it when 'tis kindly[1] ripened.

DORIMANT Else so many deserving women, madam, would not be so untimely neglected.

LADY WOODVILL I protest, Mr. Courtage, a dozen such good men as you would be enough to atone for that wicked Dorimant and all the under-debauchees of the town.

    Harriet, Emilia, Young Bellair, Medley, *and* Lady Townley *break out into a laughter.*

What's the matter there?

MEDLEY A pleasant mistake, madam, that a lady has made occasions a little laughter.

OLD BELLAIR [to Dorimant *and* Lady Woodvill] Come, come, you keep 'em idle! They are impatient till the fiddles play again.

DORIMANT You are not weary, madam?

LADY WOODVILL One dance more. I cannot refuse you, Mr. Courtage.

    They dance. After the dance, Old Bellair *singing and dancing up to Emilia.*

EMILIA You are very active, sir.

OLD BELLAIR Adod, sirrah, when I was a young fellow, I could ha' capered up to my woman's gorget.[2]

DORIMANT [to Lady Woodvill] You are willing to rest yourself, madam?

1. Naturally.
2. "I could have kicked as high as my partner's neck-scarf."

LADY TOWNLEY [to Dorimant and Lady Woodvill] We'll walk into my chamber and sit down.

MEDLEY Leave us Mr. Courtage; he's a dancer, and the young ladies are not weary yet.

LADY WOODVILL We'll send him out again.

HARRIET If you do not quickly, I know where to send for Mr. Dorimant.

LADY WOODVILL This girl's head, Mr. Courtage, is ever running on that wild fellow.

DORIMANT 'Tis well you have got her a good husband, madam. That will settle it.

Exeunt Lady Townley, Lady Woodvill, *and* Dorimant.

OLD BELLAIR [to Emilia] Adod, sweetheart, be advised and do not throw thyself away on a young idle fellow.

EMILIA I have no such intention, sir.

OLD BELLAIR Have a little patience! Thou shalt have the man I spake of. Adod, he loves thee and will make a good husband. But no words—

EMILIA But, sir—

OLD BELLAIR No answer, out a pize! Peace, and think on't.

Enter Dorimant.

DORIMANT Your company is desired within, sir.

OLD BELLAIR I go, I go! Good Mr. Courtage, fare you well. [To Emilia.] Go, I'll see you no more!

EMILIA What have I done, sir?

OLD BELLAIR You are ugly, you are ugly!—Is she not, Mr. Courtage?

EMILIA Better words, or I shan't abide you!

OLD BELLAIR Out a pize! Adod, what does she say?—Hit her a pat for me there.

Exit Old Bellair.

MEDLEY [to Dorimant] You have charms for the whole family.

DORIMANT You'll spoil all with some unseasonable jest, Medley.

MEDLEY You see I confine my tongue and am content to be a bare spectator, much contrary to my nature.

EMILIA Methinks, Mr. Dorimant, my Lady Woodvill is a little fond of you.

DORIMANT Would her daughter were.

MEDLEY It may be you may find her so. Try her. You have an opportunity.

DORIMANT And I will not lose it.—Bellair, here's a lady has something to say to you.

YOUNG BELLAIR I wait upon her.—Mr. Medley, we have both business with you.

DORIMANT Get you all together, then.

He bows to Harriet; *she curtsies.*

[To Harriet.] That demure curtsy is not amiss in jest, but do not think in earnest it becomes you.

HARRIET Affectation is catching, I find. From your grave bow I got it.

DORIMANT Where had you all that scorn and coldness in your look?

HARRIET From nature, sir; pardon my want of art. I have not learnt those softnesses and languishings which now in faces are so much in fashion.

DORIMANT You need 'em not. You have a sweetness of your own, if you would but calm your frowns and let it settle.

HARRIET My eyes are wild and wand'ring like my passions, and cannot yet be tied to rules of charming.

DORIMANT Women, indeed, have commonly a method of managing those messengers of love. Now they will look as if they would kill, and anon they will look as if they were dying. They point and rebate³ their glances, the better to invite us.

HARRIET I like this variety well enough, but hate the set face that always looks as it would say, "Come love me"—a woman who at plays makes the *doux yeux*⁴ to a whole audience and at home cannot forbear 'em to her monkey.

DORIMANT Put on a gentle smile and let me see how well it will become you.

HARRIET I am sorry my face does not please you as it is; but I shall not be complacent and change it.

DORIMANT Though you are obstinate, I know 'tis capable of improvement, and shall do you justice, madam, if I chance to be at court when the critics of the circle pass their judgment; for thither you must come.

HARRIET And expect to be taken in pieces, have all my features examined, every motion censured, and on the whole be condemned to be but pretty—or a beauty of the lowest rate. What think you?

DORIMANT The women—nay, the very lovers who belong to the drawing room—will maliciously allow you more than that. They always grant what is apparent, that they may the better be believed when they name concealed faults they cannot easily be disproved in.

HARRIET Beauty runs as great a risk exposed at court as wit does on the stage, where the ugly and the foolish all are free to censure.

DORIMANT [*aside*] I love her and dare not let her know it. I fear sh'as an ascendant o'er me and may revenge the wrongs I have done her sex. [*To her.*] Think of making a party, madam; love will engage.

HARRIET You make me start. I did not think to have heard of love from you.

DORIMANT I never knew what 'twas to have a settled ague yet, but now and then have had irregular fits.

HARRIET Take heed; sickness after long health is commonly more violent and dangerous.

DORIMANT [*aside*] I have took the infection from her and feel the disease now spreading in me. [*To her.*] Is the name of love so frightful that you dare not stand it?

HARRIET 'Twill do little execution out of your mouth on me, I am sure.

DORIMANT It has been fatal—

3. Blunt.   4. Makes eyes at.

HARRIET To some easy women, but we are not all born to one destiny. I was informed you use to laugh at love, and not make it.
DORIMANT The time has been, but now I must speak.
HARRIET If it be on that idle subject, I will put on my serious look, turn my head carelessly from you, drop my lip, let my eyelids fall and hang half o'er my eyes—thus, while you buzz a speech of an hour long in my ear and I answer never a word. Why do you not begin?
DORIMANT That the company may take notice how passionately I made advances of love and how disdainfully you receive 'em.
HARRIET When your love's grown strong enough to make you bear being laughed at, I'll give you leave to trouble me with it. Till when, pray forbear, sir.
Enter Sir Fopling *and others in masks.*
DORIMANT What's here—masquerades?
HARRIET I thought foppery had been left off, and people might have been in private with a fiddle.
DORIMANT 'Tis endeavored to be kept on foot still by some who find themselves more acceptable, the less they are known.
YOUNG BELLAIR This must be Sir Fopling.
MEDLEY That extraordinary habit[5] shows it.
YOUNG BELLAIR What are the rest?
MEDLEY A company of French rascals whom he picked up in Paris and has brought over to be his dancing equipage on these occasions. Make him own himself; a fool is very troublesome when he presumes he is incognito.
SIR FOPLING [*to* Harriet] Do you know me?
HARRIET Ten to one but I guess at you.
SIR FOPLING Are you women as fond of a vizard as we men are?
HARRIET I am very fond of a vizard that covers a face I do not like, sir.
YOUNG BELLAIR Here are no masks, you see, sir, but those which came with you. This was intended a private meeting; but because you look like a gentleman, if you will discover yourself and we know you to be such, you shall be welcome.
SIR FOPLING [*pulling off his mask*] Dear Bellair.
MEDLEY Sir Fopling! How came you hither?
SIR FOPLING Faith, as I was coming late from Whitehall, after the King's *couchée*,[6] one of my people told me he had heard fiddles at my Lady Townley's, and—
DORIMANT You need not say any more, sir.
SIR FOPLING Dorimant, let me kiss thee.
DORIMANT Hark you, Sir Fopling—
Whispers.
SIR FOPLING Enough, enough, Courtage. —[*Glancing at* Harriet.] A pretty kind of young woman that, Medley. I observed her in the Mall, more *eveliè*[7] than our English women commonly are.

5. Clothing.
6. Evening reception.

7. Sprightly. Sir Fopling mispronounces *éveillée.*

Prithee, what is she?

MEDLEY The most noted *coquetté*[8] in town. Beware of her.

SIR FOPLING Let her be what she will, I know how to take my measures. In Paris the mode is to flatter the *prudè*, laugh at the *faux-prudè*, make serious love to the *demi-prudè*, and only rally with the *coquetté*. Medley, what think you?

MEDLEY That for all this smattering of the mathematics, you may be out in your judgment at tennis.

SIR FOPLING What a *coq-à-l'âne*[9] is this? I talk of women, and thou answer'st tennis.

MEDLEY Mistakes will be, for want of apprehension.

SIR FOPLING I am very glad of the acquaintance I have with this family.

MEDLEY My lady truly is a good woman.

SIR FOPLING Ah, Dorimant—Courtage, I would say—would thou hadst spent the last winter in Paris with me. When thou wert there, La Corneus and Sallyes[1] were the only habitudes we had; a comedian would have been a *bonne fortune*.[2] No stranger ever passed his time so well as I did some months before I came over. I was well received in a dozen families, where all the women of quality used to visit. I have intrigues to tell thee more pleasant than ever thou read'st in a novel.

HARRIET Write 'em, sir, and oblige us women. Our language wants such little stories.

SIR FOPLING Writing, madam, 's a mechanic part of wit. A gentleman should never go beyond a song or a *billet*.

HARRIET Bussy was a gentleman.

SIR FOPLING Who, d'Ambois?[3]

MEDLEY [*aside*] Was there ever such a brisk blockhead?

HARRIET Not d'Ambois, sir, but Rabutin: he who writ the *Loves of France*.

SIR FOPLING That may be, madam; many gentlemen do things that are below 'em. —Damn your authors, Courtage. Women are the prettiest things we can fool away our time with.

HARRIET I hope ye have wearied yourself tonight at court, sir, and will not think of fooling with anybody here.

SIR FOPLING I cannot complain of my fortune there, madam.— Dorimant—

DORIMANT Again!

SIR FOPLING Courtage, a pox on't! I have something to tell thee. When I had made my court within, I came out and flung myself upon the mat under the state[4] i' th' outward room, i' th' midst of half a dozen beauties who were withdrawn to jeèr among themselves, as they called it.

8. Medley mocks Sir Fopling by accenting the final *e*. See Sir Fopling's next speech.
9. Lot of nonsense.
1. Probably Mesdames Cornuel and Selles, literary ladies.
2. Piece of good luck.

3. Sir Fopling confuses Bussy d'Ambois, hero of a play by George Chapman, with the French author Roger de Rabutin, Comte de Bussy.
4. Canopy.

DORIMANT Did you know 'em?

SIR FOPLING Not one of 'em, by heav'ns, not I! But they were all your friends.

DORIMANT How are you sure of that?

SIR FOPLING Why, we laughed at all the town—spared nobody but yourself. They found me a man for their purpose.

DORIMANT I know you are malicious to your power.

SIR FOPLING And, faith, I had occasion to show it; for I never saw more gaping fools at a ball or on a birthday.

DORIMANT You learned who the women were?

SIR FOPLING No matter; they frequent the drawing room.

DORIMANT And entertain themselves at the expense of all the fops who come there.

SIR FOPLING That's their bus'ness. Faith, I sifted 'em and find they have a sort of wit among them.
      Pinches a tallow candle.
      Ah, filthy!

DORIMANT Look, he has been pinching the tallow candle.

SIR FOPLING How can you breathe in a room where there's grease frying? Dorimant, thou art intimate with my lady: advise her, for her own sake and the good company that comes hither, to burn wax lights.

HARRIET What are these masquerades who stand so obsequiously at a distance?

SIR FOPLING A set of balladines, whom I picked out of the best in France and brought over with a *flute douce* or two—my servants. They shall entertain you.

HARRIET I had rather see you dance yourself, Sir Fopling.

SIR FOPLING And I had rather do it—all the company knows it. But, madam—

MEDLEY Come, come, no excuses, Sir Fopling!

SIR FOPLING By heav'ns, Medley—

MEDLEY Like a woman I find you must be struggled with before one brings you what you desire.

HARRIET [*aside*] Can he dance?

EMILIA And fence and sing too, if you'll believe him.

DORIMANT He has no more excellence in his heels than in his head. He went to Paris a plain, bashful English blockhead and is returned a fine, undertaking French fop.

MEDLEY [*to* Harriet] I cannot prevail.

SIR FOPLING Do not think it want of complaisance, madam.

HARRIET You are too well-bred to want that, Sir Fopling. I think it want of power.

SIR FOPLING By heav'ns, and so it is! I have sat up so damned late and drunk so cursed hard since I came to this lewd town that I am fit for nothing but low dancing now—a *courante*, a *bourrée* or a *menuet*.[5] But St. André[6] tells me, if I will but be regular, in one month I shall rise again.

---

5. Stately dances, lacking capers.   6. French dancing master.

Endeavors at a caper.

Pox on this debauchery!

EMILIA I have heard your dancing much commended.

SIR FOPLING It had the good fortune to please in Paris. I was judged to rise within an inch as high as the basqué[7] in an entry I danced there.

HARRIET [*to* Emilia] I am mightily taken with this fool. Let us sit. —Here's a seat, Sir Fopling.

SIR FOPLING At your feet, madam. I can be nowhere so much at ease. —By your leave, gown.

Sits.

HARRIET, EMILIA Ah, you'll spoil it!

SIR FOPLING No matter, my clothes are my creatures. I make 'em to make my court to you ladies.—Hey, *qu'on commencè*![8]

Dance.

To an English dancer, English motions! I was forced to entertain[9] this fellow [*pointing to* John Trott], one of my set miscarrying. —Oh, horrid! Leave your damned manner of dancing and put on the French air. Have you not a pattern before you?—Pretty well! Imitation in time may bring him to something.

After the dance, enter Old Bellair, Lady Woodvill, *and* Lady Townley.

OLD BELLAIR Hey, adod, what have we here? A mumming?

LADY WOODVILL Where's my daughter? —Harriet!

DORIMANT Here, here, madam. I know not but under these disguises there may be dangerous sparks. I gave the lady warning.

LADY WOODVILL Lord, I am so obliged to you, Mr. Courtage.

HARRIET Lord, how you admire this man!

LADY WOODVILL What have you to except against him?

HARRIET He's a fop.

LADY WOODVILL He's not a Dorimant, a wild, extravagant fellow of the times.

HARRIET He's a man made up of forms and commonplaces, sucked out of the remaining lees of the last age.

LADY WOODVILL He's so good a man that were you not engaged—

LADY TOWNLEY You'll have but little night to sleep in.

LADY WOODVILL Lord, 'tis perfect day!

DORIMANT [*aside*] The hour is almost come I appointed Bellinda, and I am not so foppishly in love here to forget. I am flesh and blood yet.

LADY TOWNLEY I am very sensible, madam.

LADY WOODVILL Lord, madam—

HARRIET Look, in what a struggle is my poor mother yonder!

YOUNG BELLAIR She has much ado to bring out the compliment.

DORIMANT She strains hard for it.

HARRIET See, see—her head tottering, her eyes staring, and her underlip trembling.

7. Skirt of a coat.   9. Hire.
8 Begin.

DORIMANT Now, now she's in the very convulsions of her civility. [*Aside.*] 'Sdeath, I shall lose Bellinda! I must fright her hence. She'll be an hour in this fit of good manners else. [*To* Lady Woodvill.] Do you not know Sir Fopling, madam?

LADY WOODVILL I have seen that face. Oh heav'n, 'tis the same we met in the Mall! How came he here?

DORIMANT A fiddle in this town is a kind of fop-call. No sooner it strikes up, but the house is besieged with an army of masquerades straight.

LADY WOODVILL Lord, I tremble, Mr. Courtage. For certain Dorimant is in the company.

DORIMANT I cannot confidently say he is not. You had best begone; I will wait upon you. Your daughter is in the hands of Mr. Bellair.

LADY WOODVILL I'll see her before me. —Harriet, come away!

Exeunt Lady Woodville *and* Harriet.

YOUNG BELLAIR Lights, lights!

LADY TOWNLEY Light, down there!

OLD BELLAIR Adod, it needs not—

Exeunt Lady Townley *and* Young Bellair.

DORIMANT [*calling to the servants outside*] Call my Lady Woodvill's coach to the door! Quickly!

Exit Dorimant.

OLD BELLAIR Stay, Mr. Medley; let the young fellows do that duty. We will drink a glass of wine together. 'Tis good after dancing. [*Looks at* Sir Fopling.] What mumming spark is that?

MEDLEY He is not to be comprehended in few words.

SIR FOPLING Hey, La Tour!

MEDLEY Whither away, Sir Fopling?

SIR FOPLING I have bus'ness with Courtage.

MEDLEY He'll but put the ladies into their coach and come up again.

OLD BELLAIR In the meantime I'll call for a bottle.

Exit Old Bellair.

Enter Young Bellair.

MEDLEY Where's Dorimant?

YOUNG BELLAIR Stol'n home. He has had business waiting for him there all this night, I believe, by an impatience I observed in him.

MEDLEY Very likely. 'Tis but dissembling drunkenness, railing at his friends, and the kind soul will embrace the blessing and forget the tedious expectation.

SIR FOPLING I must speak with him before I sleep.

YOUNG BELLAIR [*to* Medley] Emilia and I are resolved on that business.

MEDLEY Peace, here's your father.

Enter Old Bellair *and* butler *with a bottle of wine.*

OLD BELLAIR The women are all gone to bed. Fill, boy! —Mr. Medley, begin a health.

MEDLEY [*whispers*] To Emilia.

OLD BELLAIR Out a pize! She's a rogue, and I'll not pledge you.

MEDLEY I know you will.

OLD BELLAIR Adod, drink it, then!

SIR FOPLING Let us have the new bachique.

OLD BELLAIR Adod, that is a hard word! What does it mean, sir?

MEDLEY A catch or drinking song.

OLD BELLAIR Let us have it, then.

SIR FOPLING Fill the glasses round, and draw up in a body. —Hey, music!

> *They sing.*

> The pleasures of love and the joys of good wine,
> To perfect our happiness wisely we join.
> We to beauty all day
> Give the sovereign sway
> And her favorite nymphs devoutly obey;
> At the plays we are constantly making our court,
> And when they are ended, we follow the sport
> To the Mall and the Park,
> Where we love till 'tis dark.
> Then sparkling champagne
> Puts an end to their reign:
> It quickly recovers
> Poor languishing lovers,
> Makes us frolic and gay, and drowns all our sorrow;
> But alas, we relapse again on the morrow.
>   Let every man stand
>   With his glass in his hand,
> And briskly discharge at the word of command.
>   Here's a health to all those
>   Whom tonight we depose.
> Wine and beauty by turns great souls should inspire;
> Present all together; and now, boys, give fire!

> *They drink.*

OLD BELLAIR Adod, a pretty bus'ness and very merry!

SIR FOPLING Hark you, Medley, let you and I take the fiddles and go waken Dorimant.

MEDLEY We shall do him a courtesy, if it be as I guess. For after the fatigue of this night, he'll quickly have his belly full and be glad of an occasion to cry, "Take away, Handy!"

YOUNG BELLAIR I'll go with you; and there we'll consult about affairs, Medley.

OLD BELLAIR [*looks on his watch*] Adod, 'tis six o'clock!

SIR FOPLING Let's away, then.

OLD BELLAIR Mr. Medley, my sister tells me you are an honest man. And, adod, I love you. —Few words and hearty, that's the way with old Harry, old Harry.

SIR FOPLING [*to his servants*] Light your flambeaux![1] Hey!

OLD BELLAIR What does the man mean?

1. Torches.

MEDLEY 'Tis day, Sir Fopling.

SIR FOPLING No matter; our serenade will look the greater.

Exeunt omnes.

> Act IV. Scene ii. Dorimant's *lodging; a table, a candle, a toilet, etc.*
>
> Handy *tying up linen.* Enter Dorimant *in his gown, and* Bellinda.

DORIMANT Why will you be gone so soon?

BELLINDA Why did you stay out so late?

DORIMANT Call a chair, Handy.

Exit Handy.

—What makes you tremble so?

BELLINDA I have a thousand fears about me. Have I not been seen, think you?

DORIMANT By nobody but myself and trusty Handy.

BELLINDA Where are all your people?

DORIMANT I have dispersed 'em on sleeveless[2] errands. What does that sigh mean?

BELLINDA Can you be so unkind to ask me? Well [*sighs*], were it to do again—

DORIMANT We should do it, should we not?

BELLINDA I think we should: the wickeder man you, to make me love so well. Will you be discreet now?

DORIMANT I will.

BELLINDA You cannot.

DORIMANT Never doubt it.

BELLINDA I will not expect it.

DORIMANT You do me wrong.

BELLINDA You have no more power to keep the secret than I had not to trust you with it.

DORIMANT By all the joys I have had and those you keep in store—

BELLINDA —You'll do for my sake what you never did before.

DORIMANT By that truth thou hast spoken, a wife shall sooner betray herself to her husband.

BELLINDA Yet I had rather you should be false in this than in another thing you promised me.

DORIMANT What's that?

BELLINDA That you would never see Loveit more but in public places—in the Park, at court and plays.

DORIMANT 'Tis not likely a man should be fond of seeing a damned old play when there is a new one acted.

BELLINDA I dare not trust your promise.

DORIMANT You may.

BELLINDA This does not satisfy me. You shall swear you never will see her more.

DORIMANT I will, a thousand oaths. By all—

BELLINDA Hold! You shall not, now I think on't better.

DORIMANT I will swear!

2. Useless.

BELLINDA I shall grow jealous of the oath and think I owe your truth to that, not to your love.

DORIMANT Then, by my love! No other oath I'll swear.

Enter Handy.

HANDY Here's a chair.

BELLINDA Let me go.

DORIMANT I cannot.

BELLINDA Too willingly, I fear.

DORIMANT Too unkindly feared. When will you promise me again?

BELLINDA Not this fortnight.

DORIMANT You will be better than your word.

BELLINDA I think I shall. Will it not make you love me less?

Fiddles without.

[*Starting.*] Hark, what fiddles are these?

DORIMANT Look out, Handy.

Exit Handy *and returns.*

HANDY Mr. Medley, Mr. Bellair, and Sir Fopling. They are coming up.

DORIMANT How got they in?

HANDY The door was open for the chair.

BELLINDA Lord, let me fly!

DORIMANT Here, here, down the back stairs. I'll see you into your chair.

BELLINDA No, no, stay and receive 'em. And be sure you keep your word and never see Loveit more. Let it be a proof of your kindness.

DORIMANT It shall. —Handy, direct her. —[*Kissing her hand.*] Everlasting love go along with thee.

Exeunt Bellinda *and* Handy.

Enter Young Bellair, Medley, *and* Sir Fopling *with his* page.

YOUNG BELLAIR Not abed yet?

MEDLEY You have had an irregular fit, Dorimant.

DORIMANT I have.

YOUNG BELLAIR And it is off already?

DORIMANT Nature has done her part, gentlemen. When she falls kindly to work, great cures are effected in little time, you know.

SIR FOPLING We thought there was a wench in the case, by the chair that waited. Prithee, make us a *confidencé.*

DORIMANT Excuse me.

SIR FOPLING *Lè sagè*[3] Dorimant. Was she pretty?

DORIMANT So pretty she may come to keep her coach and pay parish duties, if the good humour of the age continue.

MEDLEY And be of the number of ladies kept by public-spirited men for the good of the whole town.

SIR FOPLING Well said, Medley.

Sir Fopling *dancing by himself.*

YOUNG BELLAIR See Sir Fopling dancing.

DORIMANT You are practicing and have a mind to recover, I see.

3. Prudent.

SIR FOPLING Prithee, Dorimant, why hast not thou a glass hung up here? A room is the dullest thing without one.

YOUNG BELLAIR Here is company to entertain you.

SIR FOPLING But I mean in case of being alone. In a glass a man may entertain himself—

DORIMANT The shadow of himself, indeed.

SIR FOPLING —Correct the errors of his motions and his dress.

MEDLEY I find, Sir Fopling, in your solitude you remember the saying of the wise man, and study yourself.

SIR FOPLING 'Tis the best diversion in our retirements. Dorimant, thou art a pretty fellow and wear'st thy clothes well, but I never saw thee have a handsome cravat. Were they made up like mine, they'd give another air to thy face. Prithee, let me send my man to dress thee but one day. By heav'ns, an Englishman cannot tie a ribbon!

DORIMANT They are something clumsy-fisted.

SIR FOPLING I have brought over the prettiest fellow that ever spread a toilet. He served some time under Merille,[4] the greatest genie in the world for a *valet de chambré*.

DORIMANT What, he who formerly belonged to the Duke of Candale?[5]

SIR FOPLING The same, and got him his immortal reputation.

DORIMANT Y' have a very fine brandenburgh on, Sir Fopling.

SIR FOPLING It serves to wrap me up, after the fatigue of a ball.

MEDLEY I see you often in it, with your periwig tied up.

SIR FOPLING We should not always be in a set dress. 'Tis more *en cavalier* to appear now and then in a *déshabillé*.[6]

MEDLEY Pray, how goes your business with Loveit?

SIR FOPLING You might have answered yourself in the Mall last night. —Dorimant, did you not see the advances she made me? I have been endeavoring at a song.

DORIMANT Already?

SIR FOPLING 'Tis my *coup d'essai*[7] in English. I would fain have thy opinion of it.

DORIMANT Let's see it.

SIR FOPLING Hey, page, give me my song. —Bellair, here. Thou hast a pretty voice; sing it.

YOUNG BELLAIR Sing it yourself, Sir Fopling.

SIR FOPLING Excuse me.

YOUNG BELLAIR You learnt to sing in Paris.

SIR FOPLING I did—of Lambert,[8] the greatest master in the world; but I have his own fault, a weak voice, and care not to sing out of a *ruelle*.[9]

DORIMANT A *ruelle* is a pretty cage for a singing fop, indeed.

Young Bellair *reads the song.*

4. Valet to the Duke of Orléans.
5. Famous French general and courtier.
6. " 'Tis more dashing to appear now and then casually dressed."
7. First effort.
8. Musician in the court of Louis XIV.
9. Lady's bedchamber.

How charming Phillis is, how fair!
Ah, that she were as willing
To ease my wounded heart of care,
And make her eyes less killing.
I sigh, I sigh, I languish now,
And love will not let me rest;
I drive about the Park and bow,
Still as I meet my dearest.

SIR FOPLING Sing it, sing it, man! It goes to a pretty new tune which I am confident was made by Baptiste.[1]

MEDLEY Sing it yourself, Sir Fopling. He does not know the tune.

SIR FOPLING I'll venture.

Sir Fopling sings.

DORIMANT Ay, marry, now 'tis something. I shall not flatter you, Sir Fopling: there is not much thought in't, but 'tis passionate and well-turned.

MEDLEY After the French way.

SIR FOPLING That I aimed at. Does it not give you a lively image of the thing? Slap, down goes the glass,[2] and thus we are at it.

DORIMANT It does indeed. I perceive, Sir Fopling, you'll be the very head of the sparks who are lucky in compositions of this nature.

Enter Sir Fopling's Footman.

SIR FOPLING La Tour, is the bath ready?

FOOTMAN Yes, sir.

SIR FOPLING *Adieu donc, mes chers.*

Exit Sir Fopling *with attendants.*

MEDLEY When have you your revenge on Loveit, Dorimant?

DORIMANT I will but change my linen and about it.

MEDLEY The powerful considerations which hindered have been removed, then?

DORIMANT Most luckily, this morning. You must along with me; my reputation lies at stake there.

MEDLEY I am engaged to Bellair.

DORIMANT What's your business?

MEDLEY Ma-tri-mony, an't like you.

DORIMANT It does not, sir.

YOUNG BELLAIR It may in time, Dorimant. What think you of Mrs. Harriet?

DORIMANT What does she think of me?

YOUNG BELLAIR I am confident she loves you.

DORIMANT How does it appear?

YOUNG BELLAIR Why, she's never well but when she's talking of you, but then she finds all the faults in you she can. She laughs at all who commend you; but then she speaks ill of all who do not.

DORIMANT Women of her temper betray themselves by their over-cunning. I had once a growing love with a lady who would always

1. Another musician to Louis XIV.   2. Coach window.

quarrel with me when I came to see her, and yet was never quiet if I stayed a day from her.

YOUNG BELLAIR My father is in love with Emilia.

DORIMANT That is a good warrant for your proceedings. Go on and prosper; I must to Loveit. —Medley, I am sorry you cannot be a witness.

MEDLEY Make her meet Sir Fopling again in the same place and use him ill before me.

DORIMANT That may be brought about, I think. —I'll be at your aunt's anon and give you joy, Mr. Bellair.

YOUNG BELLAIR You had best not think of Mrs. Harriet too much. Without church security, there's no taking up there.

DORIMANT I may fall into the snare, too. But,

> The wise will find a difference in our fate:
> You wed a woman, I a good estate.

Exeunt.

Act IV. Scene iii. The Mall; in front of Mrs. Loveit's.
Enter the chair with Bellinda; *the men set it down and open it.* Bellinda *starting.*

BELLINDA [*surprised*] Lord, where am I? In the Mall! Whither have you brought me?

FIRST CHAIRMAN You gave us no directions, madam.

BELLINDA [*aside*] The fright I was in made me forget it.

FIRST CHAIRMAN We used to carry a lady from the squire's hither.

BELLINDA [*aside*] This is Loveit! I am undone if she sees me. —Quickly, carry me away!

FIRST CHAIRMAN Whither, an't like your honor?

BELLINDA Ask no questions!

Enter Mrs. Loveit's Footman.

FOOTMAN Have you seen my lady, madam?

BELLINDA I am just come to wait upon her.

FOOTMAN She will be glad to see you, madam. She sent me to you this morning to desire your company, and I was told you went out by five o'clock.

BELLINDA [*aside*] More and more unlucky!

FOOTMAN Will you walk in, madam?

BELLINDA I'll discharge my chair and follow. Tell your mistress I am here.

Exit Footman.

Gives the Chairmen *money.*
Take this; and if ever you should be examined, be sure you say you took me up in the Strand, over against the Exchange—as you will answer it to Mr. Dorimant.

CHAIRMEN We will, an't like your honor.

Exeunt Chairmen.

BELLINDA Now to come off, I must on:

> In confidence and lies some hope is left;
> 'Twere hard to be found out in the first theft.

Act V. *Scene i.* Mrs. Loveit's.
Enter Mrs. Loveit *and* Pert, *her woman.*

PERT Well! In my eyes, Sir Fopling is no such despicable person.

MRS. LOVEIT You are an excellent judge.

PERT He's as handsome a man as Mr. Dorimant, and as great a gallant.

MRS. LOVEIT Intolerable! Is't not enough I submit to his impertinences, but must I be plagued with yours too?

PERT Indeed, madam—

MRS. LOVEIT 'Tis false, mercenary malice—

Enter her Footman.

FOOTMAN Mrs. Bellinda, madam.

MRS. LOVEIT What of her?

FOOTMAN She's below.

MRS. LOVEIT How came she?

FOOTMAN In a chair; ambling Harry brought her.

MRS. LOVEIT [*aside*] He bring her! His chair stands near Dorimant's door and always brings me from thence. —Run and ask him where he took her up. Go!

Exit Footman.

There is no truth in friendship neither. Women as well as men, all are false, or all are so to me at least.

PERT You are jealous of her too?

MRS. LOVEIT You had best tell her I am. 'Twill become the liberty you take of late. [*Aside.*] This fellow's bringing of her, her going out by five o'clock—I know not what to think.

Enter Bellinda.

Bellinda, you are grown an early riser, I hear.

BELLINDA Do you not wonder, my dear, what made me abroad so soon?

MRS. LOVEIT You do not use to be so.

BELLINDA The country gentlewomen I told you of—Lord, they have the oddest diversions—would never let me rest till I promised to go with them to the markets this morning to eat fruit and buy nosegays.

MRS. LOVEIT Are they so fond of a filthy nosegay?

BELLINDA They complain of the stinks of the town and are never well but when they have their noses in one.

MRS. LOVEIT There are essences and sweet waters.

BELLINDA Oh, they cry out upon perfumes, they are unwholesome. One of 'em was falling into a fit with the smell of these *narolii.*[3]

MRS. LOVEIT Methinks, in complaisance you should have had a nosegay too.

BELLINDA Do you think, my dear, I could be so loathsome to trick myself up with carnations and stock-gillyflowers? I begged their pardon and told them I never wore anything but orange-flowers and tuberose. That which made me willing to go was a strange desire I had to eat some fresh nectarines.

3. Essences of orange.

MRS. LOVEIT And had you any?

BELLINDA The best I ever tasted.

MRS LOVEIT Whence came you now?

BELLINDA From their lodgings, where I crowded out of a coach and took a chair to come and see you, my dear.

MRS. LOVEIT Whither did you send for that chair?

BELLINDA 'Twas going by empty.

MRS. LOVEIT Where do these country gentlewomen lodge, I pray?

BELLINDA In the Strand, over against the Exchange.

PERT That place is never without a nest of 'em. They are always, as one goes by, fleering in balconies or staring out of windows.

Enter Footman.

MRS. LOVEIT [*to the* Footman] Come hither.

Whispers.

BELLINDA [*aside*] This fellow by her order has been questioning the chairmen. I threatened 'em with the name of Dorimant. If they should have told truth, I am lost forever.

MRS. LOVEIT In the Strand, said you?

FOOTMAN Yes, madam, over against the Exchange.

Exit Footman.

MRS. LOVEIT She's innocent, and I am much to blame.

BELLINDA [*aside*] I am so frighted, my countenance will betray me.

MRS. LOVEIT Bellinda, what makes you look so pale?

BELLINDA Want of my usual rest and jolting up and down so long in an odious hackney.

Footman *returns.*

FOOTMAN Madam, Mr. Dorimant.

Exit Footman.

MRS. LOVEIT What makes him here?

BELLINDA [*aside*] Then I am betrayed indeed. H' has broke his word, and I love a man that does not care for me.

MRS. LOVEIT Lord, you faint, Bellinda.

BELLINDA I think I shall—such an oppression here on the sudden.

PERT She has eaten too much fruit, I warrant you.

MRS. LOVEIT Not unlikely.

PERT 'Tis that lies heavy on her stomach.

MRS. LOVEIT Have her into my chamber, give her some surfeit-water, and let her lie down a little.

PERT Come, madam. I was a strange devourer of fruit when I was young—so ravenous.

Exeunt Bellinda *and* Pert, *leading her off.*

MRS. LOVEIT Oh, that my love would but be calm awhile, that I might receive this man with all the scorn and indignation he deserves!

Enter Dorimant.

DORIMANT Now for a touch of Sir Fopling to begin with. —Hey, page! Give positive order that none of my people stir. Let the *canaille*[4] wait, as they should do. —Since noise and nonsense have such pow'rful charms,

4. Rabble.

"I, that I may successful prove,
Transform myself to what you love."[5]

MRS. LOVEIT If that would do, you need not change from what you are: you can be vain and loud enough.

DORIMANT But not with so good a grace as Sir Fopling. —"Hey, Hampshire!"—Oh, that sound! That sound becomes the mouth of a man of quality.

MRS. LOVEIT Is there a thing so hateful as a senseless mimic?

DORIMANT He's a great grievance, indeed, to all who—like yourself, madam—love to play the fool in quiet.

MRS. LOVEIT A ridiculous animal, who has more of the ape than the ape has of the man in him.

DORIMANT I have as mean an opinion of a sheer mimic as yourself; yet were he all ape, I should prefer him to the gay, the giddy, brisk, insipid, noisy fool you dote on.

MRS. LOVEIT Those noisy fools, however you despise 'em, have good qualities which weigh more (or ought, at least) with us women than all the pernicious wit you have to boast of.

DORIMANT That I may hereafter have a just value of their merit, pray do me the favor to name 'em.

MRS. LOVEIT You'll despise 'em as the dull effects of ignorance and vanity, yet I care not if I mention some. First, they really admire us, while you at best but flatter us well.

DORIMANT Take heed; fools can dissemble too.

MRS. LOVEIT They may—but not so artificially as you. There is no fear they should deceive us. Then, they are assiduous, sir. They are ever offering us their service and always waiting on our will.

DORIMANT You owe that to their excessive idleness. They know not how to entertain themselves at home, and find so little welcome abroad, they are fain to fly to you who countenance 'em, as a refuge against the solitude they would be otherwise condemned to.

MRS. LOVEIT Their conversation, too, diverts us better.

DORIMANT Playing with your fan, smelling to your gloves, commending your hair, and taking notice how 'tis cut and shaded after the new way—

MRS. LOVEIT Were it sillier than you can make it, you must allow 'tis pleasanter to laugh at others than to be laughed at ourselves, though never so wittily. Then, though they want skill to flatter us, they flatter themselves so well, they save us the labor. We need not take that care and pains to satisfy 'em of our love, which we so often lose on you.

DORIMANT They commonly, indeed, believe too well of themselves —and always better of you than you deserve.

MRS. LOVEIT You are in the right: they have an implicit faith in us, which keeps 'em from prying narrowly into our secrets and saves us the vexatious trouble of clearing doubts which your subtle and causeless jealousies every moment raise.

5. From Waller's "To the Mutable Fair," lines 5–6.

DORIMANT There is an inbred falsehood in women which inclines 'em still to them whom they may most easily deceive.

MRS. LOVEIT The man who loves above his quality does not suffer more from the insolent impertinence of his mistress than the woman who loves above her understanding does from the arrogant presumptions of her friend.

DORIMANT You mistake the use of fools: they are designed for properties and not for friends. You have an indifferent stock of reputation left yet. Lose it all like a frank gamester on the square. 'Twill then be time to turn rook and cheat it up again on a good, substantial bubble.[6]

MRS. LOVEIT The old and the ill-favored are only fit for properties, indeed; but young and handsome fools have met with kinder fortunes.

DORIMANT They have, to the shame of your sex be it spoken. 'Twas this, the thought of this, made me by a timely jealousy endeavor to prevent the good fortune you are providing for Sir Fopling. But against a woman's frailty all our care is vain.

MRS. LOVEIT Had I not with a dear experience bought the knowledge of your falsehood, you might have fooled me yet. This is not the first jealousy you have feigned to make a quarrel with me, and get a week to throw away on some such unknown, inconsiderable slut as you have been lately lurking with at plays.

DORIMANT Women, when they would break off with a man, never want th'address to turn the fault on him.

MRS. LOVEIT You take a pride of late in using of me ill, that the town may know the power you have over me, which now (as unreasonably as yourself) expects that I, do me all the injuries you can, must love you still.

DORIMANT I am so far from expecting that you should, I begin to think you never did love me.

MRS. LOVEIT Would the memory of it were so wholly worn out in me that I did doubt it too. What made you come to disturb my growing quiet?

DORIMANT To give you joy of your growing infamy.

MRS. LOVEIT Insupportable! Insulting devil! This from you, the only author of my shame! This from another had been justice; but from you, 'tis a hellish and inhuman outrage. What have I done?

DORIMANT A thing that puts you below my scorn and makes my anger as ridiculous as you have made my love.

MRS. LOVEIT I walked last night with Sir Fopling.

DORIMANT You did, madam; and you talked and laughed aloud, "Ha, ha, ha." Oh, that laugh! That laugh becomes the confidence of a woman of quality.

MRS. LOVEIT You, who have more pleasure in the ruin of a woman's reputation than in the endearments of her love, reproach me not with yourself and I defy you to name the man can lay a blemish on my fame.

6. Dupe.

DORIMANT To be seen publicly so transported with the vain follies of that notorious fop, to me is an infamy below the sin of prostitution with another man.

MRS. LOVEIT Rail on! I am satisfied in the justice of what I did: you had provoked me to it.

DORIMANT What I did was the effect of a passion whose extravagancies you have been willing to forgive.

MRS. LOVEIT And what I did was the effect of a passion you may forgive if you think fit.

DORIMANT Are you so indifferent grown?

MRS. LOVEIT I am.

DORIMANT Nay, then 'tis time to part. I'll send you back your letters you have so often asked for. [*Looks in his pockets.*] I have two or three of 'em about me.

MRS. LOVEIT Give 'em me.

DORIMANT You snatch as if you thought I would not.
     Gives her the letters.
There. And may the perjuries in 'em be mine if e'er I see you more.
     Offers to go; she catches him.

MRS. LOVEIT Stay!

DORIMANT I will not.

MRS. LOVEIT You shall!

DORIMANT What have you to say?

MRS. LOVEIT I cannot speak it yet.

DORIMANT Something more in commendation of the fool. Death, I want patience! Let me go.

MRS. LOVEIT I cannot. [*Aside.*] I can sooner part with the limbs that hold him. —I hate that nauseous fool, you know I do.

DORIMANT Was it the scandal you were fond of, then?

MRS. LOVEIT Y' had raised my anger equal to my love, a thing you ne'er could do before; and in revenge I did—I know not what I did. Would you would not think on't any more.

DORIMANT Should I be willing to forget it, I shall be daily minded of it. 'Twill be a commonplace for all the town to laugh at me, and Medley, when he is rhetorically drunk, will ever be declaiming on it in my ears.

MRS. LOVEIT 'Twill be believed a jealous spite. Come, forget it.

DORIMANT Let me consult my reputation; you are too careless of it. [*Pauses.*] You shall meet Sir Fopling in the Mall again tonight.

MRS. LOVEIT What mean you?

DORIMANT I have thought on it, and you must. 'Tis necessary to justify my love to the world. You can handle a coxcomb as he deserves when you are not out of humour, madam.

MRS. LOVEIT Public satisfaction for the wrong I have done you? This is some new device to make me more ridiculous.

DORIMANT Hear me.

MRS. LOVEIT I will not.

DORIMANT You will be persuaded.

MRS. LOVEIT Never!

DORIMANT Are you so obstinate?

MRS. LOVEIT Are you so base?

DORIMANT You will not satisfy my love?

MRS. LOVEIT I would die to satisfy that; but I will not, to save you from a thousand racks, do a shameless thing to please your vanity.

DORIMANT Farewell, false woman.

MRS. LOVEIT Do! Go!

DORIMANT You will call me back again.

MRS. LOVEIT Exquisite fiend! I knew you came but to torment me.
    Enter Belinda *and* Pert.

DORIMANT [*surprised*] Bellinda here!

BELLINDA [*aside*] He starts and looks pale. The sight of me has touched his guilty soul.

PERT 'Twas but a qualm, as I said, a little indigestion. The surfeit-water did it, madam, mixed with a little mirabilis.[7]

DORIMANT [*aside*] I am confounded, and cannot guess how she came hither.

MRS. LOVEIT 'Tis your fortune, Bellinda, ever to be here when I am abused by this prodigy of ill nature.

BELLINDA I am amazed to find him here. How has he the face to come near you?

DORIMANT [*aside*] Here is fine work towards! I never was at such a loss before.

BELLINDA One who makes a public profession of breach of faith and ingratitude—I loathe the sight of him.

DORIMANT [*aside*] There is no remedy. I must submit to their tongues now and some other time bring myself off as well as I can.

BELLINDA Other men are wicked, but then they have some sense of shame. He is never well but when he triumphs—nay, glories—to a woman's face in his villainies.

MRS. LOVEIT You are in the right, Bellinda; but methinks your kindness for me makes you concern yourself too much with him.

BELLINDA It does indeed, my dear. His barbarous carriage to you yesterday made me hope you ne'er would see him more, and the very next day to find him here again provokes me strangely. But because I know you love him, I have done.

DORIMANT You have reproached me handsomely, and I deserve it for coming hither, but—

PERT You must expect it, sir. All women will hate you for my lady's sake.

DORIMANT [*aside*] Nay, if she begins too, 'tis time to fly. I shall be scolded to death, else. [*To* Bellinda.] I am to blame in some circumstances, I confess; but as to the main, I am not so guilty as you imagine. [*Aloud.*] I shall seek a more convenient time to clear myself.

MRS. LOVEIT Do it now! What impediments are here?

DORIMANT I want time, and you want temper.

MRS. LOVEIT These are weak pretenses.

7. Drink made with wine and spices.

DORIMANT You were never more mistaken in your life; and so farewell.

Dorimant flings off.

MRS. LOVEIT Call a footman, Pert. Quickly! I will have him dogged.

PERT I wish you would not, for my quiet and your own.

MRS. LOVEIT I'll find out the infamous cause of all our quarrels, pluck her mask off, and expose her bare-faced to the world!

Exit Pert.

BELLINDA [*aside*] Let me but escape this time, I'll never venture more.

MRS. LOVEIT Bellinda, you shall go with me.

BELLINDA I have such a heaviness hangs on me with what I did this morning, I would fain go home and sleep, my dear.

MRS. LOVEIT Death and eternal darkness! I shall never sleep again. Raging fevers seize the world and make mankind as restless all as I am!

Exit Mrs. Loveit.

BELLINDA I knew him false and helped to make him so. Was not her ruin enough to fright me from the danger? It should have been, but love can take no warning.

Exit Bellinda.

Act V. *Scene ii.* Lady Townley's *house.*
Enter Medley, Young Bellair, Lady Townley, Emilia, *and* Smirk, *a chaplain.*

MEDLEY Bear up, Bellair, and do not let us see that repentance in thine we daily do in married faces.

LADY TOWNLEY This wedding will strangely surprise my brother when he knows it.

MEDLEY Your nephew ought to conceal it for a time, madam. Since marriage has lost its good name, prudent men seldom expose their own reputations till 'tis convenient to justify their wives'.

OLD BELLAIR [*without*] Where are you all there? Out, adod, will nobody hear?

LADY TOWNLEY My brother! Quickly, Mr. Smirk, into this closet. You must not be seen yet.

Smirk goes into the closet.
Enter Old Bellair *and* Lady Townley's Page.

OLD BELLAIR [*to* Page] Desire Mr. Fourbe to walk into the lower parlor. I will be with him presently.

Exit Page.

[*To* Young Bellair.] Where have you been, sir, you could not wait on me today?

YOUNG BELLAIR About a business.

OLD BELLAIR Are you so good at business? Adod, I have a business too, you shall dispatch out of hand, sir. —Send for a parson, sister. My Lady Woodvill and her daughter are coming.

LADY TOWNLEY What need you huddle up[8] things thus?

OLD BELLAIR Out a pize! Youth is apt to play the fool, and 'tis not good it should be in their power.

LADY TOWNLEY You need not fear your son.

8. Rush.

OLD BELLAIR H' has been idling this morning, and adod, I do not like him. [*to* Emilia.] How dost thou do, sweetheart?

EMILIA You are very severe, sir. Married in such haste!

OLD BELLAIR Go to, thou'rt a rogue, and I will talk with thee anon.
Enter Lady Woodvill, Harriet, *and* Busy.
Here's my Lady Woodvill come. —Welcome, madam. Mr. Fourbe's below with the writings.

LADY WOODVILL Let us down and make an end, then.

OLD BELLAIR Sister, show the way. [*To* Young Bellair, *who is talking to* Harriet.] Harry, your business lies not there yet. —Excuse him till we have done, lady, and then, adod, he shall be for thee. —Mr. Medley, we must trouble you to be a witness.

MEDLEY I luckily came for that purpose, sir.
Exeunt Old Bellair, Medley, Young Bellair, Lady Townley, *and* Lady Woodvill.

BUSY [*to* Harriet] What will you do, madam?

HARRIET Be carried back and mewed up in the country again, run away here—anything rather than be married to a man I do not care for. —Dear Emilia, do thou advise me.

EMILIA Mr. Bellair is engaged, you know.

HARRIET I do, but know not what the fear of losing an estate may fright him to.

EMILIA In the desp'rate conditions you are in, you should consult with some judicious man. What think you of Mr. Dorimant?

HARRIET I do not think of him at all.

BUSY [*aside*] She thinks of nothing else, I am sure.

EMILIA How fond your mother was of Mr. Courtage.

HARRIET Because I contrived the mistake to make a little mirth, you believe I like the man.

EMILIA Mr. Bellair believes you love him.

HARRIET Men are seldom in the right when they guess at a woman's mind. Would she whom he loves loved him no better!

BUSY [*aside*] That's e'en well enough, on all conscience.

EMILIA Mr. Dorimant has a great deal of wit.

HARRIET And takes a great deal of pains to show it.

EMILIA He's extremely well-fashioned.

HARRIET Affectedly grave, or ridiculously wild and apish.

BUSY You defend him still against your mother.

HARRIET I would not, were he justly rallied; but I cannot hear anyone undeservedly railed at.

EMILIA Has your woman learnt the song you were so taken with?

HARRIET I was fond of a new thing. 'Tis dull at second hearing.

EMILIA Mr. Dorimant made it.

BUSY She knows it, madam, and has made me sing it at least a dozen times this morning.

HARRIET Thy tongue is as impertinent as thy fingers.

EMILIA [*to* Busy] You have provoked her.

BUSY 'Tis but singing the song and I shall appease her.

EMILIA Prithee, do.

HARRIET She has a voice will grate your ears worse than a catcall, and dresses so ill she's scarce fit to trick up a yeoman's daughter on a holiday.

Busy *sings.*

Song, by Sir C. S.[9]

As Amoret with Phillis sat
    One evening on the plain,
And saw the charming Strephon wait
    To tell the nymph his pain,

The threat'ning danger to remove,
    She whispered in her ear,
"Ah, Phillis, if you would not love,
    This shepherd do not hear:

None ever had so strange an art,
    His passion to convey
Into a list'ning virgin's heart
    And steal her soul away.

Fly, fly betimes, for fear you give
    Occasion for your fate."
"In vain," said she, "in vain I strive.
    Alas, 'tis now too late."

Enter Dorimant.

DORIMANT

    "Music so softens and disarms the mind—"

HARRIET

    "That not one arrow does resistance find."[1]

DORIMANT Let us make use of the lucky minute, then.

HARRIET [*aside, turning from* Dorimant] My love springs with my blood into my face. I dare not look upon him yet.

DORIMANT What have we here—the picture of celebrated beauty giving audience in public to a declared lover?

HARRIET Play the dying fop and make the piece complete, sir.

DORIMANT What think you if the hint were well improved—the whole mystery of making love pleasantly designed and wrought in a suit of hangings?

HARRIET 'Twere needless to execute fools in effigy who suffer daily in their own persons.

DORIMANT [*to* Emilia, *aside*] Mrs. Bride, for such I know this happy day has made you—

EMILIA Defer the formal joy you are to give me, and mind your business with her. [*Aloud.*] Here are dreadful preparations, Mr. Dorimant—writings sealing, and a parson sent for.

DORIMANT To marry this lady?

BUSY Condemned she is; and what will become of her I know not,

---

9. Either Sir Car Scroope (who wrote the prologue) or Sir Charles Sedley.

1. From Waller's "Of my Lady Isabella, Playing on the Lute," lines 11–12.

without you generously engage in a rescue.

DORIMANT In this sad condition, madam, I can do no less than offer you my service.

HARRIET The obligation is not great: you are the common sanctuary for all young women who run from their relations.

DORIMANT I have always my arms open to receive the distressed. But I will open my heart and receive you where none yet did ever enter. You have filled it with a secret, might I but let you know it.

HARRIET Do not speak it if you would have me believe it. Your tongue is so famed for falsehood, 'twill do the truth an injury.
Turns away her head.

DORIMANT Turn not away, then, but look on me and guess it.

HARRIET Did you not tell me there was no credit to be given to faces—that women nowadays have their passions as much at will as they have their complexions, and put on joy and sadness, scorn and kindness, with the same ease they do their paint and patches? Are they the only counterfeits?

DORIMANT You wrong your own while you suspect my eyes. By all the hope I have in you, the inimitable color in your cheeks is not more free from art than are the sighs I offer.

HARRIET In men who have been long hardened in sin, we have reason to mistrust the first signs of repentance.

DORIMANT The prospect of such a heav'n will make me persevere and give you marks that are infallible.

HARRIET What are those?

DORIMANT I will renounce all the joys I have in friendship and in wine, sacrifice to you all the interest I have in other women—

HARRIET Hold! Though I wish you devout, I would not have you turn fanatic. Could you neglect these a while and make a journey into the country?

DORIMANT To be with you, I could live there and never send one thought to London.

HARRIET Whate'er you say, I know all beyond High Park's a desert to you, and that no gallantry can draw you farther.

DORIMANT That has been the utmost limit of my love; but now my passion knows no bounds, and there's no measure to be taken of what I'll do for you from anything I ever did before.

HARRIET When I hear you talk thus in Hampshire, I shall begin to think there may be some little truth enlarged upon.

DORIMANT Is this all? Will you not promise me—

HARRIET I hate to promise. What we do then is expected from us and wants much of the welcome it finds when it surprises.

DORIMANT May I not hope?

HARRIET That depends on you and not on me; and 'tis to no purpose to forbid it.
Turns to Busy.

BUSY Faith, madam, now I perceive the gentleman loves you too. E'en let him know your mind, and torment yourselves no longer.

HARRIET Dost think I have no sense of modesty?

BUSY Think, if you lose this, you may never have another opportunity.

HARRIET May he hate me—a curse that frights me when I speak it —if ever I do a thing against the rules of decency and honor.

DORIMANT [*to* Emilia] I am beholding to you for your good intentions, madam.

EMILIA I thought the concealing of our marriage from her might have done you better service.

DORIMANT Try her again.

EMILIA [*to* Harriet] What have you resolved, madam? The time draws near.

HARRIET To be obstinate and protest against this marriage.

    Enter Lady Townley *in haste.*

LADY TOWNLEY [*to* Emilia] Quickly, quickly, let Mr. Smirk out of the closet!

    Smirk *comes out of the closet.*

HARRIET A parson! [*To* Dorimant.] Had you laid him in here?

DORIMANT I knew nothing of him.

HARRIET Should it appear you did, your opinion of my easiness may cost you dear.

    Enter Old Bellair, Young Bellair, Medley, *and* Lady Woodvill.

OLD BELLAIR Out a pize, the canonical hour[2] is almost past! Sister, is the man of God come?

LADY TOWNLEY He waits your leisure.

OLD BELLAIR [*to* Smirk] By your favor, sir. —Adod, a pretty spruce fellow. What may we call him?

LADY TOWNLEY Mr. Smirk—my Lady Biggot's chaplain.

OLD BELLAIR A wise woman, adod she is; the man will serve for the flesh as well as the spirit. —Please you, sir, to commission a young couple to go to bed together a God's name? —Harry!

YOUNG BELLAIR Here, sir.

OLD BELLAIR Out a pize! Without your mistress in your hand?

SMIRK Is this the gentleman?

OLD BELLAIR Yes, sir.

SMIRK Are you not mistaken, sir?

OLD BELLAIR Adod, I think not, sir!

SMIRK Sure you are, sir.

OLD BELLAIR You look as if you would forbid the banns, Mr. Smirk. I hope you have no pretension to the lady.

SMIRK Wish him joy, sir. I have done him the good office today already.

OLD BELLAIR Out a pize! What do I hear?

LADY TOWNLEY Never storm, brother. The truth is out.

OLD BELLAIR How say you, sir? Is this your wedding day?

YOUNG BELLAIR It is, sir.

OLD BELLAIR And, adod, it shall be mine too. [*To* Emilia.] Give

2. When marriages could be legally performed.

me thy hand, sweetheart. [*She refuses.*] What dost thou mean? Give me thy hand, I say!

Emilia *kneels and* Young Bellair.

LADY TOWNLEY Come, come, give her your blessing. This is the woman your son loved and is married to.

OLD BELLAIR Ha! Cheated! Cozened! And by your contrivance, sister!

LADY TOWNLEY What would you do with her? She's a rogue, and you can't abide her.

MEDLEY Shall I hit her a pat for you, sir?

OLD BELLAIR Adod, you are all rogues, and I never will forgive you. [*Flinging away.*]

LADY TOWNLEY Whither? Whither away?

MEDLEY Let him go and cool awhile.

LADY WOODVILL [*to* Dorimant] Here's a business broke out now, Mr. Courtage. I am made a fine fool of.

DORIMANT You see the old gentleman knew nothing of it.

LADY WOODVILL I find he did not. I shall have some trick put upon me, if I stay in this wicked town any longer. —Harriet, dear child, where art thou? I'll into the country straight.

OLD BELLAIR Adod, madam, you shall hear me first.

Enter Mrs. Loveit *and* Bellinda.

MRS. LOVEIT Hither my man dogged him.

BELLINDA Yonder he stands, my dear.

MRS. LOVEIT I see him, [*aside*] and with him the face that has undone me. Oh, that I were but where I might throw out the anguish of my heart! Here it must rage within and break it.

LADY TOWNLEY Mrs. Loveit! Are you afraid to come forward?

MRS. LOVEIT I was amazed to see so much company here in a morning. The occasion sure is extraordinary.

DORIMANT [*aside*] Loveit and Bellinda! The devil owes me a share today, and I think never will have done paying it.

MRS. LOVEIT Married! Dear Emilia, how am I transported with the news!

HARRIET [*to* Dorimant] I little thought Emilia was the woman Mr. Bellair was in love with. I'll chide her for not trusting me with the secret.

DORIMANT How do you like Mrs. Loveit?

HARRIET She's a famed mistress of yours, I hear.

DORIMANT She has been, on occasion.

OLD BELLAIR [*to* Lady Woodvill] Adod, madam, I cannot help it.

LADY WOODVILL You need make no more apologies, sir.

EMILIA [*to* Mrs. Loveit] The old gentleman's excusing himself to my Lady Woodvill.

MRS. LOVEIT Ha, ha, ha! I never heard of anything so pleasant.

HARRIET [*to* Dorimant] She's extremely overjoyed at something.

DORIMANT At nothing. She is one of those hoiting[3] ladies who gaily fling themselves about and force a laugh when their aching hearts are full of discontent and malice.

3. Romping.

MRS. LOVEIT Oh heav'n, I was never so near killing myself with laughing. —Mr. Dorimant, are you a brideman?

LADY WOODVILL Mr. Dorimant! Is this Mr. Dorimant, madam?

MRS. LOVEIT If you doubt it, your daughter can resolve you, I suppose.

LADY WOODVILL I am cheated too, basely cheated!

OLD BELLAIR Out a pize, what's here? More knavery yet?

LADY WOODVILL Harriet! On my blessing, come away, I charge you.

HARRIET Dear mother, do but stay and hear me.

LADY WOODVILL I am betrayed! And thou art undone, I fear.

HARRIET Do not fear it. I have not, nor never will, do anything against my duty. Believe me, dear mother, do!

DORIMANT [to Mrs. Loveit] I had trusted you with this secret but that I knew the violence of your nature would ruin my fortune— as now unluckily it has. I thank you, madam.

MRS. LOVEIT She's an heiress, I know, and very rich.

DORIMANT To satisfy you, I must give up my interest wholly to my love. Had you been a reasonable woman, I might have secured 'em both and been happy.

MRS. LOVEIT You might have trusted me with anything of this kind; you know you might. Why did you go under a wrong name?

DORIMANT The story is too long to tell you now. Be satisfied; this is the business, this is the mask has kept me from you.

BELLINDA [aside] He's tender of my honor, though he's cruel to my love.

MRS. LOVEIT Was it no idle mistress, then?

DORIMANT Believe me—a wife, to repair the ruins of my estate that needs it.

MRS. LOVEIT The knowledge of this makes my grief hang lighter on my soul, but I shall never more be happy.

DORIMANT Bellinda—

BELLINDA Do not think of clearing yourself with me. It is impossible. Do all men break their words thus?

DORIMANT Th'extravagant words they speak in love. 'Tis as unreasonable to expect we should perform all we promise then, as do all we threaten when we are angry. When I see you next—

BELLINDA Take no notice of me, and I shall not hate you.

DORIMANT How came you to Mrs. Loveit?

BELLINDA By a mistake the chairmen made for want of my giving them directions.

DORIMANT 'Twas a pleasant one. We must meet again.

BELLINDA Never.

DORIMANT Never?

BELLINDA When we do, may I be as infamous as you are false.

LADY TOWNLEY [to Lady Woodvill] Men of Mr. Dorimant's character always suffer in the general opinion of the world.

MEDLEY You can make no judgment of a witty man from common fame, considering the prevailing faction, madam.

OLD BELLAIR Adod, he's in the right.

MEDLEY Besides, 'tis a common error among women to believe too well of them they know and too ill of them they don't.

OLD BELLAIR Adod, he observes well.

LADY TOWNLEY Believe me, madam, you will find Mr. Dorimant as civil a gentleman as you thought Mr. Courtage.

HARRIET If you would but know him better—

LADY WOODVILL You have a mind to know him better? Come away! You shall never see him more.

HARRIET Dear mother, stay!

LADY WOODVILL I wo' not be consenting to your ruin.

HARRIET Were my fortune in your power—

LADY WOODVILL Your person is.

HARRIET Could I be disobedient, I might take it out of yours and put it into his.

LADY WOODVILL 'Tis that you would be at! You would marry this Dorimant!

HARRIET I cannot deny it. I would, and never will marry any other man.

LADY WOODVILL Is this the duty that you promised?

HARRIET But I will never marry him against your will.

LADY WOODVILL [*aside*] She knows the way to melt my heart. [*To* Harriet.] Upon yourself light your undoing.

MEDLEY [*to* Old Bellair] Come, sir, you have not the heart any longer to refuse your blessing.

OLD BELLAIR Adod, I ha' not. —Rise, and God bless you both. Make much of her, Harry; she deserves thy kindness. [*To* Emilia.] Adod, sirrah, I did not think it had been in thee.

Enter Sir Fopling *and's* Page.

SIR FOPLING 'Tis a damned windy day. Hey, page! Is my periwig right?

PAGE A little out of order, sir.

SIR FOPLING Pox o' this apartment! It wants an antechamber to adjust oneself in. [*To* Mrs. Loveit.] Madam, I came from your house, and your servants directed me hither.

MRS. LOVEIT I will give order hereafter they shall direct you better.

SIR FOPLING The great satisfaction I had in the Mall last night has given me much disquiet since.

MRS. LOVEIT 'Tis likely to give me more than I desire.

SIR FOPLING [*aside*] What the devil makes her so reserved?—Am I guilty of an indiscretion, madam?

MRS. LOVEIT You will be of a great one, if you continue your mistake, sir.

SIR FOPLING Something puts you out of humour.

MRS. LOVEIT The most foolish, inconsiderable thing that ever did.

SIR FOPLING Is it in my power?

MRS. LOVEIT To hang or drown it. Do one of 'em, and trouble me no more.

SIR FOPLING So *fieré*? *Serviteur*, madam.[4] —Medley, where's Dorimant?

4. "So haughty? Your servant, madam."

MEDLEY Methinks the lady has not made you those advances today she did last night, Sir Fopling.

SIR FOPLING Prithee, do not talk of her.

MEDLEY She would be a *bonne fortune.*

SIR FOPLING Not to me at present.

MEDLEY How so?

SIR FOPLING An intrigue now would be but a temptation to me to throw away that vigor on one which I mean shall shortly make my court to the whole sex in a ballet.

MEDLEY Wisely considered, Sir Fopling.

SIR FOPLING No one woman is worth the loss of a cut in a caper.

MEDLEY Not when 'tis so universally designed.

LADY WOODVILL Mr. Dorimant, everyone has spoke so much in your behalf that I can no longer doubt but I was in the wrong.

MRS. LOVEIT [*to* Bellinda] There's nothing but falsehood and impertinence in this world. All men are villains or fools. Take example from my misfortunes. Bellinda, if thou wouldst be happy, give thyself wholly up to goodness.

HARRIET [*to* Mrs. Loveit] Mr. Dorimant has been your God almighty long enough. 'Tis time to think of another.

MRS. LOVEIT [*to* Bellinda] Jeered by her! I will lock myself up in my house and never see the world again.

HARRIET A nunnery is the more fashionable place for such a retreat and has been the fatal consequence of many a *belle passion.*

MRS. LOVEIT [*aside*] Hold, heart, till I get home! Should I answer, 'twould make her triumph greater.

Is going out.

DORIMANT Your hand, Sir Fopling—

SIR FOPLING Shall I wait upon you, madam?

MRS. LOVEIT Legion of fools, as many devils take thee!

Exit Mrs. Loveit.

MEDLEY Dorimant, I pronounce thy reputation clear; and henceforward, when I would know anything of woman, I will consult no other oracle.

SIR FOPLING Stark mad, by all that's handsome! —Dorimant, thou hast engaged me in a pretty business.

DORIMANT I have not leisure now to talk about it.

OLD BELLAIR Out a pize, what does this man of mode do here again?

LADY TOWNLEY He'll be an excellent entertainment within, brother, and is luckily come to raise the mirth of the company.

LADY WOODVILL Madam, I take my leave of you.

LADY TOWNLEY What do you mean, madam?

LADY WOODVILL To go this afternoon part of my way to Hartly.

OLD BELLAIR Adod, you shall stay and dine first! Come, we will all be good friends; and you shall give Mr. Dorimant leave to wait upon you and your daughter in the country.

LADY WOODVILL If his occasions bring him that way, I have now so good an opinion of him, he shall be welcome.

HARRIET To a great, rambling, lone house that looks as it were not inhabited, the family's so small. There you'll find my mother, an old lame aunt, and myself, sir, perched up on chairs at a distance in a large parlor, sitting moping like three or four melancholy birds in a spacious volary.[5] Does not this stagger your resolution?

DORIMANT Not at all, madam. The first time I saw you, you left me with the pangs of love upon me; and this day my soul has quite given up her liberty.

HARRIET This is more dismal than the country. —Emilia, pity me who am going to that sad place. Methinks I hear the hateful noise of rooks already—kaw, kaw, kaw. There's music in the worst cry[6] in London. "My dill and cucumbers to pickle."

OLD BELLAIR Sister, knowing of this matter, I hope you have provided us some good cheer.

LADY TOWNLEY I have, brother, and the fiddles too.

OLD BELLAIR Let 'em strike up then. The young lady shall have a dance before she departs.

Dance.

[*After the dance.*] So now we'll in, and make this an arrant wedding day.

To the pit.

And if these honest gentlemen rejoice,
Adod, the boy has made a happy choice.

Exeunt omnes.

The Epilogue

By Mr. Dryden

Most modern wits such monstrous fools have shown,
They seemed not of heav'n's making, but their own.
Those nauseous harlequins in farce may pass,
But there goes more to a substantial ass;
Something of man must be exposed to view,
That, gallants, they may more resemble you.
Sir Fopling is a fool so nicely writ,
The ladies would mistake him for a wit
And when he sings, talks loud, and cocks,[7] would cry:
"I vow, methinks he's pretty company—
So brisk, so gay, so traveled, so refined,
As he took pains to graft upon his kind."[8]
True fops help nature's work, and go to school
To file and finish God a'mighty's fool.
Yet none Sir Fopling him, or him, can call:
He's knight o' th' shire[9] and represents ye all.

5. Aviary.
6. Street-vendor's cry.
7. Struts.

8. "To improve his natural type."
9. Member of Parliament.

From each he meets, he culls whate'er he can;
Legion's his name, a people in a man.
His bulky folly gathers, as it goes,
And, rolling o'er you, like a snowball grows.
His various modes from various fathers follow;
One taught the toss,[1] and one the new French wallow.[2]
His sword-knot, this; his cravat, this designed;
And this, the yard-long snake[3] he twirls behind.
From one, the sacred periwig he gained,
Which wind ne'er blew, nor touch of hat prophaned;
Another's diving bow he did adore,
Which with a shog[4] casts all the hair before,
Till he with full decorum brings it back
And rises with a water spaniel shake.
As for his songs (the ladies' dear delight),
Those sure he took from most of you who write.
Yet every man is safe from what he feared,
For no one fool is hunted from the herd.

FINIS

1. Toss of the head.
2. Rolling gait.
3. Curl or tail of a wig.
4. Shake.

WILLIAM CONGREVE

The Way of the World†

Audire est operae pretium, procedere recte
Qui maechis non vultis—
—Metuat doti deprensa.—[1]

To the Right Honorable

Ralph, Earl of Montague, &.

My Lord,

Whether the world will arraign me of vanity or not, that I have presumed to dedicate this comedy to your Lordship, I am yet in doubt, though it may be it is some degree of vanity even to doubt of it. One who has at any time had the honor of your Lordship's conversation, cannot be supposed to think very meanly of that which he would prefer to your perusal; yet it were to incur the imputation of too much sufficiency, to pretend to such a merit as might abide that test of your Lordship's censure.

Whatever value may be wanting to this play while yet it is mine, will be sufficiently made up to it when it is once become your Lordship's; and it is my security that I cannot have overrated it more by my dedication than your Lordship will dignify it by your patronage.

That it succeeded on the stage was almost beyond my expectation; for but little of it was prepared for that general taste which seems now to be predominant in the palates of our audience.

Those characters which are meant to be ridiculous in most of our comedies are of fools so gross that, in my humble opinion, they should rather disturb than divert the well-natured and reflecting part of an audience; they are rather objects of charity than contempt; and instead of moving our mirth, they ought very often to excite our compassion.

This reflection moved me to design some characters which should appear ridiculous, not so much through a natural folly (which is

---

† First performed in 1700 and published in the same year.
1. Horace, *Satires*, II.i.37–38 and 131: "You who wish trouble to the affairs of adulterers, it is worth your while to hear how they fare badly on every side.— Seized in the act, she fears for her dowry."

153

incorrigible, and therefore not proper for the stage) as through an affected wit; a wit, which, at the same time that it is affected, is also false. As there is some difficulty in the formation of a character of this nature, so there is some hazard which attends the progress of its success upon the stage; for many come to a play so overcharged with criticism that they very often let fly their censure, when through their rashness they have mistaken their aim. This I had occasion lately to observe; for this play had been acted two or three days before some of these hasty judges could find the leisure to distinguish betwixt the character of a Witwoud and a Truewit.[2]

I must beg your Lordship's pardon for this digression from the true course of this epistle; but that it may not seem altogether impertinent, I beg that I may plead the occasion of it, in part of that excuse of which I stand in need, for recommending this comedy to your protection. It is only by the countenance of your Lordship, and the *few* so qualified, that such who write with care and pains can hope to be distinguished; for the prostituted name of *poet* promiscuously levels all that bear it.

Terence, the most correct writer in the world, had a Scipio and a Laelius,[3] if not to assist him, at least to support him in his reputation; and notwithstanding his extraordinary merit, it may be their countenance was not more than necessary.

The purity of his style, the delicacy of his turns, and the justness of his characters were all of them beauties which the greater part of his audience were incapable of tasting; some of the coarsest strokes of Plautus, so severely censured by Horace, were more likely to affect the multitude, such who come with expectation to laugh out the last act of a play, and are better entertained with two or three unseasonable jests than with the artful solution of the *fable*.

As Terence excelled in his performances, so had he great advantages to encourage his undertakings, for he built most on the foundations of Menander;[4] his plots were generally modeled, and his characters ready drawn to his hand. He copied Menander, and Menander had no less light in the formation of his characters from the observations of Theophrastus,[5] of whom he was a disciple; and Theophrastus, it is known, was not only the disciple, but the immediate successor of Aristotle, the first and greatest judge of poetry. These were great models to design by; and the further advantage which Terence possessed, towards giving his plays the due ornaments of purity of style and justness of manners, was not less considerable from the freedom of conversation which was permitted him with Laelius and Scipio, two of the greatest and most polite men of his age. And

2. Witwoud, a pretender to wit, appears in this play. Truewit, a possessor of wit, appears in Ben Jonson's *Epicoene*.
3. Patrons of the Roman comic dramatist Terence.
4. Greek comic dramatist.
5. Greek author, known for "character writing."

indeed the privilege of such a conversation is the only certain means of attaining to the perfection of dialogue.

If it has happened in any part of this comedy that I have gained a turn of style or expression more correct, or at least more corrigible, than in those which I have formerly written, I must, with equal pride and gratitude, ascribe it to the honor of your Lordship's admitting me into your conversation, and that of a society where everybody else was so well worthy of you, in your retirement last summer from the town; for it was immediately after that this comedy was written. If I have failed in my performance, it is only to be regretted, where there were so many not inferior either to a Scipio or a Laelius, that there should be one wanting equal to the capacity of a Terence.

If I am not mistaken, poetry is almost the only art which has not yet laid claim to your Lordship's patronage. Architecture and painting, to the great honor of our country, have flourished under your influence and protection. In the meantime, poetry, the eldest sister of all arts, and parent of most, seems to have resigned her birthright, by having neglected to pay her duty to your Lordship, and by permitting others of a later extraction to prepossess that place in your esteem to which none can pretend a better title. Poetry, in its nature, is sacred to the good and great; the relation between them is reciprocal, and they are ever propitious to it. It is the privilege of poetry to address to them, and it is their prerogative alone to give it protection.

This received maxim is a general apology for all writers who consecrate their labors to great men; but I could wish at this time that this address were exempted from the common pretense of all dedications; and that, as I can distinguish your Lordship even among the most deserving, so this offering might become remarkable by some particular instance of respect, which should assure your Lordship that I am, with all due sense of your extreme worthiness and humanity,

My Lord,
Your Lordship's most obedient
and most obliged humble servant
WILL. CONGREVE

Prologue

Spoken by Mr. Betterton[6]

Of those few fools, who with ill stars are cursed,
Sure scribbling fools, called poets, fare the worst;
For they're a sort of fools which Fortune makes,

6. Who played Fainall.

And after she has made 'em fools, forsakes.
With Nature's oafs 'tis quite a different case.
For Fortune favors all her idiot race;
In her own nest the cuckoo eggs we find,
O'er which she brooks to hatch the changeling kind.[7]
No portion for her own she has to spare,
So much she dotes on her adopted care.

Poets are bubbles,[8] by the town drawn in,
Suffered at first some trifling stakes to win;
But what unequal hazards do they run!
Each time they write they venture all they've won;
The squire that's buttered still is sure to be undone.
This author, heretofore, has found your favor,
But pleads no merit from his past behavior.
To build on that might prove a vain presumption,
Should grants to poets made admit resumption;
And in Parnassus[9] he must lose his seat
If that be found a forfeited estate.

He owns, with toil he wrote the following scenes,
But if they're naught ne'er spare him for his pains.
Damn him the more; have no commiseration
For dullness on mature deliberation.
He swears he'll not resent one hissed-off scene,
Nor, like those peevish wits, his play maintain,
Who, to assert their sense, your taste arraign.
Some plot we think he has, and some new thought,
Some humour too, no farce—but that's a fault.
Satire, he thinks, you ought not to expect;
For so reformed a town who dares correct?[1]
To please this time has been his sole pretense;
He'll not instruct, lest it should give offense.
Should he by chance a knave or fool expose
That hurts none here; sure here are none of those.
In short, our play shall (with your leave to show it)
Give you one instance of a passive poet,
Who to your judgments yields all resignation;
So save or damn, after your own discretion.

Dramatis Personae

Men

FAINALL, in love with MRS. MARWOOD	Mr. Betterton
MIRABELL, in love with MRS. MILLAMANT	Mr. Verbruggen
WITWOUD, PETULANT, Followers of MRS. MILLAMANT	{ Mr. Bowen Mr. Bowman

7. The cuckoo was known to lay eggs in the nests of other birds. *Changeling* means (1) *an idiot*, and (2) *a child substituted for another*.
8. Dupes.
9. Greek mountain, sacred to Apollo and the Muses.
1. A reference to moralistic efforts to reform manners; more particularly to Jeremy Collier's attack on the licentiousness of the stage—see p. 391.

Sir Wilfull Witwoud, Half-brother to Witwoud, and Nephew to Lady Wishfort	*Mr. Underhill*
Waitwell, Servant to Mirabell	*Mr. Bright*

Women

Lady Wishfort, Enemy to Mirabell, for having falsely pretended love to her	*Mrs. Leigh*
Mrs. Millamant, A fine Lady, Niece to Lady Wishfort, and loves Mirabell	*Mrs. Bracegirdle*
Mrs. Marwood, Friend to Mr. Fainall, and likes Mirabell	*Mrs. Barry*
Mrs. Fainall, Daughter to Lady Wishfort, and Wife to Fainall, formerly Friend to Mirabell	*Mrs. Bowman*
Foible, Woman to Lady Wishfort	*Mrs. Willis*
Mincing, Woman to Mrs. Millamant	*Mrs. Prince*

Dancers, Footmen, and Attendants

SCENE—LONDON

The time equal to that of the presentation.

The Way of the World

Act I. A Chocolate-house.
Mirabell *and* Fainall, *rising from cards*; Betty *waiting*.

MIRABELL You are a fortunate man, Mr. Fainall.

FAINALL Have we done?

MIRABELL What you please. I'll play on to entertain you.

FAINALL No, I'll give you your revenge another time, when you are not so indifferent; you are thinking of something else now, and play too negligently. The coldness of a losing gamester lessens the pleasure of the winner. I'd no more play with a man that slighted his ill fortune than I'd make love to a woman who undervalued the loss of her reputation.

MIRABELL You have a taste extremely delicate and are for refining on your pleasures.

FAINALL Prithee, why so reserved? Something has put you out of humour.

MIRABELL Not at all; I happen to be grave today, and you are gay; that's all.

FAINALL Confess, Millamant and you quarreled last night, after I left you; my fair cousin has some humours that would tempt the patience of a stoic. What, some coxcomb came in, and was well received by her, while you were by.

MIRABELL Witwoud and Petulant, and what was worse, her aunt, your wife's mother, my evil genius; or to sum up all in her own name, my old Lady Wishfort came in.

FAINALL Oh, there it is then! She has a lasting passion for you, and with reason. What, then my wife was there?

MIRABELL Yes, and Mrs. Marwood and three or four more, whom I
never saw before. Seeing me, they all put on their grave faces,
whispered one another; then complained aloud of the vapors,[2]
and after fell into a profound silence.

FAINALL They had a mind to be rid of you.

MIRABELL For which reason I resolved not to stir. At last the good
old lady broke through her painful taciturnity, with an invective against long visits. I would not have understood her, but
Millamant joining in the argument, I rose and with a con-
strained smile told her, I thought nothing was so easy as to know
when a visit began to be troublesome. She reddened and I withdrew, without expecting her reply.

FAINALL You were to blame to resent what she spoke only in compliance with her aunt.

MIRABELL She is more mistress of herself than to be under the
necessity of such a resignation.

FAINALL What? though half her fortune depends upon her marrying with my lady's approbation?

MIRABELL I was then in such a humour, that I should have been
better pleased if she had been less discreet.

FAINALL Now I remember, I wonder not they were weary of you.
Last night was one of their cabal-nights; they have 'em three
times a week, and meet by turns, at one another's apartments,
where they come together like the coroner's inquest, to sit upon
the murdered reputations of the week. You and I are excluded;
and it was once proposed that all the male sex should be
excepted; but somebody moved that, to avoid scandal, there
might be one man of the community; upon which motion Witwoud and Petulant were enrolled members.

MIRABELL And who may have been the foundress of this sect? My
Lady Wishfort, I warrant, who publishes her detestation of mankind, and full of the vigor of fifty-five, declares for a friend and
ratafia;[3] and let posterity shift for itself, she'll breed no more.

FAINALL The discovery of your sham addresses to her, to conceal
your love to her niece, has provoked this separation. Had you dissembled better, things might have continued in the state of
nature.

MIRABELL I did as much as a man could, with any reasonable conscience. I proceeded to the very last act of flattery with her, and
was guilty of a song in her commendation. Nay, I got a friend to
put her into a lampoon, and compliment her with the imputation of an affair with a young fellow, which I carried so far, that I
told her the malicious town took notice that she was grown fat of
a sudden; and when she lay in of a dropsy, persuaded her she was
reported to be in labor. The devil's in't, if an old woman is to be
flattered further, unless a man should endeavor downright personally to debauch her; and that my virtue forbade me. But for the

2. Depression.   3. A liqueur, fruit flavored.

discovery of that amour, I am indebted to your friend, or your wife's friend, Mrs. Marwood.

FAINALL What should provoke her to be your enemy, unless she has made you advances, which you have slighted? Women do not easily forgive omissions of that nature.

MIRABELL She was always civil to me, till of late. I confess I am not one of those coxcombs who are apt to interpret a woman's good manners to her prejudice, and think that she who does not refuse 'em everything can refuse 'em nothing.

FAINALL You are a gallant man, Mirabell; and though you may have cruelty enough not to satisfy a lady's longing, you have too much generosity not to be tender of her honor. Yet you speak with an indifference which seems to be affected, and confesses you are conscious of a negligence.

MIRABELL You pursue the argument with a distrust that seems to be unaffected, and confesses you are conscious of a concern for which the lady is more indebted to you than your wife.

FAINALL Fie, fie, friend! If you grow censorious, I must leave you. I'll look upon the gamesters in the next room.

MIRABELL Who are they?

FAINALL Petulant and Witwoud. [*To Betty.*] Bring me some chocolate.

Exit.

MIRABELL Betty, what says your clock?

BETTY Turned of the last canonical hour, sir.[4]

MIRABELL How pertinently the jade answers me! [*Looking on his watch.*] Ha? almost one o'clock! Oh, y'are come!

Enter a Servant.

Well, is the grand affair over? You have been something tedious.

SERVANT Sir, there's such coupling at Pancras,[5] that they stand behind one another, as 'twere in a country dance. Ours was the last couple to lead up; and no hopes appearing of dispatch, besides the parson growing hoarse, we were afraid his lungs would have failed before it came to our turn; so we drove round to Duke's Place, and there they were riveted in a trice.

MIRABELL So, so, you are sure they are married.

SERVANT Married and bedded, sir; I am witness.

MIRABELL Have you the certificate?

SERVANT Here it is, sir.

MIRABELL Has the tailor brought Waitwell's clothes home, and the new liveries?

SERVANT Yes, sir.

MIRABELL That's well. Do you go home again, d'ye hear, and adjourn the consummation till farther order; bid Waitwell shake his ears, and Dame Partlet[6] rustle up her feathers, and meet me

4. Noon, the last hour when marriages could be legally performed.

5. At St. Pancras Church (and at St. James's Church in Duke's Place, mentioned later in this speech) weddings were quick and a license was not always required.

6. Pertelote, a hen (and wife of Chaunte-cleer in Chaucer's *Nun's Priest's Tale*).

at one o'clock by Rosamond's Pond,[7] that I may see her before she returns to her lady; and as you tender your ears, be secret.

Exit Servant.

Re-enter Fainall *and* Betty.

FAINALL Joy of your success, Mirabell; you look pleased.

MIRABELL Aye, I have been engaged in a matter of some sort of mirth, which is not yet ripe for discovery. I am glad this is not a cabal-night. I wonder, Fainall, that you who are married, and of consequence should be discreet, will suffer your wife to be of such a party.

FAINALL Faith, I am not jealous. Besides, most who are engaged are women and relations; and for the men, they are of a kind too contemptible to give scandal.

MIRABELL I am of another opinion. The greater the coxcomb, always the more scandal; for a woman who is not a fool can have but one reason for associating with a man that is.

FAINALL Are you jealous as often as you see Witwoud entertained by Millamant?

MIRABELL Of her understanding I am, if not of her person.

FAINALL You do her wrong; for, to give her her due, she has wit.

MIRABELL She has beauty enough to make any man think so, and complaisance enough not to contradict him who shall tell her so.

FAINALL For a passionate lover, methinks you are a man somewhat too discerning in the failings of your mistress.

MIRABELL And for a discerning man, somewhat too passionate a lover; for I like her with all her faults; nay, like her for her faults. Her follies are so natural, or so artful, that they become her; and those affectations which in another woman would be odious, serve but to make her more agreeable. I'll tell thee, Fainall, she once used me with that insolence, that in revenge I took her to pieces; sifted her and separated her failings; I studied 'em, and got 'em by rote. The catalogue was so large that I was not without hopes one day or other to hate her heartily: to which end I so used myself to think of 'em that at length, contrary to my design and expectation, they gave me every hour less and less disturbance; till in a few days it became habitual to me to remember 'em without being displeased. They are now grown as familiar to me as my own frailties; and in all probability, in a little time longer I shall like 'em as well.

FAINALL Marry her, marry her! Be half as well acquainted with her charms as you are with her defects, and my life on't, you are your own man again.

MIRABELL Say you so?

FAINALL Aye, aye, I have experience: I have a wife, and so forth.

Enter Messenger.

MESSENGER Is one Squire Witwoud here?

BETTY Yes; what's your business?

MESSENGER I have a letter for him, from his brother Sir Wilfull,

7. A pond in St. James's Park.

which I am charged to deliver into his own hands.

BETTY He's in the next room, friend; that way.

Exit Messenger.

MIRABELL What, is the chief of that noble family in town, Sir Wilfull Witwoud?

FAINALL He is expected today. Do you know him?

MIRABELL I have seen him. He promises to be an extraordinary person; I think you have the honor to be related to him.

FAINALL Yes, he is half brother to this Witwoud by a former wife, who was sister to my Lady Wishfort, my wife's mother. If you marry Millamant, you must call cousins too.

MIRABELL I had rather be his relation than his acquaintance.

FAINALL He comes to town in order to equip himself for travel.

MIRABELL For travel! Why the man I mean is above forty.

FAINALL No matter for that; 'tis for the honor of England that all Europe should know we have blockheads of all ages.

MIRABELL I wonder there is not an act of parliament to save the credit of the nation, and prohibit the exportation of fools.

FAINALL By no means; 'tis better as 'tis. 'Tis better to trade with a little loss, than to be quite eaten up with being overstocked.

MIRABELL Pray, are the follies of this knight-errant and those of the squire his brother anything related?

FAINALL Not at all; Witwoud grows by the knight, like a medlar grafted on a crab.[8] One will melt in your mouth, and t'other set your teeth on edge; one is all pulp, and the other all core.

MIRABELL So one will be rotten before he be ripe, and the other will be rotten without ever being ripe at all.

FAINALL Sir Wilfull is an odd mixture of bashfulness and obstinancy. But when he's drunk, he's as loving as the monster in *The Tempest*,[9] and much after the same manner. To give t'other his due, he has something of good nature and does not always want wit.

MIRABELL Not always; but as often as his memory fails him, and his commonplace of comparisons.[1] He is a fool with a good memory and some few scraps of other folks' wit. He is one whose conversation can never be approved, yet it is now and then to be endured. He has indeed one good quality, he is not exceptious;[2] for he so passionately affects the reputation of understanding raillery, that he will construe an affront into a jest, and call downright rudeness and ill language satire and fire.

FAINALL If you have a mind to finish his picture, you have an opportunity to do it at full length. Behold the original!

Enter Witwoud.

WITWOUD Afford me your compassion, my dears! Pity me, Fainall! Mirabell, pity me!

MIRABELL I do from my soul.

8. A pulpy, overripe fruit grafted on a crab-apple.
9. Caliban, in Dryden and D'Avenant's adaptation of *The Tempest*.
1. Commonplace book, for copying witty remarks.
2. Quarrelsome.

FAINALL Why, what's the matter?

WITWOUD No letters for me, Betty?

BETTY Did not the messenger bring you one but now, sir?

WITWOUD Aye, but no other?

BETTY No, sir.

WITWOUD That's hard, that's very hard. A messenger, a mule, a beast of burden! He has brought me a letter from the fool my brother, as heavy as a panegyric in a funeral sermon, or a copy of commendatory verses from one poet to another. And what's worse, 'tis as sure a forerunner of the author as an epistle dedicatory.

MIRABELL A fool, and your brother, Witwoud!

WITWOUD Aye, aye, my half brother. My half brother he is, no nearer upon honor.

MIRABELL Then 'tis possible he may be but half a fool.

WITWOUD Good, good, Mirabell, *le drôle!*[3] Good, good; hang him, don't let's talk of him. Fainall, how does your lady? Gad, I say anything in the world to get this fellow out of my head. I beg pardon that I should ask a man of pleasure, and the town, a question at once so foreign and domestic. But I talk like an old maid at a marriage, I don't know what I say; but she's the best woman in the world.

FAINALL 'Tis well you don't know what you say, or else your commendation would go near to make me either vain or jealous.

WITWOUD No man in town lives well with a wife but Fainall. Your judgment, Mirabell.

MIRABELL You had better step and ask his wife, if you would be credibly informed.

WITWOUD Mirabell.

MIRABELL Aye.

WITWOUD My dear, I ask ten thousand pardons. Gad, I have forgot what I was going to say to you!

MIRABELL I thank you heartily, heartily.

WITWOUD No, but prithee excuse me: my memory is such a memory.

MIRABELL Have a care of such apologies, Witwoud; for I never knew a fool but he affected to complain, either of the spleen or his memory.

FAINALL What have you done with Petulant?

WITWOUD He's reckoning his money, my money it was. I have no luck today.

FAINALL You may allow him to win of you at play, for you are sure to be too hard for him at repartee; since you monopolize the wit that is between you, the fortune must be his of course.

MIRABELL I don't find that Petulant confesses the superiority of wit to be your talent, Witwoud.

WITWOUD Come, come, you are malicious now, and would breed debates. Petulant's my friend, and a very honest fellow, and a very pretty fellow, and has a smattering—faith and troth, a pretty

3. The amusing fellow.

deal of an odd sort of a small wit: nay, I'll do him justice. I'm his friend, I won't wrong him neither. And if he had but any judgment in the world, he would not be altogether contemptible. Come, come, don't detract from the merits of my friend.

FAINALL You don't take your friend to be over-nicely bred?

WITWOUD No, no, hang him, the rogue has no manners at all, that I must own. No more breeding than a bum-baily,[4] that I grant you. 'Tis pity, faith; the fellow has fire and life.

MIRABELL What, courage?

WITWOUD Hum, faith, I don't know as to that, I can't say as to that. Yes, faith, in a controversy he'll contradict anybody.

MIRABELL Though 'twere a man whom he feared, or a woman whom he loved.

WITWOUD Well, well, he does not always think before he speaks; we have all our failings. You're too hard upon him, you are, faith. Let me excuse him. I can defend most of his faults, except one or two. One he has, that's the truth on't; if he were my brother, I could not acquit him. That, indeed, I could wish were otherwise.

MIRABELL Aye, marry, what's that, Witwoud?

WITWOUD Oh, pardon me! Expose the infirmities of my friend! No, my dear, excuse me there.

FAINALL What, I warrant he's unsincere, or 'tis some such trifle.

WITWOUD No, no, what if he be? 'Tis no matter for that, his wit will excuse that. A wit should no more be sincere than a woman constant; one argues a decay of parts, as t'other of beauty.

MIRABELL Maybe you think him too positive?

WITWOUD No, no, his being positive is an incentive to argument, and keeps up conversation.

FAINALL Too illiterate?

WITWOUD That! that's his happiness; his want of learning gives him the more opportunities to show his natural parts.

MIRABELL He wants words?

WITWOUD Aye, but I like him for that now; for his want of words gives me the pleasure very often to explain his meaning.

FAINALL He's impudent?

WITWOUD No, that's not it.

MIRABELL Vain?

WITWOUD No.

MIRABELL What! he speaks unseasonable truths sometimes, because he has not wit enough to invent an evasion?

WITWOUD Truths! ha! ha! ha! No, no, since you will have it, I mean he never speaks truth at all, that's all. He will lie like a chambermaid, or a woman of quality's porter. Now that is a fault.

Enter Coachman.

COACHMAN Is Master Petulant here, mistress?

BETTY Yes.

COACHMAN Three gentlewomen in the coach would speak with him.

FAINALL Oh brave Petulant! Three!

4. Low-ranking bailiff.

BETTY I'll tell him.

COACHMAN You must bring two dishes of chocolate and a glass of cinnamon-water.

Exeunt Betty *and* Coachman.

WITWOUD That should be for two fasting strumpets, and a bawd troubled with wind. Now you may know what the three are.

MIRABELL You are very free with your friend's acquaintance.

WITWOUD Aye, aye, friendship without freedom is as dull as love without enjoyment, or wine without toasting; but to tell you a secret, these are trulls that he allows coach-hire, and something more by the week, to call on him once a day at public places.

MIRABELL How!

WITWOUD You shall see he won't go to 'em because there's no more company here to take notice of him. Why, this is nothing to what he used to do: before he found out this way, I have known him call for himself.

FAINALL Call for himself? What dost thou mean?

WITWOUD Mean! Why, he would slip you out of this chocolate-house, just when you had been talking to him. As soon as your back was turned, whip, he was gone! Then trip to his lodging, clap on a hood and scarf, and mask, slap into a hackney-coach, and drive hither to the door again in a trice, where he would send in for himself; that I mean, call for himself, wait for himself; nay, and what's more, not finding himself, sometimes leave a letter for himself.

MIRABELL I confess this is something extraordinary. I believe he waits for himself now, he is so long a-coming. Oh! I ask his pardon.

Enter Petulant *and* Betty.

BETTY Sir, the coach stays.

PETULANT Well, well; I come. 'Sbud, a man had as good be a professed midwife as a professed whoremaster, at this rate! To be knocked up and raised at all hours, and in all places! Pox on 'em, I won't come! D'ye hear, tell 'em I won't come. Let 'em snivel and cry their hearts out.

FAINALL You are very cruel, Petulant.

PETULANT All's one, let it pass. I have a humour to be cruel.

MIRABELL I hope they are not persons of condition that you use at this rate.

PETULANT Condition! Condition's a dried fig, if I am not in humour! By this hand, if they were your—a—a—your what'd'ye-call-'ems themselves, they must wait or rub off, if I want appetite.

MIRABELL What-d'ye-call-'ems! What are they, Witwoud?

WITWOUD Empresses, my dear; by your what-d'ye-call-'ems he means sultana queens.

PETULANT Aye, Roxolanas.[5]

MIRABELL Cry you mercy.

---

5. Prostitutes. So for "Empresses" and "sultana queens" above. D'Avenant's *The* *Siege of Rhodes* made the name Roxolana famous.

FAINALL Witwoud says they are—

PETULANT What does he say th'are?

WITWOUD I? Fine ladies, I say.

PETULANT Pass on, Witwoud. Harkee, by this light his relations: two co-heiresses his cousins, and an old aunt, that loves cater-wauling better than a conventicle.[6]

WITWOUD Ha! ha! ha! I had a mind to see how the rogue would come off. Ha! ha! ha! Gad, I can't be angry with him, if he had said they were my mother and my sisters.

MIRABELL No!

WITWOUD No; the rogue's wit and readiness of invention charm me. Dear Petulant!

BETTY They are gone, sir, in great anger.

PETULANT Enough, let 'em trundle. Anger helps complexion, saves paint.

FAINALL This continence is all dissembled; this is in order to have something to brag of the next time he makes court to Millamant, and swear he has abandoned the whole sex for her sake.

MIRABELL Have you not left off your impudent pretensions there yet? I shall cut your throat some time or other, Petulant, about that business.

PETULANT Aye, aye, let that pass. There are other throats to be cut.

MIRABELL Meaning mine, sir?

PETULANT Not I. I mean nobody; I know nothing. But there are uncles and nephews in the world, and they may be rivals. What then? All's one for that.

MIRABELL How! Harkee Petulant, come hither. Explain, or I shall call your interpreter.[7]

PETULANT Explain! I know nothing. Why, you have an uncle, have you not, lately come to town, and lodges by my Lady Wishfort's?

MIRABELL True.

PETULANT Why, that's enough. You and he are not friends; and if he should marry and have a child, you may be disinherited, ha?

MIRABELL Where hast thou stumbled upon all this truth?

PETULANT All's one for that; why, then say I know something.

MIRABELL Come, thou art an honest fellow, Petulant, and shalt make love to my mistress, thou sha't, faith. What hast thou heard of my uncle?

PETULANT I? Nothing I. If throats are to be cut, let swords clash! Snug's the word; I shrug and am silent.

MIRABELL Oh, raillery, raillery! Come, I know thou art in the women's secrets. What, you're a cabalist; I know you stayed at Millamant's last night, after I went. Was there any mention made of my uncle or me? Tell me. If thou hadst but good nature equal to thy wit, Petulant, Tony Witwoud, who is now thy competitor in fame, would show as dim by thee as a dead whiting's eye by a pearl of orient; he would no more be seen by thee than Mercury is by the sun. Come, I'm sure thou wo't tell me.

6. Meeting of nonconformists.
7. One who explains difficult texts. Witwoud, ironically.

PETULANT If I do, will you grant me common sense then for the future?

MIRABELL Faith, I'll do what I can for thee; and I'll pray that Heaven may grant it thee in the meantime.

PETULANT Well, harkee.

Mirabell and Petulant talk apart.

FAINALL Petulant and you both will find Mirabell as warm a rival as a lover.

WITWOUD Pshaw! pshaw! That she laughs at Petulant is plain. And for my part, but that it is almost a fashion to admire her, I should—harkee, to tell you a secret, but let it go no further; between friends, I shall never break my heart for her.

FAINALL How!

WITWOUD She's handsome; but she's a sort of an uncertain woman.

FAINALL I thought you had died for her.

WITWOUD Umh—no—

FAINALL She has wit.

WITWOUD 'Tis what she will hardly allow anybody else. Now, demme,[8] I should hate that, if she were as handsome as Cleopatra. Mirabell is not so sure of her as he thinks for.

FAINALL Why do you think so?

WITWOUD We stayed pretty late there last night, and heard something of an uncle to Mirabell, who is lately come to town, and is between him and the best part of his estate. Mirabell and he are at some distance, as my Lady Wishfort has been told; and you know she hates Mirabell worse than a Quaker hates a parrot, or than a fishmonger hates a hard frost. Whether this uncle has seen Mrs. Millamant or not, I cannot say; but there were items of such a treaty being in embryo, and if it should come to life, poor Mirabell would be in some sort unfortunately fobbed,[9] i'faith.

FAINALL 'Tis impossible Millamant should hearken to it.

WITWOUD Faith, my dear, I can't tell; she's a woman and a kind of a humorist.[1] And is this the sum of what you could collect last night?

MIRABELL And is this the sum of what you could collect last night?

PETULANT The quintessence. Maybe Witwoud knows more; he stayed longer. Besides, they never mind him; they say anything before him.

MIRABELL I thought you had been the greatest favorite.

PETULANT Aye, *tête à tête*, but not in public, because I make remarks.

MIRABELL You do?

PETULANT Aye, aye, pox, I'm malicious, man! Now he's soft, you know, they are not in awe of him. The fellow's well-bred, he's what you call a—what-d'ye-call-'em, a fine gentleman, but he's silly withal.

MIRABELL I thank you. I know as much as my curiosity requires. Fainall, are you for the Mall?[2]

8. Damn me.
9. Tricked.
1. Whimsical person.

2. A fashionable promenade adjoining St. James's Park.

FAINALL Aye, I'll take a turn before dinner.

WITWOUD Aye, we'll all walk in the park; the ladies talked of being there.

MIRABELL I thought you were obliged to watch for your brother Sir Wilfull's arrival.

WITWOUD No, no, he comes to his aunt's, my Lady Wishfort. Pox on him! I shall be troubled with him too; what shall I do with the fool?

PETULANT Beg him for his estate, that I may beg you afterwards; and so have but one trouble with you both.

WITWOUD Oh, rare Petulant! Thou art as quick as a fire in a frosty morning; thou shalt to the Mall with us, and we'll be very severe.

PETULANT Enough, I'm in a humour to be severe.

MIRABELL Are you? Pray then walk by yourselves. Let not us be accessory to your putting the ladies out of countenance with your senseless ribaldry, which you roar out aloud as often as they pass by you; and when you have made a handsome woman blush, then you think you have been severe.

PETULANT What, what? Then let 'em show their innocence by not understanding what they hear, or else show their discretion by not hearing what they would not be thought to understand.

MIRABELL But hast not thou then sense enough to know that thou ought'st to be most ashamed thyself, when thou hast put another out of countenance?

PETULANT Not I, by this hand! I always take blushing either for a sign of guilt or ill-breeding.

MIRABELL I confess you ought to think so. You are in the right, that you may plead the error of your judgment in defense of your practice.

> Where modesty's ill manners, 'tis but fit
> That impudence and malice pass for wit.

Exeunt.

Act II. St. James's Park.
Enter Mrs. Fainall *and* Mrs. Marwood.

MRS. FAINALL Aye, aye, dear Marwood, if we will be happy, we must find the means in ourselves, and among ourselves. Men are ever in extremes, either doting or averse. While they are lovers, if they have fire and sense, their jealousies are insupportable. And when they cease to love (we ought to think at least) they loathe; they look upon us with horror and distaste; they meet us like the ghosts of what we were, and as such, fly from us.

MRS. MARWOOD True, 'tis an unhappy circumstance of life, that love should ever die before us; and that the man so often should outlive the lover. But say what you will, 'tis better to be left than never to have been loved. To pass our youth in dull indifference, to refuse the sweets of life because they once must leave us, is as preposterous as to wish to have been born old, because we one day must be old. For my part, my youth may wear and waste, but it shall never rust in my possession.

MRS. FAINALL Then it seems you dissemble an aversion to mankind, only in compliance with my mother's humour.

MRS. MARWOOD Certainly. To be free, I have no taste of those insipid dry discourses with which our sex of force must entertain themselves, apart from men. We may affect endearments to each other, profess eternal friendships, and seem to dote like lovers; but 'tis not in our natures long to persevere. Love will resume his empire in our breasts; and every heart, or soon or late, receive and readmit him as its lawful tyrant.

MRS. FAINALL Bless me, how have I been deceived! Why you profess a libertine!

MRS. MARWOOD You see my friendship by my freedom. Come, be as sincere, acknowledge that your sentiments agree with mine.

MRS. FAINALL Never!

MRS. MARWOOD You hate mankind?

MRS. FAINALL Heartily, inveterately.

MRS. MARWOOD Your husband?

MRS. FAINALL Most transcendently; aye, though I say it, meritoriously.

MRS. MARWOOD Give me your hand upon it.

MRS. FAINALL There.

MRS. MARWOOD I join with you; what I have said has been to try you.

MRS. FAINALL Is it possible? Dost thou hate those vipers, men?

MRS. MARWOOD I have done hating 'em, and am now come to despise 'em; the next thing I have to do, is eternally to forget 'em.

MRS. FAINALL There spoke the spirit of an Amazon, a Penthesilea.[3]

MRS. MARWOOD And yet I am thinking sometimes to carry my aversion further.

MRS. FAINALL How?

MRS. MARWOOD Faith, by marrying; if I could but find one that loved me very well and would be thoroughly sensible of ill usage, I think I should do myself the violence of undergoing the ceremony.

MRS. FAINALL You would not make him a cuckold?

MRS. MARWOOD No, but I'd make him believe I did, and that's as bad.

MRS. FAINALL Why had not you as good do it?

MRS. MARWOOD Oh, if he should ever discover it, he would then know the worst, and be out of his pain; but I would have him ever to continue upon the rack of fear and jealousy.

MRS. FAINALL Ingenious mischief! Would thou wert married to Mirabell.

MRS. MARWOOD Would I were!

MRS. FAINALL You change color.

MRS. MARWOOD Because I hate him.

MRS. FAINALL So do I; but I can hear him named. But what reason have you to hate him in particular?

3. Queen of the Amazons, a legendary race of female warriors.

MRS. MARWOOD I never loved him; he is, and always was, insufferably proud.

MRS. FAINALL By the reason you give for your aversion, one would think it dissembled; for you have laid a fault to his charge of which his enemies must acquit him.

MRS. MARWOOD Oh, then it seems you are one of his favorable enemies! Methinks you look a little pale, and now you flush again.

MRS. FAINALL Do I? I think I am a little sick o' the sudden.

MRS. MARWOOD What ails you?

MRS. FAINALL My husband. Don't you see him? He turned short upon me unawares, and has almost overcome me.

Enter Fainall *and* Mirabell.

MRS. MARWOOD Ha! ha! ha! He comes opportunely for you.

MRS. FAINALL For you, for he has brought Mirabell with him.

FAINALL My dear!

MRS. FAINALL My soul!

FAINALL You don't look well today, child.

MRS. FAINALL D'ye think so?

MIRABELL He is the only man that does, madam.

MRS. FAINALL The only man that would tell me so at least; and the only man from whom I could hear it without mortification.

FAINALL Oh my dear, I am satisfied of your tenderness; I know you cannot resent anything from me, especially what is an effect of my concern.

MRS. FAINALL Mr. Mirabell, my mother interrupted you in a pleasant relation last night; I would fain hear it out.

MIRABELL The persons concerned in that affair have yet a tolerable reputation. I am afraid Mr. Fainall will be censorious.

MRS. FAINALL He has a humour more prevailing than his curiosity, and will willingly dispense with the hearing of one scandalous story, to avoid giving an occasion to make another by being seen to walk with his wife. This way, Mr. Mirabell, and I dare promise you will oblige us both.

Exeunt Mrs. Fainall *and* Mirabell.

FAINALL Excellent creature! Well, sure if I should live to be rid of my wife, I should be a miserable man.

MRS. MARWOOD Aye!

FAINALL For having only that one hope, the accomplishment of it, of consequence must put an end to all my hopes; and what a wretch is he who must survive his hopes! Nothing remains when that day comes, but to sit down and weep like Alexander, when he wanted other worlds to conquer.

MRS. MARWOOD Will you not follow 'em?

FAINALL Faith, I think not.

MRS. MARWOOD Pray let us; I have a reason.

FAINALL You are not jealous?

MRS. MARWOOD Of whom?

FAINALL Of Mirabell.

MRS. MARWOOD If I am, is it inconsistent with my love to you that I am tender of your honor?

FAINALL You would intimate then, as if there were a fellow-feeling between my wife and him.

MRS. MARWOOD I think she does not hate him to that degree she would be thought.

FAINALL But he, I fear, is too insensible.

MRS. MARWOOD It may be you are deceived.

FAINALL It may be so. I do now begin to apprehend it.

MRS. MARWOOD What?

FAINALL That I have been deceived, madam, and you are false.

MRS. MARWOOD That I am false? What mean you?

FAINALL To let you know I see through all your little arts. Come, you both love him; and both have equally dissembled your aversion. Your mutual jealousies of one another have made you clash till you have both struck fire. I have seen the warm confession reddening on your cheeks, and sparkling from your eyes.

MRS. MARWOOD You do me wrong.

FAINALL I do not. 'Twas for my ease to oversee[4] and wilfully neglect the gross advances made him by my wife; that by permitting her to be engaged, I might continue unsuspected in my pleasures, and take you oftener to my arms in full security. But could you think, because the nodding husband would not wake, that e'er the watchful lover slept?

MRS. MARWOOD And wherewithal can you reproach me?

FAINALL With infidelity, with loving of another, with love of Mirabell.

MRS. MARWOOD 'Tis false. I challenge you to show an instance that can confirm your groundless accusation. I hate him.

FAINALL And wherefore do you hate him? He is insensible, and your resentment follows his neglect. An instance? The injuries you have done him are a proof, your interposing in his love. What cause had you to make discoveries of his pretended passion? To undeceive the credulous aunt, and be the officious obstacle of his match with Millamant?

MRS. MARWOOD My obligations to my lady urged me; I had professed a friendship to her, and could not see her easy nature so abused by that dissembler.

FAINALL What, was it conscience then? Professed a friendship! Oh, the pious friendships of the female sex!

MRS. MARWOOD More tender, more sincere, and more enduring, than all the vain and empty vows of men, whether professing love to us, or mutual faith to one another.

FAINALL Ha! ha! ha! you are my wife's friend too.

MRS. MARWOOD Shame and ingratitude! Do you reproach me? You, you upbraid me! Have I been false to her, through strict fidelity to you, and sacrificed my friendship to keep my love inviolate? And have you the baseness to charge me with the guilt, unmindful of the merit! To you it should be meritorious, that I have

4. Overlook.

been vicious; and do you reflect that guilt upon me, which should lie buried in your bosom?

FAINALL You misinterpret my reproof. I meant but to remind you of the slight account you once could make of strictest ties, when set in comparison with your love to me.

MRS. MARWOOD 'Tis false; you urged it with deliberate malice! 'Twas spoke in scorn, and I never will forgive it.

FAINALL Your guilt, not your resentment, begets your rage. If yet you loved, you could forgive a jealousy; but you are stung to find you are discovered.

MRS. MARWOOD It shall be all discovered. You too shall be discovered; be sure you shall. I can but be exposed. If I do it myself, I shall prevent[5] your baseness.

FAINALL Why, what will you do?

MRS. MARWOOD Disclose it to your wife; own what has passed between us.

FAINALL Frenzy!

MRS. MARWOOD By all my wrongs I'll do't! I'll publish to the world the injuries you have done me, both in my fame and fortune! With both I trusted you, you bankrupt in honor, as indigent of wealth.

FAINALL Your fame I have preserved. Your fortune has been bestowed as the prodigality of your love would have it, in pleasures which we both have shared. Yet had not you been false, I had ere this repaid it. 'Tis true, had you permitted Mirabell with Millamant to have stolen their marriage, my lady had been incensed beyond all means of reconcilement; Millamant had forfeited the moiety[6] of her fortune, which then would have descended to my wife. And wherefore did I marry, but to make a lawful prize of a rich widow's wealth, and squander it on love and you?

MRS. MARWOOD Deceit and frivolous pretense!

FAINALL Death, am I not married? What's pretense? Am I not imprisoned, fettered? Have I not a wife? Nay a wife that was a widow, a young widow, a handsome widow; and would be again a widow, but that I have a heart of proof, and something of a constitution to bustle through the ways of wedlock and this world. Will you yet be reconciled to truth and me?

MRS. MARWOOD Impossible. Truth and you are inconsistent. I hate you, and shall for ever.

FAINALL For loving you?

MRS. MARWOOD I loathe the name of love after such usage; and next to the guilt with which you would asperse me, I scorn you most. Farewell!

FAINALL Nay, we must not part thus.

MRS. MARWOOD Let me go.

FAINALL Come, I'm sorry.

5. Anticipate.   6. Half.

MRS. MARWOOD I care not, let me go. Break my hands, do! I'd leave 'em to get loose.

FAINALL I would not hurt you for the world. Have I no other hold to keep you here?

MRS. MARWOOD Well, I have deserved it all.

FAINALL You know I love you.

MRS. MARWOOD Poor dissembling! Oh, that—Well, it is not yet—

FAINALL What? what is it not? What is it not yet? It is not yet too late—

MRS. MARWOOD No, it is not yet too late; I have that comfort.

FAINALL It is, to love another.

MRS. MARWOOD But not to loathe, detest, abhor mankind, myself, and the whole treacherous world.

FAINALL Nay, this is extravagance, Come, I ask your pardon. No tears. I was to blame; I could not love you and be easy in my doubts. Pray, forbear. I believe you. I'm convinced I've done you wrong; and any way, every way will make amends. I'll hate my wife yet more, damn her! I'll part with her, rob her of all she's worth, and we'll retire somewhere, anywhere, to another world. I'll marry thee; be pacified. 'Sdeath, they come; hide your face, your tears. You have a mask; wear it a moment. This way, this way. Be persuaded.

Exeunt.

Enter Mirabell *and* Mrs. Fainall.

MRS. FAINALL They are here yet.

MIRABELL They are turning into the other walk.

MRS. FAINALL While I only hated my husband, I could bear to see him; but since I have despised him, he's too offensive.

MIRABELL Oh, you should hate with prudence.

MRS. FAINALL Yes, for I have loved with indiscretion.

MIRABELL You should have just so much disgust for your husband as may be sufficient to make you relish your lover.

MRS. FAINALL You have been the cause that I have loved without bounds, and would you set limits to that aversion of which you have been the occasion? Why did you make me marry this man?

MIRABELL Why do we daily commit disagreeable and dangerous actions? To save that idol, reputation. If the familiarities of our loves had produced that consequence of which you were apprehensive, where could you have fixed a father's name with credit, but on a husband? I knew Fainall to be a man lavish of his morals, an interested[7] and professing friend, a false and a designing lover; yet one whose wit and outward fair behavior have gained a reputation with the town enough to make that woman stand excused who has suffered herself to be won by his addresses. A better man ought not to have been sacrificed to the occasion; a worse had not answered to the purpose. When you are weary of him, you know your remedy.

MRS. FAINALL I ought to stand in some degree of credit with you, Mirabell.

---

7. **Self-interested.**

MIRABELL In justice to you, I have made you privy to my whole design, and put it in your power to ruin or advance my fortune.

MRS. FAINALL Whom have you instructed to represent your pretended uncle?

MIRABELL Waitwell, my servant.

MRS. FAINALL He is an humble servant to Foible, my mother's woman, and may win her to your interest.

MIRABELL Care is taken for that. She is won and worn by this time. They were married this morning.

MRS. FAINALL Who?

MIRABELL Waitwell and Foible. I would not tempt my servant to betray me by trusting him too far. If your mother, in hopes to ruin me, should consent to marry my pretended uncle, he might, like Mosca in *The Fox*, stand upon terms;[8] so I made him sure beforehand.

MRS. FAINALL So, if my poor mother is caught in a contract, you will discover the imposture betimes, and release her by producing a certificate of her gallant's former marriage.

MIRABELL Yes, upon condition she consent to my marriage with her niece, and surrender the moiety of her fortune in her possession.

MRS. FAINALL She talked last night of endeavoring at a match between Millamant and your uncle.

MIRABELL That was by Foible's direction, and my instruction, that she might seem to carry it more privately.

MRS. FAINALL Well, I have an opinion of your success, for I believe my lady will do anything to get a husband; and when she has this, which you have provided for her, I suppose she will submit to anything to get rid of him.

MIRABELL Yes, I think the good lady would marry anything that resembled a man, though 'twere no more than what a butler could pinch out of a napkin.

MRS. FAINALL Female frailty! We must all come to it, if we live to be old and feel the craving of a false appetite when the true is decayed.

MIRABELL An old woman's appetite is depraved like that of a girl. 'Tis the green sickness[9] of a second childhood; and like the faint offer of a latter spring, serves but to usher in the fall, and withers in an affected bloom.

MRS. FAINALL Here's your mistress.

Enter Mrs. Millamant, Witwoud, *and* Mincing.

MIRABELL Here she comes, i'faith, full sail, with her fan spread and her streamers out, and a shoal of fools for tenders. Ha, no, I cry her mercy!

MRS. FAINALL I see but one poor empty sculler; and he tows her woman after him.

MIRABELL You seem to be unattended, madam. You used to have

8. Mosca is the scheming servant in Ben Jonson's *Volpone, or The Fox*; "standing upon terms" in that play amounts to blackmail.
9. The anemia that sometimes affects girls at puberty.

the beau monde throng after you, and a flock of gay fine perukes[1] hovering round you.

WITWOUD Like moths about a candle. I had like to have lost my comparison for want of breath.

MILLAMANT Oh, I have denied myself airs today. I have walked as fast through the crowd—

WITWOUD As a favorite in disgrace, and with as few followers.

MILLAMANT Dear Mr. Witwoud, truce with your similitudes; for I am as sick of 'em—

WITWOUD As a physician of a good air. I cannot help it, madam, though 'tis against myself.

MILLAMANT Yet again! Mincing, stand between me and his wit.

WITWOUD Do, Mrs. Mincing, like a screen before a great fire. I confess I do blaze today; I am too bright.

MRS. FAINALL But, dear Millamant, why were you so long?

MILLAMANT Long! Lord, have I not made violent haste? I have asked every living thing I met for you; I have inquired after you, as after a new fashion.

WITWOUD Madam, truce with your similitudes. No, you met her husband, and did not ask him for her.

MIRABELL By your leave, Witwoud, that were like inquiring after an old fashion, to ask a husband for his wife.

WITWOUD Hum, a hit! a hit! a palpable hit![2] I confess it.

MRS. FAINALL You were dressed before I came abroad.

MILLAMANT Aye, that's true. Oh, but then I had—Mincing, what had I? Why was I so long?

MINCING O mem, your la'ship stayed to peruse a pecquet[3] of letters.

MILLAMANT Oh, aye, letters; I had letters. I am persecuted with letters. I hate letters. Nobody knows how to write letters; and yet one has 'em, one does not know why. They serve one to pin up one's hair.

WITWOUD Is that the way? Pray, madam, do you pin up your hair with all your letters? I find I must keep copies.

MILLAMANT Only with those in verse, Mr. Witwoud. I never pin up my hair with prose. I fancy one's hair would not curl if it were pinned up with prose. I think I tried once, Mincing.

MINCING O mem, I shall never forget it.

MILLAMANT Aye, poor Mincing tift[4] and tift all the morning.

MINCING 'Till I had the cremp in my fingers, I'll vow, mem. And all to no purpose. But when your la'ship pins it up with poetry, it sits so pleasant the next day as anything, and is so pure and so crips.[5]

WITWOUD Indeed, so crips?

MINCING You're such a critic, Mr. Witwoud.

MILLAMANT Mirabell, did not you take exceptions last night? Oh, aye, and went away. Now I think on't, I'm angry. No, now I

1. Wigs.
2. From the dueling scene in *Hamlet*, V.ii.
3. Packet. Mincing's speech is affected.
4. Arranged, set the hair.
5. A variation of "crisp."

think on't, I'm pleased; for I believe I gave you some pain.

MIRABELL Docs that please you?

MILLAMANT Infinitely; I love to give pain.

MIRABELL You would affect a cruelty which is not in your nature; your true vanity is in the power of pleasing.

MILLAMANT Oh, I ask your pardon for that. One's cruelty is one's power; and when one parts with one's cruelty, one parts with one's power; and when one has parted with that, I fancy one's old and ugly.

MIRABELL Aye, aye, suffer your cruelty to ruin the object of your power, to destroy your lover, and then how vain, how lost a thing you'll be! Nay, 'tis true: you are no longer handsome when you've lost your lover; your beauty dies upon the instant. For beauty is the lover's gift; 'tis he bestows your charms, your glass is all a cheat. The ugly and the old, whom the looking glass mortifies, yet after commendation can be flattered by it, and discover beauties in it; for that reflects our praises, rather than your face.

MILLAMANT Oh, the vanity of these men! Fainall, d'ye hear him? If they did not commend us, we were not handsome! Now you must know they could not commend one, if one was not handsome. Beauty the lover's gift! Lord, what is a lover, that it can give? Why, one makes lovers as fast as one pleases, and they live as long as one pleases, and they die as soon as one pleases; and then, if one pleases, one makes more.

WITWOUD Very pretty. Why, you make no more of making of lovers, madam, than of making so many card-matches.[6]

MILLAMANT One no more owes one's beauty to a lover than one's wit to an echo. They can but reflect what we look and say; vain empty things if we are silent or unseen, and want a being.

MIRABELL Yet to those two vain empty things you owe two [of] the greatest pleasures of your life.

MILLAMANT How so?

MIRABELL To your lover you owe the pleasure of hearing yourselves praised; and to an echo the pleasure of hearing yourselves talk.

WITWOUD But I know a lady that loves talking so incessantly, she won't give an echo fair play; she has that everlasting rotation of tongue, that an echo must wait till she dies, before it can catch her last words.

MILLAMANT Oh, fiction! Fainall, let us leave these men.

MIRABELL Draw off Witwoud. [*Aside to* Mrs. Fainall.]

MRS. FAINALL Immediately. I have a word or two for Mr. Witwoud.

Exeunt Witwoud *and* Mrs. Fainall.

MIRABELL I would beg a little private audience too. You had the tyranny to deny me last night, though you knew I came to impart a secret to you that concerned my love.

MILLAMANT You saw I was engaged.

MIRABELL Unkind! You had the leisure to entertain a herd of fools;

6. Matches made by dipping cardboard strips in melted sulphur.

things who visit you from their excessive idleness, bestowing on
your easiness that time which is the incumbrance of their lives.
How can you find delight in such society? It is impossible they
should admire you; they are not capable. Or if they were, it
should be to you as a mortification, for sure to please a fool is
some degree of folly.

MILLAMANT I please myself. Besides, sometimes to converse with
fools is for my health.

MIRABELL Your health! Is there a worse disease than the conversation of fools?

MILLAMANT Yes, the vapors; fools are physic for it, next to
assafoetida.[7]

MIRABELL You are not in a course of fools?

MILLAMANT Mirabell, if you persist in this offensive freedom, you'll
displease me. I think I must resolve, after all, not to have you; we
shan't agree.

MIRABELL Not in our physic, it may be.

MILLAMANT And yet our distemper, in all likelihood, will be the
same; for we shall be sick of one another. I shan't endure to be
reprimanded nor instructed; 'tis so dull to act always by advice,
and so tedious to be told of one's faults—I can't bear it. Well, I
won't have you, Mirabell—I'm resolved—I think—you may go.
—Ha! ha! ha! What would you give that you could help loving
me?

MIRABELL I would give something that you did not know I could
not help it.

MILLAMANT Come, don't look grave then. Well, what do you say
to me?

MIRABELL I say that a man may as soon make a friend by his wit,
or a fortune by his honesty, as win a woman with plain dealing
and sincerity.

MILLAMANT Sententious Mirabell! Prithee, don't look with that
violent and inflexible wise face, like Solomon at the dividing of
the child in an old tapestry hanging.[8]

MIRABELL You are merry, madam, but I would persuade you for
one moment to be serious.

MILLAMANT What, with that face? No, if you keep your countenance, 'tis impossible I should hold mine. Well, after all, there is
something very moving in a love-sick face. Ha! ha! ha! —Well, I
won't laugh, don't be peevish—Heighho! Now I'll be melancholy, as melancholy as a watch-light.[9] Well, Mirabell, if ever
you will win me, woo me now. —Nay, if you are so tedious, fare
you well. —I see they are walking away.

MIRABELL Can you not find in the variety of your disposition one
moment—

MILLAMANT To hear you tell me Foible's married, and your plot
like to speed? —No.

MIRABELL But how came you to know it?

7. A sort of smelling salts.
8. From 1 Kings iii.16–28.

9. Night-light, as in a sickroom.

MILLAMANT Unless by the help of the devil, you can't imagine; unless she should tell me herself. Which of the two it may have been, I will leave you to consider; and when you have done thinking of that, think of me.

Exit with Mincing.

MIRABELL I have something more—Gone! Think of you! To think of a whirlwind, though 'twere in a whirlwind, were a case of more steady contemplation; a very tranquility of mind and mansion. A fellow that lives in a windmill has not a more whimsical dwelling than the heart of a man that is lodged in a woman. There is no point of the compass to which they cannot turn, and by which they are not turned; and by one as well as another, for motion, not method, is their occupation. To know this, and yet continue to be in love, is to be made wise from the dictates of reason, and yet persevere to play the fool by the force of instinct. —Oh, here come my pair of turtles![1] —What, billing so sweetly! Is not Valentine's Day over with you yet?

Enter Waitwell *and* Foible.

Sirrah, Waitwell, why sure you think you were married for your own recreation, and not for my conveniency.

WAITWELL Your pardon, sir. With submission, we have indeed been solacing in lawful delights; but still with an eye to business, sir. I have instructed her as well as I could. If she can take your directions as readily as my instructions, sir, your affairs are in a prosperous way.

MIRABELL Give you joy, Mrs. Foible.

FOIBLE O las, sir, I'm so ashamed! I'm afraid my lady has been in a thousand inquietudes for me. But I protest, sir, I made as much haste as I could.

WAITWELL That she did indeed, sir. It was my fault that she did not make more.

MIRABELL That I believe.

FOIBLE But I told my lady as you instructed me, sir, that I had a prospect of seeing Sir Rowland, your uncle; and that I would put her ladyship's picture in my pocket to show him, which I'll be sure to say has made him so enamored of her beauty, that he burns with impatience to lie at her ladyship's feet and worship the original.

MIRABELL Excellent Foible! Matrimony has made you eloquent in love.

WAITWELL I think she has profited, sir. I think so.

FOIBLE You have seen Madam Millamant, sir?

MIRABELL Yes.

FOIBLE I told her, sir, because I did not know that you might find an opportunity; she had so much company last night.

MIRABELL Your diligence will merit more. In the meantime—

Gives money.

FOIBLE O dear sir, your humble servant.

---

1. Turtledoves.

WAITWELL Spouse.

MIRABELL Stand off, sir, not a penny! Go on and prosper, Foible; the lease shall be made good and the farm stocked, if we succeed.

FOIBLE I don't question your generosity, sir; and you need not doubt of success. If you have no more commands, sir, I'll be gone; I'm sure my lady is at her toilet and can't dress till I come. —Oh dear, I'm sure that [*looking out*] was Mrs. Marwood that went by in a mask; if she has seen me with you I'm sure she'll tell my lady. I'll make haste home and prevent her. Your servant, sir. B'w'y,[2] Waitwell.

Exit.

WAITWELL Sir Rowland, if you please. The jade's so pert upon her preferment she forgets herself.

MIRABELL Come, sir, will you endeavor to forget yourself, and transform into Sir Rowland?

WAITWELL Why, sir, it will be impossible I should remember myself. Married, knighted, and attended all in one day! 'Tis enough to make any man forget himself. The difficulty will be how to recover my acquaintance and familiarity with my former self, and fall from my transformation to a reformation into Waitwell. Nay, I shan't be quite the same Waitwell neither; for now I remember me, I am married and can't be my own man again.

> Aye, there's the grief; that's the sad change of life,
> To lose my title, and yet keep my wife.

Exeunt.

Act III. A *Room in* Lady Wishfort's *House.*
Lady Wishfort *at her toilet,* Peg *waiting.*

LADY WISHFORT Merciful! no news of Foible yet?

PEG No, madam.

LADY WISHFORT I have no more patience. If I have not fretted myself till I am pale again, there's no veracity in me! Fetch me the red; the red, do you hear, sweetheart? An arrant ash-color, as I'm a person! Look you how this wench stirs! Why dost thou not fetch me a little red? Didst thou not hear me, mopus?

PEG The red ratafia does your ladyship mean, or the cherry brandy?

LADY WISHFORT Ratafia, fool! No, fool! Not the ratafia, fool. Grant me patience! I mean the Spanish paper,[3] idiot; complexion, darling. Paint, paint, paint, dost thou understand that, changeling, dangling thy hands like bobbins before thee? Why dost thou not stir, puppet? thou wooden thing upon wires!

PEG Lord, madam, your ladyship is so impatient! I cannot come at the paint, madam; Mrs. Foible has locked it up and carried the key with her.

LADY WISHFORT A pox take you both! Fetch me the cherry brandy then. [*Exit* Peg.] I'm as pale and as faint, I look like Mrs. Qualmsick, the curate's wife, that's always breeding. Wench, come, come, wench, what art thou doing? sipping? tasting? Save thee, dost thou not know the bottle?

2. Good-by.   3. For applying rouge.

Re-enter Peg *with a bottle and china cup.*

PEG Madam, I was looking for a cup.

LADY WISHFORT A cup, save thee! and what a cup hast thou brought! Dost thou take me for a fairy, to drink out of an acorn? Why didst thou not bring thy thimble? Hast thou ne'er a brass thimble clinking in thy pocket with a bit of nutmeg? I warrant thee. Come, fill, fill! So; again. [*One knocks.*] See who that is. Set down the bottle first. Here, here, under the table. What, wouldst thou go with the bottle in thy hand, like a tapster? As I'm a person, this wench has lived in an inn upon the road, before she came to me, like Maritornes the Asturian in *Don Quixote*![4] No Foible yet?

PEG No, madam, Mrs. Marwood.

LADY WISHFORT Oh, Marwood, let her come in. Come in, good Marwood.

Enter Mrs. Marwood.

MRS. MARWOOD I'm surprised to find your ladyship in dishabillé at this time of day.

LADY WISHFORT Foible's a lost thing; has been abroad since morning, and never heard of since.

MRS. MARWOOD I saw her but now, as I came masked through the park, in conference with Mirabell.

LADY WISHFORT With Mirabell! You call my blood into my face with mentioning that traitor. She durst not have the confidence! I sent her to negotiate an affair in which, if I'm detected, I'm undone. If that wheedling villain has wrought upon Foible to detect me, I'm ruined. Oh my dear friend, I'm a wretch of wretches if I'm detected.

MRS. MARWOOD O madam, you cannot suspect Mrs. Foible's integrity.

LADY WISHFORT Oh, he carries poison in his tongue that would corrupt integrity itself! If she has given him an opportunity, she has as good as put her integrity into his hands. Ah, dear Marwood, what's integrity to an opportunity? Hark! I hear her! Go, you thing, and send her in. [*Exit* Peg.] Dear friend, retire into my closet,[5] that I may examine her with more freedom. You'll pardon me, dear friend; I can make bold with you. There are books over the chimney. Quarles and Prynne, and the *Short View of the Stage*, with Bunyan's works, to entertain you.[6]

Exit Mrs. Marwood.

Enter Foible.

Oh Foible, where hast thou been? What hast thou been doing?

FOIBLE Madam, I have seen the party.

LADY WISHFORT But what hast thou done?

FOIBLE Nay, 'tis your ladyship has done, and are to do; I have only promised. But a man so enamored, so transported! Well, here it

---

4. Chambermaid in *Dox Quixote*, Part I, xvi.

5. Small, private room.

6. Lady Wishfort's bookshelf seems to include such Puritan works as Francis Quarles's *Emblems, Divine and Moral* (1635) and William Prynne's *Histriomastix* (1632), along with Jeremy Collier's *Short View of the Immorality and Profaneness of the English Stage* (1698).

is, all that is left; all that is not kissed away. Well, if worshiping of pictures be a sin, poor Sir Rowland, I say.

LADY WISHFORT The miniature has been counted like. But hast thou not betrayed me, Foible? Hast thou not detected me to that faithless Mirabell? What hadst thou to do with him in the Park? Answer me, has he got nothing out of thee?

FOIBLE [*aside*] So the devil has been beforehand with me. What shall I say? —Alas, madam, could I help it, if I met that confident thing? Was I in fault? If you had heard how he used me, and all upon your ladyship's account, I'm sure you would not suspect my fidelity. Nay, if that had been the worst, I could have borne; but he had a fling at your ladyship too. And then I could not hold; but i'faith I gave him his own.

LADY WISHFORT Me? What did the filthy fellow say?

FOIBLE O madam! 'tis a shame to say what he said, with his taunts and his fleers, tossing up his nose. Humph! (says he), what, you are a hatching some plot (says he), you are so early abroad, or catering (says he), ferreting for some disbanded officer, I warrant. Half-pay is but thin subsistence (says he). Well, what pension does your lady propose? Let me see (says he), what, she must come down pretty deep now, she's superannuated (says he) and —

LADY WISHFORT Ods my life, I'll have him, I'll have him murdered. I'll have him poisoned. Where does he eat? I'll marry a drawer to have him poisoned in his wine. I'll send for Robin from Locket's[7] immediately.

FOIBLE Poison him? Poisoning's too good for him. Starve him, madam, starve him; marry Sir Rowland and get him disinherited. Oh, you would bless yourself to hear what he said!

LADY WISHFORT A villain! superannuated!

FOIBLE Humph! (says he), I hear you are laying designs against me too (says he), and Mrs. Millamant is to marry my uncle (he does not suspect a word of your ladyship); but (says he) I'll fit you for that. I warrant you (says he), I'll hamper you for that (says he), you and your old frippery[8] too (says he), I'll handle you—

LADY WISHFORT Audacious villain! Handle me! would he durst! Frippery? old frippery! Was there ever such a foulmouthed fellow? I'll be married tomorrow; I'll be contracted tonight.

FOIBLE The sooner the better, madam.

LADY WISHFORT Will Sir Rowland be here, say'st thou? When, Foible?

FOIBLE Incontinently, madam. No new sheriff's wife expects the return of her husband after knighthood with that impatience in which Sir Rowland burns for the dear hour of kissing your ladyship's hands after dinner.

LADY WISHFORT Frippery? superannuated frippery! I'll frippery the villain; I'll reduce him to frippery and rags! A tatterdemalion! I hope to see him hung with tatters, like a Long Lane penthouse[9]

7. A fashionable tavern.
8. Cast-off clothes.

9. Stall in Long Lane, Smithfield, where old clothes and rags were sold.

or a gibbet thief. A slander-mouthed railer! I warrant the spendthrift prodigal's in debt as much as the million lottery,[1] or the whole court upon a birthday. I'll spoil his credit with his tailor. Yes, he shall have my niece with her fortune, he shall!

FOIBLE He! I hope to see him lodge in Ludgate[2] first, and angle into Blackfriars for brass farthings with an old mitten.

LADY WISHFORT Aye, dear Foible; thank thee for that, dear Foible. He has put me out of all patience. I shall never recompose my features to receive Sir Rowland with any economy of face. This wretch has fretted me that I am absolutely decayed. Look, Foible.

FOIBLE Your ladyship has frowned a little too rashly, indeed, madam. There are some cracks discernible in the white varnish.

LADY WISHFORT Let me see the glass. Cracks, say'st thou? Why I am arrantly flayed; I look like an old peeled wall. Thou must repair me, Foible, before Sir Rowland comes, or I shall never keep up to my picture.

FOIBLE I warrant you, madam, a little art once made your picture like you; and now a little of the same art must make you like your picture. Your picture must sit for you, madam.

LADY WISHFORT But art thou sure Sir Rowland will not fail to come? Or will he not fail when he does come? Will he be importunate, Foible, and push? For if he should not be importunate, I shall never break decorums. I shall die with confusion, if I am forced to advance. Oh no, I can never advance! I shall swoon if he should expect advances. No, I hope Sir Rowland is better bred than to put a lady to the necessity of breaking her forms. I won't be too coy neither. I won't give him despair; but a little disdain is not amiss, a little scorn is alluring.

FOIBLE A little scorn becomes your ladyship.

LADY WISHFORT Yes, but tenderness becomes me best, a sort of a dyingness. You see that picture has a short of a—ha, Foible? a swimminess in the eyes. Yes, I'll look so. My niece affects it; but she wants features. Is Sir Rowland handsome? Let my toilet be removed. I'll dress above. I'll receive Sir Rowland here. Is he handsome? Don't answer me. I won't know; I'll be surprised, I'll be taken by surprise.

FOIBLE By storm, madam. Sir Rowland's a brisk man.

LADY WISHFORT Is he! Oh, then he'll importune, if he's a brisk man. I shall save decorums if Sir Rowland importunes. I have a mortal terror at the apprehension of offending against decorums. Nothing but importunity can surmount decorums. Oh, I'm glad he's a brisk man. Let my things be removed, good Foible.

Exit.

Enter Mrs. Fainall.[3]

MRS. FAINALL O Foible, I have been in a fright, lest I should come

---

1. A government lottery of 1694 to raise a million pounds.
2. Debtors' prison. Prisoners would beg by dropping a mitten on a string from their gratings to the street below.
3. Sometimes staged so that Mrs. Marwood is visible, overhearing the following from one of the stage doors.

too late! That devil Marwood saw you in the Park with Mirabell, and I'm afraid will discover it to my lady.

FOIBLE Discover what, madam?

MRS. FAINALL Nay, nay, put not on that strange face. I am privy to the whole design, and know that Waitwell, to whom thou wert this morning married, is to personate Mirabell's uncle, and as such, winning my lady, to involve her in those difficulties from which Mirabell only must release her, by his making his conditions to have my cousin and her fortune left to her own disposal.

FOIBLE O dear madam, I beg your pardon. It was not my confidence in your ladyship that was deficient; but I thought the former good correspondence between your ladyship and Mr. Mirabell might have hindered his communicating this secret.

MRS. FAINALL Dear Foible, forget that.

FOIBLE O dear madam, Mr. Mirabell is such a sweet, winning gentleman, but your ladyship is the pattern of generosity. Sweet lady, to be so good! Mr. Mirabell cannot choose but be grateful. I find your ladyship has his heart still. Now, madam, I can safely tell your ladyship our success. Mrs. Marwood had told my lady; but I warrant I managed myself. I turned it all for the better. I told my lady that Mr. Mirabell railed at her. I laid horrid things to his charge, I'll vow; and my lady is so incensed that she'll be contracted to Sir Rowland tonight, she says. I warrant I worked her up, that he may have her for asking for, as they say of a Welsh maidenhead.

MRS. FAINALL O rare Foible!

FOIBLE Madam, I beg your ladyship to acquaint Mr. Mirabell of his success. I would be seen as little as possible to speak to him; besides, I believe Madame Marwood watches me. She has a month's mind;[4] but I know Mr. Mirabell can't abide her. [Enter Footman.] John, remove my lady's toilet. Madam, your servant. My lady is so impatient, I fear she'll come for me, if I stay.

MRS. FAINALL I'll go with you up the backstairs, lest I should meet her.

Exeunt.

Enter Mrs. Marwood.

MRS. MARWOOD Indeed, Mrs. Engine, is it thus with you? Are you become a go-between of this importance? Yes, I shall watch you. Why this wench is the *passe-partout*, a very master key to everybody's strongbox. My friend Fainall, have you carried it so swimmingly? I thought there was something in it; but it seems it's over with you. Your loathing is not from a want of appetite then, but from a surfeit. Else you could never be so cool to fall from a principal to be an assistant; to procure for him! A pattern of generosity, that I confess. Well, Mr. Fainall, you have met with your match. O man, man! woman, woman! The devil's an ass; if I were a painter, I would draw him like an idiot, a driveler with a bib and bells. Man should have his head and horns, and woman

4. Strong inclination.

the rest of him. Poor simple fiend! Madam Marwood has a month's mind, but he can't abide her. 'Twere better for him you had not been his confessor in that affair, without you could have kept his counsel closer. I shall not prove another pattern of generosity and stalk for him, till he takes his stand to aim at a fortune. He has not obliged me to that, with those excesses of himself; and now I'll have none of him. Here comes the good lady, panting ripe; with a heart full of hope, and a head full of care, like any chemist upon the day of projection.[5]

Enter Lady Wishfort.

LADY WISHFORT O dear Marwood, what shall I say, for this rude forgetfulness? But my dear friend is all goodness.

MRS. MARWOOD No apologies, dear madam. I have been very well entertained.

LADY WISHFORT As I'm a person, I am in a very chaos to think I should so forget myself; but I have such an olio[6] of affairs, really I know not what to do. —[*Calls.*] Foible! —I expect my nephew, Sir Wilfull, every moment too. —Why, Foible! —He means to travel for improvement.

MRS. MARWOOD Methinks Sir Wilfull should rather think of marrying than traveling at his years. I hear he is turned of forty.

LADY WISHFORT Oh, he's in less danger of being spoiled by his travels. I am against my nephew's marrying too young. It will be time enough when he comes back and has acquired discretion to choose for himself.

MRS. MARWOOD Methinks Mrs. Millamant and he would make a very fit match. He may travel afterwards. 'Tis a thing very usual with young gentlemen.

LADY WISHFORT I promise you I have thought on't; and since 'tis your judgment, I'll think on't again. I assure you I will; I value your judgment extremely. On my word, I'll propose it.

Enter Foible.

Come, come, Foible, I had forgot my nephew will be here before dinner. I must make haste.

FOIBLE Mr. Witwoud and Mr. Petulant are come to dine with your ladyship.

LADY WISHFORT Oh dear, I can't appear till I'm dressed. Dear Marwood, shall I be free with you again, and beg you to entertain 'em? I'll make all imaginable haste. Dear friend, excuse me.

Exeunt Lady Wishfort *and* Foible.

Enter Mrs. Millamant *and* Mincing.

MILLAMANT Sure never anything was so unbred as that odious man! Marwood, your servant.

MRS. MARWOOD You have a color, what's the matter?

MILLAMANT That horrid fellow, Petulant, has provoked me into a flame. I have broke my fan. Mincing, lend me yours; is not all the powder out of my hair?

MRS. MARWOOD No, what has he done?

---

5. When an alchemist added the final element in hopes of changing base metal to gold.

6. Hodgepodge.

MILLAMANT Nay, he has done nothing; he has only talked. Nay, he has said nothing neither; but he has contradicted everything that has been said. For my part, I thought Witwoud and he would have quarreled.

MINCING I vow, mem, I thought once they would have fit.[7]

MILLAMANT Well, 'tis a lamentable thing, I'll swear, that one has not the liberty of choosing one's acquaintance as one does one's clothes.

MRS. MARWOOD If we had the liberty, we should be as weary of one set of acquaintance, though never so good, as we are of one suit, though never so fine. A fool and a doily stuff[8] would now and then find days of grace, and be worn for variety.

MILLAMANT I could consent to wear 'em, if they would wear alike; but fools never wear out—they are such *drap-de-Berry*[9] things without one could give 'em to one's chambermaid after a day or two!

MRS. MARWOOD 'Twere better to indeed. Or what think you of the playhouse? A fine, gay, glossy fool should be given there, like a new masking habit, after the masquerade is over, and we have done with the disguise. For a fool's visit is always a disguise, and never admitted by a woman of wit, but to blind her affair with a lover of sense. If you would but appear barefaced now, and own Mirabell, you might as easily put off Petulant and Witwoud as your hood and scarf. And indeed 'tis time, for the town has found it; the secret is grown too big for the pretense. 'Tis like Mrs. Primly's great belly; she may lace it down before, but it burnishes on her hips. Indeed, Millamant, you can no more conceal it than my Lady Strammel can her face, that goodly face, which, in defiance of her Rhenish wine tea,[1] will not be comprehended in a mask.

MILLAMANT I'll take my death, Marwood, you are more censorious than a decayed beauty, or a discarded toast.[2] Mincing, tell the men they may come up. My aunt is not dressing.—Their folly is less provoking than your malice. [*Exit* Mincing.] The town has found it! What has it found? That Mirabell loves me is no more a secret than it is a secret that you discovered it to my aunt, or than the reason why you discovered it is a secret.

MRS. MARWOOD You are nettled.

MILLAMANT You're mistaken. Ridiculous!

MRS. MARWOOD Indeed, my dear, you'll tear another fan, if you don't mitigate those violent airs.

MILLAMANT O silly! Ha! ha! ha! I could laugh immoderately. Poor Mirabell! His constancy to me has quite destroyed his complaisance for all the world beside. I swear, I never enjoined it him to be so coy. If I had the vanity to think he would obey me, I would command him to show more gallantry. 'Tis hardly well-bred to be so particular on one hand, and so insensible on the

7. Fought.
8. Cheap woolen cloth.
9. Heavy, coarse woolens.
1. White Rhenish wine was supposed to benefit the figure and complexion.
2. Lady to whom toasts are no longer drunk.

other. But I despair to prevail, and so let him follow his own
way. Ha! ha! ha! Pardon me, dear creature, I must laugh, ha! ha!
ha!—though I grant you 'tis a little barbarous, ha! ha! ha!

MRS. MARWOOD What pity 'tis, so much fine raillery, and delivered
with so significant gesture, should be so unhappily directed to
miscarry.

MILLAMANT Ha? Dear creature, I ask your pardon. I swear I did not
mind you.

MRS. MARWOOD Mr. Mirabell and you both may think it a thing
impossible, when I shall tell him by telling you—

MILLAMANT Oh dear, what? For it is the same thing, if I hear it,
ha! ha! ha!

MRS. MARWOOD That I detest him, hate him, madam.

MILLAMANT O madam, why so do I—and yet the creature loves
me, ha! ha! ha! How can one forbear laughing to think of it! I
am a sybil if I am not amazed to think what he can see in me.
I'll take my death, I think you are handsomer—and within a year
or two as young. If you could but stay for me, I should overtake
you—but that cannot be. —Well, that thought makes me melancholy. —Now I'll be sad.

MRS. MARWOOD Your merry note may be changed sooner than you
think.

MILLAMANT D'ye say so? Then I'm resolved to have a song to keep
up my spirits.

    Enter Mincing.

MINCING The gentlemen stay but to comb, madam, and will wait
on you.

MILLAMANT Desire Mrs. ——, that is in the next room, to sing the
song I would have learned yesterday. You shall hear it, madam,
not that there's any great matter in it, but 'tis agreeable to my
humour.

SONG

Set by Mr. John Eccles *and sung by* Mrs. Hodgson.

I

Love's but the frailty of the mind,
When 'tis not with ambition joined;
A sickly flame, which, if not fed, expires,
And feeding, wastes in self-consuming fires.

II

'Tis not to wound a wanton boy
Or amorous youth, that gives the joy;
But 'tis the glory to have pierced a swain,
For whom inferior beauties sighed in vain.

III

Then I alone the conquest prize,
When I insult a rival's eyes;
If there's delight in love, 'tis when I see
That heart, which others bleed for, bleed for me.

Enter Petulant *and* Witwoud.

MILLAMANT Is your animosity composed, gentlemen?

WITWOUD Raillery, raillery, madam; we have no animosity. We hit off a little wit now and then, but no animosity. The falling-out of wits is like the falling-out of lovers; we agree in the main,[3] like treble and bass. Ha, Petulant?

PETULANT Aye, in the main, but when I have a humour to contradict.

WITWOUD Aye, when he has a humour to contradict, then I contradict too. What, I know my cue. Then we contradict one another like two battledores;[4] for contradictions beget one another like Jews.

PETULANT If he says black's black, if I have a humour to say 'tis blue, let that pass; all's one for that. If I have a humour to prove it, it must be granted.

WITWOUD Not positively must, but it may, it may.

PETULANT Yes, it positively must, upon proof positive.

WITWOUD Aye, upon proof positive it must; but upon proof presumptive it only may. That's a logical distinction now, madam.

MRS. MARWOOD I perceive your debates are of importance and very learnedly handled.

PETULANT Importance is one thing, and learning's another; but a debate's a debate, that I assert.

WITWOUD Petulant's an enemy to learning; he relies altogether on his parts.

PETULANT No, I'm no enemy to learning; it hurts not me.

MRS. MARWOOD That's a sign indeed it's no enemy to you.

PETULANT No, no, it's no enemy to anybody but them that have it.

MILLAMANT Well, an illiterate man's my aversion. I wonder at the impudence of any illiterate man to offer to make love.

WITWOUD That I confess I wonder at too.

MILLAMANT Ah! to marry an ignorant that can hardly read or write!

PETULANT Why should a man be ever the further from being married, though he can't read, any more than he is from being hanged? The ordinary's[5] paid for setting the psalm, and the parish priest for reading the ceremony. And for the rest which is to follow in both cases, a man may do it without book; so all's one for that.

MILLAMANT D'ye hear the creature? Lord, here's company, I'll be gone.

Exeunt Millamant *and* Mincing.

WITWOUD In the name of Bartlemew and his fair,[6] what have we here?

MRS. MARWOOD 'Tis your brother, I fancy. Don't you know him?

WITWOUD Not I. Yes, I think it is he. I've almost forgot him; I have not seen him since the Revolution.[7]

---

3. Mainly. Also a musical term for the middle voice in a song.
4. Small rackets in a game of shuttlecock (badminton).
5. Clergyman who ministered to condemned prisoners.
6. Bartholomew Fair, held annually in Smithfield around 24 August.
7. Bloodless Revolution of 1688.

Enter Sir Wilfull Witwoud *in a country riding habit, and a* Servant *to* Lady Wishfort.

SERVANT Sir, my lady's dressing. Here's company; if you please to walk in, in the meantime.

SIR WILFULL Dressing! What, it's but morning here, I warrant, with you in London; we should count it towards afternoon in our parts, down in Shropshire. Why then, belike my aunt han't dined yet, ha, friend?

SERVANT Your aunt, sir?

SIR WILFULL My aunt, sir! Yes, my aunt, sir, and your lady, sir; your lady is my aunt, sir. Why, what, dost thou not know me, friend? Why then, send somebody here that does. How long hast thou lived with thy lady, fellow, ha?

SERVANT A week, sir; longer than anybody in the house, except my lady's woman.

SIR WILFULL Why then, belike thou dost not know thy lady, if thou seest her, ha, friend?

SERVANT Why truly, sir, I cannot safely swear to her face in a morning, before she is dressed. 'Tis like I may give a shrewd guess at her by this time.

SIR WILFULL Well, prithee try what thou canst do; if thou canst not guess, inquire her out, dost hear, fellow? And tell her, her nephew, Sir Wilfull Witwoud, is in the house.

SERVANT I shall, sir.

SIR WILFULL Hold ye, hear me, friend; a word with you in your ear. Prithee who are these gallants?

SERVANT Really, sir, I can't tell; here come so many here, 'tis hard to know 'em all.

Exit Servant.

SIR WILFULL Oons, this fellow knows less than a starling; I don't think a' knows his own name.

MRS. MARWOOD Mr. Witwoud, your brother is not behindhand in forgetfulness; I fancy he has forgot you too.

WITWOUD I hope so. The devil take him that remembers first, I say.

SIR WILFULL Save you, gentlemen and lady!

MRS. MARWOOD For shame, Mr. Witwoud; why won't you speak to him? And you, sir.

WITWOUD Petulant, speak.

PETULANT And you, sir.

SIR WILFULL No offense, I hope.

Salutes Marwood.

MRS. MARWOOD No sure, sir.

WITWOUD This is a vile dog, I see that already. No offense! Ha! ha! ha! to him; to him, Petulant, smoke him.

PETULANT It seems as if you had come a journey, sir; hem, hem.

Surveying him round.

SIR WILFULL Very likely, sir, that it may seem so.

PETULANT No offense, I hope, sir.

WITWOUD Smoke the boots, the boots; Petulant, the boots, ha! ha! ha!

SIR WILFULL May be not, sir; thereafter as 'tis meant, sir.

PETULANT Sir, I presume upon the information of your boots.

SIR WILFULL Why, 'tis like you may, sir. If you are not satisfied with the information of my boots, sir, if you will step to the stable, you may inquire further of my horse, sir.

PETULANT Your horse, sir! Your horse is an ass, sir!

SIR WILFULL Do you speak by way of offense, sir?

MRS. MARWOOD The gentleman's merry, that's all, sir. —[*Aside.*] 'Slife, we shall have a quarrel betwixt an horse and an ass, before they find one another out. —[*Aloud.*] You must not take anything amiss from your friends, sir. You are among your friends here, though it may be you don't know it. If I am not mistaken, you are Sir Wilfull Witwoud.

SIR WILFULL Right, lady; I am Sir Wilfull Witwoud, so I write myself; no offense to anybody, I hope; and nephew to the Lady Wishfort of this mansion.

MRS. MARWOOD Don't you know this gentleman, sir?

SIR WILFULL Hum! What, sure 'tis not—yea by'r Lady, but 'tis. 'Sheart, I know not whether 'tis or no. Yea, but 'tis, by the Wrekin.[8] Brother Anthony! What, Tony, i'faith! What, dost thou not know me? By'r Lady, nor I thee, thou art so be-cravated and be-periwigged. 'Sheart, why dost not speak? Art thou o'erjoyed?

WITWOUD Ods, brother, is it you? Your servant, brother.

SIR WILFULL Your servant! Why, yours, sir. Your servant again, 'sheart, and your friend and servant to that, and a—[*puff*] and a flapdragon for your service, sir! and a hare's foot, and a hare's scut for your service, sir, an you be so cold and so courtly!

WITWOUD No offense, I hope, brother.

SIR WILFULL 'Sheart, sir, but there is, and much offense! A pox, is this your Inns o' Court[9] breeding, not to know your friends and your relations, your elders and your betters?

WITWOUD Why, brother Wilfull of Salop,[1] you may be as short as a Shrewsbury cake, if you please. But I tell you, 'tis not modish to know relations in town. You think you're in the country, where great lubberly brothers slabber and kiss one another when they meet, like a call of serjeants. 'Tis not the fashion here; 'tis not indeed, dear brother.

SIR WILFULL The fashion's a fool; and you're a fop, dear brother. 'Sheart, I've suspected this. By'r Lady, I conjectured you were a fop, since you began to change the style of your letters and write in a scrap of paper, gilt round the edges, no broader than a subpoena. I might expect this when you left off Honored Brother, and hoping you are in good health, and so forth—to begin with a Rat me,[2] knight, I'm so sick of a last night's debauch—ods heart, and then tell a familiar tale of a cock and a bull, and a whore and a bottle, and so conclude. You could write news before you were out of your time,[3] when you lived with honest Pumple

8. A famous hill in Shropshire.
9. The legal societies in London.
1. Shropshire.

2. Contraction of *may God rot me.*
3. While you were still apprentice to an attorney.

Nose, the attorney of Furnival's Inn;[4] you could entreat to be remembered then to your friends round the Wrekin. We could have gazettes then, and *Dawks's Letter,* and the *Weekly Bill,*[5] till of late days.

PETULANT 'Slife, Witwoud, were you ever an attorney's clerk? of the family of the Furnivals? Ha! ha! ha!

WITWOUD Aye, aye, but that was for a while, not long, not long. Pshaw! I was not in my own power then; an orphan, and this fellow was my guardian. Aye, aye, I was glad to consent to that man to come to London. He had the disposal of me then. If I had not agreed to that, I might have been bound prentice to a felt-maker in Shrewsbury; this fellow would have bound me to a maker of felts.

SIR WILFULL 'Sheart, and better than to be bound to a maker of fops, where, I suppose, you have served your time; and now you may set up for yourself.

MRS. MARWOOD You intend to travel, sir, as I'm informed.

SIR WILFULL Belike I may, madam. I may chance to sail upon the salt seas, if my mind hold.

PETULANT And the wind serve.

SIR WILFULL Serve or not serve, I shan't ask license of you, sir; nor the weathercock your companion. I direct my discourse to the lady, sir. 'Tis like my aunt may have told you, madam. Yes, I have settled my concerns, I may say now, and am minded to see foreign parts. If an how that the peace holds,[6] whereby, that is, taxes abate.

MRS. MARWOOD I thought you had designed for France at all adventures.

SIR WILFULL I can't tell that; 'tis like I may, and 'tis like I may not. I am somewhat dainty in making a resolution, because when I make it, I keep it. I don't stand shill I, shall I, then; if I say't, I'll do't. But I have thoughts to tarry a small matter in town, to learn somewhat of your lingo first, before I cross the seas. I'd gladly have a spice of your French, as they say, whereby to hold discourse in foreign countries.

MRS. MARWOOD Here is an academy in town for that use.

SIR WILFULL There is? 'Tis like there may.

MRS. MARWOOD No doubt you will return very much improved.

WITWOUD Yes, refined, like a Dutch skipper from a whale-fishing.
Enter Lady Wishfort *and* Fainall.

LADY WISHFORT Nephew, you are welcome.

SIR WILFULL Aunt, your servant.

FAINALL Sir Wilfull, your most faithful servant.

SIR WILFULL Cousin Fainall, give me your hand.

LADY WISHFORT Cousin Witwoud, your servant; Mr. Petulant, your servant. Nephew, you are welcome again. Will you drink any-

---

4. A subordinate Inn of Court.
5. Newspapers. *Dawks's Letter* was a weekly news-sheet; the *Weekly Bill* was the official list of deaths in and around London.
6. The Peace of Ryswick in 1697 interrupted war with France.

thing after your journey, nephew, before you eat? Dinner's almost ready.

SIR WILFULL I'm very well, I thank you, aunt; however, I thank you for your courteous offer. 'Sheart, I was afraid you would have been in the fashion too, and have remembered to have forgot your relations. Here's your cousin Tony; belike I mayn't call him brother for fear of offense.

LADY WISHFORT Oh, he's a rallier, nephew. My cousin's a wit; and your great wits always rally their best friends to choose.[7] When you have been abroad, nephew, you'll understand raillery better.

Fainall and Mrs. Marwood *talk apart.*

SIR WILFULL Why then, let him hold his tongue in the meantime, and rail when that day comes.

Enter Mincing.

MINCING Mem, I come to acquaint your la'ship that dinner is impatient.

SIR WILFULL Impatient? Why then, belike it won't stay till I pull off my boots. Sweetheart, can you help me to a pair of slippers? My man's with his horses, I warrant.

LADY WISHFORT Fie, fie, nephew, you would not pull off your boots here. Go down into the hall; dinner shall stay for you. My nephew's a little unbred; you'll pardon him, madam. Gentlemen, will you walk? Marwood?

MRS. MARWOOD I'll follow you, madam, before Sir Wilfull is ready.

Exeunt all but Mrs. Marwood *and* Fainall.

FAINALL Why then, Foible's a bawd, an arrant, rank, matchmaking bawd. And I, it seems, am a husband, a rank husband; and my wife a very arrant, rank wife, all in the way of the world. 'Sdeath, to be an anticipated cuckold, a cuckold in embryo! Sure I was born with budding antlers, like a young satyr, or a citizen's child.[8] 'Sdeath, to be outwitted, to be out-jilted, out-matrimonied! If I had kept my speed like a stag, 'twere somewhat; but to crawl after, with my horns like a snail, and outstripped by my wife, 'tis scurvy wedlock.

MRS. MARWOOD Then shake it off. You have often wished for an opportunity to part; and now you have it. But first prevent their plot; the half of Millamant's fortune is too considerable to be parted with, to a foe, to Mirabell.

FAINALL Damn him! that had been mine, had you not made that fond discovery. That had been forfeited, had they been married. My wife had added luster to my horns by that increase of fortune; I could have worn 'em tipt with gold, though my forehead had been furnished like a deputy lieutenant's hall.[9]

MRS. MARWOOD They may prove a cap of maintenance[1] to you still, if you can away with[2] your wife. And she's no worse than when

---

7. Make fun of their friends at will.
8. Fainall would think that the child of a citizen (a London merchant) was born to be cuckolded by rakes of higher social class.

9. With antlers—i.e., the cuckold's horns.
1. In heraldry, a cap with two points (i.e., the cuckold's horns again), worn as a sign of dignity.
2. Endure.

you had her. I dare swear she had given up her game before she was married.

FAINALL Hum! That may be. She might throw up her cards; but I'll be hanged if she did not put Pam in her pocket.[3]

MRS. MARWOOD You married her to keep you; and if you can contrive to have her keep you better than you expected, why should you not keep her longer than you intended?

FAINALL The means, the means.

MRS. MARWOOD Discover to my lady your wife's conduct; threaten to part with her. My lady loves her, and will come to any composition to save her reputation. Take the opportunity of breaking it, just upon the discovery of this imposture. My lady will be enraged beyond bounds, and sacrifice niece and fortune and all, at that conjuncture. And let me alone to keep her warm; if she should flag in her part, I will not fail to prompt her.

FAINALL Faith, this has an appearance.

MRS. MARWOOD I'm sorry I hinted to my lady to endeavor a match between Millamant and Sir Wilfull; that may be an obstacle.

FAINALL Oh, for that matter leave me to manage him; I'll disable him for that. He will drink like a Dane; after dinner, I'll set his hand in.

MRS. MARWOOD Well, how do you stand affected towards your lady?

FAINALL Why, faith, I'm thinking of it. Let me see. I am married already, so that's over. My wife has played the jade with me; well, that's over too. I never loved her, or if I had, why that would have been over too by this time. Jealous of her I cannot be, for I am certain; so there's an end of jealousy. Weary of her I am, and shall be. No, there's no end of that; no, no, that were too much to hope. Thus far concerning my repose; now for my reputation. As to my own, I married not for it; so that's out of the question. And as to my part in my wife's, why she had parted with hers before; so bringing none to me, she can take none from me. 'Tis against all rule of play that I should lose to one who has not wherewithal to stake.

MRS. MARWOOD Besides, you forget, marriage is honorable.

FAINALL Hum! Faith, and that's well thought on. Marriage is honorable, as you say; and if so, wherefore should cuckoldom be a discredit, being derived from so honorable a root?

MRS. MARWOOD Nay, I know not; if the root be honorable, why not the branches?[4]

FAINALL So, so; why this point's clear. Well, how do we proceed?

MRS. MARWOOD I will contrive a letter which shall be delivered to my lady at the time when that rascal who is to act Sir Rowland is with her. It shall come as from an unknown hand, for the less I appear to know of the truth, the better I can play the incendiary. Besides, I would not have Foible provoked if I could help it, because you know she knows some passages. Nay, I expect all will come out; but let the mine be sprung first, and then I care not if I'm discovered.

FAINALL If the worst came to the worst, I'll turn my wife to grass.[5] I have already a deed of settlement of the best part of her estate, which I have wheedled out of her; and that you shall partake at least.

MRS. MARWOOD I hope you are convinced that I hate Mirabell; now you'll be no more jealous.

FAINALL Jealous! No, by this kiss. Let husbands be jealous; but let the lover still believe. Or if he doubt, let it be only to endear his pleasure, and prepare the joy that follows, when he proves his mistress true. But let husbands' doubts convert to endless jealousy; or if they have belief, let it corrupt to superstition and blind credulity. I am single, and will herd no more with 'em. True, I wear the badge, but I'll disown the order. And since I take my leave of 'em, I care not if I leave 'em a common motto to their common crest:

> All husbands must or pain or shame endure;
> The wise too jealous are, fools too secure.

Exeunt.

Act IV. Scene continues.
Enter Lady Wishfort *and* Foible.

LADY WISHFORT Is Sir Rowland coming, say'st thou, Foible? and are things in order?

FOIBLE Yes, madam, I have put wax lights in the sconces, and placed the footmen in a row in the hall, in their best liveries, with the coachman and postilion to fill up the equipage.

LADY WISHFORT Have you pulvilled[6] the coachman and postilion that they may not stink of the stable when Sir Rowland comes by?

FOIBLE Yes, madam.

LADY WISHFORT And are the dancers and the music ready, that he may be entertained in all points with correspondence to his passion?

FOIBLE All is ready, madam.

LADY WISHFORT And—well—and how do I look, Foible?

FOIBLE Most killing well, madam.

LADY WISHFORT Well, and how shall I receive him? In what figure shall I give his heart the first impression? There is a great deal in the first impression. Shall I sit? —No, I won't sit—I'll walk—aye, I'll walk from the door upon his entrance; and then turn full upon him. —No, that will be too sudden. I'll lie down—aye, I'll receive him in my little dressing-room; there's a couch —yes, yes, I'll give the first impression on a couch. —I won't lie neither, but loll and lean upon one elbow, with one foot a little dangling off, jogging in a thoughtful way—yes—and then as soon as he appears, start, aye, start and be surprised, and rise to meet

---

5. Turn her out to pasture.   6. Powdered with scent.

him in a pretty disorder—yes—oh, nothing is more alluring than a levee[7] from a couch in some confusion. —It shows the foot to advantage, and furnishes with blushes, and recomposing airs beyond comparison. Hark! There's a coach.

FOIBLE 'Tis he, madam.

LADY WISHFORT Oh dear, has my nephew made his addresses to Millamant? I ordered him.

FOIBLE Sir Wilfull is set in to drinking, madam, in the parlor.

LADY WISHFORT Ods my life, I'll send him to her. Call her down, Foible; bring her hither. I'll send him as I go. When they are together, then come to me, Foible, that I may not be too long alone with Sir Rowland.

Exit.

Enter Mrs. Millamant *and* Mrs. Fainall.

FOIBLE Madam, I stayed here, to tell your ladyship that Mr. Mirabell has waited this half hour for an opportunity to talk with you, though my lady's orders were to leave you and Sir Wilfull together. Shall I tell Mr. Mirabell that you are at leisure?

MILLAMANT No—what would the dear man have? I am thoughtful and would amuse myself—bid him come another time.

> There never yet was woman made,
> Nor shall, but to be cursed.[8]

Repeating and walking about.
That's hard!

MRS. FAINALL You are very fond of Sir John Suckling today, Millamant, and the poets.

MILLAMANT He? Aye, and filthy verses; so I am.

FOIBLE Sir Wilfull is coming, madam. Shall I send Mr. Mirabell away?

MILLAMANT Aye, if you please, Foible, send him away—or send him hither—just as you will, dear Foible —I think I'll see him—shall I? Aye, let the wretch come.

Exit Foible.

> Thyrsis, a youth of the inspired train.[9]

Repeating.
Dear Fainall, entertain Sir Wilfull. Thou hast philosophy to undergo a fool; thou art married and hast patience. I would confer with my own thoughts.

MRS. FAINALL I am obliged to you, that you would make me your proxy in this affair; but I have business of my own.

Enter Sir Wilfull.

O Sir Wilfull, you are come at the critical instant. There's your mistress up to the ears in love and contemplation; pursue your point, now or never.

---

7. A rising.
8. The opening lines of an untitled poem by Sir John Suckling. The poems which Millamant calls to mind—on the brevity of love and the falseness of men—reflect concern for her own situation and perhaps the depth of her feeling for Mirabell.
9. The first line of Edmund Waller's *The Story of Phoebus and Daphne, Applied.*

SIR WILFULL Yes; my aunt would have it so. I would gladly have been encouraged with a bottle or two, because I'm somewhat wary at first, before I am acquainted. [*This while* Millamant *walks about repeating to herself.*] But I hope, after a time, I shall break my mind; that is, upon further acquaintance. So for the present, cousin, I'll take my leave. If so be you'll be so kind to make my excuse, I'll return to my company.

MRS. FAINALL Oh, fie, Sir Wilfull! What, you must not be daunted.

SIR WILFULL Daunted! No, that's not it. It is not so much for that; for if so be that I set on't, I'll do't. But only for the present; 'tis sufficient till further acquaintance, that's all. Your servant.

MRS. FAINALL Nay, I'll swear you shall never lose so favorable an opportunity, if I can help it. I'll leave you together and lock the door.

Exit.

SIR WILFULL Nay, nay, cousin. I have forgot my gloves. What d'ye do? 'Sheart, 'a has locked the door indeed, I think. Nay, Cousin Fainall, open the door! Pshaw, what a vixen trick is this? Nay, now 'a has seen me too. Cousin, I made bold to pass through as it were. I think this door's enchanted!

MILLAMANT [*repeating*]

> I prithee spare me, gentle boy,
> Press me no more for that slight toy—[1]

SIR WILFULL Anan?[2] Cousin, your servant.

MILLAMANT [*repeating*]

> That foolish trifle of a heart—

Sir Wilfull!

SIR WILFULL Yes. Your servant. No offense, I hope, cousin.

MILLAMANT [*repeating*]

> I swear it will not do its part,
> Though thou dost thine, employ'st thy power and art.

Natural, easy Suckling!

SIR WILFULL Anan? Suckling! No such suckling neither, cousin, nor stripling; I thank heaven, I'm no minor.

MILLAMANT Ah, rustic! ruder than Gothic!

SIR WILFULL Well, well, I shall understand your lingo one of these days, cousin; in the meanwhile, I must answer in plain English.

MILLAMANT Have you any business with me, Sir Wilfull?

SIR WILFULL Not at present, cousin. Yes, I made bold to see, to come and know if that how you were disposed to fetch a walk this evening, if so be that I might not be troublesome, I would have fought[3] a walk with you.

MILLAMANT A walk! What then?

SIR WILFULL Nay, nothing. Only for the walk's sake, that's all.

---

1. The opening lines of an untitled song by Suckling.
2. "How's that?" A provincial term.
3. A provincial form of *fetched*.

MILLAMANT I nauseate walking; 'tis a country diversion. I loathe the country and everything that relates to it.

SIR WILFULL Indeed! Ha! Look ye, look ye, you do? Nay, 'tis like you may. Here are choice of pastimes here in town, as plays and the like; that must be confessed indeed.

MILLAMANT Ah, *l'étourdie!*[4] I hate the town too.

SIR WILFULL Dear heart, that's much. Ha! that you should hate 'em both! Ha! 'tis like you may; there are some can't relish the town, and others can't away with the country. 'Tis like you may be one of those, cousin.

MILLAMANT Ha! ha! ha! Yes, 'tis like I may. You have nothing further to say to me?

SIR WILFULL Not at present, cousin. 'Tis like when I have an opportunity to be more private, I may break my mind in some measure. I conjecture you partly guess. —However, that's as time shall try; but spare to speak and spare to speed, as they say.

MILLAMANT If it is of no great importance, Sir Wilfull, you will oblige me to leave me; I have just now a little business—

SIR WILFULL Enough, enough, cousin, yes, yes, all a case; when you're disposed, when you're disposed. Now's as well as another time; and another time as well as now. All's one for that. Yes, yes, if your concerns call you, there's no haste; it will keep cold, as they say. Cousin, your servant. I think this door's locked.

MILLAMANT You may go this way, sir.

SIR WILFULL Your servant; then with your leave I'll return to my company.

Exit.

MILLAMANT Aye, aye; ha! ha! ha!

Like Phoebus sung the no less amorous boy.[5]

Enter Mirabell.

MIRABELL

Like Daphne she, as lovely and as coy.

Do you lock yourself up from me, to make my search more curious?[6] Or is this pretty artifice contrived, to signify that here the chase must end and my pursuit be crowned, for you can fly no further?

MILLAMANT Vanity! No. I'll fly and be followed to the last moment. Though I am upon the very verge of matrimony, I expect you should solicit me as much as if I were wavering at the grate of a monastery, with one foot over the threshold. I'll be solicited to the very last, nay and afterwards.

MIRABELL What, after the last?

MILLAMANT Oh, I should think I was poor and had nothing to bestow, if I were reduced to an inglorious ease and freed from the agreeable fatigues of solicitation.

MIRABELL But do not you know that when favors are conferred

---

4. "Ah, the giddy town!"
5. From Waller's *Phoebus and Daphne*, line 3. Mirabell completes the couplet in

the next line.
6. Complicated.

upon instant and tedious solicitation, that they diminish in their value, and that both the giver loses the grace, and the receiver lessens his pleasure?

MILLAMANT It may be in things of common application; but never sure in love. Oh, I hate a lover that can dare to think he draws a moment's air independent on the bounty of his mistress. There is not so impudent a thing in nature as the saucy look of an assured man, confident of success. The pedantic arrogance of a very husband has not so pragmatical an air. Ah! I'll never marry, unless I am first made sure of my will and pleasure.

MIRABELL Would you have 'em both before marriage? Or will you be contented with the first now, and stay for the other till after grace?

MILLAMANT Ah! don't be impertinent. —My dear liberty, shall I leave thee? My faithful solitude, my darling contemplation, must I bid you then adieu? Ay-h adieu—my morning thoughts, agreeable wakings, indolent slumbers, all ye *douceurs*, ye *sommeils du matin*,[7] adieu? —I can't do't, 'tis more than impossible. Positively, Mirabell, I'll lie abed in a morning as long as I please.

MIRABELL Then I'll get up in a morning as early as I please.

MILLAMANT Ah! Idle creature, get up when you will. —And d'ye hear, I won't be called names after I'm married; positively I won't be called names.

MIRABELL Names!

MILLAMANT Aye, as wife, spouse, my dear, joy, jewel, love, sweetheart, and the rest of that nauseous cant, in which men and their wives are so fulsomely familiar—I shall never bear that. —Good Mirabell, don't let us be familiar or fond, nor kiss before folks, like my Lady Fadler and Sir Francis; nor go to Hyde Park together the first Sunday in a new chariot, to provoke eyes and whispers; and then never to be seen there together again; as if we were proud of one another the first week, and ashamed of one another ever after. Let us be very strange and well-bred; let us be as strange[8] as if we had been married a great while, and as well-bred as if we were not married at all.

MIRABELL Have you any more conditions to offer? Hitherto your demands are pretty reasonable.

MILLAMANT Trifles! —As liberty to pay and receive visits to and from whom I please; to write and receive letters, without interrogatories or wry faces on your part; to wear what I please; and choose conversation with regard only to my own taste; to have no obligation upon me to converse with wits that I don't like, because they are your acquaintance; or to be intimate with fools, because they may be your relations. Come to dinner when I please; dine in my dressing room when I'm out of humour, without giving a reason. To have my closet inviolate; to be sole empress of my tea table, which you must never presume to approach without first asking leave. And lastly, wherever I am, you shall always knock at the door before you come in. These

7. Sweetnesses and morning naps.   8. Reserved.

articles subscribed, if I continue to endure you a little longer, I may by degrees dwindle into a wife.

MIRABELL Your bill of fare is something advanced in this latter account. Well, have I liberty to offer conditions—that when you are dwindled into a wife, I may not be beyond measure enlarged into a husband?

MILLAMANT You have free leave. Propose your utmost; speak and spare not.

MIRABELL I thank you. *Imprimis*[9] then, I covenant that your acquaintance be general; that you admit no sworn confidante, or intimate of your own sex; no she-friend to screen her affairs under your countenance, and tempt you to make trial of a mutual secrecy. No decoy-duck to wheedle you a fop, scrambling to the play in a mask; then bring you home in a pretended fright, when you think you shall be found out, and rail at me for missing the play, and disappointing the frolic which you had, to pick me up and prove my constancy.

MILLAMANT Detestable *imprimis*! I go to the play in a mask!

MIRABELL *Item*, I article that you continue to like your own face as long as I shall; and while it passes current with me, that you endeavor not to new-coin it. To which end, together with all vizards[1] for the day, I prohibit all masks for the night, made of oiled skins and I know not what—hog's bones, hare's gall, pig-water, and the marrow of a roasted cat. In short, I forbid all commerce with the gentlewoman in What-d'ye-call-it Court. *Item*, I shut my doors against all bawds with baskets, and pennyworths of muslin, china, fans, atlases,[2] etc. —*Item*, when you shall be breeding—

MILLAMANT Ah! name it not.

MIRABELL Which may be presumed, with a blessing on our endeavors—

MILLAMANT Odious endeavors!

MIRABELL I denounce against all strait-lacing, squeezing for a shape, till you mold my boy's head like a sugar loaf, and instead of a man-child, make me the father to a crooked billet.[3] Lastly, to the dominion of the tea table I submit, but with proviso, that you exceed not in your province, but restrain yourself to native and simple tea-table drinks, as tea, chocolate, and coffee. As likewise to genuine and authorized tea-table talk—such as mending of fashions, spoiling reputations, railing at absent friends, and so forth; but that on no account you encroach upon the men's prerogative, and presume to drink healths, or toast fellows; for prevention of which, I banish all foreign forces, all auxiliaries to the tea table, as orange brandy, all aniseed, cinnamon, citron, and Barbadoes waters, together with ratafia and the most noble spirit of clary.[4] But for cowslip-wine, poppy-water, and all dormitives, those I allow. These provisos admitted, in other things I may prove a tractable and complying husband.

---

9. *In the first place*; the phrasing of legal documents.
1. Masks.
2. Satins.
3. Stick of wood.
4. These are all alcoholic drinks.

MILLAMANT Oh, horrid provisos! filthy strong waters! I toast fellows, odious men! I hate your odious provisos.

MIRABELL Then we're agreed. Shall I kiss your hand upon the contract? And here comes one to be a witness to the sealing of the deed.

Enter Mrs. Fainall.

MILLAMANT Fainall, what shall I do? Shall I have him? I think I must have him.

MRS. FAINALL Aye, aye, take him, take him, what should you do?

MILLAMANT Well then—I'll take my death I'm in a horrid fright —Fainall, I shall never say it—well—I think—I'll endure you.

MRS. FAINALL Fie, fie! have him, have him, and tell him so in plain terms; for I am sure you have a mind to him.

MILLAMANT Are you? I think I have—and the horrid man looks as if he thought so too. —Well, you ridiculous thing you, I'll have you—I won't be kissed, nor I won't be thanked—here, kiss my hand though. —So, hold your tongue now, and don't say a word.

MRS. FAINALL Mirabell, there's a necessity for your obedience; you have neither time to talk nor stay. My mother is coming; and in my conscience, if she should see you, would fall into fits and maybe not recover time enough to return to Sir Rowland, who, as Foible tells me, is in a fair way to succeed. Therefore spare your ecstasies for another occasion, and slip down the backstairs, where Foible waits to consult you.

MILLAMANT Aye, go, go. In the meantime I suppose you have said something to please me.

MIRABELL I am all obedience.

Exit.

MRS. FAINALL Yonder Sir Wilfull's drunk, and so noisy that my mother has been forced to leave Sir Rowland to appease him; but he answers her only with singing and drinking. What they have done by this time I know not; but Petulant and he were quarreling as I came by.

MILLAMANT Well, if Mirabell should not make a good husband, I am a lost thing—for I find I love him violently.

MRS. FAINALL So it seems, when you mind not what's said to you. If you doubt him, you had best take up with Sir Wilfull.

MILLAMANT How can you name that superannuated lubber? foh!

Enter Witwoud *from drinking.*

MRS. FAINALL So, is the fray made up, that you left 'em?

WITWOUD Left 'em? I could stay no longer. I have laughed like ten christenings; I am tipsy with laughing. If I had stayed any longer I should have burst; I must have been let out and pieced in the sides like an unsized camlet.[5] Yes, yes, the fray is composed; my lady came in like a *nolle prosequi*[6] and stopped their proceedings.

MILLAMANT What was the dispute?

WITWOUD That's the jest; there was no dispute. They could neither

---

5. An unstiffened fabric.   6. Legal phrase for ending a lawsuit.

of 'em speak for rage, and so fell a-sputtering at one another like two roasting apples.

Enter Petulant *drunk.*

Now Petulant, all's over, all's well. Gad, my head begins to whim it about. Why dost thou not speak? Thou art both as drunk and as mute as a fish.

PETULANT Look you, Mrs. Millamant, if you can love me, dear nymph, say it, and that's the conclusion. Pass on, or pass off; that's all.

WITWOUD Thou hast uttered volumes, folios, in less than *decimo sexto,* my dear Lacedemonian.[7] Sirrah Petulant, thou art an epitomizer of words.

PETULANT Witwoud, you are an annihilator of sense.

WITWOUD Thou art a retailer of phrases and dost deal in remnants of remnants, like a maker of pincushions; thou art in truth (metaphorically speaking) a speaker of shorthand.

PETULANT Thou are (without a figure) just one half of an ass, and Baldwin[8] yonder, thy half brother, is the rest. A gemini[9] of asses split would make just four of you.

WITWOUD Thou dost bite, my dear mustard seed; kiss me for that.

PETULANT Stand off! I'll kiss no more males. I have kissed your twin yonder in a humour of reconciliation, till he [*hiccup*] rises upon my stomach like a radish.

MILLAMANT Eh! filthy creature! What was the quarrel?

PETULANT There was no quarrel; there might have been a quarrel.

WITWOUD If there had been words enow between 'em to have expressed provocation, they had gone together by the ears like a pair of castanets.

PETULANT You were the quarrel.

MILLAMANT Me!

PETULANT If I have a humour to quarrel, I can make less matters conclude premises. If you are not handsome, what then, if I have a humour to prove it? If I shall have my reward, say so; if not, fight for your face the next time yourself. I'll go sleep.

WITWOUD Do, wrap thyself up like a wood louse, and dream revenge; and hear me, if thou canst learn to write by tomorrow morning, pen me a challenge. I'll carry it for thee.

PETULANT Carry your mistress's monkey a spider! Go flea dogs, and read romances! I'll go to bed to my maid.

Exit.

MRS. FAINALL He's horridly drunk. How came you all in this pickle?

WITWOUD A plot! a plot! to get rid of the knight. Your husband's advice; but he sneaked off.

Enter Lady Wishfort, *and* Sir Wilfull *drunk.*

LADY WISHFORT Out upon't, out upon't! At years of discretion, and comport yourself at this rantipole[1] rate!

---

7. *Decimo sexto* means *a small book.* Lacedemonians (Spartans) were men of few words.
8. The ass in the beast epic *Reynard the* Fox.
9. Twins, from the Roman deities Castor and Pollux.
1. Ill-mannered.

SIR WILFULL No offense, aunt.

LADY WISHFORT Offense! As I'm a person, I'm ashamed of you—
foh! how you stink of wine! D'ye think my niece will ever endure
such a borachio! you're an absolute borachio.[2]

SIR WILFULL Borachio!

LADY WISHFORT At a time when you should commence an amour
and put your best foot foremost—

SIR WILFULL 'Sheart, an you grutch me your liquor, make a bill.
Give me more drink, and take my purse.

> *Sings.*

> Prithee fill me the glass,
> Till it laugh in my face,
> With ale that is potent and mellow;
> He that whines for a lass
> Is an ignorant ass,
> For a bumper has not its fellow.

But if you would have me marry my cousin, say the word, and I'll
do't. Wilfull will do't; that's the word. Wilfull will do't; that's
my crest. My motto I have forgot.

LADY WISHFORT My nephew's a little overtaken, cousin, but 'tis
with drinking your health. O' my word you are obliged to him.

SIR WILFULL *In vino veritas*,[3] aunt. If I drunk your health today,
cousin, I am a borachio. But if you have a mind to be married,
say the word, and send for the piper; Wilfull will do't. If not,
dust it away, and let's have t'other round. —Tony! —Odsheart,
where's Tony? —Tony's an honest fellow; but he spits after a
bumper, and that's a fault.

> *Sings.*

> We'll drink, and we'll never ha' done, boys,
> Put the glass then around with the sun, boys;
> Let Apollo's example invite us;
> For he's drunk every night,
> And that makes him so bright,
> That he's able next morning to light us.

The sun's a good pimple,[4] an honest soaker; he has a cellar at
your Antipodes. If I travel, aunt, I touch at your Antipodes; your
Antipodes are a good, rascally sort of topsy-turvy fellows. If I had
a bumper, I'd stand upon my head and drink a health to 'em. A
match, or no match, cousin with the hard name? Aunt, Wilfull
will do't. If she has her maidenhead, let her look to't; if she has
not, let her keep her own counsel in the meantime, and cry out
at the nine months' end.

MILLAMANT Your pardon, madam, I can stay no longer. Sir Wilfull
grows very powerful. Egh! how he smells! I shall be overcome if I
stay. Come, cousin.

> *Exeunt* Millamant *and* Mrs. Fainall.

---

2. Drunkard.
3. "In wine there is truth."
4. Good friend.

LADY WISHFORT Smells! he would poison a tallow chandler[5] and his family. Beastly creature, I know not what to do with him! Travel, quotha! aye, travel, travel, get thee gone, get thee but far enough, to the Saracens, or the Tartars, or the Turks, for thou art not fit to live in a Christian commonwealth, thou beastly pagan!

SIR WILFULL Turks, no; no Turks, aunt; your Turks are infidels, and believe not in the grape. Your Mahometan, your Mussulman, is a dry stinkard. No offense, aunt. My map says that your Turk is not so honest a man as your Christian. I cannot find by the map that your Mufti[6] is orthodox; whereby it is a plain case that orthodox is a hard word, aunt, and [*hiccup*] Greek for claret.
Sings.

> To drink is a Christian diversion,
> Unknown to the Turk and the Persian:
>   Let Mahometan fools
>   Live by heathenish rules,
> And be damned over tea cups and coffee!
>   But let British lads sing,
>   Crown a health to the king,
> And a fig for your sultan and sophy![7]

Ah, Tony!
Enter Foible, *and whispers* Lady Wishfort.

LADY WISHFORT [*aside to* Foible] Sir Rowland impatient? Good lack! what shall I do with this beastly tumbril?[8] [*Aloud.*] Go lie down and sleep, you sot! or, as I'm a person, I'll have you bastinadoed[9] with broomsticks. Call up the wenches.
Exit Foible.

SIR WILFULL Ahey! Wenches, where are the wenches?

LADY WISHFORT Dear Cousin Witwoud, get him away, and you will bind me to you inviolably. I have an affair of moment that invades me with some precipitation. You will oblige me to all futurity.

WITWOUD Come, knight. Pox on him, I don't know what to say to him. Will you go to a cock-match?

SIR WILFULL With a wench, Tony? Is she a shake-bag,[1] Sirrah? Let me bite your cheek for that.

WITWOUD Horrible! He has a breath like a bagpipe! Aye, aye, come, will you march, my Salopian?[2]

SIR WILFULL Lead on, little Tony; I'll follow thee, my Anthony, my Tantony.[3] Sirrah, thou shalt be my Tantony, and I'll be thy pig.

And a fig for your sultan and sophy.

Exit singing with Witwoud.

LADY WISHFORT This will never do. It will never make a match—at least before he has been abroad.
Enter Waitwell, *disguised as for* Sir Rowland.

---

5. A maker or seller of candles.
6. Mohammedan priest.
7. The Shah of Persia.
8. Dung cart.
9. Beaten on the soles of the feet.
1. Gamecock.
2. Native of Shropshire.
3. St. Anthony, the patron of swineherds.

Dear Sir Rowland, I am confounded with confusion at the retrospection of my own rudeness! I have more pardons to ask than the Pope distributes in the Year of Jubilee. But I hope, where there is likely to be so near an alliance, we may unbend the severity of decorum and dispense with a little ceremony.

WAITWELL My impatience, madam, is the effect of my transport; and till I have the possession of your adorable person, I am tantalized on a rack, and do but hang, madam, on the tenter of expectation.

LADY WISHFORT You have an excess of gallantry, Sir Rowland, and press things to a conclusion with a most prevailing vehemence. But a day or two for decency of marriage—

WAITWELL For decency of funeral, madam! The delay will break my heart; or, if that should fail, I shall be poisoned. My nephew will get an inkling of my designs and poison me; and I would willingly starve him before I die; I would gladly go out of the world with that satisfaction. That would be some comfort to me, if I could but live so long as to be revenged on that unnatural viper.

LADY WISHFORT Is he so unnatural, say you? Truly I would contribute much both to the saving of your life, and the accomplishment of your revenge. Not that I respect[4] myself, though he has been a perfidious wretch to me.

WAITWELL Perfidious to you!

LADY WISHFORT O Sir Rowland, the hours that he has died away at my feet, the tears that he has shed, the oaths that he has sworn, the palpitations that he has felt, the trances and the tremblings, the ardors and the ecstasies, the kneelings and the risings, the heart-heavings, and the hand-grippings, the pangs and the pathetic regards of his protesting eyes! Oh, no memory can register.

WAITWELL What, my rival! Is the rebel my rival? 'A dies.

LADY WISHFORT No, don't kill him at once, Sir Rowland; starve him gradually, inch by inch.

WAITWELL I'll do't. In three weeks he shall be barefoot; in a month out at knees with begging an alms. He shall starve upward and upward, till he has nothing living but his head, and then go out in a stink like a candle's end upon a save-all.[5]

LADY WISHFORT Well, Sir Rowland, you have the way. You are no novice in the labyrinth of love; you have the clue. But as I am a person, Sir Rowland, you must not attribute my yielding to any sinister appetite, or indigestion of widowhood; nor impute my complacency to any lethargy of continence. I hope you do not think me prone to any iteration of nuptials.

WAITWELL Far be it from me—

LADY WISHFORT If you do, I protest I must recede, or think that I have made a prostitution of decorums; but in the vehemence of compassion, and to save the life of a person of so much importance—

4. Consider. end.
5. A device for burning candles to the

WAITWELL I esteem it so.

LADY WISHFORT Or else you wrong my condescension.

WAITWELL I do not, I do not!

LADY WISHFORT Indeed you do.

WAITWELL I do not, fair shrine of virtue!

LADY WISHFORT If you think the least scruple of carnality was an ingredient—

WAITWELL Dear madam, no. You are all camphire[6] and frankincense, all chastity and odor.

LADY WISHFORT Or that—

Enter Foible.

FOIBLE Madam, the dancers are ready, and there's one with a letter, who must deliver it into your own hands.

LADY WISHFORT Sir Rowland, will you give me leave? Think favorably, judge candidly, and conclude you have found a person who would suffer racks in honor's cause, dear Sir Rowland, and will wait on you incessantly.[7]

WAITWELL Fie, fie! What a slavery have I undergone! Spouse, hast thou any cordial! I want spirits.

FOIBLE What a washy rogue art thou, to pant thus for a quarter of an hour's lying and swearing to a fine lady!

WAITWELL Oh, she is the antidote to desire! Spouse, thou wilt fare the worse for't. I shall have no appetite to iteration of nuptials this eight-and-forty hours. By this hand I'd rather be a chairman in the dog-days[8] than act Sir Rowland till this time tomorrow!

Enter Lady Wishfort, *with a letter.*

LADY WISHFORT Call in the dancers. Sir Rowland, we'll sit, if you please, and see the entertainment.

Dance.

Now, with your permission, Sir Rowland, I will peruse my letter. I would open it in your presence, because I would not make you uneasy. If it should make you uneasy, I would burn it. Speak, if it does. But you may see by the superscription it is like a woman's hand.

FOIBLE [*aside to* Waitwell] By heaven! Mrs. Marwood's; I know it. My heart aches. Get it from her.

WAITWELL A woman's hand? No, madam, that's no woman's hand; I see that already. That's somebody whose throat must be cut.

LADY WISHFORT Nay, Sir Rowland, since you give me a proof of your passion by your jealousy, I promise you I'll make you a return, by a frank communication. You shall see it; we'll open it together. Look you here. [*Reads.*] "Madam, though unknown to you"—Look you there, 'tis from nobody that I know—"I have that honor for your character, that I think myself obliged to let you know you are abused. He who pretends to be Sir Rowland is a cheat and a rascal." —Oh, heavens! what's this?

FOIBLE [*aside*] Unfortunate! all's ruined!

WAITWELL How, how, let me see, let me see! [*Reading.*] "A rascal,

6. Camphor was supposed to reduce sexual desire.
7. Instantly.

8. Bearer of a sedan chair in the hottest time of summer.

and disguised and suborned for that imposture."—O villainy! O villainy —"by the contrivance of —"

LADY WISHFORT I shall faint. I shall die, I shall die, oh!

FOIBLE [*aside to* Waitwell] Say 'tis your nephew's hand. Quickly, his plot, swear, swear it!

WAITWELL Here's a villain! Madam, don't you perceive it? don't you see it?

LADY WISHFORT Too well, too well! I have seen too much.

WAITWELL I told you at first I knew the hand. A woman's hand? The rascal writes a sort of a large hand, your Roman hand. I saw there was a throat to be cut presently. If he were my son, as he is my nephew, I'd pistol him!

FOIBLE Oh, treachery! But are you sure, Sir Rowland, it is his writing?

WAITWELL Sure? Am I here? Do I live? Do I love this pearl of India? I have twenty letters in my pocket from him in the same character.

LADY WISHFORT How!

FOIBLE Oh, what luck it is, Sir Rowland, that you were present at this juncture! This was the business that brought Mr. Mirabell disguised to Madam Millamant this afternoon. I thought something was contriving, when he stole by me and would have hid his face.

LADY WISHFORT How, how! I heard the villain was in the house indeed; and now I remember, my niece went away abruptly, when Sir Wilfull was to have made his addresses.

FOIBLE Then, then, madam, Mr. Mirabell waited for her in her chamber, but I would not tell your ladyship to discompose you when you were to receive Sir Rowland.

WAITWELL Enough, his date is short.

FOIBLE No, good Sir Rowland, don't incur the law.

WAITWELL Law? I care not for law. I can but die, and 'tis in a good cause. My lady shall be satisfied of my truth and innocence, though it cost me my life.

LADY WISHFORT No, dear Sir Rowland, don't fight; if you should be killed, I must never show my face; or hanged—oh, consider my reputation, Sir Rowland! No, you shan't fight. I'll go in and examine my niece; I'll make her confess. I conjure you, Sir Rowland, by all your love, not to fight.

WAITWELL I am charmed, madam; I obey. But some proof you must let me give you; I'll go for a black box, which contains the writings of my whole estate, and deliver that into your hands.

LADY WISHFORT Aye, dear Sir Rowland, that will be some comfort; bring the black box.

WAITWELL And may I presume to bring a contract to be signed this night? May I hope so far?

LADY WISHFORT Bring what you will; but come alive, pray come alive. Oh, this is a happy discovery!

WAITWELL Dead or alive I'll come, and married we will be in spite of treachery; aye, and get an heir that shall defeat the last remaining glimpse of hope in my abandoned nephew. Come, my buxom widow.

> Ere long you shall substantial proof receive
> That I'm an errant knight—

FOIBLE [*aside*]

> Or arrant knave.

Exeunt.

Act V. Scene continues.
Enter Lady Wishfort *and* Foible.

LADY WISHFORT Out of my house, out of my house, thou viper! thou serpent, that I have fostered! thou bosom traitress that I raised from nothing! Begone! begone! begone! go! go! That I took from washing of old gauze and weaving of dead hair,[9] with a bleak blue nose, over a chafing dish of starved embers, and dining behind a traverse rag, in a shop no bigger than a birdcage! Go, go! starve again, do, do!

FOIBLE Dear madam, I'll beg pardon on my knees.

LADY WISHFORT Away! out! out! Go set up for yourself again! Do, drive a trade, do, with your three-pennyworth of small ware, flaunting upon a pack-thread, under a brandy-seller's bulk, or against a dead wall by a ballad-monger! Go, hang out an old frisoneer gorget, with a yard of yellow colberteen again.[1] Do! an old gnawed mask, two rows of pins, and a child's fiddle; a glass necklace with the beads broken, and a quilted nightcap with one ear. Go, go, drive a trade! These were your commodities, you treacherous trull! This was your merchandise you dealt in, when I took you into my house, placed you next myself, and made you governante of my whole family! You have forgot this, have you, now you have feathered your nest?

FOIBLE No, no, dear madam. Do but hear me; have but a moment's patience. I'll confess all. Mr. Mirabell seduced me; I am not the first that he has wheedled with his dissembling tongue. Your ladyship's own wisdom has been deluded by him; then how should I, a poor ignorant, defend myself? O madam, if you knew but what he promised me, and how he assured me your ladyship should come to no damage! Or else the wealth of the Indies should not have bribed me to conspire against so good, so sweet, so kind a lady as you have been to me.

LADY WISHFORT No damage? What, to betray me, to marry me to a cast servingman? to make me a receptacle, an hospital for a decayed pimp? No damage? O thou frontless[2] impudence, more than a big-bellied actress.

FOIBLE Pray do but hear me, madam; he could not marry your ladyship, madam. No indeed; his marriage was to have been void in law, for he was married to me first, to secure your ladyship. He could not have bedded your ladyship; for if he had consummated with your ladyship, he must have run the risk of the law and

9. Wig-making.
1. *Gorget*, a woolen neckpiece; *colber-*
teen, cheap lace.
2. Shameless.

been put upon his clergy.[3] Yes indeed; I inquired of the law in that case before I would meddle or make.

LADY WISHFORT What, then I have been your property, have I? I have been convenient to you, it seems! While you were catering for Mirabell, I have been broker for you? What, have you made a passive bawd of me? This exceeds all precedent; I am brought to fine uses, to become a botcher of secondhand marriages between Abigails and Andrews![4] I'll couple you! Yes, I'll baste you together, you and your Philander![5] I'll Duke's Place you, as I'm a person! Your turtle is in custody already; you shall coo in the same cage, if there be constable or warrant in the parish.

Exit.

FOIBLE Oh, that ever I was born! Oh, that I was ever married! A bride! aye, I shall be a Bridewell-bride.[6] Oh!

Enter Mrs. Fainall.

MRS. FAINALL Poor Foible, what's the matter?

FOIBLE O madam, my lady's gone for a constable. I shall be had to a justice, and put to Bridewell to beat hemp. Poor Waitwell's gone to prison already.

MRS. FAINALL Have a good heart, Foible; Mirabell's gone to give security for him. This is all Marwood's and my husband's doing.

FOIBLE Yes, yes, I know it, madam; she was in my lady's closet, and overheard all that you said to me before dinner. She sent the letter to my lady; and that missing effect, Mr. Fainall laid this plot to arrest Waitwell, when he pretended to go for the papers; and in the meantime Mrs. Marwood declared all to my lady.

MRS. FAINALL Was there no mention made of me in the letter? My mother does not suspect my being in the confederacy? I fancy Marwood has not told her, though she has told my husband.

FOIBLE Yes, madam; but my lady did not see that part. We stifled the letter before she read so far. Has that mischievous devil told Mr. Fainall of your ladyship then?

MRS. FAINALL Aye, all's out, my affair with Mirabell, everything discovered. This is the last day of our living together; that's my comfort.

FOIBLE Indeed, madam, and so 'tis a comfort if you knew all. He has been even with your ladyship; which I could have told you long enough since, but I love to keep peace and quietness by my good will. I had rather bring friends together than set 'em at distance. But Mrs. Marwood and he are nearer related than ever their parents thought for.

MRS. FAINALL Say'st thou so, Foible? Canst thou prove this?

FOIBLE I can take my oath of it, madam; so can Mrs. Mincing. We have had many a fair word from Madam Marwood, to conceal something that passed in our chamber one evening when you

---

3. First offenders could sometimes escape penal sentence by showing an ability to read and write. The privilege was called "benefit of clergy" because it had originally been restricted to clergymen.
4. *Botcher*, a mender of old clothes. *Abi-*

gails and Andrews, generic names for maids and servants.
5. Lover.
6. Bridewell was the women's prison in London.

were at Hyde Park and we were thought to have gone a-walking;
but we went up unawares, though we were sworn to secrecy too.
Madam Marwood took a book and swore us upon it, but it was a
book of verses and poems. So as long as it was not a Bible oath,
we may break it with a safe conscience.

MRS. FAINALL This discovery is the most opportune thing I could
wish. Now, Mincing?

Enter Mincing.

MINCING My lady would speak with Mrs. Foible, mem. Mr. Mirabell is with her; he has set your spouse at liberty, Mrs. Foible,
and would have you hide yourself in my lady's closet till my old
lady's anger is abated. Oh, my old lady is in a perilous passion at
something Mr. Fainall has said; he swears, and my old lady cries.
There's a fearful hurricane, I vow. He says, mem, how that he'll
have my lady's fortune made over to him, or he'll be divorced.

MRS. FAINALL Does your lady or Mirabell know that?

MINCING Yes, mem; they have sent me to see if Sir Wilfull be sober
and to bring him to them. My lady is resolved to have him, I
think, rather than lose such a vast sum as six thousand pound.
Oh, come, Mrs. Foible, I hear my lady.

MRS. FAINALL Foible, you must tell Mincing that she must prepare
to vouch when I call her.

FOIBLE Yes, yes, madam.

MINCING O yes, mem, I'll vouch anything for your ladyship's service, be what it will.

Exeunt Mincing *and* Foible.

Enter Lady Wishfort *and* Marwood.

LADY WISHFORT O my dear friend, how can I enumerate the bene-
fits that I have received from your goodness? To you I owe the
timely discovery of the false vows of Mirabell; to you the detection of the imposter Sir Rowland. And now you are become an
intercessor with my son-in-law, to save the honor of my house,
and compound[7] for the frailties of my daughter. Well, friend,
you are enough to reconcile me to the bad world, or else I would
retire to deserts and solitudes, and feed harmless sheep by groves
and purling streams. Dear Marwood, let us leave the world, and
retire by ourselves and be shepherdesses.

MRS. MARWOOD Let us first dispatch the affair in hand, madam.
We shall have leisure to think of retirement afterwards. Here is
one who is concerned in the treaty.

LADY WISHFORT O daughter, daughter, is it possible thou shouldst
be my child, bone of my bone, and flesh of my flesh, and, as I
may say, another me, and yet transgress the most minute particle
of severe virtue? Is it possible you should lean aside to iniquity,
who have been cast in the direct mold of virtue? I have not only
been a mold but a pattern for you, and a model for you, after you
were brought into the world.

MRS. FAINALL I don't understand your ladyship.

7. Make a settlement, often in monetary terms.

LADY WISHFORT Not understand? Why, have you not been naught?[8] Have you not been sophisticated? Not understand? Here I am ruined to compound for your caprices and your cuckoldoms. I must pawn my plate and my jewels, and ruin my niece, and all little enough.

MRS. FAINALL I am wronged and abused, and so are you. 'Tis a false accusation, as false as hell, as false as your friend here, aye, or your friend's friend, my false husband.

MRS. MARWOOD My friend, Mrs. Fainall? Your husband my friend? What do you mean?

MRS. FAINALL I know what I mean, madam, and so do you; and so shall the world at a time convenient.

MRS. MARWOOD I am sorry to see you so passionate, madam. More temper[9] would look more like innocence. But I have done. I am sorry my zeal to serve your ladyship and family should admit of misconstruction, or make me liable to affronts. You will pardon me, madam, if I meddle no more with an affair in which I am not personally concerned.

LADY WISHFORT O dear friend, I am so ashamed that you should meet with such returns! [*To* Mrs. Fainall.] You ought to ask pardon on your knees, ungrateful creature; she deserves more from you than all your life can accomplish. [*To* Mrs. Marwood.] Oh, don't leave me destitute in this perplexity! No, stick to me, my good genius.

MRS. FAINALL I tell you, madam, you're abused. Stick to you! Aye, like a leech, to suck your best blood; she'll drop off when she's full. Madam, you shan't pawn a bodkin,[1] nor part with a brass counter, in composition for me. I defy 'em all. Let 'em prove their aspersions; I know my own innocence, and dare stand by a trial.

Exit.

LADY WISHFORT Why, if she should be innocent, if she should be wronged after all, ha? I don't know what to think—and, I promise you, her education has been unexceptionable. I may say it; for I chiefly made it my own care to initiate her very infancy in the rudiments of virtue, and to impress upon her tender years a young odium and aversion to the very sight of men—aye, friend, she would ha' shrieked if she had but seen a man, till she was in her teens. As I'm a person, 'tis true. She was never suffered to play with a male child, though but in coats; nay, her very babies[2] were of the feminine gender. Oh, she never looked a man in the face but her own father, or the chaplain, and him we made a shift to put upon her for a woman, by the help of his long garments and his sleek face, till she was going in her fifteen.

MRS. MARWOOD 'Twas much she should be deceived so long.

LADY WISHFORT I warrant you, or she would never have borne to have been catechized by him; and have heard his long lectures against singing and dancing, and such debaucheries; and going to

8. Immoral. *Sophisticated* means *corrupted.*
9. Moderation.

1. Ornamental hairpin. *Brass counter,* an imitation coin.
2. Dolls.

filthy plays, and profane music-meetings, where the lewd trebles squeak nothing but bawdy, and the basses roar blasphemy. Oh, she would have swooned at the sight or name of an obscene play-book! And can I think, after all this, that my daughter can be naught? What, a whore? And thought it excommunication to set her foot within the door of a playhouse! O my dear friend, I can't believe it, no, no! As she says, let him prove it, let him prove it.

MRS. MARWOOD Prove it, madam? What, and have your name pros-tituted in a public court! Yours and your daughter's reputation worried at the bar by a pack of bawling lawyers! To be ushered in with an *Oyez*[3] of scandal, and have your case opened by an old fumbling lecher in a quoif[4] like a man midwife; to bring your daughter's infamy to light; to be a theme for legal punsters and quibblers by the statute, and become a jest against a rule of court, where there is no precedent for a jest in any record, not even in Doomsday Book;[5] to discompose the gravity of the bench, and provoke naughty interrogatories in more naughty law Latin, while the good judge, tickled with the proceeding, simpers under a gray beard, and fidges off and on his cushion as if he had swallowed cantharides, or sat upon cow-itch.[6]

LADY WISHFORT Oh, 'tis very hard!

MRS. MARWOOD And then to have my young revelers of the Temple[7] take notes, like prentices at a conventicle; and after, talk it all over again in commons, or before drawers in an eating house.

LADY WISHFORT Worse and worse!

MRS. MARWOOD Nay, this is nothing; if it would end here, 'twere well. But it must, after this, be consigned by the shorthand writ-ers to the public press; and from thence be transferred to the hands, nay into the throats and lungs of hawkers, with voices more licentious than the loud flounder-man's, or the woman that cries gray peas. And this you must hear till you are stunned; nay, you must hear nothing else for some days.

LADY WISHFORT Oh, 'tis insupportable! No, no, dear friend; make it up, make it up; aye, aye, I'll compound. I'll give up all, myself and my all, my niece and her all, anything, everything for compo-sition.

MRS. MARWOOD Nay, madam, I advise nothing; I only lay before you, as a friend, the inconveniences which perhaps you have overseen.[8] Here comes Mr. Fainall. If he will be satisfied to huddle up all in silence, I shall be glad. You must think I would rather congratulate than condole with you.

    Enter Fainall.

LADY WISHFORT Aye, aye, I do not doubt it, dear Marwood; no, no, I do not doubt it.

3. "Hear ye" (French), a court-cry to gain silence.
4. Cap of a sergeant-at-law.
5. In which a survey of English lands was recorded in 1085–86.
6. Cantharides (Spanish fly) and cow-itch (the plant cowhage) would both cause the judge to "fidge" (fidget).
7. Law students. The Inner and Middle Temples were Inns of the Court.
8. Overlooked.

FAINALL Well, madam, I have suffered myself to be overcome by the importunity of this lady your friend, and am content that you shall enjoy your own proper estate during life, on condition you oblige yourself never to marry, under such penalty as I think convenient.

LADY WISHFORT Never to marry?

FAINALL No more Sir Rowlands; the next imposture may not be so timely detected.

MRS. MARWOOD That condition, I dare answer, my lady will consent to, without difficulty; she has already but too much experienced the perfidiousness of men. Besides, madam, when we retire to our pastoral solitude, we shall bid adieu to all other thoughts.

LADY WISHFORT Aye, that's true; but in case of necessity, as of health, or some such emergency—

FAINALL Oh, if you are prescribed marriage, you shall be considered; I will only reserve to myself the power to choose for you. If your physic be wholesome, it matters not who is your apothecary. Next, my wife shall settle on me the remainder of her fortune, not made over already; and for her maintenance depend entirely on my discretion.

LADY WISHFORT This is inhumanly savage, exceeding the barbarity of a Muscovite husband.

FAINALL I learned it from his Czarish majesty's retinue,[9] in a winter evening's conference over brandy and pepper, amongst other secrets of matrimony and policy, as they are at present practiced in the northern hemisphere. But this must be agreed unto, and that positively. Lastly, I will be endowed, in right of my wife, with that six thousand pound, which is the moiety of Mrs. Millamant's fortune in your possession; and which she has forfeited (as will appear by the last will and testament of your deceased husband, Sir Jonathan Wishfort) by her disobedience in contracting herself against your consent or knowledge, and by refusing the offered match with Sir Wilfull Witwoud, which you, like a careful aunt, had provided for her.

LADY WISHFORT My nephew was *non compos*,[1] and could not make his addresses.

FAINALL I come to make demands. I'll hear no objections.

LADY WISHFORT You will grant me time to consider?

FAINALL Yes, while the instrument is drawing, to which you must set your hand till more sufficient deeds can be perfected; which I will take care shall be done with all possible speed. In the meanwhile, I will go for the said instrument, and till my return you may balance this matter in your own discretion.

Exit.

LADY WISHFORT This insolence is beyond all precedent, all parallel. Must I be subject to this merciless villain?

MRS. MARWOOD 'Tis severe indeed, madam, that you should smart for your daughter's wantonness.

LADY WISHFORT 'Twas against my consent that she married this

9. Peter the Great had visited London in 1698. 1. Not in his right mind.

barbarian, but she would have him, though her year was not out.[2]—Ah! her first husband, my son Languish, would not have carried it thus. Well, that was my choice, this is hers; she is matched now with a witness.[3] I shall be mad! Dear friend, is there no comfort for me? Must I live to be confiscated at this rebel rate? —Here come two more of my Egyptian plagues, too.[4]

Enter Millamant *and* Sir Wilfull Witwoud.

SIR WILFULL Aunt, your servant.

LADY WISHFORT Out, caterpillar, call me not aunt! I know thee not!

SIR WILFULL I confess I have been a little in disguise,[5] as they say. 'Sheart! and I'm sorry for't. What would you have? I hope I committed no offense, aunt, and, if I did, I am willing to make satisfaction; and what can a man say fairer? If I have broke anything, I'll pay for't, an it cost a pound. And so let that content for what's past, and make no more words. For what's to come, to pleasure you I'm willing to marry my cousin. So pray let's all be friends; she and I are agreed upon the matter before a witness.

LADY WISHFORT How's this, dear niece? Have I any comfort? Can this be true?

MILLAMANT I am content to be a sacrifice to your repose, madam; and to convince you that I had no hand in the plot, as you were misinformed, I have laid my commands on Mirabell to come in person, and be a witness that I give my hand to this flower of knighthood; and for the contract that passed between Mirabell and me, I have obliged him to make a resignation of it in your ladyship's presence. He is without, and waits your leave for admittance.

LADY WISHFORT Well, I'll swear I am something revived at this testimony of your obedience; but I cannot admit that traitor. I fear I cannot fortify myself to support his appearance. He is as terrible to me as a Gorgon;[6] if I see him, I fear I shall turn to stone, petrify incessantly.

MILLAMANT If you disoblige him, he may resent your refusal and insist upon the contract still. Then 'tis the last time he will be offensive to you.

LADY WISHFORT Are you sure it will be the last time? If I were sure of that! Shall I never see him again?

MILLAMANT Sir Wilfull, you and he are to travel together, are you not?

SIR WILFULL 'Sheart, the gentleman's a civil gentleman, aunt; let him come in. Why, we are sworn brothers and fellow travelers. We are to be Pylades and Orestes,[7] he and I. He is to be my interpreter in foreign parts. He has been overseas once already; and with proviso that I marry my cousin, will cross 'em once again, only to bear me company. 'Sheart, I'll call him in. An I set on't once, he shall come in; and see who'll hinder him.

Exit.

---

2. Her first year of widowhood, the conventional period of mourning.
3. With a vengeance.
4. Plagues were visited upon Pharaoh until he agreed to release the Israelites

(Exodus vii–xii).
5. Drunk.
6. Whose glance turned men to stone.
7. Devoted friends, especially in hard traveling.

MRS. MARWOOD This is precious fooling, if it would pass; but I'll know the bottom of it.

LADY WISHFORT O dear Marwood, you are not going?

MRS. MARWOOD Not far, madam; I'll return immediately.

Exit.

Re-enter Sir Wilfull *and* Mirabell.

SIR WILFULL Look up, man, I'll stand by you; 'sbud an she do frown, she can't kill you; besides—harkee, she dare not frown desperately, because her face is none of her own. 'Sheart, an she should, her forehead would wrinkle like the coat of a cream cheese; but mum for that, fellow traveler.

MIRABELL If a deep sense of the many injuries I have offered to so good a lady, with a sincere remorse and a hearty contrition, can but obtain the least glance of compassion, I am too happy. Ah, madam, there was a time! But let it be forgotten. I confess I have deservedly forfeited the high place I once held, of sighing at your feet. Nay, kill me not, by turning from me in disdain. I come not to plead for favor; nay, not for pardon. I am a suppliant only for your pity. I am going where I never shall behold you more.

SIR WILFULL How, fellow traveler! You shall go by yourself then.

MIRABELL Let me be pitied first, and afterwards forgotten—I ask no more.

SIR WILFULL By'r Lady, a very reasonable request, and will cost you nothing, aunt. Come, come, forgive and forget, aunt; why you must, an you are a Christian.

MIRABELL Consider, madam, in reality you could not receive much prejudice; it was an innocent device, though I confess it had a face of guiltiness. It was at most an artifice which love contrived, and errors which love produces have ever been accounted venial. At least think it is punishment enough that I have lost what in my heart I hold most dear, that to your cruel indignation I have offered up this beauty, and with her my peace and quiet; nay, all my hopes of future comfort.

SIR WILFULL An he does not move me, would I might never be o' the quorum![8] An it were not as good a deed as to drink, to give her to him again, I would I might never take shipping! Aunt, if you don't forgive quickly, I shall melt, I can tell you that. My contract went no farther than a little mouth-glue, and that's hardly drp; one doleful sigh more from my fellow traveler, and 'tis dissolved.

LADY WISHFORT Well, nephew, upon your account—ah, he has a false insinuating tongue! Well, sir, I will stifle my just resentment at my nephew's request. I will endeavor what I can to forget, but on proviso that you resign the contract with my niece immediately.

MIRABELL It is in writing and with papers of concern; but I have sent my servant for it, and will deliver it to you, with all acknowledgments for your transcendent goodness.

LADY WISHFORT [*aside*] Oh, he has witchcraft in his eyes and

8. The quorum of justices of the peace at   a court session.

tongue! When I did not see him, I could have bribed a villain to his assassination; but his appearance rakes the embers which have so long lain smothered in my breast.

Enter Fainall and Mrs. Marwood.

FAINALL Your date of deliberation, madam, is expired. Here is the instrument; are you prepared to sign?

LADY WISHFORT If I were prepared, I am not empowered. My niece exerts a lawful claim, having matched herself by my direction to Sir Wilfull.

FAINALL That sham is too gross to pass on me, though 'tis imposed on you, madam.

MILLAMANT Sir, I have given my consent.

MIRABELL And, sir, I have resigned my pretensions.

SIR WILFULL And, sir, I assert my right; and will maintain it in defiance of you, sir, and of your instrument. 'Sheart, an you talk of an instrument, sir, I have an old fox[9] by my thigh shall hack your instrument of ram vellum to shreds, sir! It shall not be sufficient for a mittimus[1] or a tailor's measure. Therefore, withdraw your instrument, sir, or by'r Lady, I shall draw mine.

LADY WISHFORT Hold, nephew, hold!

MILLAMANT Good Sir Wilfull, respite your valor.

FAINALL Indeed? Are you provided of a guard, with your single beefeater[2] there? But I'm prepared for you, and insist upon my first proposal. You shall submit your own estate to my management and absolutely make over my wife's to my sole use, as pursuant to the purport and tenor of this other covenant. [*To Millamant.*] I suppose, madam, your consent is not requisite in this case; nor, Mr. Mirabell, your resignation; nor, Sir Wilfull, your right. You may draw your fox if you please, sir, and make a bear-garden[3] flourish somewhere else; for here it will not avail. This, my Lady Wishfort, must be subscribed, or your darling daughter's turned adrift, like a leaky hulk, to sink or swim, as she and the current of this lewd town can agree.

LADY WISHFORT Is there no means, no remedy to stop my ruin? Ungrateful wretch! dost thou not owe thy being, thy subsistence, to my daughter's fortune?

FAINALL I'll answer you when I have the rest of it in my possession.

MIRABELL But that you would not accept of a remedy from my hands—I own I have not deserved you should owe any obligation to me; or else perhaps I could advise—

LADY WISHFORT Oh, what? what? to save me and my child from ruin, from want, I'll forgive all that's past; nay, I'll consent to anything to come, to be delivered from this tyranny.

MIRABELL Aye, madam, but that is too late; my reward is intercepted. You have disposed of her who only could have made me a compensation for all my services. But be it as it may, I am resolved I'll serve you; you shall not be wronged in this savage manner.

LADY WISHFORT How! Dear Mr. Mirabell, can you be so generous at

9. Sword.
1. Warrant of arrest.
2. Yeoman of the guard.
3. Arena for bear-baiting.

last? But it is not possible. Harkee, I'll break my nephew's match; you shall have my niece yet, and all her fortune, if you can but save me from this imminent danger.

MIRABELL Will you? I take you at your word. I ask no more. I must have leave for two criminals to appear.

LADY WISHFORT Aye, aye; anybody, anybody!

MIRABELL Foible is one, and a penitent.

Enter Mrs. Fainall, Foible, *and* Mincing.

MRS. MARWOOD [*to* Fainall] Oh, my shame! These corrupt things are bought and brought hither to expose me.

Mirabell *and* Lady Wishfort *go to* Mrs. Fainall *and* Foible.

FAINALL If it must all come out, why let 'em know it; 'tis but the way of the world. That shall not urge me to relinquish or abate one title of my terms; no, I will insist the more.

FOIBLE Yes indeed, madam; I'll take my Bible oath of it.

MINCING And so will I, mem.

LADY WISHFORT O Marwood, Marwood, art thou false? my friend deceive me? Hast thou been a wicked accomplice with that profligate man?

MRS. MARWOOD Have you so much ingratitude and injustice, to give credit against your friend to the aspersions of two such mercenary trulls?

MINCING Mercenary, mem? I scorn your words. 'Tis true we found you and Mr. Fainall in the blue garret; by the same token, you swore us to secrecy upon Messalina's poems[4]. Mercenary? No, if we would have been mercenary, we should have held our tongues; you would have bribed us sufficiently.

FAINALL Go, you are an insignificant thing! Well, what are you the better for this? Is this Mr. Mirabell's expedient? I'll be put off no longer. You thing, that was a wife, shall smart for this! I will not leave thee wherewithal to hide thy shame; your body shall be as naked as your reputation.

MRS. FAINALL I despise you, and defy your malice! You have aspersed me wrongfully. I have proved your falsehood. Go you and your treacherous—I will not name it, but starve together, perish!

FAINALL Not while you are worth a groat, indeed, my dear. Madam, I'll be fooled no longer.

LADY WISHFORT Ah, Mr. Mirabell, this is small comfort, the detection of this affair.

MIRABELL Oh, in good time. Your leave for the other offender and penitent to appear, madam.

Enter Waitwell *with a box of writings.*

LADY WISHFORT O Sir Rowland! Well, rascal?

WAITWELL What your ladyship pleases. I have brought the black box at last, madam.

MIRABELL Give it to me. Madam, you remember your promise.

4. Mincing misunderstands the term "Miscellany," a collection of poems by various writers.

LADY WISHFORT Aye, dear sir.

MIRABELL Where are the gentlemen?

WAITWELL At hand, sir, rubbing their eyes; just risen from sleep.

FAINALL 'Sdeath, what's this to me? I'll not wait your private concerns.

Enter Petulant *and* Witwoud.

PETULANT How now? What's the matter? Whose hand's out?

WITWOUD Heyday! what, are you all got together, like players at the end of the last act?

MIRABELL You may remember, gentlemen, I once requested your hands as witnesses to a certain parchment.

WITWOUD Aye, I do; my hand I remember. Petulant set his mark.

MIRABELL You wrong him; his name is fairly written, as shall appear. You do not remember, gentlemen, anything of what that parchment contained?

Undoing the box.

WITWOUD No.

PETULANT Not I. I writ. I read nothing.

MIRABELL Very well; now you shall know. Madam, your promise.

LADY WISHFORT Aye, aye, sir, upon my honor.

MIRABELL Mr. Fainall, it is now time that you should know that your lady, while she was at her own disposal, and before you had by your insinuations wheedled her out of a pretended settlement of the greatest part of her fortune—

FAINALL Sir! pretended!

MIRABELL Yes, sir. I say that this lady, while a widow, having, it seems, received some cautions respecting your inconstancy and tyranny of temper, which from her own partial opinion and fondness of you she could never have suspected—she did, I say, by the wholesome advice of friends and of sages learned in the laws of this land, deliver this same as her act and deed to me in trust, and to the uses within mentioned. You may read if you please [*Holding out the parchment.*]—though perhaps what is inscribed on the back may serve your occasions.

FAINALL Very likely, sir. What's here? Damnation! [*Reads.*] "A deed of conveyance of the whole estate real of Arabella Languish, widow, in trust to Edward Mirabell." Confusion!

MIRABELL Even so, sir; 'tis the way of the world, sir, of the widows of the world. I suppose this deed may bear an elder date than what you have obtained from your lady.

FAINALL Perfidious fiend! then thus I'll be revenged.

Offers to run at Mrs. Fainall.

SIR WILFULL Hold, sir! Now you may make your bear-garden flourish somewhere else, sir.

FAINALL Mirabell, you shall hear of this, sir; be sure you shall. Let me pass, oaf!

Exit.

MRS. FAINALL Madam, you seem to stifle your resentment; you had better give it vent.

MRS. MARWOOD Yes, it shall have vent, and to your confusion; or I'll perish in the attempt.

Exit.

LADY WISHFORT O daughter, daughter, 'tis plain thou hast inherited thy mother's prudence.

MRS. FAINALL Thank Mr. Mirabell, a cautious friend, to whose advice all is owing.

LADY WISHFORT Well, Mr. Mirabell, you have kept your promise, and I must perform mine. First, I pardon, for your sake, Sir Rowland there and Foible. The next thing is to break the matter to my nephew, and how to do that—

MIRABELL For that, madam, give yourself no trouble; let me have your consent. Sir Wilfull is my friend; he has had compassion upon lovers, and generously engaged a volunteer in this action for our service, and now designs to prosecute his travels.

SIR WILFULL 'Sheart, aunt, I have no mind to marry. My cousin's a fine lady, and the gentleman loves her, and she loves him, and they deserve one another; my resolution is to see foreign parts. I have set on't, and when I'm set on't, I must do't. And if these two gentlemen would travel too, I think they may be spared.

PETULANT For my part, I say little; I think things are best off or on.

WITWOUD I gad, I understand nothing of the matter; I'm in a maze yet, like a dog in a dancing school.

LADY WISHFORT Well, sir, take her, and with her all the joy I can give you.

MILLAMANT Why does not the man take me? Would you have me give myself to you over again?

MIRABELL Aye, and over and over again; for I would have you as often as possibly I can. [*Kisses her hand.*] Well, heaven grant I love you not too well; that's all my fear.

SIR WILFULL 'Sheart, you'll have time enough to toy after you're married; or if you will toy now, let us have a dance in the meantime, that we who are not lovers may have some other employment besides looking on.

MIRABELL With all my heart, dear Sir Wilfull. What shall we do for music?

FOIBLE Oh, sir, some that were provided for Sir Rowland's entertainment are yet within call.

A dance.

LADY WISHFORT As I am a person, I can hold out no longer. I have wasted my spirits so today already that I am ready to sink under the fatigue; and I cannot but have some fears upon me yet that my son Fainall will pursue some desperate course.

MIRABELL Madam, disquiet not yourself on that account; to my knowledge his circumstances are such, he must of force comply. For my part, I will contribute all that in me lies to a reunion. In the meantime, madam [*to* Mrs. Fainall], let me before these witnesses restore to you this deed of trust; it may be a means, well-managed, to make you live easily together.

From hence let those be warned, who mean to wed,
Lest mutual falsehood stain the bridal bed;
For each deceiver to his cost may find,
That marriage frauds too oft are paid in kind.

Exeunt omnes.

Epilogue

Spoken by Mrs. Bracegirdle[5]

After our Epilogue this crowd dismisses,
I'm thinking how this play'll be pulled to pieces.
But pray consider, ere you doom its fall,
How hard a thing 'twould be to please you all.
There are some critics so with spleen diseased,
They scarcely come inclining to be pleased;
And sure he must have more than mortal skill,
Who pleases any one against his will.
Then, all bad poets we are sure are foes,
And how their number's swelled, the town well knows;
In shoals I've marked 'em judging in the pit;
Though they're on no pretense for judgment fit,
But that they have been damned for want of wit.
Since when, they, by their own offenses taught,
Set up spies on plays, and finding fault.
Others there are whose malice we'd prevent;
Such who watch plays with scurrilous intent
To mark out who by characters are meant.
And though no perfect likeness they can trace,
Yet each pretends to know the copied face.
These with false glosses feed their own ill nature,
And turn to libel what was meant a satire.
May such malicious fops this fortune find,
To think themselves alone the fools designed;
If any are so arrogantly vain,
To think they singly can support a scene,
And furnish fool enough to entertain.
For well the learned and the judicious know
That satire scorns to stoop so meanly low
As any one abstracted fop to show.
For, as when painters form a matchless face,
They from each fair one catch some different grace;
And shining features in one portrait blend,
To which no single beauty must pretend;
So poets oft do in one piece expose
Whole *belles assemblées* of coquettes and beaux.

5. Who played Millamant.

RICHARD STEELE

The Conscious Lovers†

Illud genus narrationis quod in personis positum est debet habere ser-
monis festivitatem, animorum dissimilitudinem, gravitatem lenitatem,
spem metum, suspicionem disiderium, dissimulationem misericordiam,
rerum varietates, fortunae commutationem, insperatum incommodum,
subitam laetitiam, iucundum exitum rerum.[1]

To the King[2]

May it please your Majesty,

After having aspired to the highest and most laudable ambition,
that of following the cause of liberty, I should not have humbly
petitioned your Majesty for a direction of the theater[3] had I not
believed success in that province an happiness much to be wished
by an honest man and highly conducing to the prosperity of the
Commonwealth. It is in this view I lay before your Majesty a
comedy, which the audience, in justice to themselves, has supported
and encouraged, and is the prelude of what, by your Majesty's influence and favor, may be attempted in future representations.

The imperial mantle, the royal vestment, and the shining diadem
are what strike ordinary minds; but your Majesty's native goodness,
your passion for justice and her constant assessor mercy is what continually surrounds you, in the view of intelligent spirits, and gives
hope to the suppliant, who sees he has more than succeeded in
giving Your Majesty an opportunity of doing good. Our King is
above the greatness of royalty, and every act of his will which makes
another man happy has ten times more charms in it than one that
makes himself appear raised above the condition of others. But even
this carries unhappiness with it; for calm dominion, equal[4] grandeur, and familiar greatness do not easily affect the imagination of
the vulgar, who cannot see power but in terror; and as fear moves
mean spirits and love prompts great ones to obey, the insinuations

---

† First performed in 1722 and published
in the same year (with *1723* on the title
page).
1. *Rhetorica ad Herennium* (formerly attributed to Cicero), I.viii: "A narrative
based on characters should have a lively
style and diverse traits of personality,
such as gravity and gentleness, hope and
fear, distrust and desire, hypocrisy and
compassion, and a variety of events,
such as reversal of fortune, unexpected
disaster, sudden joy, and a happy ending."
2. George I.
3. Steele was governor of Drury Lane
Theatre, where the play was first produced.
4. Calm.

of malcontents are directed accordingly, and the unhappy people are ensnared, from want of reflection, into disrespectful ideas of their gracious and amiable Sovereign, and then only begin to apprehend the greatness of their master when they have incurred his displeasure.

As your Majesty was invited to the throne of a willing people for their own sakes and has ever enjoyed it with contempt of the ostentation of it, we beseech you to protect us who revere your title as we love your person. 'Tis to be a savage to be a rebel, and they who have fallen from you have not so much forfeited their allegiance as lost their humanity. And therefore, if it were only to preserve myself from the imputation of being amongst the insensible and abandoned, I would beg permission in the most public manner possible to profess myself, with the utmost sincerity and zeal.

> SIRE,
> *Your* MAJESTY'S
> *Most Devoted Subject and Servant,*
> RICHARD STEELE

The Preface

This comedy has been received with universal acceptance, for it was in every part excellently performed; and there needs no other applause of the actors but that they excelled according to the dignity and difficulty of the character they represented. But this great favor done to the work in acting renders the expectation still the greater from the author to keep up the spirit in the representation of the closet[5] or any other circumstance of the reader, whether alone or in company. To which I can only say that it must be remembered a play is to be seen and is made to be represented with the advantage of action nor can appear but with half the spirit without it; for the greatest effect of a play in reading is to excite the reader to go see it; and when he does so, it is then a play has the effect of example and precept.

The chief design of this was to be an innocent performance, and the audience have abundantly showed how ready they are to support what is visibly intended that way; nor do I make any difficulty to acknowledge that the whole was writ for the sake of the scene of the fourth act, wherein Mr. Bevil evades the quarrel with his friend, and hope it may have some effect upon the Goths and Vandals that frequent the theaters, or a more polite audience may supply their absence.

But this incident and the case of the father and daughter are

5. Small room or study.

esteemed by some people no subjects of comedy; but I cannot be of their mind, for anything that has its foundation in happiness and success must be allowed to be the object of comedy, and sure it must be an improvement of it to introduce a joy too exquisite for laughter, that can have no spring but in delight, which is the case of this young lady. I must therefore contend that the tears which were shed on that occasion flowed from reason and good sense and that men ought not to be laughed at for weeping till we are come to a more clear notion of what is to be imputed to the hardness of the head and the softness of the heart; and I think it was very politely said of Mr. Wilks[6] to one who told him there was a general[7] weeping for Indiana, "I'll warrant he'll fight ne'er the worse for that." To be apt to give way to the impressions of humanity is the excellence of a right disposition and the natural working of a well-turned spirit. But as I have suffered by critics who are got no farther than to inquire whether they ought to be pleased or not, I would willingly find them properer matter for their employment, and revive here a song which was omitted for want of a performer and designed for the entertainment of Indiana; Signor Carbonelli[8] instead of it played on the fiddle, and it is for want of a singer that such advantageous things are said of an instrument which were designed for a voice. The song is the distress of a love-sick maid and may be a fit entertainment for some small critics to examine whether the passion is just or the distress male or female.

I

From place to place forlorn I go,
With downcast eyes, a silent shade;
Forbidden to declare my woe;
To speak, till spoken to, afraid.

II

My inward pangs, my secret grief,
My soft consenting looks betray:
He loves, but gives me no relief:
Why speaks not he who may?

It remains to say a word concerning Terence, and I am extremely surprised to find what Mr. Cibber[9] told me prove a truth, that what I valued myself so much upon, the translation of him,[1] should be imputed to me as a reproach. Mr. Cibber's zeal for the work, his care and application in instructing the actors and altering the disposition of the scenes when I was, through sickness, unable to cultivate such things myself, has been a very obliging favor and friend-

6. Actor-manager of Drury Lane who played the role of Myrtle.
7. General Charles Churchill. Indiana was played by his mistress, Anne Oldfield.
8. A virtuoso violinist.
9. Actor-manager at Drury Lane.
1. Steele's play is an adaptation of Terence's *Andria*.

ship to me. For this reason, I was very hardly persuaded to throw away Terence's celebrated funeral and take only the bare authority of the young man's character,[2] and how I have worked it into an Englishman and made use of the same circumstances of discovering a daughter when we least hoped for one is humbly submitted to the learned reader.

Prologue

By Mr. Welsted[3]

Spoken by Mr. Wilks

To win your hearts, and to secure your praise,
The comic-writers strive by various ways:
By subtle stratagems they act their game,
And leave untried no avenue to fame.
One writes the spouse a beating from his wife;
And says, "Each stroke was copied from the life."
Some fix all wit and humour in grimace,
And make a livelihood of Pinkey's[4] face.
Here one gay show and costly habits tries,
Confiding to the judgment of your eyes.
Another smuts his scene, a cunning shaver,
Sure of the rakes' and of the wenches' favor.
Oft have these arts prevailed; and one may guess,
If practiced o'er again, would find success.
But the bold sage, the poet of tonight,
By new and desp'rate rules resolved to write;
Fain would he give more just applauses rise,
And please by wit that scorns the aids of vice;
The praise he seeks, from worthier motives springs,
Such praise as praise to those that give it brings.
    Your aid, most humbly sought, then, Britons, lend,
And lib'ral mirth like lib'ral men defend:
No more let ribaldry, with license writ,
Usurp the name of eloquence or wit;
No more let lawless farce uncensured go,
The lewd dull gleanings of a Smithfield show.[5]
'Tis yours with breeding to refine the age,
To chasten wit, and moralize the stage.
    Ye modest, wise and good, ye fair, ye brave,
Tonight the champion of your virtues save,
Redeem from long contempt the comic name,
And judge politely for your country's fame.

2. "Terence's celebrated funeral" is a scene in the *Andria*. The "young man's character" refers to Terence's Pamphilus, who slightly resembles Bevil Junior.

3. Leonard Welsted, a contemporary poet.
4. William Pinkethman, a comedian.
5. An amusement at the annual Bartholomew Fair.

Dramatis Personae

Men

SIR JOHN BEVIL	*Mr. Mills*
MR. SEALAND	*Mr. Williams*
BEVIL JUNIOR, in love with Indiana	*Mr. Booth*
MYRTLE, in love with Lucinda	*Mr. Wilks*
CIMBERTON, a coxcomb	*Mr. Griffin*
HUMPHREY, an old servant to Sir John	*Mr. Shepard*
TOM, servant to Bevil Junior	*Mr. Cibber*
DANIEL, a country boy, servant to Indiana	*Mr. Theophilus Cibber*

Women

MRS. SEALAND, second wife to Sealand	*Mrs. Moore*
ISABELLA, sister to Sealand	*Mrs. Thurmond*
INDIANA, Sealand's daughter by his first wife	*Mrs. Oldfield*
LUCINDA, Sealand's daughter by his second wife	*Mrs. Booth*
PHILLIS, maid to Lucinda	*Mrs. Younger*

Scene: *London*

The Conscious Lovers

Act I. Scene i.
Scene, Sir John Bevil's *house.*
Enter Sir John Bevil *and* Humphrey.

SIR JOHN BEVIL Have you ordered that I should not be interrupted while I am dressing?

HUMPHREY Yes, sir. I believed you had something of moment to say to me.

SIR JOHN BEVIL Let me see, Humphrey; I think it is now full forty years since I first took thee to be about myself.

HUMPHREY I thank you, sir, it has been an easy forty years, and I have passed 'em without much sickness, care, or labor.

SIR JOHN BEVIL Thou hast a brave constitution; you are a year or two older than I am, sirrah.

HUMPHREY You have ever been of that mind, sir.

SIR JOHN BEVIL You knave, you know it; I took thee for thy gravity and sobriety in my wild years.

HUMPHREY Ah sir, our manners were formed from our different fortunes, not our different age. Wealth gave a loose to your youth, and poverty put a restraint upon mine.

SIR JOHN BEVIL Well, Humphrey, you know I have been a kind master to you; I have used you, for the ingenuous nature I observed in you from the beginning, more like an humble friend than a servant.

HUMPHREY I humbly beg you'll be so tender of me as to explain your commands, sir, without any farther preparation.

SIR JOHN BEVIL I'll tell thee then. In the first place, this wedding of my son's, in all probability—shut the door—will never be at all.

HUMPHREY How, sir! Not be at all? For what reason is it carried on in appearance?

SIR JOHN BEVIL Honest Humphrey, have patience, and I'll tell thee all in order. I have myself, in some part of my life, lived, indeed, with freedom, but, I hope, without reproach. Now I thought liberty would be as little injurious to my son; therefore, as soon as he grew towards man, I indulged him in living after his own manner. I knew not how, otherwise, to judge of his inclination; for what can be concluded from a behavior under restraint and fear? But what charms me above all expression is that my son has never in the least action, the most distant hint or word, valued himself upon that great estate of his mother's, which, according to our marriage settlement, he has had ever since he came to age.

HUMPHREY No, sir; on the contrary, he seems afraid of appearing to enjoy it before you or any belonging to you. He is as dependent and resigned to your will as if he had not a farthing but what must come from your immediate bounty. You have ever acted like a good and generous father, and he like an obedient and grateful son.

SIR JOHN BEVIL Nay, his carriage is so easy to all with whom he converses that he is never assuming, never prefers himself to others, nor ever is guilty of that rough sincerity which a man is not called to and certainly disobliges most of his acquaintance. To be short, Humphrey, his reputation was so fair in the world that old Sealand, the great India merchant, has offered his only daughter and sole heiress to that vast estate of his as a wife for him. You may be sure I made no difficulties, the match was agreed on, and this very day named for the wedding.

HUMPHREY What hinders the proceeding?

SIR JOHN BEVIL Don't interrupt me. You know I was last Thursday at the masquerade; my son, you may remember, soon found us out. He knew his grandfather's habit, which I then wore; and though it was the mode in the last age, yet the maskers, you know, followed us as if we had been the most monstrous figures in that whole assembly.

HUMPHREY I remember indeed a young man of quality in the habit of a clown that was particularly troublesome.

SIR JOHN BEVIL Right. He was too much what he seemed to be. You remember how impertinently he followed, and teased us, and would know who we were.

HUMPHREY [aside] I know he has a mind to come into that particular.

SIR JOHN BEVIL Ay, he followed us till the gentlemen who led the lady in the Indian mantle presented that gay creature to the

rustic and bid him like Cymon in the fable[6] grow polite by falling in love and let that worthy old gentleman alone, meaning me.
The clown was not reformed but rudely persisted and offered to
force off my mask; with that the gentleman, throwing off his
own, appeared to be my son, and in his concern for me tore off
that of the nobleman. At this they seized each other, the company called the guards, and in the surprise the lady swooned
away, upon which my son quitted his adversary and had now no
care but of the lady, when raising her in his arms, "Art thou
gone," cried he, "forever? —Forbid it heaven!" She revives at his
known voice, and with the most familiar though modest gesture
hangs in safety over his shoulder weeping, but wept as in the
arms of one before whom she could give herself a loose were she
not under observation. While she hides her face in his neck, he
carefully conveys her from the company.

HUMPHREY I have observed this accident has dwelt upon you very
strongly.

SIR JOHN BEVIL Her uncommon air, her noble modesty, the dignity
of her person, and the occasion itself drew the whole assembly
together; and I soon heard it buzzed about, she was the adopted
daughter of a famous sea-officer, who had served in France. Now
this unexpected and public discovery of my son's so deep concern
for her—

HUMPHREY Was what I suppose alarmed Mr. Sealand, in behalf of
his daughter, to break off the match.

SIR JOHN BEVIL You are right. He came to me yesterday and said
he thought himself disengaged from the bargain, being credibly
informed my son was already married, or worse, to the lady at the
masquerade. I palliated matters and insisted on our agreement,
but we parted with little less than a direct breach between us.

HUMPHREY Well, sir, and what notice have you taken of all this to
my young master?

SIR JOHN BEVIL That's what I wanted to debate with you. I have
said nothing to him yet. But look you, Humphrey, if there is so
much in this amour of his that he denies upon my summons to
marry, I have cause enough to be offended; and then by my
insisting upon his marrying today, I shall know how far he is
engaged to this lady in masquerade and from thence only shall be
able to take my measures. In the meantime I would have you
find out how far that rogue his man is let into his secret. He, I
know, will play tricks, as much to cross me as to serve his master.

HUMPHREY Why do you think so of him, sir? I believe he is no
worse than I was for you, at your son's age.

SIR JOHN BEVIL I see it in the rascal's looks. But I have dwelt on
these things too long; I'll go to my son immediately, and while
I'm gone, your part is to convince his rogue Tom that I am in
earnest. I'll leave him to you.

6. Cymon, a slow-witted fellow who
learned politeness when he fell in love
with the sleeping Iphigenia. The tale appears in Boccaccio's *Decameron and*
Dryden's *Fables*.

Exit Sir John Bevil.

HUMPHREY Well, though this father and son live as well together as possible, yet their fear of giving each other pain is attended with constant mutual uneasiness. I'm sure I have enough to do to be honest and yet keep well with them both. But they know I love 'em, and that makes the task less painful however.

Enter Tom, *singing.*

Oh, here's the prince of poor coxcombs, the representative of all the better fed than taught. —Ho! ho! Tom, whither so gay and so airy this morning?

TOM Sir, we servants of single gentlemen are another kind of people than you domestic ordinary drudges that do business. We are raised above you. The pleasures of board-wages, tavern-dinners, and many a clear gain—vails,[7] alas, you never heard or dreamt of.

HUMPHREY Thou hast follies and vices enough for a man of ten thousand a year, though 'tis but as t'other day that I sent for you to town, to put you into Mr. Sealand's family, that you might learn a little before I put you to my young master, who is too gentle for training such a rude thing as you were into proper obedience. You then pulled off your hat to everyone you met in the street, like a bashful great awkward cub as you were. But your great oaken cudgel when you were a booby became you much better than that dangling stick at your button now you are a fop.[8] That's fit for nothing, except it hangs there to be ready for your master's hand when you are impertinent.

TOM Uncle Humphrey, you know my master scorns to strike his servants. You talk as if the world was now just as it was when my old master and you were in your youth—when you went to dinner because it was so much a clock, when the great blow[9] was given in the hall at the pantry-door, and all the family came out of their holes in such strange dresses and formal faces as you see in the pictures in our long gallery in the country.

HUMPHREY Why, you wild rogue!

TOM You could not fall to your dinner till a formal fellow in a black gown said something over the meat, as if the cook had not made it ready enough.

HUMPHREY Sirrah, who do you prate after? Despising men of sacred characters! I hope you never heard my good young master talk so like a profligate!

TOM Sir, I say you put upon me, when I first came to town, about being orderly, and the doctrine of wearing shams[1] to make linen last clean a fortnight, keeping my clothes fresh, and wearing a frock within doors.

HUMPHREY Sirrah, I gave you those lessons because I supposed at that time your master and you might have dined at home every day and cost you nothing; then you might have made a good

7. Tips.
8. A servant trying for fashion would sometimes attach his walking stick to a coat button.
9. Upon the dinner gong.
1. False shirt-fronts.

family servant. But the gang you have frequented since at choco-late-houses and taverns in a continual round of noise and extrava-gance—

TOM I don't know what you heavy inmates call noise and extrava-gance, but we gentlemen who are well fed and cut a figure, sir, think it a fine life, and that we must be very pretty fellows who are kept only to be looked at.

HUMPHREY Very well, sir. I hope the fashion of being lewd and extravagant, despising of decency and order, is almost at an end, since it is arrived at persons of your quality.

TOM Master Humphrey, ha! ha! you were an unhappy lad to be sent up to town in such queer days as you were. Why now, sir, the lackeys are the men of pleasure of the age, the top-gamesters and many a laced coat about town have had their education in our parti-colored regiment.[2] We are false lovers, have a taste of music, poetry, billet-doux, dress, politics, ruin damsels, and when we are weary of this lewd town and have a mind to take up,[3] whip into our masters' wigs and linen and marry fortunes.

HUMPHREY Hey-day!

TOM Nay, sir, our order is carried up to the highest dignities and distinctions; step but into the Painted Chamber,[4] and by our titles you'd take us all for men of quality. Then again, come down to the Court of Requests, and you see us all laying our broken heads together for the good of the nation. And though we never carry a question *nemine contradicente*,[5] yet this I can say with a safe conscience—and I wish every gentleman of our cloth could lay his hand upon his heart and say the same—that I never took so much as a single mug of beer for my vote in all my life.

HUMPHREY Sirrah, there is no enduring your extravagance; I'll hear you prate no longer. I wanted to see you to inquire how things go with your master, as far as you understand them; I suppose he knows he is to be married today.

TOM Ay, sir, he knows it and is dressed as gay as the sun; but, between you and I, my dear, he has a very heavy heart under all that gaiety. As soon as he was dressed, I retired, but overheard him sigh in the most heavy manner. He walked thoughtfully to and fro in the room, then went into his closet; when he came out, he gave me this for his mistress, whose maid you know—

HUMPHREY Is passionately fond of your fine person.

TOM The poor fool is so tender, and loves to hear me talk of the world, and the plays, operas, and ridottos[6] for the winter; the parks and Belsize[7] for our summer diversions; and "Lard!" says she, "You are so wild—but you have a world of humour—"

HUMPHREY Coxcomb! Well, but why don't you run with your mas-

2. I.e., of menservants.
3. Reform.
4. Room in Parliament where servants waited for their masters. The Court of Requests, mentioned below, was nearby. Servants were in the habit of imitating the roles and titles of their masters. See Steele's discussion in *The Spectator*, No. 88.
5. Unanimously.
6. Musical entertainments, popular in 1722.
7. An estate near London, used for pub-lic amusements.

ter's letter to Mrs. Lucinda, as he ordered you?

TOM Because Mrs. Lucinda is not so easily come at as you think for.

HUMPHREY Not easily come at? Why sirrah, are not her father and my old master agreed that she and Mr. Bevil are to be one flesh before tomorrow morning?

TOM It's no matter for that; her mother, it seems, Mrs. Sealand, has not agreed to it, and you must know, Mr. Humphrey, that in that family the gray mare is the better horse.

HUMPHREY What dost thou mean?

TOM In one word, Mrs. Sealand pretends to have a will of her own and has provided a relation of hers, a stiff, starched philosopher and a wise fool, for her daughter; for which reason, for these ten past days, she has suffered no message nor letter from my master to come near her.

HUMPHREY And where had you this intelligence?

TOM From a foolish fond soul, that can keep nothing from me— one that will deliver this letter too, if she is rightly managed.

HUMPHREY What? Her pretty handmaid, Mrs. Phillis?

TOM Even she, sir; this is the very hour, you know, she usually comes hither, under a pretense of a visit to your housekeeper forsooth, but in reality to have a glance at—

HUMPHREY Your sweet face, I warrant you.

TOM Nothing else in nature; you must know, I love to fret and play with the little wanton—

HUMPHREY Play with the little wanton! What will this world come to?

TOM I met her this morning in a new manteau and petticoat,[8] not a bit the worse for her lady's wearing, and she has always new thoughts and new airs with new clothes. Then she never fails to steal some glance or gesture from every visitant at their house, and is indeed the whole town of coquettes at second hand. But here she comes; in one motion she speaks and describes herself better than all the words in the world can.

HUMPHREY Then I hope, dear sir, when your own affair is over, you will be so good as to mind your master's with her.

TOM Dear Humphrey, you know my master is my friend, and those are people I never forget.

HUMPHREY Sauciness itself! But I'll leave you to do your best for him.

    Enter Phillis.

PHILLIS Oh, Mr. Thomas, is Mrs. Sugar-key at home? Lard, one is almost ashamed to pass along the streets. The town is quite empty and nobody of fashion left in it; and the ordinary people do so stare to see anything—dressed like a woman of condition —as it were on the same floor with them pass by. Alas! Alas! It is a sad thing to walk! Oh Fortune! Fortune!

TOM What? A sad thing to walk? Why, Madame Phillis, do you wish yourself lame?

8. A gown open in front, revealing an underskirt.

PHILLIS No, Mr. Tom, but I wish I were generally carried in a coach or chair, and of a fortune neither to stand nor go, but to totter, or slide, to be short-sighted, or stare, to fleer[9] in the face, to look distant, to observe, to overlook, yet all become me; and, if I was rich, I could twire[1] and loll as well as the best of them. Oh Tom! Tom! Is it not a pity that you should be so great a coxcomb and I so great a coquette and yet be such poor devils as we are?

TOM Mrs. Phillis, I am your humble servant for that—

PHILLIS Yes, Mr. Thomas, I know how much you are my humble servant, and know what you said to Mrs. Judy, upon seeing her in one of her lady's cast manteaus; that anyone would have thought her the lady, and that she had ordered the other to wear it till it sat easy, for now only it was becoming; to my lady it was only a covering, to Mrs. Judy it was a habit. This you said, after somebody or other. Oh, Tom! Tom! Thou art as false and as base as the best gentleman of them all; but, you wretch, talk to me no more on the old odious subject. Don't, I say.

TOM [*in a submissive tone, retiring*] I know not how to resist your commands, madam.

PHILLIS Commands about parting are grown mighty easy to you of late.

TOM [*aside*] Oh, I have her; I have nettled and put her into the right temper to be wrought upon, and set a-prating. —Why truly, to be plain with you, Mrs. Phillis, I can take little comfort of late in frequenting your house.

PHILLIS Pray, Mr. Thomas, what is it all of a sudden offends your nicety at our house?

TOM I don't care to speak particulars, but I dislike the whole.

PHILLIS I thank you, sir, I am a part of that whole.

TOM Mistake me not, good Phillis.

PHILLIS Good Phillis! Saucy enough. But however—

TOM I say, it is that thou art a part which gives me pain for the disposition of the whole. You must know, madam, to be serious, I am a man, at the bottom, of prodigious nice honor. You are too much exposed to company at your house. To be plain, I don't like so many that would be your mistress's lovers whispering to you.

PHILLIS Don't think to put that upon me. You say this because I wrung you to the heart when I touched your guilty conscience about Judy.

TOM Ah Phillis! Phillis! If you but knew my heart!

PHILLIS I know too much on't.

TOM Nay then, poor Crispo's[2] fate and mine are one. Therefore give me leave to say, or sing at least, as he does upon the same occasion—
　　　Sings "Se vedete," &c.

9. Smile scornfully.
1. Leer.
2. Hero of an opera by Giovanni Bonon-

cini, popular in London in 1722. Crispo sings *"Se vedete"* when he is unjustly accused of deceit.

PHILLIS What, do you think I'm to be fobbed off with a song? I don't question but you have sung the same to Mrs. Judy too.

TOM Don't disparage your charms, good Phillis, with jealousy of so worthless an object; besides, she is a poor hussy, and if you doubt the sincerity of my love, you will allow me true to my interest. You are a fortune, Phillis—

PHILLIS [*aside*] What would the fop be at now?—In good time, indeed, you shall be setting up for a fortune!

TOM Dear Mrs. Phillis, you have such a spirit that we shall never be dull in marriage when we come together. But I tell you, you are a fortune, and you have an estate in my hands.

He pulls out a purse; she eyes it.

PHILLIS What pretense have I to what is in your hands, Mr. Tom?

TOM As thus: there are hours, you know, when a lady is neither pleased or displeased, neither sick or well, when she lolls or loiters, when she's without desires from having more of everything than she knows what to do with.

PHILLIS Well, what then?

TOM When she has not life enough to keep her bright eyes quite open to look at her own dear image in the glass.

PHILLIS Explain thyself, and don't be so fond of thy own prating.

TOM There are also prosperous and good-natured moments, as when a knot or a patch is happily fixed, when the complexion particularly flourishes.

PHILLIS Well, what then? I have not patience!

TOM Why then, or on the like occasions, we servants who have skill to know how to time business, see when such a pretty folded thing as this [*shows a letter*] may be presented, laid, or dropped, as best suits the present humour. And, madam, because it is a long wearisome journey to run through all the several stages of a lady's temper, my master, who is the most reasonable man in the world, presents you this to bear your charges on the road.

Gives her the purse.

PHILLIS Now you think me a corrupt hussy.

TOM Oh fie, I only think you'll take the letter.

PHILLIS Nay, I know you do, but I know my own innocence; I take it for my mistress's sake.

TOM I know it, my pretty one, I know it.

PHILLIS Yes, I say I do it, because I would not have my mistress deluded by one who gives no proof of his passion; but I'll talk more of this, as you see me on my way home. No, Tom, I assure thee, I take this trash of thy master's, not for the value of the thing but as it convinces me he has a true respect for my mistress. I remember a verse to the purpose:

They may be false who languish and complain,
But they who part with money never feign.

Exeunt.

Act I. Scene ii.
Bevil Junior's *lodgings*.
Bevil Junior, *reading*.

BEVIL JUNIOR These moral writers practice virtue after death.[3] This charming Vision of Mirza! Such an author consulted in a morning sets the spirit for the vicissitudes of the day better than the glass does a man's person. But what a day have I to go through! To put on an easy look with an aching heart—if this lady my father urges me to marry should not refuse me, my dilemma is insupportable. But why should I fear it? Is not she in equal distress with me? Has not the letter I have sent her this morning confessed my inclination to another? Nay, have I not moral assurances of her engagements too to my friend Myrtle? It's impossible but she must give in to it, for, sure, to be denied is a favor any man may pretend to. It must be so. Well then, with the assurance of being rejected, I think I may confidently say to my father I am ready to marry her. Then let me resolve upon what I am not very good at, though it is an honest dissimulation.

Enter Tom.

TOM Sir John Bevil, sir, is in the next room.

BEVIL JUNIOR Dunce! Why did not you bring him in?

TOM I told him, sir, you were in your closet.[4]

BEVIL JUNIOR I thought you had known, sir, it was my duty to see my father anywhere.

Going himself to the door.

TOM [*aside*] The Devil's in my master! He has always more wit than I have.

Bevil Junior *introducing* Sir John Bevil.

BEVIL JUNIOR Sir, you are the most gallant, the most complaisant of all parents. Sure 'tis not a compliment to say these lodgings are yours. Why would you not walk in, sir?

SIR JOHN BEVIL I was loath to interrupt you unseasonably on your wedding day.

BEVIL JUNIOR One to whom I am beholden for my birthday might have used less ceremony.

SIR JOHN BEVIL Well, son, I have intelligence you have writ to your mistress this morning. It would please my curiosity to know the contents of a wedding-day letter, for courtship must then be over.

BEVIL JUNIOR I assure you, sir, there was no insolence in it upon the prospect of such a vast fortune's being added to our family but much acknowledgment of the lady's greater desert.

SIR JOHN BEVIL But, dear Jack, are you in earnest in all this? And will you really marry her?

BEVIL JUNIOR Did I ever disobey any command of yours, sir? Nay, any inclination that I saw you bent upon?

SIR JOHN BEVIL Why, I can't say you have, son; but methinks in this whole business you have not been so warm as I could have

3. Addison had died in 1719. His *Vision of Mirza* appeared in *The Spectator*, No. 159.   4. Small, private room.

wished you. You have visited her, it's true, but you have not been particular. Everyone knows you can say and do as handsome things as any man, but you have done nothing but lived in the general, been complaisant only.

BEVIL JUNIOR As I am ever prepared to marry if you bid me, so I am ready to let it alone if you will have me.

Humphrey *enters unobserved.*

SIR JOHN BEVIL Look you there now! Why, what am I to think of this so absolute and so indifferent a resignation?

BEVIL JUNIOR Think? That I am still your son, sir. Sir, you have been married, and I have not. And you have, sir, found the inconvenience there is when a man weds with too much love in his head. I have been told, sir, that at the time you married, you made a mighty bustle on the occasion. There was challenging and fighting, scaling walls, locking up the lady, and the gallant under an arrest for fear of killing all his rivals. Now, sir, I suppose you having found the ill consequences of these strong passions and prejudices in preference of one woman to another in case of a man's becoming a widower—

SIR JOHN BEVIL How is this?

BEVIL JUNIOR I say, sir, experience has made you wiser in your care of me. For sir, since you lost my dear mother, your time has been so heavy, so lonely, and so tasteless that you are so good as to guard me against the like unhappiness by marrying me prudentially by way of bargain and sale. For, as you well judge, a woman that is espoused for a fortune is yet a better bargain if she dies; for then a man still enjoys what he did marry, the money, and is disencumbered of what he did not marry, the woman.

SIR JOHN BEVIL But pray, sir, do you think Lucinda then a woman of such little merit?

BEVIL JUNIOR Pardon me, sir, I don't carry it so far neither; I am rather afraid I shall like her too well; she has, for one of her fortune, a great many needless and superfluous good qualities.

SIR JOHN BEVIL I am afraid, son, there's something I don't see yet, something that's smothered under all this raillery.

BEVIL JUNIOR Not in the least, sir. If the lady is dressed and ready, you see I am. I suppose the lawyers are ready too.

HUMPHREY [*aside*] This may grow warm, if I don't interpose. —Sir, Mr. Sealand is at the coffeehouse and has sent to speak with you.

SIR JOHN BEVIL Oh! That's well! Then I warrant the lawyers are ready. Son, you'll be in the way, you say—

BEVIL JUNIOR If you please, sir, I'll take a chair and go to Mr. Sealand's, where the young lady and I will wait your leisure.

SIR JOHN BEVIL By no means. The old fellow will be so vain if he sees—

BEVIL JUNIOR Ay, but the young lady, sir, will think me so indifferent—

HUMPHREY [*aside to* Bevil Junior] Ay, there you are right. Press your readiness to go to the bride—he won't let you.

BEVIL JUNIOR [*aside to* Humphrey] Are you sure of that?

HUMPHREY [*aside*] How he likes being prevented.

SIR JOHN BEVIL [*looking on his watch*] No, no. You are an hour or two too early.

BEVIL JUNIOR You'll allow me, sir, to think it too late to visit a beautiful, virtuous young woman in the pride and bloom of life, ready to give herself to my arms; and to place her happiness or misery for the future in being agreeable or displeasing to me is a —call a chair.

SIR JOHN BEVIL No, no, no, dear Jack; this Sealand is a moody old fellow. There's no dealing with some people but by managing with indifference. We must leave to him the conduct of this day. It is the last of his commanding his daughter.

BEVIL JUNIOR Sir, he can't take it ill that I am impatient to be hers.

SIR JOHN BEVIL Pray let me govern in this matter. You can't tell how humorsome old fellows are. There's no offering reason to some of 'em, especially when they are rich. [*Aside.*] If my son should see him before I've brought old Sealand into better temper, the match would be impracticable.

HUMPHREY Pray, sir, let me beg you to let Mr. Bevil go. [*Aside to* Sir John Bevil.] See whether he will or not. [*Then to* Bevil Junior.] Pray, sir, command yourself; since you see my master is positive, it is better you should not go.

BEVIL JUNIOR My father commands me as to the object of my affections, but I hope he will not as to the warmth and height of them.

SIR JOHN BEVIL [*aside*] So! I must even leave things as I found them. And in the meantime, at least, keep old Sealand out of his sight.—Well, son, I'll go myself and take orders in your affair. You'll be in the way, I suppose, if I send to you. I'll leave your old friend with you. [*Aside to* Humphrey.] Humphrey, don't let him stir, d'ye hear? —Your servant, your servant.

                              Exit Sir John Bevil.

HUMPHREY I have a sad time on't, sir, between you and my master. I see you are unwilling, and I know his violent inclinations for the match. I must betray neither and yet deceive you both for your common good. Heav'n grant a good end of this matter. But there is a lady, sir, that gives your father much trouble and sorrow—you'll pardon me.

BEVIL JUNIOR Humphrey, I know thou art a friend to both, and in that confidence, I dare tell thee—that lady—is a woman of honor and virtue. You may assure yourself I never will marry without my father's consent. But give me leave to say too, this declaration does not come up to a promise that I will take whomsoever he pleases.

HUMPHREY Come, sir, I wholly understand you. You would engage my services to free you from this woman whom my master intends you, to make way, in time, for the woman you have really a mind to.

BEVIL JUNIOR Honest Humphrey, you have always been an useful friend to my father and myself; I beg you continue your good offices, and don't let us come to the necessity of a dispute; for, if we should dispute, I must either part with more than life or lose the best of fathers.

HUMPHREY My dear master, were I but worthy to know this secret that so near concerns you, my life, my all should be engaged to serve you. This, sir, I dare promise, that I am sure I will and can be secret. Your trust, at worst, but leaves you where you were; and if I cannot serve you, I will at once be plain and tell you so.

BEVIL JUNIOR That's all I ask. Thou hast made it now my interest to trust thee. Be patient then, and hear the story of my heart.

HUMPHREY I am all attention, sir.

BEVIL JUNIOR You may remember, Humphrey, that in my last travels my father grew uneasy at my making so long a stay at Toulon.

HUMPHREY I remember it; he was apprehensive some woman had laid hold of you.

BEVIL JUNIOR His fears were just, for there I first saw this lady. She is of English birth: her father's name was Danvers, a younger brother of an ancient family, and originally an eminent merchant of Bristol, who, upon repeated misfortunes, was reduced to go privately to the Indies. In this retreat Providence again grew favorable to his industry and, in six years' time, restored him to his former fortunes. On this he sent directions over that his wife and little family should follow him to the Indies. His wife, impatient to obey such welcome orders, would not wait the leisure of a convoy, but took the first occasion of a single ship, and with her husband's sister only and this daughter, then scarce seven years old, undertook the fatal voyage. For here, poor creature, she lost her liberty, and life; she and her family, with all they had, were unfortunately taken by a privateer from Toulon. Being thus made a prisoner, though as such not ill treated, yet the fright, the shock, and cruel disappointment seized with such violence upon her unhealthy frame, she sickened, pined, and died at sea.

HUMPHREY Poor soul! Oh the helpless infant!

BEVIL JUNIOR Her sister yet survived and had the care of her. The captain too proved to have humanity and became a father to her; for having himself married an English woman, and being childless, he brought home into Toulon this her little countrywoman, presenting her, with all her dead mother's movables of value, to his wife, to be educated as his own adopted daughter.

HUMPHREY Fortune here seemed, again, to smile on her.

BEVIL JUNIOR Only to make her frowns more terrible. For, in his height of fortune, this captain too, her benefactor, unfortunately was killed at sea, and dying intestate, his estate fell wholly to an advocate, his brother, who coming soon to take possession, there found among his other riches this blooming virgin, at his mercy.

HUMPHREY He durst not, sure, abuse his power!

BEVIL JUNIOR No wonder if his pampered blood was fired at the sight of her—in short, he loved. But when all arts and gentle means had failed to move, he offered too his menaces in vain, denouncing vengeance on her cruelty, demanding her to account for all her maintenance from her childhood, seized on her little fortune as his own inheritance, and was dragging her by violence to prison when Providence at the instant interposed and sent me, by miracle, to relieve her.

HUMPHREY 'Twas Providence indeed. But pray, sir, after all this trouble, how came this lady at last to England?

BEVIL JUNIOR The disappointed advocate, finding she had so unexpected a support, on cooler thoughts descended to a composition,[5] which I, without her knowledge, secretly discharged.

HUMPHREY That generous concealment made the obligation double.

BEVIL JUNIOR Having thus obtained her liberty, I prevailed, not without some difficulty, to see her safe to England; where no sooner arrived, but my father, jealous of my being imprudently engaged, immediately proposed this other fatal match that hangs upon my quiet.

HUMPHREY I find, sir, you are irrecoverably fixed upon this lady.

BEVIL JUNIOR As my vital life dwells in my heart. And yet you see what I do to please my father: walk in this pageantry of dress, this splendid covering of sorrow. But, Humphrey, you have your lesson.

HUMPHREY Now, sir, I have but one material question—

BEVIL JUNIOR Ask it freely.

HUMPHREY Is it, then, your own passion for this secret lady or hers for you that gives you this aversion to the match your father has proposed you?

BEVIL JUNIOR I shall appear, Humphrey, more romantic in my answer than in all the rest of my story. For though I dote on her to death and have no little reason to believe she has the same thoughts for me, yet in all my acquaintance and utmost privacies with her, I never once directly told her that I loved.

HUMPHREY How was it possible to avoid it?

BEVIL JUNIOR My tender obligations to my father have laid so inviolable a restraint upon my conduct that, till I have his consent to speak, I am determined on that subject to be dumb forever.

HUMPHREY Well, sir, to your praise be it spoken, you are certainly the most unfashionable lover in Great Britain.

Enter Tom.

TOM Sir, Mr. Myrtle's at the next door, and if you are at leisure, will be glad to wait on you.

BEVIL JUNIOR Whenever he pleases—hold, Tom! Did you receive no answer to my letter?

TOM Sir, I was desired to call again; for I was told her mother would not let her be out of her sight; but about an hour hence, Mrs. Lettice said, I should certainly have one.

BEVIL JUNIOR Very well.

5. Compromise.

Exit Tom.

HUMPHREY Sir, I will take another opportunity. In the meantime, I only think it proper to tell you that from a secret I know, you may appear to your father as forward as you please to marry Lucinda, without the least hazard of its coming to a conclusion —sir, your most obedient servant.

BEVIL JUNIOR Honest Humphrey, continue but my friend in this exigence, and you shall always find me yours.

Exit Humphrey.

I long to hear how my letter has succeeded with Lucinda. But I think it cannot fail; for, at worst, were it possible she could take it ill, her resentment of my indifference may as probably occasion a delay as her taking it right. Poor Myrtle, what terrors must he be in all this while? Since he knows she is offered to me and re- fused to him, there is no conversing or taking any measures with him for his own service. But I ought to bear with my friend and use him as one in adversity:

> All his disquiets by my own I prove,
> The greatest grief's perplexity in love.

Exit.

Act II. Scene i.
Scene continues.
Enter Bevil Junior *and* Tom.

TOM Sir, Mr. Myrtle.

BEVIL JUNIOR Very well, do your step again and wait for an answer to my letter.

Exit Tom.

Enter Myrtle.

Well, Charles, why so much care in thy countenance? Is there anything in this world deserves it? You, who used to be so gay, so open, so vacant![6]

MYRTLE I think we have of late changed complexions. You, who used to be much the graver man, are now all air in your behavior. But the cause of my concern may, for aught I know, be the same object that gives you all this satisfaction. In a word, I am told that you are this very day—and your dress confirms me in it—to be married to Lucinda.

BEVIL JUNIOR You are not misinformed. Nay, put not on the ter- rors of a rival till you hear me out. I shall disoblige the best of fathers if I don't seem ready to marry Lucinda. And you know I have ever told you, you might make use of my secret resolution never to marry her, for your own service, as you please. But I am now driven to the extremity of immediately refusing or comply- ing unless you help me to escape the match.

MYRTLE Escape? Sir, neither her merit or her fortune are below your acceptance. Escaping, do you call it!

BEVIL JUNIOR Dear sir, do you wish I should desire the match?

---

6. Relaxed.

MYRTLE No—but such is my humorous and sickly state of mind, since it has been able to relish nothing but Lucinda, that though I must owe my happiness to your aversion to this marriage, I can't bear to hear her spoken of with levity or unconcern.

BEVIL JUNIOR Pardon me, sir; I shall transgress that way no more. She has understanding, beauty, shape, complexion, wit—

MYRTLE Nay, dear Bevil, don't speak of her as if you loved her, neither.

BEVIL JUNIOR Why then, to give you ease at once, though I allow Lucinda to have good sense, wit, beauty, and virtue, I know another in whom these qualities appear to me more amiable than in her.

MYRTLE There you spoke like a reasonable and good-natured friend. When you acknowledge her merit and own your prepossession for another at once, you gratify my fondness and cure my jealousy.

BEVIL JUNIOR But all this while you take no notice, you have no apprehension of another man that has twice the fortune of either of us.

MYRTLE Cimberton! Hang him, a formal, philosophical, pedantic coxcomb! For the sot, with all these crude notions of diverse things, under the direction of great vanity and very little judgment, shows his strongest bias is avarice, which is so predominant in him that he will examine the limbs of his mistress with the caution of a jockey and pays no more compliment to her personal charms than if she were a mere breeding animal.

BEVIL JUNIOR Are you sure that is not affected? I have known some women sooner set on fire by that sort of negligence than by—

MYRTLE No, no; hang him, the rogue has no art; it is pure simple insolence and stupidity.

BEVIL JUNIOR Yet, with all this, I don't take him for a fool.

MYRTLE I own the man is not a natural;[7] he has a very quick sense, though very slow understanding. He says indeed many things that want only the circumstances of time and place to be very just and agreeable.

BEVIL JUNIOR Well, you may be sure of me if you can disappoint him; but my intelligence says the mother has actually sent for the conveyancer[8] to draw articles for his marriage with Lucinda, though those for mine with her are, by her father's order, ready for signing; but it seems she has not thought fit to consult either him or his daughter in the matter.

MYRTLE Pshaw! A poor troublesome woman. Neither Lucinda nor her father will ever be brought to comply with it. Besides, I am sure Cimberton can make no settlement upon her without the concurrence of his great uncle Sir Geoffry in the West.

BEVIL JUNIOR Well sir, and I can tell you, that's the very point that is now laid before her counsel, to know whether a firm settlement can be made without his uncle's actual joining in it. Now pray consider, sir, when my affair with Lucinda comes, as it soon must, to an open rupture, how are you sure that Cimber-

7. Half-wit.   8. Lawyer.

ton's fortune may not then tempt her father too to hear his pro-
posals?

MYRTLE There you are right indeed, that must be provided against.
Do you know who are her counsel?

BEVIL JUNIOR Yes, for your service I have found out that too; they
are Serjeant Bramble and old Target. By the way, they are neither of 'em known in the family; now I was thinking why you
might not put a couple of false counsel upon her to delay and
confound matters a little. Besides, it may probably let you into
the bottom of her whole design against you.

MYRTLE As how, pray?

BEVIL JUNIOR Why, can't you slip on a black wig and a gown and
be old Bramble yourself?

MYRTLE Ha! I don't dislike it—but what shall I do for a brother in
the case?

BEVIL JUNIOR What think you of my fellow, Tom? The rogue's
intelligent and is a good mimic; all his part will be but to stutter
heartily, for that's old Target's case. Nay, it would be an immoral
thing to mock him, were it not that his impertinence is the occasion of its breaking out to that degree. The conduct of the scene
will chiefly lie upon you.

MYRTLE I like it of all things. If you'll send Tom to my chambers,
I will give him full instructions. This will certainly give me occasion to raise difficulties, to puzzle or confound her project for a
while at least.

BEVIL JUNIOR I'll warrant you success. So far we are right then.
And now, Charles, your apprehension of my marrying her is all
you have to get over.

MYRTLE Dear Bevil! Though I know you are my friend, yet when I
abstract myself from my own interest in the thing, I know no
objection she can make to you or you to her, and therefore
hope—

BEVIL JUNIOR Dear Myrtle, I am as much obliged to you for the
cause of your suspicion as I am offended at the effect. But be
assured, I am taking measures for your certain security and that
all things with regard to me will end in your entire satisfaction.

MYRTLE [*going*] Well, I'll promise you to be as easy and as confident as I can, though I cannot but remember that I have more
than life at stake on your fidelity.

BEVIL JUNIOR Then depend upon it, you have no chance against
you.

MYRTLE Nay, no ceremony, you know I must be going.

Exit Myrtle.

BEVIL JUNIOR Well! This is another instance of the perplexities
which arise too in faithful friendship. We must often, in this life,
go on in our good offices even under the displeasure of those to
whom we do them, in compassion to their weaknesses and mistakes. But all this while poor Indiana is tortured with the doubt
of me! She has no support or comfort but in my fidelity, yet sees
me daily pressed to marriage with another! How painful, in such

a crisis, must be every hour she thinks on me! I'll let her see, at least, my conduct to her is not changed. I'll take this opportunity to visit her; for though the religious vow I have made to my father restrains me from ever marrying without his approbation, yet that confines me not from seeing a virtuous woman that is the pure delight of my eyes and the guiltless joy of my heart. But the best condition of human life is but a gentler misery.

> To hope for perfect happiness is vain,
> And Love has ever its allays[9] of pain.

Exit.

Act II. Scene ii.
Enter Isabella *and* Indiana *in her own lodgings.*

ISABELLA Yes, I say 'tis artifice, dear child; I say to thee again and again, 'tis all skill and management.

INDIANA Will you persuade me there can be an ill design in supporting me in the condition of a woman of quality? Attended, dressed, and lodged like one; in my appearance abroad and my furniture at home, every way in the most sumptuous manner, and he that does it has an artifice, a design in it?

ISABELLA Yes, yes.

INDIANA And all this without so much as explaining to me that all about me comes from him?

ISABELLA Ay, ay, the more for that—that keeps the title to all you have the more in him.

INDIANA The more in him! He scorns the thought—

ISABELLA Then he—he—he—

INDIANA Well, be not so eager. If he is an ill man, let us look into his stratagems. Here is another of them. [*Showing a letter.*] Here's two hundred and fifty pound in bank notes with these words, "To pay for the set of dressing-plate, which will be brought home tomorrow." Why, dear aunt, now here's another piece of skill for you which I own I cannot comprehend; and it is with a bleeding heart I hear you say anything to the disadvantage of Mr. Bevil. When he is present, I look upon him as one to whom I owe my life and the support of it, then again, as the man who loves me with sincerity and honor. When his eyes are cast another way and I dare survey him, my heart is painfully divided between shame and love. Oh, could I tell you—

ISABELLA Ah, you need not. I imagine all this for you.

INDIANA This is my state of mind in his presence; and when he is absent, you are ever dinning my ears with notions of the arts of men; that his hidden bounty, his respectful conduct, his careful provision for me after his preserving me from utmost misery are certain signs he means nothing but to make I know not what of me.

ISABELLA Oh! You have a sweet opinion of him, truly.

INDIANA I have, when I am with him, ten thousand things besides my sex's natural decency and shame to suppress my heart that

9. Alloys.

yearns to thank, to praise, to say it loves him. I say, thus it is with me while I see him; and in his absence I am entertained with nothing but your endeavors to tear this amiable image from my heart and, in its stead, to place a base dissembler, an artful invader of my happiness, my innocence, my honor.

ISABELLA Ah, poor soul! Has not his plot taken? Don't you die for him? Has not the way he has taken been the most proper with you? Oh ho! He has sense and has judged the thing right.

INDIANA Go on then, since nothing can answer you; say what you will of him. Heigh ho!

ISABELLA Heigh ho, indeed. It is better to say so as you are now than as many others are. There are, among the destroyers of women, the gentle, the generous, the mild, the affable, the humble, who all, soon after their success in their designs, turn to the contrary of those characters. I will own to you Mr. Bevil carries his hypocrisy the best of any man living, but still he is a man and therefore a hypocrite. They have usurped an exemption from shame for any baseness, any cruelty towards us. They embrace without love; they make vows without conscience of obligation; they are partners, nay, seducers to the crime wherein they pretend to be less guilty.

INDIANA [aside] That's truly observed. —But what's all this to Bevil?

ISABELLA This it is to Bevil and all mankind. Trust not those who will think the worse of you for your confidence in them. Serpents who lie in wait for doves! Won't you be on your guard against those who would betray you? Won't you doubt those who would condemn you for believing 'em? Take it from me, fair and natural dealing is to invite injuries; 'tis bleating to escape wolves who would devour you. Such is the world—[aside] and such, since the behavior of one man to myself, have I believed all the rest of the sex.

INDIANA I will not doubt the truth of Bevil, I will not doubt it. He has not spoken it by an organ that is given to lying: his eyes are all that have ever told me that he was mine. I know his virtue, I know his filial piety, and ought to trust his management with a father to whom he has uncommon obligations. What have I to be concerned for? My lesson is very short. If he takes me forever, my purpose of life is only to please him. If he leaves me, which Heaven avert, I know he'll do it nobly, and I shall have nothing to do but to learn to die after worse than death has happened to me.

ISABELLA Ay do, persist in your credulity! Flatter yourself that a man of his figure and fortune will make himself the jest of the town and marry a handsome beggar for love.

INDIANA The town! I must tell you, madam, the fools that laugh at Mr. Bevil will but make themselves more ridiculous. His actions are the result of thinking, and he has sense enough to make even virtue fashionable.

ISABELLA O' my conscience, he has turned her head. —Come,

come; if he were the honest fool you take him for, why has he kept you here these three weeks without sending you to Bristol in search of your father, your family, and your relations?

INDIANA I am convinced he still designs it and that nothing keeps him here but the necessity of not coming to a breach with his father in regard to the match he has proposed him. Beside, has he not writ to Bristol? And has not he advice that my father has not been heard of there almost these twenty years?

ISABELLA All sham, mere evasion; he is afraid if he should carry you thither, your honest relations may take you out of his hands and so blow up all his wicked hopes at once.

INDIANA Wicked hopes! Did I ever give him any such?

ISABELLA Has he ever given you any honest ones? Can you say, in your conscience, he has ever once offered to marry you?

INDIANA No! But by his behavior I am convinced he will offer it the moment 'tis in his power or consistent with his honor to make such a promise good to me.

ISABELLA His honor!

INDIANA I will rely upon it; therefore desire you will not make my life uneasy by these ungrateful jealousies of one to whom I am and wish to be obliged. For from his integrity alone I have resolved to hope for happiness.

ISABELLA Nay, I have done my duty; if you won't see, at your peril be it—

INDIANA Let it be. This is his hour of visiting me.

ISABELLA Oh, to be sure, keep up your form; don't see him in a bedchamber. [*Apart.*] This is pure prudence when she is liable, wherever he meets her, to be conveyed where'er he pleases.

INDIANA All the rest of my life is but waiting till he comes. I live only when I'm with him.

Exit.

ISABELLA Well, go thy ways, thou willful innocent! I once had almost as much love for a man who poorly left me to marry an estate. And I am now, against my will, what they call an old maid. But I will not let the peevishness of that condition grow upon me, only keep up the suspicion of it, to prevent this creature's being any other than a virgin except upon proper terms.

Exit.

Re-enter Indiana, *speaking to a* Servant.

INDIANA Desire Mr. Bevil to walk in.

Exit Servant.

Design! Impossible! A base, designing mind could never think of what he hourly puts in practice. And yet, since the late rumor of his marriage, he seems more reserved than formerly. He sends in, too, before he sees me, to know if I am at leisure. Such new respect may cover coldness in the heart. It certainly makes me thoughtful. I'll know the worst at once; I'll lay such fair occasions in his way that it shall be impossible to avoid an explanation. For these doubts are insupportable! But see, he comes, and clears them all.

Enter Bevil Junior.

BEVIL JUNIOR Madam, your most obedient—I am afraid I broke in upon your rest last night. 'Twas very late before we parted, but 'twas your own fault: I never saw you in such agreeable humour.

INDIANA I am extremely glad we were both pleased, for I thought I never saw you better company.

BEVIL JUNIOR Me, madam! You rally. I said very little.

INDIANA But I am afraid you heard me say a great deal; and when a woman is in the talking vein, the most agreeable thing a man can do, you know, is to have patience to hear her.

BEVIL JUNIOR Then it's pity, madam, you should ever be silent, that we might be always agreeable to one another.

INDIANA If I had your talent or power to make my actions speak for me, I might indeed be silent and yet pretend to something more than the agreeable.

BEVIL JUNIOR If I might be vain of anything in my power, madam, 'tis that my understanding from all your sex has marked you out as the most deserving object of my esteem.

INDIANA Should I think I deserve this, 'twere enough to make my vanity forfeit the very esteem you offer me.

BEVIL JUNIOR How so, madam?

INDIANA Because esteem is the result of reason, and to deserve it from good sense, the height of human glory. Nay, I had rather a man of honor should pay me that than all the homage of a sincere and humble love.

BEVIL JUNIOR You certainly distinguish right, madam; love often kindles from external merit only—

INDIANA But esteem arises from a higher source, the merit of the soul—

BEVIL JUNIOR True. And great souls only can deserve it.
Bowing respectfully.

INDIANA Now I think they are greater still that can so charitably part with it.

BEVIL JUNIOR Now, madam, you make me vain since the utmost pride and pleasure of my life is that I esteem you—as I ought.

INDIANA [*aside*]. As he ought! Still more perplexing! He neither saves nor kills my hope.

BEVIL JUNIOR But madam, we grow grave methinks. Let's find some other subject. Pray, how did you like the opera last night?

INDIANA First give me leave to thank you for my tickets.

BEVIL JUNIOR Oh, your servant, madam. But pray tell me, you now who are never partial to the fashion I fancy must be the properest judge of a mighty dispute among the ladies, that is, whether *Crispo* or *Griselda*[1] is the more agreeable entertainment.

INDIANA With submission now, I cannot be a proper judge of this question.

BEVIL JUNIOR How so, madam?

INDIANA Because I find I have a partiality for one of them.

BEVIL JUNIOR Pray, which is that?

1. Operas by Giovanni Bononcini, both popular in London in 1722.

INDIANA I do not know—there's something in that rural cottage of Griselda, her forlorn condition, her poverty, her solitude, her resignation, her innocent slumbers, and that lulling *"Dolce Sogno"*[2] that's sung over her; it had an effect upon me that—in short, I never was so well deceived at any of them.

BEVIL JUNIOR Oh! Now then, I can account for the dispute: *Griselda*, it seems, is the distress of an injured innocent woman; *Crispo*, that only of a man in the same condition. Therefore the men are mostly concerned for Crispo, and, by a natural indulgence, both sexes for Griselda.

INDIANA So that judgment, you think, ought to be for one though fancy and complaisance have got ground for the other. Well, I believe you will never give me leave to dispute with you on any subject, for I own *Crispo* has its charms for me too, though in the main, all the pleasure the best opera gives us is but mere sensation. Methinks it's pity the mind can't have a little more share in the entertainment. The music's certainly fine, but in my thoughts there's none of your composers come up to old Shakespeare and Otway.

BEVIL JUNIOR How, madam! Why if a woman of your sense were to say this in the drawing room—

Enter a Servant.

SERVANT Sir, here's Signor Carbonelli says he waits your commands in the next room.

BEVIL JUNIOR A propos! You were saying yesterday, madam, you had a mind to hear him. Will you give him leave to entertain you now?

INDIANA By all means. Desire the gentleman to walk in.

Exit Servant.

BEVIL JUNIOR I fancy you will find something in this hand that is uncommon.

INDIANA You are always finding ways, Mr. Bevil, to make life seem less tedious to me.

Enter Music Master.

When the gentleman pleases.

After a sonata[3] *is played,* Bevil Junior *waits on the* Master *to the door, etc.*

BEVIL JUNIOR You smile, madam, to see me so complaisant to one whom I pay for his visit. Now I own I think it is not enough barely to pay those whose talents are superior to our own—I mean such talents as would become our condition if we had them. Methinks we ought to do something more than barely gratify them for what they do at our command only because their fortune is below us.

INDIANA You say I smile. I assure you it was a smile of approbation, for indeed I cannot but think it the distinguishing part of a gentleman to make his superiority of fortune as easy to his inferiors

2. "Sweet Dream," sung to the sleeping Griselda by her husband.
3. Originally, any composition for instru-ments (as distinguished from vocal music).

as he can. [*Aside.*] Now once more to try him. —I was saying just now I believed you would never let me dispute with you, and I dare say it will always be so. However I must have your opinion upon a subject which created a debate between my aunt and me just before you came hither. She would needs have it that no man ever does any extraordinary kindness or service for a woman but for his own sake.

BEVIL JUNIOR Well, madam! Indeed I can't but be of her mind.

INDIANA What, though he should maintain and support her without demanding anything of her on her part?

BEVIL JUNIOR Why, madam, is making an expense in the service of a valuable woman—for such I must suppose her—though she should never do him any favor, nay, though she should never know who did her such service, such a mighty heroic business?

INDIANA Certainly! I should think he must be a man of an uncommon mold.

BEVIL JUNIOR Dear madam, why so? 'Tis but, at best, a better taste in expense. To bestow upon one whom he may think one of the ornaments of the whole creation, to be conscious that from his superfluity an innocent, a virtuous spirit is supported above the temptations and sorrows of life! That he sees satisfaction, health, and gladness in her countenance while he enjoys the happiness of seeing her—as that I will suppose too, or he must be too abstracted, too insensible. I say, if he is allowed to delight in that prospect, alas, what mighty matter is there in all this?

INDIANA No mighty matter in so disinterested a friendship!

BEVIL JUNIOR Disinterested! I can't think him so. Your hero, madam, is no more than what every gentleman ought to be, and I believe very many are. He is only one who takes more delight in reflections than in sensations. He is more pleased with thinking than eating. That's the utmost you can say of him. Why, madam, a greater expense than all this men lay out upon an unnecessary stable of horses.

INDIANA Can you be sincere in what you say?

BEVIL JUNIOR You may depend upon it, if you know any such man, he does not love dogs inordinately.

INDIANA No, that he does not.

BEVIL JUNIOR Nor cards, nor dice.

INDIANA No.

BEVIL JUNIOR Nor bottle companions.

INDIANA No.

BEVIL JUNIOR Nor loose women.

INDIANA No, I'm sure he does not.

BEVIL JUNIOR Take my word then, if your admired hero is not liable to any of these kinds of demands, there's no such pre-eminence in this as you imagine. Nay, this way of expense you speak of is what exalts and raises him that has a taste for it. And at the same time his delight is incapable of satiety, disgust, or penitence.

INDIANA But still I insist his having no private interest in the action makes it prodigious, almost incredible.

BEVIL JUNIOR Dear madam, I never knew you more mistaken. Why, who can be more an usurer than he who lays out his money in such valuable purchases? If pleasure be worth purchasing, how great a pleasure is it to him who has a true taste of life to ease an aching heart, to see the human countenance lighted up into smiles of joy on the receipt of a bit of ore which is superfluous and otherwise useless in a man's own pocket? What could a man do better with his cash? This is the effect of an humane disposition where there is only a general tie of nature and common necessity. What then must it be when we serve an object of merit, of admiration!

INDIANA Well, the more you argue against it, the more I shall admire the generosity.

BEVIL JUNIOR Nay, nay. Then, madam, 'tis time to fly, after a declaration that my opinion strengthens my adversary's argument. I had best hasten to my appointment with Mr. Myrtle and begone while we are friends and—before things are brought to an extremity—

Exit carelessly.

Enter Isabella.

ISABELLA Well, madam, what think you of him now, pray?

INDIANA I protest I begin to fear he is wholly disinterested in what he does for me. On my heart, he has no other view but the mere pleasure of doing it and has neither good or bad designs upon me.

ISABELLA Ah, dear niece! Don't be in fear of both! I'll warrant you, you will know time enough that he is not indifferent.

INDIANA You please me when you tell me so. For if he has any wishes towards me, I know he will not pursue them but with honor.

ISABELLA I wish I were as confident of one as t'other. I saw the respectful downcast of his eye when you catcht him gazing at you during the music. He, I warrant, was surprised, as if he had been taken stealing your watch. Oh, the undissembled guilty look!

INDIANA But did you observe any such thing, really? I thought he looked most charmingly graceful! How engaging is modesty in a man when one knows there is a great mind within. So tender a confusion! And yet, in other respects, so much himself, so collected, so dauntless, so determined!

ISABELLA Ah, niece! There is a sort of bashfulness which is the best engine to carry on a shameless purpose. Some men's modesty serves their wickedness, as hypocrisy gains the respect due to piety. But I will own to you, there is one hopeful symptom, if there could be such a thing as a disinterested lover. But it's all a perplexity, till—till—till—

INDIANA Till what?

ISABELLA Till I know whether Mr. Myrtle and Mr. Bevil are really friends or foes. And that I will be convinced of before I sleep, for you shall not be deceived.

INDIANA I'm sure I never shall if your fears can guard me. In the meantime, I'll wrap myself up in the integrity of my own heart, nor dare to doubt of his.

As conscious honor all his actions steers:
So conscious innocence dispels my fears.

Exeunt.

Act III. Scene i.
Scene, Sealand's *house.*
Enter Tom *meeting* Phillis.

TOM Well, Phillis! What, with a face as if you had never seen me before? [*Aside.*] What a work have I to do now! She has seen some new visitant at their house whose airs she has catched and is resolved to practice them upon me. Numberless are the changes she'll dance through before she'll answer this plain question, *videlicit*, have you delivered my master's letter to your lady? Nay, I know her too well to ask an account of it in an ordinary way; I'll be in my airs as well as she. —Well, madam, as unhappy as you are at present pleased to make me, I would not, in the general, be any other than what I am. I would not be a bit wiser, a bit richer, a bit taller, a bit shorter than I am at this instant.
Looking steadfastly at her.

PHILLIS Did ever anybody doubt, Master Thomas, but that you were extremely satisfied with your sweet self?

TOM I am indeed. The thing I have least reason to be satisfied with is my fortune, and I am glad of my poverty. Perhaps if I were rich, I should overlook the finest woman in the world that wants nothing but riches to be thought so.

PHILLIS [*aside*] How prettily was that said! But I'll have a great deal more before I'll say one word.

TOM I should, perhaps, have been stupidly above her, had I not been her equal; and by not being her equal, never had opportunity of being her slave. I am my master's servant for hire; I am my mistress's from choice, would she but approve my passion.

PHILLIS I think it's the first time I ever heard you speak of it with any sense of the anguish, if you really do suffer any.

TOM Ah, Phillis, can you doubt, after what you have seen?

PHILLIS I know not what I have seen, nor what I have heard. But since I'm at leisure, you may tell me when you fell in love with me, how you fell in love with me, and what you have suffered or are ready to suffer for me.

TOM [*aside*] Oh, the unmerciful jade! When I'm in haste about my master's letter! But I must go through it. —Ah! Too well I remember when and how and on what occasion I was first surprised. It was on the first of April, one thousand seven hundred and fifteen, I came into Mr. Sealand's service. I was then a hobbledehoy, and you a pretty little tight⁴ girl, a favorite handmaid of the housekeeper. At that time, we neither of us knew what was in us. I remember I was ordered to get out of the window, one

4. Trim.

pair of stairs,[5] to rub the sashes clean. The person employed on the innerside was your charming self, whom I had never seen before.

PHILLIS I think I remember the silly accident. What made ye, you oaf, ready to fall down into the street?

TOM You know not, I warrant you. You could not guess what surprised me. You took no delight when you immediately grew wanton in your conquest and put your lips close and breathed upon the glass, and when my lips approached, a dirty cloth you rubbed against my face and hid your beauteous form; when I again drew near, you spit and rubbed and smiled at my undoing.

PHILLIS What silly thoughts you men have!

TOM We were Pyramus and Thisbe. But ten times harder was my fate. Pyramus could peep only through a wall; I saw her, saw my Thisbe in all her beauty but as much kept from her as if a hundred walls between, for there was more, there was her will against me. Would she but yet relent! Oh, Phillis! Phillis! Shorten my torment and declare you pity me.

PHILLIS I believe it's very sufferable; the pain is not so exquisite but that you may bear it a little longer.

TOM Oh, my charming Phillis, if all depended on my fair one's will, I could with glory suffer. But, dearest creature, consider our miserable state.

PHILLIS How! Miserable!

TOM We are miserable to be in love and under the command of others than those we love—with that generous passion in the heart, to be sent to and fro on errands, called, checked and rated for the meanest trifles. Oh, Phillis! You don't know how many china cups and glasses my passion for you has made me break. You have broke my fortune as well as my heart.

PHILLIS Well, Mr. Thomas, I cannot but own to you that I believe your master writes and you speak the best of any men in the world. Never was woman so well pleased with a letter as my young lady was with his, and this is an answer to it.

    Gives him a letter.

TOM This was well done, my dearest. Consider, we must strike out some pretty livelihood for ourselves by closing their affairs. It will be nothing for them to give us a little being of our own, some small tenement out of their large possessions. Whatever they give us, 'twill be more than what they keep for themselves: one acre, with Phillis, would be worth a whole country without her.

PHILLIS O, could I but believe you!

TOM If not the utterance, believe the touch of my lips.

    Kisses her.

PHILLIS There's no contradicting you. How closely you argue, Tom!

TOM And will closer, in due time. But I must hasten with this letter, to hasten toward the possession of you. Then, Phillis, consider how I must be revenged, look to it, of all your skittishness,

5. On the second floor.

shy looks, and at best but coy compliances.

PHILLIS Oh, Tom, you grow wanton and sensual, as my lady calls it; I must not endure it. Oh! Foh! You are a man, an odious filthy male creature. You should behave, if you had a right sense or were a man of sense like Mr. Cimberton, with distance and indifference, or, let me see, some other becoming hard word, with seeming in-in-inadvertency, and not rush on one as if you were seizing a prey. But hush—the ladies are coming. Good Tom, don't kiss me above once and be gone. Lard, we have been fooling and toying and not considered the main business of our masters and mistresses.

TOM Why, their business is to be fooling and toying as soon as the parchments[6] are ready.

PHILLIS Well remembered—parchments. My lady, to my knowledge, is preparing writings between her coxcomb cousin Cimberton and my mistress though my master has an eye to the parchments already prepared between your master Mr. Bevil and my mistress; and I believe my mistress herself has signed and sealed, in her heart, to Mr. Myrtle—did I not bid you kiss me but once and be gone? But I know you won't be satisfied.

TOM No, you smooth creature, how should I!
Kissing her hand.

PHILLIS Well, since you are so humble, or so cool, as to ravish my hand only, I'll take my leave of you like a great lady, and you a man of quality.
They salute[7] formally.

TOM Pox of all this state.
Offers to kiss her more closely.

PHILLIS No, prithee, Tom, mind your business. We must follow that interest which will take, but endeavor at that which will be most for us and we like most. Oh, here's my young mistress! [Tom *taps her neck behind and kisses his fingers.*] Go, ye liquorish[8] fool.
Exit Tom.

Enter Lucinda.

LUCINDA Who was that you was hurrying away?

PHILLIS One that I had no mind to part with.

LUCINDA Why did you turn him away then?

PHILLIS For your ladyship's service, to carry your ladyship's letter to his master. I could hardly get the rogue away.

LUCINDA Why, has he so little love for his master?

PHILLIS No, but he has so much love for his mistress.

LUCINDA But I thought I heard him kiss you. Why do you suffer that?

PHILLIS Why, madam, we vulgar take it to be a sign of love. We servants, we poor people that have nothing but our persons to bestow or treat for are forced to deal and bargain by way of sample. And therefore, as we have no parchments or wax necessary in our agreements, we squeeze with our hands and seal with our lips to ratify vows and promises.

LUCINDA But can't you trust one another without such earnest down?[9]

PHILLIS We don't think it safe, any more than you gentry, to come together without deeds executed.

LUCINDA Thou art a pert, merry hussy.

PHILLIS I wish, madam, your lover and you were as happy as Tom and your servant are.

LUCINDA You grow impertinent.

PHILLIS I have done, madam, and I won't ask you what you intend to do with Mr. Myrtle, what your father will do with Mr. Bevil, nor what you all, especially my lady, mean by admitting Mr. Cimberton as particularly here as if he were married to you already. Nay, you are married actually as far as people of quality are.

LUCINDA How's that?

PHILLIS You have different beds in the same house.

LUCINDA Pshaw! I have a very great value for Mr. Bevil but have absolutely put an end to his pretensions in the letter I gave you for him. But my father, in his heart, still has a mind to him, were it not for this woman they talk of. And I am apt to imagine he is married to her, or never designs to marry at all.

PHILLIS Then Mr. Myrtle—

LUCINDA He had my parents' leave to apply to me, and by that has won me and my affections; who is to have this body of mine without 'em, it seems, is nothing to me. My mother says it's indecent for me to let my thoughts stray about the person of my husband. Nay, she says a maid rigidly virtuous, though she may have been where her lover was a thousand times, should not have made observations enough to know him from another man when she sees him in a third place.

PHILLIS That is more than the severity of a nun, for not to see when one may is hardly possible; not to see when one can't is very easy. At this rate, madam, there are a great many whom you have not seen who—

LUCINDA Mamma says the first time you see your husband should be at that instant he is made so, when your father with the help of the minister gives you to him; then you are to see him, then you are to observe and take notice of him, because then you are to obey him.

PHILLIS But does not my lady remember you are to love as well as obey?

LUCINDA To love is a passion, 'tis a desire, and we must have no desires. Oh, I cannot endure the reflection! With what insensibility on my part, with what more than patience have I been exposed and offered to some awkward booby or other in every county of Great Britain!

9. Partial payment.

PHILLIS Indeed, madam, I wonder I never heard you speak of it before with this indignation.

LUCINDA Every corner of the land has presented me with a wealthy coxcomb. As fast as one treaty has gone off, another has come on, till my name and person have been the tittle-tattle of the whole town. What is this world come to? No shame left! To be bartered for like the beasts of the fields, and that in such an instance as coming together to an entire familiarity and union of soul and body. Oh! And this without being so much as well-wishers to each other but for increase of fortune.

PHILLIS But, madam, all these vexations will end very soon in one for all. Mr. Cimberton is your mother's kinsman and three hundred years an older gentleman than any lover you ever had, for which reason, with that of his prodigious large estate, she is resolved on him and has sent to consult the lawyers accordingly. Nay, has, whether you know it or no, been in treaty with Sir Geoffry, who, to join in the settlement, has accepted of a sum to do it and is every moment expected in town for that purpose.

LUCINDA How do you get all this intelligence?

PHILLIS By an art I have, I thank my stars, beyond all the waiting-maids in Great Britain, the art of list'ning, madam, for your ladyship's service.

LUCINDA I shall soon know as much as you do. Leave me, leave me, Phillis, be gone. Here, here, I'll turn you out. My mother says I must not converse with my servants, though I must converse with no one else.

Exit Phillis.

How unhappy are we who are born to great fortunes! No one looks at us with indifference or acts towards us on the foot of plain dealing. Yet, by all I have been heretofore offered to or treated for, I have been used with the most agreeable of all abuses, flattery; but now, by this phlegmatic fool I am used as nothing or a mere thing. He, forsooth, is too wise, too learned to have any regard to desires, and I know not what the learned oaf calls sentiments of love and passion. Here he comes with my mother. It's much if he looks at me. Or if he does, takes no more notice of me than of any other movable in the room.

Enter Mrs. Sealand *and* Mr. Cimberton.

MRS. SEALAND How do I admire this noble, this learned taste of yours and the worthy regard you have to our own ancient and honorable house in consulting a means to keep the blood as pure and as regularly descended as may be.

CIMBERTON Why, really, madam, the young women of this age are treated with discourses of such a tendency and their imaginations so bewildered in flesh and blood that a man of reason can't talk to be understood. They have no ideas of happiness but what are more gross than the gratification of hunger and thirst.

LUCINDA [*aside*] With how much reflection he is a coxcomb!

CIMBERTON And in truth, madam, I have considered it as a most brutal custom that persons of the first character in the world should go as ordinarily and with as little shame to bed as to dinner with one another. They proceed to the propagation of the species as openly as to the preservation of the individual.

LUCINDA [*aside*] She that willingly goes to bed to thee must have no shame, I'm sure.

MRS. SEALAND Oh, Cousin Cimberton! Cousin Cimberton! How abstracted, how refined is your sense of things! But, indeed, it is too true, there is nothing so ordinary as to say in the best governed families, "My master and lady are gone to bed." One does not know but it might have been said of one's self.

Hiding her face with her fan.

CIMBERTON Lycurgus,[1] madam, instituted otherwise. Among the Lacedemonians, the whole female world was pregnant, but none but the mothers themselves knew by whom. Their meetings were secret and the amorous congress always by stealth, and no such professed doings between the sexes as are tolerated among us under the audacious word marriage.

MRS. SEALAND Oh, had I lived in those days and been a matron of Sparta, one might with less indecency have had ten children according to that modest institution that one under the confusion of our modern, barefaced manner.

LUCINDA [*aside*] And yet, poor woman, she has gone through the whole ceremony, and here I stand a melancholy proof of it.

MRS. SEALAND We will talk then of business. That girl walking about the room there is to be your wife. She has, I confess, no ideas, no sentiments that speak her born of a thinking mother.

CIMBERTON I have observed her. Her lively look, free air, and disengaged countenance speak her very—

LUCINDA Very what?

CIMBERTON If you please, madam, to set her a little that way.

MRS. SEALAND Lucinda, say nothing to him; you are not a match for him. When you are married, you may speak to such a husband when you're spoken to. But I am disposing of you above yourself every way.

CIMBERTON Madam, you cannot but observe the inconveniences I expose myself to in hopes that your ladyship will be the consort of my better part. As for the young woman, she is rather an impediment than a help to a man of letters and speculation. Madam, there is no reflection, no philosophy can at all times subdue the sensitive life, but the animal shall sometimes carry away the man. Ha! Ay, the vermilion of her lips.

LUCINDA Pray, don't talk of me thus.

CIMBERTON The pretty enough—pant of her bosom.

LUCINDA Sir! Madam, don't you hear him?

CIMBERTON Her forward chest.

LUCINDA Intolerable!

CIMBERTON High health.

LUCINDA The grave, easy impudence of him!

1. The lawgiver of Lacedemonia.

CIMBERTON Proud heart.

LUCINDA Stupid coxcomb!

CIMBERTON I say, madam, her impatience while we are looking at her throws out all attractions—her arms—her neck—what a spring in her step!

LUCINDA Don't you run me over thus, you strange unaccountable!

CIMBERTON What an elasticity in her veins and arteries!

LUCINDA I have no veins, no arteries.

MRS. SEALAND Oh, child, hear him, he talks finely, he's a scholar, he knows what you have.

CIMBERTON The speaking invitation of her shape, the gathering of herself up, and the indignation you see in the pretty little thing —now I am considering her on this occasion but as one that is to be pregnant.

LUCINDA [aside] The familiar, learned, unseasonable puppy!

CIMBERTON And pregnant undoubtedly she will be yearly. I fear I shan't for many years have discretion enough to give her one fallow season.

LUCINDA Monster! There's no bearing it. The hideous sot! There's no enduring it, to be thus surveyed like a steed at sale.

CIMBERTON At sale! She's very illiterate. But she's very well limbed too. Turn her in.[2] I see what she is.

MRS. SEALAND Go, you creature, I am ashamed of you.

Exit Lucinda *in a rage.*

CIMBERTON No harm done. You know, madam, the better sort of people, as I observed to you, treat by their lawyers of weddings [adjusting himself at the glass], and the woman in the bargain, like the mansion-house in the sale of the estate, is thrown in, and what that is, whether good or bad, is not at all considered.

MRS. SEALAND I grant it, and therefore make no demand for her youth and beauty and every other accomplishment, as the common world think 'em, because she is not polite.

CIMBERTON Madam, I know your exalted understanding, abstracted as it is from vulgar prejudices, will not be offended when I declare to you I marry to have an heir to my estate and not to beget a colony or a plantation. This young woman's beauty and constitution will demand provision for a tenth child at least.

MRS. SEALAND [aside] With all that wit and learning, how considerate! What an economist!—Sir, I cannot make her any other than she is, or say she is much better than the other young women of this age or fit for much besides being a mother. But I have given directions for the marriage settlements, and Sir Geoffry Cimberton's counsel is to meet ours here, at this hour, concerning his joining in the deed, which, when executed, makes you capable of settling what is due to Lucinda's fortune. Herself, as I told you, I say nothing of.

CIMBERTON No, no, no, indeed, madam, it is not usual, and I must depend upon my own reflection and philosophy not to overstock my family.

2. Drive her in (as an animal).

MRS. SEALAND I cannot help her, Cousin Cimberton, but she is, for aught I see, as well as the daughter of anybody else.

CIMBERTON That is very true, madam.

Enter a Servant, *who whispers* Mrs. Sealand.

MRS. SEALAND The lawyers are come, and now we are to hear what they have resolved as to the point whether it's necessary that Sir Geoffry should join in the settlement as being what they call in the remainder. But, good cousin, you must have patience with 'em. These lawyers, I am told, are of a different kind. One is what they call a chamber-counsel, the other a pleader.[3] The conveyancer is slow from an imperfection in his speech, and therefore shunned the bar, but extremely passionate and impatient of contradiction. The other is as warm as he but has a tongue so voluble and a head so conceited he will suffer nobody to speak but himself.

CIMBERTON You mean old Serjeant Target and Counsellor Bramble? I have heard of 'em.

MRS. SEALAND The same. Show in the gentlemen.

Exit Servant.

Re-enter Servant, *introducing* Myrtle *and* Tom *disguised as* Bramble *and* Target.

MRS. SEALAND Gentlemen, this is the party concerned, Mr. Cimberton. And I hope you have considered of the matter.

TARGET [TOM] Yes, madam, we have agreed that it must be by indent—dent—dent—dent—

BRAMBLE [MYRTLE] Yes, madam, Mr. Serjeant and myself have agreed, as he is pleased to inform you, that it must be an indenture tripartite, and tripartite let it be, for Sir Geoffry must needs be a party. Old Cimberton, in the year 1619, says in that ancient roll in Mr. Serjeant's hands, "as recourse thereto being had—will more at large appear—"

TARGET Yes, and by the deeds in your hands it appears that—

BRAMBLE Mr. Serjeant, I beg of you to make no inferences upon what is in our custody, but speak to the titles in your own deeds. I shall not show that deed till my client is in town.

CIMBERTON You know best your own methods.

MRS. SEALAND The single question is whether the entail is such that my cousin Sir Geoffry is necessary in this affair?

MYRTLE Yes, as to the lordship of Tretriplet but not as to the messuage of Grimgribber.[4]

TARGET I say that Gr—gr—that Gr—gr—Grimgribber, Grimgribber is in us. That is to say the remainder thereof, as well as that of Tr—tr—Triplet.

BRAMBLE You go upon the deed of Sir Ralph, made in the middle of the last century, precedent to that in which old Cimberton made over the remainder and made it pass to the heirs general, by which your client comes in; and I question whether the

3. The chamber-counsel gives opinions in private but does not argue in court. The pleader is a trial lawyer.

4. Steele invented "Grimgribber," but it later came to mean *legal jargon.*

remainder even of Tretriplet is in him. But we are willing to waive that and give him a valuable consideration. But we shall not purchase what is in us forever, as Grimgribber is, at the rate as we guard against the contingent of Mr. Cimberton having no son. Then we know Sir Geoffry is the first of the collateral male line in this family. Yet—

TARGET Sir, Gr—gr—ber is—

BRAMBLE I apprehend you very well, and your argument might be of force, and we would be inclined to hear that in all its parts. But sir, I see very plainly what you are going into. I tell you, it is as probable a contingent that Sir Geoffry may die before Mr. Cimberton as that he may outlive him.

TARGET Sir, we not ripe for that yet, but I must say—

BRAMBLE Sir, I allow you the whole extent of that argument, but that will go no farther than as to the claimants under old Cimberton. I am of opinion that according to the instruction of Sir Ralph, he could not dock the entail and then create a new estate for the heirs general.

TARGET Sir, I have not patience to be told that, when Gr—gr—ber—

BRAMBLE I will allow it you, Mr. Serjeant, but there must be the word "heirs forever" to make such an estate as you pretend.

CIMBERTON I must be impartial, though you are counsel for my side of the question. Were it not that you are so good as to allow him what he has not said, I should think it very hard you should answer him without hearing him. But gentlemen, I believe you have both considered this matter and are firm in your different opinions. 'Twere better therefore you proceeded according to the particular sense of each of you and gave your thoughts distinctly in writing. And do you see, sirs, pray let me have a copy of what you say, in English.

BRAMBLE Why, what is all we have been saying? In English! Oh! But I forgot myself, you're a wit. But however, to please you sir, you shall have it in as plain terms as the law will admit of.

CIMBERTON But I would have it, sir, without delay.

BRAMBLE That, sir, the law will not admit of. The courts are sitting at Westminster, and I am this moment obliged to be at every one of them, and 'twould be wrong if I should not be in the Hall to attend one of 'em at least; the rest would take it ill else. Therefore, I must leave what I have said to Mr. Serjeant's consideration, and I will digest his arguments on my part, and you shall hear from me again, sir.

Exit Bramble [Myrtle].

TARGET Agreed, agreed.

CIMBERTON Mr. Bramble is very quick. He parted a little abruptly.

TARGET He could not bear my argument; I pinched him to the quick about that Gr—gr—ber.

MRS. SEALAND I saw that, for he durst not so much as hear you—I shall send to you, Mr. Serjeant, as soon as Sir Geoffry comes to town, and then I hope all may be adjusted.

TARGET I shall be at my chambers at my usual hours.

Exit.

CIMBERTON Madam, if you please, I'll now attend you to the tea table, where I shall hear from your ladyship reason and good sense, after all this law and gibberish.

MRS. SEALAND 'Tis a wonderful thing, sir, that men of professions do not study to talk the substance of what they have to say in the language of the rest of the world. Sure, they'd find their account[5] in it.

CIMBERTON They might, perhaps, madam, with people of your good sense; but, with the generality 'twould never do. The vulgar would have no respect for truth and knowledge if they were exposed to naked view.

> Truth is too simple, of all art bereaved:
> Since the world will—why, let it be deceived.

Exeunt.

Act iv. Scene i.
Scene, Bevil Junior's *lodgings.*
Bevil Junior *with a letter in his hand, followed by* Tom.

TOM Upon my life, sir, I know nothing of the matter; I never opened my lips to Mr. Myrtle about anything of your honor's letter to Madam Lucinda.

BEVIL JUNIOR [*aside*] What's the fool in such a fright for? —I don't suppose you did. What I would know is whether Mr. Myrtle showed any suspicion or asked you any questions to lead you to say casually that you had carried any such letter for me this morning.

TOM Well, sir, if he did ask me any questions, how could I help it?

BEVIL JUNIOR I don't say you could, oaf! I am not questioning you, but him. What did he say to you?

TOM Why, sir, when I came to his chambers to be dressed for the lawyer's part your honor was pleased to put me upon, he asked me if I had been at Mr. Sealand's this morning. So I told him, sir, I often went thither, because, sir, if I had not said that, he might have thought there was something more in my going now than at another time.

BEVIL JUNIOR Very well. [*Aside.*] The fellow's caution, I find, has given him this jealousy. —Did he ask you no other questions?

TOM Yes sir, now I remember, as we came away in the hackney coach from Mr. Sealand's, "Tom," says he, "as I came in to your master this morning he bade you go for an answer to a letter he had sent. Pray did you bring him any?" says he. "Ah!" says I, "Sir, your honor is pleased to joke with me; you have a mind to know whether I can keep a secret or no?"

BEVIL JUNIOR And so, by showing him you could, you told him you had one?

TOM [*confused*] Sir—

BEVIL JUNIOR [*aside*] What mean actions does jealousy make a

5. Profit.

man stoop to! How poorly has he used art with a servant to make him betray his master!—Well! And when did he give you this letter for me?

TOM Sir, he writ it before he pulled off his lawyer's gown at his own chambers.

BEVIL JUNIOR Very well; and what did he say when you brought him my answer to it?

TOM He looked a little out of humour, sir, and said it was very well.

BEVIL JUNIOR I knew he would be grave upon't. Wait without.

TOM [*aside*] Humh! 'Gad, I don't like this; I am afraid we are all in the wrong box here.

Exit Tom.

BEVIL JUNIOR I put on a serenity while my fellow was present, but I have never been more thoroughly disturbed. This hot man! To write me a challenge on supposed artificial dealing when I professed myself his friend! I can live contented without glory, but I cannot suffer shame. What's to be done? But first, let me consider Lucinda's letter again.

Reads.

"Sir,

I hope it is consistent with the laws a woman ought to impose upon herself to acknowledge that your manner of declining a treaty of marriage in our family and desiring the refusal may come from hence has something more engaging in it than the courtship of him, who, I fear, will fall to my lot except your friend exerts himself for our common safety and happiness. I have reasons for desiring Mr. Myrtle may not know of this letter till hereafter and am your most obliged humble servant,

LUCINDA SEALAND."

Well, but the postscript.

Reads.

"I won't, upon second thoughts, hide anything from you. But my reason for concealing this is that Mr. Myrtle has a jealousy in his temper which gives me some terrors. But my esteem for him inclines me to hope that only an ill effect which sometimes accompanies a tender love, and what may be cured by a careful and unblamable conduct."

Thus has this lady made me her friend and confidant and put herself in a kind under my protection. I cannot tell him immediately the purport of her letter except I could cure him of the violent and untractable passion of jealousy and so serve him and her by disobeying her in the article of secrecy more than I should by complying with her directions. But then this dueling, which custom has imposed upon every man who would live with reputation and honor in the world—how must I preserve myself from imputations there? He'll, forsooth, call it, or think it fear if I explain without fighting. But his letter—I'll read it again.

Reads.

"Sir,

You have used me basely in corresponding and carrying on a treaty where you told me you were indifferent. I have changed my sword since I saw you, which advertisement I thought proper to send you against the next meeting between you and the injured

CHARLES MYRTLE."

Enter Tom.

TOM Mr. Myrtle, sir. Would your honor please to see him?

BEVIL JUNIOR Why you stupid creature! Let Mr. Myrtle wait at my lodgings! Show him up.

Exit Tom.

Well, I am resolved upon my carriage to him. He is in love, and in every circumstance of life a little distrustful, which I must allow for. But here he is.

Enter Tom *introducing* Myrtle.

Sir, I am extremely obliged to you for this honor. [*To* Tom.] But, sir, you, with your very discerning face, leave the room.

Exit Tom.

Well, Mr. Myrtle, your commands with me?

MYRTLE The time, the place, our long acquaintance, and many other circumstances which affect me on this occasion oblige me, without farther ceremony or conference, to desire you would not only, as you already have, acknowledge the receipt of my letter, but also comply with the request in it. I must have farther notice taken of my message than these half lines, "I have yours—I shall be at home—"

BEVIL JUNIOR Sir, I own I have received a letter from you in a very unusual style. But as I design everything in this matter shall be your own action, your own seeking, I shall understand nothing but what you are pleased to confirm face to face, and I have already forgot the contents of your epistle.

MYRTLE This cool manner is very agreeable to the abuse you have already made of my simplicity and frankness, and I see your moderation tends to your own advantage and not mine, to your own safety, not consideration of your friend.

BEVIL JUNIOR My own safety, Mr. Myrtle!

MYRTLE Your own safety, Mr. Bevil.

BEVIL JUNIOR Look you, Mr. Myrtle, there's no disguising that I understand what you would be at, but, sir, you know, I have often dared to disapprove of the decisions a tyrant custom has introduced to the breach of all laws, both divine and human.

MYRTLE Mr. Bevil, Mr. Bevil, it would be a good first principle in those who have so tender a conscience that way to have as much abhorrence of doing injuries as—

BEVIL JUNIOR As what?

MYRTLE As fear of answering for 'em.

BEVIL JUNIOR As fear of answering for 'em! But that apprehension is just or blamable according to the object of that fear. I have often told you in confidence of heart I abhorred the daring to defend the Author of Life and rushing into his presence—I say, by the very same act to commit the crime against him and immediately to urge on his tribunal.

MYRTLE Mr. Bevil, I must tell you, this coolness, this gravity, this show of conscience shall never cheat me of my mistress. You have, indeed, the best excuse for life, the hopes of possessing Lucinda. But consider, sir, I have as much reason to be weary of it if I am to lose her. And my first attempt to recover her shall be to let her see the dauntless man who is to be her guardian and protector.

BEVIL JUNIOR Sir, show me but the least glimpse of argument that I am authorized by my own hand to vindicate any lawless insult of this nature, and I will show thee—to chastise thee—hardly deserves the name of courage—slight, inconsiderate man! There is, Mr. Myrtle, no such terror in quick anger; and you shall, you know not why, be cool, as you have, you know not why, been warm.

MYRTLE Is the woman one loves so little an occasion of anger? You, perhaps, who know not what it is to love, who have your ready, your commodious, your foreign trinket for your loose hours, and from your fortune, your specious outward carriage, and other lucky circumstances, as easy a way to the possession of a woman of honor, you know nothing of what it is to be alarmed, to be distracted with anxiety and terror of losing more than life. Your marriage, happy man, goes on like common business, and in the interim you have your rambling captive, your Indian princess for your soft moments of dalliance, your convenient, your ready Indiana.

BEVIL JUNIOR You have touched me beyond the patience of a man, and I'm excusable, in the guard of innocence—or from the infirmity of human nature which can bear no more—to accept your invitation and observe your letter. Sir, I'll attend you.

Enter Tom.

TOM Did you call, sir? I thought you did; I heard you speak aloud.

BEVIL JUNIOR Yes, go call a coach.

TOM Sir—master—Mr. Myrtle—friends—gentlemen—what d'ye mean? I am but a servant, or—

BEVIL JUNIOR Call a coach.

Exit Tom.

A long pause, walking sullenly by each other.

[*Aside.*] Shall I, though provoked to the uttermost, recover myself at the entrance of a third person, and that my servant too, and not have respect enough to all I have ever been receiving from infancy, the obligation to the best of fathers, to an unhappy virgin too, whose life depends on mine?

Shutting the door.

[*To* Myrtle.] I have, thank Heaven, had time to recollect myself, and shall not, for fear of what such a rash man as you think of me, keep longer unexplained the false appearances under which your infirmity of temper makes you suffer, when, perhaps, too much regard to a false point of honor makes me prolong that suffering.

MYRTLE I am sure Mr. Bevil cannot doubt but I had rather have satisfaction from his innocence than his sword.

BEVIL JUNIOR Why then would you ask it first that way?

MYRTLE Consider, you kept your temper yourself no longer than till I spoke to the disadvantage of her you loved.

BEVIL JUNIOR True. But let me tell you, I have saved you from the most exquisite distress though you had succeeded in the dispute. I know you so well that I am sure to have found this letter about a man you had killed would have been worse than death to yourself. Read it. [*Aside.*] When he is thoroughly mortified and shame has got the better of jealousy, when he has seen himself throughly,[6] he will deserve to be assisted towards obtaining Lucinda.

MYRTLE [*aside*] With what a superiority has he turned the injury on me as the aggressor! I begin to fear I have been too far transported. "A treaty in our family!" Is not that saying too much? I shall relapse. But, I find, on the postscript, "something like jealousy"—with what face can I see my benefactor, my advocate, whom I have treated like a betrayer? —Oh! Bevil, with what words shall I—

BEVIL JUNIOR There needs none; to convince is much more than to conquer.

MYRTLE But can you—

BEVIL JUNIOR You have o'erpaid the inquietude you gave me in the change I see in you towards me. Alas, what machines are we! Thy face is altered to that of another man, to that of my companion, my friend.

MYRTLE That I could be such a precipitant wretch!

BEVIL JUNIOR Pray, no more.

MYRTLE Let me reflect how many friends have died by the hands of friends for want of temper. And you must give me leave to say again and again how much I am beholden to that superior spirit you have subdued me with. What had become of one of us, or perhaps both, had you been as weak as I was and as incapable of reason?

BEVIL JUNIOR I congratulate to us both the escape from ourselves and hope the memory of it will make us dearer friends than ever.

MYRTLE Dear Bevil, your friendly conduct has convinced me that there is nothing manly but what is conducted by reason and agreeable to the practice of virtue and justice. And yet, how many have been sacrificed to that idol, the unreasonable opinion of men! Nay, they are so ridiculous in it that they often use their swords against each other with dissembled anger and real fear.

> Betrayed by honor, and compelled by shame,
> They hazard being, to preserve a name:
> Nor dare inquire into the dread mistake,
> Till plunged in sad eternity they wake.   *Exeunt.*

Act IV. Scene ii.

Scene, St. James's Park. Enter Sir John Bevil *and* Mr. Sealand.

SIR JOHN BEVIL Give me leave, however, Mr. Sealand, as we are upon a treaty for uniting our families, to mention only the busi-

6. Thoroughly.

ness of an ancient house. Genealogy and descent are to be of some consideration in an affair of this sort—

MR. SEALAND Genealogy and descent! Sir, there has been in our family a very large one. There was Galfrid, the father of Edward, the father of Ptolemy, the father of Crassus, the father of Earl Richard, the father of Henry the Marquis, the father of Duke John—

SIR JOHN BEVIL What, do you rave, Mr. Sealand? All these great names in your family?

MR. SEALAND These? Yes sir, I have heard my father name 'em all, and more.

SIR JOHN BEVIL Ay, sir? And did he say they were all in your family?

MR. SEALAND Yes sir, he kept 'em all, he was the greatest cocker[7] in England. He said Duke John won him many battles and never lost one.

SIR JOHN BEVIL Oh sir, your servant, you are laughing at my laying any stress upon descent. But I must tell you, sir, I never knew anyone but he that wanted that advantage, turn it into ridicule.

MR. SEALAND And I never knew anyone who had many better advantages put that into his account. But, Sir John, value yourself as you please upon your ancient house, I am to talk freely of everything you are pleased to put into your bill of rates on this occasion. Yet, sir, I have made no objections to your son's family. 'Tis his morals that I doubt.

SIR JOHN BEVIL Sir, I can't help saying that what might injure a citizen's credit may be no stain to a gentleman's honor.

MR. SEALAND Sir John, the honor of a gentleman is liable to be tainted by as small a matter as the credit of a trader. We are talking of a marriage, and in such a case, the father of a young woman will not think it an addition to the honor or credit of her lover—that he is a keeper—

SIR JOHN BEVIL Mr. Sealand, don't take upon you to spoil my son's marriage with any woman else.

MR. SEALAND Sir John, let him apply to any woman else and have as many mistresses as he pleases—

SIR JOHN BEVIL My son, sir, is a discreet and sober gentleman—

MR. SEALAND Sir, I never saw a man that wenched soberly and discreetly that ever left it off. The decency observed in the practice hides even from the sinner the iniquity of it. They pursue it, not that their appetites hurry 'em away, but, I warrant you, because 'tis their opinion they may do it.

SIR JOHN BEVIL Were what you suspect a truth, do you design to keep your daughter a virgin till you find a man unblemished that way?

MR. SEALAND Sir, as much a cit[8] as you take me for, I know the town and the world. And give me leave to say that we merchants

7. Breeder of fighting cocks. for a middle-class merchant.
8. City tradesman; a contemptuous term

are a species of gentry that have grown into the world this last century, and are as honorable, and almost as useful, as you landed folks that have always thought yourselves so much above us. For your trading, forsooth, is extended no farther than a load of hay or a fat ox. You are pleasant people, indeed, because you are generally bred up to be lazy; therefore, I warrant you, industry is dishonorable.

SIR JOHN BEVIL Be not offended, sir; let us go back to our point.

MR. SEALAND Oh, not at all offended—but I don't love to leave any part of the account unclosed. Look you, Sir John, comparisons are odious, and more particularly so on occasions of this kind when we are projecting races that are to be made out of both sides of the comparisons.

SIR JOHN BEVIL But my son, sir, is, in the eye of the world, a gentleman of merit.

MR. SEALAND I own to you, I think him so. But, Sir John, I am a man exercised and experienced in chances and disasters. I lost, in my earlier years, a very fine wife, and with her a poor little infant; that makes me, perhaps, over-cautious to preserve the second bounty of Providence to me, and be as careful as I can of this child. You'll pardon me, my poor girl, sir, is as valuable to me as your boasted son to you.

SIR JOHN BEVIL Why, that's one very good reason, Mr. Sealand, why I wish my son had her.

MR. SEALAND There is nothing but this strange lady here, this *incognita,* that can be objected to him. Here and there a man falls in love with an artful creature and gives up all the motives of life to that one passion.

SIR JOHN BEVIL A man of my son's understanding cannot be supposed to be one of them.

MR. SEALAND Very wise men have been so enslaved; and when a man marries with one of them upon his hands, whether moved from the demand of the world or slighter reasons, such a husband soils[9] with his wife for a month perhaps, then good b'w'y', madam—the show's over. Ah! John Dryden points out such a husband to a hair where he says,

"And while abroad so prodigal the dolt is,
Poor spouse at home as ragged as a colt is."[1]

Now in plain terms, sir, I shall not care to have my poor girl turned a-grazing, and that must be the case when—

SIR JOHN BEVIL But pray consider, sir, my son—

MR. SEALAND Look you, sir, I'll make the matter short. This unknown lady, as I told you, is all the objection I have to him. But, one way or other, he is, or has been, certainly engaged to her. I am therefore resolved this very afternoon to visit her. Now

9. Cohabits.
1. From Dryden's epilogue to Vanbrugh's *The Pilgrim,* 1700. A similar couplet occurs in his prologue to Southerne's *The Disappointment,* 1684.

from her behavior or appearance, I shall soon be let into what I may fear or hope for.

SIR JOHN BEVIL Sir, I am very confident there can be nothing inquired into, relating to my son, that will not, upon being understood, turn to his advantage.

MR. SEALAND I hope that as sincerely as you believe it. Sir John Bevil, when I am satisfied in this great point, if your son's conduct answers the character you give him, I shall wish your alliance more than that of any gentleman in Great Britain, and so your servant.

Exit.

SIR JOHN BEVIL He is gone in a way but barely civil. But his great wealth and the merit of his only child, the heiress of it, are not to be lost for a little peevishness.

Enter Humphrey.

Oh, Humphrey, you are come in a seasonable minute. I want to talk to thee and to tell thee that my head and heart are on the rack about my son.

HUMPHREY Sir, you may trust his discretion; I am sure you may.

SIR JOHN BEVIL Why, I do believe I may, and yet I'm in a thousand fears when I lay this vast wealth before me. When I consider his prepossessions, either generous to a folly in an honorable love or abandoned past redemption in a vicious one, and from the one or the other, his insensibility to the fairest prospect towards doubling our estate, a father, who knows how useful wealth is, and how necessary, even to those who despise it, I say a father, Humphrey, a father cannot bear it.

HUMPHREY Be not transported, sir; you will grow incapable of taking any resolution in your perplexity.

SIR JOHN BEVIL Yet, as angry as I am with him, I would not have him surprised in anything. This mercantile rough man may go grossly into the examination of this matter and talk to the gentlewoman so as to—

HUMPHREY No, I hope, not in an abrupt manner.

SIR JOHN BEVIL No, I hope not. Why, dost thou know anything of her, or of him, or of anything of it, or all of it?

HUMPHREY My dear master, I know so much; that I told him this very day you had reason to be secretly out of humour about her.

SIR JOHN BEVIL Did you go so far? Well, what said he to that?

HUMPHREY His words were, looking upon me steadfastly, "Humphrey," says he, "that woman is a woman of honor."

SIR JOHN BEVIL How! Do you think he is married to her or designs to marry her?

HUMPHREY I can say nothing to the latter. But he says he can marry no one without your consent while you are living.

SIR JOHN BEVIL If he said so much, I know he scorns to break his word with me.

HUMPHREY I am sure of that.

SIR JOHN BEVIL You are sure of that—well, that's some comfort. Then I have nothing to do but to see the bottom of this matter during this present ruffle—oh, Humphrey—

HUMPHREY You are not ill, I hope, sir.

SIR JOHN BEVIL Yes, a man is very ill that's in a very ill humour. To be a father is to be in care for one whom you oftener disoblige than please by that very care. Oh, that sons could know the duty to a father before they themselves are fathers! But, perhaps, you'll say now that I am one of the happiest fathers in the world; but, I assure you, that of the very happiest is not a condition to be envied.

HUMPHREY Sir, your pain arises not from the thing itself but your particular sense of it—you are overfond, nay, give me leave to say, you are unjustly apprehensive from your fondness. My master Bevil never disobliged you, and he will, I know he will, do everything you ought to expect.

SIR JOHN BEVIL He won't take all this money with this girl. For aught I know, he will, forsooth, have so much moderation as to think he ought not to force his liking for any consideration.

HUMPHREY He is to marry her, not you; he is to live with her, not you, sir.

SIR JOHN BEVIL I know not what to think. But I know nothing can be more miserable than to be in this doubt. Follow me; I must come to some resolution.

Exeunt.

Act IV. Scene iii.

Scene, Bevil Junior's *lodgings. Enter* Tom *and* Phillis.

TOM Well, madam, if you must speak with Mr. Myrtle, you shall. He is now with my master in the library.

PHILLIS But you must leave me alone with him, for he can't make me a present, nor I so handsomely take anything from him before you; it would not be decent.

TOM It will be very decent, indeed, for me to retire and leave my mistress with another man.

PHILLIS He is a gentleman and will treat me properly.

TOM I believe so. But, however, I won't be far off and therefore will venture to trust you. I'll call him to you.

Exit Tom.

PHILLIS What a deal of pother and sputter here is between my mistress and Mr. Myrtle from mere punctilio![2] I could any hour of the day get her to her lover and would do it, but she, forsooth, will allow no plot to get him. But if he can come to her, I know she would be glad of it. I must therefore do her an acceptable violence and surprise her into his arms. I am sure I go by the best rule imaginable—if she were my maid, I should think her the best servant in the world for doing so by me.

Enter Myrtle *and* Tom.

Oh sir, you and Mr. Bevil are fine gentlemen to let a lady remain under such difficulties as my poor mistress, and no attempt to set her at liberty or release her from the danger of being instantly married to Cimberton.

2. Detail of conduct.

MYRTLE Tom has been telling. But what is to be done?

PHILLIS What is to be done—when a man can't come at his mistress! Why, can't you fire our house or the next house to us, to make us run out and you take us?

MYRTLE How, Mrs. Phillis—

PHILLIS Ay, let me see that rogue [*indicating* Tom] deny to fire a house, make a riot, or any other little thing, when there were no other way to come at me.

TOM I am obliged to you, madam.

PHILLIS Why, don't we hear every day of people's hanging themselves for love, and won't they venture the hazard of being hanged for love? Oh! Were I a man—

MYRTLE What manly thing would you have me undertake, according to your ladyship's notion of a man?

PHILLIS Only be at once what, one time or other, you may be, and wish to be, or must be.

MYRTLE Dear girl, talk plainly to me, and consider, I, in my condition, can't be in very good humour. You say, to be at once what I must be.

PHILLIS Ay, ay, I mean no more than to be an old man. I saw you do it very well at the masquerade. In a word, old Sir Geoffry Cimberton is every hour expected in town to join in the deeds and settlements for marrying Mr. Cimberton. He is half blind, half lame, half deaf, half dumb; though as to his passions and desires, he is as warm and ridiculous as when in the heat of youth—

TOM Come to the business, and don't keep the gentleman in suspense for the pleasure of being courted, as you serve me.

PHILLIS I saw you at the masquerade act such a one to perfection. Go and put on that very habit, and come to our house as Sir Geoffry. There is not one there but myself knows his person. I was born in the parish where he is lord of the manor. I have seen him often and often at church in the country. Do not hesitate, but come thither. They will think you bring a certain security against Mr. Myrtle, and you bring Mr. Myrtle. Leave the rest to me, I leave this with you, and expect— They don't, I told you, know you; they think you out of town, which you had as good be forever, if you lose this opportunity. I must be gone; I know I am wanted at home.

MYRTLE My dear Phillis!

Catches and kisses her, and gives her money.

PHILLIS Oh fie! My kisses are not my own; you have committed violence, but I'll carry 'em to the right owner.

Tom kisses her.

[*To* Tom.] Come, see me downstairs, and leave the lover to think of his last game for the prize.

Exeunt Tom *and* Phillis.

MYRTLE I think I will instantly attempt this wild expedient. The extravagance of it will make me less suspected, and it will give me opportunity to assert my own right to Lucinda, without whom I cannot live. But I am so mortified at this conduct of mine towards poor Bevil. He must think meanly of me. I know not how to reassume myself and be in spirit enough for such an adventure as this. Yet I must attempt it, if it be only to be near Lucinda under her present perplexities. And sure—

> The next delight to transport with the fair
> Is to relieve her in her hours of care. *Exit.*

Act V. *Scene i.*
Scene, Sealand's house. Enter Phillis *with lights before* Myrtle, *disguised like old Sir Geoffry, supported by* Mrs. Sealand, Lucinda, *and* Cimberton.

MRS. SEALAND Now I have seen you thus far, Sir Geoffry, will you excuse me a moment while I give my necessary orders for your accommodation?

Exit Mrs. Sealand.

MYRTLE I have not seen you, Cousin Cimberton, since you were ten years old, and as it is incumbent on you to keep up our name and family, I shall upon very reasonable terms join with you in a settlement to that purpose. Though I must tell you, cousin, this is the first merchant that has married into our house.

LUCINDA [*aside*] Deuce on 'em! Am I a merchant because my father is?

MYRTLE But is he directly a trader at this time?

CIMBERTON There's no hiding the disgrace, sir; he trades to all parts of the world.

MYRTLE We never had one of our family before who descended from persons that did anything.

CIMBERTON Sir, since it is a girl that they have, I am, for the honor of my family, willing to take it in again and to sink her into our name and no harm done.

MYRTLE 'Tis prudently and generously resolved. Is this the young thing?

CIMBERTON Yes sir.

PHILLIS [*aside to Lucinda*] Good madam, don't be out of humour but let them run to the utmost of their extravagance. Hear them out.

MYRTLE Can't I see her nearer? My eyes are but weak.

PHILLIS [*aside to* Lucinda] Besides, I am sure the uncle has something worth your notice, I'll take care to get off the young one and leave you to observe what may be wrought out of the old one for your good.

Exit.

CIMBERTON Madam, this old gentleman, your great-uncle, desires to be introduced to you and to see you nearer. Approach, sir.

MYRTLE By your leave, young lady— [*Puts on spectacles.*] Cousin Cimberton! She has exactly that sort of neck and bosom for which my sister Gertrude was so much admired in the year sixty-one before the French dresses first discovered anything in women below the chin.

LUCINDA [*aside*] What a very odd situation am I in! Though I cannot but be diverted at the extravagance of their humours, equally unsuitable to their age—chin, quotha—I don't believe my passionate lover there knows whether I have one or not. Ha! Ha!

MYRTLE Madam. I would not willingly offend, but I have a better glass—[3]
   Pulls out a large one.
   Enter Phillis *to* Cimberton.

PHILLIS Sir, my lady desires to show the apartment to you that she intends for Sir Geoffry.

CIMBERTON Well sir, by that time you have sufficiently gazed and sunned yourself in the beauties of my spouse there, I will wait on you again.
   Exit Cimberton *and* Phillis.

MYRTLE Were it not, madam, that I might be troublesome, there is something of importance, though we are alone, which I would say more safe from being heard.

LUCINDA [*aside*] There is something in this old fellow, methinks, that raises my curiosity.

MYRTLE To be free, madam, I as heartily condemn this kinsman of mine as you do and am sorry to see so much beauty and merit devoted by your parents to so insensible a possessor.

LUCINDA [*aside*] Surprising —I hope then, sir, you will not contribute to the wrong you are so generous as to pity, whatever may be the interest of your family.

MYRTLE This hand of mine shall never be employed to sign anything against your good and happiness.

LUCINDA I am sorry, sir, it is not in my power to make you proper acknowledgements, but there is a gentleman in the world whose gratitude will, I am sure, be worthy of the favor.

MYRTLE All the thanks I desire, madam, are in your power to give.

LUCINDA Name them, and command them.

MYRTLE Only, madam, that the first time you are alone with your lover, you will, with open arms, receive him.

LUCINDA As willingly as his heart could wish it.

MYRTLE Thus then he claims your promise! Oh, Lucinda!

LUCINDA Oh! A cheat! A cheat! A cheat!

MYRTLE Hush! 'Tis I, 'tis I, your lover, Myrtle himself, madam.

LUCINDA Oh bless me! What a rashness and folly to surprise me so —But hush—my mother—
   Enter Mrs. Sealand, Cimberton, *and* Phillis.

MRS. SEALAND How now! What's the matter?

LUCINDA Oh madam! As soon as you left the room, my uncle fell into a sudden fit, and—and—so I cried out for help, to support him, and conduct him to his chamber.

MRS. SEALAND That was kindly done! Alas! Sir, how do you find yourself?

MYRTLE Never was taken in so odd a way in my life. Pray lead me!

3. Optical instrument.

Oh! I was talking here—pray carry me—to my Cousin Cimberton's young lady—

MRS. SEALAND [*aside*] My Cousin Cimberton's young lady! How zealous he is, even in his extremity, for the match! A right Cimberton!

Cimberton *and* Lucinda *lead him, as one in pain, etc.*

CIMBERTON Pox! Uncle, you will pull my ear off.

LUCINDA Pray uncle! You will squeeze me to death.

MRS. SEALAND No matter, no matter, he knows not what he does. Come, sir, shall I help you out?

MYRTLE By no means; I'll trouble nobody but my young cousins here.

They lead him off.

PHILLIS But pray, madam, does your ladyship intend that Mr. Cimberton shall really marry my young mistress at last? I don't think he likes her.

MRS. SEALAND That's not material! Men of his speculation[4] are above desires. But be it as it may, now I have given old Sir Geoffry the trouble of coming up to sign and seal, with what countenance can I be off?

PHILLIS As well as with twenty others, madam. It is the glory and honor of a great fortune to live in continual treaties and still to break off. It looks great, madam.

MRS. SEALAND True, Phillis. Yet to return our blood again into the Cimbertons is an honor not to be rejected. But were not you saying that Sir John Bevil's creature Humphrey has been with Mr. Sealand?

PHILLIS Yes, madam: I overheard them agree that Mr. Sealand should go himself and visit this unknown lady that Mr. Bevil is so great with; and if he found nothing there to fright him, that Mr. Bevil should still marry my young mistress.

MRS. SEALAND How! Nay then, he shall find she is my daughter as well as his: I'll follow him this instant and take the whole family along with me. The disputed power of disposing of my own daughter shall be at an end this very night. I'll live no longer in anxiety for a little hussy that hurts my appearance wherever I carry her and for whose sake I seem to be not at all regarded, and that in the best of my days.

PHILLIS Indeed, madam, if she were married, your ladyship might very well be taken for Mr. Sealand's daughter.

MRS. SEALAND Nay, when the chit has not been with me, I have heard the men say as much. I'll no longer cut off the greatest pleasure of a woman's life, the shining in assemblies, by her forward anticipation of the respect that's due to her superior—she shall down to Cimberton-Hall—she shall—she shall.

PHILLIS I hope, madam, I shall stay with your ladyship.

MRS. SEALAND Thou shalt, Phillis, and I'll place thee then more about me. But order chairs immediately; I'll be gone this minute.

Exeunt.

4. Vision.

Act V. Scene ii.
Scene, Charing Cross. Enter Mr. Sealand *and* Humphrey.

MR. SEALAND I am very glad, Mr. Humphrey, that you agree with me that it is for our common good I should look thoroughly into this matter.

HUMPHREY I am indeed of that opinion, for there is no artifice, nothing concealed in our family which ought in justice to be known. I need not desire you, sir, to treat the lady with care and respect.

MR. SEALAND Master Humphrey, I shall not be rude, though I design to be a little abrupt and come into the matter at once to see how she will bear upon a surprise.

HUMPHREY That's the door, sir, I wish you success.

While Humphrey *speaks,* Mr. Sealand *consults his table-book.*[5]

[*Aside.*] I am less concerned what happens there because I hear Mr. Myrtle is well-lodged as old Sir Geoffry, so I am willing to let this gentleman employ himself here to give them time at home, for I am sure 'tis necessary for the quiet of our family Lucinda were disposed of out of it, since Mr. Bevil's inclination is so much otherwise engaged.

Exit.

MR. SEALAND I think this is the door.

Knocks.

I'll carry this matter with an air of authority to inquire, though I make an errand to begin discourse.

Knocks again, and enter a Footboy.

So young man! Is your lady within?

BOY Alack, sir! I am but a country boy—I dan't know whether she is or noa. But an you'll stay a bit, I'll goa and ask the gentle-woman that's with her.

MR. SEALAND Why, sirrah, though you are a country boy, you can see, can't you? You know whether she is at home when you see her, don't you?

BOY Nay, nay, I'm not such a country lad neither, master, to think she's at home because I see her. I have been in town but a month, and I lost one place already for believing my own eyes.

MR. SEALAND Why, sirrah! Have you learnt to lie already?

BOY Ah, master, things that are lies in the country are not lies at London—I begin to know my business a little better than so. But an you please to walk in, I'll call a gentlewoman to you that can tell you for certain; she can make bold to ask my lady herself.

MR. SEALAND O, then, she is within, I find, though you dare not say so.

BOY Nay, nay! That's neither here nor there. What's matter whether she is within or no if she has not a mind to see anybody?

MR. SEALAND I can't tell, sirrah, whether you are arch or simple, but however get me a direct answer and here's a shilling for you.

BOY Will you please to walk in? I'll see what I can do for you.

5. Notebook.

MR. SEALAND I see you will be fit for your business in time, child. But I expect to meet with nothing but extraordinaries in such a house.

BOY Such a house! Sir, you han't seen it yet. Pray walk in.

MR. SEALAND Sir, I'll wait upon you.

Exeunt.

Act V. Scene iii.

Scene, Indiana's *house. Enter* Isabella.

ISABELLA What anxiety do I feel for this poor creature! What will be the end of her? Such a languishing, unreserved passion for a man that at last must certainly leave or ruin her, and perhaps both! Then the aggravation of the distress is that she does not believe he will—not but, I must own, if they are both what they would seem, they are made for one another as much as Adam and Eve were, for there is no other of their kind but themselves.

Enter Boy.

So, Daniel! What news with you?

BOY Madam, there's a gentleman below would speak with my lady.

ISABELLA Sirrah, don't you know Mr. Bevil yet?

BOY Madam, 'tis not the gentleman who comes every day and asks for you and won't go in till he knows whether you are with her or no.

ISABELLA [*aside*] Ha! That's a particular I did not know before. —Well! Be it who it will, let him come up to me.

Exit Boy *and re-enters with* Mr. Sealand. Isabella *looks amazed.*

MR. SEALAND Madam, I can't blame your being a little surprised to see a perfect stranger make a visit and—

ISABELLA I am indeed surprised! [*Aside.*] I see he does not know me.

MR. SEALAND You are very prettily lodged here, madam; in troth, you seem to have everything in plenty. [*Aside, and looking about.*] A thousand a year, I warrant you, upon this pretty nest of rooms, and the dainty one within them.

ISABELLA [*aside*] Twenty years, it seems, have less effect in the alteration of a man of thirty than of a girl of fourteen; he's almost still the same. But alas! I find, by other men as well as himself, I am not what I was. As soon as he spoke, I was convinced 'twas he. How shall I contain my surprise and satisfaction? He must not know me yet.

MR. SEALAND Madam, I hope I don't give you any disturbance, but there is a young lady here with whom I have a particular business to discourse, and I hope she will admit me to that favor.

ISABELLA Why, sir, have you had any notice concerning her? I wonder who could give it you.

MR. SEALAND That, madam, is fit only to be communicated to herself.

ISABELLA Well, sir, you shall see her. [*Aside.*] I find he knows nothing yet nor shall from me. I am resolved I will observe this interlude, this sport of nature and of fortune. —You shall see her presently, sir; for now I am as a mother and will trust her with you.

Exit.

MR. SEALAND As a mother! Right; that's the old phrase for one of those commode⁶ ladies who lend out beauty for hire to young gentlemen that have pressing occasions. But here comes the precious lady herself. In troth, a very sightly woman—

Enter Indiana.

INDIANA I am told, sir, you have some affair that requires your speaking with me.

MR. SEALAND Yes, madam. There came to my hands a bill drawn by Mr. Bevil which is payable tomorrow, and he, in the intercourse of business, sent it to me, who have cash of his, and desired me to send a servant with it, but I have made bold to bring you the money myself.

INDIANA Sir, was that necessary?

MR. SEALAND No, madam; but, to be free with you, the fame of your beauty and the regard which Mr. Bevil is a little too well known to have for you excited my curiosity.

INDIANA Too well known to have for me! Your sober appearance, sir, which my friend described, made me expect no rudeness or absurdity at least—who's there? Sir, if you pay the money to a servant, 'twill be as well.

MR. SEALAND Pray, madam, be not offended. I came hither on an innocent, nay a virtuous design; and, if you will have patience to hear me, it may be as useful to you, as you are in a friendship with Mr. Bevil, as to my only daughter, whom I was this day disposing of.

INDIANA You make me hope, sir, I have mistaken you; I am composed again. Be free, say on— [*aside*] what I am afraid to hear—

MR. SEALAND I feared, indeed, an unwarranted passion here, but I did not think it was in abuse of so worthy an object, so accomplished a lady as your sense and mien bespeak. But the youth of our age care not what merit and virtue they bring to shame, so they gratify—

INDIANA Sir, you are going into very great errors. But, as you are pleased to say you see something in me that has changed, at least, the color of your suspicions, so has your appearance altered mine and made me earnestly attentive to what has any way concerned you to inquire into my affairs and character.

MR. SEALAND [*aside*] How sensibly, with what an air she talks!

INDIANA Good sir, be seated, and tell me tenderly—keep all your suspicions concerning me alive that you may in a proper and prepared way—acquaint me why the care of your daughter obliges a person of your seeming worth and fortune to be thus inquisitive about a wretched, helpless, friendless— [*Weeping.*] But I beg your pardon—though I am an orphan, your child is not; and your concern for her, it seems, has brought you hither. I'll be composed. Pray go on, sir.

6. Accommodating.

MR. SEALAND How could Mr. Bevil be such a monster to injure such a woman?

INDIANA No, sir, you wrong him. He has not injured me; my support is from his bounty.

MR. SEALAND Bounty! When gluttons give high prices for delicates, they are prodigious bountiful.

INDIANA Still, still you will persist in that error. But my own fears tell me all: you are the gentleman, I suppose, for whose happy daughter he is designed a husband by his good father, and he has, perhaps, consented to the overture. He was here this morning dressed beyond his usual plainness, nay, most sumptuously, and he is to be, perhaps, this night a bridegroom.

MR. SEALAND I own he was intended such. But, madam, on your account I have determined to defer my daughter's marriage till I am satisfied from your own mouth of what nature are the obligations you are under to him.

INDIANA His actions, sir, his eyes have only made me think he designed to make me the partner of his heart. The goodness and gentleness of his demeanor made me misinterpret all. 'Twas my own hope, my own passion, that deluded me. He never made one amorous advance to me. His large heart and bestowing hand have only helped the miserable. Nor know I why but from his mere delight in virtue that I have been his care, the object on which to indulge and please himself with pouring favors.

MR. SEALAND Madam, I know not why it is, but I, as well as you, am methinks afraid of entering into the matter I came about; but 'tis the same thing as if we had talked never so distinctly—he ne'er shall have a daughter of mine.

INDIANA If you say this from what you think of me, you wrong yourself and him. Let not me, miserable though I may be, do injury to my benefactor. No, sir, my treatment ought rather to reconcile you to his virtues. If to bestow, without a prospect of return, if to delight in supporting what might, perhaps, be thought an object of desire with no other view than to be her guard against those who would not be so disinterested, if these actions, sir, can in a careful parent's eye commend him to a daughter, give yours, sir, give her to my honest, generous Bevil. What have I to do but sigh, and weep, to rave, run wild, a lunatic in chains, or, hid in darkness, mutter in distracted starts and broken accents my strange, strange story!

MR. SEALAND Take comfort, madam.

INDIANA All my comfort must be to expostulate in madness, to relieve with frenzy my despair, and, shrieking, to demand of fate why—why was I born to such variety of sorrows?

MR. SEALAND If I have been the least occasion—

INDIANA No, 'twas Heaven's high will I should be such—to be plundered in my cradle! Tossed on the seas! And even there, an infant captive! To lose my mother, hear but of my father! To be adopted! Lose my adopter! Then plunged again in worse calamities!

MR. SEALAND An infant captive!

INDIANA Yet then to find the most charming of mankind once more to set me free from what I thought the last distress, to load me with his services, his bounties, and his favors; to support my very life in a way that stole at the same time my very soul itself from me.

MR. SEALAND And has young Bevil been this worthy man?

INDIANA Yet then again, this very man to take another! Without leaving me the right, the pretense of easing my fond heart with tears! For oh, I can't reproach him, though the same hand that raised me to this height now throws me down the precipice.

MR. SEALAND Dear lady! Oh, yet one moment's patience. My heart grows full with your affliction. But yet, there's something in your story that—

INDIANA My portion here is bitterness and sorrow.

MR. SEALAND Do not think so. Pray answer me, does Bevil know your name and family?

INDIANA Alas, too well! Oh, could I be any other thing than what I am—I'll tear away all traces of my former self, my little ornaments, the remains of my first state, the hints of what I ought to have been—

In her disorder she throws away a bracelet, which Mr. Sealand *takes up, and looks earnestly on it.*

MR. SEALAND Ha! What's this? My eyes are not deceived? It is, it is the same! The very bracelet which I bequeathed my wife at our last mournful parting.

INDIANA What said you, sir? Your wife! Whither does my fancy carry me? What means this unfelt motion at my heart? And yet again my fortune but deludes me, for if I err not, sir, your name is Sealand, but my lost father's name was—

MR. SEALAND Danvers! Was it not?

INDIANA What new amazement! That is indeed my family.

MR. SEALAND Know then, when my misfortunes drove me to the Indies, for reasons too tedious now to mention, I changed my name of Danvers into Sealand.

Enter Isabella.

ISABELLA If yet there wants an explanation of your wonder, examine well this face—yours, sir, I well remember—gaze on, and read, in me, your sister Isabella!

MR. SEALAND My sister!

ISABELLA But here's a claim more tender yet—your Indiana, sir, your long lost daughter.

MR. SEALAND Oh, my child! My child!

INDIANA All-gracious Heavens! Is it possible? Do I embrace my father?

MR. SEALAND And do I hold thee—these passions are too strong for utterance—rise, rise, my child, and give my tears their way—Oh, my sister!

Embracing her.

ISABELLA Now, dearest niece, my groundless fears, my painful cares no more shall vex thee. If I have wronged thy noble lover with too hard suspicions, my just concern for thee, I hope, will plead my pardon.

MR. SEALAND Oh! Make him then the full amends and be yourself the messenger of joy. Fly this instant! Tell him all these wondrous turns of Providence in his favor! Tell him I have now a daughter to bestow which he no longer will decline, that this day he still shall be a bridegroom, nor shall a fortune, the merit which his father seeks, be wanting. Tell him the reward of all his virtues waits on his acceptance.

Exit Isabella.

My dearest Indiana!
Turns, and embraces her.

INDIANA Have I then at last a father's sanction on my love? His bounteous hand to give and make my heart a present worthy of Bevil's generosity?

MR. SEALAND Oh my child! How are our sorrows past o'erpaid by such a meeting! Though I have lost so many years of soft paternal dalliance with thee, yet, in one day, to find thee thus, and thus bestow thee in such perfect happiness is ample, ample reparation! And yet again the merit of thy lover—

INDIANA Oh! Had I spirits left to tell you of his actions, how strongly filial duty has suppressed his love, and how concealment still has doubled all his obligations, the pride, the joy of his alliance, sir, would warm your heart as he has conquered mine.

MR. SEALAND How laudable is love when born of virtue! I burn to embrace him—

INDIANA See, sir, my aunt already has succeeded and brought him to your wishes.

Enter Isabella, *with* Sir John Bevil, Bevil Junior, Mrs. Sealand, Cimberton, Myrtle, *and* Lucinda.

SIR JOHN BEVIL [*entering*] Where? Where's this scene of wonder? Mr. Sealand, I congratulate, on this occasion, our mutual happiness. Your good sister, sir, has, with the story of your daughter's fortune, filled us with surprise and joy. Now all exceptions are removed. My son has now avowed his love and turned all former jealousies and doubts to approbation, and, I am told, your goodness has consented to reward him.

MR. SEALAND If, sir, a fortune equal to his father's hopes can make this object worthy his acceptance.

BEVIL JUNIOR I hear your mention, sir, of fortune with pleasure only as it may prove the means to reconcile the best of fathers to my love. Let him be provident, but let me be happy. —My everdestined, my acknowledged wife!
Embracing Indiana.

INDIANA Wife! Oh, my ever loved, my lord, my master!

SIR JOHN BEVIL [*to* Indiana] I congratulate myself as well as you that I had a son who could, under such disadvantages, discover your great merit.

MR. SEALAND Oh, Sir John, how vain, how weak is human prudence!

What care, what foresight, what imagination could contrive such blest events to make our children happy as Providence in one short hour has laid before us?

CIMBERTON [*to Mrs. Sealand*] I am afraid, madam, Mr. Sealand is a little too busy for our affair. If you please, we'll take another opportunity.

MRS. SEALAND Let us have patience, sir.

CIMBERTON But we make Sir Geoffry wait, madam.

MYRTLE Oh, sir! I am not in haste.

During this, Bevil Junior *presents* Lucinda *to* Indiana.

MR. SEALAND But here! Here's our general benefactor. Excellent young man that could be at once a lover to her beauty and a parent to her virtue.

BEVIL JUNIOR If you think that an obligation, sir, give me leave to overpay myself in the only instance that can now add to my felicity, by begging you to bestow this lady on Mr. Myrtle.

MR. SEALAND She is his without reserve; I beg he may be sent for. Mr. Cimberton, notwithstanding you never had my consent, yet there is, since I last saw you, another objection to your marriage with my daughter.

CIMBERTON I hope, sir, your lady has concealed nothing from me.

MR. SEALAND Troth, sir, nothing but what was concealed from myself—another daughter, who has an undoubted title to half my estate.

CIMBERTON How, Mr. Sealand! Why then if half Mrs. Lucinda's fortune is gone, you can't say that any of my estate is settled upon her. I was in treaty for the whole, but if that is not to be come at, to be sure, there can be no bargain. Sir, I have nothing to do but to take my leave of your good lady, my cousin, and beg pardon for the trouble I have given this old gentleman.

MYRTLE That you have, Mr. Cimberton, with all my heart.

Discovers himself.

OMNES Mr. Myrtle!

MYRTLE And I beg pardon of the whole company that I assumed the person of Sir Geoffry only to be present at the danger of this lady's being disposed of and in her utmost exigence to assert my right to her. Which if her parents will ratify, as they once favored my pretensions, no abatement of fortune shall lessen her value to me.

LUCINDA Generous man!

MR. SEALAND If, sir, you can overlook the injury of being in treaty with one who as meanly left her as you have generously asserted your right in her, she is yours.

LUCINDA Mr. Myrtle, though you have ever had my heart, yet now I find I love you more because I bring you less.

MYRTLE We have much more than we want, and I am glad any event has contributed to the discovery of our real inclinations to each other.

MRS. SEALAND [*aside*] Well! However I'm glad the girl's disposed of any way.

BEVIL JUNIOR Myrtle! No longer rivals now, but brothers.

MYRTLE Dear Bevil! You are born to triumph over me! But now our competition ceases. I rejoice in the pre-eminence of your virtue and your alliance adds charms to Lucinda.

SIR JOHN BEVIL Now, ladies and gentlemen, you have set the world a fair example. Your happiness is owing to your constancy and merit, and the several difficulties you have struggled with evidently show

> Whate'er the generous mind itself denies
> The secret care of Providence supplies.

Exeunt.

Epilogue[7]

Spoken by Mrs. Oldfield[8]

Now, I presume, our moralizing knight
Is heartily convinced my sense was right:
  I told him, flat, his Conscious Lovers' passion
Had, many ages past, been out of fashion.
That all attempts to mend the mode were shallow,
Our man in favor now's a pretty fellow
That talks and laughs and sings, fights, dances, dresses,
Rakes with an air, and keeps his string of misses,
Then to his fame such courage too belongs
That when by rivals called to account for wrongs,
Ne'er stands to talk but—hah—whips 'em through the lungs.
  Not like his Bevil—coolly waits his season,
And traps determined courage into reason;
Nor loves like him, poor soul, confined to one!
And is at vast expense—for nothing done!
To pass whole days alone and never meddle,
Treat her with senseless solo—on the fiddle!
And all this chaste restraint, forsooth, to flow
From strait obedience to a father due!
T'have shown his modern breeding, he should rather
Not have obeyed, but bit the put,[9] his father;
Or, in compliance to his daddy's courting,
Have starved his dear, and fairly took the fortune.
But to maintain her, and not let her know it—
Oh! the wild—crack-brained notions of a poet!
What though his hero never loved before,
He might have, sure, done less for her—or more.
  With scenes of this coarse kind, he owns that plays

7. This epilogue, spoken on the opening night, was not printed with the play and first appeared in Benjamin Victor's *Epistle to Sir Richard Steele* (2nd edition, 1722). Welsted's epilogue, which follows, was originally published with the play.
8. Who played Indiana.
9. "Bit the put" means "fooled the blockhead."

Too often have beguiled you of your praise:
Where sense and virtue were allowed no part,
That only touched the loose and wanton heart.
If then a diff'rent way of thinking might   ⎱
Incline the chaste to hear, the learned to write, ⎰
On you it rests—to make your profit your delight. ⎰

Epilogue

By Mr. Welsted
Intended to be Spoken by Indiana

Our author, whom entreaties cannot move,
Spite of the dear coquetry that you love,
Swears he'll not frustrate, so he plainly means,
By a loose epilogue his decent scenes.
Is it not, sirs, hard fate I meet today,   ⎱
To keep me rigid[1] still beyond the play? ⎰
And yet I'm saved a world of pains that way. ⎰
I now can look, I now can move at ease,
Nor need I torture these poor limbs to please;
Nor with the hand or foot attempt surprise,
Nor wrest my features, nor fatigue my eyes.
Bless me! What freakish gambols have I played!
What motions tried and wanton looks betrayed!
Out of pure kindness all! to over-rule
The threatened hiss, and screen some scribbling fool.
With more respect I'm entertained tonight:
Our author thinks I can with ease delight.
My artless looks while modest graces arm,
He says, I need but to appear, and charm.
A wife so formed, by these examples bred,
Pours joy and gladness 'round the marriage bed;
Soft source of comfort, kind relief from care,
And 'tis her least perfection to be fair.
The nymph with Indiana's worth who vies
A nation will behold with Bevil's eyes.

1. Strait-laced, moral.

RICHARD BRINSLEY SHERIDAN

The School for Scandal†

Prologue

Spoken by Mr. King[1]

Written by D. Garrick, Esq.[2]

A School for Scandal! tell me, I beseech you,
Needs there a school this modish art to teach you?
No need of lessons now, the knowing think—
We might as well be taught to eat and drink.
Caused by a dearth of scandal, should the vapors
Distress our fair ones—let 'em read the papers;
Their pow'rful mixtures such disorders hit;
Crave what they will, there's *quantum sufficit.*[3]
   "Lord!" cries my Lady Wormwood (who loves tattle,
And puts much salt and pepper in her prattle),
Just ris'n at noon, all night at cards when threshing
Strong tea and scandal—"Bless me, how refreshing!
Give me the papers, Lisp—how bold and free! (*Sips.*)
Last night Lord L——(sips) was caught with Lady D——
For aching heads what charming sal volatile! (*Sips.*)
If Mrs. B.——will still continue flirting,
We hope she'll DRAW, *or we'll* UNDRAW *the curtain.*
Fine satire, poz[4]—in public all abuse it,
But, by ourselves (*sips*), our praise we can't refuse it.
Now, Lisp, *read you*—there, at that dash and star."[5]
   "Yes, ma'am.—*A certain Lord had best beware,*
Who lives not twenty miles from Grosv'nor Square;
For should he Lady W——find willing,
WORMWOOD *is bitter"*—"Oh! that's me! the villain!
Throw it behind the fire, and never more

---

† First performed in 1777. Sheridan did not authorize publication, and the versions printed during his lifetime were in various degrees spurious. The most authoritative texts occur in manuscripts with corrections in Sheridan's hand, especially in a copy which Sheridan presented to Lady Crewe in 1777.
1. Who played Sir Peter Teazle.
2. David Garrick, the most famous actor of his age.
3. As much as suffices.
4. Slang for "positively."
5. With a dash and star the middle letters of a person's name were obscured in published gossip columns, as a way of avoiding libel suits.

Let that vile paper come within my door."—
    Thus at our friends we laugh, who feel the dart;
    To reach our feelings, we ourselves must smart.
    Is our young bard so young, to think that he
    Can stop the full spring-tide of calumny?
    Knows he the world so little, and its trade?
    Alas! the devil is sooner raised than laid.
    So strong, so swift, the monster there's no gagging:
    Cut Scandal's head off—still the tongue is wagging.
    Proud of your smiles once lavishly bestow'd,
    Again your young Don Quixote takes the road:
    To show his gratitude, he draws his pen,
    And seeks this hydra,[6] Scandal, in his den.
For your applause all perils he would through—
He'll fight—that's *write*—a cavalliero true,
Till every drop of blood—that's *ink*—is spilt for you.

Dramatis Personae

Men

SIR PETER TEAZLE	*Mr. King*
SIR OLIVER SURFACE	*Mr. Yates*
JOSEPH SURFACE	*Mr. Palmer*
CHARLES SURFACE	*Mr. Smith*
CRABTREE	*Mr. Parsons*
SIR BENJAMIN BACKBITE	*Mr. Dodd*
ROWLEY	*Mr. Aickin*
TRIP	*Mr. LaMash*
MOSES	*Mr. Baddeley*
SNAKE	*Mr. Packer*
CARELESS	*Mr. Farren*

and other Companions to CHARLES [SURFACE],
Servants, etc.

Women

LADY TEAZLE	*Mrs. Abington*
MARIA	*Miss P. Hopkins*
LADY SNEERWELL	*Miss Sherry*
MRS. CANDOUR	*Miss Pope*

The School for Scandal

Act I. Scene 1.
[Lady Sneerwell's *house*.]

---

6. A fabled snake whose many heads grew again as soon as they were cut off.

Lady Sneerwell *at the dressing-table*—Snake *drinking chocolate.*

LADY SNEERWELL The paragraphs, you say, Mr. Snake, were all inserted?

SNAKE They were, madam, and as I copied them myself in a feigned hand, there can be no suspicion whence they came.

LADY SNEERWELL Did you circulate the reports of Lady *Brittle's* intrigue with Captain *Boastall?*

SNAKE That is in as fine a train as your ladyship could wish,—in the common sense of things, I think it must reach Mrs. *Clackit's* ears within four-and-twenty hours; and then, you know, the business is as good as done.

LADY SNEERWELL Why, truly, Mrs. *Clackit* has a very pretty talent, and a great deal of industry.

SNAKE True, madam, and has been tolerably successful in her day: —to my knowledge, she has been the cause of six matches being broken off, and three sons being disinherited, of four forced elopements, as many close confinements, nine separate maintenances, and two divorces;—nay, I have more than once traced her causing a *Tête-à-Tête* in the *Town and Country Magazine,*[7] when the parties perhaps had never seen each other's faces before in the course of their lives.

LADY SNEERWELL She certainly has talents, but her manner is gross.

SNAKE 'Tis very true,—she generally designs well, has a free tongue, and a bold invention; but her coloring is too dark, and her outline often extravagant. She wants that *delicacy* of *hint,* and *mellowness* of *sneer,* which distinguish your ladyship's scandal.

LADY SNEERWELL Ah! you are partial, Snake.

SNAKE Not in the least; everybody allows that Lady *Sneerwell* can do more with a *word* or a *look* than many can with the most labored detail, even when they happen to have a little truth on their side to support it.

LADY SNEERWELL Yes, my dear Snake; and I am no hypocrite to deny the satisfaction I reap from the success of my efforts. Wounded myself, in the early part of my life, by the envenomed tongue of slander, I confess I have since known no pleasure equal to the reducing others to the level of my own injured reputation.

SNAKE Nothing can be more natural. But, Lady Sneerwell, there is one affair in which you have lately employed me, wherein, I confess, I am at a loss to guess your motives.

LADY SNEERWELL I conceive you mean with respect to my neighbor, Sir Peter Teazle, and his family?

SNAKE I do; here are two young men, to whom Sir Peter has acted as a kind of guardian since their father's death; the elder possessing the most amiable character, and universally well spoken of; the youngest, the most dissipated and extravagant young fellow in the kingdom, without friends or character,—the former an avowed admirer of your ladyship, and apparently your favorite;

---

7. The scandal column in this magazine was entitled "Tête-à-Tête."

the latter attached to Maria, Sir Peter's ward, and confessedly beloved by her. Now, on the face of these circumstances, it is utterly unaccountable to me, why you, the widow of a city knight, with a good jointure,[8] should not close with the passion of a man of such character and expectations as Mr. *Surface*; and more so why you should be so uncommonly earnest to destroy the mutual attachment subsisting between his brother *Charles* and *Maria*.

LADY SNEERWELL Then, at once to unravel this mystery, I must inform you that love has no share whatever in the intercourse between Mr. *Surface* and me.

SNAKE No!

LADY SNEERWELL His real attachment is to *Maria*, or her fortune; but, finding in his brother a favored rival, he has been obliged to mask his pretensions, and profit by my assistance.

SNAKE Yet still I am more puzzled why you should interest yourself in his success.

LADY SNEERWELL Heav'ns! how dull you are! Cannot you surmise the weakness which I hitherto, through shame, have concealed even from *you*? Must I confess that *Charles*—that libertine, that extravagant, that bankrupt fortune and reputation—that he it is for whom I am thus anxious and malicious, and to gain whom I would sacrifice everything?

SNAKE Now, indeed, your conduct appears consistent; but how came you and Mr. *Surface* so confidential?

LADY SNEERWELL For our mutual interest. I have found him out a long time since—I know him to be artful, selfish, and malicious—in short, a sentimental knave.

SNAKE Yet, Sir Peter vows he has not his equal in England—and, above all, he praises him as a man of sentiment.

LADY SNEERWELL True; and with the assistance of his sentiment and hypocrisy he has brought him [Sir Peter] entirely into his interest with regard to *Maria*.

Enter Servant.

SERVANT Mr. Surface.

LADY SNEERWELL Show him up.

Exit Servant.

He generally calls about this time. I don't wonder at people's giving him to me for a lover.

Enter Joseph Surface.

JOSEPH SURFACE My dear Lady Sneerwell, how do you do to-day? Mr. Snake, your most obedient.

LADY SNEERWELL Snake has just been arraigning me on our mutual attachment, but I have informed him of our real views; you know how useful he has been to us; and, believe me, the confidence is not ill placed.

JOSEPH SURFACE Madam, it is impossible for me to suspect a man of Mr. *Snake's* sensibility and discernment.

8. Property settled upon a woman at marriage which becomes hers in widowhood.

LADY SNEERWELL Well, well, no compliments now;—but tell me when you saw your mistress, *Maria*—or, what is more material to me, your brother.

JOSEPH SURFACE I have not seen either since I left you; but I can inform you that they never meet. Some of your stories have taken a good effect on Maria.

LADY SNEERWELL Ah, my dear Snake! the merit of this belongs to you. But do your brother's distresses increase?

JOSEPH SURFACE Every hour;—I am told he has had another execution[9] in the house yesterday; in short, his dissipation and extravagance exceed any thing I ever heard of.

LADY SNEERWELL Poor Charles!

JOSEPH SURFACE True, madam;—notwithstanding his vices, one can't help feeling for him.—Aye, poor Charles! I'm sure I wish it was in *my* power to be of any essential service to him.—For the man who does not share in the distress of a brother, even though merited by his own misconduct, deserves——

LADY SNEERWELL O lud! you are going to be moral, and forget that you are among friends.

JOSEPH SURFACE Egad, that's true!—I'll keep that sentiment till I see Sir Peter. However, it is certainly a charity to rescue *Maria* from such a libertine, who, if he is to be reclaimed, can be so only by a person of your ladyship's superior accomplishments and understanding.

SNAKE I believe, Lady Sneerwell, here's company coming,—I'll go and copy the letter I mentioned to you.—Mr. Surface, your most obedient.

Exit Snake.

JOSEPH SURFACE Sir, your very devoted.—Lady Sneerwell, I am very sorry you have put any further confidence in that fellow.

LADY SNEERWELL Why so?

JOSEPH SURFACE I have lately detected him in frequent conference with old *Rowley*, who was formerly my father's steward, and has never, you know, been a friend of mine.

LADY SNEERWELL And do you think he would betray us?

JOSEPH SURFACE Nothing more likely: take my word for't, Lady Sneerwell, that fellow hasn't virtue enough to be faithful even to his own villainy.—Hah! Maria!

Enter Maria.

LADY SNEERWELL Maria, my dear, how do you do?—What's the matter?

MARIA Oh! there is that disagreeable lover of mine, Sir *Benjamin Backbite*, has just called at my guardian's, with his odious uncle, *Crabtree*; so I slipped out, and ran hither to avoid them.

LADY SNEERWELL Is that all?

JOSEPH SURFACE If my brother *Charles* had been of the party, ma'am, perhaps you would not have been so much alarmed.

LADY SNEERWELL Nay, now you are severe; for I dare swear the truth of the matter is, Maria heard *you* were here;—but, my dear,

9. Legal seizure of a debtor's goods in default of payment.

what has Sir Benjamin done, that you should avoid him so?

MARIA Oh, he has done nothing—but 'tis for what he has said,—his conversation is a perpetual libel on all his acquaintance.

JOSEPH SURFACE Aye, and the worst of it is, there is no advantage in not knowing him; for he'll abuse a stranger just as soon as his best friend—and his uncle's as bad.

LADY SNEERWELL Nay, but we should make allowance; Sir Benjamin is a wit and a poet.

MARIA For my part, I own, madam, wit loses its respect with me, when I see it in company with malice.—What do you think, Mr. Surface?

JOSEPH SURFACE Certainly, madam; to smile at the jest which plants a thorn in another's breast is to become a principal in the mischief.

LADY SNEERWELL Pshaw! there's no possibility of being witty without a little ill nature: the malice of a good thing is the barb that makes it stick.—What's your opinion, Mr. Surface?

JOSEPH SURFACE To be sure, madam, that conversation, where the spirit of raillery is suppressed, will ever appear tedious and insipid.

MARIA Well, I'll not debate how far scandal may be allowable; but in a man, I am sure, it is always contemptible.—We have pride, envy, rivalship, and a thousand motives to depreciate each other; but the male slanderer must have the cowardice of a woman before he can traduce one.

Enter Servant.

SERVANT Madam, Mrs. Candour is below, and, if your ladyship's at leisure, will leave her carriage.

LADY SNEERWELL Beg her to walk in.

Exit Servant.

Now Maria, however here is a character to your taste; for though Mrs. Candour is a little talkative, everybody allows her to be the best-natured and best sort of woman.

MARIA Yes, with a very gross affectation of good nature and benevolence, she does more mischief than the direct malice of old Crabtree.

JOSEPH SURFACE I'faith 'tis very true, Lady Sneerwell; whenever I hear the current running against the characters of my friends, I never think them in such danger as when Candour undertakes their defence.

LADY SNEERWELL Hush!—here she is!

Enter Mrs. Candour.

MRS. CANDOUR My dear Lady Sneerwell, how have you been this century?—Mr. Surface, what news do you hear?—though indeed it is no matter, for I think one hears nothing else but scandal.

JOSEPH SURFACE Just so, indeed, madam.

MRS. CANDOUR Ah, Maria! child,—what, is the whole affair off between you and Charles? His extravagance, I presume—the town talks of nothing else.

MARIA I am very sorry, ma'am, the town has so little to do.

MRS. CANDOUR True, true, child: but there is no stopping people's tongues.—I own I was hurt to hear it, as indeed I was to learn, from the same quarter, that your guardian, Sir Peter, and Lady Teazle have not agreed lately so well as could be wished.

MARIA 'Tis strangely impertinent for people to busy themselves so.

MRS. CANDOUR Very true, child, but what's to be done? People will talk—there's no preventing it.—Why, it was but yesterday I was told that Miss Gadabout had eloped with Sir Filigree Flirt.—But, Lord! there's no minding what one hears—though, to be sure, I had this from very good authority.

MARIA Such reports are highly scandalous.

MRS. CANDOUR So they are, child—shameful, shameful! But the world is so censorious, no character escapes.—Lord, now who would have suspected your friend, Miss Prim, of an indiscretion? Yet such is the ill-nature of people, that they say her uncle stopped her last week, just as she was stepping into the York Diligence[1] with her dancing-master.

MARIA I'll answer for't there are no grounds for the report.

MRS. CANDOUR Oh, no foundation in the world, I dare swear; no more, probably, than for the story circulated last month, of Mrs. Festino's affair with Colonel Cassino;—though, to be sure, that matter was never rightly cleared up.

JOSEPH SURFACE The license of invention some people take is monstrous indeed.

MARIA 'Tis so.—But, in my opinion, those who report such things are equally culpable.

MRS. CANDOUR To be sure they are; tale-bearers are as bad as the tale-makers—'tis an old observation, and a very true one—but what's to be done, as I said before? how will you prevent people from talking?—To-day, Mrs. Clackit assured me Mr. and Mrs. Honeymoon were at last become mere man and wife, like the rest of their acquaintances.—She likewise hinted that a certain widow, in the next street, had got rid of her dropsy and recovered her shape in a most surprising manner. And at the same time Miss Tattle, who was by, affirmed that Lord Buffalo had discovered his lady at a house of no extraordinary fame—and that Sir Harry Bouquet and Tom Saunter were to measure swords on a similar provocation. But, Lord, do you think I would report these things! No, no! tale-bearers, as I said before, are just as bad as tale-makers.

JOSEPH SURFACE Ah! Mrs. Candour, if everybody had your forbearance and good nature!

MRS. CANDOUR I confess, Mr. Surface, I cannot bear to hear people attacked behind their backs, and when ugly circumstances come out against one's acquaintance I own I always love to think the best.—By the bye, I hope it is not true that your brother is absolutely ruined?

JOSEPH SURFACE I am afraid his circumstances are very bad indeed, ma'am.

MRS. CANDOUR Ah!—I heard so—but you must tell him to keep up his spirits—everybody almost is in the same way! Lord Spindle,

1. The stagecoach to York.

Sir Thomas Splint, Captain Quinze, and Mr. Nickit—all up, I hear, within this week; so, if Charles is undone, he'll find half his acquaintances ruined too—and that, you know, is a consolation.

JOSEPH SURFACE Doubtless, ma'am—a very great one.

Enter Servant.

SERVANT Mr. Crabtree and Sir Benjamin Backbite.

LADY SNEERWELL So, Maria, you see your lover pursues you; positively you shan't escape.

Enter Crabtree *and* Sir Benjamin Backbite.

CRABTREE Lady Sneerwell, I kiss your hands. Mrs. Candour, I don't believe you are acquainted with my nephew, Sir Benjamin Backbite? Egad, ma'am, he has a pretty wit, and is a pretty poet too; isn't he, Lady Sneerwell?

SIR BENJAMIN O fie, uncle!

CRABTREE Nay, egad it's true—I'll back him at a rebus[2] or a charade against the best rhymer in the kingdom. Has your ladyship heard the epigram he wrote last week on Lady Frizzle's feather catching fire?—Do, Benjamin, repeat it—or the charade you made last night extempore at Mrs. Drowzie's conversazione.— Come now; your *first* is the name of a fish, your *second* a great naval commander, and——

SIR BENJAMIN Uncle, now—prithee——

CRABTREE I'faith, ma'am, 'twould surprise you to hear how ready he is at these things.

LADY SNEERWELL I wonder, Sir Benjamin, you never publish anything.

SIR BENJAMIN To say truth, ma'am, 'tis very vulgar to print; and, as my little productions are mostly satires and lampoons on particular people, I find they circulate more by giving copies in confidence to the friends of the parties—however, I have some love elegies, which, when favored with this lady's smiles, I mean to give to the public.

CRABTREE 'Fore heav'n, ma'am, they'll immortalize you!—you'll be handed down to posterity like Petrarch's Laura, or Waller's Sacharissa.[3]

SIR BENJAMIN Yes, madam, I think you will like them, when you shall see them on a beautiful quarto page, where a neat rivulet of text shall murmur through a meadow of margin. 'Fore gad, they will be the most elegant things of their kind!

CRABTREE But, ladies, that's true—have you heard the news?

MRS. CANDOUR What, sir, do you mean the report of—

CRABTREE No, ma'am, that's not it.—Miss Nicely is going to be married to her own footman.

MRS. CANDOUR Impossible!

CRABTREE Ask Sir Benjamin.

SIR BENJAMIN 'Tis very true, ma'am—everything is fixed, and the wedding liveries bespoke.

---

2. A riddle in which pictures represent the syllables of a word to be guessed.
3. Laura inspired the love poems of Pe-
trarch. "Sacharissa" was Lady Dorothy Sidney, to whom Edmund Waller addressed his love poems.

CRABTREE Yes—and they *do* say there were pressing reasons for it.

LADY SNEERWELL Why, I *have* heard something of this before.

MRS. CANDOUR It can't be—and I wonder any one should believe such a story of so prudent a lady as Miss Nicely.

SIR BENJAMIN O lud! ma'am, that's the very reason 'twas believed at once. She has always been so *cautious* and so *reserved*, that everybody was sure there was some reason for it at bottom.

MRS. CANDOUR Why, to be sure, a tale of scandal is as fatal to the credit of a prudent lady of her stamp as a fever is generally to those of the strongest constitutions; but there is a sort of puny, sickly reputation that is always ailing, yet will outlive the robuster characters of a hundred prudes.

SIR BENJAMIN True, madam, there are valetudinarians in reputation as well as constitution, who, being conscious of their weak part, avoid the least breath of air, and supply their want of stamina by care and circumspection.

MRS. CANDOUR Well, but this may be all a mistake. You know, Sir Benjamin, very trifling circumstances often give rise to the most injurious tales.

CRABTREE That they do, I'll be sworn, ma'am. Did you ever hear how Miss Piper came to lose her lover and her character last summer at Tunbridge?[4]—Sir Benjamin, you remember it?

SIR BENJAMIN Oh, to be sure!—the most whimsical circumstance—

LADY SNEERWELL How was it, pray?

CRABTREE Why, one evening, at Mrs. Ponto's assembly, the conversation happened to turn on the difficulty of breeding Nova Scotia sheep in this country. Says a young lady in company, "I have known instances of it; for Miss Letitia Piper, a first cousin of mine, had a Nova Scotia sheep that produced her twins." "What!" cries the old Dowager Lady Dundizzy (who you know is as deaf as a post), "has Miss Piper had twins?" This mistake, as you may imagine, threw the whole company into a fit of laughing. However, 'twas the next morning everywhere reported, and in a few days believed by the whole town, that Miss Letitia Piper had actually been brought to bed of a fine boy and a girl—and in less than a week there were people who could name the father, and the farm-house where the babies were put out to nurse!

LADY SNEERWELL Strange, indeed!

CRABTREE Matter of fact, I assure you.—O lud! Mr. Surface, pray is it true that your uncle, Sir Oliver, is coming home?

JOSEPH SURFACE Not that I know of, indeed, sir.

CRABTREE He has been in the East Indias a long time. You can scarcely remember him, I believe.—Sad comfort, whenever he returns, to hear how your brother has gone on!

JOSEPH SURFACE Charles has been imprudent, sir, to be sure; but I hope no busy people have already prejudiced Sir Oliver against him,—he may reform.

SIR BENJAMIN To be sure he may—for my part I never believed him to be so utterly void of principle as people say—and though

4. A fashionable resort in Kent.

he has lost all his friends, I am told nobody is better spoken of by the Jews.[5]

CRABTREE That's true, egad, nephew. If the old Jewry were a ward, I believe Charles would be an alderman; no man more popular there, 'fore gad! I hear he pays as many annuities as the Irish tontine;[6] and that, whenever he's sick, they have prayers for the recovery of his health in the Synagogue.

SIR BENJAMIN Yet no man lives in greater splendor.—They tell me, when he entertains his friends, he can sit down to dinner with a dozen of his own securities;[7] have a score [of] tradesmen waiting in the antechamber, and an officer behind every guest's chair.

JOSEPH SURFACE This may be entertainment to you, gentlemen, but you pay very little regard to the feelings of a brother.

MARIA [*Aside.*] Their malice is intolerable!—Lady Sneerwell, I must wish you a good morning—I'm not very well.

Exit Maria.

MRS. CANDOUR O dear! She changes color very much!

LADY SNEERWELL Do, Mrs. Candour, follow her—she may want assistance.

MRS. CANDOUR That I will, with all my soul, ma'am.—Poor dear girl! who knows what her situation may be!

Exit Mrs. Candour.

LADY SNEERWELL 'Twas nothing but that she could not bear to hear Charles reflected on, notwithstanding their difference.

SIR BENJAMIN The young lady's *penchant* is obvious.

CRABTREE But, Benjamin, you mustn't give up the pursuit for that; follow her, and put her into good humour. Repeat her some of your own verses.—Come, I'll assist you.

SIR BENJAMIN Mr. Surface, I did not mean to hurt you; but depend upon't your brother is utterly undone. [*Going.*]

CRABTREE O, lud, aye! undone as ever man was—can't raise a guinea. [*Going.*]

SIR BENJAMIN And everything sold, I'm told, that was movable. [*Going.*]

CRABTREE I have seen one that was at his house—not a thing left but some empty bottles that were overlooked, and the family pictures, which I believe are framed in the wainscot. [*Going.*]

SIR BENJAMIN And I am very sorry to hear also some bad stories against him. [*Going.*]

CRABTREE Oh, he has done many mean things, that's certain. [*Going.*]

SIR BENJAMIN But, however, as he's your brother—[*Going.*]

CRABTREE We'll tell you all, another opportunity.

Exeunt Crabtree *and* Sir Benjamin.

LADY SNEERWELL Ha, ha! ha! 'tis very hard for them to leave a subject they have not quite run down.

JOSEPH SURFACE And I believe the abuse was no more acceptable to your ladyship than to Maria.

---

5. I.e., the moneylenders.
6. A life annuity plan established in 1773 by the Irish government.
7. Men who have endorsed his notes.

LADY SNEERWELL I doubt[8] her affections are farther engaged than we imagined; but the family are to be here this evening, so you may as well dine where you are, and we shall have an opportunity of observing farther;—in the meantime, I'll go and plot mischief, and you shall study sentiments.

Exeunt.

Act I. Scene ii.
Sir Peter Teazle's *house.*
Enter Sir Peter.

SIR PETER When an old bachelor takes a young wife, what is he to expect?—'Tis now six months since Lady Teazle made me the happiest of men—and I have been the miserablest dog ever since that ever committed wedlock! We tift a little going to church, and came to a quarrel before the bells were done ringing. I was more than once nearly choked with gall during the honeymoon, and had lost all comfort in life before my friends had done wishing me joy! Yet I chose with caution—a girl bred wholly in the country, who never knew luxury beyond one silk gown, nor dissipation above the annual gala of a race ball. Yet now she plays her part in all the extravagant fopperies of the fashion and the town, with as ready a grace as if she had never seen a bush nor a grass-plat out of Grosvenor Square! I am sneered at by my old acquaintance—paragraphed in the newspapers. She dissipates my fortune, and contradicts all my humours; yet the worst of it is, I doubt I love her, or I should never bear all this. However, I'll never be weak enough to own it.

Enter Rowley.

ROWLEY Oh! Sir Peter, your servant,—how is it with you, sir?

SIR PETER Very bad, Master Rowley, very bad;—I meet with nothing but crosses and vexations.

ROWLEY What can have happened to trouble you since yesterday?

SIR PETER A good question to a married man!

ROWLEY Nay, I'm sure your lady, Sir Peter, can't be the cause of your uneasiness.

SIR PETER Why, has anyone told you she was dead?

ROWLEY Come, come, Sir Peter, you love her, notwithstanding your tempers don't exactly agree.

SIR PETER But the fault is entirely hers, Master Rowley. I am, myself, the sweetest-tempered man alive, and hate a teasing temper—and so I tell her a hundred times a day.

ROWLEY Indeed!

SIR PETER Aye; and what is very extraordinary, in all our disputes she is always in the wrong! But Lady Sneerwell, and the set she meets at her house, encourage the perverseness of her disposition. Then, to complete my vexations, Maria, my ward, whom I ought to have the power of a father over, is determined to turn rebel too, and absolutely refuses the man whom I have long resolved on for her husband; —meaning, I suppose, to bestow herself on his profligate brother.

8. Fear.

ROWLEY You know, Sir Peter, I have always taken the liberty to differ with you on the subject of these two young gentlemen. I only wish you may not be deceived in your opinion of the elder. For Charles, my life on't! he will retrieve his errors yet. Their worthy father, once my honored master, was, at his years, nearly as wild a spark; yet, when he died, he did not leave a more benevolent heart to lament his loss.

SIR PETER You are wrong, Master Rowley. On their father's death, you know, I acted as a kind of guardian to them both, till their uncle Sir Oliver's Eastern liberality gave them an early independence; of course, no person could have more opportunities of judging of their hearts, and I was never mistaken in my life. Joseph is indeed a model for the young men of the age. He is a man of sentiment, and acts up to the sentiments he professes; but, for the other, take my word for't, if he had any grains of virtue by descent, he has dissipated them with the rest of his inheritance. Ah! my old friend, Sir Oliver, will be deeply mortified when he finds how part of his bounty has been misapplied.

ROWLEY I am sorry to find you so violent against the young man, because this may be the most critical period of his fortune. I came hither with news that will surprise you.

SIR PETER What! let me hear.

ROWLEY Sir Oliver *is* arrived, and at this moment in town.

SIR ROWLEY How! you astonish me! I thought you did not expect him this month.

ROWLEY I did not; but his passage has been remarkably quick.

SIR PETER Egad, I shall rejoice to see my old friend,—'tis sixteen years since we met—we have had many a day together; but does he still enjoin us not to inform his nephews of his arrival?

ROWLEY Most strictly. He means, before it is known, to make some trial of their dispositions.

SIR PETER Ah! There needs no art to discover their merits—however, he shall have his way; but, pray, does he know I am married?

ROWLEY Yes, and will soon wish you joy.

SIR PETER What, as we drink health of a friend in a consumption! Ah, Oliver will laugh at me—we used to rail at matrimony together—but he has been steady to his text. Well, he must be at my house, though—I'll instantly give orders for his reception. But, Master Rowley, don't drop a word that Lady Teazle and I ever disagree.

ROWLEY By no means.

SIR PETER For I should never be able to stand Noll's jokes; so I'd have him think, Lord forgive me! that we are a very happy couple.

ROWLEY I understand you—but then you must be very careful not to differ while he's in the house with you.

SIR PETER Egad, and so we must—and that's impossible. Ah! Master Rowley, when an old bachelor marries a young wife, he deserves—no—the crime carries the punishment along with it.

Exeunt.

Act II. Scene i.

Sir Peter Teazle's *house.*

Enter Sir Peter *and* Lady Teazle.

SIR PETER Lady Teazle, Lady Teazle, I'll not bear it!

LADY TEAZLE Sir Peter, Sir Peter, you may bear it or not, as you please; but I ought to have my own way in everything, and what's more, I *will* too.—What! though I was educated in the country, I know very well that women of fashion in London are accountable to nobody after they are married.

SIR PETER Very well, ma'am, very well,—so a husband is to have no influence, no authority?

LADY TEAZLE Authority! No, to be sure—if you wanted authority over me, you should have adopted me, and not married me; I am sure you were old enough.

SIR PETER Old enough!—aye, there it is!—Well, well, Lady Teazle, though my life may be made unhappy by your temper, I'll not be ruined by your extravagance.

LADY TEAZLE My extravagance! I'm sure I'm not more extravagant than a woman of fashion ought to be.

SIR PETER No, no, madam, you shall throw away no more sums on such unmeaning luxury. 'Slife! to spend as much to furnish your dressing-room with flowers in a winter as would suffice to turn the Pantheon[9] into a greenhouse, and give a *fête champêtre*[1] at Christmas!

LADY TEAZLE Lord, Sir Peter, am I to blame because flowers are dear in cold weather? You should find fault with the climate, and not with me. For my part, I am sure I wish it was spring all the year round, and that roses grew under one's feet!

SIR PETER Oons! madam—if you had been born to this, I shouldn't wonder at your talking thus.—But you forget what your situation was when I married you.

LADY TEAZLE No, no, I don't; 'twas a very disagreeable one, or I should never have married *you.*

SIR PETER Yes, yes, madam, you were then in somewhat an humbler style—the daughter of a plain country squire. Recollect, Lady Teazle, when I saw you first, sitting at your tambour,[2] in a pretty figured linen gown, with a bunch of keys by your side, your hair combed smooth over a roll, and your apartment hung round with fruits in worsted, of your own working.

LADY TEAZLE O, yes! I remember it very well, and a curious life I led—my daily occupation to inspect the dairy, superintend the poultry, make extracts from the family receipt-book, and comb my aunt Deborah's lapdog.

SIR PETER Yes, yes, ma'am, 'twas so indeed.

LADY TEAZLE And then, you know, my evening amusements! To draw patterns for ruffles, which I had not the materials to make; to play Pope Joan[3] with the curate; to read a novel to my aunt; or

9. A concert hall in London.
1. Outdoor entertainment.
2. Frame for embroidery.
3. A card game.

to be stuck down to an old spinet to strum my father to sleep after a fox-chase.

SIR PETER I am glad you have so good a memory. Yes, madam, these were the recreations I took you from; but now you must have your coach—*vis-à-vis*[4]—and three powdered footmen before your chair and, in summer, a pair of white cats[5] to draw you to Kensington Gardens.—No recollection, I suppose, when you were content to ride double, behind the butler, on a docked coach-horse?

LADY TEAZLE No—I swear I never did that—I deny the butler and the coach-horse.

SIR PETER This, madam, was your situation—and what have I not done for you? I have made you a woman of fashion, of fortune, of rank—in short, I have made you my wife.

LADY TEAZLE Well, then, and there is but one thing more you can make me to add to the obligation—and that is——

SIR PETER My widow, I suppose?

LADY TEAZLE Hem! hem!

SIR PETER Thank you, madam—but don't flatter yourself; for though your ill-conduct may disturb my peace, it shall never break my heart, I promise you: however, I am equally obliged to you for the hint.

LADY TEAZLE Then why will you endeavor to make yourself so disagreeable to me, and thwart me in every little elegant expense?

SIR PETER 'Slife, madam, I say, had you any of these elegant expenses when you married me?

LADY TEAZLE Lud, Sir Peter! would you have me be out of the fashion?

SIR PETER The fashion, indeed! what had you to do with the fashion before you married me?

LADY TEAZLE For my part, I should think you would like to have your wife thought a woman of taste.

SIR PETER Aye—there again—taste! Zounds! madam, you had no taste when you married *me!*

LADY TEAZLE That's very true, indeed, Sir Peter! and *after* having married you, I am sure I should never pretend to taste again! But now, Sir Peter, if we have finished our daily jangle, I presume I may go to my engagement of Lady Sneerwell's?

SIR PETER Aye—there's another precious circumstance!—a charming set of acquaintance you have made there!

LADY TEAZLE Nay, Sir Peter, they are people of rank and fortune, and remarkably tenacious of reputation.

SIR PETER Yes, egad, they are tenacious of reputation with a vengeance; for they don't choose anybody should have a character but themselves! Such a crew! Ah! many a wretch has rid on a hurdle[6] who has done less mischief than those utterers of forged tales, coiners of scandal,—and clippers of reputation.

4. A fashionable coach in which passengers could face each other.
5. Probably ponies.
6. Cart or sledge on which traitors were hauled to execution.

LADY TEAZLE What! would you restrain the freedom of speech?

SIR PETER Oh! they have made you just as bad as any one of the society.

LADY TEAZLE Why, I believe I do bear a part with a tolerable grace. But I vow I have no malice against the people I abuse; when I say an ill-natured thing, 'tis out of pure good humour—and I take it for granted they deal exactly in the same manner with me. But, Sir Peter, you know you promised to come to Lady Sneerwell's too.

SIR PETER Well, well, I'll call in just to look after my own character.

LADY TEAZLE Then, indeed, you must make haste after me or you'll be too late.—So good-bye to ye.

Exit Lady Teazle.

SIR PETER So—I have gained much by my intended expostulations! Yet with what a charming air she contradicts everything I say, and how pleasingly she shows her contempt of my authority. Well, though I can't make her love me, there is a great satisfaction in quarreling with her; and I think she never appears to such advantage as when she's doing everything in her power to plague me.

Exit.

Act II. Scene ii.

Lady Sneerwell's.

Lady Sneerwell, Mrs. Candour, Crabtree, Sir Benjamin Backbite, *and* Joseph Surface.

LADY SNEERWELL Nay, positively, we will hear it.

JOSEPH SURFACE Yes, yes, the epigram, by all means.

SIR BENJAMIN Pleague on't, uncle! 'tis mere nonsense.

CRABTREE No, no; 'fore gad, very clever for an extempore!

SIR BENJAMIN But, ladies, you should be acquainted with the circumstance,—you must know, that one day last week, as Lady Betty Curricle was taking the dust in Hyde Park, in a sort of duodecimo phaëton,[7] she desired me to write some verses on her ponies; upon which, I took out my pocket-book, and in one moment produced the following:

> Sure never were seen two such beautiful ponies!
> Other horses are clowns, and these macaronies!
> Nay, to give 'em this title I'm sure isn't wrong—
> Their legs are so slim, and their tails so long.

CRABTREE There, ladies—done in the smack of a whip, and on horseback too!

JOSEPH SURFACE A very Phoebus, mounted—indeed, Sir Benjamin.

SIR BENJAMIN O dear sir—trifles—trifles.

Enter Lady Teazle *and* Maria.

MRS. CANDOUR I must have a copy.

LADY SNEERWELL Lady Teazle, I hope we shall see Sir Peter.

7. A light open carriage. "Duodecimo" (a very small book) indicates its size.

LADY TEAZLE I believe he'll wait on your ladyship presently.

LADY SNEERWELL Maria, my love, you look grave. Come, you shall sit down to cards with Mr. Surface.

MARIA I take very little pleasure in cards—however, I'll do as your ladyship pleases.

LADY TEAZLE [*Aside.*] I am surprised Mr. Surface should sit down with *her.*—I thought he would have embraced this opportunity of speaking to me before Sir Peter came.

MRS. CANDOUR [*coming forward*] Now, I'll die but you are so scandalous, I'll forswear your society.

LADY TEAZLE What's the matter, Mrs. Candour?

MRS. CANDOUR They'll not allow our friend Miss Vermilion to be handsome.

LADY SNEERWELL Oh, surely, she's a pretty woman.

CRABTREE I am very glad you think so, ma'am.

MRS. CANDOUR She has a charming fresh color.

LADY TEAZLE Yes, when it is fresh put on.

MRS. CANDOUR O fie! I'll swear her color is natural—I have seen it come and go.

LADY TEAZLE I dare swear you have, ma'am—it goes of a night, and comes again in the morning.

MRS. CANDOUR Ha! ha! ha! how I hate to hear you talk so! But surely, now, her sister *is*, or *was*, very handsome.

CRABTREE Who? Mrs. Evergreen?—O Lord! she's six-and-fifty if she's an hour!

MRS. CANDOUR Now positively you wrong her; fifty-two or fifty-three is the utmost—and I don't think she looks more.

SIR BENJAMIN Ah! there is no judging by her looks, unless one could see her face.

LADY SNEERWELL Well, well, if Mrs. Evergreen *does* take some pains to repair the ravages of time, you must allow she effects it with great ingenuity; and surely that's better than the careless manner in which the widow Ochre caulks her wrinkles.

SIR BENJAMIN Nay, now, Lady Sneerwell, you are severe upon the widow. Come, come, it is not that she paints so ill—but, when she has finished her face, she joins it on so badly to her neck, that she looks like a mended statue, in which the connoisseur sees at once that the head's modern, though the trunk's antique!

CRABTREE Ha! ha! ha! Well said, nephew!

MRS. CANDOUR Ha! ha! ha! Well, you make me laugh, but I vow I hate you for't.—What do you think of Miss Simper?

SIR BENJAMIN Why, she has very pretty teeth.

LADY TEAZLE Yes; and on that account, when she is neither speaking nor laughing (which very seldom happens), she never absolutely shuts her mouth, but leaves it always on a jar, as it were.

MRS. CANDOUR How can you be so ill-natured?

LADY TEAZLE Nay, I allow even that's better than the pains Mrs. Prim takes to conceal her losses in front. She draws her mouth till it positively resembles the aperture of a poor's-box,[8] and all

8. A box for contributions to charity.

her words appear to slide out edgeways.

LADY SNEERWELL Very well, Lady Teazle; I see you can be a little severe.

LADY TEAZLE In defence of a friend it is but justice;—but here comes Sir Peter to spoil our pleasantry.

Enter Sir Peter Teazle.

SIR PETER Ladies, your most obedient—Mercy on me, here is the whole set! a character dead at every word, I suppose. [*Aside.*]

MRS. CANDOUR I am rejoiced you are come, Sir Peter. They have been *so* censorious. They will allow good qualities to nobody— not even good nature to our friend Mrs. Pursy.

LADY TEAZLE What, the fat dowager who was at Mrs. Codille's last night?

MRS. CANDOUR Nay, her bulk is her misfortune; and, when she takes such pains to get rid of it, you ought not to reflect on her.

LADY SNEERWELL That's very true, indeed.

LADY TEAZLE Yes, I know she almost lives on acids and small whey;[9] laces herself by pulleys; and often, in the hottest noon of summer, you may see her on a little squat pony, with her hair platted up behind like a drummer's, and puffing round the Ring[1] on a full trot.

MRS. CANDOUR I thank you, Lady Teazle, for defending her.

SIR PETER Yes, a good defense, truly.

MRS. CANDOUR But Sir Benjamin is as censorious as Miss Sallow.

CRABTREE Yes, and she is a curious being to pretend to be censorious!—an awkward gawky, without any one good point under heaven.

MRS. CANDOUR Positively you shall not be so very servere. Miss Sallow is a relation of mine by marriage, and, as for her person, great allowance is to be made; for, let me tell you, a woman labors under many disadvantages who tries to pass for a girl at six-and-thirty.

LADY SNEERWELL Though, surely, she is handsome still—and for the weakness in her eyes, considering how much she reads by candle-light, it is not to be wondered at.

MRS. CANDOUR True; and then as to her manner, upon my word I think it is particularly graceful, considering she never had the least education; for you know her mother was a Welch milliner, and her father a sugar-baker at Bristol.

SIR BENJAMIN Ah! you are both of you too good-natured!

SIR PETER Yes, damned good-natured! This their own relation! mercy on me! [*Aside.*]

SIR BENJAMIN And Mrs. Candour is of so moral a turn she can sit for an hour to hear Lady Stucco talk sentiment.

LADY TEAZLE Nay, I vow Lady Stucco is very well with the dessert after dinner; for she's just like the French fruit one cracks for mottoes—made up of paint and proverb.

MRS. CANDOUR Well, I never will join in ridiculing a friend; and so I constantly tell my cousin Ogle, and you all know what preten-

9. The watery part of milk.   1. Circular drive in Hyde Park.

sions she has to be critical in beauty.

CRABTREE Oh, to be sure! she has herself the oddest countenance that ever was seen; 'tis a collection of features from all the different countries of the globe.

SIR BENJAMIN So she has, indeed—an Irish front!

CRABTREE Caledonian locks!

SIR BENJAMIN Dutch nose!

CRABTREE Austrian lip!

SIR BENJAMIN Complexion of a Spaniard!

CRABTREE And teeth *à la Chinoise!*

SIR BENJAMIN In short, her face resembles a *table d'hôte* at Spa[2]—where no two guests are of a nation——

CRABTREE Or a congress at the close of a general war—wherein all the members, even to her eyes, appear to have a different interest, and her nose and chin are the only parties likely to join issue.

MRS. CANDOUR Ha! ha! ha!

SIR PETER Mercy on my life!—a person they dine with twice a week! [*Aside.*]

MRS. CANDOUR Nay, but I vow you shall not carry the laugh off so —for give me leave to say, that Mrs. Ogle—

SIR PETER Madam, madam, I beg your pardon—there's no stopping these good gentlemen's tongues. But when I tell *you*, Mrs. Candour, that the lady they are abusing is a particular friend of mine —I hope you'll not take her part.

LADY SNEERWELL Well said, Sir Peter! but you are a cruel creature —too phlegmatic yourself for a jest, and too peevish to allow wit on others.

SIR PETER Ah, madam, true wit is more nearly allied to good nature than your ladyship is aware of.

LADY TEAZLE True, Sir Peter; I believe they are so near akin that they can never be united.

SIR BENJAMIN Or rather, madam, suppose them man and wife, because one so seldom sees them together.

LADY TEAZLE But Sir Peter is such an enemy to scandal, I believe he would have it put down by parliament.

SIR PETER 'Fore heaven, madam, if they were to consider the sporting with reputation of as much importance as poaching on manors, and pass *An Act for the Preservation of Fame,* I believe many would thank them for the bill.

LADY SNEERWELL O lud! Sir Peter; would you deprive us of our privileges?

SIR PETER Aye, madam; and then no person should be permitted to kill characters or run down reputations, but qualified old maids and disappointed widows.

LADY SNEERWELL Go, you monster!

MRS. CANDOUR But sure you would not be quite so severe on those who only report what they hear.

SIR PETER Yes, madam, I would have law merchant[3] for them too;

2. The dining table at Spa, a famous resort in Belgium.
3. System of commercial law. Sir Peter continues the metaphor by playing on the fact that endorsers of notes are held responsible in cases of default of payment.

and in all cases of slander currency, whenever the drawer of the lie was not to be found, the injured parties should have a right to come on any of the endorsers.

CRABTREE Well, for my part, I believe there never was a scandalous tale without some foundation.

LADY SNEERWELL Come, ladies, shall we sit down to cards in the next room?

Enter Servant *and whispers* Sir Peter.

SIR PETER I'll be with them directly.—[*Exit* Servant.] I'll get away unperceived. [*Aside.*]

LADY SNEERWELL Sir Peter, you are not leaving us?

SIR PETER Your ladyship must excuse me; I'm called away by particular business—but I leave my character behind me.

Exit Sir Peter.

SIR BENJAMIN Well certainly, Lady Teazle, that lord of yours is a strange being; I could tell you some stories of him would make you laugh heartily, if he wasn't your husband.

LADY TEAZLE O pray don't mind that—come, do let's hear them.

They join the rest of the company, all talking as they are going into the next room.

JOSEPH SURFACE [*Rising with* Maria.] Maria, I see you have no satisfaction in this society.

MARIA How is it possible I should? If to raise malicious smiles at the infirmities and misfortunes of those who have never injured us be the province of wit or humour, heaven grant me a double portion of dulness!

JOSEPH SURFACE Yet they appear more ill-natured than they are; they have no malice at heart.

MARIA Then is their conduct still more contemptible; for, in my opinion, nothing could excuse the intemperance of their tongues but a natural and ungovernable bitterness of mind.

JOSEPH SURFACE But can you, Maria, feel thus for others, and be unkind to me alone? Is hope to be denied the tenderest passion?

MARIA Why will you distress me by renewing this subject?

JOSEPH SURFACE Ah, Maria! you would not treat me thus, and oppose your guardian, Sir Peter's will, but that I see that profligate *Charles* is still a favored rival.

MARIA Ungenerously urged! But, whatever my sentiments of that unfortunate young man are, be assured I shall not feel more bound to give him up, because his distresses have lost him the regard even of a brother.

Lady Teazle *returns.*

JOSEPH SURFACE Nay, but, Maria, do not leave me with a frown— by all that's honest, I swear—Gad's life, here's Lady Teazle. [*Aside.*]—You must not—no, you shall not—for, though I have the greatest regard for Lady Teazle——

MARIA Lady Teazle!

JOSEPH SURFACE Yet were Sir Peter to suspect——

LADY TEAZLE [*Coming forward.*] What's this, pray? Do you take her for me?—Child, you are wanted in the next room.—

Exit Maria.

What is all this, pray?

JOSEPH SURFACE Oh, the most unlucky circumstance in nature! Maria has somehow suspected the tender concern I have for your happiness, and threatened to acquaint Sir Peter with her suspicions, and I was just endeavoring to reason with her when you came.

LADY TEAZLE Indeed! but you seemed to adopt a very tender mode of reasoning—do you *usually* argue on your knees?

JOSEPH SURFACE Oh, she's a child—and I thought a little bombast ——but, Lady Teazle, when are you to give me your judgment on my library, as you promised?

LADY TEAZLE No, no,—I begin to think it would be imprudent, and you know I admit you as a lover no further than *fashion* requires.

JOSEPH SURFACE True—a mere Platonic cicisbeo,[4] what every London wife is *entitled* to.

LADY TEAZLE Certainly, one must not be out of the fashion; however, I have so much of my country prejudices left, that, though Sir Peter's ill humour may vex me ever so, it never shall provoke me to——

JOSEPH SURFACE The only revenge in your power. Well, I applaud your moderation.

LADY TEAZLE Go—you are an insinuating wretch! But we shall be missed—let us join the company.

JOSEPH SURFACE But we had best not return together.

LADY TEAZLE Well, don't stay—for Maria shan't come to hear any more of your *reasoning,* I promise you.

Exit Lady Teazle.

JOSEPH SURFACE A curious dilemma, truly, my politics have run me into! I wanted, at first, only to ingratiate myself with Lady Teazle, that she might be my enemy with Maria; and I have, I don't know how, become her serious lover. Sincerely I begin to wish I had never made such a point of gaining so *very good* a character, for it has led me into so many cursed rogueries that I doubt I shall be exposed at last.

Exit.

Act II. Scene iii.
Sir Peter's.
Enter Sir Oliver Surface *and* Rowley.

SIR OLIVER Ha! ha! ha! and so my old friend is married, hey?— a young wife out of the country.— Ha! ha! ha!—that he should have stood bluff[5] to old bachelor so long, and sink into a husband at last!

ROWLEY But you must not rally him on the subject, Sir Oliver; 'tis a tender point, I assure you, though he has been married only seven months.

SIR OLIVER Then he has been just half a year on the stool of repentance![6] Poor Peter! But you say he has entirely given up

4. The recognized gallant of a married woman.
5. Firm.
6. A seat in church where offenders do penance.

Charles—never sees him, hey?

ROWLEY His prejudice against him is astonishing, and I am sure greatly increased by a jealousy of him with Lady Teazle, which he has been industriously led into by a scandalous society in the neighborhood, who have contributed not a little to Charles's ill name; whereas the truth is, I believe, if the lady is partial to either of them, his brother is the favorite.

SIR OLIVER Aye,—I know there are a set of malicious, prating, prudent gossips, both male and female, who murder characters to kill time, and will rob a young fellow of his good name before he has years to know the value of it,—but I am not to be prejudiced against my nephew by such, I promise you! No, no;—if Charles has done nothing false or mean, I shall compound for his extravagance.

ROWLEY Then, my life on't, you will reclaim him.—Ah, sir, it gives me new life to find that *your* heart is not turned against him, and that the son of my good old master has one friend, however, left.

SIR OLIVER What! shall I forget, Master Rowley, when I was at his years myself? Egad, my brother and I were neither of us very *prudent* youths—and yet, I believe, you have not seen many better men than your old master was?

ROWLEY Sir, 'tis this reflection gives me assurance that Charles may yet be a credit to his family.—But here comes Sir Peter.

SIR OLIVER Egad, so he does!—Mercy on me, he's greatly altered, and seems to have a settled married look! One may read husband in his face at this distance!

Enter Sir Peter Teazle.

SIR PETER Hah! Sir Oliver—my old friend! Welcome to England a thousand times!

SIR OLIVER Thank you, thank you, Sir Peter! and i'faith I am glad to find you well, believe me!

SIR PETER Ah! 'tis a long time since we met—sixteen years, I doubt, Sir Oliver, and many a cross accident in the time.

SIR OLIVER Aye, I have had my share—but, what! I find you are married, hey, my old boy?—Well, well, it can't be helped—and so I wish you joy with all my heart!

SIR PETER Thank you, thank you, Sir Oliver.—Yes, I have entered into the happy state—but we'll not talk of that now.

SIR OLIVER True, true, Sir Peter; old friends should not begin on grievances at first meeting. No, no, no.

ROWLEY [*to* Sir Oliver.] Take care, pray, sir.

SIR OLIVER Well, so one of my nephews is a wild rogue, hey?

SIR PETER Wild! Ah! my old friend, I grieve for your disappointment there—he's a lost young man, indeed; however, his brother will make you amends; *Joseph* is, indeed, what a youth should be —everybody in the world speaks well of him.

SIR OLIVER I am sorry to hear it—he has too good a character to be an honest fellow.—Everybody speaks well of him! Psha! then he has bowed as low as knaves and fools as to the honest dignity of genius or virtue.

SIR PETER What, Sir Oliver! do you blame him for not making enemies?

SIR OLIVER Yes, if he has merit enough to deserve them.

SIR PETER Well, well—you'll be convinced when you know him. 'Tis edification to hear him converse—he professes the noblest sentiments.

SIR OLIVER Ah, plague of his sentiments! If he salutes me with a scrap of morality in his mouth, I shall be sick directly. But, however, don't mistake me, Sir Peter; I don't mean to defend Charles's errors—but, before I form my judgment of either of them, I intend to make a trial of their hearts—and my friend Rowley and I have planned something for the purpose.

ROWLEY And Sir Peter shall own for once he has been mistaken.

SIR PETER Oh, my life on Joseph's honor!

SIR OLIVER Well, come, give us a bottle of good wine, and we'll drink the lad's health, and tell you our scheme.

SIR PETER *Allons,*[7] then!

SIR OLIVER And don't, Sir Peter, be so severe against your old friend's son. Odds my life! I am not sorry that he has run out of the course a little; for my part, I hate to see prudence clinging to the green succors of youth; 'tis like ivy round a sapling, and spoils the growth of the tree.

Exeunt.

Act III. Scene i.
Sir Peter's.
Sir Peter Teazle, Sir Oliver Surface, *and* Rowley.

SIR PETER Well, then—we will see this fellow first, and have our wine afterwards. But how is this, Master Rowley? I don't see the jet[8] of your scheme.

ROWLEY Why, sir, this Mr. Stanley, whom I was speaking of, is nearly related to them, by their mother; he was once a merchant in Dublin, but has been ruined by a series of undeserved misfortunes. He has applied, by letter, since his confinement, both to Mr. Surface and Charles—from the former he has received nothing but evasive promises of future service, while Charles has done all that his extravagance has left him power to do; and he is, at this time, endeavoring to raise a sum of money, part of which, in the midst of his own distresses, I know he intends for the service of poor Stanley.

SIR OLIVER Ah! he is my brother's son.

SIR PETER Well, but how is Sir Oliver personally to——

ROWLEY Why, sir, I will inform Charles and his brother that Stanley has obtained permission to apply in person to his friends, and, as they have neither of them ever seen him, let Sir Oliver assume his character, and he will have a fair opportunity of judging at least of the benevolence of their dispositions; and believe me, sir, you will find in the youngest brother one who, in the midst of folly and dissipation, has still, as our immortal bard expresses it,—

7. "Let's go."   8. Point.

a tear for pity, and a hand
Open as day, for melting charity.⁹

SIR PETER Psha! What signifies his having an open hand or purse either, when he has nothing left to give? Well, well, make the trial, if you please; but where is the fellow whom you brought for Sir Oliver to examine, relative to Charles's affairs?

ROWLEY Below, waiting his commands, and no one can give him better intelligence.—This, Sir Oliver, is a friendly Jew, who, to do him justice, has done everything in his power to bring your nephew to a proper sense of his extravagance.

SIR PETER Pray let us have him in.

ROWLEY Desire Mr. Moses to walk upstairs.

SIR PETER But why should you suppose he will speak the truth?

ROWLEY Oh, I have convinced him that he has no chance of recovering certain sums advanced to Charles but through the bounty of Sir Oliver, who he knows is arrived; so that you may depend on his fidelity to his interest. I have also another evidence in my power, one Snake, whom I have detected in a matter little short of forgery, and shall shortly produce to remove some of *your* prejudices, Sir Peter, relative to Charles and Lady Teazle.

SIR PETER I have heard too much on that subject.

ROWLEY Here comes the honest Israelite.

Enter Moses.

—This is Sir Oliver.

SIR OLIVER Sir, I understand you have lately had great dealings with my nephew Charles.

MOSES Yes, Sir Oliver—I have done all I could for him, but he was ruined before he came to me for assistance.

SIR OLIVER That was unlucky, truly—for you have had no opportunity of showing your talents.

MOSES None at all—I hadn't the pleasure of knowing his distresses —till he was some thousands worse than nothing.

SIR OLIVER Unfortunate, indeed! But I suppose you have done all in your power for him, honest Moses?

MOSES Yes, he knows that. This very evening I was to have brought him a gentleman from the city, who doesn't know him, and will, I believe, advance him some money.

SIR PETER What, one Charles has never had money from before?

MOSES Yes; Mr. Premium, of Crutched Friars¹—formerly a broker.

SIR PETER Egad, Sir Oliver, a thought strikes me!—Charles, you say, doesn't know Mr. Premium?

MOSES Not at all.

SIR PETER Now then, Sir Oliver, you may have a better opportunity of satisfying yourself than by an old romancing tale of a poor relation;—go with my friend Moses, and represent Mr. *Premium,* and then, I'll answer for't, you will see your nephew in all his glory.

9. Shakespeare's *2 Henry IV*, IV.iv.31– 32.   1. A street in London. *Crutched* means *having or bearing a cross.*

SIR OLIVER Egad, I like this idea better than the other, and I may
visit *Joseph* afterwards, as old *Stanley*.

SIR PETER True—so you may.

ROWLEY Well, this is taking Charles rather at a disadvantage, to be
sure. However, Moses—you understand Sir Peter, and will be
faithful?

MOSES You may depend upon me,—this is near the time I was to
have gone.

SIR OLIVER I'll accompany you as soon as you please, Moses; but
hold! I have forgot one thing—how the plague shall I be able to
pass for a Jew?

MOSES There's no need—the principal is Christian.

SIR OLIVER Is he?—I'm sorry to hear it—but, then again, an't I
rather too smartly dressed to look like a money-lender?

SIR PETER Not at all; 'twould not be out of character, if you went
in your own carriage—would it, Moses?

MOSES Not in the least.

SIR OLIVER Well, but how must I talk? there's certainly some cant
of usury, and mode of treating, that I ought to know.

SIR PETER Oh, there's not much to learn—the great point, as I
take it, is to be exorbitant enough in your demands—hey, Moses?

MOSES Yes, that's a very great point.

SIR OLIVER I'll answer for't I'll not be wanting in that. I'll ask him
eight or ten per cent on the loan, at least.

MOSES If you ask him no more than that, you'll be discovered
immediately.

SIR OLIVER Hey! what the plague! how much then?

MOSES That depends upon the circumstances. If he appears not
very anxious for the supply, you should require only forty or fifty
per cent; but if you find him in great distress, and want the
moneys very bad—you may ask double.

SIR PETER A good honest trade you're learning, Sir Oliver!

SIR OLIVER Truly I think so—and not unprofitable.

MOSES Then, you know, you haven't the moneys yourself, but are
forced to borrow them for him of a friend.

SIR OLIVER Oh! I borrow it of a friend, do I?

MOSES Yes, and your friend is an unconscionable dog, but you can't
help it.

SIR OLIVER My friend is an unconscionable dog, is he?

MOSES Yes, and he himself has not the moneys by him—but is
forced to sell stock at a great loss.

SIR OLIVER He is forced to sell stock, is he, at a great loss, is he?
Well, that's very kind of him.

SIR PETER I'faith, Sir Oliver—Mr. Premium, I mean—you'll soon
be master of the trade. But, Moses! wouldn't you have him run
out a little against the Annuity Bill?[2] That would be in character, I should think.

MOSES Very much.

2. A bill to protect the property of minors. It became law during the first run of
the play.

ROWLEY And lament that a young man now must be at years of discretion before he is suffered to ruin himself?

MOSES Aye, great pity!

SIR PETER And abuse the public for allowing merit to an act whose only object is to snatch misfortune and imprudence from the rapacious relief of usury, and give the minor a chance of inheriting his estate without being undone by coming into possession.

SIR OLIVER So, so—Moses shall give me further instructions as we go together.

SIR PETER You will not have much time, for your nephew lives hard by.

SIR OLIVER Oh, never fear! my tutor appears so able, that though Charles lived in the next street, it must be my own fault if I am not a complete rogue before I turn the corner.

Exeunt Sir Oliver *and* Moses.

SIR PETER So now I think Sir Oliver will be convinced;—you are partial, Rowley, and would have prepared Charles for the other plot.

ROWLEY No, upon my word, Sir Peter.

SIR PETER Well, go bring me this Snake, and I'll hear what he has to say presently.—I see Maria, and want to speak with her.—

Exit Rowley.

I should be glad to be convinced my suspicions of Lady Teazle and Charles were unjust. I have never yet opened my mind on this subject to my friend *Joseph*—I'm determined I will do it—*he* will give me his opinion sincerely.

Enter Maria.

So, child, has Mr. Surface returned with you?

MARIA No, sir—he was engaged.

SIR PETER Well, Maria, do you not reflect, the more you converse with that amiable young man, what return his partiality for you deserves?

MARIA Indeed, Sir Peter, your frequent importunity on this subject distresses me extremely—you compel me to declare, that I know no man who has ever paid me a particular attention whom I would not prefer to Mr. Surface.

SIR PETER So—here's perverseness! No, no, Maria, 'tis Charles only whom you would prefer—'tis evident his vices and follies have won your heart.

MARIA This is unkind, sir—you know I have obeyed you in neither seeing nor corresponding with him; I have heard enough to convince me that he is unworthy my regard. Yet I cannot think it culpable, if, while my understanding severely condemns his vices, my heart suggests some pity for his distresses.

SIR PETER Well, well, pity him as much as you please, but give your heart and hand to a worthier object.

MARIA Never to his brother!

SIR PETER Go, perverse and obstinate! But take care, madam; you have never yet known what the authority of a guardian is—don't compel me to inform you of it.

MARIA I can only say, you shall not have *just* reason. 'Tis true, by my father's will, I am for a short period bound to regard you as his substitute, but must cease to think you so, when you compel me to be miserable.

Exit Maria.

SIR PETER Was ever man so crossed as I am! everything conspiring to fret me!—I had not been involved in matrimony a fortnight, before her father, a hale and hearty man, died—on purpose, I believe, for the pleasure of plaguing me with the care of his daughter. But here comes my helpmate! She appears in great good humour.|How happy I should be if I could tease her into loving me, though but a little!

Enter Lady Teazle.

LADY TEAZLE Lud! Sir Peter, I hope you haven't been quarreling with Maria—it isn't using me well to be ill humoured when I am not by.

SIR PETER Ah, Lady Teazle, you might have the power to make me good humoured at all times.

LADY TEAZLE I am sure I wish I had—for I want you to be in charming sweet temper at this moment. Do be good humoured now, and let me have two hundred pounds, will you?

SIR PETER Two hundred pounds! what, an't I to be in a good humour without paying for it! But speak to me thus, and i'faith there's nothing I could refuse you. You shall have it; but seal me a bond for the repayment.

LADY TEAZLE O, no—there—my note of hand will do as well.

SIR PETER [*Kissing her hand.*] And you shall no longer reproach me with not giving you an independent settlement,—I mean shortly to surprise you; shall we always live thus, hey?

LADY TEAZLE If you please. I'm sure I don't care how soon we leave off quarrelling, provided you'll own *you* were tired first.

SIR PETER Well—then let our future contest be, who shall be most obliging.

LADY TEAZLE I assure you, Sir Peter, good nature becomes you. You look now as you did before we were married!—when you used to walk with me under the elms, and tell me stories of what a gallant you were in your youth, and chuck me under the chin, you would, and ask me if I thought I could love an old fellow, who would deny me nothing—didn't you?

SIR PETER Yes, yes, and you were as kind and attentive.

LADY TEAZLE Aye, so I was, and would always take your part, when my acquaintance used to abuse you, and turn you into ridicule.

SIR PETER Indeed!

LADY TEAZLE Aye, and when my cousin Sophy has called you a stiff, peevish old bachelor, and laughed at me for thinking of marrying one who might be my father, I have always defended you—and said, I didn't think you so ugly by any means, and that I dared say you'd make a very good sort of a husband.

SIR PETER And you prophesied right—and we shall certainly now be the happiest couple——

LADY TEAZLE And never differ again!

SIR PETER No, never!—though at the same time, indeed, my dear Lady Teazle, you must watch your temper very narrowly; for in all our little quarrels, my dear, if you recollect, my love, you always began first.

LADY TEAZLE I beg your pardon, my dear Sir Peter: indeed, you always gave the provocation.

SIR PETER Now, see, my angel! take care—*contradicting* isn't the way to keep friends.

LADY TEAZLE Then, don't *you* begin it, my love!

SIR PETER There, now! you—you are going on—you don't perceive, my life, that you are just doing the very thing which you know always makes me angry.

LADY TEAZLE Nay, you know if you will be angry without any reason—

SIR PETER There now! you want to quarrel again.

LADY TEAZLE No, I am sure I don't—but, if you will be so peevish——

SIR PETER There now! who begins first?

LADY TEAZLE Why, you, to be sure. I said nothing—but there's no bearing your temper.

SIR PETER No, no, madam, the fault's in your own temper.

LADY TEAZLE Aye, you are just what my cousin Sophy said you would be.

SIR PETER Your cousin Sophy is a forward, impertinent gipsy.

LADY TEAZLE You are a great bear, I'm sure, to abuse my relations.

SIR PETER Now may all the plagues of marriage be doubled on me, if ever I try to be friends with you any more!

LADY TEAZLE So much the better.

SIR PETER No, no, madam; 'tis evident you never cared a pin for me, and I was a madman to marry you—a pert, rural coquette, that had refused half the honest squires in the neighborhood!

LADY TEAZLE And I am sure, I was a fool to marry you—an old dangling bachelor, who was single at fifty, only because he never could meet with any one who would have him.

SIR PETER Aye, aye, madam; but you were pleased enough to listen to me—*you* never had such an offer before.

LADY TEAZLE No! didn't I refuse Sir Twivy Tarrier, who everybody said would have been a better match—for his estate is just as good as yours—and he has broke his neck since we have been married.

SIR PETER I have done with you, madam! You are an unfeeling, ungrateful—but there's an end of everything. I believe you capable of anything that's bad. Yes, madam, I now believe the reports relative to you and Charles, madam—yes, madam, you and Charles—are not without grounds——

LADY TEAZLE Take care, Sir Peter! you had better not insinuate any such thing! I'll not be suspected with*out cause*, I promise you.

SIR PETER Very well, madam! very well! a separate maintenance as soon as you please. Yes, madam, or a divorce! I'll make an example of myself for the benefit of all old bachelors. Let us separate, madam.

LADY TEAZLE Agreed! agreed! And now, my dear Sir Peter, we are of a mind once more, we may be the *happiest couple*, and *never differ again*, you know: ha! ha! Well, you are going to be in a passion, I see, and I shall only interrupt you—so, bye! bye!

Exit.

SIR PETER Plagues and tortures! can't I make her angry neither? Oh, I am the miserablest fellow! But I'll not bear her presuming to keep her temper—no! she may break my heart, but she shan't keep her temper.

Exit.

Act III. Scene ii.
Charles's *house.*
Enter Trip, Moses, *and* Sir Oliver Surface.

TRIP Here, Master Moses! if you'll stay a moment, I'll try whether —what's the gentleman's name?

SIR OLIVER Mr. Moses, what *is* my name? [*Aside.*]

MOSES Mr. Premium.

TRIP Premium—very well.

Exit Trip, taking snuff.

SIR OLIVER To judge by the servants one wouldn't believe the master was ruined. But what!—sure, this was my brother's house?

MOSES Yes, sir; Mr. Charles bought it of Mr. Joseph, with the furniture, pictures, &c., just as the old gentleman left it—Sir Peter thought it a great piece of extravagance in him.

SIR OLIVER In my mind, the other's economy in *selling* it to him was more reprehensible by half.

Re-enter Trip.

TRIP My master says you must wait, gentlemen; he has company, and can't speak with you yet.

SIR OLIVER If he knew *who* it was wanted to see him, perhaps he wouldn't have sent such a message?

TRIP Yes, yes, sir; he knows *you* are here—I didn't forget little Premium—no, no, no.

SIR OLIVER Very well—and I pray, sir, what may be your name?

TRIP Trip, sir—my name is Trip, at your service.

SIR OLIVER Well, then, Mr. Trip, you have a pleasant sort of a place here, I guess.

TRIP Why, yes—here are three or four of us pass our time agreeably enough; but then our wages are sometimes a little in arrear— and not very great either—but fifty pounds a year, and find our own bags and bouquets.[3]

SIR OLIVER [*Aside.*] Bags and bouquets! halters and bastinadoes![4]

TRIP But *à propos*, Moses, have you been able to get me that little bill discounted?

SIR OLIVER [*Aside.*] Wants to raise money, too!—mercy on me!

3. Footmen's dress.   4. Cudgels.

Has his distresses, I warrant, like a lord,—and affects creditors and duns.

MOSES 'Twas not to be done, indeed, Mr. Trip.
> *Gives the note.*

TRIP Good lack, you surprise me! My friend *Brush* has endorsed it, and I thought when he put his mark on the back of a bill 'twas as good as cash.

MOSES No, 'twouldn't do.

TRIP A small sum—but twenty pounds. Hark'ee, Moses, do you think you couldn't get it me by way of annuity?

SIR OLIVER [*Aside.*] An annuity! ha! ha! a footman raise money by way of annuity! Well done, luxury, egad!

MOSES But you must insure your place.

TRIP Oh, with all my heart! I'll insure my place, and my life too, if you please.

SIR OLIVER [*Aside.*] It's more than I would your neck.

TRIP But then, Moses, it must be done before this d——d register[5] takes place—one wouldn't like to have one's name made public, you know.

MOSES No, certainly. But is there nothing you could deposit?

TRIP Why, nothing capital of my master's wardrobe has dropped lately; but I could give you a mortgage on some of his winter clothes, with equity of redemption before November—or you shall have the reversion of the French velvet, or a post-obit[6] on the blue and silver;—these, I should think, Moses, with a few pair of point ruffles, as a collateral security—hey, my little fellow?

MOSES Well, well.
> *Bell rings.*

TRIP Gad, I heard the bell! I believe, gentlemen, I can now introduce you. Don't forget the annuity, little Moses! This way, gentlemen, insure my place, you know.

SIR OLIVER [*Aside.*] If the man be a shadow of his master, this is the temple of dissipation indeed!
> *Exeunt.*

Act III. Scene iii.
Charles [Surface], Careless, &c., &c. at a table with wine, &c.

CHARLES 'Fore heaven, 'tis true!—there's the great degeneracy of the age. Many of our acquaintance have taste, spirit, and politeness; but, plague on't, they won't drink.

CARELESS It is so, indeed, Charles! they give in to all the substantial luxuries of the table, and abstain from nothing but wine and wit.

CHARLES Oh, certainly society suffers by it intolerably! for now, instead of the social spirit of raillery that used to mantle over a glass of bright Burgundy, their conversation is become just like the Spa-water they drink, which has all the pertness and flatulence of champagne, without its spirit or flavor.

---

5. The record of annuities granted according to the Annuity Bill.   6. A bond to take effect after death.

1 GENT But what are *they* to do who love play better than wine?

CARELESS True! there's Harry diets himself for gaming, and is now under a hazard[7] regimen.

CHARLES Then he'll have the worst of it. What! you wouldn't train a horse for the course by keeping him from corn! For my part, egad, I am now never so successful as when I am a little merry— let me throw on a bottle of champagne, and I never lose—at least I never feel my losses, which is exactly the same thing.

2 GENT Aye, that I believe.

CHARLES And, then, what man can pretend to be a believer in love, who is an abjurer of wine? 'Tis the test by which the lover knows his own heart. Fill a dozen bumpers to a dozen beauties, and she that floats at top is the maid that has bewitched you.

CARELESS Now then, Charles, be honest, and give us your real favorite.

CHARLES Why, I have withheld her only in compassion to you. If I toast her, you must give a round of her peers—which is impossible—on earth.

CARELESS Oh, then we'll find some canonised vestals or heathen goddesses that will do, I warrant!

CHARLES Here then, bumpers, you rogues! bumpers! Maria! Maria—

> *Drink.*

1 GENT Maria who?

CHARLES O, damn the surname!—'tis too formal to be registered in Love's calendar—but now, Sir Toby Bumper, beware—we must have beauty superlative.

CARELESS Nay, never study, Sir Toby: we'll stand to the toast, though your mistress should want an eye—and you know you have a song will excuse you.

SIR TOBY Egad, so I have! and I'll give him the song instead of the lady.

SONG AND CHORUS

Here's to the maiden of bashful fifteen;
    Here's to the widow of fifty;
Here's to the flaunting extravagant quean,[8]
    And here's to the housewife that's thrifty.
Chorus.   Let the toast pass—
        Drink to the lass—
I'll warrant she'll prove an excuse for the glass.

Here's to the charmer whose dimples we prize;
    Now to the maid who has none, sir;
Here's to the girl with a pair of blue eyes,
    And here's to the nymph with but one, sir.
Chorus.   Let the toast pass, &c.

Here's to the maid with a bosom of snow:
    Now to *her* that's as brown as a berry:

---

7. A dice game.   8. Harlot or hussy.

Here's to the wife with a face full of woe,
    And now for the damsel that's merry.
Chorus.   Let the toast pass, &c.

For let 'em be clumsy, or let 'em be slim,
    Young or ancient, I care not a feather:
So fill a pint bumper quite up to the brim,
    —And let us e'en toast 'em together.
Chorus.   Let the toast pass, &c.

ALL Bravo! Bravo!

  Enter Trip, *and whispers* Charles Surface.

CHARLES Gentlemen, you must excuse me a little.—Careless, take the chair, will you?

CARELESS Nay, prithee, Charles, what now? This is one of your peerless beauties, I suppose, has dropped in by chance?

CHARLES No, faith! To tell you the truth, 'tis a Jew and a broker, who are come by appointment.

CARELESS Oh, damn it! let's have the Jew in—

1 GENT Aye, and the broker too, by all means.

2 GENT Yes, yes, the Jew and the broker.

CHARLES Egad, with all my heart!—Trip bid the gentlemen walk in.—

            [*Exit* Trip.]

Though there's one of them a stranger, I can tell you.

CARELESS Charles, let us give them some generous Burgundy, and perhaps they'll grow conscientious.

CHARLES Oh, hang 'em, no! wine does but draw forth a man's *natural* qualities; and to make *them* drink would only be to whet their knavery.

  Enter Trip, Sir Oliver Surface, *and* Moses.

CHARLES So, honest Moses; walk in, pray, Mr. Premium—that's the gentleman's name, isn't it, Moses?

MOSES Yes, sir.

CHARLES Set chairs, Trip.—Sit down, Mr. Premium.—Glasses, Trip.—Sit down, Moses.—Come, Mr. Premium, I'll give you a sentiment; here's "Success to usury!"—Moses, fill the gentleman a bumper.

MOSES Success to usury!

CARELESS Right, Moses—usury is prudence and industry, and deserves to succeed.

SIR OLIVER Then here's— All the success it deserves!

CARELESS No, no, that won't do! Mr. Premium, you have demurred to the toast, and must drink it in a pint bumper.

1 GENT A pint bumper, at least.

MOSES Oh, pray, sir, consider—Mr. Premium's a gentleman.

CARELESS And therefore loves good wine.

2 GENT Give Moses a quart glass—this is mutiny, and a high contempt of the chair.

CARELESS Here, now for't! I'll see justice done, to the last drop of my bottle.

SIR OLIVER Nay, pray, gentlemen—I did not expect this usage.

CHARLES No, hang it, Careless, you shan't; Mr. Premium's a stranger.

SIR OLIVER [*Aside.*] Odd! I wish I was well out of this company.

CARELESS Plague on 'em then! if they won't drink, we'll not sit down with 'em. Come, Harry, the dice are in the next room.— Charles, you'll join us—when you have finished your business with these gentlemen?

CHARLES I will! I will!—

Careless! *Exeunt Gentlemen.*

CARELESS Well!

CHARLES Perhaps I may want *you.*

CARELESS Oh, you know I am always ready—word, note, or bond, 'tis all the same to me.

Exit.

MOSES Sir, this is Mr. Premium, a gentleman of the strictest honor and secrecy; and always performs what he undertakes. Mr. Premium, this is——

CHARLES Pshaw! have done! Sir, my friend Moses is a very honest fellow, but a little slow at expression; he'll be an hour giving us our titles. Mr. Premium, the plain state of the matter is this—I am an extravagant young fellow who want[s] money to borrow; you I take to be a prudent old fellow, who ha[s] got money to lend. I am blockhead enough to give fifty per cent sooner than not have it; and you, I presume, are rogue enough to take a hundred if you could get it. Now, sir, you see we are acquainted at once, and may proceed to business without farther ceremony.

SIR OLIVER Exceeding frank, upon my word. I see, sir, you are not a man of many compliments.

CHARLES Oh, no, sir! plain dealing in business I always think best.

SIR OLIVER Sir, I like you the better for't. However, you are mistaken in one thing—I have no money to lend, but I believe I could procure some of a friend; but then he's an unconscionable dog—isn't he, Moses? And must sell stock to accommodate you —mustn't he, Moses?

MOSES Yes, indeed! You know I always speak the truth, and scorn to tell a lie!

CHARLES Right! People that expect truth generally do. But these are trifles, Mr. Premium. What! I know money isn't to be bought without paying for't!

SIR OLIVER Well, but what security could you give? You have no land, I suppose?

CHARLES Not a mole-hill, nor a twig, but what's in beau-pots[9] out at the window!

OLIVER Nor any stock, I presume?

CHARLES Nothing but live stock—and that's only a few pointers and ponies. But pray, Mr. Premium, are you acquainted at all with any of my connections?

SIR OLIVER Why, to say truth, I am.

9. Flower pots.

CHARLES Then you must know that I have a devilish rich uncle in the East Indies, Sir *Oliver Surface,* from whom I have the greatest expectations.

SIR OLIVER That you have a wealthy uncle, I have heard—but how your expectations will turn out is more, I believe, than you can tell.

CHARLES Oh, no!—there can be no doubt—they tell me I'm a prodigious favorite—and that he talks of leaving me everything.

SIR OLIVER Indeed! this is the first I've heard on't.

CHARLES Yes, yes, 'tis just so.—Moses knows 'tis true; don't you, Moses?

MOSES Oh, yes! I'll swear to't.

SIR OLIVER [*Aside.*] Egad, they'll persuade me presently I'm at Bengal.

CHARLES Now I propose, Mr. Premium, if it's agreeable to you, a post-obit on Sir Oliver's life; though at the same time the old fellow has been so liberal to me that I give you my word I should be very sorry to hear anything had happened to him.

SIR OLIVER Not more than *I* should, I assure you. But the bond you mention happens to be just the worst security you could offer me —for I might live to a hundred and never recover the principal.

CHARLES Oh, yes, you would!—the moment Sir Oliver dies, you know, you'd come on me for the money.

SIR OLIVER Then I believe I should be the most unwelcome dun you ever had in your life.

CHARLES What! I suppose you are afraid now that Sir Oliver is too good a life?

SIR OLIVER No, indeed I am not—though I have heard he is as hale and healthy as any man of his years in Christendom.

CHARLES There again you are misinformed. No, no, the climate has hurt him considerably, poor uncle Oliver. Yes, he breaks apace, I'm told—and so much altered lately that his nearest relations don't know him.

SIR OLIVER No! Ha! ha! ha! so much altered lately that his relations don't know him! Ha! ha! ha! that's droll, egad—ha! ha! ha!

CHARLES Ha! ha!—you're glad to hear that, little Premium.

SIR OLIVER No, no, I'm not.

CHARLES Yes, yes, you are—ha! ha! ha!—you know that mends your chance.

SIR OLIVER But I'm told Sir Oliver is coming over—nay, some say he is actually arrived.

CHARLES Pshaw! sure I must know better than you whether he's come or not. No, no, rely on't, he is at this moment at Calcutta, isn't he, Moses?

MOSES Oh, yes, certainly.

SIR OLIVER Very true, as you say, you must know better than I, though I have it from pretty good authority—haven't I, Moses?

MOSES Yes, most undoubted!

SIR OLIVER But, sir, as I understand you want a few hundreds immediately, is there nothing you would dispose of?

CHARLES How do you mean?

SIR OLIVER For instance, now—I have heard—that your father left behind him a great quantity of massy old plate.

CHARLES O lud! that's gone long ago—Moses can tell you how better than I can.

SIR OLIVER Good lack! all the family race-cups and corporation-bowls! [*Aside.*]—Then it was also supposed that his library was one of the most valuable and complete.

CHARLES Yes, yes, so it was—vastly too much so for a private gentleman—for my part, I was always of a communicative disposition, so I thought it a shame to keep so much knowledge to myself.

SIR OLIVER [*Aside.*] Mercy on me! learning that had run in the family like an heirloom!—[*Aloud.*] Pray, what are become of the books?

CHARLES You must inquire of the auctioneer, Master Premium, for I don't believe even Moses can direct you there.

MOSES I never meddle with books.

SIR OLIVER So, so, nothing of the family property left, I suppose?

CHARLES Not much, indeed; unless you have a mind to the family pictures. I have got a room full of ancestors above—and if you have a taste for old paintings, egad, you shall have 'em a bargain!

SIR OLIVER Hey! and the devil! sure, you wouldn't sell your fore-fathers, would you?

CHARLES Every man of 'em, to the best bidder.

SIR OLIVER What! your great-uncles and aunts?

CHARLES Aye, and my great-grandfathers and grandmothers too.

SIR OLIVER Now I give him up!—[*Aside.*]—What the plague, have you no bowels for your own kindred? Odd's life! do you take me for Shylock in the play, that you would raise money of me on your own flesh and blood?

CHARLES Nay, my little broker, don't be angry: what need *you* care, if you have your money's worth?

SIR OLIVER Well, I'll be the purchaser—I think I can dispose of the family.—[*Aside.*] Oh, I'll never forgive him this! never!

Enter Careless.

CARELESS Come, Charles, what keeps you?

CHARLES I can't come yet. I'faith! we are going to have a sale above —here's little Premium will buy all my ancestors!

CARELESS Oh, burn your ancestors!

CHARLES No, he may do that afterwards, if he pleases. Stay, Careless, we want you; egad, you shall be auctioneer—so come along with us.

CARELESS Oh, have with you, if that's the case.—I can handle a hammer as well as a dice box!

SIR OLIVER [*Aside.*] Oh, the profligates!

CHARLES Come, Moses, you shall be appraiser, if we want one. —Gad's life, little Premium, you don't seem to like the business.

SIR OLIVER Oh, yes, I do, vastly! Ha! ha! yes, yes, I think it a rare joke to sell one's family by auction—ha! ha!—[*Aside.*] Oh, the prodigal!

CHARLES To be sure! when a man wants money, where the plague should he get assistance, if he can't make free with his own relations?

> Act IV. Scene i.
> Picture-room at Charles's.
> Enter Charles Surface, Sir Oliver Surface, Moses, and Careless.

CHARLES Walk in, gentlemen, pray walk in!—here they are, the family of the Surfaces, up to the Conquest.[1]

SIR OLIVER And, in my opinion, a goodly collection.

CHARLES Aye, aye, these are done in true spirit of portrait-painting —no volunteer grace or expression—not like the works of your modern Raphael, who gives you the strongest resemblance, yet contrives to make your own portrait independent of you; so that you may sink the original and not hurt the picture. No, no; the merit of these is the inveterate likeness—all stiff and awkward as the originals, and like nothing in human nature beside!

SIR OLIVER Ah! we shall never see such figures of men again.

CHARLES I hope not. Well, you see, Master Premium, what a domestic character I am—here I sit of an evening surrounded by my family. But come, get to your pulpit, Mr. Auctioneer—here's an old gouty chair of my grandfather's will answer the purpose.

CARELESS Aye, aye, this will do. But, Charles, I have ne'er a hammer; and what's an auctioneer without his hammer?

CHARLES Egad, that's true. What parchment have we here? [*Takes down a roll.*] "Richard, heir to Thomas"—our genealogy in full. Here, Careless, you shall have no common bit of mahogany— here's the family tree for you, you rogue—this shall be your hammer, and now you may knock down my ancestors with their own pedigree.

SIR OLIVER [*Aside.*] What an unnatural rogue!—an *ex post facto* parricide![2]

CARELESS Yes, yes, here's a list of your generation indeed;—faith, Charles, this is the most convenient thing you could have found for the business, for 'twill serve not only as a hammer, but a catalogue into the bargain.—But come, begin—A-going, a-going, a-going!

CHARLES Bravo, Careless! Well, here's my great uncle, Sir Richard Raviline, a marvellous good general in his day, I assure you. He served in all the Duke of Marlborough's wars, and got that cut over his eye at the battle of Malplaquet.[3] What say you, Mr. Premium? look at him—there's a hero for you! not cut out of his feathers, as your modern clipped captains are, but enveloped in wig and regimentals, as a general should be. What do you bid?

MOSES Mr. Premium would have you speak.

CHARLES Why, then, he shall have him for ten pounds, and I am sure that's not dear for a staff-officer.

---

1. The Norman conquest of England (1066).
2. In retrospect, a murderer of his fore-fathers.
3. A victory over the French in 1709.

SIR OLIVER [*Aside.*] Heaven deliver me! his famous uncle Richard for ten pounds!—Very well, sir, I take him at that.

CHARLES Careless, knock down my uncle Richard.—Here, now, is a maiden sister of his, my great-aunt Deborah, done by Kneller,[4] thought to be in his best manner, and a very formidable likeness. There she is, you see, a shepherdess feeding her flock. You shall have her for five pounds ten—the sheep are worth the money.

SIR OLIVER [*Aside.*] Ah! poor Deborah! a woman who set such a value on herself!—Five pound ten—she's mine.

CHARLES Knock down my aunt Deborah! Here, now, are two that were a sort of cousins of theirs.—You see, Moses, these pictures were done some time ago, when beaux wore wigs, and the ladies wore their own hair.

SIR OLIVER Yes, truly, head-dresses appear to have been a little lower in those days.

CHARLES Well, take that couple for the same.

MOSES 'Tis [a] good bargain.

CHARLES Careless!—This, now, is a grandfather of my mother's, a learned judge, well known on the western circuit.—What do you rate him at, Moses?

MOSES Four guineas.

CHARLES Four guineas! Gad's life, you don't bid me the price of his wig.—Mr. Premium, *you* have more respect for the woolsack;[5] do let us knock his lordship down at fifteen.

SIR OLIVER By all means.

CARELESS Gone!

CHARLES And there are two brothers of his, William and Walter Blunt, Esquires, both members of Parliament, and noted speakers; and, what's very extraordinary, I believe this is the first time they were ever bought and sold.

SIR OLIVER That's very extraordinary, indeed! I'll take them at your own price, for the honor of Parliament.

CARELESS Well said, little Premium! I'll knock 'em down at forty.

CHARLES Here's a jolly fellow—I don't know what relation, but he was mayor of Manchester; take him at eight pounds.

SIR OLIVER No, no—six will do for the mayor.

CHARLES Come, make it guineas, and I'll throw you the two aldermen there into the bargain.

SIR OLIVER They're mine.

CHARLES Careless, knock down the mayor and aldermen. But, plague on't! we shall be all day retailing in this manner; do let us deal wholesale—what say you, little Premium? Give me three hundred pounds for the rest of the family in the lump.

CARELESS Aye, aye, that will be the best way.

SIR OLIVER Well, well, anything to accommodate you; they are mine. But there is one portrait which you have always passed over.

4. Sir Godfrey Kneller, a successful portrait painter.
5. I.e., respect for judges. The Lord Chancellor, presiding over the House of Lords, is traditionally seated on a woolsack.

CARELESS What, that ill-looking little fellow over the settee?

SIR OLIVER Yes, sir, I mean that; though I don't think him so ill-looking a little fellow, by any means.

CHARLES What, that? Oh, that's my uncle Oliver! 'Twas done before he went to India.

CARELESS Your uncle Oliver! Gad, then you'll never be friends, Charles. That, now, to me, is as stern a looking rogue as ever I saw—an unforgiving eye, and a damned disinheriting countenance! an inveterate knave, depend on't. Don't you think so, little Premium?

SIR OLIVER Upon my soul, sir, I do not; I think it is as honest a looking face as any in the room, dead or alive. But I suppose your uncle Oliver goes with the rest of the lumber?

CHARLES No, hang it! I'll not part with poor Noll. The old fellow has been very good to me, and, egad, I'll keep his picture while I've a room to put it in.

SIR OLIVER The rogue's my nephew after all! [*Aside.*]—But, sir, I have somehow taken a fancy to that picture.

CHARLES I'm sorry for't, for you certainly will not have it. Oons! haven't you got enough of 'em?

SIR OLIVER I forgive him everything! [*Aside.*]—But, sir, when I take a whim in my head, I don't value money. I'll give you as much for that as for all the rest.

CHARLES Don't tease me, master broker; I tell you I'll not part with it, and there's an end on't.

SIR OLIVER How like his father the dog is!—[*Aloud.*] Well, well, I have done.—I did not perceive it before, but I think I never saw such a resemblance.—Well, sir—here is a draught for your sum.

CHARLES Why, 'tis for eight hundred pounds!

SIR OLIVER You will not let Sir Oliver go?

CHARLES Zounds! no! I tell you, once more.

SIR OLIVER Then never mind the difference; we'll balance another time. But give me your hand on the bargain; you are an honest fellow, Charles—I beg pardon, sir, for being so free.—Come, Moses.

CHARLES Egad, this is a whimsical old fellow!—but hark'ee, Premium, you'll prepare lodgings for these gentlemen.

SIR OLIVER Yes, yes, I'll send for them in a day or two.

CHARLES But hold—do now—send a genteel conveyance for them, for, I assure you, they were most of them used to ride in their own carriages.

SIR OLIVER I will, I will, for all but—Oliver.

CHARLES Aye, all but the little honest nabob.[6]

SIR OLIVER You're fixed on that?

CHARLES Peremptorily.

SIR OLIVER A dear extravagant rogue!—Good day!—Come, Moses, —Let me hear now who dares call him profligate!

Exeunt Sir Oliver *and* Moses.

CARELESS Why, this is the oddest genius of the sort I ever saw!

6. One who has made his fortune in India.

CHARLES Egad, he's the prince of brokers, I think. I wonder how the devil Moses got acquainted with so honest a fellow.—Ha! here's Rowley.—Do, Careless, say I'll join the company in a moment.

CARELESS I will—but don't let that old blockhead persuade you to squander any of that money on old musty debts, or any such nonsense; for tradesmen, Charles, are the most exorbitant fellows!

CHARLES Very true, and paying them is only encouraging them.

CARELESS Nothing else.

CHARLES Aye, aye, never fear. *Exit* Careless.

So! this was an odd fellow, indeed! Let me see, two-thirds of this is mine by right—five hundred and thirty pounds. 'Fore heaven! I find one's ancestors are more valuable relations than I took 'em for!—Ladies and gentlemen, your most obedient and very grateful humble servant.

Enter Rowley.

Ha! old Rowley! egad, you are just come in time to take leave of your old acquaintance.

ROWLEY Yes, I heard they were going. But I wonder you can have such spirits under so many distresses.

CHARLES Why, there's the point—my distresses are so many, that I can't afford to part with my spirits; but I shall be rich and splenetic, all in good time. However, I suppose you are surprised that I am not more sorrowful at parting with so many near relations; to be sure, 'tis very affecting; but, rot 'em, you see they never move a muscle, so why should I?

ROWLEY There's no making you serious a moment.

CHARLES Yes, faith: I am so now. Here, my honest Rowley, here, get me this changed, and take a hundred pounds of it immediately to old Stanley.

ROWLEY A hundred pounds! Consider only—

CHARLES Gad's life, don't talk about it! poor Stanley's wants are pressing, and, if you don't make haste, we shall have some one call that has a better right to the money.

ROWLEY Ah! there's the point! I never will cease dunning you with the old proverb——

CHARLES "Be *just* before you're *generous*," hey!—Why, so I would if I could; but Justice is an old lame hobbling beldame,[7] and I can't get her to keep pace with Generosity, for the soul of me.

ROWLEY Yet, Charles, believe me, one hour's reflection——

CHARLES Aye, aye, it's all very true; but hark'ee, Rowley, while I have, by heaven I'll give—so, damn your economy! and now for hazard.

Exeunt.

Act IV. Scene ii.
The parlor.
Enter Sir Oliver Surface *and* Moses.

MOSES Well, sir, I think, as Sir Peter said, you have seen Mr. Charles in high glory; 'tis great pity he's so extravagant.

7. Hag.

SIR OLIVER True, but he wouldn't sell my picture.

MOSES And loves wine and women so much.

SIR OLIVER But he wouldn't sell my picture!

MOSES And game[s] so deep.

SIR OLIVER But he wouldn't sell my picture. Oh, here's Rowley.
Enter Rowley.

ROWLEY So, Sir Oliver, I find you have made a purchase——

SIR OLIVER Yes, yes, our young rake has parted with his ancestors
like old tapestry.

ROWLEY And here has he commissioned me to redeliver you part of
the purchase-money—I mean, though, in your necessitous character of old *Stanley.*

MOSES Ah! there is the pity of all: he is so damned charitable.

ROWLEY And I left a hosier and two tailors in the hall, who, I'm
sure, won't be paid, and this hundred would satisfy 'em.

SIR OLIVER Well, well, I'll pay his debts—and his benevolence too;
but now I am no more a broker, and you shall introduce me to
the elder brother as old Stanley.

ROWLEY Not yet awhile; Sir Peter, I know, means to call there
about this time.
Enter Trip.

TRIP O gentlemen, I beg pardon for not showing you out; this way
—Moses, a word.

Exeunt Trip *and* Moses.

SIR OLIVER There's a fellow for you! Would you believe it, that
puppy intercepted the Jew on our coming, and wanted to raise
money before he got to his master!

ROWLEY Indeed!

SIR OLIVER Yes, they are now planning an annuity business. Ah,
Master Rowley, in my days, servants were content with the follies
of their masters, when they were worn a little threadbare—but
now they have their vices, like their birthday clothes,[8] with the
gloss on.

Exeunt.

Act IV. Scene iii.
A *library* [*in* Joseph Surface's *house.*]
Joseph Surface *and* Servant.

JOSEPH SURFACE No letter from Lady Teazle?

SERVANT No, sir.

JOSEPH SURFACE [*Aside.*] I am surprised she hasn't sent, if she is
prevented from coming. Sir Peter certainly does not suspect me.
Yet I wish I may not lose the heiress, through the scrape I have
drawn myself in with the wife; however, Charles's imprudence
and bad character are great points in my favor.
Knocking.

SERVANT Sir, I believe that must be Lady Teazle.

JOSEPH SURFACE Hold! See whether it is or not, before you go to
the door—I have a particular message for you, if it should be my
brother.

8. Worn on the King's birthday.

SERVANT 'Tis her ladyship, sir; she always leaves her chair at the milliner's in the next street.

JOSEPH SURFACE Stay, stay—draw that screen before the window —that will do;—my opposite neighbor is a maiden lady of so curious a temper.—[Servant *draws the screen, and exit.*] I have a difficult hand to play in this affair. Lady Teazle has lately suspected my views on Maria; but she must by no means be let into that secret,—at least, not till I have her more in my power.
    Enter Lady Teazle.

LADY TEAZLE What, sentiment in soliloquy! Have you been very impatient now? O lud! don't pretend to look grave. I vow I couldn't come before.

JOSEPH SURFACE O madam, punctuality is a species of constancy, a very unfashionable quality in a lady.

LADY TEAZLE Upon my word, you ought to pity me. Do you know that Sir Peter is grown so ill-tempered to me of late, and so jealous of *Charles* too—that's the best of the story, isn't it?

JOSEPH SURFACE [*Aside.*] I am glad my scandalous friends keep that up.

LADY TEAZLE I am sure I wish he would let Maria marry him, and then perhaps he would be convinced; don't you, Mr. Surface?

JOSEPH SURFACE [*Aside.*] Indeed I do not.—Oh, certainly I do! for then my dear Lady Teazle would also be convinced how wrong her suspicions were of my having any design on the silly girl.
    Sit.

LADY TEAZLE Well, well I'm inclined to believe you. But isn't it provoking, to have the most ill-natured things said to one? And there's my friend Lady Sneerwell has circulated I don't know how many scandalous tales of me! and all without any foundation, too —that's what vexes me.

JOSEPH SURFACE Aye, madam, to be sure, that *is* the provoking circumstance—without foundation! yes, yes, there's the mortification, indeed; for, when a scandalous story is believed against one, there certainly is no comfort like the consciousness of having deserved it.

LADY TEAZLE No, to be sure—then I'd forgive their malice; but to attack me, who am really so innocent, and who never say an ill-natured thing of anybody—that is, of any friend—and then Sir Peter, too, to have him so peevish, and so suspicious, when I know the integrity of my own heart—indeed 'tis monstrous!

JOSEPH SURFACE But, my dear Lady Teazle, 'tis your own fault if you suffer it. When a husband entertains a groundless suspicion of his wife, and withdraws his confidence from her, the original compact is broke, and she owes it to the honor of her sex to endeavor to outwit him.

LADY TEAZLE Indeed! So that, if he suspects me without cause, it follows that the best way of curing his jealousy is to give him reason for't?

JOSEPH SURFACE Undoubtedly—for your husband should never be deceived in you: and in that case it becomes *you* to be frail in compliment to *his* discernment.

LADY TEAZLE To be sure, what you say is very reasonable, and when the consciousness of my own innocence——

JOSEPH SURFACE Ah, my dear madam, there is the great mistake; 'tis this very conscious innocence that is of the greatest prejudice to you. What is it makes you negligent of forms, and careless of the world's opinion? why, the *consciousness* of your innocence. What makes you thoughtless in your conduct, and apt to run into a thousand little imprudences? why, the *consciousness* of your innocence. What makes you impatient of Sir Peter's temper and outrageous at his suspicions? why, the *consciousness* of your own innocence!

LADY TEAZLE 'Tis very true!

JOSEPH SURFACE Now, my dear Lady Teazle, if you would but once make a trifling *faux pas*, you can't conceive how cautious you would grow—and how ready to humour and agree with your husband.

LADY TEAZLE Do you think so?

JOSEPH SURFACE Oh, I'm sure on't; and then you would find all scandal would cease at once, for—in short, your character at present is like a person in a plethora, absolutely dying of too much health.

LADY TEAZLE So, so; then I perceive your prescription is, that I must sin in my own defence, and part with my virtue to preserve my reputation?

JOSEPH SURFACE Exactly so, upon my credit, ma'am.

LADY TEAZLE Well, certainly that is the oddest doctrine, and the newest receipt for avoiding calumny?

JOSEPH SURFACE An infallible one, believe me. *Prudence*, like *experience*, must be paid for.

LADY TEAZLE Why, if my understanding were once convinced——

JOSEPH SURFACE Oh, certainly, madam, your understanding *should* be convinced. Yes, yes—heaven forbid I should persuade you to do anything you *thought* wrong. No, no, I have too much honor to desire it.

LADY TEAZLE Don't you think we may as well leave honor out of the argument?

JOSEPH SURFACE Ah, the ill effects of your country education, I see, still remain with you.

LADY TEAZLE I doubt they do, indeed; and I will fairly own to you, that if I could be persuaded to do wrong, it would be by Sir Peter's ill-usage sooner than your honorable logic, after all.

JOSEPH SURFACE Then, by this hand, which he is unworthy of——
  [*Taking her hand.*]
        Re-enter Servant.
'Sdeath, you blockhead—what do you want?

SERVANT I beg pardon, sir, but I thought you wouldn't choose Sir Peter to come up without announcing him.

JOSEPH SURFACE Sir Peter!—Oons—the devil!

LADY TEAZLE Sir Peter! O lud! I'm ruined! I'm ruined!

318 · *Richard Brinsley Sheridan*

SERVANT Sir, 'twasn't I let him in.

LADY TEAZLE Oh! I'm undone! What will become of me, now, Mr. Logic?—Oh! mercy, he's on the stairs—I'll get behind here—and if ever I'm so imprudent again——
Goes behind the screen.

JOSEPH SURFACE Give me that book.
Sits down. Servant *pretends to adjust his hair.*
Enter Sir Peter Teazle.

SIR PETER Aye, ever improving himself!—Mr. Surface, Mr. Surface——

JOSEPH SURFACE Oh, my dear Sir Peter, I beg your pardon. [*Gaping, and throws away the book.*] I have been dozing over a stupid book. Well, I am much obliged to you for this call. You haven't been here, I believe, since I fitted up this room. Books, you know, are the only things I am a coxcomb in.

SIR PETER 'Tis very neat indeed. Well, well, that's proper; and you make even your screen a source of knowledge—hung, I perceive, with maps.

JOSEPH SURFACE Oh, yes, I find great use in that screen.

SIR PETER I dare say you must—certainly—when you want to find anything in a hurry.

JOSEPH SURFACE [*Aside.*] Aye, or to hide anything in a hurry either.

SIR PETER Well, I have a little private business——

JOSEPH SURFACE You needn't stay. [*To Servant.*]

SERVANT No, sir.

Exit.

JOSEPH SURFACE Here's a chair, Sir Peter—I beg——

SIR PETER Well, now we are alone, there is a subject, my dear friend, on which I wish to unburden my mind to you—a point of the greatest moment to my peace: in short, my good friend, Lady Teazle's conduct of late has made me extremely unhappy.

JOSEPH SURFACE Indeed! I am very sorry to hear it.

SIR PETER Yes, 'tis but too plain she has not the least regard for me; but, what's worse, I have pretty good authority to suspect she must have formed an attachment to another.

JOSEPH SURFACE You astonish me!

SIR PETER Yes! and, between ourselves, I think I have discovered the person.

JOSEPH SURFACE How! you alarm me exceedingly.

SIR PETER Aye, my dear friend, I knew you would sympathize with me!

JOSEPH SURFACE Yes, believe me, Sir Peter, such a discovery would hurt me just as much as it would you.

SIR PETER I am convinced of it.—Ah! it is a happiness to have a friend whom one can trust even with one's family secrets. But have you no guess who I mean?

JOSEPH SURFACE I haven't the most distant idea. It can't be Sir Benjamin Backbite!

SIR PETER O, no! What say you to Charles?

JOSEPH SURFACE My brother! impossible!

SIR PETER Ah, my dear friend, the goodness of your own heart misleads you—you judge of others by yourself.

JOSEPH SURFACE Certainly, Sir Peter, the heart that is conscious of its own integrity is ever slow to credit another's treachery.

SIR PETER True; but your brother has no sentiment—you never hear him talk so.

JOSEPH SURFACE Yet I can't but think Lady Teazle herself has too much principle——

SIR PETER Aye; but what's her principle against the flattery of a handsome, lively young fellow?

JOSEPH SURFACE That's very true.

SIR PETER And then, you know, the difference of our ages makes it very improbable that she should have any great affection for me; and if she were to be frail, and I were to make it public, why the town would only laugh at me, the foolish old bachelor who had married a girl.

JOSEPH SURFACE That's true, to be sure—they *would* laugh.

SIR PETER Laugh! aye, and make ballads, and paragraphs, and the devil knows what of me.

JOSEPH SURFACE No, you must never make it public.

SIR PETER But then again—that the nephew of my old friend, Sir Oliver, should be the person to attempt such a wrong, hurts me more nearly.

JOSEPH SURFACE Aye, there's the point. When ingratitude barbs the dart of injury, the wound has double danger in it.

SIR PETER Aye—I, that was, in a manner, left his guardian—in whose house he had been so often entertained—who never in my life denied him—my advice!

JOSEPH SURFACE Oh, 'tis not to be credited! There *may* be a man capable of such baseness, to be sure; but, for my part, till you can give me positive proofs, I cannot but doubt it. However, if it should be proved on him, he is no longer a brother of mine! I disclaim kindred with him—for the man who can break through the laws of hospitality, and attempt the wife of his friend, deserves to be branded as the pest of society.

SIR PETER What a difference there is between you! What noble sentiments!

JOSEPH SURFACE Yet I cannot suspect Lady Teazle's honor.

SIR PETER I am sure I wish to think well of her, and to remove all ground of quarrel between us. She has lately reproached me more than once with having made no settlement on her; and, in our last quarrel, she almost hinted that she should not break her heart if I was dead. Now, as we seem to differ in our ideas of expense, I have resolved she shall be her own mistress in that respect for the future; and if I *were* to die, she shall find that I have not been inattentive to her interest while living. Here, my friend, are the drafts of two deeds, which I wish to have your opinion on. By one, she will enjoy eight hundred a year independent while I live; and, by the other, the bulk of my fortune after my death.

JOSEPH SURFACE This conduct, Sir Peter, is indeed truly gener-

320 · *Richard Brinsley Sheridan*

ous.— [*Aside.*] I wish it may not corrupt my pupil.

SIR PETER Yes, I am determined she shall have no cause to complain, though I would not have her acquainted with the latter instance of my affection yet awhile.

JOSEPH SURFACE Nor I, if I could help it. [*Aside.*]

SIR PETER And now, my dear friend, if you please, we will talk over the situation of your hopes with *Maria*.

JOSEPH SURFACE [*Softly.*] No, no, Sir Peter; another time, if you please.

SIR PETER I am sensibly chagrined at the little progress you seem to make in her affection.

JOSEPH SURFACE I beg you will not mention it. What are my disappointments when your happiness is in debate! [*Softly.*]—'Sdeath, I shall be ruined every way! [*Aside.*]

SIR PETER And though you are so averse to my acquainting Lady Teazle with your passion, I am sure she's not your enemy in the affair.

JOSEPH SURFACE Pray, Sir Peter, now oblige me. I am really too much affected by the subject we have been speaking on to bestow a thought on my own concerns. The man who is entrusted with his friend's distresses can never——

Enter Servant.

Well, sir?

SERVANT Your brother, sir, is speaking to a gentleman in the street, and says he knows you are within.

JOSEPH SURFACE 'Sdeath, blockhead—I'm not within—I'm out for the day.

SIR PETER Stay—hold—a thought has struck me—you shall be at home.

JOSEPH SURFACE Well, well, let him up.

Exit Servant.

He'll interrupt Sir Peter—however—

SIR PETER Now, my good friend, oblige me, I entreat you. Before Charles comes, let me conceal myself somewhere; then do you tax him on the point we have been talking on, and his answers may satisfy me at once.

JOSEPH SURFACE O, fie, Sir Peter! would you have me join in so mean a trick?—to trepan[9] my brother too?

SIR PETER Nay, you tell me you are *sure* he is innocent; if so, you do him the greatest service by giving him an opportunity to clear himself, and you will set my heart at rest. Come, you shall not refuse me; here, behind the screen will be [*Goes to the screen.*] —Hey! what the devil! there seems to be *one* listener here already—I'll swear I saw a petticoat!

JOSEPH SURFACE Ha! ha! ha! Well, this is ridiculous enough. I'll tell you, Sir Peter, though I hold a man of intrigue to be a most despicable character, yet you know, it doesn't follow that one is to be an absolute Joseph[1] either! Hark'ee! 'tis a little French mil-

9. Entrap.
1. I.e., one who refuses all opportunities with women. In Genesis XXXIX.7–20, Jo-

seph refuses the adulterous invitations of Potiphar's wife.

liner, a silly rogue that plagues me—and having some character
—on your coming, she ran behind the screen.

SIR PETER Ah, you rogue!—But, egad, she has overheard all I have
been saying of my wife.

JOSEPH SURFACE Oh, 'twill never go any further, you may depend
on't!

SIR PETER No! then, i'faith, let her hear it out.— Here's a closet
will do as well.

JOSEPH SURFACE Well, go in then.

SIR PETER Sly rogue! sly rogue!
> *Goes into the closet.*

JOSEPH SURFACE A very narrow escape, indeed! and a curious situation I'm in, to part man and wife in this manner.

LADY TEAZLE [*Peeping from the screen.*] Couldn't I steal off?

JOSEPH SURFACE Keep close, my angel!

SIR PETER [*Peeping out.*] Joseph, tax him home.

JOSEPH SURFACE Back, my dear friend!

LADY TEAZLE [*Peeping.*] Couldn't you lock Sir Peter in?

JOSEPH SURFACE Be still, my life!

SIR PETER [*Peeping.*] You're sure the little milliner won't blab?

JOSEPH SURFACE In, in, my dear Sir Peter!—'Fore gad, I wish I
had a key to the door.
> *Enter* Charles Surface.

CHARLES Hollo! brother, what has been the matter? Your fellow
would not let me up at first. What! have you had a Jew or a
wench with you?

JOSEPH SURFACE Neither, brother, I assure you.

CHARLES But what has made Sir Peter steal off? I thought he had
been with you.

JOSEPH SURFACE He was, brother; but, hearing *you* were coming,
he did not choose to stay.

CHARLES What! was the old gentleman afraid I wanted to borrow
money of him!

JOSEPH SURFACE No, sir, but I am sorry to find, Charles, that you
have lately given that worthy man grounds for geat uneasiness.

CHARLES Yes, they tell me I do that to a great many worthy men.
But how so, pray?

JOSEPH SURFACE To be plain with you, brother, he thinks you are
endeavoring to gain Lady Teazle's affections from him.

CHARLES Who, I? O lud! not I, upon my word. —Ha! ha! ha! so
the old fellow has found out that he has got a young wife, has
he?—or, what's worse, has her ladyship discovered that she has
an old husband?

JOSEPH SURFACE This is no subject to jest on, brother.—He who
can laugh——

CHARLES True, true, as you were going to say—then, seriously, I
never had the least idea of what you charge me with, upon my
honor.

JOSEPH SURFACE Well, it will give Sir Peter great satisfaction to
hear this. [*Aloud.*]

CHARLES To be sure, I once thought the lady seemed to have taken a fancy to me; but, upon my soul, I never gave her the least encouragement. Besides, you know my attachment to Maria.

JOSEPH SURFACE But sure, brother, even if Lady Teazle had betrayed the fondest partiality for you——

CHARLES Why, look'ee, Joseph, I hope I shall never deliberately do a dishonorable action—but if a pretty woman were purposely to throw herself in my way—and that pretty woman married to a man old enough to be her father——

JOSEPH SURFACE Well!

CHARLES Why, I believe I should be obliged to borrow a little of your morality, that's all.—But, brother, do you know now that you surprise me exceedingly, by naming *me* with Lady Teazle; for, faith, I alway[s] understood *you* were her favorite.

JOSEPH SURFACE Oh, for shame, Charles! This retort is foolish.

CHARLES Nay, I swear I have seen you exchange such significant glances——

JOSEPH SURFACE Nay, nay, sir, this is no jest——

CHARLES Egad, I'm serious! Don't you remember—one day, when I called here——

JOSEPH SURFACE Nay, prithee, Charles——

CHARLES And found you together——

JOSEPH SURFACE Zounds, sir, I insist——

CHARLES And another time, when your servant——

JOSEPH SURFACE Brother, brother, a word with you!— [*Aside.*] Gad, I must stop him.

CHARLES Informed me, I say, that——

JOSEPH SURFACE Hush! I beg your pardon, but Sir Peter has overheard all we have been saying—I knew you would clear yourself, or I should not have consented.

CHARLES How, Sir Peter! Where is he?

JOSEPH SURFACE Softly, there! [*Points to the closet.*]

CHARLES Oh, 'fore heaven, I'll have him out.—Sir Peter, come forth!

JOSEPH SURFACE No, no——

CHARLES I say, Sir Peter, come into court.—[*Pulls in* Sir Peter.] What! my old guardian!—What—turn inquisitor, and take evidence, incog.?[2]

SIR PETER Give me your hand, Charles—I believe I have suspected you wrongfully—but you mustn't be angry with Joseph—'twas my plan!

CHARLES Indeed!

SIR PETER But I acquit you. I promise you I don't think near so ill of you as I did. What I have heard has given me great satisfaction.

CHARLES Egad, then, 'twas lucky you didn't hear any more. Wasn't it, Joseph? [*Half aside.*]

SIR PETER Ah! you would have retorted on him.

CHARLES Aye, aye, that was a joke.

SIR PETER Yes, yes, I know his honor too well.

2. Incognito.

CHARLES But you might as well have suspected him as me in this matter, for all that. Mightn't he, Joseph? [*Half aside.*]

SIR PETER Well, well, I believe you.

JOSEPH SURFACE [*Aside.*] Would they were both out of the room!

SIR PETER And in future, perhaps, we may not be such strangers.

Enter Servant *who whispers* Joseph Surface.

JOSEPH SURFACE Lady Sneerwell!—stop her by all means—[*Exit* Servant.] Gentlemen—I beg pardon—I must wait on you down-stairs—here's a person come on particular business.

CHARLES Well, you can see him in another room. Sir Peter and I haven't met a long time, and I have something to say to him.

JOSEPH SURFACE They must not be left together.—I'll send Lady Sneerwell away, and return directly.—[*Aside.*] Sir Peter, not a word of the French milliner.

Exit Joseph Surface.

SIR PETER Oh! not for the world!—Ah, Charles, if you associated more with your brother, one might indeed hope for your reforma-tion. He is a man of sentiment.—Well, there is nothing in the world so noble as a man of sentiment!

CHARLES Pshaw! he is too moral by half, and so apprehensive of his good name, as he calls it, that I suppose he would as soon let a priest into his house as a girl.

SIR PETER No, no,—come, come,—you wrong him. No, no, Joseph is no rake, but he is not such a saint in that respect either,—I have a great mind to tell him—we should have a laugh! [*Aside.*]

CHARLES Oh, hang him! he's a very anchorite, a young hermit!

SIR PETER Hark'ee—you must not abuse him; he may chance to hear of it again, I promise you.

CHARLES Why, you won't tell him?

SIR PETER No—but—this way.—[*Aside.*] Egad, I'll tell him.— Hark'ee, have you a mind to have a good laugh at Joseph?

CHARLES I should like it of all things.

SIR PETER Then, i'faith, we will!—I'll be quit with him for discov-ering me. [*Aside.*]—He had a girl with him when I called.

CHARLES What! Joseph? you jest.

SIR PETER Hush!—a little—French milliner—[*whispers*] and the best of the jest is—she's in the room now.

CHARLES The devil she is!

SIR PETER Hush! I tell you. [*Points to the screen.*]

CHARLES Behind the screen! 'Slife, let's unveil her!

SIR PETER No, no, he's coming:—you shan't, indeed!

CHARLES Oh, egad, we'll have a peep at the little milliner!

SIR PETER Not for the world!—Joseph will never forgive me.

CHARLES I'll stand by you——

SIR PETER [*Struggling with* Charles.] Odds, here he is!

Joseph Surface *enters just as* Charles *throws down the screen.*

CHARLES Lady Teazle, by all that's wonderful!

SIR PETER Lady Teazle, by all that's horrible!

CHARLES Sir Peter, this is one of the smartest French milliners I

ever saw. Egad, you seem all to have been diverting yourselves
here at hide and seek—and I don't see who is out of the secret.
Shall I beg your ladyship to inform me?—Not a word!—Brother,
will you please to explain this matter? What! Morality dumb too!
—Sir Peter, though I *found* you in the dark, perhaps you are not
so now! All mute! Well—though I can make nothing of the
affair, I suppose you perfectly understand one another; so I'll
leave you to yourselves.—[*Going.*] Brother, I'm sorry to find you
have given that worthy man so much uneasiness,—Sir Peter!
there's nothing *in the world* so *noble as a man of sentiment!*

Exit Charles.

They stand for some time looking at each other.

JOSEPH SURFACE Sir Peter—notwithstanding I confess that appearances are against me—if you will afford me your patience—I
make no doubt but I shall explain everything to your satisfaction.

SIR PETER If you please—

JOSEPH SURFACE The fact is, sir, Lady Teazle, knowing my pretensions to your ward Maria—I say, sir, Lady Teazle, being apprehensive of the jealousy of your temper—and knowing my friendship to the family—she, sir, I say—called here—in order that—I
might explain those pretensions—but on your coming—being
apprehensive—as I said—of your jealousy—she withdrew—and
this, you may depend on't is the whole truth of the matter.

SIR PETER A very clear account, upon my word; and I dare swear
the lady will vouch for every article of it.

LADY TEAZLE [*Coming forward.*] For not one word of it, Sir Peter!

SIR PETER How! don't you think it worth while to agree in the lie?

LADY TEAZLE There is not one syllable of truth in what the gentleman has told you.

SIR PETER I believe you, upon my soul, ma'am!

JOSEPH SURFACE [*Aside.*] 'Sdeath, madam, will you betray me?

LADY TEAZLE Good Mr. Hypocrite, by your leave, I will speak for
myself.

SIR PETER Aye, let her alone, sir; you'll find she'll make out a better
story than *you*, without prompting.

LADY TEAZLE Hear me, Sir Peter!—I came here on no matter relating to your ward, and even ignorant of this gentleman's pretensions to her—but I came, seduced by his insidious arguments, at
least to listen to his pretended passion, if not to sacrifice *your*
honor to his baseness.

SIR PETER Now, I believe, the truth *is* coming, indeed!

JOSEPH SURFACE The woman's mad!

LADY TEAZLE No sir; she has recovered her senses, and your own
arts have furnished her with the means.—Sir Peter, I do not
expect you to credit me—but the tenderness you expressed for
me, when I am sure you could not think I was a witness to it, has
penetrated to my heart, and had I left the place without the
shame of this discovery, my future life should have spoke[n] the
sincerity of my gratitude. As for that smooth-tongue hypocrite,
who would have seduced the wife of his too credulous friend,

while he affected honorable addresses to his ward—I behold him now in a light so truly despicable, that I shall never again respect myself for having listened to him.

Exit.

JOSEPH SURFACE Notwithstanding all this, Sir Peter, heaven knows——

SIR PETER That you are a villain!—and so I leave you to your conscience.

JOSEPH SURFACE You are too rash, Sir Peter; you shall hear me. The man who shuts out conviction by refusing to——

SIR PETER Oh!—

Exeunt, Joseph Surface *following and speaking.*

Act V. Scene i.

The library [in Joseph Surface's *house.*]

Enter Joseph Surface *and* Servant.

JOSEPH SURFACE Mr. Stanley! why should you think I would see him? you *must* know he comes to ask something.

SERVANT Sir, I should not have let him in, but that Mr. Rowley came to the door with him.

JOSEPH SURFACE Pshaw! blockhead! to suppose that I should *now* be in a temper to receive visits from poor relations!—Well, why don't you show the fellow up?

SERVANT I will, sir.—Why, sir, it was not my fault that Sir Peter discovered my lady——

JOSEPH SURFACE Go, fool!

Exit Servant.

Sure, Fortune never played a man of my policy such a trick before! My character with Sir Peter, my hopes with Maria, destroyed in a moment! I'm in a rare humour to listen to other people's distresses! I shan't be able to bestow even a benevolent sentiment on Stanley.—So! here he comes, and Rowley with him. I must try to recover myself—and put a little charity into my face, however.

Exit.

Enter Sir Oliver Surface *and* Rowley.

SIR OLIVER What! does he avoid us? That was he, was it not?

ROWLEY It was, sir—but I doubt you are come a little too abruptly —his nerves are so weak, that the sight of a poor relation may be too much for him.—I should have gone first to break you to him.

SIR OLIVER A plague of his nerves!—Yet this is he whom Sir Peter extols as a man of the most benevolent way of thinking!

ROWLEY As to his way of thinking, I cannot pretend to decide; for, to do him justice, he appears to have as much speculative benevolence as any private gentleman in the kingdom, though he is seldom so sensual as to indulge himself in the exercise of it.

SIR OLIVER Yet has a string of charitable sentiments, I suppose, at his fingers' ends!

ROWLEY Or, rather, at his tongue's end, Sir Oliver; for I believe there is no sentiment he has more faith in than that "Charity begins at home."

SIR OLIVER And his, I presume, is of that domestic sort which never stirs abroad at all.

ROWLEY I doubt you'll find it so;—but he's coming—I mustn't seem to interrupt you; and you know, immediately as you leave him, I come in to announce your arrival in your real character.

SIR OLIVER True; and afterwards you'll meet me at Sir Peter's.

ROWLEY Without losing a moment.

Exit Rowley.

SIR OLIVER So! I don't like the complaisance of his features.

Re-enter Joseph Surface.

JOSEPH SURFACE Sir, I beg you ten thousand pardons for keeping you a moment waiting—Mr. Stanley, I presume.

SIR OLIVER At your service.

JOSEPH SURFACE Sir, I beg you will do me the honor to sit down— I entreat you, sir.

SIR OLIVER Dear sir—there's no occasion.—Too civil by half! [*Aside.*]

JOSEPH SURFACE I have not the pleasure of knowing you, Mr. Stanley; but I am extremely happy to see you look so well. You were nearly related to my mother, I think, Mr. Stanley?

SIR OLIVER I was, sir—so nearly that my present poverty, I fear, may do discredit to her wealthy children—else I should not have presumed to trouble you.

JOSEPH SURFACE Dear sir, there needs no apology: he that is in distress, though a stranger, has a right to claim kindred with the wealthy;—I am sure I wish I was one of that class, and had it in my power to offer you even a small relief.

SIR OLIVER If your uncle, Sir Oliver, were here, I should have a friend.

JOSEPH SURFACE I wish he were, sir, with all my heart: you should not want an advocate with him, believe me, sir.

SIR OLIVER I should not *need* one—my distresses would recommend me; but I imagined his bounty had enabled *you* to become the agent of his charity.

JOSEPH SURFACE My dear sir, you were strangely misinformed. Sir Oliver is a worthy man, a very worthy sort of man; but—avarice, Mr. Stanley, is the vice of age. I will tell you, my good sir, in confidence, what he has done for me has been a mere nothing; though people, I know, have thought otherwise, and, for my part, I never chose to contradict the report.

SIR OLIVER What! has he never transmitted you bullion! rupees! pagodas![3]

JOSEPH SURFACE O dear sir, nothing of the kind! No, no; a few presents now and then—china—shawls—Congo tea—avadavats[4] and India crackers[5]—little more, believe me.

SIR OLIVER [*Aside.*] Here's gratitude for twelve thousand pounds! —Avadavats and Indian crackers!

JOSEPH SURFACE Then, my dear sir, you have heard, I doubt not,

3. Rupees and pagodas: Indian coins.   5. Firecrackers.
4. Small Indian songbirds.

of the extravagance of my brother; there are very few would credit what I have done for that unfortunate young man.

SIR OLIVER Not I, for one! [*Aside.*]

JOSEPH SURFACE The sums I have lent him! Indeed I have been exceedingly to blame—it was an amiable weakness: however, I don't pretend to defend it—and now I feel it doubly culpable, since it has deprived me of the pleasure of serving *you*, Mr. Stanley, as my heart dictates.

SIR OLIVER [*Aside.*] Dissembler!—Then, sir, you cannot assist me?

JOSEPH SURFACE At present, it grieves me to say, I cannot; but, whenever I have the ability, you may depend upon hearing from me.

SIR OLIVER I am extremely sorry——

JOSEPH SURFACE Not more than I am, believe me; to pity, without the power to relieve, is still more painful than to ask and be denied.

SIR OLIVER Kind sir, your most obedient humble servant.

JOSEPH SURFACE You leave me deeply affected, Mr. Stanley.—William, be ready to open the door.

SIR OLIVER O dear sir, no ceremony.

JOSEPH SURFACE Your very obedient.

SIR OLIVER Sir, your most obsequious.

JOSEPH SURFACE You may depend upon hearing from me, whenever I can be of service.

SIR OLIVER Sweet sir, you are too good.

JOSEPH SURFACE In the meantime I wish you health and spirits.

SIR OLIVER Your ever grateful and perpetual humble servant.

JOSEPH SURFACE Sir, yours as sincerely.

SIR OLIVER Now I am satisfied!

Exit.

JOSEPH SURFACE [*Solus.*] This is one bad effect of a good character; it invites applications from the unfortunate, and there needs no small degree of address to gain the reputation of benevolence without incurring the expense. The silver one of pure charity is an expensive article in the catalogue of a man's good qualities; whereas the sentimental French plate I use instead of it makes just as good a show, and pays no tax.

Enter Rowley.

ROWLEY Mr. Surface, your servant—I was apprehensive of interrupting you—though my business demands immediate attention —as this note will inform you.

JOSEPH SURFACE Always happy to see Mr. Rowley.—[*Reads.*] How! "*Oliver—Surface*"—My uncle arrived!

ROWLEY He is, indeed—we have just parted—quite well, after a speedy voyage, and impatient to embrace his worthy nephew.

JOSEPH SURFACE I am astonished!—William! stop Mr. Stanley, if he's not gone.

ROWLEY Oh! he's out of reach, I believe.

JOSEPH SURFACE Why didn't you let me know this when you came in together?

ROWLEY I thought you had particular business. But I must be gone to inform your brother, and appoint him here to meet his uncle. He will be with you in a quarter of an hour.

JOSEPH SURFACE So he says. Well, I am strangely overjoyed at his coming.—[*Aside.*] Never, to be sure, was anything so damned unlucky!

ROWLEY You will be delighted to see how well he looks.

JOSEPH SURFACE Oh! I'm rejoiced to hear it.—[*Aside.*] Just at this time!

ROWLEY I'll tell him how impatiently you expect him.

JOSEPH SURFACE Do, do; pray give my best duty and affection. Indeed, I cannot express the sensations I feel at the thought of seeing him.—[*Exit* Rowley.] Certainly his coming just at this time is the cruellest piece of ill fortune.

Exit.

Act V. Scene ii.
At Sir Peter's.
Enter Mrs. Candour *and* Maid.

MAID Indeed, ma'am, my lady will see nobody at present.

MRS. CANDOUR Did you tell her it was her friend Mrs. Candour?

MAID Yes, madam; but she begs you will excuse her.

MRS. CANDOUR Do go again; I shall be glad to see her, if it be only for a moment, for I am sure she must be in great distress.—

Exit Maid.

Dear heart, how provoking; I'm not mistress of half the circumstances! We shall have the whole affair in the newspapers, with the names of the parties at length, before I have dropped the story at a dozen houses.

Enter Sir Benjamin Backbite.

O dear Sir Benjamin! you have heard, I suppose——

SIR BENJAMIN Of Lady Teazle and Mr. Surface——

MRS. CANDOUR And Sir Peter's discovery——

SIR BENJAMIN Oh, the strangest piece of business, to be sure!

MRS. CANDOUR Well, I never was so surprised in my life. I am so sorry for all parties, indeed I am.

SIR BENJAMIN Now, I don't pity Sir Peter at all—he was so extravagantly partial to Mr. Surface.

MRS. CANDOUR Mr. Surface! Why, 'twas with Charles Lady Teazle was detected.

SIR BENJAMIN No such thing—Mr. Surface is the gallant.

MRS. CANDOUR No, no—Charles is the man. 'Twas Mr. Surface brought Sir Peter on purpose to discover them.

SIR BENJAMIN I tell you I have it from one——

MRS. CANDOUR And I have it from one——

SIR BENJAMIN Who had it from one, who had it——

MRS. CANDOUR From one immediately—— But here's Lady Sneerwell; perhaps she knows the whole affair.

Enter Lady Sneerwell.

LADY SNEERWELL So, my dear Mrs. Candour, here's a sad affair of our friend Lady Teazle!

MRS. CANDOUR Aye, my dear friend, who could have thought it——

LADY SNEERWELL Well, there's no trusting appearances; though, indeed, she was always too lively for me.

MRS. CANDOUR To be sure, her manners were a little too free—but she was very young!

LADY SNEERWELL And had, indeed, some good qualities.

MRS. CANDOUR So she had, indeed. But have you heard the particulars?

LADY SNEERWELL No; but everybody says that Mr. Surface——

SIR BENJAMIN Aye, there, I told you—Mr. Surface was the man.

MRS. CANDOUR No, no, indeed—the assignation was with Charles.

LADY SNEERWELL With Charles! You alarm me, Mrs. Candour.

MRS. CANDOUR Yes, yes, he was the lover. Mr. Surface—do him justice—was only the informer.

SIR BENJAMIN Well, I'll not dispute with you, Mrs. Candour; but, be it which it may, I hope that Sir Peter's wound will not——

MRS. CANDOUR Sir Peter's wound! Oh, mercy! I didn't hear a word of their fighting.

LADY SNEERWELL Nor I, a syllable.

SIR BENJAMIN No! what, no mention of the duel?

MRS. CANDOUR Not a word.

SIR BENJAMIN O Lord—yes, yes—they fought before they left the room.

LADY SNEERWELL Pray let us hear.

MRS. CANDOUR Aye, do oblige us with the duel.

SIR BENJAMIN "Sir," says Sir Peter—immediately after the discovery—"you are a most ungrateful fellow."

MRS. CANDOUR Aye, to Charles——

SIR BENJAMIN No, no—to Mr. Surface—"a most ungrateful fellow; and old as I am, sir," says he, "I insist on immediate satisfaction."

MRS. CANDOUR Aye, that must have been to Charles; for 'tis very unlikely Mr. Surface should go to fight in his house.

SIR BENJAMIN 'Gad's life, ma'am, not at all—"giving me immediate satisfaction."—On this, madam, Lady Teazle, seeing Sir Peter in such danger, ran out of the room in strong hysterics, and Charles after her, calling out for hartshorn[6] and water! Then, madam, they began to fight with swords——

Enter Crabtree.

CRABTREE With pistols, nephew—I have it from undoubted authority.

MRS. CANDOUR O Mr. Crabtree, then it is all true!

CRABTREE Too true, indeed, ma'am, and Sir Peter's dangerously wounded——

SIR BENJAMIN By a thrust of *in seconde*[7] quite through his left side——

CRABTREE By a bullet lodged in the thorax.

MRS. CANDOUR Mercy on me! Poor Sir Peter!

CRABTREE Yes, ma'am—though Charles would have avoided the matter, if he could.

MRS. CANDOUR I knew Charles was the person.

---

6. Smelling-salts.　　　　7. A standard position in fencing.

SIR BENJAMIN Oh, my uncle, I see, knows nothing of the matter.

CRABTREE But Sir Peter taxed him with the basest ingratitude——

SIR BENJAMIN That I told you, you know.

CRABTREE Do, nephew, let me speak!—and insisted on an immediate——

SIR BENJAMIN Just as I said.

CRABTREE Odds life, nephew, allow others to know something too! A pair of pistols lay on the bureau (for Mr. Surface, it seems, had come the night before late from Salt-Hill, where he had been to see the Montem[8] with a friend, who has a son at Eton), so, unluckily, the pistols were left charged.

SIR BENJAMIN I heard nothing of this.

CRABTREE Sir Peter forced Charles to take one, and they fired, it seems, pretty nearly together. Charles's shot took place, as I told you, and Sir Peter's missed; but, what is very extraordinary, the ball struck against a little bronze Pliny that stood over the chimney-piece, grazed out of the window at a right angle, and wounded the postman, who was just coming to the door with a double letter from Northamptonshire.

SIR BENJAMIN My uncle's account is more circumstantial, I must confess; but I believe mine is the true one, for all that.

LADY SNEERWELL [*Aside.*] I am more interested in this affair than they imagine, and must have better information.

Exit Lady Sneerwell.

SIR BENJAMIN [*After a pause looking at each other.*] Ah! Lady Sneerwell's alarm is very easily accounted for.

CRABTREE Yes, yes, they certainly *do* say—but that's neither here nor there.

MRS. CANDOUR But, pray, where is Sir Peter at present?

CRABTREE Oh! they brought him home, and he is now in the house, though the servants are ordered to deny it.

MRS. CANDOUR I believe so, and Lady Teazle, I suppose, attending him.

CRABTREE Yes, yes; I saw one of the faculty[9] enter just before me.

SIR BENJAMIN Hey! who comes here?

CRABTREE Oh, this is he—the physician, depend on't.

MRS. CANDOUR Oh, certainly! it must be the physician; and now we shall know.

Enter Sir Oliver Surface.

CRABTREE Well, doctor, what hopes?

MRS. CANDOUR Aye, doctor, how's your patient?

SIR BENJAMIN Now, doctor, isn't it a wound with a small-sword?

CRABTREE A bullet lodged in the thorax, for a hundred!

SIR OLIVER Doctor! a wound with a small-sword! and a bullet in the thorax?—Oons! are you mad, good people?

SIR BENJAMIN Perhaps, sir, you are not a doctor?

SIR OLIVER Truly, I am to thank you for my degree, if I am.

CRABTREE Only a friend of Sir Peter's, then, I presume. But, sir,

8. An annual festival by the students of Eton College. 9. A physician.

you must have heard of this accident?

SIR OLIVER Not a word!

CRABTREE Not of his being dangerously wounded?

SIR OLIVER The devil he is!

SIR BENJAMIN Run through the body——

CRABTREE Shot in the breast——

SIR BENJAMIN By one Mr. Surface——

CRABTREE Aye, the younger.

SIR OLIVER Hey! what the plague! you seem to differ strangely in your accounts—however, you agree that Sir Peter is dangerously wounded.

SIR BENJAMIN Oh, yes, we agree there.

CRABTREE Yes, yes, I believe there can be no doubt of that.

SIR OLIVER Then, upon my word, for a person in that situation, he is the most imprudent man alive—for here he comes, walking as if nothing at all were the matter.

Enter Sir Peter Teazle.

Odds heart, Sir Peter! you are come in good time, I promise you; for we had just *given you over*.

SIR BENJAMIN Egad, uncle, this is the most sudden recovery!

SIR OLIVER Why, man! what do you do out of bed with a small-sword through your body, and a bullet lodged in your thorax?

SIR PETER A small-sword and a bullet?

SIR OLIVER Aye; these gentlemen would have killed you without law or physic, and wanted to dub me a doctor—to make me an accomplice.

SIR PETER Why, what is all this?

SIR BENJAMIN We rejoice, Sir Peter, that the story of the duel is not true, and are sincerely sorry for your other misfortunes.

SIR PETER So, so; all over the town already. [*Aside.*]

CRABTREE Though, Sir Peter, you were certainly vastly to blame to marry at all, at your years.

SIR PETER Sir, what business is that of yours?

MRS. CANDOUR Though, indeed, as Sir Peter made so good a husband, he's very much to be pitied.

SIR PETER Plague on your pity, ma'am! I desire none of it.

SIR BENJAMIN However, Sir Peter, you must not mind the laughing and jests you will meet with on this occasion.

SIR PETER Sir, I desire to be master in my own house.

CRABTREE 'Tis no uncommon case, that's one comfort.

SIR PETER I insist on being left to myself: without ceremony, I insist on your leaving my house directly!

MRS. CANDOUR Well, well, we are going; and depend on't, we'll make the best report of you we can.

SIR PETER Leave my house!

CRABTREE And tell how hardly you have been treated.

SIR PETER Leave my house!

SIR BENJAMIN And how patiently you bear it.

SIR PETER Fiends! vipers! furies! Oh! that their own venom would choke them!

Exeunt Mrs. Candour, Sir Benjamin Backbite, Crabtree, &c.

SIR OLIVER They are very provoking indeed, Sir Peter.

Enter Rowley.

ROWLEY I heard high words—what has ruffled you, Sir Peter?

SIR PETER Pshaw! what signifies asking? Do I ever pass a day without my vexations?

SIR OLIVER Well, I'm not inquisitive—I come only to tell you that I have seen both my nephews in the manner we proposed.

SIR PETER A precious couple they are!

ROWLEY Yes, and Sir Oliver is convinced that your judgment was right, Sir Peter.

SIR OLIVER Yes, I find *Joseph* is indeed the man, after all.

ROWLEY Yes, as Sir Peter says, he's a man of sentiment.

SIR OLIVER And acts up to the sentiments he professes.

ROWLEY It certainly is edification to hear him talk.

SIR OLIVER Oh, he's a model for the young men of the age! But how's this, Sir Peter? you don't join in your friend Joseph's praise, as I expected.

SIR PETER Sir Oliver, we live in a damned wicked world, and the fewer we praise the better.

ROWLEY What! do *you* say so, Sir Peter, who were never mistaken in your life?

SIR PETER Pshaw! plague on you both! I see by your sneering you have heard the whole affair. I shall go mad among you!

ROWLEY Then, to fret you no longer, Sir Peter, we are indeed acquainted with it all. I met Lady Teazle coming from Mr. Surface's, so humbled that she deigned to request me to be her advocate with you.

SIR PETER And does Sir Oliver know all too?

SIR OLIVER Every circumstance.

SIR PETER What, of the closet—and the screen, hey?

SIR OLIVER Yes, yes, and the little French milliner. Oh, I have been vastly diverted with the story! ha! ha!

SIR PETER 'Twas very pleasant.

SIR OLIVER I never laughed more in my life, I assure you: ha! ha!

SIR PETER O, vastly diverting! ha! ha!

ROWLEY To be sure, Joseph with his sentiments! ha! ha!

SIR PETER Yes, yes, his sentiments! ha! ha! A hypocritical villain!

SIR OLIVER Aye, and that rogue Charles to pull Sir Peter out of the closet: ha! ha!

SIR PETER Ha! ha! 'twas devilish entertaining, to be sure!

SIR OLIVER Ha! ha! Egad, Sir Peter, I should like to have seen your face when the screen was thrown down: ha! ha!

SIR PETER Yes, yes, my face when the screen was thrown down: ha! ha! Oh, I must never show my head again!

SIR OLIVER But come, come, it isn't fair to laugh at you neither, my old friend— though, upon my soul, I can't help it.

SIR PETER Oh, pray don't restrain your mirth on my account—it does not hurt me at all! I laugh at the whole affair myself. Yes, yes, I think being a standing jest for all one's acquaintances a very happy situation. O yes, and then of a morning to read the paragraphs about Mr. S——, Lady T——, and Sir P——, will be so entertaining!

ROWLEY Without affectation, Sir Peter, you may despise the ridicule of fools. But I see Lady Teazle going towards the next room; I am sure you must desire a reconciliation as earnestly as she does.

SIR OLIVER Perhaps my being here prevents her coming to you. Well, I'll leave honest Rowley to mediate between you; but he must bring you all presently to Mr. Surface's, where I am now returning, if not to reclaim a libertine, at least to expose hypocrisy.

SIR PETER Ah! I'll be present at your discovering yourself there with all my heart—though 'tis a vile unlucky place for discoveries!

ROWLEY We'll follow.

[*Exit* Sir Oliver Surface.]

SIR PETER She is not coming here, you see, Rowley.

ROWLEY No, but she has left the door of that room open, you perceive. See, she is in tears!

SIR PETER Certainly a little mortification appears very becoming in a wife! Don't you think it will do her good to let her pine a little?

ROWLEY Oh, this is ungenerous in you!

SIR PETER Well, I know not what to think. You remember, Rowley, the letter I found of hers, evidently intended for Charles!

ROWLEY A mere forgery, Sir Peter! laid in your way on purpose. This is one of the points which I intend *Snake* shall give you conviction on.

SIR PETER I wish I were once satisfied of that. She looks this way. What a remarkably elegant turn of the head she has! Rowley, I'll go to her.

ROWLEY Certainly.

SIR PETER Though, when it is known that we are reconciled, people will laugh at me ten times more!

ROWLEY Let them laugh, and retort their malice only by showing them you are happy in spite of it.

SIR PETER I'faith, so I will! and, if I'm not mistaken, we may yet be the happiest couple in the country.

ROWLEY Nay, Sir Peter—he who once lays aside suspicion——

SIR PETER Hold, my dear Rowley! if you have any regard for me, never let me hear you utter anything like a sentiment—I have had enough of them to serve me the rest of my life.

Exeunt.

Act V. *Scene iii.*
The library [*in* Joseph Surface's *house*].
Joseph Surface *and* Lady Sneerwell.

LADY SNEERWELL Impossible! Will not Sir Peter immediately be reconciled to Charles, and of consequence no longer oppose his union with Maria? The thought is distraction to me!

JOSEPH SURFACE Can passion furnish a remedy?

LADY SNEERWELL No, nor cunning either. Oh, I was a fool, an idiot, to league with such a blunderer!

JOSEPH SURFACE Sure, Lady Sneerwell, *I* am the greatest sufferer; yet you see I bear the accident with calmness.

LADY SNEERWELL Because the disappointment doesn't reach your *heart*; your *interest* only attached you to Maria. Had you felt for *her* what *I* have for that ungrateful libertine, neither your temper nor hypocrisy could prevent your showing the sharpness of your vexation.

JOSEPH SURFACE But why should your reproaches fall on *me* for this disappointment?

LADY SNEERWELL Are you not the cause of it? What had you to do to bate in your pursuit of Maria to pervert Lady Teazle by the way? Had you not a sufficent field for your roguery in blinding Sir Peter, and supplanting your brother? I hate such an avarice of crimes; 'tis an unfair monopoly, and never prospers.

JOSEPH SURFACE Well, I admit I have been to blame. I confess I deviated from the direct road of wrong, but I don't think we're so totally defeated neither.

LADY SNEERWELL No!

JOSEPH SURFACE You tell me you have made a trial of Snake since we met, and that you still believe him faithful to us—

LADY SNEERWELL I do believe so.

JOSEPH SURFACE And that he has undertaken, should it be necessary, to swear and prove that Charles is at this time contracted by vows and honor to your ladyship—which some of his former letters to you will serve to support?

LADY SNEERWELL This, indeed, might have assisted.

JOSEPH SURFACE Come, come; it is not too late yet.— [*Knocking at the door.*] But hark! this is probably my uncle, Sir Oliver: retire to that room; we'll consult farther when he's gone.

LADY SNEERWELL Well! but if *he* should find you out too—

JOSEPH SURFACE Oh, I have no fear of that. Sir Peter will hold his tongue for his own credit['s] sake—and you may depend on't I shall soon discover Sir Oliver's weak side!

LADY SNEERWELL I have no diffidence[1] of your abilities—only be constant to one roguery at a time.

Exit.

JOSEPH SURFACE I will, I will! So! 'tis confounded hard, after such bad fortune, to be baited by one's confederate in evil. Well, at all events, my character is so much better than Charles's, that I certainly—hey!—what!—this is not *Sir Oliver*, but old *Stanley* again! Plague on't! that he should return to tease me just now! We shall have Sir Oliver come and find him here—and——

Enter Sir Oliver Surface.

Gad's life, Mr. Stanley, why have you come back to plague me just at this time? You must not stay now, upon my word.

SIR OLIVER Sir, I hear your uncle Oliver is expected here, and

1. Doubt.

though he has been so penurious to *you*, I'll try what he'll do for *me*.

JOSEPH SURFACE Sir, 'tis impossible for you to stay now, so I must beg——Come any other time, and I promise you you shall be assisted.

SIR OLIVER No: Sir Oliver and I must be acquainted.

JOSEPH SURFACE Zounds, sir! then I insist on your quitting the room directly.

SIR OLIVER Nay, sir!

JOSEPH SURFACE Sir, I insist on't!—Here, William! show this gentleman out. Since you compel me, sir—not one moment—this is such insolence!

> *Going to push him out.*
> *Enter* Charles Surface.

CHARLES Heyday! what's the matter now? What the devil, have you got hold of my little broker here? Zounds, brother, don't hurt little Premium. What's the matter, my little fellow?

JOSEPH SURFACE So! he has been with you, too, has he?

CHARLES To be sure he has! Why, 'tis as honest a little—— But sure, Joseph, you have not been borrowing money too, have you?

JOSEPH SURFACE Borrowing! no! But, brother, you know here we expect Sir Oliver every——

CHARLES O gad, that's true! Noll mustn't find the little broker here to be sure.

JOSEPH SURFACE Yet, Mr. *Stanley* insists——

CHARLES Stanley! why his name is *Premium*.

JOSEPH SURFACE No, no, *Stanley*.

CHARLES No, no, *Premium*.

JOSEPH SURFACE Well, no matter which—but—

CHARLES Aye, aye, Stanley or Premium, 'tis the same thing, as you say; for I suppose he goes by half [a] hundred names, besides A.B.'s at the coffee-houses.[2]

JOSEPH SURFACE Death! here's Sir Oliver at the door. [*Knocking again.*] Now I beg, Mr. Stanley——

CHARLES Aye, and I beg, Mr. Premium——

SIR OLIVER Gentlemen——

JOSEPH SURFACE Sir, by heaven you shall go!

CHARLES Aye, out with him, certainly.

SIR OLIVER This violence——

JOSEPH SURFACE 'Tis your own fault.

CHARLES Out with him, to be sure.

> *Both forcing* Sir Oliver *out.*
> *Enter* Sir Peter *and* Lady Teazle, Maria, *and* Rowley.

SIR PETER My old friend, Sir Oliver—hey! What in the name of wonder!—Here are dutiful nephews!—assault their uncle at the first visit!

LADY TEAZLE Indeed, Sir Oliver, 'twas well we came in to rescue you.

ROWLEY Truly it was; for I perceive, Sir Oliver, the character of old

2. Moneylenders often met their clients under assumed names at coffeehouses.

Stanley was no protection to you.

SIR OLIVER Nor of Premium either: the necessities of the *former* could not extort a shilling from *that* benevolent gentleman; and now, egad, I stood a chance of faring worse than my ancestors, and being knocked down without being bid for.

After a pause, Joseph *and* Charles *turning to each other.*

JOSEPH SURFACE Charles! [*Aside.*]

CHARLES Joseph!

JOSEPH SURFACE 'Tis now complete!

CHARLES Very!

SIR OLIVER Sir Peter, my friend, and Rowley too—look on that elder nephew of mine. You know what he has already received from my bounty; and you know also how gladly I would have regarded half my fortune as held in trust for him—judge, then, my disappointment in discovering him to be destitute of truth—charity—and gratitude!

SIR PETER Sir Oliver, I should be more surprised at this declaration, if I had not myself found him selfish, treacherous, and hypocritical!

LADY TEAZLE And if the gentleman pleads not guilty to these, pray let him call *me* to his character.

SIR PETER Then, I believe, we need add no more.—If he knows himself, he will consider it as the most perfect punishment that he is known to the world.

CHARLES [*Aside.*] If they talk this way to *Honesty,* what will they say to *me,* by and by?

Sir Peter, Lady Teazle, *and* Maria *retire.*

SIR OLIVER As for that prodigal, his brother, there——

CHARLES [*Aside.*] Aye, now comes my turn: the damned family pictures will ruin me!

JOSEPH SURFACE Sir Oliver!—uncle!—will you honor me with a hearing?

CHARLES [*Aside.*] Now if Joseph would make one of his long speeches, I might recollect myself a little.

SIR OLIVER [*to* Joseph Surface.] I suppose you would undertake to justify yourself entirely?

JOSEPH SURFACE I trust I could.

SIR OLIVER Pshaw!—Well, sir! and *you* [*to* Charles] could justify yourself too, I suppose?

CHARLES Not that I know of, Sir Oliver.

SIR OLIVER What!—Little Premium has been let too much into the secret, I presume?

CHARLES True, sir; but they were family secrets, and should never be mentioned again, you know.

ROWLEY Come, Sir Oliver, I know you cannot speak of Charles's follies with anger.

SIR OLIVER Odd's heart, no more I can—nor with gravity either. Sir Peter, do you know the rogue bargained with me for all his ancestors—sold me judges and generals by the foot—and maiden aunts as cheap as broken china.

CHARLES To be sure, Sir Oliver, I did make a little free with the family canvas, that's the truth on't. My ancestors may certainly rise in evidence against me, there's no denying it; but believe me sincere when I tell you—and upon my soul I would not say it if I was not—that if I do not appear mortified at the exposure of my follies, it is because I feel at this moment the warmest satisfaction in seeing you, my liberal benefactor.

SIR OLIVER Charles, I believe you. Give me your hand again; the ill-looking little fellow over the settee has made your peace.

CHARLES Then, sir, my gratitude to the original is still increased.

LADY TEAZLE [*Pointing to* Maria.] Yet, I believe, Sir Oliver, here is one whom Charles is still more anxious to be reconciled to.

SIR OLIVER Oh, I have heard of his attachment there; and, with the young lady's pardon, if I construe right—that blush——

SIR PETER Well, child, speak your sentiments.

MARIA Sir, I have little to say, but that I shall rejoice to hear that he is happy; for me, whatever claim I had to his affection, I willingly resign it to one who has a better title.

CHARLES How, Maria!

SIR PETER Heyday! what's the mystery now? While he appeared an incorrigible rake, you would give your hand to no one else; and now that he is likely to reform, I warrant you won't have him.

MARIA His own heart—and Lady Sneerwell know the cause.

CHARLES Lady Sneerwell!

JOSEPH SURFACE Brother, it is with great concern I am obliged to speak on this point, but my regard to justice compels me, and Lady Sneerwell's injuries can no longer be concealed.

   Goes to the door.

   Enter Lady Sneerwell.

SIR PETER So! another French milliner!—Egad, he has one in every room in the house, I suppose!

LADY SNEERWELL Ungrateful Charles! Well may you be surprised, and feel for the indelicate situation which your perfidy has forced me into.

CHARLES Pray, uncle, is this another plot of yours? For, as I have life, I don't understand it.

JOSEPH SURFACE I believe, sir, there is but the evidence of one person more necessary to make it extremely clear.

SIR PETER And that person, I imagine, is Mr. Snake.—Rowley, you were perfectly right to bring him with us, and pray let him appear.

ROWLEY Walk in, Mr. Snake.

   Enter Snake.

   I thought his testimony might be wanted; however, it happens unluckily, that he comes to confront Lady Sneerwell, and not to support her.

LADY SNEERWELL Villain! Treacherous to me at last! [*Aside.*]— Speak, fellow, have *you* too conspired against me?

SNAKE I beg your ladyship ten thousand pardons: you paid me extremely liberally for the lie in question; but I have unfortunately been offered double to speak the truth.

SIR PETER Plot and counterplot, egad—I wish your ladyship joy of the success of your negotiation.

LADY SNEERWELL The torments of shame and disappointment on you all!

LADY TEAZLE Hold, Lady Sneerwell—before you go, let me thank you for the trouble you and that gentleman have taken, in writing letters to me from Charles, and answering them yourself; and let me also request you to make my respects to the Scandalous College, of which you are president, and inform them, that Lady Teazle, licentiate,[3] begs leave to return the diploma they granted her, as she leaves off practice, and kills characters no longer.

LADY SNEERWELL You too, madam!—provoking—insolent! May your husband live these fifty years! *Exit.*

SIR PETER Oons! what a fury!

LADY TEAZLE A malicious creature, indeed!

SIR PETER Hey! not for her last wish?

LADY TEAZLE Oh, no!

SIR OLIVER Well, sir, and what have you to say now?

JOSEPH SURFACE Sir, I am so confounded, to find that Lady *Sneerwell* could be guilty of suborning Mr. *Snake* in this manner, to impose on us all, that I know not what to say; however, lest her revengeful spirit should prompt her to injure my brother, I had certainly better follow her directly. *Exit.*

SIR PETER Moral to the last drop!

SIR OLIVER Aye, and marry her, Joseph, if you can.—Oil and vinegar, egad! you'll do very well together.

ROWLEY I believe we have no more occasion for Mr. Snake at present.

SNAKE Before I go, I beg pardon once for all, for whatever uneasiness I have been the humble instrument of causing to the parties present.

SIR PETER Well, well, you have made atonement by a good deed at last.

SNAKE But I must request of the company, that it shall never be known.

SIR PETER Hey! what the plague! are you ashamed of having done a right thing once in your life?

SNAKE Ah, sir,—consider I live by the badness of my character—I have nothing but my infamy to depend on! and, if it were once known that I had been betrayed into an honest action, I should lose every friend I have in the world.

SIR OLIVER Well, well—we'll not traduce you by saying anything in your praise, never fear. *Exit Snake.*

SIR PETER There's a precious rogue! yet that fellow is a writer and a critic!

LADY TEAZLE See, Sir Oliver, there needs no persuasion now to reconcile your nephew and Maria.

Charles *and* Maria *apart.*

3. Holder of a diploma.

SIR OLIVER Aye, aye, that's as it should be, and, egad, we'll have the wedding to-morrow morning.

CHARLES Thank you, my dear uncle.

SIR PETER What, you rogue! don't you ask the girl's consent first?

CHARLES Oh, I have done that a long time—above a minute ago—and she has looked yes.

MARIA For shame, Charles!—I protest, Sir Peter, there has not been a word——

SIR OLIVER Well, then, the fewer the better—may your love for each other never know abatement.

SIR PETER And may you live as happily together as Lady Teazle and I—intend to do!

CHARLES Rowley, my old friend, I am sure you congratulate me; and I suspect that I owe you much.

SIR OLIVER You do, indeed, Charles.

ROWLEY If my efforts to serve you had not succeeded you would have been in my debt for the attempt—but deserve to be happy —and you overpay me.

SIR PETER Aye, honest Rowley always said you would reform.

CHARLES Why as to reforming, Sir Peter, I'll make no promises, and that I take to be a proof that I intend to set about it.—But here shall be my monitor—my gentle guide.—Ah! can I leave the virtuous path those eyes illumine?

> Thou thou, dear maid, shouldst waive thy *beauty's* sway,
> Thou still must rule, because I *will* obey:
> An humbled fugitive from Folly view,
> No sanctuary near but *Love* and—You;
>
> *To the audience.*
>
> *You* can, indeed, each anxious fear remove,
> For even *Scandal* dies, if *you* approve.

Finis

Epilogue

Written by G. Colman, Esq.[4]

Spoken by Mrs. Abington[5]

> I, who was late so volatile and gay,
> Like a trade-wind must now blow all one way,
> Bend all my cares, my studies, and my vows,
> To one old rusty weathercock—my spouse!
> So wills our virtuous bard—the motley Bayes[6]
> Of crying epilogues and laughing plays!

4. George Colman, playwright.
5. Who played Lady Teazle.
6. Poet—from the leading character (a caricature of Dryden) in Buckingham's *The Rehearsal*.

Old bachelors, who marry smart young wives,
Learn from our play to regulate your lives:
Each bring his dear to town, all faults upon her—
London will prove the very source of honor.
Plunged fairly in, like a cold bath it serves,
When principles relax, to brace the nerves.
    Such is my case;—and yet I might deplore
That the gay dream of dissipation's o'er;
And say, ye fair, was ever lively wife,
Born with a genius for the highest life,
Like me untimely blasted in her bloom,
Like me condemned to such a dismal doom?
Save money—when I just knew how to waste it!
Leave London—just as I began to taste it!
Must I then watch the early crowing cock,
The melancholy ticking of a clock;
In the lone rustic hall for ever pounded,
With dogs, cats, rats, and squalling brats surrounded?
With humble curates can I now retire,
(While good Sir Peter boozes with the squire,)
And at backgammon mortify my soul,
That pants for loo,[7] or flutters at a vole?[8]
Seven's the main![9] Dear sound!—that must expire,
Lost at hot cockles,[1] round a Christmas fire!
The transient hour of fashion too soon spent,
Farewell the tranquil mind, farewell content![2]
Farewell the plumèd head, the cushioned tête,
That takes the cushion from its proper seat!
That spirit-stirring drum![3]—card drums I mean,
Spadille—odd trick—pam—basto[4]—king and
    queen!
And you, ye knockers, that, with brazen throat,
The welcome visitors' approach denote;
Farewell! all quality of high renown,
Pride, pomp, and circumstance of glorious town!
Farewell! your revels I partake no more,
And Lady Teazle's occupation's o'er!
All this I told our bard—he smiled, and said 'twas clear,
I ought to play deep tragedy next year.
Meanwhile he drew wise morals from his play,
And in these solemn periods stalked away:—
"Blest were the fair like you; her faults who stopped,
And closed her follies when the curtain dropped!
No more in vice or error to engage,
Or play the fool at large on life's great stage."

7. A card game.
8. Winning all the tricks.
9. A term in hazard, a dice game.
1. A parlor game popular in the country.
2. These lines parody *Othello*, III.iii.-

348-58.
3. A fashionable card-party.
4. Spadille, pam, and basto were the names of cards.

Backgrounds

On Wit, Humour, and Laughter: 1650-1775

THOMAS HOBBES

[On Laughter]†

From On Human Nature, *Chapter IX*
(*1650*)

There is a passion that hath *no name*; but the sign of it is that
distortion of the countenance which we call *laughter*, which is
always *joy*: but what joy, what we think, and wherein we triumph
when we laugh, is not hitherto declared by any. That it consisteth
in *wit*, or, as they call it, in the *jest*, experience *confuteth*: for men
laugh at mischances and indecencies, wherein there lieth no wit nor
jest at all. And forasmuch as the same thing is no more ridiculous
when it groweth stale or usual, whatsoever it be that moveth laughter, it must be *new* and *unexpected*. Men laugh often, especially
such as are greedy of applause from every thing they do well, at
their own actions performed never so little beyond their own expectations; as also at their own *jests*: and in this case it is manifest,
that the passion of laughter proceedeth from a *sudden conception*
of some *ability* in himself that laugheth. Also men laugh at the
infirmities of others, by comparison wherewith their own abilities
are set off and illustrated. Also men laugh at *jests*, the *wit* whereof
always consisteth in the elegant *discovering* and conveying to our
minds some *absurdity* of *another*: and in this case also the passion
of laughter proceedeth from the *sudden* imagination of our own
odds and eminency: for what is else the recommending of ourselves
to our own good opinion, by comparison with another man's infirmity or absurdity? For when a jest is broken upon ourselves, or
friends of whose dishonor we participate, we never laugh thereat. I
may therefore conclude, that the passion of laughter is nothing else

† Brief definitions often prove the most
lasting, especially when offered by a controversial writer. Thomas Hobbes was
the most controversial English philosopher of his time, and his explanation of
laughter, no more than a paragraph in
his long essay *On Human Nature*, became for the next hundred years the central point of reference for other commentators—especially for those whom
Hobbes alarmed.

but *sudden glory* arising from some sudden *conception* of some *eminency* in ourselves, by *comparison* with the *infirmity* of others, or with our own formerly: for men laugh at the follies of themselves past, when they come suddenly to remembrance, except they bring with them any present dishonor. It is no wonder therefore that men take heinously to be laughed at or derided, that is, triumphed over. Laughter *without offense,* must be at *absurdities* and infirmities *abstracted* from persons, and when all the company may laugh together: for laughing to one's-self putteth all the rest into jealousy and examination of themselves. Besides, it is vain glory, and an argument of little worth, to think the infirmity of another, sufficient matter for his triumph.* * *

[On Wit] †

From Leviathan, *Part I, Chapter* VIII
(*1651*)

Virtue generally, in all sorts of subjects, is somewhat that is valued for eminence, and consists in comparison. For if all things were equal in all men, nothing would be prized. And by *virtues intellectual* are always understood such abilities of the mind as men praise, value, and desire should be in themselves and go commonly under the name of a *good wit,* though the same word *wit* be used also to distinguish one certain ability from the rest.

These *virtues* are of two sorts: *natural* and *acquired.* By natural, I mean not that which a man has from his birth, for that is nothing else but sense, wherein men differ so little one from another and from brute beasts as it is not to be reckoned among virtues. But I mean that *wit* which is gotten by use only and experience, without method, culture, or instruction. This NATURAL WIT consists principally in two things: *celerity of imagining*—that is, swift succession of one thought to another—*and steady direction* to some approved end. On the contrary, a slow imagination makes that defect or fault of the mind which is commonly called DULLNESS, *stupidity,* and sometimes by other names that signify slowness of motion or difficulty to be moved.

And this difference of quickness is caused by the difference of

† Wit is another famous Hobbesian topic, and this he treated at length in his famous *Leviathan.* Reprinted here is his basic definition, in which he divides wit into two kinds: the perception of similitudes among things commonly regarded as different (fancy); and the perception of differences among things commonly regarded as similar (judgment). Having set forth this distinction, Hobbes offers a characteristic intrigue: what causes men to have different degrees of wit is that men have different passions for power. One must know what *power* meant to Hobbes, for it is a key word in his political philosophy, and it offers some unusual implications about wit for the reader who puts things together. Part of Hobbes's discussion of power, from a different section of *Leviathan,* has therefore been joined to the section on wit.

men's passions that love and dislike, some one thing, some another; and therefore some men's thoughts run one way, some another, and are held to and observe differently the things that pass through their imagination. And whereas in this succession of men's thoughts there is nothing to observe in the things they think on but either in what they be *like one another* or in what they be *unlike, or what they serve for* or *how they serve to such a purpose*, those that observe their similitudes, in case they be such as are but rarely observed by others, are said to have a *good wit*, by which, in this occasion, is meant a *good fancy*. But they that observe their differences and dissimilitudes, which is called *distinguishing* and *discerning* and *judging* between thing and thing, in case such discerning be not easy, are said to have a *good judgment*; and particularly in matter of conversation and business wherein times, places, and persons are to be discerned, this virtue is called DISCRETION.

The former—that is, fancy—without the help of judgment, is not commended as a virtue; but the latter, which is judgment and discretion, is commended for itself without the help of fancy. Besides the discretion of times, places, and persons necessary to a good fancy, there is required also an often application of his thoughts to their end—that is to say, to some use to be made of them. This done, he that has this virtue will be easily fitted with similitudes that will please, not only by illustrations of his discourse and adorning it with new and apt metaphors, but also by the rarity of their invention. But without steadiness and direction to some end, a great fancy is one kind of madness, such as they have that, entering into any discourse, are snatched from their purpose by everything that comes in their thought into so many and so long digressions and parentheses that they utterly lose themselves; which kind of folly I know no particular name for; but the cause of it is sometimes want of experience, whereby that seems to a man new and rare which does not so to others; sometimes pusillanimity, by which that seems great to him which other men think a trifle; and whatsoever is new or great, and therefore thought fit to be told, withdraws a man by degrees from the intended way of his discourse.

In a good poem, whether it be *epic* or *dramatic*, as also in *sonnets, epigrams*, and other pieces, both judgment and fancy are required; but the fancy must be more eminent, because they please for the extravagancy, but ought not to displease by indiscretion.

In a good history the judgment must be eminent, because the goodness consists in the method, in the truth, and in the choice of the actions that are most profitable to be known. Fancy has no place, but only in adorning the style.

In orations of praise and in invectives the fancy is predominant, because the design is not truth but to honor or dishonor, which is done by noble or by vile comparisons. The judgment does not suggest what circumstances make an action laudable or culpable.

In hortatives and pleadings, as truth or disguise serves best to the design in hand, so is the judgment or the fancy most required.

In demonstration, in counsel, and all rigorous search of truth, judgment does all, except sometimes the understanding have need to be opened by some apt similitude, and then there is so much use of fancy. But for metaphors, they are in this case utterly excluded. For seeing they openly profess deceit, to admit them into counsel or reasoning were manifest folly.

And in any discourse whatsoever, if the defect of discretion be apparent, how extravagant soever the fancy be, the whole discourse will be taken for a sign of want of wit; and so will it never when the discretion is manifest, though the fancy be never so ordinary.

The secret thoughts of a man run over all things—holy, profane, clean, obscene, grave, and light—without shame or blame, which verbal discourse cannot do farther than the judgment shall approve of the time, place, and persons. An anatomist or a physician may speak or write his judgment of unclean things because it is not to please but profit; but for another man to write his extravagant and pleasant fancies of the same is as if a man, from being tumbled into the dirt, should come and present himself before good company. And it is the want of discretion that makes the difference. Again, in professed remissness of mind and familiar company, a man may play with the sounds and equivocal significations of words, and that many times with encounters of extraordinary fancy; but in a sermon, or in public, or before persons unknown or whom we ought to reverence, there is no jingling of words that will not be accounted folly; and the difference is only in the want of discretion. So that where wit is wanting, it is not fancy that is wanting but discretion. Judgment therefore without fancy is wit, but fancy without judgment not.

When the thoughts of a man that has a design in hand, running over a multitude of things, observes how they conduce to that design, or what design they may conduce unto, if his observations be such as are not easy or usual this wit of his is called PRUDENCE, and depends on much experience and memory of the like things and their consequences heretofore. In which there is not so much difference of men as there is in their fancies and judgment, because the experience of men equal in age is not much unequal as to the quantity but lies in different occasions, everyone having his private designs. To govern well a family and a kingdom are not different degrees of prudence but different sorts of business; no more than to draw a picture in little, or as great, or greater than the life are different degrees of art. A plain husbandman is more prudent in affairs

of his own house than a privy councilor in the affairs of another
man.

To prudence, if you add the use of unjust or dishonest means
such as usually are prompted to men by fear or want, you have that
crooked wisdom which is called CRAFT, which is a sign of pusillanimity. For magnanimity is contempt of unjust or dishonest helps.
And that which the Latins call *versutia*—translated into English
shifting—and is a putting off of a present danger or incommodity
by engaging into a greater, as when a man robs one to pay another,
is but a shorter-sighted craft, called *versutia* from *versura*, which signifies taking money at usury for the present payment of interest.

As for *acquired wit*—I mean acquired by method and instruction
—there is none but reason, which is grounded on the right use of
speech and produces the sciences. But of reason and science I have
already spoken in the fifth and sixth chapters.

The causes of this difference of wits are in the passions, and the
difference of passions proceeds partly from the different constitution
of the body and partly from different education. For if the difference proceeded from the temper of the brain and the organs of
sense, either exterior or interior, there would be no less difference of
men in their sight, hearing, or other senses than in their fancies and
discretions. It proceeds, therefore, from the passions, which are different not only from the difference of men's complexions, but also
from their difference of customs and education.

The passions that most of all cause the difference of wit are principally the more or less desire of power, of riches, of knowledge, and
of honor. All which may be reduced to the first—that is, desire of
power. For riches, knowledge, and honor are but several sorts of
power.* * *

[On Power]

From Leviathan, *Part I, Chapter X*

The POWER of a man, to take it universally, is his present means
to obtain some future apparent good, and is either *original* or
instrumental.

Natural power is the eminence of the faculties of body or mind,
as extraordinary strength, form, prudence, arts, eloquence, liberality,
nobility. *Instrumental* are those powers which, acquired by these or
by fortune, are means and instruments to acquire more, as riches,
reputation, friends, and the secret working of God, which men call
good luck. For the nature of power is in this point like to fame,
increasing as it proceeds; or like the motion of heavy bodies, which,
the further they go, make still the more haste.

The greatest of human powers is that which is compounded of the powers of most men united by consent in one person, natural or civil, that has the use of all their powers depending on his will, such as is the power of a commonwealth; or depending on the wills of each particular, such as is the power of a faction or of divers factions leagued. Therefore to have servants is power; to have friends is power; for they are strengths united.

Also riches joined with liberality is power, because it procures friends and servants; without liberality, not so, because in this case they defend not, but expose men to envy, as a prey.

Reputation of power is power, because it draws with it the adherence of those that need protection.

So is reputation of love of a man's country, called popularity, for the same reason.

Also, what quality soever makes a man beloved or feared of many, or the reputation of such quality, is power, because it is a means to have the assistance and service of many.

Good success is power, because it makes reputation of wisdom or good fortune, which makes men either fear him or rely on him.

Affability of men already in power is increase of power, because it gains love.

Reputation of prudence in the conduct of peace or war is power, because to prudent men we commit the government of ourselves more willingly than to others.

Nobility is power, not in all places, but only in those commonwealths where it has privileges, for in such privileges consists their power.

Eloquence is power, because it is seeming prudence.

Form is power, because, being a promise of good, it recommends men to the favor of women and strangers.

The sciences are small power, because not eminent and therefore not acknowledged in any man; nor are at all but in a few, and in them but of a few things. For science is of that nature as none can understand it to be but such as in a good measure have attained it.

Arts of public use—as fortification, making of engines, and other instruments of war—because they confer to defense and victory, are power, and though the true mother of them be science—namely, the mathematics—yet, because they are brought into the light by the hand of the artificer, they be esteemed—the midwife passing with the vulgar for the mother—as his issue.

The *value* or WORTH of a man is, as of all other things, his price —that is to say, so much as would be given for the use of his power —and therefore is not absolute but a thing dependent on the need and judgment of another. An able conductor of soldiers is of great price in time of war present or imminent, but in peace not so. A learned and uncorrupt judge is much worth in time of peace, but not so much in war. And as in other things so in men, not the seller but the buyer determines the price. For let a man, as most men do, rate themselves at the highest value they can, yet their true value is no more than it is esteemed by others.

The manifestation of the value we set on one another is that which is commonly called honoring and dishonoring. To value a man at a high rate is to *honor* him, at a low rate is to *dishonor* him. But high and low, in this case, is to be understood by comparison to the rate that each man sets on himself.

The public worth of a man, which is the value set on him by the commonwealth, is that which men commonly call DIGNITY. And this value of him by the commonwealth is understood by offices of command, judicature, public employment, or by names and titles introduced for distinction of such value.

To pray to another for aid of any kind is *to* HONOR, because a sign we have an opinion he has power to help; and the more difficult the aid is, the more is the honor.

To obey is to honor, because no man obeys them whom they think have no power to help or hurt them. And consequently to disobey is to *dishonor*.

To give great gifts to a man is to honor him, because it is buying of protection and acknowledging of power. To give little gifts is to dishonor, because it is but alms, and signifies an opinion of the need of small helps.

To be sedulous in promoting another's good, also to flatter, is to honor, as a sign we seek his protection or aid. To neglect is to dishonor.

To give way or place to another in any commodity is to honor, being a confession of greater power. To arrogate is to dishonor.

To show any sign of love or fear of another is to honor, for both to love and to fear is to value. To condemn, or less to love or fear than he expects, is to dishonor, for it is undervaluing.

To praise, magnify, or call happy is to honor, because nothing but goodness, power, and felicity is valued. To revile, mock, or pity is to dishonor.

To speak to another with consideration, to appear before him with decency and humility, is to honor him, as signs of fear to offend. To speak to him rashly, to do anything before him obscenely, slovenly, impudently, is to dishonor.

To believe, to trust, to rely on another is to honor him, sign of opinion of his virtue and power. To distrust or not believe is to dishonor.

To hearken to a man's counsel or discourse of what kind soever is to honor, as a sign we think him wise or eloquent or witty. To sleep or go forth or talk the while is to dishonor.

To do those things to another which he takes for signs of honor, or which the law or custom makes so, is to honor, because in approving the honor done by others he acknowledges the power which others acknowledge. To refuse to do them is to dishonor.

To agree with in opinion is to honor, as being a sign of approving his judgment and wisdom. To dissent is dishonor, and an upbraiding of error; and, if the dissent be in many things, of folly.

To imitate is to honor, for it is vehemently to approve. To imitate one's enemy is to dishonor.

To honor those another honors is to honor him, as a sign of approbation of his judgment. To honor his enemies is to dishonor him.

To employ in counsel or in actions of difficulty is to honor, as a sign of opinion of his wisdom or other power. To deny employment in the same cases to those that seek it is to dishonor.

All these ways of honoring are natural, and as well within as without commonwealths. But in commonwealths, where he or they that have the supreme authority can make whatsoever they please to stand for signs of honor, there be other honors.

A sovereign does honor a subject with whatsoever title or office or employment or action that he himself will have taken for a sign of his will to honor him.

The king of Persia honored Mordecai when he appointed he should be conducted through the streets in the king's garment, upon one of the king's horses, with a crown on his head, and a prince before him, proclaiming *thus shall it be done to him that the king will honor*.[1] And yet another king of Persia, or the same another time, to one that demanded for some great service to wear one of the king's robes, gave him leave so to do, but with this addition, that he should wear it as the king's fool, and then it was dishonor. So that of civil honor the fountain is in the person of the commonwealth and depends on the will of the sovereign, and is therefore temporary and called *civil honor*: such as magistracy, offices, titles, and in some places coats and scutcheons painted; and men honor such as have them as having so many signs of favor in the commonwealth, which favor is power. *Honorable* is whatsoever possession, action, or quality is an argument and sign of power.

And therefore to be honored, loved, or feared of many is honorable, as arguments of power. To be honored of few or none, *dishonorable*.

Dominion and victory is honorable, because acquired by power; and servitude, for need or fear, is dishonorable.

Good fortune, if lasting, honorable, as a sign of the favor of God. Ill fortune and losses, dishonorable. Riches are honorable, for they are power. Poverty, dishonorable. Magnanimity, liberality, hope, courage, confidence are honorable, for they proceed from the con-

1. Esther vi.11.

science of power. Pusillanimity, parsimony, fear, diffidence are dishonorable.

Timely resolution, or determination of what a man is to do, is honorable, as being the contempt of small difficulties and dangers. And irresolution dishonorable, as a sign of too much valuing of little impediments and little advantages; for when a man has weighed things as long as the time permits and resolves not, the difference of weight is but little; and therefore if he resolve not, he overvalues little things, which is pusillanimity.

All action and speeches that proceed, or seem to proceed, from much experience, science, discretion, or wit are honorable, for all these are powers. Actions or words that proceed from error, ignorance, or folly, dishonorable.

Gravity, as far forth as it seems to proceed from a mind employed on something else, is honorable, because employment is a sign of power. But if it seem to proceed from a purpose to appear grave, it is dishonorable. For the gravity of the former is like the steadiness of a ship laden with merchandise; but of the latter, like the steadiness of a ship ballasted with sand and other trash.

To be conspicuous—that is to say, to be known—for wealth, office, great actions, or any eminent good is honorable, as a sign of the power for which he is conspicuous. On the contrary, obscurity is dishonorable.

To be descended from conspicuous parents is honorable, because they the more easily attain the aids and friends of their ancestors. On the contrary, to be descended from obscure parentage is dishonorable.

Actions proceeding from equity, joined with loss, are honorable, as signs of magnanimity; for magnanimity is a sign of power. On the contrary, craft, shifting, neglect of equity is dishonorable.

Covetousness of great riches and ambition of great honors are honorable, as signs of power to obtain them. Covetousness and ambition of little gains or preferments is dishonorable.

Nor does it alter the case of honor whether an action, so it be great and difficult and consequently a sign of much power, be just or unjust, for honor consists only in the opinion of power. Therefore the ancient heathen did not think they dishonored but greatly honored the gods when they introduced them in their poems committing rapes, thefts, and other great but unjust or unclean acts; insomuch as nothing is so much celebrated in Jupiter as his adulteries, nor in Mercury as his frauds and thefts—of whose praises, in a hymn of Homer, the greatest is this: that, being born in the morning, he had invented music at noon and, before night, stolen away the cattle of Apollo from his herdsmen. * * *[2]

2. Hobbes's discussion of power continues in Chapters XI and XII of *Leviathan*, culminating in his famous statement about a "war of every man against every man."

JOHN DRYDEN

Preface to *An Evening's Love:*
or, *The Mock Astrologer*†
(1671)

I had thought, Reader, in this preface to have written somewhat
concerning the difference betwixt the plays of our age and those of
our predecessors on the English stage: to have shown in what parts
of dramatic poesy we were excelled by Ben Jonson, I mean humour
and contrivance of comedy; and in what we may justly claim prece-
dence of Shakespeare and Fletcher, namely in heroic plays. But this
design I have waived on second considerations; at least deferred it
till I publish the *Conquest of Granada,* where the discourse will be
more proper. I have also prepared to treat of the improvement of
our language since Fletcher's and Jonson's days, and consequently
of our refining the courtship, raillery, and conversation of plays: but
as I am willing to decline that envy which I should draw on myself
from some old opiniatre¹ judges of the stage; so likewise I am
pressed in time so much that I have not leisure, at present, to go
through with it.

Neither, indeed, do I value a reputation gained from comedy so
far as to concern myself about it any more than I needs must in my
own defense: for I think it, in its own nature, inferior to all sorts of
dramatic writing. Low comedy especially requires, on the writer's
part, much of conversation with the vulgar: and much of ill nature
in the observation of their follies. But let all men please themselves
according to their several tastes: that which is not pleasant to me
may be to others who judge better; and, to prevent an accusation
from my enemies, I am sometimes ready to imagine that my disgust

† Dryden's essays and prefaces form the
central body of English criticism in the
Restoration period. No writer of the age
was more influential in defining such
terms as *wit* and *humour,* or in establish-
ing criteria for evaluating dramatic
works. *An Evening's Love* was first performed in 1668, and it is important to
notice that in his preface to the published version (1671) Dryden already
felt a need to defend himself against
moralistic attacks of the sort that Jeremy
Collier was to enlarge upon a generation
later. Indeed, Collier centered a large
portion of his attack upon this essay
(see p. 391).

Along with this extended discussion of
wit and comedy, two of Dryden's brief-
est statements about wit are important
to know: wit "is no other than the faculty of imagination in the writer which,
like a nimble spaniel, beats over and
ranges through the field of memory, till
it springs the quarry it hunted after. . . .
It is some lively and apt description,
dressed in such colors of speech that it
sets before your eyes the absent object
as perfectly and more delightfully than
nature" (Preface to *Annus Mirabilis,*
1667); and wit "is a propriety of
thoughts and words; or, in other terms,
thoughts and words elegantly adapted to
the subject" ("The Author's Apology,"
prefixed to *The State of Innocence,*
1677).

1. Stubborn.

of low comedy proceeds not so much from my judgment as from my temper; which is the reason why I so seldom write it; and that when I succeed in it (I mean so far as to please the audience), yet I am nothing satisfied with what I have done; but am often vexed to hear the people laugh, and clap, as they perpetually do, where I intended 'em no jest; while they let pass the better things without taking notice of them. Yet even this confirms me in my opinion of slighting popular applause, and of condemning that approbation which those very people give, equally with me, to the zany of a mountebank; or to the appearance of an antic on the theater, without wit on the poet's part, or any occasion of laughter from the actor besides the ridiculousness of his habit and his grimaces.

But I have descended, before I was aware, from comedy to farce; which consists principally of grimaces. That I admire not any comedy equally with tragedy is, perhaps, from the sullenness of my humour; but that I detest those farces which are now the most frequent entertainments of the stage, I am sure I have reason on my side. Comedy consists, though of low persons, yet of natural actions and characters; I mean such humours, adventures, and designs as are to be found and met with in the world. Farce, on the other side, consists of forced humours and unnatural events. Comedy presents us with the imperfections of human nature. Farce entertains us with what is monstrous and chimerical: the one causes laughter in those who can judge of men and manners, by the lively representation of their folly or corruption; the other produces the same effect in those who can judge of neither, and that only by its extravagances. The first works on the judgment and fancy; the latter on the fancy only: there is more of satisfaction in the former kind of laughter, and in the latter more of scorn. But how it happens that an impossible adventure should cause our mirth, I cannot so easily imagine. Something there may be in the oddness of it, because on the stage it is the common effect of things unexpected to surprise us into a delight: and that is to be ascribed to the strange appetite, as I may call it, of the fancy; which, like that of a longing woman, often runs out into the most extravagant desires; and is better satisfied sometimes with loam, or with the rinds of trees, than with the wholesome nourishments of life. In short, there is the same difference betwixt farce and comedy as betwixt an empiric[2] and a true physician: both of them may attain their ends; but what the one performs by hazard, the other does by skill. And as the artist is often unsuccessful while the mountebank succeeds; so farces more commonly take the people than comedies. For to write unnatural things is the most probable way of pleasing them, who understand not

2. Quack.

nature. And a true poet often misses of applause because he cannot debase himself to write so ill as to please his audience.

* * *

Ben Jonson is to be admired for many excellencies; and can be taxed with fewer failings than any English poet. I know I have been accused as an enemy of his writings; but without any other reason than that I do not admire him blindly, and without looking into his imperfections. For why should he only be exempted from those frailties from which Homer and Virgil are not free? Or why should there be any *ipse dixit* in our poetry, any more than there is in our philosophy? I admire and applaud him where I ought: those who do more do but value themselves in their admiration of him; and, by telling you they extol Ben Jonson's way, would insinuate to you that they can practice it. For my part, I declare that I want judgment to imitate him; and should think it a great impudence in myself to attempt it. To make men appear pleasantly ridiculous on the stage was, as I have said, his talent; and in this he needed not the acumen of wit, but that of judgment. For the characters and representations of folly are only the effects of observation; and observation is an effect of judgment. Some ingenious men, for whom I have a particular esteem, have thought I have much injured Ben Jonson when I have not allowed his wit to be extraordinary: but they confound the notion of what is witty with what is pleasant. That Ben Jonson's plays were pleasant, he must want reason who denies: but that pleasantness was not properly wit, or the sharpness of conceit, but the natural imitation of folly: which I confess to be excellent in its kind, but not to be of that kind which they pretend. Yet if we will believe Quintilian in his chapter *De movendo risu*, he gives his opinion of both in these following words: *stulta reprehendere facillimum est; nam per se sunt ridicula: et a derisu non procul abest risus: sed rem urbanum facit aliqua ex nobis adjectio.*[3]

And some perhaps would be apt to say of Jonson as it was said of Demosthenes: *non displicuisse illi jocos, sed non contigisse.*[4]

I will not deny but that I approve most the mixed way of comedy; that which is neither all wit, nor all humour, but the result of both. Neither so little of humour as Fletcher shows, nor so little of love and wit as Jonson; neither all cheat, with which the best plays of the one are filled, nor all adventure, which is the common practice of the other. I would have the characters well chosen, and kept distant from interfering with each other; which is more than Fletcher or

3. *Institutio Oratoria*, VI.iii.71: "It is easy to make fun of folly, for folly is itself ridiculous, and our response always verges on laughter; but the joke improves when we add something of our own."
4. *Ibid.*, VI.iii.2: "Not that he disliked jokes, but that he lacked the power to make them."

Shakespeare did: but I would have more of the *urbana, venusta, salsa, faceta,*[5] and the rest which Quintilian reckons up as the ornaments of wit; and these are extremely wanting in Ben Jonson. As for repartee in particular; as it is the very soul of conversation, so it is the greatest grace of comedy, where it is proper to the characters. There may be much of acuteness in a thing well said; but there is more in a quick reply: *sunt enim longe venustiora omnia in respondendo quam in provocando.*[6] Of one thing I am sure, that no man ever will decry wit but he who despairs of it himself; and who has no other quarrel to it but that which the fox had to the grapes. Yet, as Mr Cowley (who had a greater portion of it than any man I know) tells us in his character of wit, rather than all wit let there be none.[7] I think there's no folly so great in any poet of our age as the superfluity and waste of wit was in some of our predecessors: particularly we may say of Fletcher and of Shakespeare what was said of Ovid, *in omni ejus ingenio, facilius quod rejici, quam quod adjici potest, invenies.*[8] The contrary of which was true in Virgil, and our incomparable Jonson.

Some enemies of repartee have observed to us that there is a great latitude in their characters which are made to speak it: and that it is easier to write wit than humour; because, in the characters of humour, the poet is confined to make the person speak what is only proper to it. Whereas all kind of wit is proper in the character of a witty person. But, by their favor, there are as different characters in wit as in folly. Neither is all kind of wit proper in the mouth of every ingenious person. A witty coward and a witty brave must speak differently. Falstaff and the Liar speak not like Don John in the *Chances,* and Valentine in *Wit without Money.*[9] And Jonson's Truewit in the *Silent Woman* is a character different from all of them. Yet it appears that this one character of wit was more difficult to the author than all his images of humour in the play: for those he could describe and manage from his observations of men; this he has taken, at least a part of it, from books: witness the speeches in the first act, translated *verbatim* out of Ovid *De arte amandi;* to omit what afterwards he borrowed from the sixth satire of Juvenal against women.

However, if I should grant that there were a greater latitude in characters of wit than in those of humour; yet that latitude would be of small advantage to such poets who have too narrow an imagination to write it. And to entertain an audience perpetually with

5. *Ibid.,* VI.iii.17–20. The four terms describe kinds of wit: *urbanitas,* urbanity and learning; *venustus,* grace and charm; *salsus,* the salt of wit; *facetus,* polished elegance.
6. *Ibid.,* VI.iii.13: "For wit always appears more successful in reply than in attack."
7. Cowley's "Ode: Of Wit," lines 35–36.
8. *Institutio Oratoria,* VI.iii.5: "In all his wit you will find it easier to remove than to add." The modern reading ends *possit, invenient.*
9. Comedies by John Fletcher.

humour is to carry them from the conversation of gentlemen, and treat them with the follies and extravagances of Bedlam.

I find I have launched out farther than I intended in the beginning of this preface. And that, in the heat of writing, I have touched at something which I thought to have avoided. 'Tis time now to draw homeward: and to think rather of defending myself than assaulting others. I have already acknowledged that this play is far from perfect: but I do not think myself obliged to discover the imperfections of it to my adversaries, any more than a guilty person is bound to accuse himself before his judges. 'Tis charged upon me that I make debauched persons (such as, they say, my Astrologer and Gamester are) my protagonists, or the chief persons of the drama; and that I make them happy in the conclusion of my play; against the law of comedy, which is to reward virtue and punish vice. I answer first, that I know no such law to have been constantly observed in comedy, either by the ancient or modern poets. Chaerea is made happy in the *Eunuch*, after having deflowered a virgin; and Terence generally does the same through all his plays, where you perpetually see not only debauched young men enjoy their mistresses, but even the courtesans themselves rewarded and honored in the catastrophe. The same may be observed in Plautus almost everywhere. Ben Jonson himself, after whom I may be proud to err, has given me more than once the example of it. That in the *Alchemist* is notorious, where Face, after having contrived and carried on the great cozenage of the play, and continued in it without repentance to the last, is not only forgiven by his master, but enriched by his consent with the spoils of those whom he had cheated. And, which is more, his master himself, a grave man and a widower, is introduced taking his man's counsel, debauching the widow first, in hope to marry her afterward. In the *Silent Woman*, Dauphine (who, with the other two gentlemen, is of the same character with my Celadon in the *Maiden Queen*, and with Wildblood in this) professes himself in love with all the Collegiate Ladies: and they likewise are all of the same character with each other, excepting only Madam Otter, who has something singular: yet this naughty Dauphine is crowned in the end with the possession of his uncle's estate, and with the hopes of enjoying all his mistresses; and his friend Mr Truewit (the best character of a gentleman which Ben Jonson ever made) is not ashamed to pimp for him. As for Beaumont and Fletcher, I need not allege examples out of them; for that were to quote almost all their comedies.

But now it will be objected that I patronize vice by the authority of former poets, and extenuate my own faults by recrimination. I answer that, as I defend myself by their example, so that example I defend by reason, and by the end of all dramatic poesy. In the first place, therefore, give me leave to show you their mistake who have accused me. They have not distinguished, as they ought, betwixt the rules of tragedy and comedy. In tragedy, where the actions and persons are great, and the crimes horrid, the laws of justice are more strictly to be observed; and examples of punishment to be made to deter mankind from the pursuit of vice. Faults of this kind have been rare amongst the ancient poets: for they have punished in Oedipus, and in his posterity, the sin which he knew not he had committed. Medea is the only example I remember at present who escapes from punishment after murder. Thus tragedy fulfils one great part of its institution: which is, by example, to instruct. But in comedy it is not so; for the chief end of it is divertisement and delight: and that so much, that it is disputed, I think, by Heinsius, before Horace his *Art of Poetry*, whether instruction be any part of its employment.[1] At least I am sure it can be but its secondary end: for the business of the poet is to make you laugh: when he writes humour, he makes folly ridiculous; when wit, he moves you, if not always to laughter, yet to a pleasure that is more noble. And if he works a cure on folly, and the small imperfections in mankind, by exposing them to public view, that cure is not performed by an immediate operation. For it works first on the ill nature of the audience; they are moved to laugh by the representation of deformity; and the shame of that laughter teaches us to amend what is ridiculous in our manners. This being, then, established, that the first end of comedy is delight, and instruction only the second, it may reasonably be inferred that comedy is not so much obliged to the punishment of faults which it represents, as tragedy. For the persons in comedy are of a lower quality, the action is little, and the faults and vices are but the sallies of youth, and the frailties of human nature, and not premeditated crimes: such to which all men are obnoxious, not such as are attempted only by few, and those abandoned to all sense of virtue: such as move pity and commiseration, not destestation and horror; such, in short, as may be forgiven, not such as must of necessity be punished. But, lest any man should think that I write this to make libertinism amiable, or that I cared not to debase the end and institution of comedy so I might thereby maintain my own errors, and those of better poets, I must further declare, both for them and for myself, that we make not vicious persons happy, but only as Heaven makes sinners so; that is, by reclaiming them first from vice. For so 'tis to be supposed they are, when they resolve to marry; for then enjoying what they desire in one, they cease to pursue the love of many. So Chaerea is made happy by Terence, in marrying her whom he had deflowered: and so are Wildblood and the Astrologer in this play.

There is another crime with which I am charged, at which I am

1. Daniel Heinsius was a Dutch scholar who edited Horace in 1610. Dryden is wrong to suggest that he urged delight more than teaching as the purpose of comedy.

yet much less concerned, because it does not relate to my manners, as the former did, but only to my reputation as a poet: a name of which I assure the reader I am nothing proud; and therefore cannot be very solicitous to defend it. I am taxed with stealing all my plays, and that by some who should be the last men from whom I would steal any part of 'em. There is one answer which I will not make; but it has been made for me by him to whose grace and patronage I owe all things,

et spes et ratio studiorum in Caesare tantum,[2]

and without whose command they should no longer be troubled with any thing of mine, that he only desired that they who accused me of theft would always steal him plays like mine. But though I have reason to be proud of this defense, yet I should waive it, because I have a worse opinion of my own comedies than any of my enemies can have. 'Tis true that, where ever I have liked any story in a romance, novel, or foreign play, I have made no difficulty, nor ever shall, to take the foundation of it, to build it up, and to make it proper for the English stage. And I will be so vain to say it has lost nothing in my hands: but it always cost me so much trouble to heighten it for our theater (which is incomparably more curious in all the ornaments of dramatic poesy than the French or Spanish), that when I had finished my play, it was like the hulk of Sir Francis Drake, so strangely altered that there scarcely remained any plank of the timber which first built it.[3] To witness this, I need go no farther than this play: it was first Spanish, and called *El astrologo fingido*; then made French by the younger Corneille; and is now translated into English, and in print, under the name of the *Feigned Astrologer*.[4] What I have performed in this will best appear by comparing it with those: you will see that I have rejected some adventures which I judged were not divertising; that I have heightened those which I have chosen, and that I have added others which were neither in the French nor Spanish. And besides, you will easily discover that the walk of the Astrologer is the least considerable in my play: for the design of it turns more on the parts of Wildblood and Jacinta, who are the chief persons in it. I have farther to add that I seldom use the wit and language of any romance or play, which I undertake to alter: because my own invention (as bad as it is) can furnish me with nothing so dull as what is

2. Juvenal, *Satires*, VII.1: "The hope and inducement of studies rest upon Caesar alone." *An Evening's Love* was dedicated to the Duke of Newcastle.
3. After Drake's circumnavigation of the globe, the *Golden Hind* became a museum for sightseers. By the middle of the seventeenth century, after many repairs, the ship had fallen apart and the pieces were carried away for souvenirs.
4. Calderón's play was the source of Corneille's *Le feint astrologue* (1651), anonymously adapted into English as *The Feigned Astrologer* (1668).

there. Those who have called Virgil, Terence, and Tasso plagiaries (though they much injured them), had yet a better color for their accusation; for Virgil has evidently translated Theocritus, Hesiod, and Homer, in many places; besides what he has taken from Ennius in his own language. Terence was not only known to translate Menander (which he avows also in his prologues), but was said also to be helped in those translations by Scipio the African and Laelius. And Tasso, the most excellent of modern poets, and whom I reverence next to Virgil, has taken both from Homer many admirable things which were left untouched by Virgil, and from Virgil himself where Homer could not furnish him. Yet the bodies of Virgil's and Tasso's poems were their own; and so are all the ornaments of language and elocution in them. The same (if there were any thing commendable in this play) I could say for it. But I will come nearer to our own countrymen. Most of Shakespeare's plays, I mean the stories of them, are to be found in the *Hecatommithi* or *Hundred Novels* of Cinthio.[5] I have myself read in his Italian that of *Romeo and Juliet*, the *Moor of Venice*, and many others of them. Beaumont and Fletcher had most of theirs from Spanish novels: witness the *Chances*, the *Spanish Curate*, *Rule a Wife and Have a Wife*, the *Little French Lawyer*, and so many others of them as compose the greatest part of their volume in folio. Ben Jonson, indeed, has designed his plots himself; but no man has borrowed so much from the Ancients as he has done: and he did well in it, for he has thereby beautified our language.

But these little critics do not well consider what is the work of a poet, and what the graces of a poem. The story is the least part of either: I mean the foundation of it, before it is modeled by the art of him who writes it; who forms it with more care, by exposing only the beautiful parts of it to view, than a skillful lapidary sets a jewel. On this foundation of the story the characters are raised: and, since no story can afford characters enough for the variety of the English stage, it follows that it is to be altered and enlarged with new persons, accidents, and designs, which will almost make it new. When this is done, the forming it into acts and scenes, disposing of actions and passions into their proper places, and beautifying both with descriptions, similitudes, and propriety of language, is the principal employment of the poet; as being the largest field of fancy, which is the principal quality required in him: for so much the word ποιητής implies. Judgment, indeed, is necessary in him; but 'tis fancy that gives the life-touches, and the secret graces to it; especially in the serious plays, which depend not much on observation. For to

5. Cinthio's *Hecatommithi* (1565) was a source for *Othello* and others of Shakespeare's plays, but not for *Romeo and Juliet*.

write humour in comedy (which is the theft of poets from mankind), little of fancy is required; the poet observes only what is ridiculous and pleasant folly, and by judging exactly what is so, he pleases in the representation of it.

But in general, the employment of a poet is like that of a curious gunsmith or watchmaker: the iron or silver is not his own; but they are the least part of that which gives the value: the price lies wholly in the workmanship. And he who works dully on a story, without moving laughter in a comedy, or raising concernments in a serious play, is no more to be accounted a good poet than a gunsmith of the Minories[6] is to be compared with the best workman of the town.

But I have said more of this than I intended; and more, perhaps, than I needed to have done. I shall but laugh at them hereafter who accuse me with so little reason; and withal condemn their dullness who, if they could ruin that little reputation I have got, and which I value not, yet would want both wit and learning to establish their own; or to be remembered in after ages for any thing but only that which makes them ridiculous in this.

WILLIAM CONGREVE

Concerning Humour in Comedy†
(1695)

Dear Sir. You write to me that you have entertained yourself two or three days with reading several comedies of several authors, and your observation is that there is more of Humour in our English writers than in any of the other comic poets, ancient or modern. You desire to know my opinion, and at the same time my thought of that which is generally called Humour in comedy.

I agree with you in an impartial preference of our English writers in that particular. But if I tell you my thoughts of Humour, I must at the same time confess that what I take for true Humour has not been so often written even by them as is generally believed. And some who have valued themselves and have been esteemed by others for that kind of writing have seldom touched upon it. To make this appear to the world would require a long and labored dis-

6. Location of armorers' workshops in London.
† This essay first appeared in a collection of *Letters on Several Occasions: Written By and Between Mr. Dryden, Mr. Wycherley, Mr. ——, Mr. Congreve, and Mr. Dennis,* published in

1696. Congreve, in his mid-twenties at the time, was already well known as a writer of comedies. This is his most extensive critical commentary on the subject. The letter is addressed to John Dennis.

course, and such as I neither am able nor willing to undertake. But such little remarks as may be continued within the compass of a letter, and such unpremeditated thoughts as may be communicated between friend and friend, without incurring the censure of the world, or setting up for a dictator, you shall have from me since you have enjoined it.

To define Humour, perhaps, were as difficult as to define Wit, for like that, it is of infinite variety. To enumerate the several Humours of men were a work as endless as to sum up their several opinions. And in my mind the *Quot homines tot Sententiae*[1] might have been more properly interpreted of Humour, since there are many men of the same opinion in many things who are yet quite different in Humours. But tho' we cannot certainly tell what Wit is, or, what Humour is, yet we may go near to show something which is not Wit or not Humour, and yet often mistaken for both. And since I have mentioned Wit and Humour together, let me make the first distinction between them and observe to you that *Wit is often mistaken for Humour*.

I have observed that when a few things have been wittily and pleasantly spoken by any character in a comedy it has been very usual for those who make their remarks on a play while it is acting to say, *Such a thing is very Humourously spoken. There is a great deal of Humour in that part*. Thus the character of the person speaking, maybe, surprisingly and pleasantly, is mistaken for a character of Humour which indeed is a character of Wit. But there is a great difference between a comedy wherein there are many things *humourously*, as they call it which is *pleasantly*, spoken, and one where there are several characters of Humour distinguished by the particular and different Humours appropriated to the several persons represented and which naturally arise from the different constitutions, complexions, and dispositions of men. The saying of humourous things does not distinguish characters, for every person in a comedy may be allowed to speak them. From a witty man they are expected, and even a fool may be permitted to stumble on 'em by chance. Tho' I make a difference betwixt Wit and Humour, yet I do not think that humourous characters exclude Wit. No, but the manner of Wit should be adapted to the Humour. As for instance, a character of splenetic and peevish Humour should have a satirical Wit. A jolly and sanguine Humour should have a facetious Wit. The former should speak positively; the latter, carelessly, for the former observes and shows things as they are; the latter, rather overlooks Nature and speaks things as he would have them; and his Wit and Humour have both of them a less alloy of judgment than the others.

1. As many opinions as men.

362 · William Congreve

As Wit, so its opposite, *folly, is sometimes mistaken for Humour.*
When a poet brings a character on the stage committing a thousand absurdities and talking impertinencies, roaring aloud and laughing immoderately on every, or rather, upon no occasion, this is a character of Humour.

Is anything more common than to have a pretended comedy stuffed with such grotesques, figures, and farce fools? Things that either are not in Nature, or if they are, are monsters and births of mischance, and consequently as such should be stifled and huddled out of the way like Sooterkins, that mankind may not be shocked with an appearing possibility of the degeneration of a God-like species. For my part, I am as willing to laugh as anybody, and am as easily diverted with an object truly ridiculous, but at the same time, I can never care for seeing things that force me to entertain low thoughts of my Nature. I don't know how it is with others, but I confess freely to you, I could never look long upon a monkey without very mortifying reflections, tho' I never heard anything to the contrary why that creature is not originally of a distinct species. As I don't think Humour exclusive of Wit, neither do I think it inconsistent with Folly, but I think the Follies should be only such as men's Humours may incline 'em to, and not Follies entirely abstracted from both Humour and Nature.

Sometimes *personal defects are misrepresented for Humours.*
I mean, sometimes characters are barbarously exposed on the stage, ridiculing natural deformities, casual defects in the senses, and infirmities of age. Sure the poet must both be very ill-natured himself and think his audience so when he proposes by showing a man deformed, or deaf, or blind, to give them an agreeable entertainment, and hopes to raise their mirth by what is truly an object of compassion. But much need not be said upon this head to anybody, especially to you, who in one of your letters to me concerning Mr. Jonson's *Fox*[2] have justly excepted against this immoral part of ridicule in Corbaccio's character; and there I must agree with you to blame him, whom otherwise I cannot enough admire for his great mastery of true Humour in comedy.

External habit of body is often mistaken for Humour.
By external habit I do not mean the ridiculous dress or clothing of a character, tho' that goes a good way in some received characters. (But undoubtedly a man's Humour may incline him to dress differently from other people.) But I mean a singularity of manners, speech, and behavior peculiar to all, or most, of the same country, trade, profession, or education. I cannot think that a Humour which is only a habit or disposition contracted by use or custom; for

---

2. I.e., Ben Jonson's *Volpone* (1606). Corbaccio, a foolish and greedy old man in the play, is also deaf, and Dennis had complained that turning a physical defect into ridicule is "contrary to the end of comedy, instruction."

by a disuse or compliance with other customs it may be worn off or diversified.

Affectation is generally mistaken for Humour.

These are indeed so much alike that at a distance they may be mistaken one for the other. For what is Humour in one may be Affectation in another, and nothing is more common than for some to affect particular ways of saying and doing things peculiar to others whom they admire and would imitate. Humour is the life, Affectation the picture. He that draws a character of Affectation shows Humour at the second hand; he at best but publishes a translation and his pictures are but copies.

But as these two last distinctions are the nicest, so it may be most proper to explain them by particular instances from some author of reputation. Humour I take either to be born with us, and so of a natural growth, or else to be grafted into us by some accidental change in the constitution or revolution of the internal habit of body, by which it becomes, if I may so call it, naturalized.

Humour is from Nature, Habit from custom, and Affectation from industry.

Humour shows us as we are.

Habit shows us as we appear under a forcible impression.

Affectation shows us what we would be under a voluntary disguise.

Tho' here I would observe by the way that a continued Affectation may in time become a Habit.

The character of Morose in the *Silent Woman*[3] I take to be a character of Humour. And I choose to instance this character to you from many others of the same author because I know it has been condemned by many as unnatural and farce. And you have yourself hinted some dislike of it for the same reason in a letter to me concerning some of Jonson's plays.

Let us suppose Morose to be a man naturally splenetic and melancholy; is there anything more offensive to one of such a disposition than noise and clamor? Let any man that has the spleen (and there are enough in England) be judge. We see common examples of this Humour in little every day. 'Tis ten to one but three parts in four of the company that you dine with are discomposed and startled at the cutting of a cork or scratching a plate with a knife. It is a proportion of the same Humour that makes such or any other noise offensive to the person that hears it, for there are others who will not be disturbed at all by it. Well. But Morose you will say is so extravagant he cannot bear any discourse or conversation above a whisper. Why, it is his excess of this Humour that makes him become ridiculous and qualifies his character for comedy. If the

---

3. Jonson's *Epicoene: or The Silent Woman*, 1609.

poet had given him but a moderate proportion of that Humour, 'tis odds but half the audience would have sided with the character and have condemned the author for exposing a Humour which was neither remarkable nor ridiculous. Besides, the distance of the stage requires the figure represented to be something larger than the life, and sure a picture may have features larger in proportion and yet be very like the original. If this exactness of quality were to be observed in Wit, as some would have it in Humour, what would become of those characters that are designed for men of Wit? I believe if a poet should steal a dialogue of any length from the extempore discourse of the two wittiest men upon earth, he would find the scene but coldly received by the town. But to the purpose.

The character of Sir John Daw in the same play is a character of Affectation. He everywhere discovers[4] an Affectation of learning, when he is not only conscious to himself but the audience also plainly perceives that he is ignorant. Of this kind are the characters of Thraso in the *Eunuch* of Terence, and Pyrgopolinices in the *Miles Gloriosus* of Plautus. They affect to be thought valiant when both themselves and the audience know they are not. Now such boasting of valor in men who were really valiant would undoubtedly be a Humour, for a fiery disposition might naturally throw a man into the same extravagance which is only affected in the characters I have mentioned.

The character of Cob in *Every Man in His Humour* and most of the under-characters in *Bartholomew Fair*[5] discover only a singularity of manners appropriated to the several educations and professions of the persons represented. They are not Humours but Habits contracted by custom. Under this head may be ranged all country clowns, sailors, tradesmen, jockeys, gamesters, and such like who make use of cants or peculiar dialects in their several arts and vocations. One may almost give a receipt for the composition of such a character, for the poet has nothing to do but to collect a few proper phrases and terms of art and to make the person apply them by ridiculous metaphors in his conversation with characters of different natures. Some late characters of this kind have been very successful, but in my mind they may be painted without much art or labor, since they require little more than a good memory and superficial observation. But true Humour cannot be shown without a dissection of Nature and a narrow search to discover the first seeds from whence it has its root and growth.

If I were to write to the world, I should be obliged to dwell longer upon each of these distinctions and examples, for I know that they would not be plain enough to all readers. But a bare hint is sufficient to inform you of the notions which I have on this subject. And I hope by this time you are of my opinion that Humour is nei-

4. Reveals.   5. Comedies by Jonson.

ther Wit, nor Folly, nor personal defect, nor Affectation, nor Habit, and yet that each and all of these have been both written and received for Humour.

I should be unwilling to venture even on a bare description of Humour, much more, to make a definition of it, but now my hand is in, I'll tell you what serves me instead of either. I take it to be, *A singular and unavoidable manner of doing or saying anything, peculiar and natural to one man only, by which his speech and actions are distinguished from those of other men.*

Our Humour has relation to us, and to what proceeds from us, as the accidents have to a substance; it is a color, taste, and smell diffused through all; tho' our actions are never so many and different in form, they are all splinters of the same wood and have naturally one complexion, which tho' it may be disguised by art, yet cannot be wholly changed. We may paint it with other colors, but we cannot change the grain. So the natural sound of an instrument will be distinguished, tho' the notes expressed by it are never so various and the diversions never so many. Dissimulation may, by degrees, become more easy to our practice, but it can never absolutely transubstantiate us into what we would seem. It will always be in some proportion a violence upon nature.

A man may change his opinion, but I believe he will find it a difficulty to part with his Humour, and there is nothing more provoking than the being made sensible of that difficulty. Sometimes one shall meet with those who, innocently enough, but at the same time impertinently, will ask the question, "Why are you not merry?" "Why are you not gay, pleasant, and cheerful?" Then instead of answering, could I ask such one, "Why are you not handsome? Why have you not black eyes and a better complexion?" Nature abhors to be forced.

The two famous philosophers of Ephesus and Abdera[6] have their different sects at this day. Some weep and others laugh at one and the same thing.

I don't doubt but you have observed several men laugh when they are angry, others who are silent, some that are loud. Yet I cannot suppose that it is the passion of anger which is in itself different, or more or less in one than t'other, but that it is the Humour of the man that is predominant and urges him to express it in that manner. Demonstrations of pleasure are as various; one man has a Humour of retiring from all company when anything has happened to please him beyond expectation; he hugs himself alone, and thinks it an addition to the pleasure to keep it secret. Another is upon thorns till he has made proclamation of it, and must make other people sensible of his happiness before he can be so himself.

6. Heraclitus of Ephesus was known as the "weeping philosopher"; Democritus of Abdera, as the "laughing philosopher."

So it is in grief and other passions. Demonstrations of love and the effects of that passion upon several Humours are infinitely different, but here the ladies who abound in servants[7] are the best judges. Talking of the ladies, methinks something should be observed of the Humour of the fair sex, since they are sometimes so kind as to furnish out a character for comedy. But I must confess I have never made any observation of what I apprehend to be true Humour in women. Perhaps passions are too powerful in that sex to let Humour have its course, or maybe by reason of their natural coldness, Humour cannot exert itself to that extravagant degree which it often does in the male sex. For if ever anything does appear comical or ridiculous in a woman, I think it is little more than an acquired Folly or an Affectation. We may call them the weaker sex, but I think the true reason is because our Follies are stronger and our faults more prevailing.

One might think that the diversity of Humour, which must be allowed to be diffused throughout mankind, might afford endless matter for the support of comedies. But when we come closely to consider that point, and nicely to distinguish the difference of Humours, I believe we shall find the contrary. For tho' we allow every man something of his own and a peculiar Humour, yet every man has it not in quantity to become remarkable by it. Or if many do become remarkable by their Humours, yet all those Humours may not be diverting. Nor is it only requisite to distinguish what Humour will be diverting, but also how much of it, what part of it to show in light and what to cast in shades, how to set it off by preparatory scenes, and by opposing other Humours to it in the same scene. Thro' a wrong judgment, sometimes, men's Humours may be opposed when there is really no specific difference between them, only a greater proportion of the same in one than t'other, occasioned by his having more phlegm, or choler, or whatever the constitution is, from whence their Humours derive their source.

There is infinitely more to be said on this subject, tho' perhaps I have already said too much; but I have said it to a friend, who I am sure will not expose it if he does not approve of it. I believe the subject is entirely new and was never touched upon before; and if I would have anyone to see this private essay, it should be someone who might be provoked by my errors in it to publish a more judicious treatise on the subject. Indeed I wish it were done, that the world being a little acquainted with the scarcity of true Humour, and the difficulty of finding and showing it, might look a little more favorably on the labors of them who endeavor to search into Nature for it and lay it open to the public view.

I don't say but that very entertaining and useful characters, and proper for comedy, may be drawn from Affectations and those other qualities which I have endeavored to distinguish from Humour; but

7. Lovers.

I would not have such imposed on the world for Humour, nor esteemed of equal value with it. It were perhaps the work of a long life to make one comedy true in all its parts, and to give every character in it a true and distinct Humour. Therefore, every poet must be beholding to other helps to make out his number of ridiculous characters. But I think such a one deserves to be broke who makes all false musters, who does not show one true Humour in a comedy, but entertains his audience to the end of the play with everything out of nature.

I will make but one observation to you more, and have done; and that is grounded upon an observation of your own, and which I mentioned at the beginning of my letter, *viz.*, that there is more of Humour in our English comic writers than in any others. I do not at all wonder at it, for I look upon Humour to be almost of English growth; at least, it does not seem to have found such increase on any other soil. And what appears to me to be the reason of it is the great freedom, privilege, and liberty which the common people of England enjoy. Any man that has a Humour is under no restraint or fear of giving it a vent; they have a proverb among them which, maybe, will show the bent and genius of the people as well as a longer discourse. "He that will have a May Pole shall have a May Pole." This is a maxim with them and their practice is agreeable to it. I believe something considerable too may be ascribed to their feeding so much on flesh, and the grossness of their diet in general. But I have done; let the physicians agree that. Thus you have my thoughts of Humour to my power of expressing them in so little time and compass. You will be kind to show me wherein I have erred, and as you are very capable of giving me instruction, so I think I have a very just title to demand it from you, being without reserve,

Your real Friend,
and humble Servant,
W. CONGREVE

July 10, 1695

RICHARD STEELE

Epilogue to *The Lying Lover*†
(1704)

Our too advent'rous author soared tonight ⎫
Above the little praise, mirth to excite, ⎬
And chose with pity to chastise delight. ⎭

† *The Lying Lover* (first performed in 1703 and published in the following year) was Steele's second play, and the epilogue is one of his earliest statements about the kindly feelings proper to comedy. Together with the Preface and Prologue to *The Conscious Lovers*, it offers a fairly complete definition of "sentimental" comedy.

For laughter's a distorted passion, born
Of sudden self-esteem and sudden scorn;
Which, when 'tis o'er, the men in pleasure wise
Both him that moved it and themselves despise;
While generous pity of a painted woe
Make us ourselves both more approve and know.
What is that touch within, which nature gave
For man to man, e'er fortune made a slave?
Sure it descends from that dread power alone ⎫
Who levels thunder from His awful throne,   ⎬
And shakes both worlds—yet hears the wretched groan. ⎭

'Tis what the ancient sage would ne'er define,
Wonder'd—and called, part human, part divine:
'Tis that pure joy, which guardian angels know
When timely they assist their care below,
When they the good protect, the ill oppose;
'Tis what our Sovereign feels when she bestows,
Which gives her glorious cause such high success,
That only on the stage you see distress.

RICHARD STEELE

The Tatler, No. 219†
(1710)

From my own Apartment, Sept. 1.

Never were men so perplexed as a select company of us were this
evening with a couple of possessed wits, who through our ill fortune, and their own confidence, had thought fit to pin themselves
upon a gentleman who had owned to them that he was going to
meet such and such persons, and named us one by one. These pert
puppies immediately resolved to come with him, and from the
beginning to the end of the night entertained each other with
impertinences, to which we were perfect strangers. I am come home
very much tired; for the affliction was so irksome to me, that it sur-
passes all other I ever knew, insomuch that I cannot reflect upon
this sorrow with pleasure, though it is past.

An easy manner of conversation is the most desirable quality a
man can have; and for that reason coxcombs will take upon them to

† *The Tatler* and *The Spectator*, upon
which Addison and Steele collaborated
in the years 1709–1712, often commented
on comedy and related literary subjects.
Taken together, these essays indicate the
spirit of sophisticated moralism which
informed discussions of laughter, wit,
and comedy in the early eighteenth century. Particularly for Steele, right-minded
laughter is a matter of benevolent and
social grace, a concern of "mutual
good-will." Addison's perspective is often
more formal and critical than Steele's;
but even when he appears to be following Hobbes (*Spectator* No. 249), his interests return to the generous and polite
possibilities of the comic impulse.

be familiar with people whom they never saw before. What adds to
the vexation of it is, that they will act upon the foot of knowing
you by fame, and rally with you, as they call it, by repeating what
your enemies say of you; and court you, as they think, by uttering
to your face at a wrong time all the kind things your friends speak
of you in your absence.

These people are the more dreadful, the more they have of what
is usually called wit: for a lively imagination, when it is not governed by a good understanding, makes such miserable havoc both in
conversation and business, that it lays you defenseless, and fearful to
throw the least word in its way that may give it new matter for its
further errors.

Tom Mercett has as quick a fancy as any one living; but there is no
reasonable man can bear him half-an-hour. His purpose is to entertain, and it is of no consequence to him what is said, so it be what
is called well said; as if a man must bear a wound with patience,
because he that pushed at you came up with a good air and mien.
That part of life which we spend in company, is the most pleasing
of all our moments; and therefore I think our behavior in it should
have its laws as well as the part of our being which is generally
esteemed the more important. From hence it is, that from long
experience I have made it a maxim, that however we may pretend
to take satisfaction in sprightly mirth and high jollity, there is no
great pleasure in any company where the basis of the society is not
mutual good-will. When this is in the room, every trifling circumstance, the most minute accident, the absurdity of a servant, the
repetition of an old story, the look of a man when he is telling it,
the most indifferent and the most ordinary occurrences, are matters
which produce mirth and good-humour. I went to spend an hour
after this manner with some friends who enjoy it in perfection
whenever they meet, when those destroyers above-mentioned came
in upon us. There is not a man among them has any notion of distinction of superiority to one another, either in their fortunes or
their talents, when they are in company. Or if any reflection to the
contrary occurs in their thoughts, it only strikes a delight upon their
minds, that so much wisdom and power is in possession of one
whom they love and esteem.

In these my lucubrations, I have frequently dwelt upon this one
topic. It would make short work for us reformers, for it is only want
of making this a position that renders some characters bad which
would otherwise be good. Tom Mercett means no man ill, but does
ill to everybody. His ambition is to be witty; and to carry on that
design, he breaks through all things that other people hold sacred.
If he thought wit was no way to be used but to the advantage of
society, that sprightliness would have a new turn, and we should

expect what he is going to say with satisfaction instead of fear. It is no excuse for being mischievous, that a man is mischievous without malice: nor will it be thought an atonement that the ill was done not to injure the party concerned, but to divert the indifferent.

It is, methinks, a very great error that we should not profess honesty in conversation as much as in commerce. If we consider that there is no greater misfortune than to be ill received where we love the turning a man to ridicule among his friends, we rob him of greater enjoyments than he could have purchased by his wealth; yet he that laughs at him, would perhaps be the last man who would hurt him in this case of less consequence. It has been said, the history of Don Quixote utterly destroyed the spirit of gallantry in the Spanish nation; and I believe we may say much more truly, that the humour of ridicule has done as much injury to the true relish of company in England.

Such satisfactions as arise from the secret comparison of ourselves to others, with relation to their inferior fortunes or merit, are mean and unworthy. The true and high state of conversation is when men communicate their thoughts to each other upon such subjects, and in such a manner, as would be pleasant if there were no such thing as folly in the world; for it is but a low condition of wit in one man which depends upon folly in another. * * *

JOSEPH ADDISON
The Spectator, No. 47
(1711)

Mr. Hobbes, in his "Discourse of Human Nature," which, in my humble opinion, is much the best of all his works, after some very curious observations upon laughter, concludes thus: "The passion of laughter is nothing else but sudden glory arising from some sudden conception of some eminency in ourselves, by comparison with the infirmity of others, or with our own formerly. For men laugh at the follies of themselves past, when they come suddenly to remembrance, except they bring with them any present dishonor."

According to this author therefore, when we hear a man laugh excessively, instead of saying he is very merry, we ought to tell him he is very proud. And indeed, if we look into the bottom of this matter, we shall meet with many observations to confirm us in his opinion. Every one laughs at somebody that is in an inferior state of folly to himself. It was formerly the custom for every great house in England to keep a tame fool dressed in petticoats, that the heir of the family might have an opportunity of joking upon him, and divert himself with his absurdities. For the same reason idiots are still in request in most of the courts of Germany, where there is not a prince of any great magnificence who has not two or three dressed, distinguished, undisputed fools in his retinue, whom the rest of the courtiers are always breaking their jests upon.

The Dutch, who are more famous for their industry and application than for wit and humour, hang up in several of their streets what they call the sign of the Gaper, that is, the head of an idiot dressed in a cap and bells, and gaping in a most immoderate manner. This is a standing jest at Amsterdam.

Thus every one diverts himself with some person or other that is below him in point of understanding, and triumphs in the superiority of his genius, whilst he has such objects of derision before his eyes. Mr. Dennis has very well expressed this in a couple of humorous lines, which are part of a translation of a satire in Monsieur Boileau.[1]

> Thus one fool lolls his tongue out at another,
> And shakes his empty noddle at his brother.

Mr. Hobbes's reflection gives us the reason why the insignificant people above-mentioned are stirrers up of laughter among men of a gross taste. But as the more understanding part of mankind do not find their risibility affected by such ordinary objects, it may be worth the while to examine into the several provocatives of laughter in men of superior sense and knowledge.

In the first place I must observe, that there is a set of merry drolls, whom the common people of all countries admire, and seem to love so well, that they could eat them, according to the old proverb: I mean those circumforaneous[2] wits whom every nation calls by the name of that dish of meat which it loves best. In Holland they are termed "pickled herrings"; in France, "Jean potages"; in Italy, "maccaronies"; and in Great Britain, "Jack puddings." These merry wags, from whatsoever food they receive their titles, that they may make their audiences laugh, always appear in a fool's coat, and commit such blunders and mistakes in every step they take, and every word they utter, as those who listen to them would be ashamed of.

But this little triumph of the understanding, under the disguise of laughter, is nowhere more visible than in that custom which prevails everywhere among us on the first day of the present month,[3] when everybody takes it in his head to make as many fools as he can. In proportion as there are more follies discovered, so there is more laughter raised on this day, than in any other in the whole year. A neighbor of mine, who is a haberdasher by trade, and a very

---

1. Boileau, *Satire IV*, translated by John Dennis. 2. Strolling, vagrant. 3. April.

shallow conceited fellow, makes his boasts that for these ten years successively he has not made less than a hundred "April fools." My landlady had a falling out with him about a fortnight ago, for sending every one of her children upon some "sleeveless errand," as she terms it. Her eldest son went to buy a halfpenny worth of inkle[4] at a shoemaker's; the eldest daughter was dispatched half a mile to see a monster; and, in short, the whole family of innocent children made "April fools." Nay, my landlady herself did not escape him. This empty fellow has laughed upon these conceits ever since.

This art of wit is well enough, when confined to one day in a twelvemonth; but there is an ingenious tribe of men sprung up of late years, who are for making "April fools" every day in the year. These gentlemen are commonly distinguished by the name of "biters"; a race of men that are perpetually employed in laughing at those mistakes which are of their own production.

Thus we see, in proportion as one man is more refined than another, he chooses his fool out of a lower or higher class of mankind; or, to speak in a more philosophical language, that secret elation and pride of heart which is generally called laughter, arises in him from his comparing himself with an object below him, whether it so happens that it be a natural or an artificial fool. It is indeed very possible, that the persons we laugh at may in the main of their characters be much wiser men than ourselves; but if they would have us laugh at them, they must fall short of us in those respects which stir up this passion.

I am afraid I shall appear too abstracted in my speculations, if I show that when a man of wit makes us laugh, it is by betraying some oddness or infirmity in his own character, or in the representation which he makes of others; and that when we laugh at a brute, or even at an inanimate thing, it is at some action or incident that bears a remote analogy to any blunder or absurdity in reasonable creatures.

But to come into common life: I shall pass by the consideration of those stage coxcombs that are able to shake a whole audience, and take notice of a particular sort of men who are such provokers of mirth in conversation, that it is impossible for a club or merry meeting to subsist without them; I mean those honest gentlemen that are always exposed to the wit and raillery of their well-wishers and companions; that are pelted by men, women, and children, friends and foes, and, in a word, stand as "butts" in conversation, for every one to shoot at that pleases. I know several of these "butts" who are men of wit and sense, though by some odd turn of humour, some unlucky cast in their person or behavior, they have always the misfortune to make the company merry. The truth of it is, a man is

4. Linen tape.

not qualified for a "butt," who has not a good deal of wit and vivacity, even in the ridiculous side of his character. A stupid "butt" is only fit for the conversation of ordinary people; men of wit require one that will give them play, and bestir himself in the absurd part of his behavior. A "butt" with these accomplishments frequently gets the laugh of his side, and turns the ridicule upon him that attacks him. Sir John Falstaff was an hero of this species, and gives a good description of himself in his capacity of a "butt," after the following manner: "Men of all sorts," says that merry knight,[5] "take a pride to gird at me. The brain of man is not able to invent anything that tends to laughter more than I invent, or is invented on me. I am not only witty in myself, but the cause that wit is in other men."

JOSEPH ADDISON

The Spectator, No. 62
(1711)

Mr. Locke has an admirable reflection upon the difference of wit and judgment, whereby he endeavors to show the reason why they are not always the talents of the same person. His words are as follow: "And hence, perhaps, may be given some reason of that common observation, that men who have a great deal of wit and prompt memories, have not always the clearest judgment, or deepest reason. For wit lying most in the assemblage of ideas, and putting those together with quickness and variety, wherein can be found any resemblance or congruity, thereby to make up pleasant pictures and agreeable visions in the fancy; judgment, on the contrary, lies quite on the other side, in separating carefully one from another, ideas wherein can be found the least difference, thereby to avoid being misled by similitude, and by affinity to take one thing for another. This is a way of proceeding quite contrary to metaphor and allusion; wherein, for the most part, lies that entertainment and pleasantry of wit which strikes so lively on the fancy, and is therefore so acceptable to all people."[1]

This is, I think, the best and most philosophical account that I have ever met with of wit, which generally, though not always, consists in such a resemblance and congruity of ideas as this author mentions. I shall only add to it, by way of explanation, that every resemblance of ideas is not that which we call wit, unless it be such an one that gives delight and surprise to the reader. These two

5. *2 Henry IV*, I.ii.7–12.
1. John Locke, *Essay Concerning Human*   *Understanding*, II.xi.2.

properties seem essential to wit, more particularly the last of them. In order therefore that the resemblance in the ideas be wit, it is necessary that the ideas should not lie too near one another in the nature of things; for where the likeness is obvious, it gives no surprise. To compare one man's singing to that of another, or to represent the whiteness of any object by that of milk and snow, or the variety of its colors by those of the rainbow, cannot be called wit, unless, besides this obvious resemblance, there be some further congruity discovered in the two ideas that is capable of giving the reader some surprise. Thus when a poet tells us, the bosom of his mistress is as white as snow, there is no wit in the comparison; but when he adds, with a sigh, that it is as cold too, it then grows into wit. Every reader's memory may supply him with innumerable instances of the same nature. For this reason, the similitudes in heroic poets, who endeavor rather to fill the mind with great conceptions, than to divert it with such as are new and surprising, have seldom anything in them that can be called wit. Mr. Locke's account of wit, with this short explanation, comprehends most of the species of wit, as metaphors, similitudes, allegories, enigmas, mottoes, parables, fables, dreams, visions, dramatic writings, burlesque, and all the methods of allusion: as there are many other pieces of wit (how remote soever they may appear at first sight from the foregoing description) which upon examination will be found to agree with it.

As true wit generally consists in this resemblance and congruity of ideas, false wit chiefly consists in the resemblance and congruity sometimes of single letters, as in anagrams, chronograms, lipograms, and acrostics; sometimes of syllables, as in echoes and doggerel rhymes; sometimes of words, as in puns and quibbles; and sometimes of whole sentences or poems, cast into the figures of eggs, axes, or altars: nay, some carry the notion of wit so far as to ascribe it even to external mimicry; and to look upon a man as an ingenious person, that can resemble the tone, posture, or face of another.

As true wit consists in the resemblance of ideas, and false wit in the resemblance of words, according to the foregoing instances; there is another kind of wit which consists partly in the resemblance of ideas, and partly in the resemblance of words; which for distinction's sake I shall call mixed wit. This kind of wit is that which abounds in Cowley, more than in any author that ever wrote. Mr. Waller has likewise a great deal of it. Mr. Dryden is very sparing in it. Milton had a genius much above it. Spenser is in the same class with Milton. The Italians, even in their epic poetry, are full of it. Monsieur Boileau, who formed himself upon the ancient poets, has everywhere rejected it with scorn. If we look after mixed wit among the Greek writers, we shall find it nowhere but in the epigrammatists. There are indeed some strokes of it in the little poem ascribed to Musaeus, which by that, as well as many other marks, betrays itself to be a modern composition. If we look into the Latin writers, we find none of this mixed wit in Virgil, Lucretius, or Catullus; very little in Horace, but a great deal of it in Ovid, and scarce anything else in Martial.

Out of the innumerable branches of mixed wit, I shall choose one instance which may be met with in all the writers of this class. The passion of love in its nature has been thought to resemble fire; for which reason the words fire and flame are made use of to signify love. The witty poets therefore have taken an advantage from the doubtful meaning of the word fire, to make an infinite number of witticisms. Cowley, observing the cold regard of his mistress's eyes, and at the same time their power of producing love in him, considers them as burning-glasses made of ice; and finding himself able to live in the greatest extremities of love, concludes the torrid zone to be habitable.[2] When his mistress has read his letter written in juice of lemon by holding it to the fire, he desires her to read it over a second time by love's flames. When she weeps, he wishes it were inward heat that distilled those drops from the limbec.[3] When she is absent he is beyond eighty, that is, thirty degrees nearer the pole than when she is with him. His ambitious love is a fire that naturally mounts upwards; his happy love is the beams of heaven, and his unhappy love flames of hell. When it does not let him sleep, it is a flame that sends up no smoke; when it is opposed by counsel and advice, it is a fire that rages the more by the wind's blowing upon it. Upon the dying of a tree in which he had cut his loves, he observes that his written flames had burned up and withered the tree. When he resolves to give over his passion, he tells us that one burnt like him for ever dreads the fire. His heart is an Etna, that instead of Vulcan's shop encloses Cupid's forge in it. His endeavoring to drown his love in wine, is throwing oil upon the fire. He would insinuate to his mistress, that the fire of love, like that of the sun (which produces so many living creatures) should not only warm but beget. Love in another place cooks pleasure at his fire. Sometimes the poet's heart is frozen in every breast, and sometimes scorched in every eye. Sometimes he is drowned in tears, and burnt in love, like a ship set on fire in the middle of the sea.

The reader may observe in every one of these instances, that the poet mixes the qualities of fire with those of love; and in the same sentence speaking of it both as a passion, and as real fire, surprises the reader with those seeming resemblances or contradictions that make up all the wit in this kind of writing. Mixed wit therefore is a composition of pun and true wit, and is more or less perfect as the

2. These examples come from Cowley's collection of lyric poems, *The Mistress* (1647).

3. Alembic, an apparatus used in distillation.

resemblance lies in the ideas or in the words: its foundations are laid partly in falsehood and partly in truth: reason puts in her claim for one half of it, and extravagance for the other. The only province therefore for this kind of wit, is epigram, or those little occasional poems that in their own nature are nothing else but a tissue of epigrams. I cannot conclude this head of mixed wit, without owning that the admirable poet out of whom I have taken the examples of it, had as much true wit as any author that ever writ; and indeed all other talents of an extraordinary genius.

It may be expected, since I am upon this subject, that I should take notice of Mr. Dryden's definition of wit; which, with all the deference that is due to the judgment of so great a man, is not so properly a definition of wit, as of good writing in general. Wit, as he defines it, is "a propriety of words and thoughts adapted to the subject."[4] If this be a true definition of wit, I am apt to think that Euclid was the greatest wit that ever set pen to paper: it is certain there never was a greater propriety of words and thoughts adapted to the subject, than what that author has made use of in his elements. I shall only appeal to my reader, if this definition agrees with any notion he has of wit: if it be a true one, I am sure Mr. Dryden was not only a better poet, but a greater wit than Mr. Cowley; and Virgil a much more facetious man than either Ovid or Martial.

Bouhours,[5] whom I look upon to be the most penetrating of all the French critics, has taken pains to show that it is impossible for any thought to be beautiful which is not just, and has not its foundation in the nature of things; that the basis of all wit is truth; and that no thought can be valuable, of which good sense is not the groundwork. Boileau has endeavored to inculcate the same notion in several parts of his writings, both in prose and verse. This is that natural way of writing, that beautiful simplicity, which we so much admire in the compositions of the ancients; and which nobody deviates from, but those who want strength of genius to make a thought shine in its own natural beauties. Poets who want this strength of genius to give that majestic simplicity to nature, which we so much admire in the works of the ancients, are forced to hunt after foreign ornaments and not to let any piece of wit of what kind soever escape them. I look upon these writers as Goths in poetry, who, like those in architecture, not being able to come up to the beautiful simplicity of the old Greeks and Romans, have endeavored to supply its place with all the extravagances of an irregular fancy. Mr. Dryden makes a very handsome observation on Ovid's writing a

4. Addison omits an important word. Dryden wrote ". . . thoughts and words *elegantly* adapted to the subject." See note on p. 352.

5. Dominique Bouhours, a Jesuit grammarian and critic. Addison refers to his *Manière de bien penser dans les ouvrages d'esprit* (1687).

letter from Dido to Aeneas, in the following words:[6] "Ovid (says
he, speaking of Virgil's fiction of Dido and Aeneas) takes it up after
him, even in the same age, and makes an ancient heroine of Virgil's
new-created Dido; dictates a letter for her just before her death to
the ungrateful fugitive; and, very unluckily for himself, is for measuring a sword with a man so much superior in force to him, on the
same subject. I think I may be judge of this, because I have translated both. The famous author of the art of love has nothing of his
own; he borrows all from a greater master in his own profession,
and, which is worse, improves nothing which he finds: nature fails
him, and being forced to his old shift, he has recourse to witticism.
This passes indeed with his soft admirers, and gives him the preference to Virgil in their esteem."

Were not I supported by so great an authority as that of Mr.
Dryden, I should not venture to observe, that the taste of most of
our English poets, as well as readers, is extremely Gothic. He quotes
Monsieur Segrais[7] for a threefold distinction of the readers of
poetry: in the first of which he comprehends the rabble of readers,
whom he does not treat as such with regard to their quality, but to
their numbers and the coarseness of their taste. His words are as
follow: "Segrais has distinguished the readers of poetry, according
to their capacity of judging, into three classes. (He might have said
the same of writers too, if he had pleased.) In the lowest form he
places those whom he calls *les petits esprits*, such things as are our
upper-gallery audience in a playhouse; who like nothing but the
husk and rind of wit, prefer a quibble, a conceit, an epigram, before
solid sense and elegant expression: these are mob-readers. If Virgil
and Martial stood for parliament-men, we know already who would
carry it. But though they make the greatest appearance in the field,
and cry the loudest, the best on't is they are but a sort of French
Huguenots, or Dutch boors, brought over in herds, but not naturalized; who have not lands of two pounds per annum in Parnassus,
and therefore are not privileged to poll.[8] Their authors are of the
same level, fit to represent them on a mountebank's stage, or to be
masters of the ceremonies in a bear-garden: yet these are they who
have the most admirers. But it often happens, to their mortification,
that as their readers improve their stock of sense (as they may by
reading better books, and by conversation with men of judgment)
they soon forsake them."

I must not dismiss this subject without observing, that as Mr.
Locke in the passage above mentioned has discovered the most
fruitful source of wit, so there is another of a quite contrary nature
to it, which does likewise branch itself out into several kinds. For

6. "Dedication of the Aeneis" (1697).
7. Jean Regnauld de Segrais, French
critic and poet. The quotation is from
the preface of his translation of the
Aeneid and the *Georgics*.
8. Vote.

not only the resemblance but the opposition of ideas does very often produce wit; as I could show in several little points, turns, and antitheses, that I may possibly enlarge upon in some future speculation.

JOSEPH ADDISON

The Spectator, No. 249
(1711)

When I make a choice of a subject that has not been treated of by others, I throw together my reflections on it without any order or method, so that they may appear rather in the looseness and freedom of an essay, than in the regularity of a set discourse. It is after this manner that I shall consider laughter and ridicule in my present paper.

Man is the merriest species of the creation, all above and below him are serious. He sees things in a different light from other beings, and finds his mirth rising from objects which perhaps cause something like pity or displeasure in higher natures. Laughter is indeed a very good counterpoise to the spleen; and it seems but reasonable that we should be capable of receiving joy from what is no real good to us, since we can receive grief from what is no real evil.

I have in my forty-seventh paper raised a speculation on the notion of a modern philosopher,[1] who describes the first motive of laughter to be a secret comparison which we make between ourselves and the persons we laugh at; or in other words, that satisfaction which we receive from the opinion of some pre-eminence in ourselves, when we see the absurdities of another, or when we reflect on any past absurdities of our own. This seems to hold in most cases, and we may observe that the vainest part of mankind are the most addicted to this passion.

I have read a sermon of a conventual in the Church of Rome on those words of the wise man, "I said of laughter, It is mad: and of mirth, What doeth it?"[2] Upon which he laid it down as a point of doctrine that laughter was the effect of original sin, and that Adam could not laugh before the Fall.

Laughter, while it lasts, slackens and unbraces the mind, weakens the faculties, and causes a kind of remissness and dissolution in all the powers of the soul. And thus far it may be looked upon as a weakness in the composition of human nature. But if we consider the frequent reliefs we receive from it, and how often it breaks the

1. Hobbes. See p. 370.   2. Ecclesiastes ii.2.

gloom which is apt to depress the mind and damp our spirits, with transient unexpected gleams of joy, one would take care not to grow too wise for so great a pleasure of life.

The talent of turning men into ridicule, and exposing to laughter those one converses with, is the qualification of little ungenerous tempers. A young man with this cast of mind cuts himself off from all manner of improvement. Every one has his flaws and weaknesses; nay, the greatest blemishes are often found in the most shining characters; but what an absurd thing is it to pass over all the valuable parts of a man, and fix our attention on his infirmities; to observe his imperfections more than his virtues; and to make use of him for the sport of others, rather than for our own improvement.

We therefore very often find that persons the most accomplished in ridicule, are those who are very shrewd in hitting a blot, without exerting anything masterly in themselves. As there are many eminent critics who never wrote a good line, there are many admirable buffoons that animadvert upon every single defect in another, without ever discovering the least beauty of their own. By this means these unlucky little wits often gain reputation in the esteem of vulgar minds, and raise themselves above persons of much more laudable characters.

If the talent of ridicule were employed to laugh men out of vice and folly, it might be of some use to the world; but instead of this, we find that it is generally made use of to laugh men out of virtue and good sense, by attacking everything that is solemn and serious, decent and praiseworthy in human life.

We may observe that in the first ages of the world, when the great souls and masterpieces of human nature were produced, men shined by a noble simplicity of behavior, and were strangers to those little embellishments which are so fashionable in our present conversation. And it is very remarkable, that notwithstanding we fall short at present of the ancients in poetry, painting, oratory, history, architecture, and all the noble arts and sciences which depend more upon genius than experience, we exceed them as much in doggerel, humour, burlesque, and all the trivial arts of ridicule. We meet with more raillery among the moderns, but more good sense among the ancients.

The two great branches of ridicule in writing are comedy and burlesque. The first ridicules persons by drawing them in their proper characters, the other by drawing them quite unlike themselves. Burlesque is therefore of two kinds, the first represents mean persons in the accoutrements of heroes; the other describes great persons acting and speaking like the basest among the people. Don Quixote is an instance of the first, and Lucian's gods of the second. It is a dispute among the critics, whether burlesque poetry runs best in heroic verse, like that of the "Dispensary," or in doggerel like that of "Hudibras."[3] I think where the low character is to be raised the heroic is the proper measure, but when an hero is to be pulled down and degraded, it is done best in doggerel.

If Hudibras had been set out with as much wit and humour in heroic verse as he is in doggerel, he would have made a much more agreeable figure than he does; though the generality of his readers are so wonderfully pleased with the double rhymes, that I do not expect many will be of my opinion in this particular.

I shall conclude this essay upon laughter with observing that the metaphor of laughing, applied to fields and meadows when they are in flower, or to trees when they are in blossom, runs through all languages; which I have not observed of any other metaphor, excepting that of fire and burning when they are applied to love. This shows that we naturally regard laughter as what is both in itself amiable and beautiful. For this reason likewise Venus has gained the title of φιλομμειδής (the laughter-loving dame, as Waller has translated it), and is represented by Horace as the goddess who delights in laughter. Milton, in a joyous assembly of imaginary persons, has given us a very poetical figure of laughter. His whole band of mirth is so finely described that I shall set the passage down at length:[4]—

> But come thou goddess fair and free,
> In heaven y-cleped Euphrosyne,
> And by men, heart-easing Mirth,
> Whom lovely Venus at a birth
> With two sister graces more
> To ivy-crownèd Bacchus bore:
> Haste thee nymph, and bring with thee
> Jest and youthful jollity,
> Quips and cranks, and wanton wiles,
> Nods, and becks, and wreathèd smiles,
> Such as hang on Hebe's cheek,
> And love to live in dimple sleek;
> Sport that wrinkled Care derides,
> And Laughter holding both his sides.
> Come, and trip it as you go
> On the light fantastic toe,
> And in thy right hand lead with thee,
> The mountain nymph, sweet Liberty;
> And if I give thee honor due,
> Mirth, admit me of thy crew,
> To live with her, and live with thee,
> In unreprovèd pleasures free.

3. Sir Samuel Garth, *The Dispensary* (1699); Samuel Butler, *Hudibras* (1663). 4. *L'Allegro*, lines 11–16, 25–40.

FRANCIS HUTCHESON

Reflections Upon Laughter, III†
(1725)

To treat this subject of laughter gravely may subject the author to a censure like to that which Longinus makes upon a prior treatise of the sublime, because wrote in a manner very unsuitable to the subject. But yet it may be worth our pains to consider the effects of laughter and the ends for which it was implanted in our nature, that thence we may know the proper use of it; which may be done in the following observations.

First, we may observe that laughter, like many other dispositions of our mind, is necessarily pleasant to us when it begins in the natural manner, from some perception in the mind of something ludicrous, and does not take its rise unnaturally from external motions in the body. Every one is conscious that a state of laughter is an easy and agreeable state, that the recurring or suggestion of ludicrous images tends to dispel fretfulness, anxiety, or sorrow, and to reduce the mind to an easy, happy state; as on the other hand, an easy and happy state is that in which we are most lively and acute in perceiving the ludicrous in objects. Anything that gives us pleasure puts us also in a fitness for laughter when something ridiculous occurs; and ridiculous objects occurring to a soured temper will be apt to recover it to easiness. The implanting then a sense of the ridiculous in our nature was giving us an avenue to pleasure and an easy remedy for discontent and sorrow.

Again, laughter, like other affections, is very contagious; our whole frame is so sociable that one merry countenance may diffuse cheerfulness to many; nor are they all fools who are apt to laugh before they know the jest, however curiosity in wise men may restrain it, that their attention may be kept awake.

We are disposed by laughter to a good opinion of the person who raises it, if neither ourselves nor our friends are made the butt. Laughter is none of the smallest bonds of common friendships, though it be of less consequence in great heroic friendships. If an object, action, or event be truly great in every respect, it will have

† Hutcheson, a philosopher whose best-known work is *An Inquiry into the Original of our Ideas of Beauty and Virtue,* published three essays on laughter in the *Dublin Journal* in 1725. The first is an answer to Hobbes's theory that laughter is an exercise of self-eminency; the second relates laughter psychologically to the association of ideas. (These two essays have been reprinted in *Eighteenth-Century Critical Essays,* edited by Scott Elledge, Vol. I [Ithaca, N.Y.: Cornell University Press, 1961].) The third essay, here reprinted in abridged form, concerns the moral uses of ridicule.

no natural relation or resemblance to anything mean or base; and consequently no mean idea can be joined to it with any natural resemblance. If we make some forced remote jests upon such subjects, they can never be pleasing to a man of sense and reflection, but raise contempt of the ridiculer, as void of just sense of those things which are truly great. As to any great and truly sublime sentiments, we may perhaps find that, by a playing upon words, they may be applied to a trifling or mean action or object; but this application will not diminish our high idea of the great sentiment. * * * Let any of our wits try their mettle in ridiculing the opinion of a good and wise mind governing the whole universe; let them try to ridicule integrity and honesty, gratitude, generosity, or the love of one's country, accompanied with wisdom. All their art will never diminish the admiration which we must have for such dispositions, wherever we observe them pure and unmixed with any low views, or any folly in the exercise of them.

When in any object there is a mixture of what is truly great along with something weak or mean, ridicule may, with a weak mind which cannot separate the great from the mean, bring the whole into disesteem, or make the whole appear weak or contemptible. But with a person of just discernment and reflection it will have no other effect but to separate what is great from what is not so.

When any object either good or evil is aggravated and increased by the violence of our passions, or an enthusiastic admiration or fear, the application of ridicule is the readiest way to bring down our high imaginations to a conformity to the real moment or importance of the affair. Ridicule gives our minds as it were a bend to the contrary side, so that upon reflection they may be more capable of settling in a just conformity to nature.

Laughter is received in a different manner by the person ridiculed, according as he who uses the ridicule evidences good nature, friendship, and esteem of the person whom he laughs at, or the contrary.

The enormous crime or grievous calamity of another is not of itself a subject which can be naturally turned into ridicule. The former raises horror in us and hatred; and the latter pity. When laughter arises on such occasions, it is not excited by the guilt or the misery. To observe the contortions of the human body in the air upon the blowing up of an enemy's ship may raise laughter in those who do not reflect on the agony and distress of the sufferers, but the reflecting on this distress could never move laughter of itself. So some fantastic circumstances accompanying a crime may raise laughter, but a piece of cruel barbarity or treacherous villainy of itself must raise very contrary passions. A jest is not ordinary in

an impeachment of a criminal or an invective oration. It rather
diminishes than increases the abhorrence in the audience and may
justly raise contempt of the orator for an unnatural affectation of
wit. Jesting is still more unnatural in discourses designed to move
compassion toward the distressed. A forced unnatural ridicule on
either of these occasions must be apt to raise in the guilty or the
miserable hatred against the laughter, since it must be supposed to
flow from hatred in him toward the object of his ridicule, or from
want of all compassion. The guilty will take laughter to be a
triumph over him as contemptible; the miserable will interpret it as
hardness of heart and insensibility of the calamities of another. This
is the natural effect of joining to either of these objects mean ludicrous ideas.

*   *   *

From this consideration of the effects of laughter it may be easy
to see for what cause or end a sense of the ridiculous was implanted
in human nature and how it ought to be managed.

It is plainly of considerable moment in human society. It is often
a great occasion of pleasure and enlivens our conversation exceedingly when it is conducted by good nature. It spreads a pleasantry
of temper over multitudes at once; and one merry easy mind may
by this means diffuse a like disposition over all who are in company.
There is nothing of which we are more communicative than of a
good jest. And many a man who is incapable of obliging us otherwise can oblige us by his mirth and really insinuate himself into our
kind affections and good wishes.

But this is not all the use of laughter. It is well known that our
passions of every kind lead us into wild enthusiastic apprehensions
of their several objects. When any object seems great in comparison
of ourselves, our minds are apt to run into a perfect veneration.
When an object appears formidable, a weak mind will run into a
panic, an unreasonable, impotent horror. Now in both these cases,
by our sense of the ridiculous, we are made capable of relief from
any pleasant, ingenious well-wisher by more effectual means than
the most solemn, sedate reasoning. Nothing is so properly applied
to the false grandeur, either of good or evil, as ridicule. Nothing
will sooner prevent our excessive admiration of mixed grandeur, or
hinder our being led by that which is, perhaps, really great in such
an object to imitate also and approve what is really mean.

I question not but the jest of Elijah upon the false Deity,[1]
whom his countrymen had set up, has been very effectual to rectify
their notions of the divine nature; as we find that like jests have

1. See I Kings xviii, where Elijah confounds the worshippers of Baal. The
quotation below ("Cry aloud . . .") is
Elijah's taunt about the failure of the
worshippers to draw a response from
Baal.

been very seasonable in other nations. Baal, no doubt, had been represented as a great personage of unconquerable power. But how ridiculous does the image appear when the prophet sets before them, at once, the poor ideas which must arise from such a limitation of nature as could be represented by their statues and the high ideas of omniscience and omnipotence with which the people declared themselves possessed by their invocation. *Cry aloud, either he is talking, or pursuing, or he is on a journey, or he is asleep.*

This engine of ridicule, no doubt, may be abused and have a bad effect upon a weak mind; but with men of any reflection, there is little fear that it will ever be very pernicious. An attempt of ridicule before such men, upon a subject every way great, is sure to return upon the author of it. One might dare the boldest wit in company with men of sense to make a jest upon a completely great action or character. Let him try the story of Scipio and his fair captive, upon the taking of Cartagena; or the old story of Pylades and Orestes. I fancy he would sooner appear in a fool's coat himself than he could put either of these characters in such a dress. The only danger is in objects of a mixed nature before people of little judgment, who by jests upon the weak side are sometimes led into neglect or contempt of that which is truly valuable in any character, institution, or office. And this may show us the impertinence and pernicious tendency of general undistinguished jests upon any character or office which has been too much over-rated. But that ridicule may be abused does not prove it useless or unnecessary more than a like possibility of abuse would prove all our senses and passions impertinent or hurtful. Ridicule, like other edged tools, may do good in a wise man's hands, though fools may cut their fingers with it or be injurious to an unwary bystander.

The rules to avoid abuse of this kind of ridicule are, first, *either never to attempt ridicule upon what is every way great, whether it be any great being, character, or sentiments.* Or, if our wit must sometimes run into allusions on low occasions to the expressions of great sentiments, *let it not be in weak company who have not a just discernment of true grandeur.* And secondly, concerning objects of a mixed nature, partly great and partly mean, *let us never turn the meanness into ridicule, without acknowledging what is truly great and paying a just veneration to it.* In this sort of jesting we ought to be cautious of our company.

> *Discit enim citius, meminitque libentius illud,*
> *Quod quis deridet, quam quod probat et veneratur.*[2]

Another valuable purpose of ridicule is with relation to smaller vices, which are often more effectually corrected by ridicule than by

---

2. Horace, *Epistles*, II.i.262–63: "For men more quickly learn, and more gladly remember, what they mock than what they approve and respect."

grave admonition. Men have been laughed out of faults which a sermon could not reform; nay, there are many little indecencies which are improper to be mentioned in such solemn discourses. Now ridicule with contempt or ill-nature is indeed always irritating and offensive; but we may, by testifying a just esteem for the good qualities of the person ridiculed, and our concern for his interests, let him see that our ridicule of his weakness flows from love to him, and then we may hope for a good effect. This then is another necessary rule, *that along with our ridicule of smaller faults we should always join evidences of good nature and esteem.*

As to jests upon imperfections which one cannot amend, I cannot see of what use they can be. Men of sense cannot relish such jests; foolish trifling minds may by them be led to despise the truest merit, which is not exempted from the casual misfortunes of our mortal state. If these imperfections occur along with a vicious character, against which people should be alarmed and cautioned, it is below a wise man to raise aversions to bad men from their necessary infirmities when they have a juster handle from their vicious dispositions. * * *

ANONYMOUS

[On Wit] †
(1732)

Wit in King Charles II's reign seemed to be the fashion of the times; in the next reign it gave way to politics and religion; while King William was on the throne, it revived under the protection of Lord Somers and some other noblemen, and then those geniuses received that tincture of elegance and politeness which afterwards made such a figure in the *Tatlers, Spectators, etc.*, through the greatest part of the reign of Queen Anne. But, since, it has broke out only by fits and starts. Few people of distinction trouble themselves about the name of wit, fewer understand it, and hardly any have honored it with their example. In the next class of people[1] it seems best known, most admired, and most frequently practiced; but their stations in life are not eminent enough to dazzle us into imitation.

Wit is a start of imagination in the speaker that strikes the imagination of the hearer with an idea of beauty common to both; and

† Daily and weekly journalism, nourished by a growing middle-class reading public, was a flourishing trade during the early eighteenth century. This brief comment on wit, one of many on similar subjects in the journals, appeared in *The Weekly Register* of 22 July 1732.
1. The middle class.

the immediate result of the comparison is the flash of joy that attends it; it stands in the same regard to sense or wisdom as lightning to the sun, suddenly kindled and as suddenly gone; it as often arises from the defect of the mind as from its strength and capacity. This is evident in those who are wits only, without being grave or wise. Just, solid, and lasting wit is the result of fine imagination, finished study, and a happy temper of body. As no one pleases more than the man of wit, none is more liable to offend; therefore he should have a fancy quick to conceive, knowledge, good humour, and discretion to direct the whole. Wit often leads a man into misfortunes that his prudence would have avoided; as it is the means of raising a reputation, so it sometimes destroys it. He who affects to be always witty renders himself cheap, and, perhaps, ridiculous.

The great use and advantage of wit is to render the owner agreeable by making him instrumental to the happiness of others. When such a person appears among his friends, an air of pleasure and satisfaction diffuses itself over every face. Wit, so used, is an instrument of the sweetest music in the hands of an artist, commanding, soothing, and modulating the passions into harmony and peace. Neither is this the only use of it; 'tis a sharp sword, as well as a musical instrument, and ought to be drawn against folly and affectation. There is at the same time an humble ignorance, a modest weakness that ought to be spared; they are unhappy already in the consciousness of their own defects, and 'tis fighting with the lame and sick to be severe upon them. The wit that genteelly glances at a foible is smartly retorted, or generously forgiven, because the merit of the reprover is as well known as the merit of the reproved. In such delicate conversations, mirth, tempered with good manners, is the only point in view, and we grow gay and polite together; perhaps there's no moment of our lives so sincerely happy, certainly none so innocent.

Wit is a quality which some possess and all covet: youth affects it, folly dreads it, age despises it, and dullness abhors it. Some authors would persuade us that wit is owing to a double cause; one, the desire of pleasing others, and one of recommending ourselves. The first is made a merit in the owners and is therefore ranged among the virtues. The last is styled vanity and therefore a vice, though this is an erroneous distinction, as wit was never possessed by any without both: for no man endeavors to excel without being conscious of it, and that consciousness will produce vanity, let us disguise it how we please. Upon the whole, vanity is inseparable from the heart of man; where there is excellency, it may be endured; where there is none, it may be censured but never removed.

OLIVER GOLDSMITH

An Essay on the Theater; or, A Comparison between Laughing and Sentimental Comedy†
(1773)

The theater, like all other amusements, has its fashions and its prejudices; and, when satiated with its excellence, mankind begin to mistake change for improvement. For some years tragedy was the reigning entertainment, but of late it has entirely given way to comedy, and our best efforts are now exerted in these lighter kinds of composition. The pompous train, the swelling phrase, and the unnatural rant are displaced for that natural portrait of human folly and frailty, of which all are judges, because all have sat for the picture.

But as in describing nature it is presented with a double face, either of mirth or sadness, our modern writers find themselves at a loss which chiefly to copy from; and it is now debated, whether the exhibition of human distress is likely to afford the mind more entertainment than that of human absurdity?

Comedy is defined by Aristotle to be a picture of the frailties of the lower part of mankind, to distinguish it from tragedy, which is an exhibition of the misfortunes of the great. When comedy, therefore, ascends to produce the characters of princes or generals upon the stage, it is out of its walk, since low life and middle life are entirely its object. The principal question, therefore, is, whether, in describing low or middle life, an exhibition of its follies be not preferable to a detail of its calamities? Or, in other words, which deserves the preference—the weeping sentimental comedy so much in fashion at present, or the laughing, and even low comedy, which seems to have been last exhibited by Vanbrugh and Cibber?[1]

If we apply to authorities, all the great masters in the dramatic art have but one opinion. Their rule is, that as tragedy displays the calamities of the great, so comedy should excite our laughter by ridiculously exhibiting the follies of the lower part of mankind. Boileau, one of the best modern critics, asserts that comedy will not admit of tragic distress:—

---

† Goldsmith's attack on sentimental comedy appeared in the *Westminster Magazine* in 1773. Within the year, his own play *She Stoops to Conquer* had scored a success; within five years, it had been joined by the major comedies of Sheridan to form a revival of what Goldsmith in his essay calls "laughing comedy."

1. Sir John Vanbrugh and Colley Cibber, dramatists of the 1690s and earlier eighteenth century.

Le comique, ennemi des soupirs et des pleurs,
N'admet point dans ses vers de tragiques douleurs.[2]

Nor is this rule without the strongest foundation in nature, as the distresses of the mean by no means affect us so strongly as the calamities of the great. When tragedy exhibits to us some great man fallen from his height and struggling with want and adversity, we feel his situation in the same manner as we suppose he himself must feel, and our pity is increased in proportion to the height from which he fell. On the contrary, we do not so strongly sympathize with one born in humbler circumstances, and encountering accidental distress: so that while we melt for Belisarius,[3] we scarcely give halfpence to the beggar who accosts us in the street. The one has our pity, the other our contempt. Distress, therefore, is the proper object of tragedy, since the great excite our pity by their fall; but not equally so of comedy, since the actors employed in it are originally so mean that they sink but little by their fall.

Since the first origin of the stage, tragedy and comedy have run in distinct channels, and never till of late encroached upon the provinces of each other. Terence, who seems to have made the nearest approaches, always judiciously stops short before he comes to the downright pathetic; and yet he is even reproached by Caesar for wanting the *vis comica*. All the other comic writers of antiquity aim only at rendering folly or vice ridiculous, but never exalt their characters into buskined pomp, or make what Voltaire humourously calls *a tradesmen's tragedy*.

Yet notwithstanding this weight of authority, and the universal practice of former ages, a new species of dramatic composition has been introduced, under the name of *sentimental* comedy, in which the virtues of private life are exhibited, rather than the vices exposed; and the distresses rather than the faults of mankind make our interest in the piece. These comedies have had of late great success, perhaps from their novelty, and also from their flattering every man in his favorite foible. In these plays almost all the characters are good, and exceedingly generous; they are lavish enough of their *tin* money on the stage: and though they want humour, have abundance of sentiment and feeling. If they happen to have faults or foibles, the spectator is taught not only to pardon but to applaud them, in consideration of the goodness of their hearts; so that folly, instead of being ridiculed, is commended, and the comedy aims at touching our passions without the power of being truly pathetic. In this manner we are likely to lose one great source of entertainment on the stage; for while the comic poet is invading the province of

2. *L'Art Poétique*, III.401–02: "Comedy, the foe of sighs and tears/ Prevents all tragic sorrows from its lines."
3. A famous Roman general under the emperor Justinian. According to legend, he was disgraced, blinded, and forced to beg in the streets.

the tragic muse, he leaves her lovely sister quite neglected. Of this, however, he is no way solicitous, as he measures his fame by his profits.

But it will be said that the theater is formed to amuse mankind, and that it matters little, if this end be answered, by what means it is obtained. If mankind find delight in weeping at comedy, it would be cruel to abridge them in that or any other innocent pleasure. If those pieces are denied the name of comedies, yet call them by any other name, and if they are delightful, they are good. Their success, it will be said, is a mark of their merit, and it is only abridging our happiness to deny us an inlet to amusement.

These objections, however, are rather specious than solid. It is true that amusement is a great object of the theater, and it will be allowed that these sentimental pieces do often amuse us, but the question is whether the true comedy would not amuse us more? The question is whether a character supported throughout a piece, with its ridicule still attending, would not give us more delight than this species of bastard tragedy, which only is applauded because it is new?

A friend of mine, who was sitting unmoved at one of these sentimental pieces, was asked how he could be so indifferent? "Why, truly," says he, "as the hero is but a tradesman, it is indifferent to me whether he be turned out of his counting-house on Fish Street Hill, since he will still have enough left to open shop in St. Giles's."

The other objection is as ill-grounded; for though we should give those pieces another name, it will not mend their efficacy. It will continue a kind of *mulish* production, with all the defects of its opposite parents, and marked with sterility. If we are permitted to make comedy weep, we have an equal right to make tragedy laugh and to set down in blank verse the jests and repartees of all the attendants in a funeral procession.

But there is one argument in favor of sentimental comedy, which will keep it on the stage in spite of all that can be said against it. It is, of all others, the most easily written. Those abilities that can hammer out a novel are fully sufficient for the production of a sentimental comedy. It is only sufficient to raise the characters a little; to deck out the hero with a riband, or give the heroine a title; then to put an insipid dialogue, without character or humour, into their mouths, give them mighty good hearts, very fine clothes, furnish a new set of scenes, make a pathetic scene or two, with a sprinkling of tender melancholy conversation through the whole, and there is no doubt but all the ladies will cry and all the gentlemen applaud.

Humour at present seems to be departing from the stage, and it will soon happen that our comic players will have nothing left for it but a fine coat and a song. It depends upon the audience whether they will actually drive those poor merry creatures from the stage, or sit at a play as gloomy as at the Tabernacle.[4] It is not easy to recover an art when once lost; and it will be but a just punishment, that when, by our being too fastidious, we have banished humour from the stage, we should ourselves be deprived of the art of laughing.

4. A Methodist chapel in London.

The Collier Controversy: 1698

JEREMY COLLIER

A Short View of the Immorality and Profaneness of the English Stage†
(1698)

Introduction

The business of plays is to recommend virtue and discountenance vice; to show the uncertainty of human greatness, the sudden turns of fate, and the unhappy conclusions of violence and injustice; 'tis to expose the singularities of pride and fancy, to make folly and falsehood contemptible, and to bring everything that is ill under infamy and neglect. This design has been oddly pursued by the English stage. Our poets write with a different view and are gone into another interest. 'Tis true, were their intentions fair, they might be serviceable to this purpose. They have in a great measure the springs of thought and inclination in their power. Show, music, action, and rhetoric are moving entertainments; and, rightly employed, would be very significant. But force and motion are things indifferent, and the use lies chiefly in the application. These advantages are now in the enemy's hand and under a very dangerous management. Like cannon seized, they are pointed the wrong way; and by the strength of the defense, the mischief is made the greater. That this complaint is not unreasonable I shall endeavor to prove by showing the misbehavior of the stage with respect to morality and religion. Their liberties in the following particulars are intolerable, *viz.*, their smuttiness of expression; their swearing, profaneness, and lewd application of Scripture; their abuse of the clergy, their making their top characters libertines and giving them success in their debauchery. This charge, with some other irregulari-

† Collier was something of an outlaw by the time he published his *Short View*. As a non-juror (that is, a clergyman who refused to swear allegiance to William and Mary after the "bloodless revolution" of 1688), he had been deprived of his offices and briefly imprisoned; and in 1696 he became a fugitive from another charge, that of absolving on the scaffold two prisoners convicted of an assassination plot against the king. Compared to these adventures, an attack on the indecency of the stage was rather a popular effort, and Collier did not stop with one volley. Within the next decade he wrote *A Defense of the Short View* (1698), *A Second Defense of the Short View* (1700), *A Dissuasive from the Playhouse* (1703), and *A Farther Vindication of the Short View* (1707).

ties, I shall make good against the stage and show both the novelty and scandal of the practice. And, first, I shall begin with the rankness and indecency of their language.

Chapter I: The Immodesty of the Stage

In treating this head, I hope the reader does not expect that I should set down chapter and page and give him the citations at length. To do this would be a very unacceptable and foreign employment. Indeed the passages, many of them, are in no condition to be handled. He that is desirous to see these flowers, let him do it in their own soil. 'Tis my business rather to kill the root than transplant it. But that the poets may not complain of injustice, I shall point to the infection at a distance, and refer in general to play and person.

Now among the curiosities of this kind we may reckon Mrs. Pinchwife, Horner, and Lady Fidget in the *Country Wife*; Widow Blackacre and Olivia in the *Plain Dealer*.[1] These, though not all the exceptionable characters, are the most remarkable. I'm sorry the author should stoop his wit thus low and use his understanding so unkindly. Some people appear coarse and slovenly out of poverty. They can't well go to the charge of sense. They are offensive, like beggars, for want of necessaries. But this is none of the *Plain Dealer's* case; he can afford his Muse a better dress when he pleases. But then the rule is, where the motive is the less, the fault is the greater. To proceed. Jacinta, Elvira, Dalinda, and Lady Pliant, in the *Mock Astrologer*, *Spanish Friar*, *Love Triumphant*, and *Double Dealer*,[2] forget themselves extremely; and almost all the characters in the *Old Bachelor*[3] are foul and nauseous. *Love for Love* and the *Relapse* strike sometimes upon this sand, and so likewise does *Don Sebastian*.[4]

I don't pretend to have read the stage through; neither am I particular to my utmost. Here is quoting enough unless 'twere better. Besides, I may have occasion to mention somewhat of this kind afterwards. But from what has been hinted already, the reader may be over-furnished. Here is a large collection of debauchery; such pieces are rarely to be met with. 'Tis sometimes painted at length too and appears in great variety of progress and practice. It wears almost all sorts of dresses to engage the fancy and fasten upon the memory and keep up the charm from languishing. Sometimes you have it in image and description; sometimes by way of allusion; sometimes in disguise; and sometimes without it. And what can be the meaning of such a representation unless it be to tincture the audience, to

1. Both plays are by Wycherley.
2. The first three plays are by Dryden, the fourth by Congreve.
3. By Congreve.
4. By Congreve, Vanbrugh, and Dryden, respectively.

extinguish shame, and make lewdness a diversion? This is the natural consequence, and therefore one would think 'twas the intention too. Such licentious discourse tends to no point but to stain the imagination, to awaken folly, and to weaken the defenses of virtue. It was upon the account of these disorders that Plato banished poets his Commonwealth. And one of the Fathers calls poetry, *Vinum Daemonum*, an intoxicating draught made up of the Devil's dispensatory.

I grant the abuse of a thing is no argument against the use of it. However, young people particularly should not entertain themselves with a lewd picture, especially when 'tis drawn by a masterly hand. For such a liberty may probably raise those passions which can neither be discharged without trouble, nor satisfied without a crime. 'Tis not safe for a man to trust his virtue too far, for fear it should give him the slip! But the danger of such an entertainment is but part of the objection; 'tis all scandal and meannesss into the bargain. It does in effect degrade human nature; sinks reason into appetite, and breaks down the distinctions between man and beast. Goats and monkeys, if they could speak, would express their brutality in such language as this.

To argue the matter more at large.

Smuttiness is a fault in behavior as well as in religion. 'Tis a very coarse diversion, the entertainment of those who are generally least both in sense and station. The looser part of the mob have no true relish of decency and honor, and want education and thought to furnish out a genteel conversation. Barrenness of fancy makes them often take up with those scandalous liberties. A vicious imagination may blot a great deal of paper at this rate with ease enough. And 'tis possible convenience may sometimes invite to the expedient. The modern poets seem to use smut as the old ones did machines, to relieve a fainting invention. When Pegasus is jaded and would stand still, he is apt like other tits to run into every puddle.

Obscenity in any company is a rustic, uncreditable talent, but among women 'tis particularly rude. Such talk would be very affrontive in conversation and not endured by any lady of reputation. Whence then comes it to pass that those liberties which disoblige so much in conversation should entertain upon the stage? Do women leave all the regards to decency and conscience behind them when they come to the playhouse? Or does the place transform their inclinations and turn their former aversions into pleasure? Or were their pretenses to sobriety elsewhere nothing but hypocrisy and grimace? Such suppositions as these are all satire and invective. They are rude imputations upon the whole sex. To treat the ladies with such stuff is no better than taking their money to abuse them. It supposes their imagination vicious and their memories ill-furnished, that they are practiced in the language of the stews and pleased with the scenes of brutishness. When at the same time the customs of education and the laws of decency are so very cautious and reserved in regard to women—I say so very reserved—that 'tis almost a fault for them to understand they are ill-used. They can't discover their disgust without disadvantage, nor blush without disservice to their modesty. To appear with any skill in such cant looks as if they had fallen upon ill conversation or managed their curiosity amiss. In a word, he that treats the ladies with such discourse must conclude either that they like it or they do not. To suppose the first is a gross reflection upon their virtue. And as for the latter case, it entertains them with their own aversion, which is ill-nature, and ill-manners enough in all conscience. And in this particular custom and conscience, the forms of breeding and the maxims of religion are on the same side. In other instances vice is often too fashionable. But here a man can't be a sinner without being a clown.

In this respect the stage is faulty to a scandalous degree of nauseousness and aggravation. For:

1. The poets make women speak smuttily. Of this the places before-mentioned are sufficient evidence, and if there was occasion they might be multiplied to a much greater number. Indeed the comedies are seldom clear of these blemishes. And sometimes you have them in tragedy. For instance, the *Orphan's*[5] Monimia makes a very improper description, and the Royal Leonora in the *Spanish Friar* runs a strange length in the history of love. And do princesses use to make their reports with such fulsome freedoms? Certainly this Leonora was the first queen of her family. Such raptures are too luscious for Joan of Naples. Are these the tender things Mr. Dryden says the ladies call on him for? I suppose he means the ladies that are too modest to show their faces in the pit.[6] This entertainment can be fairly designed for none but such. Indeed it hits their palate exactly. It regales their lewdness, graces their character, and keeps up their spirits for their vocation. Now to bring women under such misbehavior is violence to their native modesty, and a misrepresentation of their sex. For modesty, as Mr. Rapin observes,[7] is the character of women. To represent them without this quality is to make monsters of them and throw them out of their kind. Euripides, who was no negligent observer of human nature, is always careful of this Decorum. Thus Phaedra,[8] when possessed with an infamous passion, takes all imaginable pains to conceal it. She is as regular and reserved in her language as the most virtuous matron. 'Tis true, the force of shame and desire, the scandal of satisfying,

5. A play by Thomas Otway.
6. Prostitutes sometimes wore masks to the theater.
7. René Rapin, a seventeenth-century French commentator on Aristotle.
8. In Euripides' *Hippolitus*.

and the difficulty of parting with her inclinations disorder her to distraction. However, her frenzy is not lewd; she keeps her modesty even after she has lost her wits. Had Shakespeare secured this point for his young virgin, Ophelia, the play had been better contrived. Since he was resolved to drown the lady like a kitten, he should have set her a swimming a little sooner. To keep her alive only to sullen her reputation and discover the rankness of her breath was very cruel. But it may be said the freedoms of distraction go for nothing, a fever has no faults, and a man *non compos* may kill without murder. It may be so; but then such people ought to be kept in dark rooms and without company. To show them or let them loose is somewhat unreasonable. But after all, the modern stage seems to depend upon this expedient. Women are sometimes represented silly, and sometimes mad, to enlarge their liberty and screen their impudence from censure. This politic contrivance we have in Marcella, Hoyden, and Miss Prue.[9] However, it amounts to this confession, that women, when they have their understanding about them, ought to converse otherwise. In fine, modesty is the distinguishing virtue of that sex and serves both for ornament and defense; modesty was designed by providence as a guard to virtue, and that it might be always at hand 'tis wrought into the mechanism of the body. 'Tis likewise proportioned to the occasions of life and strongest in youth when passion is so too. 'Tis a quality as true to innocence as the senses are to health; whatever is ungrateful to the first is prejudicial to the latter. The enemy no sooner approaches, but the blood rises in opposition and looks defiance to an indecency. It supplies the room of reasoning and collection. Intuitive knowledge can scarcely make a quicker impression; and what, then, can be a surer guide to the unexperienced? It teaches by sudden instinct and aversion. This is both a ready and a powerful method of instruction. The tumult of the blood and spirits and the uneasiness of the sensation are of singular use. They serve to awaken reason and prevent surprise. Thus the distinctions of good and evil are refreshed, and the temptation kept at a proper distance.

2. They represent their single ladies and persons of condition under these disorders of liberty. This makes the irregularity still more monstrous and a greater contradiction to Nature and probability. But rather than not be vicious, they will venture to spoil a character. This mismanagement we have partly seen already. Jacinta and Belinda[1] are farther proof; and the *Double Dealer* is particularly remarkable. There are but four Ladies in this play, and three of the biggest of them are whores. A great compliment to quality to tell

9. Characters in, respectively, Thomas D'Urfey's *Don Quixote*, Vanbrugh's *The Relapse*, and Dryden's *An Evening's Love; or, The Mock Astrologer*.

1. Characters in Dryden's *The Mock Astrologer* and Congreve's *The Old Bachelor*.

them there is not above a quarter of them honest! This was not the Roman breeding. Terence and Plautus his strumpets were little people; but of this more hereafter.

3. They have oftentimes not so much as the poor refuge of a double meaning to fly to. So that you are under a necessity either of taking ribaldry or nonsense. And when the sentence has two handles, the worst is generally turned to the audience. The matter is so contrived that the smut and scum of the thought now arises uppermost, and, like a picture drawn to sight, looks always upon the company.

4. And which is still more extraordinary, the prologues and epilogues are sometimes scandalous to the last degree. I shall discover them for once, and let them stand like rocks in the margin.[2] Now here, properly speaking, the actors quit the stage and remove from fiction into life. Here they converse with the boxes and pit and address directly to the audience. These preliminary and concluding parts are designed to justify the conduct of the play, and bespeak the favor of the company. Upon such occasions one would imagine, if ever, the ladies should be used with respect and the measures of decency observed. But here we have lewdness without shame or example. Here the poet exceeds himself. Here are such strains as would turn the stomach of an ordinary debauchee and be almost nauseous in the stews. And to make it the more agreeable, women are commonly picked out for this service. Thus the poet courts the good opinion of the audience. This is the dessert he regales the ladies with at the close of the entertainment. It seems, he thinks, they have admirable palates! Nothing can be a greater breach of manners than such liberties as these. If a man would study to outrage quality and virtue, he could not do it more effectually. But:

5. Smut is still more insufferable with respect to religion. The heathen religion was in a great measure a mystery of iniquity. Lewdness was consecrated in the temples as well as practiced in the stews. Their deities were great examples of vice and worshipped with their own inclination. 'Tis no wonder therefore their poetry should be tinctured with their belief, and that the stage should borrow some of the liberties of their theology. This made Mercury's procuring and Jupiter's adultery the more passable in *Amphytrion*.[3] Upon this score, Gimnausium is less monstrous in praying the gods to send her store of gallants. And thus Chaerea defends his adventure by the precedent of Jupiter and Danae. But the Christian religion is quite of another complexion. Both its precepts and authorities are the highest discouragement to licentiousness. It forbids the remotest tendencies to evil, banishes the follies of conversation, and

2. In the margin Collier lists *The Mock Astrologer, The Country Wife,* Dryden's *Cleomenes* (*The Spartan Hero*), and *The Old Bachelor.*
3. Collier mentions Roman comedies by Plautus and Terence.

obliges up to sobriety of thought. That which might pass for raillery and entertainment in heathenism is detestable in Christianity. The restraint of the precept and the quality of the Deity and the expectations of futurity quite alter the case.

* * *

From Chapter IV. The Stage-Poets Make Their Principal Persons Vicious and Reward Them at the End of the Play

The lines of virtue and vice are struck out by nature in very legible distinctions; they tend to a different point, and in the greater instances the space between them is easily perceived. Nothing can be more unlike than the original forms of these qualities: the first has all the sweetness, charms, and graces imaginable; the other has the air of a post ill carved into a monster, and looks both foolish and frightful together. These are the native appearances of Good and Evil. And they that endeavor to blot the distinctions, to rub out the colors or change the marks, are extremely to blame. 'Tis confessed as long as the mind is awake and conscience goes true there's no fear of being imposed on. But when vice is varnished over with pleasure and comes in the shape of convenience, then the case grows somewhat dangerous; for the fancy may be gained and the guards corrupted and reason suborned against itself. And thus a disguise often passes when the person would otherwise be stopped. To put lewdness into a thriving condition, to give it an equipage of quality, and to treat it with ceremony and respect is the way to confound the understanding, to fortify the charm, and to make the mischief invincible. Innocence is often owing to fear, and appetite is kept under by shame; but when these restraints are once taken off, when profit and liberty lie on the same side, and a man can debauch himself into credit, what can be expected in such a case, but that pleasure should grow absolute and madness carry all before it? The stage seems eager to bring matters to this issue; they have made a considerable progress and are still pushing their point with all the vigor imaginable. If this be not their aim, why is lewdness so much considered in character and success? Why are their favorites atheistical and their fine gentlemen debauched? To what purpose is vice thus preferred, thus ornamented and caressed, unless for imitation? That matter of fact stands thus, I shall make good by several instances. To begin then with their men of breeding and figure. Wildblood[4] sets up for debauchery, ridicules marriage, and swears by Mahomet. Bellamy makes sport with the Devil, and Lorenzo[5] is vicious and calls his father bawdy magistrate. Horner is horridly

4. In Dryden's *The Mock Astrologer*, as is Bellamy, below.

5. In Dryden's *The Spanish Friar*.

smutty, and Harcourt false to his friend who used him kindly. In
The Plain Dealer, Freeman talks coarsely, cheats the widow,
debauches her son, and makes him undutiful. Bellmour[6] is lewd
and profane, and Mellefont[7] puts Careless in the best way he can
to debauch Lady Plyant. These sparks generally marry the top
ladies, and those that do not are brought to no penance, but go off
with the character of fine gentlemen. In *Don Sebastian*,[8] Antonio,
an atheistical bully, is rewarded with the Lady Moraima and half
the Mufti's estate. Valentine in *Love for Love* is (if I may so call
him) the hero of the play. This spark the poet would pass for a
person of virtue, but he speaks too late. 'Tis true, he was hearty in
his affection to Angelica. Now without question, to be in love with
a fine lady of 30,000 Pounds is a great virtue! But then abating this
single commendation, Valentine is altogether compounded of vice.
He is a prodigal debauchee, unnatural and profane, obscene, saucy
and undutiful, and yet this libertine is crowned for the man of
merit, has his wishes thrown into his lap, and makes the happy exit.
I perceive we should have a rare set of virtues if these poets had the
making of them! How they hug a vicious character, and how profuse are they in their liberalities to lewdness! In *The Provoked
Wife*,[9] Constant swears at length, solicits Lady Brute, confesses
himself lewd, and prefers debauchery to marriage. He handles the
last subject very notably and worth the hearing. *There is* (says he)
*a poor sordid slavery in marriage that turns the flowing tide of
honor and sinks it to the lowest ebb of infamy. 'Tis a corrupted
soil; ill nature, avarice, sloth, cowardice, and dirt are all its product
—but then constancy (alias whoring) is a brave, free, haughty, generous agent.* This is admirable stuff both for the rhetoric and the
reason! The character of Young Fashion in *The Relapse* is of the
same staunchness, but this the reader may have in another place.

To sum up the evidence. A fine gentleman is a fine whoring,
swearing, smutty, atheistical man. These qualifications, it seems,
complete the idea of honor. They are the top improvements of fortune and the distinguishing glories of birth and breeding! This is
the stage-test for quality, and those that can't stand it ought to be
disclaimed. The restraints of conscience and the pendantry of virtue
are unbecoming a cavalier. Future securities and reaching beyond
life are vulgar provisions. If he falls a-thinking at this rate, he for-
feits his honor; for his head was only made to run against a post!
Here you have a man of breeding and figure that burlesques the
Bible, swears, and talks smut to ladies, speaks ill of his friend
behind his back, and betrays his interest. A fine gentleman that has
neither honesty nor honor, conscience nor manners, good nature

6. In Congreve's *The Old Bachelor*.   8. By Dryden.
7. In Congreve's *The Double-Dealer*.   9. By Vanbrugh.

nor civil hypocrisy; fine only in the insignificancy of life, the abuse
of religion, and the scandals of conversation. These worshipful things
are the poet's favorites. They appear at the head of the fashion and
shine in character and equipage. If there is any sense stirring, they
must have it, though the rest of the stage suffer never so much by
the partiality. And what can be the meaning of this wretched distribution of honor? Is it not to give credit and countenance to vice
and to shame young people out of all pretense to conscience and
regularity? They seem forced to turn lewd in their own defense.
They can't otherwise justify themselves to the fashion, nor keep up
the character of gentlemen. Thus people not well-furnished with
thought and experience are debauched both in practice and principle. And thus religion grows uncreditable and passes for ill education. The stage seldom gives quarter to any thing that's serviceable
or significant, but persecutes worth and goodness under every appearance. He that would be safe from their satire must take care to
disguise himself in vice and hang out the colors of debauchery. How
often is learning, industry, and frugality ridiculed in comedy? The
rich citizens are often misers and cuckolds, and the universities,
schools of pedantry upon this score. In short, libertinism and profaneness, dressing, idleness, and gallantry, are the only valuable
qualities. As if people were not apt enough of themselves to be lazy,
lewd, and extravagant unless they were pricked forward and provoked by glory and reputation. Thus the marks of honor and infamy
are misapplied, and the ideas of virtue and vice confounded. Thus
monstrousness goes for proportion, and the blemishes of human
nature make up the beauties of it.

The fine ladies are of the same cut with the gentlemen. Moraima
is scandalously rude to her father, helps him to a beating, and runs
away with Antonio.[1] Angelica talks saucily to her uncle,[2] and
Belinda confesses her inclination for a gallant.[3] And, as I have
observed already, the topping ladies in *The Mock Astrologer, Spanish Friar, Country Wife, Old Bachelor, Orphan, Double Dealer,*
and *Love Triumphant* are smutty and sometimes profane.

* * *

Thus we see what a fine time lewd people have on the English
stage. No censure, no mark of infamy, no mortification must touch
them. They keep their honor untarnished and carry off the advantage of their character. They are set up for the standard of behavior
and the masters of ceremony and sense. And at last, that the example may work the better they generally make them rich and happy
and reward them with their own desires.

Mr. Dryden, in the Preface to his *Mock Astrologer,*[4] confesses

1. In Dryden's *Don Sebastian.*
2. In Congreve's *Love for Love.*
3. In Vanbrugh's *The Provoked Wife.*
4. Reprinted on p. 352.

himself blamed for this practice: *for making debauched persons his protagonists or chief persons of the drama; and for making them happy in the conclusion of the play, against the law of comedy, which is to reward virtue and punish vice.* To this objection he makes a lame defense. And answers, *that he knows no such law constantly observed in comedy by the ancient or modern poets.* What then? Poets are not always exactly in rule. It may be a good law though 'tis not constantly observed; some laws are constantly broken and yet ne'er the worse for all that. He goes on and pleads the authorities of Plautus and Terence. I grant there are instances of favor to vicious young people in those authors, but to this I reply:

1. That those poets had a greater compass of liberty in their religion. Debauchery did not lie under those discouragements of scandal and penalty with them, as it does with us. Unless, therefore, he can prove heathenism and Christianity the same, his precedents will do him little service.

2. Horace, who was as good a judge of the stage as either of those comedians, seems to be of another opinion.[5] He condemns the obscenities of Plautus and tells you men of fortune and quality in his time would not endure immodest satire. He continues, that poets were formerly admired for the great services they did: for teaching matters relating to religion and government; for refining the manners, tempering the passions, and improving the understandings of mankind; for making them more useful in domestic relations and the public capacities of life. This is a demonstration that vice was not the inclination of the muses in those days, and that Horace believed the chief business of a poet was to instruct the audience. * * *

Lastly, Horace having expressly mentioned the beginning and progress of comedy, discovers himself more fully. He advises a poet to form his work upon the precepts of Socrates and Plato and the models of moral philosophy. This was the way to preserve decency and to assign a proper fate and behavior to every character. Now if Horace would have his poet governed by the maxims of morality, he must oblige him to sobriety of conduct and a just distribution of rewards and punishments.

Mr. Dryden makes homewards and endeavors to fortify himself in modern authority. He lets us know that *Ben Jonson, after whom he may be proud to err, gives him more than one example of this conduct; that in The Alchemist is notorious,* where neither Face nor his master are corrected according their demerits. But how proud soever Mr. Dryden may be of an error, he has not so much of Ben Jonson's comedy as he pretends. His instance of Face *etc.* in *The Alchemist* is rather notorious against his purpose than for it.

5. Collier refers to Horace's *Ars Poetica.*

For Face did not counsel his master Lovewit to debauch the widow; neither is it clear that the matter went thus far. He might gain her consent upon terms of honor for aught appears to the contrary. 'Tis true, Face, who was one of the principal cheats, is pardoned and considered. But then his master confesses himself kind to a fault. He owns this indulgence was a breach of justice and unbecoming the gravity of an old man. And then desires the audience to excuse him upon the score of the temptation. But *Face continued in the cozenage till the last without repentance.* Under favor, I conceive this is a mistake. For does not Face make an apology before he leaves the stage? Does he not set himself at the bar, arraign his own practice, and cast the cause upon the clemency of the company? And are not all these signs of the dislike of what he had done? Thus careful the poet is to prevent the ill impressions of his play! He brings both man and master to confession; he dismisses them like malefactors and moves for their pardon before he gives them their discharge. But the Mock Astrologer has a gentler hand: Wildblood and Jacinta are more generously used. There is no acknowledgment exacted, no hardship put upon them. They are permitted to talk on in their libertine way to the last and take leave without the least appearance of reformation. The Mock Astrologer urges Ben Jonson's *Silent Woman* as another precedent to his purpose. For *there Dauphine confesses himself in love with all the collegiate ladies. And yet this naughty Dauphine is crowned in the end with the possession of his uncle's estate, and with the hopes of all his mistresses.* This charge, as I take it, is somewhat too severe. I grant Dauphine professes himself in love with the collegiate ladies at first. But when they invite him to a private visit, he makes them no promise, but rather appears tired and willing to disengage. Dauphine therefore is not altogether so naughty as this author represents him.

Ben Jonson's *Fox*[6] is clearly against Mr. Dryden. And here I have his own confession for proof. He declares the *poet's end in this play was the punishment of vice and the reward of virtue.* Ben was forced to strain for this piece of justice and break through the unity of design. This Mr. Dryden remarks upon him. However, he is pleased to commend the performance and calls it an excellent fifth act.

Ben Jonson shall speak for himself afterwards in the character of a critic; in the meantime I shall take a testimony or two from Shakespeare. And here we may observe the admired Falstaff goes off in disappointment. He is thrown out of favor as being a rake and dies like a rat behind the hangings. The pleasure he had given would not excuse him. The poet was not so partial as to let his

6. I.e., *Volpone.*

humour compound for his lewdness. If 'tis objected that this remark is wide of the point, because Falstaff is represented in tragedy, where the laws of justice are more strictly observed. To this I answer, that you may call *Henry the Fourth* and *Fifth* tragedies if you please; but for all that, Falstaff wears no buskins; his character is perfectly comical from end to end.

The next instance shall be in Flowerdale the prodigal.[7] This spark, notwithstanding his extravagance, makes a lucky hand on't at last and marries up a rich lady. But then the poet qualifies him for his good fortune and mends his manners with his circumstances. He makes him repent and leave off his intemperance, swearing, *etc.* And when his father warned him against a relapse, he answers very soberly: *Heaven helping me, I'll hate the course of Hell.*

I could give some instances of this kind out of Beaumont and Fletcher, but there's no need of any farther quotation: for Mr. Dryden is not satisfied with his apology from authority. He does as good as own that this may be construed no better than defending one ill practice by another. To prevent this very reasonable objection he endeavors to vindicate his precedents from the reason of the thing. To this purpose he *makes a wide difference between the rules of tragedy and comedy. That vice must be impartially prosecuted in the first, because the persons are great, etc.*

It seems then executions are only for greatness and quality. Justice is not to strike much lower than a prince. Private people may do what they please. They are too few for mischief and too little for punishment! This would be admirable doctrine for Newgate and give us a general Gaol-Delivery without more ado. But in *tragedy* (says the Mock Astrologer) *the crimes are likewise horrid*, so that there is a necessity for severity and example. And how stands the matter in comedy? Quite otherwise. There the *faults are but the sallies of youth and the frailties of human nature.* For instance. There is nothing but a little whoring. pimping, gaming, profaneness, etc. And who could be so hard hearted to give a man any trouble for this? Such rigors would be strangely inhumane! A poet is a better natured thing I can assure you. These little miscarriages *move pity and commiseration and are not such as must of necessity be punished.* This is comfortable casuistry! But to be serious. Is dissolution of manners such a peccadillo? Does a profligate conscience deserve nothing but commiseration? And are people damned only for human frailties? I perceive the laws of religion and those of the stage differ extremely! The strength of his defense lies in this choice maxim, that the *chief end of comedy is delight.* He questions *whether instruction has any thing to do in comedy.* If it has, he is sure *'tis no more than its secondary end; for the business of the*

---

7. Collier refers to *The London Prodigal*, once thought to be Shakespeare's.

poet is to make you laugh. Granting the truth of this principle, I somewhat question the serviceableness of it. For is there no diversion to be had unless vice appears prosperous and rides at the head of success? One would think such a preposterous distribution of rewards should rather shock the reason and raise the indignation of the audience. To laugh without reason is the pleasure of fools, and against it, of something worse. The exposing of knavery and making lewdness ridiculous is a much better occasion for laughter. And this, with submission, I take to be the end of comedy. And therefore it does not differ from tragedy in the end, but in the means. Instruction is the principal design of both. The one works by terror, the other by infamy. 'Tis true, they don't move in the same line, but they meet in the same point at last.

* * *

Indeed to make delight the main business of comedy is an unreasonable and dangerous principle, opens the way to all licentiousness, and confounds the distinction between mirth and madness. For if diversion is the chief end, it must be had at any price. No serviceable expedient must be refused, though never so scandalous. And thus the worst things are said, and the best abused; religion is insulted, and the most serious matters turned into ridicule! As if the blind side of an audience ought to be caressed, and their folly and atheism entertained in the first place. Yes, if the palate is pleased, no matter though the body is poisoned! For can one die of an easier disease than diversion? But raillery apart, certainly mirth and laughing without respect to the cause are not such supreme satisfactions! A man has sometimes pleasure in losing his wits. Frenzy and possession will shake the lungs and brighten the face; and yet I suppose they are not much to be coveted. However, now we know the reason of the profaneness and obscenity of the stage, of their hellish cursing and swearing, and in short of their great industry to make God and Goodness contemptible. 'Tis all to satisfy the company and make people laugh! A most admirable justification. What can be more engaging to an audience than to see a poet thus atheistically brave? To see him charge up to the cannon's mouth and defy the vengeance of Heaven to serve them? Besides, there may be somewhat of convenience in the case. To fetch diversion out of innocence is no such easy matter. There's no succeeding, it may be, in this method, without sweat and drudging. Clean wit, inoffensive humour, and handsome contrivance require time and thought. And who would be at this expense when the purchase is so cheap another way? 'Tis possible a poet may not always have sense enough by him for such an occasion. And since we are upon supposals, it may be the audience is not to be gained without straining a point and giving a loose to conscience. And when people are sick, are they not to be humoured? In fine, we must not make them laugh, right or wrong, for delight is the *chief end of comedy*. Delight! He should have said debauchery. That's the English of the word and the consequence of the practice. But the original design of comedy was otherwise. And granting it was not so, what then? If the ends of things were naught, they must be mended. Mischief is the chief end of malice, would it be then a blemish in ill nature to change temper and relent into goodness? The chief end of a madman, it may be, is to fire a house; must we not therefore bind him in his bed? To conclude. If delight without restraint or distinction, without conscience or shame, is the supreme law of comedy, 'twere well if we had less on't. Arbitrary pleasure is more dangerous than arbitrary power. Nothing is more brutal than to be abandoned to appetite; and nothing more wretched than to serve in such a design. * * *

ANONYMOUS
A Vindication of the Stage†
(1698)

* * * In his introduction [Mr. Collier] tells us, "the business of the stage is to recommend virtue and discourage vice." Now whether or no plays (comedies I mean) have any business at all, or whether their chief and prime business is not to divert the audience, and relieve the mind fatigued with the business of the foregoing part of the day, is yet a disputable point. Nor shall I easily grant his proposition. For my part, when I go to the theaters, it is with this intention alone, *viz.* to unbend my thoughts from all manner of business and by this relaxation to raise again my wearied spirits and fit them for the affairs of the next day. The mirth and jollity of the place, like a well prescribed cordial, performs its operation, enlivens my drooping thoughts, and passes clearly off, working a pleasing cure and leaving no impression behind it. This is my opinion of comedy, and not only mine, but also of several very famous and learned persons; however, there are but few of our comedies that will not afford some moral instructions too, and our tragedies may stand the test, even by his rule, with any of the ancients.

His chief objections against our plays are, that they are immodest, profane, and immoral; and that the sacred order of the clergy is abused and ill treated. I shall endeavor to say something on each of these heads.

First, he tells us they are immodest and generally smutty. I shall give him an answer from the celebrated Sir Philip Sidney:[1]

† Published in May 1698, just a month after Collier's *Short View* appeared.
1. In *An Apology for Poetry.*

"Comedy [saith he] is an imitation of the common errors of life; now as in geometry the oblique must be known, as well as the right, and in arithmetic the odd as well as the even, so in the actions of our life who seeth not the filthiness of evil wanteth a great foil to perceive the beauty of virtue; and little reason hath any man to say that men learn the evil by seeing it so set out, since there is no man living, but by the force truth hath in nature, no sooner seeth these men play their parts but he wisheth them in *Pristinum*." And Cicero tells us *comedia est imitatio vitae*, where every one might see himself hit in some part or other. So that I know not how they can avoid giving descriptions of debauchery till the world has left the practice of it. When men no longer swear, you will hear no oaths in the playhouse, and so of all other vices. Besides, if delight be the end of comedy, the charge will fall on the people and not on the poets, so that at least Mr. Collier has laid his arguments wrong, for if the spectators were displeased with the representation, the poets would quickly change it. This, granting his charge were true, but Mr. Collier perhaps may fancy a bad meaning where there is none; this heavy condemnation may be only a bugbear of his own raising to fright away the fairest and best part of the audience, I mean the ladies. How has it happened that he has made such discoveries? When others, as clear sighted as himself, nay, and as modest too, never found any such faults. Further, his dwelling so long on the subject of debauchery argues something of delight and pleasure in the case. It puts me in mind of a custom common among the native Irish, which is that they cannot endure to go dry in their feet, but when they travel run into every puddle they find, and are very angry if for want of a bog or ditch they are forced to be cleanly, though ne'er so short a time. Mr. Collier may apply the story at his leisure.

And here I can't but think the ladies have great cause to thank him for his kind instructions; they, harmless innocents, found nothing amiss before, but Mr. Collier has taken care they shall not be so ignorant hereafter; for he, in his great wisdom, has pointed out the places where he promises they may be furnished with smut in abundance.

His way of complimenting them on this account is something odd; but that's not to be regarded in him. He well knows that several of those plays he condemns are immediately dedicated to ladies of the highest quality, and almost all of them have gained the approbation of the fair sex. Now, by his pretending to find these faults of smuttiness and obscenity, he very boldly asserts that they encourage and are pleased with the crimes. This every one must own is very obliging, civil, and well-bred.

But perhaps, to excuse himself, he will say that the ladies did not observe any ill in what they encouraged and that if they had they would have showed their dislike of it. But this he shall answer himself in page 11, where speaking of women's modesty he tells us, "it is wrought in the mechanism of their bodies, that intuitive knowledge scarce makes a quicker impression; and that the enemy no sooner approaches, but the blood rises in opposition and looks defiance to an indecency." So that if there had been the enemy which he pretends, the ladies would have found it out without his interposing in the business, and if there was no enemy, we must imagine him a little allied to Quixotism, or troubled with something like a windmill in his brains, that for the sake of quarrelling only, he will combat with the air. But the ladies have not found this enemy; therefore, we must think his needless assistance impertinence, and his charge vain and frivolous.

* * *

We will now examine his next charge, which is their immorality, their making debauchees their top characters and rewarding them in the end.

And upon this head, this critical gentleman is very severe, though if delight be the chief end of comedy, as I think no one need to question, the business will be found to bear much harder upon those of his own order than upon the poets. For, the poet's business being to please his audience, he must study their humours and fancies and not his own; for, though the drama be never so regularly writ, yet everything represented will seem nauseous and insipid unless it is conformable to the sentiments and relish of the spectators. Whatever poet follows not this rule exactly will quickly be sensible of his error, by his bad harvest of fame and profit. And if the audience will not be pleased with anything but immorality, *etc.*, pray why have not the clergy, whose business it is to instruct the people, taught them better? Which if they had, they would have found the poets to have followed the steps of their audience. So that we see it is rather the clergy's fault than the poet's crime that our dramas are irregular on this head. And Mr. Collier has laid his argument just wrong, for if the world be good, plays would be good also; but if the world be bad, plays will be bad too. And I am sure the ancients were fully as guilty, if not more criminal, on this account. In Sophocles and Aristophanes we may find several instances of vice rewarded and escaping unpunished. In almost every play of Terence we may see vice rewarded: Chaerea is made happy in the *Eunuch* after having debauched a virgin, and he generally does the same in all his plays; nay, you will not only see profligate lewd sparks enjoy their mistresses, but the common courtesans themselves rewarded and honored. Plautus will afford several examples to our purpose. However, granting we do sometimes see on our theaters instances of vice rewarded, or at least unpunished, yet it ought not to be an argument against the art, any more than the extravagancies and ill practices of *some in orders* can be against the whole body of the clergy. And here I cannot but call to mind a sentence I have somewhere met with: "That much of ill nature, and a very little judgment, go far in finding the faults of others." How nearly this may affect Mr. Collier I leave himself to consider.

* * *

[The usefulness of the stage] is so manifest, that I wonder anyone can question it who considers how well adapted it is to the intentions of human life, profit, and delight. Who can express the charms of a well wrought scene lively represented? The motions of the actor charm our outward senses, while the pleasing words steal into our souls and mix with our very blood and spirits, so that we are carried by an irresistless but pleasing violence into the very passion we behold. What heart can forbear relenting to see an unfortunate person, for some unhappy mistakes in his conduct, fall into irreparable misfortunes? This strikes deep into our breasts, by a tender insinuation steals into our souls, and draws a pity from us; so consequently making us ready to assist all that we meet within a like condition. It teaches us to judge charitably of the miserable when we see a small error ignorantly committed may be the cause of heavy misfortunes. It teaches us at the same time caution and circumspection in the management of our selves. And who that sees a vicious person severely punished will not tremble at vice? I think the *Libertine Destroyed*[2] cannot fail to put serious thoughts into the most hardened and profligate atheist and rouse him from his diabolical lethargy as powerfully as the loudest denunciations from the pulpit. Nor is comedy without its excellencies, which being a lower and more natural representation than tragedy, discovers to us the daily affairs we meet with in the world; and if tragedy scares us out of our vices, comedy will no less shame us out of our follies. Tragedy, like a severe master, keeps a heavy hand over us; but comedy, like an indulgent parent, mixes something to please when it reproves. Who can forbear blushing that sees some darling folly exposed? And though its ridiculousness tickles him into a laughter, yet at the same time he feels a secret shame for the guilt. Aristophanes kept all the Athenians in awe by his satire; a person was no sooner guilty of a crime in the city but it stared him full in the face on the stage, and by this means he regulated the commonwealth better than their greatest philosophers with their empty sophisms, or the laws with their blunted edge. Comedy is also useful to instruct us in our dealings in the world; when we see a friend false and treacherous, this teaches us to stand upon our guard and be very

2. Alternate title for Thomas Shadwell's *The Libertine.*

cautious whom we trust. When we see a young gentleman ruined
by the subtle and deluding arts of some cunning courtesan, it bids
us beware of the like danger. The *Squire of Alsatia*³ gives more
effectual instructions to the country gentleman for the avoiding his
ruin both in person and estate by the town-sharpers, by exposing
their shifts and cheats, than the best advice of the ablest divines.
Thus seeing of what worth and value dramatic poetry is for the
forming our manners and regulating our lives, besides the great
delight and pleasure it affords us, I think I need not urge much
more for its recommendation. * * *

JOHN DENNIS

The Usefulness of the Stage†
(1698)

*Part I, Chapter I. That the Stage is Instrumental
to the Happiness of Mankind.*

Nothing can more strongly recommend any thing to us than the
assuring us that it will improve our happiness. For the chief end
and design of man is to make himself happy. 'Tis what he constantly has in his eye, and in order to which he takes every step that
he makes. In whatever he does, or he does not, he designs to
improve or maintain his happiness. And it is by this universal principle that God maintains the harmony and order and quiet of the
reasonable world. It had indeed been an inconsistency in Providence to have made a thinking and reasoning creature that had been
indifferent as to misery and happiness; for God had made such a
one only to disturb the rest and, consequently, had acted against his
own design.

If then I can say enough to convince the reader that the stage is
instrumental to the happiness of mankind, and to his own by consequence, it is evident that I need say no more to make him espouse
its interest.

I shall proceed then to the proving these two things.

First, that the stage is instrumental to the happiness of mankind
in general.

Secondly, that it is more particularly instrumental to the happiness of Englishmen.

3. A play by Thomas Shadwell.
† Published in June 1698, the first
large-scale answer to Collier. Dennis's
introduction, not included here, argues
that Collier's real purpose was not to reform the stage but to abolish it. Reform
is necessary, Dennis allows, but for him
the theater has a civilizing power, "instrumental to the instruction of mankind," and must be defended as an institution in the face of attacks such as Collier's.

The stage is instrumental to the happiness of mankind in general. And here it will be necessary to declare what is meant by happiness, and to proceed upon that.

By happiness, then, I never could understand any thing else but pleasure; for I never could have any notion of happiness that did not agree with pleasure, or any notion of pleasure that did not agree with happiness. I could never possibly conceive how any one can be happy without being pleased, or pleased without being happy. 'Tis universally acknowledged by mankind that happiness consists in pleasure, which is evident from this, that whatever a man does, whether in spiritual or temporal affairs, whether in matters of profit or diversion, pleasure is, at least, the chief and the final motive to it, if it is not the immediate one. And Providence seems to have sufficiently declared that pleasure was intended for our spring and fountain of action when it made it the incentive to those very acts by which we propagate our kind and preserve ourselves. As if self-love without pleasure were insufficient for either; for, as I myself have known several who have chosen rather to die than to go through tedious courses of physic, so, I make no doubt, but several would have taken the same resolution rather than have supported life by a perpetual course of eating, which had differed in nothing from a course of physic if eating and pleasure had not been things inseparable. Now as it is pleasure that obliges man to preserve himself, it is the very same that has sometimes the force to prevail upon him to his own destruction. For, as Monsieur Pascal[1] observes, the very men who hang and who drown themselves are instigated by the secret pleasure which they have from the thought that they shall be freed from pain.

Since, therefore, man in every thing that he does proposes pleasure to himself, it follows that in pleasure consists his happiness. But though he always proposes it, he very often falls short of it; for pleasure is not in his own power, since, if it were, it would follow from thence that happiness were in his power. The want of which has been always the complaint of men both sacred and secular, in all ages, in all countries, and in all conditions. "Man that is born of a woman is but of few days, and full of trouble" says Job, ch. xiv, ver. 1. Of the same nature are the two complaints of Horace, which are so fine and so poetical and so becoming of the best antiquity.

> *Scandit aeratas vitiosa naves*
> *Cura; nec turmas equitum relinquit,*
> *Ocior cervis et agente nimbos*
> *Ocior Euro.*   Hor., Ode 16, Lib. 2.[2]

---

1. Blaise Pascal, seventeenth-century French philosopher.
2. "Morbid care boards even the bronze-beaked ship, nor abandons the troops of horse, swifter than stags, swifter than the east wind driving the storm."

And that other, in the first ode of the third book.

> ————————*Timor et Minae*
> *Scandunt eodem quo dominus: neque*
> *Decedit aerata triremi et*
> *Post equitem sedet atra Cura.*[3]

In short, they who have made the most reflections on it have been the most satisfied of it; and above all, philosophers who, by the voluminous instructions, by the laborious directions, which they have left to posterity, have declared themselves sensible that to be happy is a very difficult thing.

And the reason why they, of all men, have always found it so difficult is because they always propounded to owe their happiness to reason, though one would think that experience might have convinced them of the folly of such a design, because they had seen that the most thinking and the most reasonable had always most complained.

For reason may often afflict us and make us miserable by setting our impotence or our guilt before us; but that which it generally does is the maintaining us in a languishing state of indifference, which, perhaps, is more removed from pleasure than it is from affliction, and which may be said to be the ordinary state of men.

It is plain then that reason, by maintaining us in that state, is an impediment to our pleasure which is our happiness: for to be pleased a man must come out of his ordinary state; now nothing in this life can bring him out of it but passion alone, which reason pretends to combat.

Nothing but passion, in effect, can please us, which every one may know by experience. For when any man is pleased he may find by reflection that at the same time he is moved. The pleasure that any man meets with oftenest is the pleasure of sense. Let anyone examine himself in that and he will find that the pleasure is owing to passion; for the pleasure vanishes with the desire and is succeeded by loathing, which is a sort of grief.

Since nothing but pleasure can make us happy, it follows that to be very happy we must be much pleased; and since nothing but passion can please us, it follows that to be very much pleased, we must be very much moved. This needs no proof, or, if it did, experience would be a very convincing one; since anyone may find, when he has a great deal of pleasure. that he is extremely moved.

And that very height and fullness of pleasure which we are promised in another life must, we are told, proceed from passion or something which resembles passion. At least no man has so much as

---

3. "Fear and Threats climb to the place of the master: nor does black Care with-draw from the bronze-beaked galley and even settles behind the horseman."

pretended that it will be the result of reason. For we shall then be delivered from these mortal organs, and reason shall then be no more. We shall then no more have occasion from premises to draw conclusions and a long train of consequences; for, becoming all spirit and all knowledge, we shall see things as they are: we shall lead the glorious life of angels, a life exalted above all reason, a life consisting of ecstasy and intelligence.

Thus is it plain that the happiness, both of this life and the other, is owing to passion and not to reason. But though we can never be happy by the force of reason, yet, while we are in this life, we cannot possibly be happy without it, or against it. For since man is by his nature a reasonable creature, to suppose man happy against reason is to suppose him happy against nature, which is absurd and monstrous. We have shown that a man must be pleased to be happy and must be moved to be pleased; and that to please him to a height, you must move him in proportion. But then the passions must be raised after such a manner as to take reason along with them. If reason is quite overcome, the pleasure is neither long, nor sincere, nor safe. For how many that have been transported beyond their reason have never more recovered it? If reason resists, a man's breast becomes the seat of civil war, and the combat makes him miserable. For the passions, which are in their natures so very troublesome, are only so because their motions are always contrary to the motions of the will; as grief, sorrow, shame and jealousy. And that which makes some passions in their natures pleasant is because they move with the will, as love, joy, pity, hope, terror, and sometimes anger. But this is certain, that no passion can move in a full consent with the will, unless at the same time it be approved of by the understanding. And no passion can be allowed of by the understanding that is not raised by its true springs and augmented by its just degrees. Now in the world it is so very rare to have our passions thus raised, and so improved, that that is the reason why we are so seldom thoroughly and sincerely pleased. But in the drama the passions are false and abominable unless they are moved by their true springs and raised by their just degrees. Thus are they moved, thus are they raised in every well-written tragedy, till they come to as great a height as reason can very well bear. Besides, the very motion has a tendency to the subjecting them to reason, and the very raising purges and moderates them. So that the passions are seldom anywhere so pleasing and nowhere so safe as they are in tragedy. Thus have I shown that to be happy is to be pleased and to be pleased is to be moved in such a manner as is allowed of by reason. I have shown too that tragedy moves us thus, and consequently pleases us, and consequently makes us happy. Which was the thing to be proved.

Part I, Chapter III. The Objections from Reason Answered.

* * * The corruption of manners upon the Restoration appeared with all the fury of libertinism even before the playhouse was reëstablished, and long before it could have any influence on manners; so that another cause of that corruption is to be inquired after than the reestablishment of the drama; and that can be nothing but that beastly Reformation which, in the time of the late civil wars, was begun at the tail instead of the head and the heart; and which oppressed and persecuted men's inclinations instead of correcting and converting them, which afterwards broke out with the same violence that a raging fire does upon its first getting vent. And that which gave it so licentious a vent was not only the permission but the example of the court, which, for the most part, was just arrived from abroad with the king, where it had endeavored by foreign corruption to sweeten, or at least to soften, adversity, and having sojourned for a considerable time both at Paris and in the Low Countries, united the spirit of the French whoring to the fury of the Dutch drinking. So that the poets who wrote immediately after the Restoration were obliged to humour the depraved tastes of their audience. For as an impenitent sinner that should be immediately transported to heaven would be incapable of partaking of the happiness of the place, because his inclinations and affections would not be prepared for it; so if the poets of these times had written in a manner purely instructive, without any mixture of lewdness, the appetites of the audience were so far debauched that they would have judged the entertainment insipid; so that the spirit of libertinism which came in with the court and for which the people were so well prepared by the sham reformation of manners caused the lewdness of their plays, and not the lewdness of the plays the spirit of libertinism. For it is ridiculous to assign a cause of so long a standing to so new, so sudden, and so extraordinary an effect, when we may assign a cause so new, so probable, and unheard of before, as the inclinations of the people, returning with violence to their natural bent upon the encouragement and example of a court that was come home with all the corruptions of a foreign luxury; so that the sham Reformation being, in a great measure, the cause of that spirit of libertinism which with so much fury came in with King Charles the Second, and the putting down the playhouse being part of that Reformation, it is evident that the corruption of the nation is so far from proceeding from the playhouse, that it partly proceeds from having no plays at all.

That the corruption of manners is not to be attributed to the licentiousness of the drama may appear from the consideration of the reigning vices, I mean those moral vices which have more immediate influence upon men's conduct and consequently upon their happiness. And those are chiefly four.

1. The Love of Women.
2. Drinking.
3. Gaming.
4. Unnatural Sins.

For drinking and gaming, their excesses cannot be reasonably charged upon the stage for the following reasons.

First, because it cannot possibly be conceived that so reasonable a diversion as the drama can encourage or incline men to so unreasonable a one as gaming or so brutal a one as drunkenness.

Secondly, because these two vices have been made odious and ridiculous by our plays instead of being shown agreeable. As for drunkenness, to show the sinner is sufficient to discredit the vice; for a drunkard, of necessity, always appears either odious or ridiculous. And for a gamester, I never knew one shown in a play but either as a fool or a rascal.

Thirdly, because those two vices flourish in places that are too remote and in persons that are too abject to be encouraged or influenced by the stage. There is drinking and gaming in the furthest north and the furthest west among peasants as well as among dukes and peers. But here, perhaps, some visionary zealot will urge that these two vices, even in these remote places and these abject persons, proceed from the influence of that irreligion which is caused by the corruptions of the stage and will, with as much reason, and as much modesty, deduce the lewdness which is transacted in the tin-mines in Cornwall and the coal-pits of Newcastle from the daily abominations of the pits of the two play houses as he would derive the brutality of the High-Dutch drinking from the profaneness of our English drama.

But what will they say then to those gentlemen who neither are supposed to go to our theaters, nor to converse much with those who do, nor to be liable to be corrupted by them? What will they say to these gentlemen if they can be proved to have a considerable share in the two afore-mentioned vices? What can they answer? For it would be ridiculously absurd to reply that the clergy are corrupted by the laity, whom it is their business to convert. But here I think myself obliged to declare that I by no means design this as a reflection upon the Church of England, who, I am satisfied, may more justly boast of its clergy than any other church whatsoever; a clergy that are equally illustrious for their piety and for their learning. Yet may I venture to affirm that there are some among them who can never be supposed to have been corrupted by playhouses, who yet turn up a bottle oftener than they do an hour glass; who box about a pair of tables with more fervor than they do their cushions, contemplate a pair of dice more frequently than the Fathers or Councils, and meditate and depend upon hazard more than they do upon Providence.

And as for that unnatural sin which is another growing vice of the age, it would be monstrous to urge that it is, in the least, encouraged by the stage; for it is either never mentioned there or mentioned with the last detestation.

And now, lastly, for the love of women, fomented by the corruption and not by the genuine art of the stage; though the augmenting and nourishing of it cannot be defended, yet it may be in some measure excused.

1. Because it has more of nature, and consequently more temptation and consequently less malice, than the preceding three, which the drama does not encourage.

2. Because it has a check upon the other vices and peculiarly upon that unnatural sin, in the restraining of which the happiness of mankind is, in so evident a manner, concerned.

So that of the four moral reigning vices, the stage encourages but one, which as it has been proved to be the least of them all, so it is the least contagious and the least universal. For in the country fornication and adultery are seldom heard of, whereas drunkenness rages in almost every house there: from all which it appears how very unreasonable it is to charge the lewdness of the times upon the stage when it is evident that of the four reigning moral vices the stage encourages but one, and that the least of the four and the least universal and a vice which has a check upon the other three, and particularly upon that amongst them which is most opposite and most destructive to the happiness of mankind.

Part I, Chapter IV. The Objections from Authority Answered.

* * * While I am pleading in defense of the stage I am defending and supporting poetry, the best and the noblest kind of writing. For all other writers are made by precept and are formed by art; but a poet prevails by the force of nature; is excited by all that's powerful in humanity, and is, sometimes, by a spirit not his own exalted to divinity.

For if poetry in other countries has flourished with the stage and been with that neglected, what must become of it here in England if the stage is ruined; For foreign poets have found their public and their private patrons. They who excelled in Greece were encouraged by the Athenian state, nay and by all Greece, assembled at their Olympian, Istmean, Nemean, Pythian games. Rome had its Scipios, its Caesars, and its Maecenases. France had its magnanimous Richelieu, and its greater Lewis; but the protection that poetry has found in England has been from the stage alone. Some few indeed of our private men have had souls that have been large enough, and wanted only power. But of our princes how few have had any taste of arts! Nay, and of them who had some, have had their heads too full, and some their souls too narrow!

As then in maintaining the cause of the stage, I am defending poetry in general; so in defending that I am pleading for eloquence, for history, and philosophy. I am pleading for the reasonable pleasures of mankind, the only harmless, the only cheap, the only universal pleasures; the nourishments of youth and the delights of age; the ornaments of prosperity and the surest sanctuaries of adversity; now insolently attempted by furious zeal, too wretchedly blind to see their beauties or discern their innocence. For unless the stage be encouraged in England, poetry cannot subsist; for never was any man a great poet who did not make it his business as well as pleasure and solely abandon himself to that. And as poetry would be crushed by the ruins of the stage, so eloquence would be miserably maimed by them; for which, if action be confessed the life of it, the theater is certainly the best of schools; and if action be not the life of it, Demosthenes was much mistaken. * * *

WILLIAM CONGREVE

Amendments of Mr. Collier's False and Imperfect Citations†
(1698)

I have been told by some that they should think me very idle if I threw away any time in taking notice even of so much of Mr. Collier's late treatise of the Immorality, *etc.* of the English stage as related to myself, in respect of some plays written by me; for that his malicious and strained interpretations of my words were so gross and palpable that any indifferent and unprejudiced reader would immediately condemn him upon his own evidence and acquit me before I could make any defense.

On the other hand, I have been taxed of laziness, and too much security, in neglecting thus long to do my self a necessary right, which might be effected with so very little pains; since very little

† Published in July 1698, just after the initial flurry of pamphlets on the subject had reached a peak in June. Congreve's reluctance to enter an argument of this kind is clear; but Collier had reserved his plays (except *The Way of the World*, not yet written) for especially severe treatment, and Congreve, obviously angered, felt it necessary to defend himself. Most of his reply is spent in explaining specific passages by placing them in the context from which Collier had sometimes wrenched them. These portions are omitted here in favor of the more general comments with which Congreve introduced his essay.

more is requisite in my vindication than to represent truly and at length those passages which Mr. Collier has shown imperfectly and for the most part by halves. I would rather be thought idle than lazy; and so the last advice prevailed with me.

I have no intention to examine all the absurdities and falsehoods in Mr. Collier's book; to use the gentleman's own metaphor in his preface, *an inventory of such a warehouse would be a large work.* My detection of his malice and ignorance, of his sophistry and vast assurance, will lie within a narrow compass, and only bear a proportion to so much of his book as concerns myself.

Least of all would I undertake to defend the corruptions of the stage; indeed if I were so inclined, Mr. Collier has given me no occasion, for the greater part of those examples which he has produced are only demonstrations of his own impurity, they only savor of his utterance, and were sweet enough till tainted by his breath.

I will not justify any of my own errors; I am sensible of many, and if Mr. Collier has by any accident stumbled on one or two, I will freely give them up to him, *nullum unquam ingenium placuit sine venia.*[1] But I hope I have done nothing that can deprive me of the benefit of my clergy; and though Mr. Collier himself were the ordinary, I may hope to be acquitted.

My intention, therefore, is to do little else but to restore those passages to their primitive station which have suffered so much in being transplanted by him. I will remove 'em from his dunghill and replant 'em in the field of nature; and when I have washed 'em of that filth which they have contracted in passing through his very dirty hands, let their own innocence protect them.

Mr. Collier, in the high vigor of his obscenity, first commits a rape upon my words, and then arraigns 'em of immodesty; he has barbarity enough to accuse the very virgins that he has deflowered, and to make sure of their condemnation he has himself made 'em guilty. But he forgets that while he publishes their shame he divulges his own.

His artifice to make words guilty of profaneness is of the same nature; for where the expression is unblameable in its own clear and genuine signification, he enters into it himself like the evil spirit; he possesses the innocent phrase and makes it bellow forth his own blasphemies; so *that one would think the muse was legion.*

To reprimand him a little in his own words, if these passages produced by Mr. Collier are obscene and profane, *why were they raked in and disturbed unless it were to conjure up vice and revive impurities? Indeed Mr. Collier has a very untoward way with him; his pen has such a libertine stroke that 'tis a question whether the practice or the reproof be the more licentious.*

1. From Seneca, *Epistles*, CXIV.12: "No man's talent has ever been approved   without pardon of something."

He teaches those vices he would correct and writes more like a pimp than a p———. Since the business must be undertaken, why was not the thought blanched, the expression made remote, and the ill features cast into shadows? So far from this, which is his own instruction in his own words, is Mr. Collier's way of proceeding, that he has blackened the thoughts with his own smut; the expression that was remote, he has brought nearer; and lest by being brought near its native innocence might be more invisible, he has frequently varied it, he has new-molded it, and stamped his own image on it; so that it at length is become current deformity and fit to be paid into the devil's exchequer.

I will therefore take the liberty to exorcise this evil spirit and whip him out of my plays wherever I can meet with him. Mr. Collier has reversed the story which he relates from Tertullian; and after his visitation of the playhouse, returns, having left the devil behind him.[2]

If I do not return his civilities in calling him names, it is because I am not very well versed in his nomenclatures; therefore, for his *foot pads*, which he calls us in his preface, and for his *buffoons* and *slaves in the Saturnalia*, which he frequently bestows on us in the rest of his book, I will only call him Mr. Collier, and that I will call him as often as I think he shall deserve it.

Before I proceed, for method's sake, I must premise some few things to the reader, which if he thinks in his conscience are too much to be granted me, I desire he would proceed no further in his perusal of these animadversions, but return to Mr. Collier's *Short View*, etc.

First, I desire that I may lay down Aristotle's definition of comedy, which has been the compass by which all the comic poets since his time have steered their course. I mean them whom Mr. Collier so very frequently calls *comedians;* for the distinction between *comicus* and *comoedus* and *tragicus* and *tragoedus*[3] is what he has not met with in the long progress of his reading.

Comedy (says Aristotle) is an imitation of the worse sort of people. Μίμησις φαυλοτέρων, *imitatio pejorum.* He does not mean the worse sort of people in respect to their quality, but in respect to their manners. This is plain from his telling you immediately after, that he does not mean κατὰ πάσαν κακίαν, relating to all kinds of vice; there are crimes too daring and too horrid for comedy. But the vices most frequent, and which are the common practice of the looser sort of livers, are the subject matter of comedy. He tells us farther, that they must be exposed after a ridiculous manner. For men are to be laughed out of their vices in comedy; the business of

2. Collier had cited Tertullian's story (*De Spectaculis*, XXVI) about a woman who brought the devil home with her from the theater.
3. I.e., between tragic actor and tragic poet, etc.

comedy is to delight as well as to instruct; and as vicious people are made ashamed of their follies or faults by seeing them exposed in a ridiculous manner, so are good people at once both warned and diverted at their expense.

Thus much I though necessary to premise, that by showing the nature and end of comedy we may be prepared to expect characters agreeable to it.

Secondly, since comic poets are obliged by the laws of comedy, and to the intent that comedy may answer its true end and purpose above-mentioned, to represent vicious and foolish characters—in consideration of this, I desire that it may not be imputed to the persuasion or private sentiments of the author if at any time one of these vicious characters in any of his plays shall behave himself foolishly or immorally in word or deed. I hope I am not yet unreasonable; it were very hard that a painter should be believed to resemble all the ugly faces that he draws.

Thirdly, I must desire the impartial reader not to consider any expression or passage cited from any play as it appears in Mr. Collier's book, nor to pass any sentence or censure upon it out of its proper scene, or alienated from the character by which it is spoken; for in that place alone, and in his mouth alone, can it have its proper and true signification.

I cannot think it reasonable, because Mr. Collier is pleased to write one chapter of *Immodesty* and another of *Profaneness*, that therefore every expression traduced by him under those heads shall be condemned as obscene and profane immediately, and without any further inquiry. Perhaps Mr. Collier is acquainted with the *deceptio visus*, and presents objects to the view through a stained glass; things may appear seemingly profane, when in reality they are only seen through a profane medium, and the true color is dissembled by the help of a sophistical varnish. Therefore, I demand the privilege of the *habeas corpus* act, that the prisoners may have liberty to remove and to appear before a just judge in an open and an uncounterfeit light.

Fourthly, because Mr. Collier in his chapter of the profaneness of the stage has founded great part of his accusation upon the liberty which poets take of using some words in their plays which have been sometimes employed by the translators of the Holy Scriptures, I desire that the following distinction may be admitted, *viz.* that when words are applied to sacred things and with a purpose to treat of sacred things, they ought to be understood accordingly; but when they are otherwise applied, the diversity of the subject gives a diversity of signification. And in truth he might as well except against the common use of the alphabet in poetry because the same letters are necessary to the spelling of words which are mentioned in sacred writ.

Though I have thought it requisite and but reasonable to premise these few things, to which, as to so many *postulata*, I may when occasion offers refer myself, yet if the reader should have any objection to the latitude which at first sight they may seem to comprehend, I dare venture to assure him that it shall be removed by the caution which I shall use, and those limits by which I shall restrain myself, when I shall judge it proper for me to refer to them.

It may not be impertinent in this place to remind the reader of a very common expedient which is made use of to recommend the instruction of our plays, which is this. After the action of the play is over and the delight of the representation at an end, there is generally care taken that the moral of the whole shall be summed up and delivered to the audience in the very last and concluding lines of the poem. The intention of this is that the delight of the representation may not so strongly possess the minds of the audience as to make them forget or oversee the instruction. It is the last thing said, that it may make the last impression; and it is always comprehended in a few lines and put into rhyme, that it may be easy and engaging to the memory. * * *

Steele and Dennis:
On *The Man of Mode* and
The Conscious Lovers

RICHARD STEELE

The Spectator, No. 65 †
(1711)

After having at large explained what wit is, and described the false appearances of it,[1] all that labor seems but an useless inquiry, without some time be spent in considering the application of it. The seat of wit, when one speaks as a man of the town and the world, is the playhouse; I shall therefore fill this paper with reflections upon the use of it in that place. The application of wit in the theater has as strong an effect upon the manners of our gentlemen as the taste of it has upon the writings of our authors. It may, perhaps, look like a very presumptuous work, though not foreign from the duty of a Spectator, to tax the writings of such as have long had the general applause of a nation. But I shall always make reason, truth, and nature the measures of praise and dispraise; if those are for me, the generality of opinion is of no consequence against me; if they are against me, the general opinion cannot long support me.

Without further preface, I am going to look into some of our most applauded plays, and see whether they deserve the figure they at present bear in the imaginations of men, or not.

In reflecting upon these works, I shall chiefly dwell upon that for which each respective play is most celebrated. The present paper shall be employed upon Sir Fopling Flutter. The received character

† Steele's attack in 1711 upon *The Man of Mode*, by then a well-known play of the previous generation, was part of his extensive effort to establish a new mode of comedy which would present virtuous behavior as a pattern for imitation. His earlier plays, such as *The Lying Lover* (1703) and *The Tender Husband* (1705), had already indicated his interest in moral drama, and not long after his essay on *The Man of Mode* he began work on a play intended to serve as the complete formulation of the new comic mode. This was *The Conscious Lovers* (1722), and it was preceded by a sly publicity campaign, largely of Steele's own composition and represented here by the selections from his periodical *The Theatre*.

1. Numbers 58–63 of *The Spectator* concerned the subject of wit.

of this play is that it is the pattern of genteel comedy. Dorimant and Harriet are the characters of greatest consequence, and if these are low and mean, the reputation of the play is very unjust.

I will take for granted that a fine gentleman should be honest in his actions and refined in his language. Instead of this, our hero in this piece is a direct knave in his designs and a clown in his language. Bellair is his admirer and friend; in return for which, because he is forsooth a greater wit than his said friend, he thinks it reasonable to persuade him to marry a young lady, whose virtue, he thinks, will last no longer than till she is a wife, and then she cannot but fall to his share, as he is an irresistible fine gentleman. The false-hood to Mrs. Loveit, and the barbarity of triumphing over her anguish for losing him, is another instance of his honesty, as well as his good nature. As to his fine language, he calls the orange-woman, who, it seems, is inclined to grow fat, "an overgrown jade, with a flasket of guts before her;" and salutes her with a pretty phrase of, "How now, double tripe!" Upon the mention of a country gentle-woman, whom he knows nothing of (no one can imagine why), he "will lay his life she is some awkward, ill-fashioned country toad, who not having above four dozen of hairs on her head, has adorned her baldness with a large white fruz, that she may look sparkishly in the forefront of the king's box at an old play." Unnatural mixture of senseless commonplace!

As to the generosity of his temper, he tells his poor footman, "If he did not wait better——" he would turn him away, in the insolent phrase of "I'll uncase you."

Now for Mrs. Harriet: she laughs at obedience to an absent mother, whose tenderness Busy describes to be very exquisite, for "that she is so pleased with finding Harriet again, that she cannot chide her for being out of the way." This witty daughter and fine lady has so little respect for this good woman that she ridicules her air in taking leave, and cries, "In what struggle is my poor mother yonder? See, see! her head tottering, her eyes staring, and her under lip trembling." But all this is atoned for, because "she has more wit than is usual in her sex, and as much malice, though she is as wild as you would wish her, and has a demureness in her looks that makes it so surprising!" Then to recommend her as a fit spouse for his hero, the poet makes her speak her sense of marriage very ingeniously. "I think," says he, "I might be brought to endure him, and that is all a reasonable woman should expect in an husband." It is, methinks, unnatural that we are not made to understand how she that was bred under a silly pious old mother, that would never trust her out of her sight, came to be so polite.

It cannot be denied but that the negligence of everything which engages the attention of the sober and valuable part of mankind appears very well drawn in this piece; but it is denied that it is necessary to the character of a fine gentleman that he should in that manner trample upon all order and decency. As for the character of Dorimant, it is more of a coxcomb than that of Fopling. He says of one of his companions that a good correspondence between them is their mutual interest. Speaking of that friend, he declares their being much together "makes the women think the better of his understanding, and judge more favorably of my reputation. It makes him pass upon some for a man of very good sense, and me upon others for a very civil person."

This whole celebrated piece is a perfect contradiction to good manners, good sense, and common honesty; and as there is nothing in it but what is built upon the ruin of virtue and innocence, according to the notion of merit in this comedy, I take the shoemaker to be, in reality, the fine gentleman of the play; for it seems he is an atheist, if we may depend upon his character as given by the orange-woman, who is herself far from being the lowest in the play. She says of a fine man who is Dorimant's companion, "There is not such another heathen in the town, except the shoemaker." His pretension to be the hero of the drama appears still more in his own description of his way of living with his lady. "There is," says he, "never a man in town lives more like a gentleman with his wife than I do; I never mind her motions; she never inquires into mine. We speak to one another civilly, hate one another heartily; and because it is vulgar to lie and soak together, we have each of us our several settle-bed." That of "soaking together" is as good as if Dorimant had spoken it himself; and I think, since he puts human nature in as ugly a form as the circumstance will bear, and is a staunch unbeliever, he is very much wronged in having no part of the good fortune bestowed in the last act.

To speak plainly of this whole work, I think nothing but being lost to a sense of innocence and virtue can make any one see this comedy without observing more frequent occasion to move sorrow and indignation than mirth and laughter. At the same time I allow it to be nature, but it is nature in its utmost corruption and degeneracy.

RICHARD STEELE

The Theatre, No. 1†
(1720)

In the beginning of a work which I design to publish twice a week, it is necessary to explain myself to the town and make them

† *The Theatre* appeared twice weekly for three months in 1720. The fictional scheme of the early numbers, which included characters from *The Conscious Lovers*, was not consistently carried through; instead, Steele turned the journal to his own purposes in the internal politics of the theater.

understand why I attempt to entertain them under this title. When I have informed my reader that I am in the sixty-first year of my age[1] and have been induced to frequent the theater by the persuasion of my son, it will perhaps raise attention and curiosity to know what are the particular circumstances which make the father ductile to his child, instead of the son's governing himself by the example of his father.

I have always abhorred living at distance with him, and ever gave him his freedom in all his words and actions, so that I have seldom expostulated with him concerning them; but of late years, observed him mighty conversant at the theater and living in occasional familiarity with the chief actors. This turn was so particular that I inquired what he could find thus delightful to him among persons singularly remarked to their disadvantage. He begged of me (as I had formerly advised him) to judge for myself in those matters, and prevailed with me to go with him to the play very frequently; where I soon recovered the taste I had had for those entertainments in my youth, and reflected that this, above all other diversions, was proper and pleasing rather to the young or old than to the middle-aged. The middle of our days, thought I, is generally taken up in the hurry and eagerness of business; but the days we pass before we mingle with the world, and after we are retired from it, are the seasons wherein plays well acted give greatest pleasure. Young men learn from the stage the knowledge of that world they are scarce yet acquainted with; old men look back on the road which they have passed through with equal delight and satisfaction.

My son *Harry* is a gentleman of a discernment above his years and affects the company of elder men. He has a vivacity in his manner and a good-natured quickness of spirit that renders him very agreeable to his acquaintance. When he comes into a room, I have observed the company look upon him with the aspect which people usually have when one enters from some place whence they expect news. His manner is uncommon and his thoughts on any subject give that sort of pleasure which we receive by fresh intelligence from some scene of action. His imagination dispenses new reflections on any subject, and he is always a great addition to the entertainment by the pleasant and peculiar relish he has of it.

This boy of mine who brought me back to the play-house is as proud of his good-humoured old man, as the pert thing calls me, as I am of him, and never makes a new acquaintance, though with a young lady, but the first thing he promises is that the party shall be acquainted with his father. He has introduced me to a particular friend of his, a lady of great quality and merit, with whom, and her visitants, I am often very well entertained, and the theater is no

---

1. Steele is writing in the guise of "Sir John Edgar," a fictional personage who was to become "Sir John Bevil" in *The Conscious Lovers*.

small part of our conversation. *Sophronia*, for that shall be her name, is, according to the course of nature, in a stage of this life not far from a better being, but under no manner of decay as to her senses and understanding. From experience added to her great wit and good humour, you would take her, by her discourse, to be only a very wise young woman. She has always encouraged theatrical diversions and admitted the eminent performers (from *Hart* and *Mohun*, to those of our time) to her presence and conversation, and has a very excellent taste both of the composition and performance of a good play.

At this lady's house, elegance and decency, not licentiousness and luxury, are consulted as the most inviting entertainment of the company that meet there. There is a purity in their manners and a kind of chastity in their very dress. Their mirth has no noise, their joy little laughter; but freedom is bounded by respect, and their familiarity rendered more agreeable by good breeding. A romp would there look like a prostitute, and a rake would be as terrible as a ruffian.

There are but very few of either sex who are capable of being well pleased at her assemblies; for as 'tis said, the vicious could not be happy were they to be translated to Heaven; so (with reverence in the comparison) may I aver that the ordinary people of fashion would be there very much at a loss, and those who pass for fine gentlemen and ladies in other conversations would be in the apartment of *Sophronia* uninformed savages.

Deviation from reason and good sense is there the only error, and uninstructed innocence is pitied and assisted, while studied faults and assumed singularities are banished or discountenanced.

* * *

The Theatre, No. 3
(1720)

Upon my producing my second paper[1] at *Sophronia's* tea-table, the ladies had the goodness to express a delight in that they now began to be convinced of my being determined to go on with the work. And in order to it, I had leave to lay before them a new scheme for the government of the public diversions. I told them that it had long been a great cause of distress to the actors to know who were properly the town and who not; they having been often under the nicest perplexities from the very different opinions of people of quality and condition.

There is, they tell me, scarce any play put up in their bills, or

---

1. I.e., the second issue of *The Theatre*, here omitted.

that they propose to revive, but has as much the dislike of some as the approbation of others, even before it comes on, and that the same happens in most of their private affairs. Whenever they fall into public company, it is very difficult to preserve that deference due to the opinion of their superiors and at the same time to pursue their own measures, and what their experience convinces them will most probably contribute to the public entertainment. Therefore, that the players may be better justified in what they shall do hereafter, I have proposed:

1. That a select number of persons shall be chosen as real representatives of a *British* audience.

2. These persons so elected shall be styled *Auditors of the Drama*.

3. No persons to have free voices in these elections but such as shall produce certificates from the respective door-keepers of the theater that they never refused to pay for their places.

4. The players shall choose two of their own society, *viz.* one male and one female, to take care of their interest, and for the better information of these *Auditors*, in matters immediately relating to their customs and private economy.

5. One dramatic poet to serve for the liberties of *Parnassus*; to be chosen only by tragic or comic writers.

6. Three of the fair sex shall represent the front-boxes.

7. Two gentlemen of wit and pleasure for the side-boxes.

8. Three substantial citizens for the pit.

9. One lawyer's clerk and one *valet de chambre* for the first gallery. One journeyman-baker for the upper-gallery.

10. And one footman that can write and read shall be *Mercury* to the Board.

11. This body so chosen shall have full power, in the right of the audiences of *Great Britain*, to approve, condemn, or rectify whatever shall be exhibited on the *English* theater.

And the players guiding themselves by their laws shall not be accountable to or controlled by any other opinions or suggestions whatever, nor ever appeal from the judgments of these duly elected *Auditors*. Provided notwithstanding, that any daily spectators shall have reserved to them and their successors for ever their full right of applauding or disliking the performance of any particular actor whenever his care or negligence shall appear to deserve either the one or the other. But in matters merely relating to the conduct of the theater, the said elected *Auditors*, from time to time, shall be deemed able, and to have right, to give laws for ever.

This scheme was approved by the whole assembly at the Lady *Sophronia's*, and they desired me accordingly to appoint the day of the election of *Auditors*. I am therefore to acquaint the town that due notice shall be given of some play to be acted, after which the audience will proceed to choose representatives for the *British* theater by way of ballot; which every door-keeper is hereby impowered to receive at the same time he takes their money.

This matter has already taken air, and there are candidates who already appear and have desired my interest and recommendation. The first who addressed me with a modest discovery of that ambition is *Lucinda*, who hopes to be chosen for the boxes.

Lucinda is the daughter of Mr. *Sealand*, an eminent merchant; she is a young woman of a most unaffected, easy, and engaging behavior, which has brought her much into fashion among all the great families she visits. She is conversant in books and no stranger to household affairs, of a discerning and quick spirit in conversation, and has a mortal aversion to all coxcombs; she has the modesty, in the account of herself, to pretend only to a judgment in the dresses and habits of the theater. But as I love to be fair in all representations, I must give the electors notice (who may act accordingly) that she is a great favorer of the woollen manufactures; and she intends on the election-day to appear in a white stuff suit, lined with cherry-colored silk, in the second row of the front-boxes. For, besides the consideration of her country's good, she has skill enough to know that no woman is the better dressed for being in rich clothes, and that 'tis the fancy and elegance of an habit, and not the cost, that makes it always becoming to the wearer. She is in hopes too, as I am privately informed, to introduce, even on the stage, dresses of our own growth and labor, which shall be as good, as cheap, and becoming, as any imported from abroad. This method, she imagines, will give the world a very advantageous opportunity of judging of the commodiousness, beauty, and ease of those habits by the appearance they make upon the players in parts proper to them. She concludes that the theater should be made serviceable to all parts of life and all trades and professions, that it may the better deserve the support of the public.

Mr. *Charles Myrtle* stands for the side-box. He is a gentleman of a very plentiful fortune; a student, or rather an inhabitant of the *Temple*; he has a fine taste of letters, and from thence bears some reputation of a scholar, which makes him much more valuable in that of a gentleman. He has many agreeable qualities, besides the distinction of a good understanding and more good nature. But he has little imperfections that frequently indispose his temper; and when jealousy takes hold of him, he becomes untractable and unhappily positive in his opinions and resolutions; but I must not say too much on the less side of his character, because my son *Harry Edgar* offers himself at the same time to the town, and hopes for their votes and interest for the side-box.

We have a candidate for the pit, an eminent *East India* merchant, Mr. *Sealand*, father of *Lucinda*. This gentleman was formerly what is called a man of pleasure about the town; and having, when young, lavished a small estate, retired to *India*, where by marriage, and falling into the knowledge of trade, he laid the foundation of the great fortune of which he is now master. I am in great hopes he will carry his election, for his thoughts and sentiments against the unworthy representations of citizens on the stage may highly contribute to the abolition of such ridiculous images for the future. His knowledge and experience, by living in mixed company as well as in the busy world here, balanced him against approving what is either too frivolous or too abstracted for public entertainments. He is a true pattern of that kind of third gentry which has arose in the world this last century; I mean the great and rich families of merchants and eminent traders, who in their furniture, their equipage, their manner of living, and especially their economy, are so far from being below the gentry that many of them are now the best representatives of the ancient ones and deserve the imitation of the modern nobility. If this gentleman should carry his election (as from his having the whole city-interest of *Jews*, as well as Gentiles, in the pit, it is very likely he will), we shall have great assistance from him with relation both to the real and imaginary world. He is a man that does business with the candor of a gentleman, and performs his engagements with the exactness of a citizen.

The players are in much hurry about the election of their proper representatives, there being but two female candidates, who are both remarkable for their great merit and industry in their profession. My son tells me he finds by their discourse about the playhouse that every one, consulted apart, speaks of them in different modes. I'll vote, says one, for a lady that values her self only as she is eminent in the theater, that never when she is in her part has her hero in the sidebox instead of on the stage, but is acting as well when another is speaking as when she speaks herself; who expresses in her countenance as much what she hears as what she utters. This description could relate to but two of all the house; but it is thought the actors will choose the less handsome out of their complaisance to those ladies who are candidates for the audience, because it is remarkable that people of quality bear to see their inferiors in fortune their equals in wit and knowledge, with patience enough, provided they do not also come up to them in their manners and beauty.

The first gallery has offered to it a representative who is an underling of the law, one who knows a great deal, as the quirks of it may perplex, but not a word as the reason of it may protect and serve mankind. I hope he will not carry it, because such a creature can be in no place where he does not consider rather how he can, as he is situated, disturb his neighbor than enjoy his own. And this kind of creature will show himself as much during his term in a seat at a play as in the possession of an estate for ever and ever.

My man *Humphrey*, who has lived with me for many years, proposes himself for the first gallery. He is a diligent, careful, sensible man and has had a right in all that comes off my person these forty years; for so long has he been my *valet de chambre*, or gentleman, as they call it. I cannot accuse him but of one ungentlemanly thing during our whole time together; and that was, he brought a tailor to see me as I walked in *Lincoln's-Inn* Garden, and sold him the coat I had then on my back, while I was musing concerning the course of human affairs in the upper walk. This I cannot call an injustice, for I had given him the suit, and he put me in it, because it was warm, the day after I gave it him being cold. However, I may call it an unpoliteness and an *indecorum*, because his master had it on while he was making the bargain. After I have said all this, I think I may put up a man for the gallery whose greatest offense he ever committed was only against decency.

I had, when I proposed this scheme, a journeyman-baker in my eye, as well that in case of danger of famine from any outward cause, the house might bake for themselves, as also that he is a robust critic, and can by way of cudgel keep silence about him in the upper-gallery, where the wit and humour of the play will not always command attention.

I have not yet heard of any other candidates; but when I do, shall give timely notice. In the meantime shall rest with great content in the hopes I conceive from the assistance of a well chosen board. The election of a poet for the landed interest of *Parnassus*, as well as the choice of the actors who are to accompany the *Auditors* of the *Drama*, are matters that deserve to be treated of distinctly; but the qualification of so much *per annum*,[2] in order to be deemed a man of capacity for this service, I cannot allow to be necessary, though I have very good friends of another mind, who will also take upon them to say that for the dignity and safety of *Arcadia* a comic or tragic poet should have three hundred pounds a-year; and an epic poet cannot be truly such, except he have six hundred a-year. From which worthy gentlemen I must beg leave to differ; and I take the liberty to say that there is no such accomplishment mentioned by *Aristotle, Horace* or any other Critic, ancient or modern.

2. Steele is joking about the Landed Property Qualifications Act of 1711, which set requirements of landed wealth for candidates to the House of Commons.

JOHN DENNIS

A Defense of *Sir Fopling Flutter* †
(1722)

* * * How little do they know of the nature of true comedy, who believe that its proper business is to set us patterns for imitation. For all such patterns are serious things, and laughter is the life and the very soul of comedy. 'Tis its proper business to expose persons to our view whose views we may shun and whose follies we may despise; and by showing us what is done upon the comic stage, to show us what ought never to be done upon the stage of the world.

All the characters in *Sir Fopling Flutter*, and especially the principal characters, are admirably drawn, both to please and to instruct. First, they are drawn to please, because they are drawn in the truth of nature; but to be drawn in the truth of nature, they must be drawn with those qualities that are proper to each respective season of life.[1]

* * *

A comic poet who gives to a young man the qualities that belong to a middle-aged man or to an old man can answer neither of the ends of his art. He cannot please, because he writes out of nature, of which all poetry is an imitation, and without which no poem can possibly please. And as he cannot please, he cannot instruct; because, by showing such a young man as is not to be seen in the world, he shows a monster and not a man, sets before us a particular character instead of an allegorical and universal one, as all his characters, and especially his principal characters, ought to be; and therefore can give no general instruction, having no moral, no fable, and therefore no comedy.

Now if any one is pleased to compare the character of Dorimant, to which the knight[2] has taken so much absurd exception, with the two forementioned descriptions, he will find in his character all the chief distinguishing strokes of them. For such is the force of nature, and so admirable a talent had she given Sir George for comedy, that, though to my certain knowledge he understood neither Greek nor Latin, yet one would swear that in drawing his Dorimant, he copied the foresaid drafts, and especially that of Aristotle. Dorimant is a young courtier, haughty, vain, and prone to anger, amorous, false, and inconstant. He debauches Loveit and betrays her; loves Bellinda, and so soon as he enjoys her is false to her.

† Published as a pamphlet on 2 November 1722, just five days before the opening of Steele's *The Conscious Lovers*.
1. Dennis goes on to quote Horace, Aristotle, and the French critic André Da-cier to support his argument that each character should possess traits appropriate to his years.
2. "The knight" is Sir Richard Steele.

But secondly, the characters in *Sir Fopling* are admirably contrived to please, and more particularly the principal ones, because
we find in those characters a true resemblance of the persons both
in court and town who lived at the time when that comedy was
written. For Rapin[3] tells us with a great deal of judgment: "That
comedy is as it ought to be when an audience is apt to imagine that
instead of being in the pit and boxes they are in some assembly of
the neighborhood or in some family meeting and that we see
nothing done in it but what is done in the world. For it is [says he]
not worth one farthing if we do not discover ourselves in it, and do
not find in it both our own manners and those of the persons with
whom we live and converse."

The reason of this rule is manifest, for as it is the business of a
comic poet to cure his spectators of vice and folly by the apprehension of being laughed at, it is plain that his business must be with
the reigning follies and vices. The violent passions which are the
subjects of tragedy are the same in every age and appear with the
same face; but those vices and follies which are the subjects of
comedy are seen to vary continually. Some of those that belonged
to our ancestors have no relation to us, and can no more come
under the cognizance of our present comic poets than the sweating
and sneezing sickness can come under the practice of our contemporary physicians. What vices and follies may infect those who are to
come after us, we know not; it is the present, the reigning vices and
follies, that must be the subjects of our present comedy. The comic
poet therefore must take characters from such persons as are his
contemporaries and are infected with the foresaid follies and vices.
* * *

Now I remember very well that upon the first acting this comedy,
it was generally believed to be an agreeable representation of the
persons of condition of both sexes, both in court and town; and
that all the world was charmed with Dorimant; and that it was
unanimously agreed that he had in him several of the qualities of
Wilmot Earl of Rochester, as his wit, his spirit, his amorous
temper, the charms that he had for the fair sex, his falsehood, and
his inconstancy; the agreeable manner of his chiding his servants,
which the late Bishop of Salisbury takes notice of in his life; and
lastly, his repeating on every occasion the verses of Waller, for
whom that noble lord had a very particular esteem; witness his imitation of the Tenth Satire of the First Book of Horace:

> Waller, by nature for the bays design'd,
> With spirit, force, and fancy unconfin'd,
> In panegyric is above mankind.

3. René Rapin, a seventeenth-century French commentator on Aristotle.

Now, as several of the qualities in Dorimant's character were taken from the Earl of Rochester, so they who were acquainted with the late Sir Fleetwood Shepherd knew very well that not a little of that gentleman's character is to be found in Medley.

But the characters in this comedy are very well formed to instruct as well as to please, especially those of Dorimant and of Loveit; and they instruct by the same qualities to which the knight has taken so much whimsical exception; as Dorimant instructs by his insulting and his perfidiousness, and Loveit by the violence of her resentment and her anguish. For Loveit has youth, beauty, quality, wit, and spirit. And it was depending upon these that she reposed so dangerous a trust in Dorimant, which is a just caution to the fair sex never to be so conceited of the power of their charms or their other extraordinary qualities as to believe they can engage a man to be true to them to whom they grant the best favor without the only sure engagement, without which they can never be certain that they shall not be hated and despised by that very person whom they have done everything to oblige.

To conclude with one general observation, that comedy may be qualified in a powerful manner both to instruct and to please, the very constitution of its subject ought always to be ridiculous. Comedy, says Rapin, is an image of common life and its end is to expose upon the stage the defects of particular persons in order to cure the defects of the public and to correct and amend the people by the fear of being laughed at. That therefore, says he, which is most essential to comedy is certainly the ridicule.

Every poem is qualified to instruct and to please most powerfully by that very quality which makes the forte and the characteristic of it, and which distinguishes it from all other kinds of poems. As tragedy is qualified to instruct and to please by terror and compassion, which two passions ought always to be predominant in it and to distinguish it from all other poems, epic poetry pleases and instructs chiefly by admiration, which reigns throughout it and distinguishes it from poems of every other kind. Thus comedy instructs and pleases most powerfully by the ridicule, because that is the quality which distinguishes it from every other poem. The subject, therefore, of every comedy ought to be ridiculous by its constitution; the ridicule ought to be of the very nature and essence of it. Where there is none of that, there can be no comedy. It ought to reign both in the incidents and in the characters, and especially in the principal characters, which ought to be ridiculous in themselves, or so contrived as to show and expose the ridicule of others. In all the masterpieces of Ben Jonson, the principal character has the ridicule in himself, as Morose in *The Silent Woman*, Volpone in *The*

Fox, and Subtle and Face in *The Alchemist*; and the very ground and foundation of all these comedies is ridiculous. 'Tis the very same thing in the masterpieces of Molière: *The Misanthrope, The Imposter, The Avare,* and the *Femmes Savantes.* Nay, the reader will find that in most of his other pieces the principal characters are ridiculous; as, *L'Étourdi, Les Précieuses Ridicules, Le Cocu Imaginaire, Les Fâcheux,* and *Monsieur de Pourceaugnac, Le Bourgeois Gentilhomme, L'École des Maris, L'École des Femmes, L'Amour Médecin, Le Médecin Malgré lui, Le Mariage Forcé, George Dandin, Les Fourberies de Scapin, Le Malade Imaginaire.* The reader will not only find upon reflection that in all these pieces the principal characters are ridiculous, but that in most of them there is the ridicule of comedy in the very titles.

'Tis by the ridicule that there is in the character of Sir Fopling, which is one of the principal ones of this comedy, and from which it takes its name, that he is so very well qualified to please and to instruct. What true Englishman is there but must be pleased to see this ridiculous knight made the jest and the scorn of all the other characters for showing, by his foolish aping foreign customs and manners, that he prefers another country to his own? And of what important instruction must it be to all our youth who travel to show them that, if they so far forget the love of their country as to declare by their espousing foreign customs and manners that they prefer France or Italy to Great Britain, at their return they must justly expect to be the jest and the scorn of their own countrymen.

Thus, I hope I have convinced the reader that this comical knight, Sir Fopling, has been justly formed by the knight his father to instruct and please, whatever may be the opinion to the contrary of the knight his brother.

Whenever *The Fine Gentleman*[4] of the latter comes upon the stage, I shall be glad to see that it has all the shining qualities which recommend *Sir Fopling,* that his characters are always drawn in nature, and that he never gives to a young man the qualities of a middle-aged man or an old one; that they are the just images of our contemporaries, and of what we every day see in the world; that instead of setting us patterns for our imitation, which is not the proper business of comedy, he makes those follies and vices ridiculous which we ought to shun and despise; that the subject of his comedy is comical by its constitution; and that the ridicule is particularly in the grand incidents and in the principal characters. For a true comic poet is a philosopher who, like old Democritus, always instructs us laughing.

---

4. I.e., *The Conscious Lovers.*

JOHN DENNIS

Remarks on *The Conscious Lovers*†
(1723)

* * * When Sir Richard says that anything that has its foundation in happiness and success must be the subject of comedy, he confounds comedy with that species of tragedy which has a happy catastrophe. When he says that 'tis an improvement of comedy to introduce a joy too exquisite for laughter, he takes all the care that he can to show that he knows nothing of the nature of comedy. Does he really believe that Molière, who, in the opinion of all Europe, excepting that small portion of it which is acquainted with Ben Jonson, had borne away the prize of comedy from all nations and from all ages if for the sake of his profit he had not descended sometimes too much to buffoonry? Let Sir Richard or anyone look into that little piece of Molière called *La Critique de l'école des femmes*, and he shall find there that in Molière's opinion 'tis the business of a comic poet to enter into the ridicule of men and to expose the blind sides of all sorts of people agreeably; that he does nothing at all if he does not draw the pictures of his contemporaries and does not raise the mirth of the sensible part of an audience, which, says he, 'tis no easy matter to do. This is the sense of Molière, though the words are not his exactly.

When Sir Richard talks of a joy too exquisite for laughter, he seems not to know that joy, generally taken, is common, like anger, indignation, love, to all sorts of poetry: to the epic, the dramatic, the lyric; but that that kind of joy which is attended with laughter is the characteristic of comedy, as terror or compassion, according as the one or the other is predominant, makes the characteristic of tragedy, as admiration does of epic poetry.

When Sir Richard says that weeping upon the sight of a deplorable object is not a subject for laughter but that 'tis agreeable to good sense and to humanity, he says nothing but what all the sensible part of the world has always granted; but then all that sensible part of the world have always denied that a deplorable object is fit to be shown in comedy. When Sir George Etherege, in his comedy of *Sir Fopling Flutter*, shows Loveit in all the height and violence of grief and rage, the judicious poet takes care to give those passions a ridiculous turn by the mouth of Dorimant. Besides that, the subject is at the bottom ridiculous; for Loveit is a mistress who has

---

† Published as a pamphlet on 24 January 1723, about two months after   Steele's play had appeared in print.

abandoned herself to Dorimant, and by falling into these violent passions only because she fancies that something of which she is very desirous has gone beside her makes herself truly ridiculous. Thus is the famous scene in the second act of *Sir Fopling* by the character of Loveit and the dextrous handling of the subject kept within the bounds of comedy. But the scene of the discovery in the *Conscious Lovers* is truly tragical. Indiana was strictly virtuous. She had indeed conceived a violent passion for Bevil, but all young people in full health are liable to such a passion, and perhaps the most sensible and the most virtuous are more than others liable. But besides that she kept this passion within the bounds of honor, it was the natural effect of her esteem for her benefactor and of her gratitude; that is, of her virtue. These considerations rendered her case deplorable and the catastrophe downright tragical, which of a comedy ought to be the most comical part for the same reason that it ought to be the most tragical part of a tragedy.

* * *

The filial obedience of young Bevil is carried a great deal too far. He is said to be one of a great estate and a great understanding; and yet he makes a promise to his father not to marry without his consent, which is a promise that can do his father only a vain imaginary good and may do him real hurt. A young man of a great understanding cannot but know that if he makes such a promise he may be obliged to break it, or perish, or at least be unhappy all the rest of his life. Such a one cannot but know that he may possibly be seized with a passion so resistless and so violent that he must possess or perish; and consequently if the woman who inspires this passion be a woman of strict virtue, he must marry, or perish, or at least be mortally uneasy for the rest of his life. Children, indeed, before they come to years of discretion are obliged to pay a blind obedience to their parents. But after they are come to the full use of their reason they are only bound to obey them in what is reasonable. Indeed, if a son is in expectation of an estate from his father, he is engaged to a good deal of compliance, even after he comes to years of discretion. But that was not Bevil's case: he enjoyed a very good one of his mother's, by virtue of a marriage article; and therefore it was unreasonable in him to make such a promise to his father, as it was unreasonable in his father to urge him of it, especially upon so sordid a motive as the doubling a great estate. This is acting in a manner something arbitrary. And it ill becomes an author who would be thought a patron of liberty to suppose that fathers are absolute when kings themselves are limited. If he had not an understanding of his own to tell him this, he might have learned from Mr. Locke, in his sixth chapter of his admirable *Essay on Government:*

> That every man has a right to his natural freedom, without being subjected to the will or authority of any other man. Children, I confess, are not born in this full state of equality, though they are born to it. Their parents have a sort of rule and jurisdiction over them when they come into the world, and for some time after; but it is but a temporary one. The bonds of this subjection are like the swaddling clothes which they are wrapped up in, and supported by in the weakness of their infancy. Age and reason, as they grow up, lessen them, till at length they drop quite off, and leave a man at his own free disposal.

*   *   *

From what I have quoted from so judicious and so penetrating an author, I think it is pretty plain that young Bevil, who disposed of part of his estate without, nay, and as he might reasonably suppose, against the consent of his father, might *a fortiori* have disposed of his person too if it had not been for his unreasonable promise; and that it is highly improbable that one of the estate and understanding which he is said to have should absurdly make a promise which might possibly endanger the happiness of his whole life. 'Tis said, indeed, in more than one place of the play that the son has uncommon obligations to his father; but we are neither told, nor are we able to guess, what those obligations are. What uncommon obligations can a son who has a great estate in possession have to a father of so sordid a nature as Sir John Bevil shows himself? Act IV. Besides, what obligations can be binding enough to make a man of a great estate part with liberty, with the very liberty of his choice, in the most important action of his life, upon which the happiness of all the rest depends?

But as unreasonable as this promise is, which young Bevil made to his father, by which he gave away his birthright, his liberty, yes, the very liberty of his choice, in an affair upon which his happiness most depended, his behavior to Indiana is still more unaccountable. He loves her and is beloved by her; makes constant visits and profuse presents to her; and yet conceals his passion from her; which may be perhaps a clumsy expedient for the author's preparing the discovery, but is neither agreeable to nature nor reason. For it is impossible that any young man in nature, in health and vigor, and in the height of a violent passion, can so far command himself by the mere force of reason. I am willing, indeed, to allow that he may be able to do it by the assistance of the true religion. But the business of a comic poet is only to teach morality; Grace is not taught, but inspired. The dreadful mysteries of Christianity are but ill compatible with the lightness and mirth of comedy, or with the obscenity and profaneness of a degenerate stage, or with the dispositions of an assembly composed of persons who have some of them no religion and some of them not the true one. Besides that, nothing but a doctrine taken from the moral law can be a just foundation of a fable, which every true comedy is.

Nor is such a behavior any more agreeable to reason than it is to nature. Bevil loves Indiana and is beloved by her; she adores him, she dies for him, and he knows it; he observes it, and observes at the same time that so violent a passion is attended with equal anxiety; and that anxiety is entirely caused by the perplexing doubt she is in, whether she is beloved or not, as appears by what he says himself, Act II. Why then doth he not declare himself and by that declaration compose her mind and qualify her to expect with patience the benefit of time? 'Tis indeed true that he had promised his father never to marry without his consent while his father lived; but he had not promised him never to love without his consent; for that would have been a ridiculous promise; a promise the performance or nonperformance of which was not in his own power and would depend entirely on what the people call chance and what philosophers call providence. What could he mean then by not declaring himself? As the love he had conceived for Indiana was no breach of the promise he had made to his father, so neither could he violate it by any declaration of that passion! What then, once more, can he mean by his silence? His only reasonable way of proceeding had been to acquaint not only his mistress, but his father and all the world, with the passion which he felt for her and with the necessity he was in to marry her, or to be forever miserable. Such a declaration was not at all inconsistent with his duty; and if his father had either reason or compassion, would have caused him to relent and to release his son from a promise, the persevering in which must prove unhappy or fatal to him. If it should be said that such a concealment of his passion was necessary that he might make a retreat with honor in case his father should still be obstinate; to this I answer that there was no retreat for him unless he would at the same time retreat from virtue and honor; that his behavior had fixed and determined him; that by his generosity and constant visits he had raised the passion of Indiana to such a height that his leaving her would in all likelihood be followed by madness, or by self-murder, or by dreadful hysterical symptoms as deplorable as either; of which, what passes between her father and her in the fifth act is a sufficient proof. Beside, that such a retreat would prove as fatal to her honor as to her person. He had for some time made constant visits; he had made very extravagant presents to her; he had made no declaration of the affection he had for her, either to

her or to her Aunt Isabella, or acquainted any one with his design
to marry her if he could obtain his father's consent. Now can anything be more plain than that such a behavior, if he left her, would
ruin the reputation of the poor lady and cause all the world to
entertain such thoughts of her as Sealand and Myrtle had already
expressed? And thus I have endeavored to show that the behavior of
Bevil to Indiana, in his concealing his passion from her, is as ridiculously whimsical as that of Cimberton to her sister Lucinda.

The catastrophe, I must confess, is very moving, but it would be
more so if it were rightly and reasonably handled, because it would
be much more surprising. For the surprise is, in a good measure,
prevented by the behavior of Isabella upon the first appearance of
Sealand; which, if it had not been out of all probability and nature,
would have prevented it more. It was highly in nature and probability that Isabella, upon the first discovering her brother, should fly
into an excessive transport of joy and have run to embrace him; for
when she is made to say that her brother must not know her yet,
she is made to give no reasons for it, nor can the audience imagine
any. 'Tis not Isabella who says that, but the author, who clumsily
uses it to serve a turn; for if she had discovered herself to her
brother at his first appearance, it had prevented the audience's
sorrow and compassion for the imaginary distress of Indiana and,
consequently, their return to joy. But as Aristotle and all the great
critics after him have taught us, that there is to be no incident in a
dramatic poem but what must be founded on reason, it happens, as
we observed above, very unluckily here, that there is no incident in
the *Conscious Lovers* but what is attended by some great absurdity.
For the action of Indiana in throwing away her bracelet is of the
same stamp and is entirely the author's and not the dramatic person's; for it was neither necessary nor profitable that Indiana, in the
height of her agony, should so much as think of her bracelet, or if
she did think of it, should resolve to throw away the greatest token
that she had to remember her dead mother, for whose memory her
grief and distress ought naturally to renew and redouble her tenderness. But the author is obliged to have recourse to this as an awkward expedient, though the best he could find, to bring on the discovery. But had he known anything of the art of the stage, he
would have known that those discoveries are but dully made which
are made by tokens; that they ought necessarily or probably to
spring from the whole train of the incidents contrary to our expectation. And how easy was it to bring that about here? For such a
discovery had been very well prepared by what young Bevil says to
Humphrey in the first act and by the hint Indiana gives to Sealand
in the fifth act, which hint the old gentleman readily takes; for
when she tells him she had been made an infant captive on the

seas, he immediately cries out, "An infant captive!" and after some
interruption given by Indiana, he says, "Dear lady! O yet one
moment's patience, my heart grows full with your affliction, but yet
there is something in your story that ——————". She answers
as if she were at cross purposes, "My portion here is bitterness and
sorrow." To which he replies, "Do not think so. Pray answer me,
does Bevil know your name and family?" So that a few questions
more, pertinently answered, would have brought on the discovery.
Now if the discovery had been made this way and Isabella had not
known her brother at her first seeing him, but had come in to Sealand and Indiana just after the discovery had been made, there
would have been two surprises, both greater and more agreeable
than now they are and both of them without absurdity. * * *

Stages, Actors, and Audiences

EMMET L. AVERY AND

ARTHUR H. SCOUTEN

The Theatrical World, 1660–1700†

Rarely does an art form have its professional development interrupted for a generation. In some respects, however, this happened to the public theaters in London from the prohibition against acting passed late in 1642 by the Commonwealth[1] to the restoration of the monarchy in 1660. For twenty years the Commonwealth, opposed in principle and practice to theatrical entertainments, kept the playhouses under relatively tight rein and frequently reduced acting in the public theaters so severely as to make financially unprofitable the operations of a company and the composing of plays for public presentation. Although plays did not wholly disappear from the stage, the eighteen years from 1642 to 1660 represent an unusual hiatus in the public practice of the various forms of dramatic art, a situation especially unusual for a country which in the preceding century had had a glorious dramatic renaissance.

With the restoration of Charles II early in 1660, an opportunity arose for the theatrical world to begin anew and the player, manager, playwright, and spectator to restore the drama to its former position in England's culture. By 1660 the principal actors of the days of James I and Charles I had died or had so drifted out of touch with dramatic enterprise that the continuity of acting had been impaired, though certainly not lost. Furthermore, most of the pre-Commonwealth theaters had been closed, destroyed, or converted to purposes other than theatrical. In addition, the playwrights of the old regime no longer were productive. And a new generation had appeared in London, one which had little intimate knowledge of acting, the drama, or the playhouse. One can note this frame of mind in Samuel Pepys, who in 1660 and for some years later found the reopened theatrical scene a dazzling sight

† From *The London Stages: 1600–1800*, Part I, edited by William Van Lennep (Carbondale, Ill.: Southern Illinois University Press, 1965), xxi–xxviii. Footnotes are Avery and Scouten's unless otherwise noted. Reprinted by permission of the publisher.

1. See Leslie Hotson, *The Commonwealth and Restoration Stage* (Cambridge, Mass., 1928), pp. 5–6.

and who occasionally mentioned, as though it was interesting but not exceptional, taking to the theater a friend who had never before seen a staged play and was therefore vague concerning the traditions of the drama. During the Commonwealth the drama had not, of course, been extinguished, for old plays had been given (sometimes in public, often in private) and new ones, such as Sir William Davenant's operatic works, had been composed and staged. Nevertheless, the professional theater, experienced actors, and knowledgeable spectators had to be re-created. In bringing the theater to life again, the managers, playwrights, performers, and the public developed after 1660 many practices, including some striking innovations, which set the pattern for the London professional theaters for the next hundred and fifty years.

Although it is difficult to determine the relative importance of the innovations and alterations, it is not difficult to select those which had important effects upon the English stage to the end of the eighteenth century: (1) The creation of a monopoly of theatrical enterprises, ordinarily restricted to two patent companies, sometimes compressed into a single company; (2) the introduction of women to act upon the stage, altering the old custom of the boy actor in female roles; (3) the altered design of the playhouses, with the development of the pit as a main seating area, the stage-boxes, front-boxes, and side-boxes as the more expensive and, theoretically, more desirable locations, and the first and second galleries for less expensive tastes; (4) the greatly increased use of scenes, especially changeable scenery, and machines, with an accompanying emphasis upon spectacle in both dramatic and operatic productions; (5) an increasing enlargement of the day's program by means of entr'acte entertainments of singing and dancing, accompanied by a correspondingly greater emphasis in the public concert halls upon vocal and instrumental music. During the forty years from 1660 and 1700 and during most of the eighteenth century, these practices, both singly and in unison, had extremely important effects upon the course of English drama and stagecraft.

Although the first of these events—the creation of a two-company monopoly—apparently came about without extended discussion of the wisdom of a theatrical monopoly, it did not materialize without opposition. Because the continuity of management had been interrupted by the Commonwealth, a mild scramble for power occurred in 1659 and 1660. The energy and prestige of two men, Sir William Davenant and Thomas Killigrew, as well as their access to Charles II's ear, gave them an exceptional opportunity to secure exclusive rights to form companies and to present plays. At first, however, they were opposed by John Rhodes, Michael Mohun, and William Beeston, theatrical entrepreneurs who wished to form their

own companies, and by Sir Henry Herbert, who, as Master of the
Revels, opposed the grants to Davenant and Killigrew not because
he objected to a monopoly in principle but because he desired that
all grants be put directly under his control. Within a short time,
Davenant and Killigrew won the struggle against other competitors
by securing patents to form a monopoly of two companies, and they
succeeded in securing considerable, though not complete, independence of the Office of the Revels. Although legal measures had to be
taken occasionally to suppress upstart companies and although some
leniency was allowed to a series of Nurseries for relatively untrained
actors, control by Davenant and Killigrew rapidly became effective.
The Duke's Company and the King's Company, the names by
which these groups were familiarly known, dominated London's
theatrical enterprises; and when they had erected two new theaters,
Dorset Garden and the Theatre Royal in Bridges Street, they made
it virtually impossible for any other company to achieve equality in
London. The patent houses strengthened their control by securing
regulations which prevented an actor from exercising easy freedom
of movement from one position to another.

Nevertheless, monopoly by two companies did not necessarily
guarantee financial success. By 1682 the King's Company, weak-
ened by internal dissensions, misfortunes (including the burning of
the Bridges Street playhouse a few years earlier), and poor patronage,
made overtures to the Duke's Company to form a united enterprise.
This amalgamation, essentially an absorption of the weaker King's
by the more powerful Duke's Company, exercised until 1695 a virtually unchallenged control over theatrical offerings. In the season
of 1694–95, however, fresh internal dissension caused a secession by
the best actors, with the result that from 1695 to the close of the
century London again had two companiess. This pattern—a two-
company structure altering to a single-company monopoly—occurred again in the early years of the next century. In fact, the
kinds of monopoly established in 1660 and 1661 set the pattern
for limiting the number of legally-operating theatrical companies
to two for a great many decades, with the exception of several
seasons in the first third of the eighteenth century, when the authorities closed their eyes to violations of this principle. The Li-
censing Act of 1737 restored a rigorous legalization of a two-company monopoly of dramatic offerings in the regular winter season.

A second innovation, the admission of women to act in the
public theaters, also occurred within a year after the reopening of
the playhouses in 1660. No doubt, the employment of actresses
would have come about in due time as a result of social change, but
the interruption in dramatic continuity provided both a stimulus
and an occasion. For a very brief time the playhouses retained the

employment of boy actors for female roles: for example, Edward Kynaston, William Betterton, and James Nokes. Nevertheless, the dissolution of the repertory companies during the Commonwealth had inhibited the training of boys as female impersonators at the same time that the sojourn of the English court in France had demonstrated the practicality of having women perform upon the stage. Andrew Newport, writing to Sir Richard Leveson upon the new practices in London, 15 December 1660, reflected the influence of the Continent: "Upon our stages we have women actors, as beyond seas."[2] In fact, by the early autumn of 1660, during the formation of the patent houses, a petition (13 October 1660) indicates that the companies had in prospect the engaging of women.[3] We do not know just when the first actress played a major role or who she was, but a woman certainly acted Desdemona in *Othello* in late 1660.[4] Thereafter, although the stage was not a proper place for proper young gentlewomen, many actresses gained recognition and fame— Nell Gwynn is a shining example—even if, in the words of John Downes, prompter to the Duke's Company, they often "by force of Love were Erept the Stage."[5]

The impact of the introduction of actresses is immeasurable. Early in the 1660's it was argued that their presence in the companies would improve the moral tone of the playhouses and the drama. In the patent issued to Killigrew, 25 April 1662, the argument runs as follows:

> for as much as many plays formerly acted doe conteine severall prophane, obscene, and scurrulous passages, and the women's part therein have byn acted by men in the habit of women, at which some have taken offence, for the preventing of these abuses for the future . . . wee do likewise permit and give leave, that all of the woemen's part . . . may be performed by woemen soe long as their recreacones, which by reason of the abuses aforesaid were scandalous and offensive, may by such reformation be esteemed not onely harmless delight, but useful and instructive.[6]

That this pious hope was not fully realized requires no demonstration, for numerous commentators deplored the private and public lives of the actresses and the fact that the immoral tone of the stage was not genuinely improved by the presence of women. John Evelyn, for example, frequently referred in his diary to the corrupting influences of actresses upon the Court. (See his strongly-worded

2. HMC [Historical Manuscript Commission], Fifth Report, Part I (1876), p. 158.
3. Hotson, *Commonwealth and Restoration Stage*, p. 204. See also *The Dramatic Records of Sir Henry Herbert*, ed. J. Q. Adams (New Haven, Conn., 1917), pp. 94–96, where a petition by several actors states that they "had by convenant obliged [themselves] to act with woemen."
4. For a comprehensive account of Restoration actresses, see John Harold Wilson, *All the King's Ladies* (Chicago, 1958).
5. *Roscius Anglicanus*, edited by Montague Summers (London, n.d.), p. 35.
6. See Percy Fitzgerald, *A New History of the English Stage* (London, 1882), I, 80.

disapproval in the entry for 18 October 1666.) On the other hand, the delight with which Pepys followed the acting and careers of such actresses as Nell Gwynn and Mary Knepp testifies to the pleasure as well as to the more effective acting which the abilities of women brought to the stage. The actresses, nevertheless, did not fully achieve equality in position, for among the early sharing groups there are no women sharers, although in 1695 actresses and actors became equal sharers in a new company. In numbers, also, the proportion of actors to actresses usually was at least two to one, although this inequality reflected primarily the needs of the companies, as the number of male to female roles in most plays was a disproportionate one. On the other hand, by the end of the seventeenth century the London theaters had trained several women of considerable talent and great proficiency: Nell Gwynn, Katherine Corey, Mary Saunderson Betterton, Frances Knight, Elinor Leigh, Anne Bracegirdle, Elizabeth Barry, and Susanna Percival Mountfort Verbruggen. These women established the actress as an integral part of English theatrical enterprises.

Another result of the long closure of the theaters was an alteration in the physical accommodations. When acting resumed, not all of the older theaters were available, although the old Cockpit in Drury Lane sufficed for a while. Temporarily, Gibbons' Tennis Court, constructed much earlier, was converted into a not wholly satisfactory playhouse. In these circumstances, both the Duke's and King's companies early planned to build new theaters, and these new structures set the characteristic features of the playhouses for several generations. First of all, the principal new ones—the two in Drury Lane and the theater in Dorset Garden—were of moderate size, permitting an intimate atmosphere. The stage extended in front of the proscenium arch into the pit, which was fitted with benches (backless), continuing the growing practice of seating nearly all of the spectators and eliminating the large proportion of standees which had been characteristic of some earlier playhouses. Extending from the stage on both sides of the pit were tiers of boxes, commonly referred to as stage-boxes (often a double tier); side boxes (those extending along both sides of the interior); and front-boxes (those facing or fronting the stage, at the rear of the pit). Rising above the front boxes and pit was a gallery or (in some theaters) a lower gallery as well as a smaller upper one. With benches rather than individual seats as the prevailing mode, particularly in the pit, the playhouses had a flexible rather than a fixed capacity. If the performance was sparsely attended, spectators might sit comfortably upon the benches; but if the attendance was very large, the increase was accommodated in part by crowding. At all times, in spite of a tendency for the socially or financially elite to sit apart from those of lesser quality, the spectators talked and listened in an atmosphere of conviviality, as Pepys makes abundantly clear in many entries in his diary. These types of accommodation and the informal, intimate atmosphere essentially prevailed until, in the second half of the eighteenth century, the proprietors embarked upon a steady enlargement of the playhouses, an alteration which affected not only the cohesion of the audience but also its relationship to the actors on stage.

Another change in the technical operations of the playhouses was a vastly increased emphasis upon changeable scenery and devices ("machines") for creating such special effects as flyings of persons and objects. Much of the impetus for this movement came from the imagination and ingenuity of Sir William Davenant, who, some years before the restoration of Charles II, had envisioned public theaters with elaborate embellishments to the action. Although he had experimented in this vein in a few productions during the five years preceding 1660, he lacked a genuine opportunity to develop his theories until he secured a patent and formed a company to act in Lincoln's Inn Fields.[7] John Downes, prompter to Davenant's company, stressed these innovations when he described the opening of that theater (probably on 28 June 1661) with *The Siege of Rhodes,* an operatic work "having new Scenes and Decorations, being the first that e're were Introduc'd in England."[8] Pepys' first glimpse of this play (2 July 1661) much impressed him, for he found the opening "indeed is very fine and magnificent." By the summer of 1662 Davenant's reliance upon these devices was sufficiently on record that a poem characterizing recent dramatic events referred to the progress of this theater, "Where the Knight with his Scenes doth keep much adoe."[9]

Davenant constantly improved his stock of scenery, and although the King's Company, Davenant's rival, somewhat slowly followed his lead, within ten years both companies had invested large sums in this phase of their operations and had set the London theaters upon a venture leading to more and more elaborate and costly creations. Although Davenant did not live to see the new theater in Dorset Garden which his company constructed, he would have been delighted with the attention given to settings and contrivances in this elegant playhouse. As was true of other innovations, there was no turning back from Davenant's pioneering; thereafter, for many decades, the companies vied with each other in colorful scenes, startling machines, realistic properties and embellishments to the dramas and entr'acte entertainments. In fact, they occasionally praised their own initiative, as did the speaker in the Second Prologue to Shadwell's revision of *The Tempest,* 1674:

7. For a full discussion of the history of scenes in the English theaters, see Richard Southern, *Changeable Scenery: Its Origin and Development in the British Theatre* (London, 1952).

8. *Roscius Anglicanus,* p. 20.

9. Hotson, *Commonwealth and Restoration Stage,* p. 246.

Had we not for y^r pleasure found new wayes
You still had rusty Arras had, & thredbare playes;
Nor Scenes nor Woomen had they had their will,
But some with grizl'd Beards had acted Woomen still.

Alterations in the daily program accompanied these changes. Possessing increasingly elaborate gear, the management placed greater emphasis upon spectacle. Although the play remained the center of the day's offerings, spectacular staging provided a drawing attraction. Shakespeare's *The Tempest*, for example, owed much of its popularity to its transformation into a dramatic opera or musical drama in which flyings, sinkings, and machines augmented the appeal. Each burst of applause for an operatic spectacle, even if sometimes the receipts did not equal the large expenses, caused the rival companies to launch still more expensive productions. In addition, these spectacles stimulated a taste for musical and terpsichorean novelties, and the managements larded many comedies and even some tragedies with songs, dances, and "vocal and instrumental entertainments," some of which, though not all, were thematically related to the action. The fresh faces, engaging talents, and novelty of actresses popularized these augmentations. Pepys, for example, often expressed his delight in the singing and dancing of Nell Gwynn and Mary Knepp, sometimes being so engrossed by them that he failed to mention his response to the play proper; he occasionally found the incidental music so ravishing that he secured a copy of it for his own collection. Further proof of the drawing power of this new trend appears in the Preface to Thomas Shadwell's *The Humorists* (10 December 1670), where he credits the triumph of his play over its enemies to the delightful dancing of Mrs. Johnson, whose talents drew both friends and foes and silenced the loud critics. By the end of the century the newspaper announcements make it evident that song and dance as entr'acte entertainments had begun to assume the dominant position which they were to make secure in the first half of the eighteenth century.

* * *

HUGH HUNT

Restoration Acting†

The patents granted by the king to Thomas Killigrew and Sir William Davenant in 1660 stipulated that not only should they be

† From *Restoration Theatre*, ed. John Russell Brown and Bernard Harris (Edward Arnold Ltd., 1965), pp. 179–82, 185–92. Reprinted by permission of the publisher.

allowed to build their own playhouses and form their own companies, but they should henceforth only permit women to play women's parts to the end that plays might "be esteemed not only harmless delights but useful and instructive representations of human life."

The high hopes expressed in the Royal Warrants were realized in a somewhat ironic sense. One wonders whether the official who drew them up, knowing the frailty of his royal master, had his tongue in his cheek. But the introduction of actresses in the place of boy actors together with the introduction of movable scenery were the two most significant conventions adopted by the resurrected theaters and were to have far-reaching results on the style of performance. Neither of these conventions can strictly be called novelties to the English stage. Scenic elements, housed behind proscenium frames together with machines to change them, had graced with elaborate splendor the court masques devised by Inigo Jones. French acting companies employing actresses had been seen on the public stages in the pre-Commonwealth period, and that alliterative Puritan, William Prynne, reported with pleasure that "they were hissed, hooted, and pippin-pelted off the stage." Even in the dark years of the Puritan Commonwealth, Sir William Davenant had prevailed on the authorities to allow him to present private performances of opera, and in *The Siege of Rhodes* (1656) both an actress and scenery made their appearance. The significance of the adoption of these two conventions by the acting companies licensed by Charles II lies in the fact that they were adopted as a rule and not as a rarity.

The time was ripe for the substitution of actresses for boy actors. The voice of Puritanism was temporarily muffled; feminism both in costume and social influence had never achieved such freedom, and a considerable percentage of the new audience had grown accustomed to seeing actresses in the French theater during the exile of the king. The new actresses had, however, to be selected and trained for the stage. And, although it seems likely that the first professional British actress may have made her appearance as early as November or December 1660, in the part of Desdemona, it was some years before the full influence of women made itself felt. But even in the earliest days when the newcomers to the stage had little more than their youth and beauty to rely on, it is clear that their impact on the public was considerable. The play-going public during the years following the emancipation from Puritanism was a minute fraction of society confined almost entirely to those who frequented the court with an occasional country cousin up for a visit to town and, of course, the inevitable prostitutes, or vizard-masks, who plied their trade in the galleries and boxes. The majority of the merchant classes, even if they were of the Royalist party, were nervous of frequenting this exotic and unfamiliar meeting place of fashionable society with its strange dress and manners and its disdainful attitude to the homely citizens. This small, exclusive audience would have been incapable of supporting the two patent playhouses had there not been a strong attraction to induce them to do so. One of those inducements was the appearance of actresses. It is, therefore, not to be wondered at that the companies exploited the charms of their female recruits to the full, and exercised the greatest care in their selection; not without success both with regard to their future histrionic powers and to their immediate physical attractions.

The problem of recruitment must have been considerable. First, because none of the candidates had previous experience of acting; not even in an amateur capacity. Secondly, because no lady of education and breeding would deign to accept a job on the stage. This entailed training the raw recruits in manners, deportment, and elocution in order to meet the demands of acting parts that were almost exclusively aristocratic. From the little that is known of the family or social origins of the first actresses, it would seem that the principle was to choose them from an impecunious middle stratum of society which might be expected to have some pretensions to literacy and refinement, such as the daughter of a "decayed knight," like Charlotte Butler, or of a notary, like Mrs. Shadwell, or Mrs. Pepys' personal maid, whose mother was a widow with genteel connections. Some may have been gentlemen's bastards, like Moll Davis, or orphans, like Mrs. Barry who, having been brought up in the household of Sir William Davenant. would have been steeped in the traditions of the stage. Probably the exceptions were the totally illiterate cockney wenches, like Nell Gwynn. But there were other attributes which the new managers must have looked for in making their selection. Little time was available for preliminary training; once the first actresses had appeared on the stage to the considerable delight of spectators like Pepys, it was clearly impossible to carry on with the boy actors without considerable losses at the box office. Consequently, quickness of wit, a good sense of mimicry, an immediately engaging manner and a pert and impudent approach could do much to compensate for inexperience. It is precisely these characteristics which Nell Gwynn, Moll Davis and many of their sisterhood must have possessed, that appear most frequently in the parts written for young ladies of Restoration comedy. It must not be forgotten that the dramatists of the new age had only two companies to whom they could sell their plays; indeed from 1682 to 1695, during which period the two theaters were amalgamated, there was only one. As a result playwrights were forced to write plays with the particular characteristics of the actors and actresses in mind, and this gave rise to a certain similarity of characterization both in tragedy and in comedy throughout the period. This tendency was emphasized by the audience's attitude toward the players. Association between the private life of the players and their stage impersonations became inevitable in so small a world of theater; doubly inevitable when the private lives of the players—more especially of the actresses—were so intimately entangled with those of the audience.

As a result of the success of the new actresses—success which was not only dependent on the possession of histrionic talents—the career of an actress became attractive to ladies whose main concern was the acquisition of a rich husband or "keeper." Husbands were hard to obtain in a society which placed greater emphasis on social and financial advantages in matrimonial arrangements than on mutual affection, but potential "keepers" abounded. The determined and skillful female practitioners of this age-old profession could beguile the lecherous admirers who thronged the green rooms and wings into providing handsome settlements. The success of Mrs. Davenport who, after some difficulties and an irregular marriage ceremony, managed to persuade Parliament into forcing the Earl of Oxford in 1662 into granting her a handsome pension, was more than matched in subsequent years by a whole series of successes of this kind with the most renowned and powerful of the land, culminating in the triumphs of Moll Davis and Nell Gwynn with the king himself. Whilst it can be rightly said that such affairs had nothing to do with theatrical art, they had an important bearing on the whole attitude of the audience toward the theater and of the theatrical companies towards their public. There is no need to pursue the salacious stories of the lives of most, though not all, of the actresses; we can accept the ample evidence that the tiring rooms of the playhouses were commonly used to pave the way for future adventures.

* * *

Just as the novelty of the actress was filtered through to the public playhouses of the Restoration from the private playhouses of the Carolean stages by way of Davenant's opera, *The Siege of Rhodes,* so, too was the novelty of "scenes." In Rutland House, the private residence of Sir William Davenant, the first English opera was presented in the month of September 1656; for political reasons it was announced as "A Representation by the Art of Prospective in Scenes, and the Story sung in Recitative Musick." The scenes framed by a frontispiece, or proscenium arch, were painted by John Webb, the pupil and collaborator of Inigo Jones, who was later to be employed in the Restoration playhouses. Thus the stream of theatrical style, both with regard to the employment of actresses and the use of scenes, flowed directly from the court masques of the pre-Restoration stage through the Commonwealth "Representations" to the public theaters of 1660. Whatever elaborations of machinery and refinements of scenic techniques may have been later introduced from France, it was the English traditions themselves which led directly to these novelties on our public stages.

To call the new scenery realistic, as we understand the term today, would be ludicrous. The scenes themselves, which were formed by the bringing together of two painted canvas flats or shutters running in grooves, were framed by side wings and borders. They were, in fact, flat pictures or panoramas on which rooms, prisons, streets, landscapes and, when occasion demanded it, battles and crowds were painted. Richard Southern, whose book *Changeable Scenery* is a mine of information on this subject, concludes that there were four grooves carrying the shutter-like scenes in the two fully developed Restoration playhouses. These grooves were spaced so as to allow room between each set of scenes for setting furniture and for assembling actors in a tableau, such as a company assembled round a dining table. By drawing the two halves of the scene apart such discoveries were revealed against the succeeding scene. Not all these "discoveries" were flat paintings running in grooves; "relieve" scenes, consisting of cut-out ground-rows set one behind the other, provided vistas extending to a back-scene which was set up in a recess behind the space occupied by the grooves themselves, thus giving an illusion of great depth to the scenic area. A distant vista could also be revealed by drawing aside the upper portions of a scene which, when painted as a cloud formation, could discover succeeding cut-outs of billowing clouds terminating in a distant vision of an enthroned deity, or a heaven filled with allegorical figures.

Such elaborate scenic displays together with the use of traps in the stage floor to bring up set-pieces from below or to provide descents into the nether regions, as well as flying devices, added greatly to the spectacle, but can hardly be said to have contributed to realism in the naturalistic sense; nor were they so intended.

Just as the charms of the actresses were exploited to induce the small audience to make frequent visits to the theater, so were the spectacular scenes. Rivalry between the two patent playhouses in scenic "shows" was intense, and on more than one occasion an eye-catching spectacle in one playhouse resulted in the emptying of the other. In opera, tragedy, and heroic plays, the scenes were not only elaborate and, consequently, expensive (the scenes of one opera alone cost £800—a considerable sum), they must have been, on occasions, extremely beautiful. In Act V of Shadwell's opera, *Psyche*, the scene changes to a heaven:

> In the highest part is the Palace of *Jupiter*; the Columns and all the Ornaments of it of Gold. The lower part is all fill'd with *Angels* and *Cupids*, with a round open *Temple* in the midst of it.

This *Temple* is just before the *Sun,* whose Beams break fiercely
through it in divers places: Below the Heav'ns, several Semi-circu-
lar Clouds, of the breadth of the whole House, descend. In these
Clouds sit the Musicians, richly Habited. On the front-Cloud sits
Apollo alone. While the Musicians are descending, they play a
Symphony till *Apollo* begins, and sings.

The full flavor of Baroque taste bursts forth in this description.

Spectacular scenery, however, was generally confined to operas,
tragedies, and heroic plays; comedies and revivals of pre-Restoration
plays were normally performed in whatever scenery the theaters possessed. This was hardly surprising since a failure might only run one
night, and even a success could not be expected to run for more
than eight to ten performances in a season. This limitation of the
available scenery was a factor to be taken into account by the
author of a comedy and affected the style in which plays were conceived and constructed. It cannot, then, be argued that spectacular
or original scenery was characteristic of Restoration staging. What
was characteristic, and is highly important from the point of view of
contemporary staging, was the relation of the scenery to the action.

Before considering this relationship a word must be said about
the use of the front curtain and of the all-important forestage area.

Apart from some early experiments with painted curtains in the
pre-Commonwealth masques, a front curtain was unknown in British theatrical tradition. To the mind of the Restoration player the
front curtain, which he inherited from the French and Italian theaters, was merely a cover for the stage; the raising of which was the
signal for the play to commence. It was not used to conceal changes
of scenery, nor to denote a passage of time, nor to provide full-stops
in the action. Once raised the curtain did not fall again until the
epilogue had been spoken. Exceptions to this rule were sometimes
made in opera which was derived directly from the continental traditions, but the dropping of the curtain during a play was, I suggest, considered in very much the same way as the French neo-class-
ical theater regarded a breach in the rules of the unities of action,
time, and place—it was bad stage-craft. The Earl of Orrery, who
used the front curtain for the discovery of tableaux in some of his
plays, was severely satirized for this practice by Buckingham in *The
Rehearsal*. This deliberate refusal to punctuate the action by using
the front curtain was not merely a quaint convention, nor was it
due to failure to realize its possibilities as a means of concealing a
scene-change. It would be ridiculous to suggest that the players were
too stupid not to realize that the use of the curtain for this purpose
in the operas might also serve for the same purpose in the plays.
The point that the players were making in refusing to use the curtain, as we use it today, was a deliberate stylistic point; namely that

the action of a play is a continuous action which must flow onwards without breaks within each act in exactly the same way as it did on the open stage of the Elizabethan period, or as it does in the cinema. Scene changes, then, had to take place within sight of the audience and were not allowed to halt the action.

The method the players employed was the use of the sliding scenes operating in the grooves, and this simple and swift way of changing the location could not only take place within full view, but its operation provided, just as it does in a pantomime transformation scene, an important part of the entertainment. Apart from the visual entertainment provided by this "play of the moving scenery," the more important stylistic point of the flow of the action was emphasized by the use of the forestage and its doors.

The Restoration forestage. as shown in Wren's design for the second Theater Royal, which took the place of the former building destroyed by fire in 1672, was serviced by two doors on each side. There is evidence that during the early part of the period there were three doors a side leading on to the forestage. These doors were the main entrances to the stage, and entry through the scenes was sufficiently rare to require a stage-direction to this effect to be included in the prompter's script. The size of the forestage itself, which in Wren's design is seventeen feet deep, was almost equal to the entire area that lay behind the proscenium arch and which housed the scenery and the grooves. Thus the stage was divided into two areas, the one serving the scenery and the other the action. The action area, or forestage, was not only provided with its own entrances, but also with its own lighting system. The footlights, or "floats," which could be raised or lowered in a trough located in the front of the forestage to control their intensity, were the main source for lighting the actors' faces. Chandeliers located above the forestage, or within the scenic area, provided supplementary lighting, but were by themselves inadequate for displaying facial mimicry. Similarly any candles or oil lamps located in the wings of the scenic area were only adequate for lighting the scenery. Consequently almost the whole action of the play took place on the forestage, and when the action required that actors be discovered within the scenic area at the drawing apart of the sliding scenes, a stage-direction usually bids them "to come forward." The action area was, like the Elizabethan platform stage, a neutral area; it was not considered necessary for an actor to leave this area if the action required him to be present at the end of one scene and also at the beginning of the next one. Instead of the actor leaving the room, the room left the actor, revealing him in a new location. In these cases the stage direction *"manet"* usually takes the place of the familiar *"exit."*

The flexibility provided by the sliding scenes behind the proscenium arch and the neutral acting area in front of it offered the playwright far greater opportunities to maneuver his action through a variety of locations without overtaxing the imagination of his audience than either the older conventions of the Elizabethan stage or our contemporary proscenium stage when it is used to house box-settings. From the point of view of our contemporary productions of Restoration plays the vital point is to preserve this flexibility and to maintain the continuous flow of the action; both are an integral part of the style of the plays themselves. Too often contemporary directors either destroy the unity of each act by breaking it up into a sequence of heavily built scenes, separated from each other by pauses filled out with recorded music; or—what is no less harmful—adapt the text so as to allow a variety of locations to be played in the same set. To preserve the stylistic requirements of the "play of the moving scenery" and its relation to the action we do not, of course, have to reproduce the conventions of grooves and sliding scenes. The convention of changing the scenery in view of the audience by means of modern stage-devices is now a commonplace in Shakesperian productions, and we have discarded our reliance on naturalistic box-settings. But wherever possible the contemporary director should, I think, construct or make use of a forestage and doors if he is to recapture the flavor of the acting style in which the play was intended to be performed.

The principles of the acting style were taught in the "nurseries," or acting schools, maintained by the two acting companies. In these the older actors were the tutors, and Betterton himself was awarded fifty guineas a year for this work. Private coaching was also given, and John Wilmot, Earl of Rochester, is said to have transformed Elizabeth Barry in six months of intensive training from a complete failure who was three times rejected by the Duke's Company into one of the greatest actresses of her age. Needless to add that in the course of training he is also said to have made her his mistress.

The basic training of a Restoration player covered speech, singing, dancing, stance, gesture, and walking; all were equally important. Walking or standing on the stage may seem to the layman to require no training, but to the acting student this often proves the most difficult lesson to master. Never more so than to the young players of the Restoration who had to learn all the arts of deportment in order to emulate a society in which the upper classes were immediately recognizable by a strict code of mannerisms. These mannerisms included the mincing steps, later known as the stage "strut," the typical stance with chest thrust forward and hips forced back, the prescribed elegancies of the curtsy and the bow, the manipulation of the long tragedienne's train, usually held up by a page, the various symbolic uses of the fan, the veiled looks and languid glances, or "doux yeux," which signaled the lover, and the "black disorder'd Look" of the villain.

The acme of theatrical style was centered in tragic acting. Here the set of rules attributed to Betterton emphasize the importance placed on control of the voice, and the tragedian's success was judged in particular by his ability to rouse enthusiasm through the delivery of the great tirades, commonly known as "rants." Musical speech was assiduously cultivated, and was generally known as the "heroic tone." This tone, or series of tones, was codified in Betterton's rules which had to be learned by rote. The young player had to learn to

> express Love by a gay, soft, charming Voice, his Hate, by a sharp, sullen and severe one; his Joy, by a full flowing and brisk Voice, his Grief, by a sad dull and languishing Tone; not without sometimes interrupting the Continuity of the Sound with a sigh or Groan, drawn from the very inmost of the Bosom.

To these tones were added a whole range of gestures. The tragedian was required to point to his head and his heart to indicate reason and passion, to raise his eyes and hands upwards when invoking the Gods, to extend his arms forward with palms extended to indicate horror or surprise. In short his arms, hands, head, and features seem to have been in almost continual motion, "For indeed," said Betterton, "Action is the Business of the Stage, and an Error is more pardonable on the right, than on the Wrong side."

Today it would be impossible to induce our actors to adopt such mannerisms, and even more impossible to expect our audiences to accept them. The path of naturalism has been trodden too far, and only in opera or ballet can we accept symbolic acting. Peter Brook's recent revival of Otway's *Venice Preserved* made little attempt to recapture the style of Restoration tragic acting, but although the production had much merit, one felt it belonged to the Elizabethan or Jacobean period, rather than to the age of Dryden and Congreve. If a director is bold enough to attempt to bridge the wide gap between the Baroque style and the taste of a modern audience, it is clear that a great deal of study would have to be given to the question of acting style. It is a sad fact that the acting student today is given too little training in musical speech and graceful gesture and, consequently, he has little basis on which to develop Restoration style. An overdose of contemporary naturalism coupled with a mistaken belief that acting is necessarily based on psychology has resulted in an all-too-ready condemnation of the emotional appeal of the grand manner, which is commonly derided as "ham" acting.

The French theater with its strong neo-classic traditions and wealth of fine tragic drama has been careful to ensure that its student-actors are trained to speak the verse of Racine and Corneille in a way which, with intelligent direction, will illuminate without anachronism the style of the epoch of Louis XIV to a contemporary audience.

Between the styles of tragic acting and comic acting there was a wide gulf fixed; the one was frankly artificial, the other sought to provide an imitation of life. The two styles are effectively juxtaposed in Dryden's *Marriage à la Mode*. But whilst the tragic conventions could be lampooned, as they are in Buckingham's satire, *The Rehearsal*, the real art of the stage, at least in the view of the Restoration actors, lay in the tragic rather than the comic style. Amongst actors, Grammont explained, it was

> a standing and incontrovertible principle, that a tragedian always takes the place of a Commedian; and 'tis very well known that Merry Drolls who make us laugh are always placed at the lower end of the table, and in every Entertainment give way to the Dignity of the Buskin.

But, whilst it was easier for the "Merry Drolls" of the Restoration companies to imitate life than for the tragedians to master the difficult techniques of their artificial conventions, we must not forget that the life they imitated was not our life. The modern actor will require just as much training to acquire the essentials of the comic style as he will to acquire the essentials of the tragic; both are equally foreign to him. Once again the emphasis of our dramatic training on contemporary naturalism and especially on psychological realism are against him.

When we talk of realism in relation to Restoration style, either in the matter of scenery or comic acting, we must not confuse what we mean by the theatrical realism of the epoch with what we mean by theatrical realism today. Both forms are real in that they are true to the spirit of their period, but both are theatrical since their truth is expressed through their respective theatrical conventions. Archaic reproduction of theatrical conventions is not the business of a live theater; but illumination of the truth, or realism, of the playwright's intention is very much its concern. Congreve is the most realistic of the comic playwrights of his period, but the realism he aimed at is not expressed in terms of psychological realism, though his attitude towards sex and marriage is entirely realistic. His characterization may have been based on observation of life, but it was an imitation of the externals only; to this extent Restoration comedy is truly named the Comedy of Manners. It is the technical mastery of these manners, and manners includes phrasing, timing, and diction, that requires the attention of our teachers of acting, but technique is only the bare bones of style. I mentioned earlier that it is the fault of some directors to cloak their productions with an air of unreality in which scenery, costumes, fans, and snuff-boxes assume such importance that reality is overlooked. The director and the actor will only be able to breathe life into the style of Restoration plays if they can make the audience feel that what they see and hear on the stage is a true reflection of life as it was lived and as it was understood. To do this requires more than the bare bones, it also requires an instinctive understanding of the stage of the period and its relation to the audience who frequented it.

EMMET L. AVERY AND
ARTHUR H. SCOUTEN

The Audience†

The common assumption is that the Restoration audience was essentially of upper-class composition by contrast with the greater diversity of classes, education, and taste of the Elizabethan era. Nevertheless, the Restoration audience was not of the single complexion which some subsequent theatrical historians have emphasized. The range of social classes, professions, and cultural attainments was fairly great, and the taste of the spectators as well as their motives in attending the playhouses varied considerably. Some, like Pepys, were fascinated by the stage, by the sense of illusion, and by the social structure of the spectators. Others, like James Brydges, in the closing decade, apparently regarded the theater as a port of call on the social round, where Brydges might look in and quickly withdraw if the atmosphere did not attract him. Many men of letters attended frequently, sometimes as arbiters of taste, sometimes because the theater was, except for the Court, the coffee-houses, and private homes, a center where intellectuals met and kept abreast of literary tendencies, the old and new drama, and the climate of acting. To it also came many wits, gentlemen, Persons of Quality, citizens, Templars, and others of varying social and financial status.

In fact, the audience seems to have been of almost unceasing interest to itself, to playwrights, to authors of prologues and epilogues, and to pamphleteers. They tended to categorize the spectators and to define their habitats. Pepys, an observant man, often responded to the composition of the audience, partly because he

† From *The London Stage: 1660-1800*, Part I, edited by William Van Lennep (Carbondale, Ill.: Southern Illinois Uni- versity Press, 1965), clxii–clxxi. Reprinted by permission of the publisher.

was delighted when interesting wits and lovely ladies attended, and disappointed when lower social groups dominated. He also enjoyed a play more when there was a full house, for a meager one had a desolate air. In fact, the social atmosphere of the theater was rarely better captured than by Pepys, attending *Heraclius* on 4 February 1666/7; he had

> [an] extraordinary content; and the more from the house being very full, and great company; among others, Mrs Steward, very fine, with her locks done up with puffs . . . and several other great ladies, had their hair so. . . . Here I saw my Lord Rochester and his lady, Mrs Mallet, who hath after all this ado married him; and, as I hear some say in the pit, it is a great act of charity; for he hath no estate. But it was pleasant to see how everybody rose up when my Lord John Butler, the Duke of Ormond's son, come into the pit towards the end of the play, who was a servant to Mrs Mallet, and now smiled upon her, and she on him. I had sitting next to me a woman, the likest my Lady Castlemayne that ever I saw anybody like another; but she is a whore, I believe, for she is acquainted with every fine fellow, and called them by their name, Jacke, and Tom, and before the end of the play frisked to another place.

How like a social afternoon, lacking only tea to make the gossipy atmosphere complete. In other vignettes Pepys suggests the informality of the auditors. On 16 September 1667 he recorded that "one of the best parts of our sport was a mighty pretty lady that sat behind us, that did laugh so heartily and constantly, that it did me good to hear her." Or a touchingly sentimental scene, at *The Mad Couple*, 28 December 1667: "It pleased us mightily to see the natural affection of a poor woman, the mother of one of the children brought upon the stage: the child crying, she by force got upon the stage and took up her child and carried it away off of the stage from Hart [the actor]." Or a moment of near tragedy, averted skillfully, on 2 November 1667 at *I Henry IV*: "And it was observable how a gentleman of good habit, sitting just before us, eating of some fruit in the midst of the play, did drop down as dead, being choked; but with much ado Orange Moll did thrust her finger down his throat, and brought him to life again."

Some contemporary writers attempted to understand the composition and alteration in the audiences during the forty years preceding 1700; usually, they made distinctions between the spectators during the reign of Charles II and those from the accession of William and Mary to the end of the century. The author of *Historia Histrionica* (1699) briefly examined conditions before the Civil Wars, during the Commonwealth, and after the Restoration. In his opinion, although London was much more populous after 1660 than before the Commonwealth, the increase in admission charges in the Restoration playhouses (which he blames upon the introduction of costly scenes) narrowed the range of individuals who could afford to attend. As a result, there was "better order kept among the Company that came; which made very good People think a Play an Innocent Diversion for an idle Hour or two." In addition, he believed that the plays after 1660 were, "for the most part, more Instructive and Moral."[1] From a vantage point in the early eighteenth century, John Dennis also looked back upon the reign of Charles II and analyzed the nature of the audience at that time. First of all, he believed that "a considerable Part" of the auditory "had that due application, which is requisite for the judging of Comedy," the leisure to attend to dramatic theory and practice, for "that was an age of Pleasure, and not of Business." Gentlemen had the financial security and leisure to be "serene enough to receive its impressions."[2] Later, Dennis returned to this subject and emphasized another factor which he thought made the audiences of the reign of Charles II superior: There "were several extraordinary men at Court who wanted neither Zeal nor Capacity, nor Authority to sett [the audiences] right again." He named, among others, George Villiers Duke of Buckingham, John Wilmot Earl of Rochester, the Earl of Dorset, Sir John Denham, and Edmund Waller. Men of their culture, knowledge, and taste could strongly influence an audience. When "these or the Majority of them Declared themselves upon any new Dramatick performance, the Town fell Immediately in with them."[3]

An examination of the known records of attendance at the theaters between 1660 and 1670 will document some of the analysis which Dennis made. The diaries and correspondence for that period show that a considerable number of literary men attended the theater, some with considerable frequency: Sir Charles Sedley, Sir George Etherege, the Earl of Dorset, George Villiers Duke of Buckingham, Thomas Shadwell, John Dryden, Roger Boyle Earl of Burlington, Sir William Coventry, the Earl of Rochester, William Cavendish Duke of Newcastle, Thomas Killigrew, Sir William Davenant. No doubt, many of the dramatists attended the opening performances of their own plays and, probably, those of rival playwrights. Pepys also gave particular attention to the nobility, gentlemen, and ladies attending the theater. He noted that Charles II attended frequently, sometimes accompanied by the Duke and Duchess of York, often with other nobles and Ladies of Honor; in addition, the Lord Chamberlain's records list many other occasions on which royalty was present. When Elizabeth, Queen of Bohemia

1. In Cibber, *Apology*, I, xxvii.
2. *Works*, I, 293–94.
3. *Ibid.*, II, 277. At this point he offered as an influence their verdict on *The Plain Dealer*, referred to earlier, which turned the opinion of the town in its favor.

visited in London, she also attended the theaters. Other frequenters during this period were Lord Brouncker and Sir William Penn, both close friends to Pepys; he often accompanied other members of the Penn family. Among other upper-class auditors were: Sir Christopher North, Sir Philip Carteret, John Evelyn, Prince Rupert, Lord Lauderdale, the Duke of Ormond, Lord Arlington, the Duke of Norfolk, the Duke of Albemarle, Lord Sandwich, Sir William Batten, Dr. Thomas Sprat, Bishop of Rochester, Lord Fauconberg, Henry Savile.

Pepys also frequently recorded in his Diary the presence of "fine ladies." He was particularly aware of Lady Castlemayne's presence in the playhouse and occasionally, seeing her carriage outside the theater, could hardly resist the temptation to go into the playhouse in spite of a resolve not to do so. He noticed also that the actresses from one company attended the opposition offerings whenever practicable, seeing Mrs. Knepp and Betty Hall of the King's Company at the Duke's Theatre on 30 March 1667. Nell Gwynn and Hester Davenport were sometimes conspicuously present, Mrs. Davenport sitting in the box at *The Villain* on 1 January 1662/3 and catching Pepys' eye. Later, as we know from the Lord Chamberlain's records, Nell Gwynn attended the theaters frequently on the King's bounty. Lady Dorset, Lady Penn, Lady Elizabeth Bodvile, Mlle Le Blanc, Queen Elizabeth of Bohemia and other ladies of fashion filled the boxes.

Attending as regularly as his conscience and purse would allow, Pepys makes it clear that some of his friends were equally attentive playgoers. Captain Ferrers and John Creed, a Deputy-Treasurer to the Fleet, often were Pepys' companions on a playgoing afternoon. On other occasions he attended with the Penn family, sometimes with Lord Brouncker, or with ladies of the circles in which Pepys moved. He refers occasionally to the presence of "gallants," sometimes as though they were a disturbing breed but rarely naming them. Much of what Pepys reports bears out Thomas Killigrew's assertions, 12 February 1666/7, concerning the improved atmosphere at the King's Theatre: earlier "the Queen seldom and the King never would come; now, not the King only for state, but all civil people do think they may come as well as any." In addition, Killigrew "tells me plainly that the City audience was as good as the Court, but now they are most gone."

Nevertheless, Pepys makes us aware that a greater diversity of persons by class, birth, and occupation attended occasionally and, apparently, with greater frequency year by year. On 27 December 1662 he was "not so well pleased with the company at the house to-day, which was full of citizens, there hardly being a gentleman or woman in the house." On 1 January 1662/3 he reported: "The house was full of citizens, and so the less pleasant." Attending *Tu Quoque*, 12 September 1667, he disliked the play, adding, "but it will please the citizens." At *I Henry IV*, 2 November 1667, he especially noted that "The house [was] full of Parliamentmen," as a result of a holiday for them. In a thoughtful mood on 1 January 1667/8 at *The Feigned Innocence*, he reflected on the changes he had seen in several years of theatergoing: "Here a mighty company of citizens, 'prentices, and others; and it makes me observe, that when I begun first to be able to bestow a play on myself, I do not remember that I saw so many by half of the ordinary 'prentices and mean people in the pit at 2s. 6d. a-piece as now."

If we turn to the last twenty years of the seventeenth century, the evidence suggests that changes had occurred in the composition of the audience. Dennis believed that the quality and taste of the spectators had seriously declined by 1700. Commenting upon the audiences of 1702, he found there "three sorts of People . . . who have had no education at all; and who were unheard of in the Reign of Charles the Second." These included (a) a "great many younger Brothers, Gentlemen born, who had been kept at home, by reason of the pressure of the Taxes"; (b) individuals "who made their Fortunes in the late War" and who had risen "from a state of obscurity" to a "condition of distinction and plenty"; and (c) "that considerable number of Foreigners, which within the last twenty years have been introduc'd among us; some of whom not being acquainted with our Language, and consequently with the sense of our Plays, and others disgusted with our extravagant, exorbitant Rambles, have been Instrumental in introducing Sound and Show." The second group, in his view, "could never attain to any higher entertainment than Tumbling and Vaulting and Ladder Dancing, and the delightful diversions of Jack Pudding . . . and encourage these noble Pastimes still upon the Stage." The third group, furthermore, like "Sound and Show, where the business of the Theatre does not require it, and particularly a sort of soft and wanton Musick, which has used the People to a delight which is independent of Reason, a delight that has gone a very great way towards the enervating and dissolving their minds." Finally, he argued that by 1702 "there are ten times more Gentlemen now in business, than there were in King Charles his Reign." They have been disturbed by war and pressed by taxes, "which make them uneasie." As a result, they "are attentive in the events of affairs, and too full of great and real events, to receive due impressions from the imaginary ones of the Theatre."[4] In a somewhat similar vein the author of

4. *Ibid.*, I, 293–94. One cannot help being reminded, at this point, of the way in which Pepys, concerned with the affairs of the navy and the state, nevertheless responded to the illusion of the stage. On 5 October 1667, dropping behind the scenes at Bridges Street, he expressed this sense of illusion: "But,

Historia Histrionica (1699) emphasized that in the late years of the seventeenth century "The Play-houses are so extremely pestered with Vizard-masks and their Trade (occasioning continual Quarrels and Abuses) that many of the more Civilized Part of the Town are uneasy in the Company, and shun the Theatre as they would a House of Scandal."[5]

An associated influence was a change in the management. In the fifteen years following 1660 management lay in the hands of individuals who, frequently, were both proprietors and dramatists (Sir William Davenant is an example), and the actor-sharers had an interest in attracting audiences who responded to the best in dramatic offerings. After 1682, and especially in the last decade, when Rich and Skipwith bought into the United Company, they catered to a diversified audience. In part, they responded to a change; in part, they broadened the range of spectators and tastes.

The writers of Prologues and Epilogues and of pamphlets also show the diversified nature of the audience, especially from 1670 to 1700. They tend also to characterize the spectators in each section of the house, from the boxes to the upper gallery. In a Prologue spoken after the King's Company had suffered a fire at Drury Lane in 1672, Dryden presented a panoramic view of the audience.

> *Here's good Accommodation in the Pit,*
> *The Grave demurely in the midst may Sit.*
> *And so the hot Burgundians on the Side,*
> *Ply Vizard Masque, and o're the Benches stride:*
> *Here are convenient upper boxes too,*
> *For those that make the most triumphant show,*
> *All that keep Coaches must not Sit below.*
> *There Gallants, You betwixt the Acts retire,*
> *And at dull Plays have something to admire.*

Examining the habituees of the pit, some writers look at them caustically, some gently. In *The Young Gallant's Academy* (1674) the satirist pictures the young man who attends the play to draw attention to himself.

> Therefore, I say, let our Gallant . . . presently advance himself into the middle of the Pit, where having made his Honor to the rest of the Company, but especially to the Vizard-Masks, let him pull out his comb, and manage his flaxen Wig with all the Grace he can. Having so done, the next step is to give a hum to the China-Orange-Wench, and give her her own rate for her Oranges (for 'tis beneath a Gentleman to stand haggling like a Citizens

Lord! to see how they [Mrs. Knepp and Nell Gwynn] were both painted would make a man mad, and did make me loath them; and what base company of men comes among them, and how lewdly they talk! and how poor the men are in clothes, and yet what a shew they make on the stage by candle-light, is very observable."

5. In Cibber, *Apology*, I, xxvii.

wife) and then to present the fairest to the next Vizard-mask. And that I may incourage our Gallant not like the Tradesman to save a shilling, and so sit but in the Middle-Gallery, let him but consider what large comings-in are pursued up sitting in the Pit.

The Gallant, the satirist continues, can thus gain a "conspicuous Eminence," and, if he is a knight, secure a mistress. In addition, "It shall frown you with rich Commendations, to laugh aloud in the midst of the most serious and sudden Scene of the terriblest Tragedy, and to let the Clapper (your Tongue) be tossed so high, that all the House may ring of it." Further, the Gallant can "publish your tempera . . . to the world, in that you seem not to resort thither to taste vain Pleasures with a hungry Appetite; but only as a Gentleman to spend a foolish hour or two, because you can do nothing else."[6]

From 1660 to 1700 the writers of prologues and epilogues emphasize the conspicuous behavior of the young-man-about-town in the pit. According to the Prologue to *The Comical Revenge*, March 1664:

> And Gallants, as for you, talk loud i'th' Pit,
> Divert your selves and Friends with your own Wit.

More caustic is the Prologue to *The Ordinary*, ca. January 1670/1.

> Some come with lusty Burgundy half-drunk,
> T'eat China Oranges, make love to Punk;
> And briskly mount a bench when th' Act is done,
> And comb their much-lov'd Periwigs to the tune
> And can sit out a Play of three hours long,
> Minding no part of't but the Dance or Song.

That for *The Rival Queens*, 17 March 1676/7, ridicules the gallants who "with loud Nonsense drown the Stages Wit," a point reiterated in the Epilogue to *Sertorius*, ca. March 1679: "[Our Poet] scorns those little Vermin in the Pit, / Who noise and nonsense vent instead of Wit."[7] They tended to put on a show of their own

(Epilogue to Mrs. Behn's *The False Count*):

> You Sparks better Comedians are than we;
> You every day out-fool ev'n Nokes and Lee.
> They're forc'd to stop, and their own Farces quit,
> T'admire the Merry-Andrews of the Pit.

Although many commentators lashed the gallants and fops in the Pit, the boxes commonly held more sedate and, theoretically, more sympathetic spectators. Here frequently sat the Ladies to whom the writers of Epilogues turned with requests that the warm-hearted

6. Pp. 56–58.
7. The Prologue to *Bellamira*, 12 May 1687, also criticized the excessive noise in the Pit: "Tho the shrill Pit be louder than the Stage."

"Fair Sex" lead the spectators to a favorable verdict. Here, too, sat the upper classes, a fact which attracted Pepys on 1 May 1667: "We sat at the upper bench next the boxes; and I find it do pretty well, and have the advantage of seeing and hearing the great people." Even Robert Gould's caustic satire, *The Play-House* (1685), acknowledged the gentility of the boxes: "And for the Muse a Nobler Scene prepare, / And let Her breathe in Milder air." Even so, the side-boxes irritated commentators by inattentiveness to the play and by devotion to flirtation. As Lord Foppington in *The Relapse*, December 1696, remarked: "But a Man must endeavour to look wholesome, lest he makes so nauseous a Figure in the Side-box, the Ladies shou'd be compell'd to turn their Eyes upon the Play."

For the Galleries, however, the commentators often saved their sharpest barbs. Just as the fops sometimes turned to the side-boxes for intrigue, so they, as the Prologue to Shadwell's *Woman Captain*, September 1679, states, "Whom mounting from the Pit we use to see / (For dangerous Intrigues) to th'Gallery." In the Epilogue to the opening of the theater, 16 November 1682, Dryden vividly re-created the scene.

> *Methinks some Vizard Masque I see,*
> *Cast but her Lure from the mid Gallery.*
> *About her all the flutt'ring Sparks are rang'd;*
> *The Noise continues though the Scene is chang'd:*
> *Now growling, sputtring, wauling, such a clutter.*
> . . . .
> *Then for your Lacqueys, and your Train beside,*
> *(By what e'er Name or Title dignify'd)*
> *They roar so loud, you'd think behind the Stairs*
> *Tom Dove, and all the Brotherhood of Bears:*
> *They've grown a Nuisance, beyond all Disasters,*
> *We've none so great but their unpaying Masters.*
> *We beg you, Sirs, to beg your Men, that they*
> *Wou'd please to give you leave to hear the Play.*[8]

The Prologue to Southerne's *The Disappointment*, 5 April 1684, spoke still more sharply.

> *Last, some there are, who take their first Degrees*
> *Of Lewdness in our Middle Galleries:*
> *The Doughty Bullies enter Bloody Drunk,*
> *Invade and grabble one another's Punk:*
> *They Caterwoul, and make a dismal Rout,*
> *Call Sons of Whores, and strike, but ne're lugg-out.*

The Playhouse (1685), consistently caustic, was most severe in castigating the galleries.

8. The problem of footmen in the galleries was to become a serious one in the eighteenth century.

The Middle Galle'ry first demands our View;
The filth of Jakes, and stench of ev'ry Stew!
Here reeking Punks like Ev'ning Insects swarm;
The Polecat's Perfume much the Happier Charm.
Their very Scent gives Apoplectick Fits,
And yet they're thought all Civit by the Cits;
Nor can we blame 'em; for the Truth to tell,
The want of Brains may be the Want of Smell.
Here ev'ry Night they sit three Hours for Sale;
The Night-rail always cleanlier than the Tayl.

If one believed the exaggeration of the commentators, the theater would appear to be a place wholly inimical to the art of the drama. In fact, a disparaging view was summed up by Jovial, speaking in James Wright's *The Humours and Conversations of the Town* (1693), who replied to a question concerning the value of attending plays:

> What wou'd you go to the Play for? . . . to be dun'd all round with the impertinent Discourse of Beardless Fops to the Orange-Wenches, with Commodes an Ell high; and to the Vizor-Masks: of the Rake-Hells, talking loud to one another; or the perpetual Chat of the Noisy Coquets, that come there to get Cullies, and to disturb, not mind the Play. Or to what Effect has all the Plays upon you? Are not your Fops in the Pit and Boxes incorrigible to all the Endeavours of your Writers, in their Prologues and Epilogues, or the variety of Characters that have been made to reform them? Tho a Play be an generous Diversion, yet 'tis better to read than see, unless one cou'd see it without these Inconveniences.[9]

Obviously, these views are extremist, an exaggeration of the worst elements in the theaters, for no playhouse could exist if all the audiences at all times were composed of spectators like those described in these vignettes. Nevertheless, the satirists strike at characteristics of audiences lamented by all players and playwrights: their inability to be quiet, to lend full attention to the play, and to subordinate their personal interests to the serious aims of author and actor, who had a good deal of right on their side. After all, quarrels and disturbances sometimes made the pit a noisy place and disrupted the play. The orangewomen bargained for their goods and charms not only in the intervals but sometimes during the action on stage. The intrigues of the gallants almost never ceased. And the gentlemen, wits, and Templars considered it their privilege to be critics, wise or witty but usually vocal. In the long run, however, the best of the drama survived and the worst died away as the judgment of the spectators surmounted temporary confusions of the moment.

9. Pp. 105–6.

ALLARDYCE NICOLL

[The Eighteenth-Century Stage] †

Apart from the opera houses, which tended to assume Italianate features (particularly the arrangement of the galleries in rows of boxes), the playhouses of the time agreed in displaying common elements and in adopting modifications by general consent. The large apron of the Restoration stage tended to become less deep, thus approaching the modern form, and the four doors in front of the proscenium arch were accordingly reduced to two. Colley Cibber describes the beginning of this change at the Theatre Royal in Drury Lane, and attributes it to the desire for additional seating accommodation. Since the passage includes an interesting comment on the resultant changes in performance, his words may be given in their entirety:

> It must be observ'd, then, that the Area, or Platform of the old Stage, projected about four Foot forwarder, in a Semi-oval Figure, parallel to the Benches of the Pit; and that the former, lower Doors of Entrance for the Actors were brought down between the two foremost (and then only) Pilasters; in the Place of which Doors, now the two Stage Boxes are fixt. That where the Doors of Entrance now are, there formerly stood two additional Side-Wings, in front to a full Set of Scenes, which had then almost a double Effect, in their Loftiness and Magnificence.
>
> By the Original Form, the usual Station of the Actors, in almost every Scene, was advanc'd at least ten foot nearer to the Audience, than they now can be; because, not only from the Stage's being shorten'd, in front, but likewise from the additional Interposition of those Stage-Boxes, the Actors (in respect to the Spectators, that fill them) are kept so much more backward from the main Audience, than they us'd to be: But when the Actors were in Possession of that forwarder Space, to advance upon, the Voice was then more in the Centre of the House, so that the most distant Ear had scarce the least Doubt, or Difficulty in hearing what fell from the weakest Utterance: All Objects were thus drawn nearer to the Sense; every painted Scene was stronger; every grand Scene and Dance more extended; every rich, or fine-coloured Habit had a more lively Lustre: Nor was the minutest Motion of a Feature (properly changing with the Passion, or Humour it suited) ever lost, as they frequently must be in the Obscurity of too great a Distance: And how valuable an Advantage that Facility of hearing distinctly, is to every well-acted Scene, every common Spectator is a Judge.[1]

† From Allardyce Nicoll, *The British Theatre* (London: Thomas Nelson and Sons Ltd., 1936), pp. 115–18, 126–29. Reprinted by permission of the publisher.

1. Quoted from *An Apology for the Life of Colley Cibber*, 3rd. ed. (London, 1750), pp. 338 ff. [Editor].

Cibber's complaints, of course, have to be interpreted in the (literal) light of his theater, when candles and oil-lamps might readily render "obscure" any objects far removed from sight. Those complaints, however, were of no avail; the apron definitely became smaller as decades advanced.

Otherwise, the playhouses of the time maintained the shape and arrangement which had been theirs in the Restoration. Pit, box, and gallery served for the auditorium; stage and apron were still used by the players. True, for the most part the houses were larger; in this age came the vogue of the enormous playhouse which, although it did not reach full proportions until the very end of the century, is to be traced back to the earlier years. Partly due to the increasing body of spectators, the movement is also to be associated with the introduction of spectacle—a frequently satirized element between 1700 and 1800.

* * *

Spectacle, of course, itself demands considerable means at the service of the manager, and it has to be confessed that, if England possessed no Bibiena, the theaters did progress in material resources. The Restoration stage had established firmly the convention of the back shutters and side wings, and this convention endured for many years—has, indeed, endured to our own times. Alongside of this, on the other hand, we find many theatrical developments, particularly in the latter half of the eighteenth century. Built up effects—that is to say, simulated rocks and castles and greenswards—often took the place of, or were used along with, the side wings. The flats became less flimsy and less patently artificial; practicable doors and windows frequently appeared in them. Fire effects were often indulged in, and lighting devices, such as the "Eidophusikon,"[2] provided thrills for an audience which had previously known only the primitive and artificial clouds painted upon flat strips of canvas.

The appearance of this "Eidophusikon" indicates the great advances which had been made in lighting. Up to the time of Garrick, the methods of illumination were primitive in the extreme. The auditorium seems to have remained in brightness during the performance of every play, the candles arranged at intervals along the edges of the galleries being left to splutter from the time that the curtain was raised to the closing of the theatre.

For the stage itself there were three main sources of illumination. The chief of these was the rings or "hoops" of candles suspended from the roof over the apron or the stage. Not shaded in any way, the candles burned in full view of the audience, providing what, we must imagine, was an eye-aching glare. By the sides of the proscenium were also set wall brackets, but the few candles there furnished

2. A scenic display making use of concealed overhead lighting to give an appearance of movement in the scenic background [Editor].

apparently little additional light. More important were the "floats" or footlights—a series of candles or lamps placed originally without a shield along the front of the apron, and later concealed by a bar of wood or placed in a trough. Footlights, be it noted, were no modern invention. They are clearly seen in the "Red Bull" engraving of 1673, and we find them referred to nearly a century earlier in Italian writings. Although references to them are scant, we are forced to believe that they formed a regular part of the lighting equipment of every post-Restoration English playhouse.

These conditions endured until the year 1765, when Garrick, after a visit to the Continent, returned full of enthusiasm in the possession of an idea for a complete reorganizing of the theater's illumination. First of all, he obtained a set of new lamps. "I have carried out your two commissions," he heard from Jean Monnet, director of the Opéra Comique,

> and with M. Boquet's designs I will send you a reflector and two different samples of the lamp you want for the footlights at your theatre. There are two kinds of reflectors: those that are placed in a niche in the wall, and which have one wick; and those which are hung up like a chandelier, and have five. . . . As to the lamps for lighting your stage, they are of two kinds: some of earthenware, and in biscuit form; they have six or eight wicks, and you put oil in them; the others are of tin, in the shape of a candle, with a spring, and you put candles in them.[3]

Further information followed in another letter concerning torches in which licopodium might be burned. That Garrick's introduction of new instruments was of importance may not be denied, but of far greater significance was his almost complete rearrangement of these and earlier instruments. Briefly, this seems to have consisted in the banishing of the rings and the placing of candles or lamps either behind the side wings or at least behind suitable shades. In itself the change does not appear so epoch-making, yet Garrick's innovation was revolutionary in its results. It meant that now the portion of the stage behind the proscenium arch was more brightly illuminated than the apron, consequently the actors tended to move back from the audience, and the already curtailed apron lost even such significance as it still retained. It meant, too, that no row of lights prevented those in the galleries from seeing the rear of the stage, so that processions and the like might more freely be exploited. And above all, it meant that the basis was now provided for more elaborate, more easily controlled, more pleasing, and more realistic effects. The path was being opened up which the theater was to tread in the following century. * * *

3. Translated from *The Private Correspondence of David Garrick*, edited by James Boaden (London, 1831–32), II, 441–42 [Editor].

CHARLES BEECHER HOGAN

[Scenery and Lighting] †

* * * Between the audience and the proscenium arch, with its large, green proscenium curtain, was the sunken pit in which the orchestra sat, and beyond which lay the area known, at least in theatrical history, as the forestage. (I am reminded by Professor Allardyce Nicoll that this part of the stage was never referred to as the "apron" until about 1900. Even the term "forestage" was seldom, possibly never, employed in the eighteenth century, i.e. everything from the footlights to the furthest upstage piece of scenery was called, and quite properly, merely "the stage.") In any event, this area was one of the first importance in every production of every evening's entertainment. From it were heard prologues, epilogues, announcements of changes of play; on it took place not only songs, monologues, incidental dances and other forms of intermediary activity, but also a considerable part of the action of the play proper. At moments of stress or tension in the unfolding of the plot the actors would want to be in as close proximity as possible to the audience, and would advance well beyond the proscenium arch to deliver an important speech, whether a soliloquy or not. On either side of the forestage stood a door, which generations of stage convention had accepted as an integral part of the scenery, as, that is, either an exterior or interior door in or near whatever kind of building the action of the play—otherwise progressing on the stage proper behind the proscenium arch—might be located. These doors were even used for entrances and exits in scenes not connected with a building at all: a scene in a park or a forest, by the seashore or on a country highway. The forestage was, in other words, for all purposes completely and intimately associated with the entire acting area from front to back.

The measurement of the depth of the forestage varied from theater to theater; an average, however, would be about twelve to fourteen feet. At the opera house it was somewhat deeper, in order to provide a larger space for the elaborate ballets produced there. The footlights, or "lamps," extended along the entire front of the forestage. At either end of the footlights it was customary to install a curved and ornamented grille-work of iron, perhaps eighteen inches in height. These grilles were known as the "spikes," and had been introduced at a much earlier time when, during serious riots, mem-

† From *The London Stage: 1660–1800*, Part V, Vol. I, edited by C. B. Hogan (Carbondale, Ill.: Southern Illinois University Press, 1968), lv–lix, lxv–lxvii. Reprinted by permission of the publisher.

bers of the audience attempted to clamber into the orchestra pit
and thence onto the stage. For the same reason rows of similar
spikes, also of an ornamental nature, were affixed upon all three
sides of the inclosure surrounding that pit. Whether these devices
ever effectively deterred a serious-minded rioter may be questioned.
As time went on they became more a matter of accepted convention in theater architecture than of genuine defense against mischief.

The curtain was, therefore, taking into account the depth of both
the orchestra pit and the forestage, situated at a distance of perhaps
twenty-five feet from the front bench in the pit proper. When, after
the playing of the last "music," it finally rose, it did so by being
pulled up in the form of three or four shallow festoons. It was never
pulled all the way out of sight, but remained at the top of the proscenium arch, and hence served as a border that helped to conceal
the flies and the grid. As it rose the audience saw a flat scene
extending all the way from one wing to its opposite wing, and
standing in a groove about an inch and a half wide and an inch and
three-quarters high. This scene was supported in like manner by a
comparable groove situated upside down underneath the flies at the
top of the stage. These grooves were used in all eighteenth-century
English theaters. They were brought to America, but, except in a
modified form developed in Holland, never found their way into
any public Continental theater. The scenes which they held, known
as "flats,"[1] consisted of two pieces, divided vertically in the middle.
These pieces were drawn on or off the stage, right and left, by scene
shifters who were working behind them. No concealment of this
operation was ever attempted; it was carried on in full view of the
audience.[2]

The grooves were arbitrarily known as the "first groove," being the
one nearest the footlights, the second, the one next upstage, the
third and so on. For moving the flats two different things therefore
happened. The opening scene of an act might be placed in the
fourth groove and the next scene in the third. When this opening
scene was concluded the flats of the following scene "closed" upon
it, and oftentimes upon the actors still remaining in that scene. Or
the situation might be reversed. At the end of the first scene, in
which the third groove had been elected for use, the actors would
make their exits, whereupon the flats would be pulled offstage,
revealing the following scene, placed in the fourth groove. But any
one of the grooves, no matter how far apart, could of course be used

1. This term first came into use about 1736. Throughout the hundred years pre-vious they were known as "shutters."
2. "The scenes visibly shifted in your sight."—Sir Joshua Reynolds, *Literary Works* (London, 1852), II. 72. For a full discussion of the mechanism of the grooves and of their operation see Ri-chard Southern, *Changeable Scenery* (London, 1953), and the same writer in *The Oxford Companion to the Theatre*, 2nd ed. (London, 1957), pp. 238–42.

successively. The choosing of them was usually dictated by the exi-
gencies of whatever play was being performed, in particular as
regards characters who appear in two consecutive scenes. For this
very reason, most eighteenth-century dramatists were careful, as far
as possible, to begin each scene with a different set of characters
than those on whom the flats of the preceding scene had just
closed. In other words, changes were always made, provided the
scene shifters were properly alert, with great rapidity.

But oftentimes it was unnecessary, again because of what was
demanded by the plot of the play, to move the scenes from upstage
to downstage, or vice versa. This was made possible because the
grooves were not constructed as individual units. They were
assembled into what were called "sets," each set consisting of anywhere from three to five grooves laid side by side. Thus, for two successive scenes that had to be played downstage, their flats would be
arranged within the same set, and operated exactly as has been
described in the preceding paragraph. An example of how the various grooves were chosen is found in connection with the property
plot for *Love in a Village* as acted at Covent Garden on 15 September 1788. It is reproduced by John Williams in his *Poems* in 1789.[3]

ACT I

Scene i. A Garden—5th groove.
Scene ii. A Hall in Woodcock's House—2nd groove.
Scene iii. A Field [this scene was in common use in many other
plays; it was known as the "Stratford"]—2nd groove.
Scene iv. A Village Green—5th groove.

ACT II

Scene i. A Parlour in Woodcock's House [this scene, like that
in *I.iii*, was known as the "Beausett"]—2nd groove.
Scene ii. As *I.i*—5th groove.
Scene iii. As *I.ii*—2nd groove.

ACT III

Scene i. As *II.i*—2nd groove.
Scene ii. A Greenhouse ["Open Cutt Wood back'd by Garden
Cloth"]—3rd groove.
Scene iii. Another Hall in Woodcock's House [this scene, like that
in *I.iii*, was known as the "Picture"]—3rd groove.

It will be observed that the first and fourth grooves were not made
use of at all, and that on two occasions (I.ii, iii and III.ii, iii) the
flats for two successive scenes were installed in the same set of
grooves. For the exterior scenes representing the Garden and the
Village Green the stage was open to its fullest extent. In order to
give a sharper effect to the scene of the Village Green—that of a

3. (London, 1789), II, 264.

busy and well-attended fair—the "Stratford" scene of the Field, which was introductory to it, was played downstage. So were all the interior scenes of the two Halls and the Parlor, in either the second or third groove.

More was called for than merely the flats. The principle underlying, and the necessity for, the use of wings had long been known. The wings were placed in the groove that, in each of the sets, lay furthest downstage. The number of the sets of grooves corresponded to the number of the wings, which, in Drury Lane and Covent Garden, were usually ten, i.e. five to a side. The reconstructed King's of 1791 had six wings to a side.[4] No line drawing of the stage of the Haymarket appears to have survived, but the number was probably also five. The sets containing the wings and grooves at all the theaters were roughly six feet apart. The wings could be called extensions of the flat scenes that ran in and out on the grooves. When pulled off the stage each flat came to rest immediately behind the wing to which it corresponded. The wings themselves were in grooves, and had to be changed to fit the scene as a whole: a "tree" wing for a park or countryside, a "palace" wing for any interior of a building, etc. Being of a more or less generalized design they were frequently, like the "Stratford" and "Beausett" flat scenes, used again and again in different plays, and would in fact be held over for several successive seasons. When on the playbills the expression, "With New Scenes," appears, the reference is almost invariably to the flats alone. The entire system lay parallel to the footlights. Had the wings been set at an angle the grooves could not then have been placed in a straight line from one side of the stage to the other.

* * *

The stages of all the London theaters received their illumination from three sources: the lighted auditorium, the footlights, and oil lamps and candles fastened at intervals behind the proscenium and behind each of the wings. Concealed lighting from behind the borders at the top of the proscenium may also have been employed, but no positive evidence of this has survived. The stage was therefore given a steady flow of undiminished light, whenever such a light was required. But years of practice and the ingenuity of more than one machinist and scene designer—notably De Loutherbourg[5]—had made possible a good deal of variety in obtaining various effects of light and dark.

The first important change had come at the beginning of the 1765–66 season when at both Drury Lane and Covent Garden the large chandeliers, or "rings," that from the time of the opening of

4. *Oracle*, 24 Feb. 1791.
5. Philippe Jacques De Loutherbourg, an Alsatian painter and scene designer who came to London in 1771 and became famous as the scenic director at Drury Lane [Editor].

the theaters in 1660 had hung suspended over the stage of every theater in London, were abolished. In his *Personal Sketches of his own Times* Sir Jonah Barrington speaks of the Dublin theaters of the eighteenth century being lit "with tallow candles, stuck into tin circles hanging from the middle of the stage, which were every now and then snuffed by some performer."[6] That London actors were obliged to do likewise was certainly the case. These chandeliers were a deterrent both to the illusion of the scene and to a complete view of the stage on the part of those seated in the upper gallery. Garrick, just returned from a long journey on the Continent, had insisted on doing away with these bothersome objects—in fact, the idea of doing so had come to him while seeing the lighting arrangements on some of the stages in the foreign countries he had visited. In any event, the Covent Garden management took up the idea, too, and in place of the chandeliers long, vertical strips, probably of tin, were installed out of sight of the audience on either side of the stage. On these strips the lights were fastened. Behind each light was a reverberator or reflector, and beside each light was a curved metal shield. These shields could be drawn slowly or rapidly, as the occasion demanded, across the lights, with somewhat the effect achieved by a modern rheostat, and, if entire darkness was desired on the stage, the footlights were so arranged that, at the same moment, they could be lowered until they were entirely out of sight.

These devices continued to be used at Drury Lane and at Covent Garden—they were presently adopted by the Haymarket as well—until the end of the century and for some years thereafter. A more simplified and efficient system was that installed in the opera house. It is described, with a fine flourish, by the *Oracle* on 10 January 1791, as follows: "Upon our theatres are generally affixed to the wings [the stage lights, which can be] darkened by folding blinds; but here the lamps are suspended before the wings upon posts, which by one mechanic power are moved together—gradually receding for the coming on of night—gradually approaching with the increasing blushes of Aurora."

De Loutherbourg went even further. By stretching silk screens of different colors working on pivots in front of bright lights he was able to obtain effects of clouds, storms, etc. that perpetually astonished and delighted the audience. Henry Angelo describes how, by this method, "a sudden transition [was brought about] in a forest scene, where the foliage varies from green to blood colors and . . . so illuminated the stage as to give the effect of enchantment."[7] Transparencies De Loutherbourg brought to a high point of beauty and of accuracy. They had long been in use in theaters everywhere, and consisted usually of a scene placed well upstage made of linen

6. (London, 1827), II, 197.   7. *Reminiscences* (London, 1830), II, 326.

or of calico and painted in transparent dye. The "Cavern of Despair," in the penultimate scene of pantomime, painted on the front side of the transparency, would be visible when light shone on it; on the back side would be painted the "Temple of Virtue," which when lighted from behind in the concluding scene, would burst suddenly into view. Effects of this nature were, as just indicated, much more commonly utilized in the Drury Lane and Covent Garden pantomimes than in anything else, but they were also seen from time to time at the opera house, especially in the elaborate allegorical ballets performed there. Another experiment with lighting at this theater aroused the admiration of a reviewer in the *Gazetteer*, 28 March 1791, who refers to the scene of the Elysian Fields in a ballet based on the legend of Orpheus. There, "by means of lights placed behind gauze, a filmy hue is thrown over the stage, and the figures assume the appearance of aerial beings."

The footlights lay at the front of the forestage, which obviously needed additional illumination, since a good deal of the action of the play took place on it. They were situated in a long metal trough, the "footlight trap," which was filled with oil, on which were floating a series of small rectangular saucers, each holding two candles which were fed by the oil. The entire contrivance could be lowered by means of a system of lines and pulleys attached to a winch in the prompter's corner whenever it was necessary to give to the stage as much darkness as possible. * * *

The "screen scene" in *The School for Scandal*, probably from the original production at Drury Lane in 1777. Photograph from Alec Clunes, The British Theatre (London: Cassel, 1964), p. 103. (Original in the Victoria and Albert Museum.

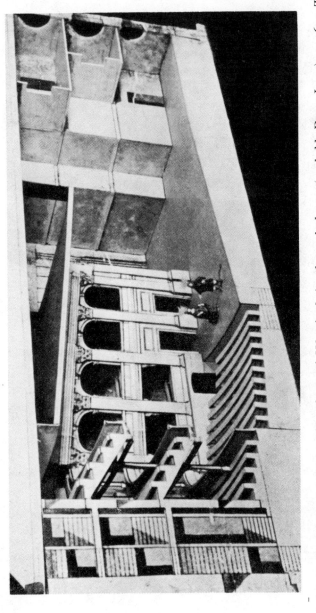

Model reconstruction by Richard Southern of Wren's design for a playhouse (probably Drury Lane), c. 1674. The actors are shown on the forestage. Entrances and exits were usually through the proscenium doors, shown stage right. The large area to the rear of the stage was used for movable scenery.

Photograph from Richard Southern, Changeable Scenery (London: Faber, 1952), Plate 28.

The interior of Drury Lane in 1775, showing the pit, boxes, and galleries after gradual enlargement during the eighteenth century.

Photograph from Allardyce Nicoll, The Development of the Theatre, 5th edition (London: Harrap, 1966), Figure 201. (Original in the Folger Shakespeare Library.)

Criticism
From Lamb to the Present

CHARLES LAMB

On the Artificial Comedy of the Last Century†

The artificial Comedy, or Comedy of Manners, is quite extinct on our stage. Congreve and Farquhar show their heads once in seven years only, to be exploded and put down instantly. The times cannot bear them. Is it for a few wild speeches, an occasional license of dialogue? I think not altogether. The business of their dramatic characters will not stand the moral test. We screw every thing up to that. Idle gallantry in a fiction, a dream, the passing pageant of an evening, startles us in the same way as the alarming indications of profligacy in a son or ward in real life should startle a parent or guardian. We have no such middle emotions as dramatic interests left. We see a stage libertine playing his loose pranks of two hours' duration, and of no after consequence, with the severe eyes which inspect real vices with their bearings upon two worlds. We are spectators to a plot or intrigue (not reducible in life to the point of strict morality) and take it all for truth. We substitute a real for a dramatic person, and judge him accordingly. We try him in our courts, from which there is no appeal to the *dramatis personæ*, his peers. We have been spoiled with—not sentimental comedy—but a tyrant far more pernicious to our pleasures which has succeeded to it, the exclusive and all devouring drama of common life; where the moral point is every thing; where, instead of the fictitious half-believed personages of the stage (the phantoms of old comedy) we recognize ourselves, our brothers, aunts, kinsfolk, allies, patrons, enemies—the same as in life—with an interest in what is going on so hearty and substantial, that we cannot afford our moral judgment, in its deepest and most vital results, to compromise or slumber for a moment. What is *there* transacting, by no modification is made to affect us in any other manner than the same events or characters would do in our relationships of life. We carry our fire-side concerns to the theater with us. We do not go thither, like our ancestors, to escape from the pressure of reality, so much as to confirm our experience of it; to make assurance double, and take a bond of fate. We must live our toilsome lives twice over, as it was the mournful privilege of Ulysses to descend twice to the shades. All that neutral ground of character, which stood between vice and virtue; or which in fact was indifferent to neither, where neither properly was called in question; that happy breathing-place from the burden of a perpetual moral questioning—the sanctuary and quiet

† First published in the *London Magazine* in 1822 and included (in the version followed here) in Lamb's collection of essays called *Elia*, 1823.

Alsatia of hunted casuistry[1]—is broken up and disfranchised, as injurious to the interests of society. The privileges of the place are taken away by law. We dare not dally with images, or names, of wrong. We bark like foolish dogs at shadows. We dread infection from the scenic representation of disorder; and fear a painted pustule. In our anxiety that our morality should not take cold, we wrap it up in a great blanket surtout of precaution against the breeze and sunshine.

I confess for myself that (with no great delinquencies to answer for) I am glad for a season to take an airing beyond the diocese of the strict conscience—not to live always in the precincts of the law-courts—but now and then, for a dream-while or so, to imagine a world with no meddling restrictions—to get into recesses, whither the hunter cannot follow me—

> ——————Secret shades
> Of woody Ida's inmost grove,
> While yet there was no fear of Jove—[2]

I come back to my cage and my restraint the fresher and more healthy for it. I wear my shackles more contentedly for having respired the breath of an imaginary freedom. I do not know how it is with others, but I feel the better always for the perusal of one of Congreve's—nay, why should I not add even of Wycherley's—comedies. I am the gayer at least for it; and I could never connect those sports of a witty fancy in any shape with any result to be drawn from them to imitation in real life. They are a world of themselves almost as much as fairy-land. Take one of their characters, male or female (with few exceptions they are alike), and place it in a modern play, and my virtuous indignation shall rise against the profligate wretch as warmly as the Catos[3] of the pit could desire; because in a modern play I am to judge of the right and the wrong. The standard of *police* is the measure of *political justice*. The atmosphere will blight it, it cannot live here. It has got into a moral world, where it has no business, from which it must needs fall headlong; as dizzy, and incapable of making a stand, as a Swedenborgian bad spirit that has wandered unawares into the sphere of one of his Good Men, or Angels. But in its own world do we feel the creature is so very bad?—The Fainalls and the Mirabels, the Dorimants and the Lady Touchwoods, in their own sphere, do not offend my moral sense; in fact they do not appeal to it at all. They seem engaged in their proper elements. They break through no laws, or conscientious restraints. They know of none. They have got out of Christendom into the land—what shall I call it?—of cuckoldry—the Utopia of

1. I.e., a haven or sanctuary for men burdened by logic and morality [Editor].
2. *Milton, Il Penseroso*, lines 28–30 [Editor].
3. Cato was known for condemning luxury and decadence in Rome [Editor].

gallantry, where pleasure is duty, and the manners perfect freedom. It is altogether a speculative scene of things, which has no reference whatever to the world that is. No good person can be justly offended as a spectator, because no good person suffers on the stage. Judged morally, every character in these plays—the few exceptions only are *mistakes*—is alike essentially vain and worthless. The great art of Congreve is especially shown in this, that he has entirely excluded from his scenes—some little generosities in the part of Angelica perhaps excepted—not only any thing like a faultless character, but any pretensions to goodness or good feelings whatsoever. Whether he did this designedly, or instinctively, the effect is as happy, as the design (if design) was bold. I used to wonder at the strange power which his *Way of the World* in particular possesses of interesting you all along in the pursuits of characters, for whom you absolutely care nothing—for you neither hate nor love his personages—and I think it is owing to this very indifference for any, that you endure the whole. He has spread a privation of moral light, I will call it, rather than by the ugly name of palpable darkness, over his creations; and his shadows flit before you without distinction or preference. Had he introduced a good character, a single gush of moral feeling, a revulsion of the judgment to actual life and actual duties, the impertinent Goshen would have only lighted to the discovery of deformities, which now are none, because we think them none.

Translated into real life, the characters of his, and his friend Wycherley's dramas, are profligates and strumpets—the business of their brief existence, the undivided pursuit of lawless gallantry. No other spring of action, or possible motive of conduct, is recognized; principles which, universally acted upon, must reduce this frame of things to a chaos. But we do them wrong in so translating them. No such effects are produced in *their* world. When we are among them, we are amongst a chaotic people. We are not to judge them by our usages. No reverend institutions are insulted by their proceedings—for they have none among them. No peace of families is violated—for no family ties exist among them. No purity of the marriage bed is stained—for none is supposed to have a being. No deep affections are disquieted—no holy wedlock bands are snapped asunder—for affection's depth and wedded faith are not of the growth of that soil. There is neither right nor wrong—gratitude or its opposite—claim or duty—paternity or sonship. Of what consequence is it to virtue, or how is she at all concerned about it, whether Sir Simon, or Dapperwit, steal away Miss Martha; or who is the father of Lord Froth's, or Sir Paul Pliant's children.

The whole is a passing pageant, where we should sit as unconcerned at the issues, for life or death, as at a battle of the frogs and mice. But, like Don Quixote, we take part against the puppets, and quite as impertinently. We dare not contemplate an Atlantis, a scheme, out of which our coxcombical moral sense is for a little transitory ease excluded. We have not the courage to imagine a state of things for which there is neither reward nor punishment. We cling to the painful necessities of shame and blame. We would indict our very dreams.

Amidst the mortifying circumstances attendant upon growing old, it is something to have seen the *School for Scandal* in its glory. This comedy grew out of Congreve and Wycherley, but gathered some allays of the sentimental comedy, which followed theirs. It is impossible that it should be now *acted*, though it continues, at long intervals, to be announced in the bills. Its hero, when Palmer[4] played it at least, was Joseph Surface. When I remember the gay boldness, the graceful solemn plausibility, the measured step, the insinuating voice—to express it in a word—the downright *acted* villany of the part, so different from the pressure of conscious actual wickedness—the hypocritical assumption of hypocrisy—which made Jack so deservedly a favorite in that character, I must needs conclude the present generation of play-goers more virtuous than myself, or more dense. I freely confess that he divided the palm with me with his better brother; that, in fact, I liked him quite as well. Not but there are passages—like that, for instance, where Joseph is made to refuse a pittance to a poor relation—incongruities which Sheridan was forced upon by the attempt to join the artificial with the sentimental comedy, either of which must destroy the other—but over these obstructions Jack's manner floated him so lightly, that a refusal from him no more shocked you, than the easy compliance of Charles gave you in reality any pleasure; you got over the paltry question as quickly as you could, to get back into the regions of pure comedy, where no cold moral reigns. The highly artificial manner of Palmer in this character counteracted every disagreeable impression which you might have received from the contrast, supposing them real, between the two brothers. You did not believe in Joseph with the same faith with which you believed in Charles. The latter was a pleasant reality, the former a no less pleasant poetical foil to it. The comedy, I have said, is incongruous; a mixture of Congreve with sentimental incompatibilities: the gaiety upon the whole is buoyant; but it required the consummate art of Palmer to reconcile the discordant elements.

A player with Jack's talents, if we had one now, would not dare to do the part in the same manner. He would instinctively avoid every turn which might tend to unrealize, and so to make the char-

4. Jack Palmer, who in the late eighteenth century was famous for his performance as Joseph Surface [Editor].

acter fascinating. He must take his cue from his spectators, who
would expect a bad man and a good man as rigidly opposed to each
other as the death-beds of those geniuses are contrasted in the
prints, which I am sorry to say have disappeared from the windows
of my old friend Carrington Bowles,[5] of St. Paul's Church-yard
memory—(an exhibition as venerable as the adjacent cathedral, and
almost coeval) of the bad and good man at the hour of death;
where the ghastly apprehensions of the former—and truly the grim
phantom with his reality of a toasting fork is not to be despised—so
finely contrast with the meek complacent kissing of the rod—taking
it in like honey and butter—with which the latter submits to the
scythe of the gentle bleeder, Time, who wields his lancet with the
apprehensive finger of a popular young ladies' surgeon. What flesh,
like loving grass, would not covet to meet half-way the stroke of
such a delicate mower?—John Palmer was twice an actor in this
exquisite part. He was playing to you all the while that he was playing upon Sir Peter and his lady. You had the first intimation of a
sentiment before it was on his lips. His altered voice was meant to
you, and you were to suppose that his fictitious co-flutterers on the
stage perceived nothing at all of it. What was it to you if that half-
reality, the husband, was over-reached by the puppetry—or the thin
thing (Lady Teazle's reputation) was persuaded it was dying of a
plethory? The fortunes of Othello and Desdemona were not concerned in it. Poor Jack has passed from the stage in good time, that
he did not live to this our age of seriousness. The pleasant old
Teazle *King*,[6] too, is gone in good time. His manner would scarce
have passed current in our day. We must love or hate—acquit or
condemn—censure or pity—exert our detestable coxcombry of
moral judgment upon every thing. Joseph Surface, to go down now,
must be a downright revolting villain—no compromise—his first
appearance must shock and give horror—his specious plausibilities,
which the pleasurable faculties of our fathers welcomed with such
hearty greetings, knowing that no harm (dramatic harm even)
could come, or was meant to come of them, must inspire a cold and
killing aversion. Charles (the real canting person of the scene—for
the hypocrisy of Joseph has its ulterior legitimate ends, but his
brother's professions of good heart center in downright self-satis-
faction) must be *loved*, and Joseph *hated*. To balance one disagreeable reality with another, Sir Peter Teazle must be no longer the
comic idea of a fretful old bachelor bridegroom, whose teasings
(while King acted it) were evidently as much played off at you, as
they were meant to concern anybody on the stage—he must be a
real person, capable in law of sustaining an injury—a person

5. A publisher of prints whose shop was at St. Paul's [Editor].

6. Thomas King, who originally played Sir Peter Teazle [Editor].

towards whom duties are to be acknowledged—the genuine crim-
con antagonist of the villainous seducer Joseph. To realize him
more, his sufferings under his unfortunate match must have the
downright pungency of life—must (or should) make you not mirth-
ful but uncomfortable, just as the same predicament would move
you in a neighbor or old friend. The delicious scenes which give the
play its name and zest, must affect you in the same serious manner
as if you heard the reputation of a dear female friend attacked in
your real presence. Crabtree and Sir Benjamin—those poor snakes
that live but in the sunshine of your mirth—must be ripened by
this hot-bed process of realization into asps or amphisbaenas; and
Mrs. Candour—O! frightful! become a hooded serpent. Oh who
that remembers Parsons and Dodd—the wasp and butterfly of the
School for Scandal—in those two characters; and charming natural
Miss Pope,[7] the perfect gentlewoman as distinguished from the fine
lady of comedy, in this latter part—would forego the true scenic
delight—the escape from life—the oblivion of consequences—the
holiday barring out of the pedant Reflection—those Saturnalia of
two or three brief hours, well won from the world—to sit instead at
one of our modern plays—to have his coward conscience (that forsooth must not be left for a moment) stimulated with perpetual
appeals—dulled rather, and blunted, as a faculty without repose
must be—and his moral vanity pampered with images of notional
justice, notional beneficence, lives saved without the spectators' risk,
and fortunes given away that cost the author nothing? * * *

JOHN PALMER

[The Comedy of Manners][†]

* * * It is a recognized principle of English law that the worst
criminal should have counsel. It has been sensibly felt that innocence is a frail barricade against a really vigorous and alert prosecu-
tion, and that it would be grossly unjust to leave a prisoner to fend
for himself against the practiced onslaught of a specialist. The
comic dramatists of the Restoration are in the position of criminals
tried for their reputation without counsel. Surely it is grossly against
even the coarse sense of justice typified in the ordinary procedure of
the courts to condemn them for having failed in these circumstances to establish their innocence.

"Art for morality's sake," said Jeremy Collier; and Congreve

---

7. Jane Pope, the original Mrs. Candour
[Editor].
† From John Palmer, *The Comedy of*
Manners (London: G. Bell and Sons,
1913), pp. 288–97. Reprinted by permis-
sion of the publisher.

accepted it. It is easy for a modern critic to say that Congreve should have refused. We have thought a good deal about art since 1698, and written even more than we have thought. We have tested formulae at the opposite extreme to Collier's. It is possible to understand how Collier was wrong and how difficult it was for Congreve to perceive exactly why and where.

Art is not primarily concerned with morality. It is not the aim or business of comedy to improve the world. Good morality is not necessarily good art, else every good man would of necessity be a great artist. We are not committing ourselves to any nonsense about "art for art's sake"—really a pleonasm. When we say that art is not primarily concerned with morality, we mean that in most cases (the exceptions prove the rule) an artist is first concerned with beautifully expressing something he has felt or seen. He endeavors to give local habitation and a name to a piece of life imaginatively realized. His art is fashioned in the heart of a desire to see life in shape and form. His impulse is not the impulse of a moralist to improve the world: it is the impulse of an artist to express it.

Here, in the art of a poet or dramatist, enters a paradox and stumbling-block. Art is not primarily concerned with morality, but morality is the stuff of the poet's art. The artist is dealing with emotions and conduct which in the world whence he draws his material are determined by a positive morality. Morality is his subject, though it is not his object. The critics of Collier's generation, and incompetent critics of every generation, invariably confuse the subject with the object—worse, they mistake the subject of a picture or a poem for the work itself.

The problem is further confused by the continuous inter-influence of subject and object. The artist's purpose is to give form and imaginative reality to a piece of life—beauty is his object. But just as the beauty which a worker in marble and bronze aims at expressing is conditioned by his material, so is the poet's work conditioned by the period in which he lives, the moral laws which his moods and characters unconsciously obey. He does not aim at enforcing or weakening the moral code; but in the result he necessarily does so. The moralist, Jeremy Collier for instance, perceives the result; and mistakes it for the intention. The artist himself, working intuitively, if he is not also a critic, is equally liable to mistake it.

The most difficult question remains. Can good art be bad morality? If Collier has proved that the result of Congreve's impulse to express beautifully the life of his time is morally vicious, has he also proved that it is bad art? First we must be quite clear as to what morality means. If it means the definite system of moral values from which Collier attacked the plays of Congreve, then it is immediately obvious that bad morality as Collier understood it is quite

486 · *John Palmer*

consistent with good art as any artist understands it. It is not necessarily bad art—nor ever was—to suggest that man and wife though
they be made one flesh will often remain two fools. If by morality is
understood the minutiae of the contemporary code, then obviously
bad morality may be not only good art but better manners.

But there is a higher morality than that of Jeremy Collier—a
plane upon which Plato and St. Francis, Confucius and Elijah may
meet. Without being a Manichee one may reasonably see in the
history of mankind an angel of darkness in conflict with an angel of
light; and without in the least circumscribing the sphere of the
artist one may confidently assert that the highest art has invariably
expressed the highest morality. A great artist does not consciously
intend to be a great prophet. His prophesying comes by the way.
His impulse is to create imaginatively in the likeness of things felt
and seen; but precisely in proportion to the strength of his artistic
impulse he sees clearer and feels deeper into life than common folk.
He aims at winning from the chaos of life one more province for
the imagination of man; but the province when put upon the map
is perceived to be in the loftiest sense a moral as well as an imaginative triumph. "Art for art's sake" is in the event, "art for morality's
sake." The greatest artists are also those who have contributed most
to the morality of the Commonwealth. Morality is an accident of
the artist's accomplishment, though it is not the intention. It is
required of the artist that he should sincerely live for his art alone.
These other things are, thereafter, added unto him.

This is the heart of the matter. The artist must himself be sincere. Only so long as he obeys an impulse to express the thing he
sees, reaching into the unconquered spaces of life, is he protected
against falsehood. Responding to a genuine inspiration he will leave
the moral result of his endeavors to look after itself. But if he is, as
an artist, immoral; if he repeats a message which he has not himself
realized imaginatively, he is then at the mercy of mischance. Congreve, though not one of the very great artists of the world, was
within his limits sincere. He is therefore saved not only artistically
but morally. Vanbrugh, who accepted without examination artistic
conventions which had no real relation to the truth he might otherwise have expressed, is, both ways, as inevitably damned.

How shall we at last decide the critical and moral questions
raised in the course of this study? The evidence is before us; and
some liberty of dogmatism may, after so long an argument, be permitted. What is the position of Etherege, Wycherley, Congreve,
Vanbrugh and Farquhar in the light of all we have been able to see
and hear?

We have looked into a period of our social history unlike any that preceded it or followed. We found in Etherege a man who in temperament and mind accurately reflected this period in his personal character, and received a sincere impulse to reflect it artistically in his comedies. His sincerity as an artist has met the inevitable reward. His plays are morally as well as artistically sound. He felt and saw the comedy of contemporary life; and he honestly sought and found the means to express it. The result of his honesty and purity of motive as an artist is that, as soon as we enter the imaginative regions of his comedy, we are sensible that the laws are harmonious and just; they will bear inspection. We are sensible of a strange land; but it does not occur to us to question the finality of its laws so long as we remain within its bounds. They are not laws with which we are familiar to-day in the homes of Kensington or Mayfair; but having submitted our imagination to the author in the act of consenting to read his comedy, that suggestion can only intrude when the comedy is put away. Moreover, when the comedy is put away, we are aware that the morality of this strange country, just because Etherege was as an artist sincerely endeavoring to see life and express it, has a positive value of its own. We have contemplated a phase of human experience; realized it imaginatively. We have explored a mood of the human spirit which is in every age, though in this particular age it was more conspicuous. Etherege, aiming at beauty, has brought down truth as well; and, if from the standpoint of the narrow morality of this or that generation, truth may often seem an angel of darkness, from the standpoint of the higher morality of all time it is seen as an angel of light.

Wycherley followed. The truth of Wycherley is in the main the truth of Etherege. He was sufficiently the man of his period to enter and possess as his artistic right the comic world which Etherege had opened up before him. His comedies admirably illustrate the main point of our argument, that in art he who would save his moral shall lose it, and he that would lose his moral for art's sake shall find it. So long as Wycherley obeys a simple impulse to express the attitude towards life of his time the reader who enters his comedy from another world instinctively accepts the picture and is not offended. But when the singleness of Wycherley's artistic purpose is confused by a malignant puritanism, inconsistent with the temper of his comedy, then we are immediately arrested. Wycherley's whole fabric tumbles about us.

Wycherley's lapses are the exception. His plays are masterpieces of sustained comedy, broken only very rarely by the intrusions of the shorter catechist. *The Country Wife*, for example, is almost perfect. With the exception of the tea-drinking scene between Mr. Horner and the Fidgets it answers the severest test of imaginative sincerity; and, in proportion as it does so, it equally satisfies the severest test of morality. So long as the laws of Mr. Horner's comic kingdom are faithfully observed, Mr. Horner is quite immune from the attacks of Collier and his successors. Mr. Horner is in another world, whence there is no treaty of extradition for his attachment. When, for instance, he is accused of indecent gallantry, those of us who are seized of his imaginative kingdom already know that gallantry cannot here be indecent. It is a first law of the cloud-cuckoo-land of *The Country Wife* that the act of sex has no more suggestion of the indecently amorous than tumbling upstairs or losing one's hat in a gale. Wycherley has already created an atmosphere where passion is unable to breathe. Mr. Horner goes after his friend's wife precisely as boys go after their neighbor's apples. Either you have accepted this convention, and without further thought of the proprieties, enter with zest into the collection of Mr. Horner's china, or the comedy is worse than nonsense. Lamb was entirely accurate in this regard when he virtually describes Mr. Horner as a fairy. He was wrong when, and if, he assumed that Mr. Horner never had a prototype in real life. Mr. Horner, in fact, is a perfect fairy for the very reason that he is also a faithful portrait. It is because Mr. Horner imaginatively expresses his period so well that he is morally immune from the censure of any other period.

Wycherley, on the other hand, is fairly open to criticism when he breaks the laws of his own comedy—when the passionate satire of *The Plain Dealer* intrudes into the dispassionate comedy of *The Country Wife*. The illusion of fairyland is lost. Everyday values intrude into our thoughts. Mr. Horner as a comic figure is spiritually lost, in whose place we seem to see an ineligible guest for a modern house-party.

Vanbrugh and Farquhar inevitably come in here. What was accidental in Wycherley was fundamental in them. They took over the comic kingdom of Mr. Horner; but administered it according to the laws of Queen Anne. They accepted as the figures of their comedy characters which had no relation to their own imaginative vision of life, or their attitude towards society. They did not obey a simple artistic impulse to express something clearly seen and vividly felt. They accepted a formula whose significance was outworn, writing entertainingly within its bounds, and slurring where it was possible inconsistencies of which they were only half aware. The result of their artistic insincerity is, as ever, a moral as well as an imaginative degeneration. So long as Mr. Horner borrows the wives of his friends in the same spirit as he would borrow their books, he may proceed unchallenged and unashamed. But when Mr. Horner seduces one particular wife of one particular friend with every circumstance of suggestive ardor the case is different. Vanbrugh and

Farquhar read romantic love into Mr. Horner's affairs. They are trying to reconcile two inconsistent attitudes. Romantic love cannot be reconciled with a comic treatment of adultery. The result upon the reader is that, driven from one convention to another, he finally retires for refuge to the conventions of his own well-regulated life of every day. He then sees Vanbrugh's Loveless and Farquhar's Mr. Archer forcibly seducing a pretty woman in his immediate presence.

Congreve, like Etherege and Wycherley at his best, is immune from any such criticism. His comedies are the perfect expression of an attitude. They are as consistent in art as in morality. All we have found in the Comedy of Etherege is expressed in Congreve upon a higher imaginative level. Congreve saw more clearly what he had to express and drew with a firmer hand.

Congreve is the summit of our theme. He produced the most perfect specimens of the comedy we have studied. Nevertheless we must end upon a statute of limitations. A critic could no more put Congreve upon a level with Shakespeare than he could put Catullus upon a level with Homer, or Scarlatti upon a level with Beethoven. But if Congreve attained the extreme limit of beauty in the artistic expression of the life of his time, whence comes this sense of his inferiority to the greatest? The obvious answer is that Shakespeare's subjects are bigger than those of Congreve; that whereas Shakespeare expressed Falstaff and Othello, Congreve expressed Mirabell and Witwoud. But this difference of subject is not the root of the matter. It is a visible token of the contrast; not the contrast itself. The contrast itself is in the creative energy of the two men. Whereas Shakespeare was ardently impelled to look quite through the shows of things, to penetrate into the depths of himself and of the life he saw, to body forth in imagination secrets he was furiously urged to discover, Congreve was mildly driven to fashion an image of existence observed at ease, incuriously, with no ambition to pursue the spirit of truth into the dark. That almost invisible curl of the lip with which he seems to follow the movements of his creatures is not of a man who could be stirred in imagination to the depths. He is not less than Shakespeare because his subjects are less; for an artist's subjects, be they what they may, are never by one jot less or greater than the artist. Congreve is less than Shakespeare, because the mood in which he wrote is not that of a man whose imagination is, like Shakespeare's, working at the limit of pressure. If after-generations had lost his work entirely, they would have lost a perfect artistic reflection of English Society at a particular period. Had they entirely lost the work of Shakespeare, they would have lost an embattled fortress upon boundaries which part the waters of chaos from the solid earth redeemed by great artists for the habitation of man.

BONAMY DOBRÉE

[Restoration Comedy]†

* * * "I could never connect these sports of a witty fancy," Lamb wrote in his famous essay upon this comedy, "in any shape with any result to be drawn from them to imitation in real life. They are a world of themselves—almost as much as fairyland. . . . They break through no laws of conscientious restraints. They know of none. They have got out of Christendom into the land of—what shall I call it?—of cuckoldry—the Utopia of gallantry, where pleasure is duty, and the manners perfect freedom. It is altogether a speculative scene of things, which has no reference whatever to the world that is."

But that this is untrue, even his admiring contemporaries had to admit. "Perhaps," Leigh Hunt commented, "he thought that he could even play his readers a child's trick, and persuade them that Congreve's fine ladies and gentlemen were doing nothing but 'making as if.' Most assuredly he was mistaken." Lamb's trick, indeed, was innocent enough; he was trying to persuade his readers to become Congreve's also, in spite of their prudish horror. For Leigh Hunt was right; and Macaulay, though his moral judgment was irrelevant, was not wrong in his facts: "A hundred little tricks are employed to make the fictitious world appear like the actual world." And Hazlitt in a brilliant passage showed that although this comedy might have no reference whatever to the world that is, it was very like a society that had been; "we are almost transported to another world, and escape from this dull age. . . ."

Lamb's delightful argument does of course contain a useful truth; we must not confuse moral and aesthetic values. But it would not be of great importance at the present day in connection with Restoration comedy were it not that many critics accept his dicta blindly; it is constantly assumed that to appreciate Restoration comedy we must accept Elia's[1] attitude. Yet if we read this comedy in Lamb's spirit, we shall certainly find it very refreshing, but we shall miss seeing what it really was.

It is admittedly tiresome, but it seems unavoidable, to have to approach this work through Collier and Swift, Johnson, Macaulay, and Taine, and excuse its "impurity." For "impurity" was its most important subject. How could it avoid dealing with sex when the distinguishing characteristic of Restoration comedy down to Con-

† From Bonamy Dobrée, *Restoration Comedy: 1660–1720* (Oxford: The Clarendon Press, 1924), pp. 22–26, 171–73. Reprinted by permission of the publisher. 1. I.e., Lamb's; he wrote under the name Elia [Editor].

greve is that it is concerned with the attempt to rationalize sexual relationships? It is this that makes it different from any other comedy that has ever been written; but if we regard it as creating a wholly fantastic world we shall not see this. It said in effect, "Here is life lived upon certain assumptions; see what it becomes." It also dealt, as no other comedy has ever done, with a subject that arose directly out of this, namely, sex-antagonism, a consequence of the experimental freedom allowed to women, which gave matter for some of its most brilliant scenes.

"Sex in Congreve," Mr. Palmer says, "is a battle of the wits. It is not a battlefield of the emotions"; but this was so in real life as well as in the plays of Congreve. "When sex laws remain rigid . . . ," writes Mr. Heape,[2] "while society becomes more and more complicated and the life led by its members more purely artificial, the probability of the growth of drastic sex-antagonism is vastly increased, becomes indeed, a certainty." But although men recognized with Hobbes that in the political world liberty and security are incompatible, and that a compromise has to be made, they did not see the necessity of applying the maxim in the social world. Men may not want the bonds of marriage, but once married they want to keep their wives to themselves. Women may be inconstant, but they want to be secure. Thus "virtue" retains its social prestige. This was perfectly understood in those days, and was exquisitely phrased by Ariana speaking to Courtal (Etherege, *She Would if She Could*, v. i). "I know you would think it as great a scandal to be thought to have an inclination for marriage, as we should be believed willing to take our freedom without it." Indeed, a woman's virtue was of great importance, unless she was one of the king's mistresses. Says Lady Fidget to Horner (Wycherley, *The Country Wife*, iv. iii): "But first, my dear sir, you must promise to have a care of my dear honor," because (v. iv) "Our reputation! Lord, why should you not think that we women make use of our reputation, as you men of yours, only to deceive the world with less suspicion?"

But if sex did indeed become a battle of the wits rather than a question of the emotions, it must not be assumed that the figures represented on the stage were any less flesh and blood than their human types. Certainly, and here is the importance for us, the audiences did not regard the actors as puppets playing at a life of their own, but as men living an existence which they were almost invited to share.[3]

But let us repeat that the object of the bawdry in these plays was not to tickle the desires of the audience. The motto of Restoration comedy was not "Thrive, lechery, thrive," nor its subject the suc-

2. *Sex Antagonism*, by W. Heape, F.R.S.   to *Marriage à la Mode*.
3. As is made quite clear by the Epilogue

cessful pursuit of the town coquette by the town gallant, though this provided many scenes. Its great joke was not "and swearing she would not consent, consented." It had a profounder philosophy. Its joke, indeed, is rather a grim one; it is more accurate to say that it is

> How nature doth compel us to lament
> Our most persisted deeds,

for having consented, she regretted; he, having instituted liberty, repented of it.

But apart from these considerations, and apart from Lamb, does not the whole question of impurity, and any attempt to justify it, seem a little absurd? For even if we abhor the idea of sexual looseness in real life, this does not preclude the possibility of turning the common facts of life into art. No one objects to "adultery being part of the action" in *Agamemnon*, *The Rape of Lucrece*, or *Anna Karenina*. And just as in these works something definite is made of the theme, so in our period the writers of comedy who were also artists, crystallized sex excitement into a comic appearance. Therefore the only questions arising are these: If we are disgusted at the "impurities" which are the material of much of this comedy, are they handled with sufficient skill to make us indifferent to the subject-matter? Or is there, in spite of much that disgusts us, enough beauty and intelligence to overbalance our revulsion in favor of delight? Or can we simply accept the life of the time, and without associating it with ourselves, derive interest and pleasure from the observation and understanding of men whose outlook on life died with their erring bodies some two centuries ago? Surely this seems the reasonable attitude. Indeed, condemnation at this distance, emotion at two hundred years, itself provides a target for the comic imps.

* * *

If we were to try to sum up what the comedy of this period as a whole achieved, it would be to say that it gave a brilliant picture of its time rather than a new insight into man. Taine has wondered why, with all its mastery of vivid description, racy idiom, and polished phrase, this English comedy did not come to a fuller perfection, did not reach the level of Molière, and, we would add, of Jonson. Apart from the fact that astonishing genius of every kind is not to be met with in every decade, the explanation perhaps lies in this: these writers never came to the condition of seeing life whole, though what they saw they perceived very clearly. They loved it with Etherege, or, like Wycherley, snatched from it a fearful joy, or, like Congreve, tried in their dissatisfaction to distill from it something exquisite: they hardly ever related it, as Molière nearly always did, to a larger world; they did not try to construct something terrific out of it as Jonson was able to do.

Their time forced them to be too critical, though it is hardly fair to blame a time for the very peculiarities that gave them their best material. But they were forced to be too moral, that is, too engaged with the immediate application of their ideas. It is in this sense that the word moral has been used throughout: nothing so foolish is suggested as that art and morality are incompatible, any more than that they are necessary to one another. Without a moral vision there would have been no *Divine Comedy*, no *War and Peace*. Without the notions of good and evil and divine justice there would have been no Greek tragedy and no *Paradise Lost*. But the morality of the Restoration dramatists, taken as a whole, was not a universal vision; it could not be. For the medieval view was dead, had died in the iron verse of Milton; eighteenth-century scepticism was being born, had made its appearance in the shattering syllogisms of Hobbes and the trenchant strokes of Shaftesbury. Modern curiosity was awakening, and the old moral order lay in ruins about the scaffold of a king. The dramatists of that day were almost necessarily forced to be content with morality as conceived by the *honnête homme*. Wycherley could never imagine, as did Goethe's *Faust*, that all experience whatsoever might be good: Congreve would never see that the art of graceful living might, by its very fineness, miss something fundamental in life, and destroy the directness he was eager to preserve.

These are limitations; but the want of an inspiring, comprehensive philosophy such as was Dante's to use, the absence of a feeling of revolt such as urged Shelley to his most sustained flights, has its advantages. For then the creative impulse is bent inwards upon the thing, it will not be satisfied until the object made has complete validity within itself: it cannot afford to slip into life. Thus lapses into realism which scarcely injure the structure of much Elizabethan comedy are ruinous here, and it is because this kind of perfection requires a more consummate and conscious artistry that so few comedies of this period are satisfactory. Even when complete in themselves they do not always include enough "spiritual nourishment," to use Synge's analytic phrase, and Etherege's perfect creation, *The Man of Mode*, compared with great comedy, is Sèvres-china painting to a canvas of El Greco. Dryden, more comprehensive, was, except in one great tragedy, always a little too swayed by his experimental curiosity to attain that unity which alone can make such work close-sealed.

But *The Country Wife* and *The Way of the World* are beyond Taine's criticism, and the former can take its place among the great masterpieces of the ages, to stand beside *Volpone*. *The Way of the*

World will always remain a trifle isolated, not because it came to so little, but because, working within such severe limits Congreve succeeded in concentrating in it matter for which others have found larger, easier mediums more convenient. It is unique—even if the comedies of Corneille may claim affinity—and likely to remain so, yet it belongs inalienably to its period: it is built upon its contemporaries, and it is by it and *The Country Wife* that the achievement of the period may be measured. It is hard to imagine that in any civilized age they will not be regarded as glories of our literature, gems of our theatrical inheritance.

L. C. KNIGHTS

Restoration Comedy: The Reality and the Myth†

* * * Apart from the presentation of incidental and unrelated "wit" (which soon becomes as tiring as the epigrams of the "good talker"), Restoration comedy has two main interests—the behavior of the polite and of pretenders to politeness, and some aspects of sexual relationships. Critics have made out a case for finding in one or other of these themes a unifying principle and a serious base for the comedy of manners. According to Miss Lynch, the "thoroughly conventionalized social mode" of the courtly circle "was discovered to have manifestly comic aspects, both when awkwardly misinterpreted, and when completely fulfilled through personalities to which, however, it could not give complete expression,"[1] and both these discrepancies were exploited by Etherege and his successors. Bonamy Dobrée, attributing to the comic dramatists "a deep curiosity, and a desire to try new ways of living," finds that "the distinguishing characteristic of Restoration comedy down to Congreve is that it is concerned with the attempt to rationalize sexual relationships. It is this that makes it different from any other comedy that has ever been written. . . . It said in effect, 'Here is life lived upon certain assumptions; see what it becomes.' It also dealt, as no other comedy has ever done, with a subject that arose directly out of this, namely sex-antagonism, a consequence of the experimental freedom allowed to women, which gave matter for some of its most brilliant scenes."[2]

† From *Explorations: Essays in Criticism Mainly on the Literature of the Seventeenth Century* (London: Chatto & Windus, 1946), pp. 135–49. Copyright 1947 by George W. Stewart Publisher, Inc. Reprinted by permission of New York University Press and Chatto & Windus Ltd.
1. K. M. Lynch, *The Social Mode of Restoration Comedy*, p. 216.
2. Bonamy Dobrée, *Restoration Comedy*, pp. 22–23.

These accounts, as developed, certainly look impressive, and if
Restoration comedy really answered to them—if it had something
fresh and penetrating to say on sex and social relations—there
would be no need to complain, even if one found the "solutions"
distasteful. But Miss Lynch's case, at all events, depends on a vigorous reading into the plays of values which are not there, values
which could not possibly be expressed, in fact, in the prose of any
of the dramatists. (The candid reader can turn up the passages
selected by Miss Lynch in support of her argument, and see if they
are not all in the factitious, superficial mode that I have described.)

We may consider, by way of illustration, Etherege's *The Man of
Mode*. When the play opens, Dorimant ("the finest of all fine gentlemen in Restoration comedy") is trying to rid himself of an old
mistress, Mrs. Loveit, before taking up with a new, Bellinda, whilst
Young Bellair, in love with Emilia, is trying to find some way out of
marrying Harriet, an heiress whom his father has brought to town
for him. The entertainment is made up of these two sets of complications, together with an exhibition of the would-be modishness of
Sir Fopling Flutter. Events move fast. After a night spent in various sociabilities Dorimant keeps an appointment with Bellinda at 5
A.M. Letting her out of his lodgings an hour or so later, and swearing to be discreet "By all the Joys I have had, and those you keep in
store," he is surprised by his companions, and in the resulting confusion Bellinda finds herself paying an unwilling visit to Mrs.
Loveit. Dorimant appears and is rated by the women before he
"flings off." Meanwhile Young Bellair and Emilia have secretly married. Dorimant, his equanimity recovered, turns up for the exposure,
followed by his mistresses. The lovers are forgiven, the mistresses
are huddled off the stage, and it is decided that Dorimant, who, the
previous day, had ingratiated himself with Harriet's mother, and
whose "soul has quite given up her liberty," shall be allowed to pay
court to the heiress.

It seems to me that what the play provides—apart from the
briskly handled intrigue—is a demonstration of the physical stamina
of Dorimant. But Miss Lynch sees further. For her, Dorimant is
"the fine flowering of Restoration culture." Illustrating her theory
of the double standard, she remarks: "We laugh at Sir Fopling
Flutter because he so clumsily parodies social fashions which Dorimant interprets with unfailing grace and distinction. We laugh at
Dorimant because his assumed affectation admits of so poor and
incomplete an expression of an attractive and vigorous
personality."[3] The "unfailing grace and distinction" are perhaps
not much in evidence in Dorimant's spiteful treatment of Mrs.

3. *The Social Mode of Restoration Comedy*, p. 181.

Loveit;[4] but even if we ignore those brutish scenes we are forced to ask, How do we know that there *is* this "attractive and vigorous personality" beneath the conventional forms? Dorimant's intrigues are of no more human significance than those of a barn-yard cock, and as for what Miss Lynch calls "his really serious affair with Harriet" (I feel this deserves a *sic*), it is purely theatrical, and the "pangs of love" are expressed in nothing but the conventional formulae: "She's gone, but she has left a pleasing Image of herself behind that wanders in my Soul." The answer to the question posed is that Miss Lynch's account is a mere assumption. Nothing that Dorimant actually *says* will warrant it—and nothing in the whole of Restoration comedy—in the words actually spoken—allows us a glimpse of those other "personalities" to which the conventional social modes "could not give complete expression." The "real values"[5] simply are not there.

A minor point can be made in passing. It is just possible to claim that Restoration comedy contains "social criticism" in its handling of "the vulgar." "Come Mr. Sharper," says Congreve's Belinda, "you and I will take a turn, and laugh at the vulgar; both the great vulgar and the small," and Etherege's Lady Townley expresses the common attitude of the polite towards the social nuisances: "We should love wit, but for variety be able to divert ourselves with the extravagancies of those who want it." The butts, unfortunately, are only shown as fools by the discrepancy between their ambitions and their achievements, not because their ambitions are puerile. The subject is hardly worth discussing, since it is obviously nothing but an easily satisfied sense of superiority that is diverted by the "variety" of a constant succession of Dapperwits, Froths and Fopling Flutters. "When a humour takes in London," Tom Brown remarked, "they ride it to death ere they leave it. The primitive Christians were not persecuted with half that variety as the poor unthinking beaus are tormented with upon the theater. . . . A huge great muff, and a gaudy ribbon hanging at a bully's backside, is an excellent jest, and new-invented curses, as, Stap my vitals, damn my diaphragm, slit my wind pipe, sink me ten thousand fathom deep, rig up a new beau, though in the main 'tis but the same everlasting coxcomb."[6]

4. See II, ii and V, i, where Dorimant, trying to force a quarrel with Mrs. Loveit, attributes to her a fondness for Sir Fopling. The first of these scenes was too much for Etherege, and he makes Bellinda say: "He's given me the proof which I desired of his love,/ But 'tis a proof of his ill nature too./ I wish I had not seen him use her so." But this is soon forgotten, and we are not, of course, called on to register an unfavorable judgment of Dorimant.

5. "The love affairs of Courtal and Ariana, Freeman and Gatty [in *She Wou'd if She Cou'd*] are similarly embarrassed by social convention. . . . The conduct of these polite lovers acquires comic vitality through the continually suggested opposition of artificial and real values."—*Op. cit.*, p. 152.
6. Tom Brown, *Works,* Vol. III, *Amusements Comical and Serious,* "At the Playhouse," p. 39.

In the matter of sexual relations Restoration comedy is entirely dominated by a narrow set of conventions. The objection that it is only certain characters, not the dramatists themselves, who accept them can be more freely encountered when the assumptions that are expressed most frequently have been briefly illustrated.

The first convention is, of course, that constancy in love, especially in marriage, is a bore. Vanbrugh, who was the most uneasy if not the most honest of the comic dramatists (I think that in *The Provok'd Wife* he shows as unusually honest), unambiguously attributes this attitude to Sir John Brute:

> What cloying meat is love—when matrimony's the sauce to it! Two years marriage has debaunch'd my five senses. . . . No boy was ever so weary of his tutor, no girl of her bib, no nun of doing penance, or old maid of being chaste, as I am of being married. Sure there's a secret curse entail'd upon the very name of wife!
>
> The woman's well enough; she has no vice that I know of, but she's a wife, and—damn a wife![7]

What Vanbrugh saw as a fit sentiment for Sir John had by that time (1697) served the Restoration stage—without change—for thirty years. In *She Wou'd if She Cou'd* Etherege had exhibited Sir Oliver Cockwood in an identical vein: "A pox of this tying man and woman together, for better, for worse." "To have a mistress love thee entirely" is "a damn'd trouble." "There are sots that would think themselves happy in such a Lady; but to a true bred Gentleman all lawful solace is abomination."[8] If Sir Oliver is a fool it is only because he is a trifle gross in his expression. 'If you did but know, Madam," says the polite Freeman, "'what an odious thing it is to be thought to love a Wife in good company."[9] And the convention is constantly turning up in Congreve. "There is no creature perfectly civil but a husband," explains Mrs. Frail, "for in a little time he grows only rude to his wife, and that is the highest good breeding, for it begets his civility to other people."[1] "Marry her! Marry her!" Fainall advises Mirabell, "Be half as well acquainted with her charms, as you are with her defects, and my life on't, you are your own man again."[2] And Witwoud: "A wit should no more be sincere than a woman constant; one argues a decay of parts, as t'other of beauty."[3] Appetite, it seems (and this is the second assumption), needs perpetually fresh stimulus. This is the faith of Rhodophil in *Marriage à la Mode* and of Constant in *The Provoked Wife*, as well as of Wycherley's old procuress, Mrs. Joyner. "If our wives would suffer us but now and then to make excursions," Rhodophil explains to Palamede, "the benefit of our

7. *The Provok'd Wife*, I, i; II, i.
8. *She Wou'd if She Cou'd*, I, i; III, iii.
9. *Ibid.*, III, iii.

1. *Love for Love*, I, ii.
2. *The Way of the World*, I, ii.
3. *Ibid.*

variety would be theirs; instead of one continued, lazy, tired love, they would, in their turns, have twenty vigorous, fresh, and active lovers."[4] "Would anything but a madman complain of uncertainty?" asks Congreve's Angelica, for "security is an insipid thing, and the overtaking and possessing of a wish, discovers the folly of the chase."[5] And Fainall, in *The Way of the World*, speaks for a large class when he hints at a liking for sauce—a little gentleman's relish—to his seductions: "I'd no more play with a man that slighted his ill fortune than I'd make love to a woman who undervalued the loss of her reputation."[6] Fainall, of course, is what he is, but the attitude that makes sexual pleasure "the bliss," that makes woman "delicious"—something to be savored—as well as "damned" and "destructive," demands, for its support, "the pleasure of a chase."[7]

> Would you long preserve your lover?
> Would you still his goddess reign?
> Never let him all discover,
> Never let him much obtain.[8]

Restoration comedy used to be considered outrageously outspoken, but such stuff as this, far from being "outspoken," hovers on the outskirts of sexual relations, and sees nothing but the titillation of appetite (" 'Tis not the success," Collier observed, "but the manner of gaining it which is all in all").[9] Sex is a hook baited with tempting morsels;[1] it is a thirst quencher;[2] it is a cordial;[3] it is a dish to feed on;[4] it is a bunch of grapes;[5] it is anything but sex. (This, of course, explains why some people can combine a delighted approval of Restoration comedy with an unbalanced repugnance for such

4. *Marriage à la Mode*, II, i. Cf. *The Provok'd Wife*, III, i: *Constant*, "There's a poor sordid slavery in marriage, that turns the flowing tide of honour, and sinks us to the lowest ebb of infamy. 'Tis a corrupted soil: Ill-nature, sloth, cowardice, and dirt, are all its product."
5. *Love for Love*, IV, iii.
6. *The Way of the World*, I, i.
7. *The Old Bachelor*, I, i; III, ii ("Oh thou delicious, damned, dear destructive woman!"); IV, ii.
8. *Ibid.*, II, ii.
9. *A Short View of the Profaneness and Immorality of the English Stage*, Fifth Edition, 1738, p. 116.
1. " 'Tis true you are so eager in pursuit of the temptation, that you save the devil the trouble of leading you into it: nor is it out of discretion that you don't swallow the very hook yourselves have baited, but . . . what you meant for a whet turns the edge of your puny stomachs."—*The Old Bachelor*, I, i. "Strike

Heartwell home, before the bait's worn off the hook. Age will come. He nibbled fairly yesterday, and no doubt will be eager enough to-day to swallow the temptation."—*Ibid.*, III, i.
2. "What was my pleasure is become my duty: and I have as little stomach to her now as if I were her husband. . . . Pox on't that a man can't drink without quenching his thirst."—*The Plain Dealer*, III, i.
3. "You must get you a mistress, Rhodophil. That indeed, is living upon cordials; but as fast as one fails, you must supply it with another." *Marriage à la Mode*, I, i.
4. Because our husbands cannot feed on one dish, therefore we must be starved."—*Ibid.*, III, i.
5. "The only way to keep us new to one another, is never to enjoy, as they keep grapes, by hanging them upon a line; they must touch nothing, if you would preserve them fresh."—*Ibid.*, V, i.

modern literature as deals sincerely and realistically with sexual relationships.)

Now the objection referred to above was that sentiments such as these are not offered for straightforward acceptance. Many of them are attributed to characters plainly marked as Wicked (Maskwell, for example, is the black-a-vised villain of melodrama), or, more frequently, as trivial, and the dramatist can therefore dissociate himself. He may even be engaged in showing his audience the explicit, logical consequences of the half-unconscious premises on which they base their own lives, saying, as Mr. Dobrée has it, "Here is life lived upon certain assumptions; see what it becomes." To this there are several answers. The first is that reflections of the kind that I have quoted are indistinguishable in tone and style from the general epigrammatic stock-in-trade (the audience was not altogether to be blamed if, as Congreve complained, they could not at first "distinguish betwixt the character of a Witwoud and a Lovewit"); and they are largely "exhibited," just as all the self-conscious witticisms are exhibited, for the sake of their immediate "comic" effect. One has only to note the laughter of a contemporary audience at a revival, and the places where the splutters occur, to realize how much of the fun provides a rather gross example of tendency wit.[6] The same attitudes, moreover, are manipulated again and again, turning up with the stale monotony of jokes on postcards, and the play that is made with them demands only the easiest, the most superficial, response. But it is, after all, useless to argue about the degree of detachment, the angle at which these attitudes and assumptions are presented. As soon as one selects a particular comedy for that exercise one realizes that all is equally grist to the mill and that the dramatist (there is no need, here, to make distinctions) has no coherent attitude of his own. A consistent artistic purpose would not be content to express itself in a style that allows so limited, so local an effect.

But it is the triviality that one comes back to. In Dryden's *Marriage à la Mode* the characters accept the usual conventions: constancy is dull, and love only thrives on variety.

> PALAMEDE. O, now I have found it! you dislike her for no other
> reason but because she's your wife.

6. The Freudian "censor" is at times projected in the form of the stage puritan. The plays written soon after the Commonwealth period appealed to Royalist prejudice by satirizing the "seemingly precise"; and even later, when "the bonfires of devotion," "the bellows of zeal," were forgotten, a good deal of the self-conscious swagger of indecency seems to have been directed against "our protestant husbands," city merchants, aldermen and the like; the "daring" effect was intensified by postulating a shockable audience somewhere—not necessarily in the theater. Not that the really obscene jokes were merely bravado: Collier quite rightly remarked that "the modern poets seem to use smut as the old ones did Machines, to relieve a fainting situation."—*A Short View*, Fifth Edition, p. 4.

RHODOPHIL. And is not that enough? All that I know of her
perfections now, is only by memory ... At last we arrived at
that point, that there was nothing left in us to make us new
to one another ...

PALAMEDE. The truth is, your disease is very desperate; but,
though you cannot be cured, you may be patched up a little:
you must get you a mistress, Rhodophil. That, indeed, is living
upon cordials; but, as fast as one fails, you must supply it with
another.

The mistress that Rhodophil selects is Melantha, whom Palamede
is to marry; Palamede falls in love with Doralice, Rhodophil's wife,
and the ensuing complications provide sufficient entertainment (the
grotto scene, III, ii, is really funny). Mr. Dobrée, however, regards
the play as a witty exposure of the impossibility of rationalizing sex
relations, as Palamede and Rhodophil attempt to rationalize them.
Dryden "laughs morality back into its rightful place, as the scheme
which ultimately makes life most comfortable."[7] But what Dryden
actually does is to *use* the conventions for the amusement they
afford, not to examine them. The level at which the play works is
fairly indicated by the opening song:

> Why should a foolish marriage vow,
> Which long ago was made,
> Oblige us to each other now,
> When passion is decayed?
> We loved, and we loved, as long as we could,
> 'Till our love was loved out in us both;
> But our marriage is dead, when the pleasure is fled:
> 'Twas pleasure first made it an oath.
>
> If I have pleasures for a friend,
> And further love in store,
> What wrong has he, whose joys did end,
> And who could give no more?
> 'Tis a madness that he should be jealous of me,
> Or that I should bar him of another:
> For all we can gain, is to give ourselves pain,
> When neither can hinder the other.

The lovers make no attempt to "rationalize sex" for the simple reason that genuine sexual feelings no more enter into the play as a
whole than feelings of any kind enter into the song. (The obviously
faked emotions of that heroic plot are, after all, relevant—and
betraying.) And according to Mr. Dobrée, "In one sense the whole
idea of Restoration comedy is summed up in the opening song of
Marriage à la Mode."[8]

In a sense, too, Mr. Dobrée is right. Restoration comedy nowhere

7. *Restoration Comedy*, p. 133. 8. *Ibid.*, p. 106.

provides us with much more of the essential stuff of human experience than we have here. Even Congreve, by common account the
best of the comic writers, is no exception. I have said that his verbal
pattern often seems to be quite unrelated to an individual mode of
perceiving. At best it registers a very limited mode. Restoration
prose is all "social" in its tone, implications and general tenor, but
Congreve's observation is *merely* of the public surface. And Congreve, too, relies on the conventional assumptions. In *The Way of
the World*, it is true, they are mainly given to the bad and the
foolish to express: it is Fainall who discourses on the pleasures of
disliking one's wife, and Witwoud who maintains that only old age
and ugliness ensure constancy. And Mirabell, who is explicitly
opposed to some aspects of contemporary manners, goes through
the common forms in a tone of rather weary aloofness: "I wonder,
Fainall, that you who are married, and of consequence should be
discreet, will suffer your wife to be of such a party." But Congreve
himself is not above raising a cheap snigger;[9] and, above all, the
characters with some life in them have nothing to fall back on—
nothing, that is, except the conventional, and conventionally limited, pleasures of sex. Millamant, who says she loathes the country
and hates the town, expects to draw vitality from the excitement
of incessant solicitation:

> I'll be solicited to the very last, nay, and afterwards ... I
> should think I was poor and had nothing to bestow, if I were
> reduced to an inglorious ease, and freed from the agreeable
> fatigues of solicitation . . . Oh, I hate a lover that can dare to
> think he draws a moment's air, independent of the bounty of his
> mistress. There is not so impudent a thing in nature, as the saucy
> look of an assured man, confident of success. The pedantic arro-
> gance of a very husband has not so pragmatical an air.

Everyone seems to have found Millamant intelligent and attractive,
but her attitude is not far removed from that expressed in

> Would you long preserve your lover?
> Would you still his goddess reign?

and she shares with characters who are decidedly not attractive a
disproportionate belief in "the pleasure of a chase." Which is not
surprising in view of her other occupations and resources; visiting,
writing and receiving letters, tea parties and small talk make up a
round that is never for a moment enlivened by the play of genuine
intelligence.[1] And although Congreve recognizes, at times, the trivi-

9. Ay there's my grief; that's the sad
change of life,/ To lose my title, and yet
keep my wife./ *The Way of the World*,
II, ii.
1. As Lady Brute remarks, "After all, a
woman's life would be a dull business, if
it were not for the men ... We shou'd
never blame Fate for the shortness of
our days; our time would hang
wretchedly upon our hands."—*The Provok'd Wife*, III, iii.

ality of his characters,[2] it is to the world whose confines were the
Court, the drawing-room, the play-house and the park—a world
completely lacking the real sophistication and self-knowledge that
might, in some measure, have redeemed it—that he limits his
appeal.

It is, indeed, hard to resist the conclusion that "society"—the
smart town society that sought entertainment at the theaters—was
fundamentally bored.[3] In *The Man of Mode* Emilia remarks of
Medley, "I love to hear him talk o' the intrigues, let 'em be never
so dull in themselves, he'll make 'em pleasant i' the relation," and
the idiotic conversation that follows (II, i), affording us a glimpse
of what Miss Lynch calls "the most brilliant society which Restoration comedy has to offer,"[4] suggests in more than one way how
badly society *needed* to be entertained. It is the boredom—the constant need for titillation—that helps to explain not only the heroic
"heightening" of emotion, but the various scenic effects, the devices
of staging and costume that became popular at this period.
(Charles II "almost died of laughing" at Nell Gwynn's enormous
hat.) The conventions—of sexual pursuit, and so on—were an
attempt to make life interesting—an impossible job for those who
were aware of so limited a range of human potentialities.

The dominating mood of Restoration comedy is, by common
account, a cynical one. But one cannot even say that there is here,
in contrast to naïve Romantic fervors, the tough strength of disillu-
sion. If—recognizing that there is a place in the educational process
for, say, La Rochefoucauld—one finds the "cynicism" of the plays
distasteful, it is because it is easy and superficial; the attitudes that
we are presented with are based on so meagre an amount of observation and experience. Thus, "Elle retrouvait dans l'adultère toutes
les platitudes du marriage" has, superficially, much the same meaning as, "I find now, by sad experience, that a mistress is much more
chargeable than a wife, and after a little time too, grows full as dull
and insignificant." But whereas the first sentence has behind it the
whole of *Madame Bovary*, the second comes from *Sir Martin
Mar-all*, which (although Dryden shares the honors with the Duke
of Newcastle) is perhaps the stupidest play I have ever read, and
the context is imbecility.

But the superficiality is betrayed at every turn—by the obvious
rhythms of the interspersed songs, as well as by the artificial ele-

<hr>

2. *Mirabell*: You had the leisure to entertain a herd of fools; things who visit
you from their excessive idleness; bestowing on your easiness that time which
is the encumbrance of their lives. How
can you find delight in such society?—
The Way of the World, II, i.
3. The constitution, habits and demands
of the theater audience are admirably il-

lustrated by Alexandre Beljame in that
neglected classic of scholarship, *Le Public et les Hommes de Lettres en Angleterre
au Dix-Huitième Siècle*, 1660–1740. See
also C. V. Deane, *Dramatic Theory and
the Rhymed Heroic Play*, Chapter I, Section 6.
4. *The Social Mode of Restoration Comedy*, p. 177.

gance of the prose. And the cynicism is closely allied with—merges into—sentimentality. One thinks of the sentimentally conceived Fidelia in the resolutely "tough" *Plain Dealer;* and there is no doubt that the audience was meant to respond sympathetically when, at the end of *Love for Love,* Angelica declared her love for Valentine: "Had I the world to give you, it could not make me worthy of so generous a passion; here's my hand, my heart was always yours, and struggled very hard to make this utmost trial of your virtue." There is, of course, a good deal of loose emotion in the heroic plays, written—it is useful to remember—for the same audience:

> I'm numbed, and fixed, and scarce my eyeballs move;
> I fear it is the lethargy of love!
> 'Tis he; I feel him now in every part:
> Like a new lord he vaunts about my heart;
> Surveys, in state, each corner of my breast,
> While poor fierce I, that was, am dispossessed.[5]
> A secret pleasure trickles through my veins:
> It works about the inlets of my soul,
> To feel thy touch, and pity tempts the pass:
> But the tough metal of my heart resists;
> 'Tis warmed with the soft fire, not melted down.[6]

"Feeling," in Dryden's serious plays, is fairly represented by such passages as these, and Dryden, we know, was not alone in admiring the Fletcherian "pathos." But it is the lyric verse of the period that provides the strongest confirmatory evidence of the kind of bad taste that is in question. It is not merely that in Etherege, Sedley, and Dorset the feeling comes from much nearer the surface than in the Metaphysicals and the Caroline poets, intellectual "wit" no longer strengthens and controls the feeling. Conventional attitudes are rigged out in a conventional vocabulary and conventional images. (The stock outfit—the "fair eyes" that "wound," the "pleasing pains," the "sighs and tears," the "bleeding hearts" and "flaming darts"—can be studied in any anthology.)[7] There is, in consequence, a pervasive strain of sentimental vulgarity.

> Farewell, ungrateful traitor!
> Farewell, my perjured swain!
> Let never injured creature
> Believe a man again.
> The pleasure of possessing
> Surpasses all expressing,

5. *The Conquest of Granada,* Part I, III, i.
6. *Don Sebastian,* III, i.
7. See, for example, Aphra Behn's "Love in fantastic triumph sate," Buckingham's *To his Mistress* ("Phyllis, though your all powerful charms"), Dryden's "Ask not the cause why sullen spring," and "Ah, how sweet it is to love," and Sedley's *To Chloris*—all in *The Oxford Book of English Verse,* or Ault's *Seventeenth Century Lyrics.*

> But 'tis too short a blessing,
>   And love too long a pain.
>
> . . . .
>
> The passion you pretended,
>   Was only to obtain;
> But when the charm is ended,
>   The charmer you disdain.
> Your love by ours we measure
> Till we have lost our treasure,
> But dying is a pleasure
>   When living is a pain.

This piece of music-hall sentiment comes from Dryden's *The Span-ish Friar*, and it does not stand alone. The mode that was to pro-duce, among other things of equal merit, "When lovely woman stoops to folly," had its origin in the lyrics of the Restoration period. Most of these were written by the group connected with the theaters, and they serve to underline the essential criticism of the plays. The criticism that defenders of Restoration comedy need to answer is not that the comedies are "immoral," but that they are trivial, gross, and dull.

THOMAS H. FUJIMURA

[*The Man of Mode* as a Comedy of Wit]†

* * * Etherege's last play, *The Man of Mode, or Sir Fopling Flutter* (1676), is one of the best examples of the comedy of wit. In the prologue Sir Car Scroope implied that one would find "Nature well drawn and Wit" in this comedy; and Langbaine commended its naturalism: "This Play is written with great Art and Judgment, and is acknowledg'd by all, to be as true Comedy, and the Charac-ters as well drawn to the Life, as any Play that has been Acted since the Restauration of the *English* Stage."[1] The contemporaries of Etherege noted particularly this fact of realistic portraiture, and there was much speculation as to the originals of characters like Dorimant, Sir Fopling, and Medley.

It is a failure to appreciate the realistic technique and the natur-alistic basis which has led to an underestimation of the play's true merits. On the one hand, we have Steele's moralistic censure of the play, in the *Spectator* #65, as "a perfect contradiction to good manners, good sense, and common honesty," and of Dorimant as "a direct knave in his designs, and a clown in his language." On the

† From Thomas H. Fujimura, *The Res-toration of Comedy of Wit* (Princeton, N.J.: Princteon University Press, 1952), pp. 104–16. Reprinted by permission of the publisher.
1. Langbaine, *An Account of the Eng-lish Dramatick Poets*, p. 187.

other hand, we have the "manners" view that the play is "a more exquisite and airy picture of the manners of that age than any other extant."[2] Neither of these estimates does justice to the comedy, for they both fail to appreciate the essential character of the play and the two main elements in it—the wit and the naturalistic characterization. *The Man of Mode* is a comedy of wit, with the usual outwitting situations involving naturalistically conceived characters.

Among the major figures, Dorimant is perhaps the least appreciated by modern readers, largely because the naturalistic characterization is not recognized. He is too often dismissed as a cruel and selfish rake; whereas he is actually a superb portrait of a Truewit. Dennis, in his defense of the play, pointed out that "*Dorimont* is a young Courtier, haughty, vain, and prone to Anger, amorous, false, and inconstant," because this is the true nature of young men as described by Aristotle in his *Rhetoric*, and the dramatist must be true to life (that is, be a naturalistic writer).[3] Dennis also pointed out that Rochester was the model for the part: "all the World was charm'd with *Dorimont*; . . . it was unanimously agreed, that he had in him several of the Qualities of *Wilmot Earl of Rochester*, as, his Wit, his spirit, his amorous Temper, the Charms that he had for the fair Sex, his Falshood, and his Inconstancy; the agreeable Manner of his chiding his Servants . . . ; and lastly, his repeating, on every Occasion, the Verses of *Waller*, for whom that noble Lord had a very particular Esteem."[4] Jacob says further that "the Character of *Dorimant* was drawn in Compliment to the Earl of Rochester."[5]

Dorimant embodies all the virtues of the masculine Truewit, and he is what Dean Lockier called "the genteel rake of wit."[6] Every term of this description deserves emphasis: Dorimant is genteel, as a Truewit who observes decorum ought to be; he is a rake, because his principles are libertine; and above all, he is a Wit, for he values intellectual distinction above other virtues. This is a far better description than Hazlitt's, which makes Dorimant "the genius of grace, gallantry, and gaiety"[7]—and sacrifices accuracy to alliteration. The gallantry of Dorimant is more predatory than courtly, in keeping with his naturalistic bias; and his gaiety is subdued, for there is a dark streak in his nature, compounded of the intellectuality, cynicism, and passion of his original. He is not easy to understand because he has considerable depth, and unlike Courtall and Freeman, he is not open and frank about his inner life. He is a man

2. Hazlitt, *Lectures on the English Comic Writers*, in *The Collected Works*, VIII, 129.
3. Dennis, "A Defense of *Sir Fopling Flutter*," *The Critical Works*, II, 245–247.
4. *Ibid.*, p. 248.
5. Giles Jacob, *The Poetical Register*, London, 1719, p. 96.
6. Rev. Joseph Spence, *Anecdotes, Observations, and Characters, of Books and Men*, London, 1858, p. 47.
7. Hazlitt, *op. cit.*, VIII, 68.

506 · *Thomas H. Fujimura*

of strong passions, but is Wit enough to have control over them; his fancy is tempered by judgment; and he possesses higher intellectual qualities than the average Truewit.

On the more superficial side, he is the embodiment of elegant ease—a ready Wit, a cultivated man who has Waller on his lips, and an easy conversationalist with "a Tongue ... would tempt the Angels to a second fall." He has histrionic talents, and can adopt the proper tone for every occasion: with Lady Woodvill, he ironically plays the role of the formally courteous Mr. Courtage; with his fellow Wits he is the railler; with Bellinda he is gallantly amorous and ardent; and with the Orange Woman and the Shoemaker, he adopts a tone of rough raillery and easy superiority. Possessing the superior perspicacity and cleverness of a Truewit, Dorimant can see through the devices of others, and at the same time, dissemble well enough so that others cannot see through him. His histrionic talents are also displayed in mimicry of others, a talent which Harriet shares with him. He does it grossly and sarcastically with Loveit, in his imitation of Sir Fopling, or ironically and maliciously, as in his mimicry of Harriet. Dorimant can please anyone when, and if, he wishes to do so, because he possesses the virtues of versatility, ease, and perspicacity.

As a truewit, he also has a tongue as sharp as a rapier—and the raillery of Dorimant is seldom gentle, since he has malice enough to be cutting. Yet it has point and originality enough to be pleasing. It can be as fine as his repartee with Harriet on their first encounter:

DOR: You were talking of Play, Madam; Pray what may be your stint?

HAR: A little harmless discourse in publick walks, or at most an appointment in a Box bare-fac'd at the Play-House; you are for Masks, and private meetings, where Women engage for all they are worth, I hear.

DOR: I have been us'd to deep Play, but I can make one at small Game, when I like my Gamester well.

HAR: And be so unconcern'd you'l ha' no pleasure in't.

DOR: Where there is a considerable sum to be won, the hope of drawing people in, makes every trifle considerable.

HAR: The sordidness of mens natures, I know, makes 'em willing to flatter and comply with the Rich, though they are sure never to be the better for 'em.

DOR: 'Tis in their power to do us good, and we despair not but at some time or other they may be willing.

HAR: To men who have far'd in this Town like you, 'twoud be a great Mortification to live on hope; could you keep a Lent for a mistress?

Dor: In expectation of a happy Easter, and though time be very precious, think forty daies well lost, to gain your favour. (iii, iii)

His raillery can also be as sarcastic as his retort to Pert, "Oh Mrs. Pert, I never knew you sullen enough to be silent" (ii, ii); or as good-naturedly rough as his remark to his servant, "take notice henceforward who's wanting in his duty, the next Clap he gets, he shall rot for an example" (i, i).

As a Truewit, Dorimant professes naturalistic principles, and he is cynical about women. He has known enough women to be certain that they are vain, hypocritical, and affected creatures; most complaisant when they seem most to resist; and jealous and demanding when won. A striking example of his raillery, malice, his libertinism, frankness, and wit is his passage with Mrs. Loveit:

Loveit: Is this the constancy you vow'd?

Dor: Constancy at my years! 'tis not a Vertue in season, you might as well expect the Fruit the Autumn ripens i'the Spring.

Loveit: Monstrous Principle!

Dor: Youth has a long Journey to go, Madam; shou'd I have set up my rest at the first Inn I lodg'd at, I shou'd never have arriv'd at the happiness I now enjoy.

Loveit: Dissembler, damn'd Dissembler!

Dor: I am so, I confess; good nature and good manners corrupt me. I am honest in my inclinations, and wou'd not, wer' not to avoid offense, make a Lady a little in years believe I think her young, wilfully mistake Art for Nature; and seem as fond of a thing I am weary of, as when I doated on't in earnest.

Loveit: False Man!

Dor: True Woman!

Loveit: Now you begin to show your self!

Dor: Love gilds us over, and makes us show fine things to one another for a time, but soon the Gold wears off, and then again the native brass appears. (ii, ii)

He is professedly libertine, and lives according to naturalistic principles.

If there is any fault in Dorimant as a Truewit, it is his oversophistication, which makes his wit a little too self-conscious; for now and then his wit is a trifle forced, as in his raillery on the young women whom the Orange Woman reports to him: "This fine Woman, I'le lay my life, is some awkward ill fashion'd Country Toad, who not having above Four Dozen of black hairs on her head, has adorn'd her baldness with a large white Fruz, that she may look sparkishly in the Fore Front of the Kings Box, at an old

Play" (i, i). Harriet, who is a keen judge of wit, observes of Dorimant, when Young Bellair praises him for his ease and naturalness, "He's agreeable and pleasant I must own, but he does so much affect being so, he displeases me" (iii, iii). Dorimant has too much judgment to indulge in fanciful wit, so that he does not provide the most natural and spontaneous display of wit. But he is a Truewit because he is libertine in his principles, perspicacious and malicious, he observes decorum in his speech and conduct, and he detests coxcombs like Sir Fopling.

His friend Medley has the more fanciful wit of the two, and he serves, therefore, as a foil to Dorimant's more solid wit. When he is "rhetorically drunk," he is a great elaborator of fancies; and he rallies the ladies with a pleasant account of a fictitious book, "written by a late beauty of Quality, teaching you how to draw up your Breasts, stretch up your neck, to thrust out your Breech, to play with your Head, to toss up your Nose, to bite your Lips, to turn up your Eyes, to speak in a silly soft tone of a Voice, and use all the Foolish French Words that will infallibly make your person and conversation charming, with a short apologie at the end, in behalf of young Ladies, who notoriously wash, and paint, though they have naturally good Complexions" (ii, i). Medley rallies everyone but with much less malice than Dorimant, and he lets his tongue run freely on everyone and everything.

It is also he, rather than Dorimant, who voices most of the skeptical wit in the play; and this is done with a much more natural, if less fine, carelessness than Dorimant is capable of. He is a skeptic in matrimony as well as religion, and he rallies Young Bellair on his intended marriage: "You have a good strong Faith, and that may contribute much towards your Salvation. I confess I am but of an untoward constitution, apt to have doubts and scruples, and in Love they are no less distracting than in Religion; were I so near Marriage, I shou'd cry out by Fits as I ride in my Coach, Cuckold, Cuckold, with no less fury than the mad Fanatick does Glory in *Bethlem*" (i, i). When Dorimant gets a letter from Molly the whore asking for a guinea to see the "Opery," Medley exclaims, "Pray let the Whore have a favorable answer, that she may spark it in a Box, and do honor to her profession" (i, i). He also gives the rallying advice to the witty Shoemaker: "I advise you like a Friend, reform your Life; you have brought the envy of the World upon you, by living above your self. Whoring and Swearing are Vices too gentile for a Shoomaker" (i, i). Though Dorimant is the finer Wit, with more malice, perspicacity, and judgment, Medley, with his fanciful and skeptical wit, is often more original and entertaining.

The one other important Truewit in the play is Harriet, who has much in common with Dorimant. Compared to her sisters Gatty, Ariana, and the Widow Rich, Harriet is endowed with a much more solid wit; and her perspicacity, sound sense, and fine self-control make her a formidable person. She is, as Dorimant says, "Wild, witty, lovesome, beautiful and young," but tempering these qualities is sound judgment and sincere feeling. Her exceptional physical beauty is the least part of her merits, and it speaks well for Dorimant that he is interested in her wit (i, i).

Like Dorimant, she has histrionic talents and the ability to dissemble, and there are excellent scenes of comic wit when she and Dorimant take each other off on their first meeting, and when she and Young Bellair dissemble before their parents, by pretending to be in love. She displays a roguish wit, as when she tells Young Bellair, "I know not what it is to love, but I have made pretty remarks by being now and then where Lovers meet" (iii, i). Or when she is merry at her mother's expense, by exclaiming in the presence of Dorimant, who is unknown to Lady Woodvill, "I would fain see that *Dorimant*, Mother, you so cry out of, for a monster; he's in the *Mail I hear*" (iii, iii). But there is good-nature at bottom in Harriet, and the occasional malice of her tongue is due to some deeper feeling which she wishes to conceal. She is a Truewit with sufficient self-control to treat her lover and her emotion playfully; and if her emotion breaks through, it is perceptible only in her shaprer and more malicious wit:

HAR: I did not think to have heard of Love from you.

DOR: I never knew what 'twas to have a settled Ague yet, but now and then have had irregular fitts.

HAR: Take heed, sickness after long health is commonly more violent and dangerous.

DOR: I have took the infection from her, and feel the disease spreading in me— (Aside.)
Is the name of love so frightful that you dare not stand it? (To her.)

HAR: 'Twill do little execution out of your mouth on me, I am sure.

DOR: It has been fatal—

HAR: To some easy Women, but we are not all born to one destiny; I was inform'd you use to laugh at Love, and not make it.

DOR: the time has been, but now I must speak—

HAR: If it be on that Idle subject, I will put on my serious look, turn my head carelessly from you, drop my lip, let my Eyelids fall and hang half o're my Eyes— Thus— while you buz a speech of an hour long in my ear, and I answer never a word! why do you not begin? (iv, i)

Such raillery is a fine weapon in her capable hands.

Her wit is charming because it springs from sincere feeling and sound judgment. She has sensible views, untainted by cynicism; and though she may say of a husband, "I think I might be brought to endure him, and that is all a reasonable Woman should expect in a Husband," she adds significantly, "but there is duty i'the case," implying thereby that were not duty involved (as there must be in an arranged marriage), a woman might reasonably dote on her husband (III, i). As a Truewit she is an enemy of all that is affected, dull, and formal, and speaking of Hyde Park, she says, "I abominate the dull diversions there, the formal bows, the Affected smiles, the silly by-Words and amorous Tweers, in passing (III, iii). She has passions, and will not conceal them under an affected softness (IV, i). In fact, she loves naturalness so much that she criticizes even Dorimant for not being natural enough in his wit (III, iii). And she exclaims against all pretenders—"That Women should set up for beauty as much in spite of nature, as some men have done for Wit!" (III, i). At its best, her wit is first-rate because it is unpretentious: her witticisms are never forced, and her speech is free of labored similitudes. Only she is capable of wit at once so sensible and whimsical as the following:

> DOR: Is this all—will you not promise me—
> HAR: I hate to promise! what we do then is expected from us, and wants much of the welcom it finds, when it surprizes.
> DOR: May I not hope?
> HAR: That depends on you, and not on me, and 'tis to no purpose to forbid it. (v, ii).

It must be her speeches in particular that Dennis had in mind when he said of *The Man of Mode*: "the Dialogue is the most charming that has been writ by the Moderns: That with Purity and Simplicity, it has Art and Elegance; and with Force and Vivacity, the utmost Grace and Delicacy."[8]

As foils to the three Wits discussed so far, there are the several characters who fall short of being Truewits. Of these Emilia and Young Bellair are the most attractive, but like Graciana and Beaufort in the first play, they belong to an honorable world which is out of harmony with the dominantly naturalistic temper of the play. Young Bellair is described by Dorimant as "Handsome, well bred, and by much the most tolerable of all the young men that do abound in wit" (I, i); and Emilia, according to Medley, "has the best reputation of any young Woman about Town, who has beauty enough to provoke detraction; her Carriage, is unaffected, her discourse modest, not at all censorious, nor pretending like the Counterfeits of the Age" (I, i). What alone makes them tolerable to the Truewits is their naturalness and lack of affectation; as lovers, they

8. Dennis, "A Defence of *Sir Fopling Flutter*," *The Critical Works*, II, 243.

lack fire and spirit and theirs is a conventional affair, with the usual obstacles and hazards of honorable courtship and marriage.

Aside from Bellinda, who is a rather foolish young woman, the other foils to the Truewits are all objects of malicious laughter in the play. Mrs. Loveit has some beauty and wit, but she is absurd because of her unnatural jealousy and affectation. Lady Woodvill and Old Bellair, "their Gravities" of a past age, are minor objects of ridicule. Old Bellair is laughable because of his unnatural love for a young girl, for such fond love at his age is a sure sign of dotage or impotent lechery. Lady Woodvill is "a great Admirer of the Forms and Civilities of the last Age," when beauties were courted in proper form, with a due regard for the conventions of Platonic love. "Lewdness is the business now," she says with regret, "Love was the bus'ness in my Time" (IV, i). She does not realize that the new world in which she is so out of place is naturalistic in its principles, and that young couples like Emilia and Young Bellair who carry on in the approved fashion of her age are passé.

The chief foil to the Truewits is Sir Fopling, but so much has been said about him by critics that further commentary seems superfluous. It is important, however, to note that he is not chiefly an object of social satire, as is commonly supposed: he is laughed at principally because he is deficient in wit. His pretension to fashion and taste in clothes reveals the poverty of his mind, and it is this mental defect that exposes him to laughter. He is such a person as the Marquess of Halifax described—a superfine gentleman whose understanding is so appropriated to his dress that his fine clothes become his sole care.[9] After the Truewits have ironically ridiculed his supposed fine taste in clothes, they mercilessly condemn him as a fool:

MED: A fine mettl'd Coxcomb.

DOR: Brisk and Insipid—

MED: Pert and dull.

EMILIA: However you despise him, Gentlemen, I'le lay my life he passes for a Wit with many.

DOR: That may very well be, Nature has her cheats, stum's a brain, and puts sophisticate dulness often on the tasteless multitude for true wit and good humour. (III, ii)

Undoubtedly there is some element of social satire in the ridicule of the fop, but the "manners" approach which makes Sir Fopling a mere conglomeration of fine clothes misses the whole point of his being Witwoud. Furthermore, the "manners" view which finds him a superfluous accessory to the plot fails to grasp the unity of the

9. Halifax, "Some Cautions offered to the Consideration of those who are to chuse *Members* to serve for the Ensuing *Parliament*," in *The Complete Works*, p. 153.

play. It is quite evident that in this comedy of wit he occupies the role of the Witwoud who is exposed by his intellectual superiors, and that he is not only a foil to the Truewits but the butt of their malicious laughter.

In his three wit comedies, Etherege shows a progressive development in his art. *The Comical Revenge*, his first attempt at the comedy of wit, shows an uncertain mastery: the heroic-moral world is not properly subordinated, Wheadle and Dufoy are not perfect Witwouds, and Sir Nicholas is not a very amusing Witless. The Truewits are also deficient: Sir Frederick, with his callow interest in frolics, and the Widow, with her over-ready show of feeling, are not yet capable of the brilliant comic wit to be found in later plays. But the naturalistic temper is prominently displayed. In the second comedy, *She Would if She Could*, Etherege successfully poked witty fun at the conventional notion of honor, in the person of Lady Cockwood, and he brought together a quartet of spirited Truewits. The wit in the play, however, seldom reaches a very high level: the repartees are characterized more by high spirits than by an original exchange of ideas; there is a preponderance of wit play over comic wit; and the Truewits are not properly distinguished in their wit, for the difference between Courtall and Freeman, for example, is that the former is the bolder of the two.

The last play, *The Man of Mode*, is superior in every respect. Not only does it have a fine Witwoud in Sir Fopling Flutter, but it has three notable Truewits, in Dorimant, Harriet, and Medley, who are carefully distinguished by Etherege in terms of their wit: Dorimant is characterized by malice and judgment, Medley by fanciful and skeptical wit, and Harriet by natural, spontaneous wit. In Dorimant and Harriet, we see to what an extent Etherege succeeded in making the wit significant and dramatic: not only does the wit of Harriet probe deeper into human absurdities; it is more thoroughly a part of the dramatic action, as well as an expression of her true character. Dorimant and Harriet also have an intellectual solidity and depth of feeling which make them far more human and substantial than their predecessors. These two Truewits are both lovers of fine wit; they have penetration enough to see through the affectation and folly of others, and wit enough to dissemble with the world; enough judgment to act sensibly at all times; a sufficiently playful attitude toward life not to be swept away by their own emotions; and an easy and elegant superiority to everyone else by virtue of these qualities. They are intelligent without being over-intellectual, worldly without being disillusioned with life, and witty without being superficial or frivolous.

Dorimant and particularly Harriet represent the finest expression of Etherege's witty attitude toward life—his good sense, elegance, and libertinism; and his scorn of fools, ceremony, and artificiality. As

Truewits they belong to a free world—and a world which is neither corrupt as the moralistic critics affirm, nor superficial as the "manners" critics would have us believe. It may not have the breadth of Dante's universe because the supernatural is excluded, but there is much in this world of the Truewit that is valuable, such as elegance, intellectual distinction, clarity of thought, absence of artificial formality, freedom from cant about honor, and a graceful and natural acceptance of this life on earth.

JOCELYN POWELL

George Etherege and the Form of a Comedy†

* * * Love and friendship in *The Man of Mode* arise out of and return to the self. The friendship of Dorimant and Medley exists because they find each other entertaining as companions, but they are as willing to be amused at each other's expense as in each other's company. They look upon each other, as upon everyone else, as cogs to the wheel of pleasure; the acquaintance helps in one way or other to make life go round.

'Tis good to have an universal taste; we should love Wit, but for Variety be able to divert ourselves with the Extravagancies of those who want it:

(III. ii. 131)

Lady Townley speaks of passing acquaintances, but one feels that the sentiment is applied by and large to all human contact. Other human beings exist, not even simply for one's entertainment—that is to put it too passively—but for one's use.

The malignant aspect of this can be seen from Dorimant's relationship with young Bellair. Bellair is presented as a frank, good-natured young man who instantly acquires our sympathy, as does Emilia, the girl he wants to marry. They are both simple, unaffected people, and our interest in them is considerable, as it should be in two persons whose plans and difficulties form a central intrigue of the play. Dorimant's first scene with Bellair bears out this impression. It is jovial, intimate, and apparently open-hearted. But no sooner has the young man gone than we are presented with a very different view of the relationship:

He's Handsome [says Dorimant], well bred, and by much the most tolerable of all the young men that do not abound in wit.

(I. i. 424)

† From *Restoration Theatre*, edited by John Russell Brown and Bernard Harris (London: Edward Arnold Ltd., 1965), pp. 61–65. Reprinted by permission of the publisher.

There is a complacency in the judgment which is displeasing, and the displeasure is increased by Dorimant's later remarks to the effect that he is interested in the young man's marriage largely because he thinks it will make possible attempts upon the lady that are ineffective while she is a virgin. The combination of real intention and libertine bravado gives a new perspective to what appeared to be a frank and open relationship. The apparent sympathy does not exist.

The emptiness of this life of isolation is given full expression in the exploration of Dorimant's relations with women. The three main affairs, of Loveit, Bellinda, and Harriet are cleverly contrasted and build up a ruthless picture of lovelessness and boredom. Dorimant is the typical erotic, spending most of his wit on retaining his independence and achieving his pleasure. He considers his affairs to be a mutual indulgence between himself and the lady, and considers there should be no obligation incurred upon either side. Each party is responsible for their own person and their own pleasure; nothing is shared. The resulting associations are scarcely worthy of the name relationship, they are casual, and quite meaningless.

The seduction of Bellinda is obviously a typical episode in the life of Dorimant, and the tone in which it is drawn scarcely gives the impression that it has been very satisfactory. Bellinda's attitude to the affair is complicated and ambiguous. She continually hesitates to give herself, wishing to make sure the performance is one of love. She demands Dorimant should throw off Loveit to prove his feeling, but though he does so she never altogether believes him. She comes to him out of a desire she has not the power to resist. When she has finally yielded, she makes all the conventional demands on him, but apparently with little expectation of success. Her very coyness is half-hearted:

BELLINDA: Were it to do again——
DORIMANT: We should do it, should we not?
BELLINDA: I think we should: the wickeder man you to make me love so well—will you be discreet now?
DORIMANT: I will——
BELLINDA: You cannot.
DORIMANT: Never doubt it.
BELLINDA: I will not expect it.
DORIMANT: You do me wrong.
BELLINDA: You have no more power to keep the secret, than I had not to trust you with it.

(IV. ii. 11)

There is nothing between them but a momentary sensual gratification, the casualness of which is neatly stressed by a visual detail. As they come out of the bedroom we are to see "Handy, *tying up Linnen.*" The touch is unsavory, and by its suggestion of the usual, the stream of such acquaintances before and after, robs the situation of any glamor. The work of the household goes on; Handy, doubtless, continues to do the laundry throughout the little passage quoted above. When the lady has gone Dorimant's friends arrive, and sum up the position on sight:

> MEDLEY: You have had an irregular fit, *Dorimant.*
> DORIMANT: I have.
> YOUNG BELLAIR: And it is off already?
> DORIMANT: Nature has done her part, Gentlemen; when she falls kindly to work, great Cures are effected in little time, you know.
>
> (IV. ii. 69)

The whole business is sordid and without hope. The almost complete lack of resistance on Bellinda's part removes the comedy that would arise from a conflict of wills, and does, indeed, do so in the case of Loveit. Bellinda has no will: simply a cynical wavering between what she would like to think love is and what she thinks she knows it to be. The disillusionment that comes to her hurts, but it was expected, and is accepted. The negatives that litter her speeches characterize her attitude, and establish the isolated nihilism of herself and her lover. It all finds expression in her injunction to him at parting:

> Take no notice of me, and I shall not hate you.
>
> (V. ii. 303)

Bellinda accepts isolation and independence, but her lack of resistance is so depressing that it sets up a curious tension with Mrs. Loveit's comic and selfish passion. We laugh at this, we find her dramatics, her pretensions, her possessiveness quite ridiculous; but at least it is positive, and at least it has something to give. Mrs. Loveit is comic because she allows Dorimant to manipulate her. She is worked on so that the effects of her actions are the contrary of those she intended. The discrepancy between her will and its effect renders her ridiculous. But this arises out of an opposition of motive. Dorimant can manage her because he is completely indifferent; he does not care what comes of the interview, and she does. She wishes to give herself to him, and the desire to submit destroys the desire to hurt. The comedy this creates is complex. We laugh with Dorimant at Loveit, because he controls her and makes her ridiculous. When she tears her fan we laugh at the impotence of the gesture to express the feeling, and her helplessness before him.

But though she is selfishly clinging, she is also genuinely passionate; there is a sense of sincerity in her actions which shows well against the frivolity of his, a warmth which reflects upon his cold destructiveness. The sympathy in the laughter is undermined as it asserts itself, for we find ourselves laughing at something to which we are emotionally sympathetic, with someone whose actions deny our sympathy. We are deriding something we feel to be ultimately of value. This creates a deep sense of insecurity that is at once comic and profound.

This insecurity, arising from a sense of the value of something we are mocking, finds its complement in the relation of Dorimant and Harriet, which, partly through its contrast with the affairs of Loveit and Bellinda, and partly from within itself, continually suggests that what we find brilliant and sympathetic is actually hollow. The selfishness of Dorimant's previous relationships gives one the impression that he is unable and unwilling to give himself to anyone, and this leaves the prospect of his marriage on a high level of difficulty. There is no doubt of the physical attraction, and of a certain sympathy arising from their equality in wit and will. The relationship is genuinely exciting: in Harriet Dorimant has met his match; but through the play we see him struggling to keep his independence, and the end shows no definitive sign that he has resigned it. The feeling is reinforced by Harriet's own doubts on the subject.

But there are also deeper grounds for disquiet. The libertine's own independence of person has, as a necessary corollary, the desire to possess others. In all Dorimant's relations with Loveit this is uppermost in his mind. He asserts his independence through her dependence; his power over her is the mark of his superiority. He tries to show this power by maneuvering her into making a fool of herself for his sake with Sir Fopling; but Loveit turns the tables by entertaining Sir Fopling at Dorimant's expense. Each is trying to prove their power over the other. And the same is true of Dorimant and Harriet:

> HARRIET: I was inform'd you use to laugh at Love, and not make it.
> DORIMANT: The time has been, but now I must speak——
> HARRIET: If it be on that Idle subject, I will put on my serious look, turn my head carelessly from you, drop my lip, let my Eyelids fall and hang half o're my Eyes—Thus—while you buz a speech of an hour long in my ear, and I answer never a word! why do you not begin?
> DORIMANT: That the company may take notice how passionately I make advances of Love! and how disdainfully you receive 'em.
> HARRIET: When your love's grown strong enough to make you

bear being laugh'd at, I'll give you leave to trouble me with it.
'Till when pray forbear, Sir.

(IV. i. 169)

This is the iron hand in the velvet glove, right enough. Harriet, with her conscious posing, is playing a game at her lover's expense. There is no equality or balance; she simply wishes to subdue. The nearest they get to sharing an experience is their joint effort to enrage Loveit and offend Sir Fopling at the end of the play; Dorimant acting out of a natural desire to revenge his own frustration, and Harriet out of one equally natural, that of displaying her triumph. It is true; it is very funny; and it is distinctly unpleasant. Their last exchange does nothing to resolve the difficulty: they are both still struggling for the last word. Harriet paints a picture of life in the country and asks if this does not stagger his resolution to ask for her:

> DORIMANT: Not at all, Madam! The first time I saw you, you left me with the pangs of Love upon me, and this day my soul has quite given up her liberty.
>
> HARRIET: This is more dismal than the Country! *Emilia!* pitty me, who am going to that sad place. Methinks I hear the hateful noise of Rooks already—Kaw, Kaw, Kaw——

(V. ii. 427)

One cannot help asking oneself who is the fool. Dorimant's line is one we have seen him at before; Loveit and Bellinda are not so easily forgotten: and Harriet's retort shows a steady persistence in demanding her pound of flesh. Their marriage is ideal in Restoration terms, being between a young wit and a fine woman with "a hugeous fortune"; but the two personalities, with their determined independence and overt possessiveness, make one question its future.

*   *   *

The particular quality of Etherege's Comedy of Manners is achieved not through a superficial, but through an actual realism. It comes from our taking his characters as real human beings and experiencing the implications of their conduct in terms of actual life.

Dorimant is a portrait of Rochester, and the mood in which he is portrayed communicates that combination of glamor and viciousness which burns so much more fiercely in Rochester's satires. The form of the play, in which one mood or attitude continually reveals the flaws in another, while our sympathies are engaged to comprehend the nature of both, creates in Dorimant a figure in which tremendous life and energy generate a sympathy which is continually frustrated by the realization that all the energy turns back upon itself. It is useless; it becomes atrophied. The whole is a tremendous display of brilliance which has no aim. Powers of expression are called forth, but there is nothing to express. The wit, the forms and manners, the pleasure that has no end beyond itself, are almost desperate means to express an energy that has nowhere to go. The end of it all is increasing isolation and emptiness.

When Dryden, in his Epilogue to *The Man of Mode*, wrote:

> *Yet none Sir* Fopling *him, or him can call;*
> *He's Knight o'th'Shire, and represents ye all*

he gave us a clue to the mood and method of the play. The fault of Dorimant is the personal equivalent of the fault of his whole society: form has become a substitute for feeling.

Sir Fopling is a comic embodiment of this idea. In him the elements of lyrical and musical life and energy that lifted *She Wou'd if She Cou'd* and *Love in a Tub* off the ground have been pared away to a rhythmic precision conveyed through the words. He is the successor of Sir Frederick and Sir Joslin, picking up the realism of the play and turning it into a dance; he occurs as they do to give a rhythmic finish to important scenes; but, with the exception of the Masquerade, he does so without any help. The whole effect comes from his own personality unaided by music or song. He creates his own accompaniment, and the effect is at once drier, and more real: exactly suited to the texture of the play. Like Sir Frederick, too, he is not one man but eight. His "equipage," like Sir Frederick's masquers, spreads his personality over the stage: the exquisite with the fatal flaw. The whole tension of this personality goes with them as they follow him about, a page, five Frenchmen, and an Englishman, like the famous centipede with the wooden leg, each exquisite ripple of movement initiated by Sir Fopling collapsing in the final and inadequate execution of the ill-fated John Trott. It is a brilliant comic device, and translates into pure spectacle the empty emotionless forms of the rest of the play. Life, for Sir Fopling, is a continual pose, as it was, or had to be, for Ariana and Gatty, and as it is with Harriet with her accurate observations of behavior designed to deceive; and, since it is so, the whole energy of his personality goes into the pastime.

The feeling is given perfectly in a little pamphlet entitled *News From Covent Garden or The Town Gallant's Vindication*. It appeared in 1675, but it might almost have been written as a portrait of Etherege's hero. The Gallant is describing the difficulties of his way of life:

> To know how to discar'd the Goloshooes in due season in their proper place: to tie the knot of one's Muff Ribbon, to the best

advantage: to walk with such pleasing Gate that your Swinging Arm may keep true time with your Feet, which must dance to the Musick of the Points, Ratling on your Pantaloons, and especially to provide that the Foot-Boy be observant in his distances, that he never stand just behind, but bearing a respectful point *East* or *West* from his Master. You know full well Gentlemen! tis no such easie business to discern how much of the *Handkerchief* ought to hang out of the Right Pocket, and how to Poise it Mathematically, with the Tortoise shell comb on the left: to apprehend what a boon Grace there is in some notable words keenly pronounced, with a neat shrug and a becoming lisp, to avoid the horrible absurdity of sitting both feet flat on the Ground, when one should always stand tottering on the toe, as waiting in readiness for a *Congee*!

It is all form and no meaning; manners have become a contradiction of themselves, for manners are really the means by which men and women, wishing to know each other, can express themselves and yet not impose upon the identity of those to whom they are speaking. They are the means of communicating one's deepest feelings and preserving at the same time a respect for the feelings of others. They arise out of consideration and respect for other people. But in the society Etherege portrays manners have become not a means to an end, but an end in themselves, and an end which denies their original purpose; that which was intended to express feeling, now dictates to it, and manners prevent the intercourse they were designed to aid. Instead of ensuring you do not impose yourself upon another, they ensure that others do not impose themselves on you. They have become a means of personal isolation rather than a means of personal communication, and what was designed as a medicine has become a weapon. To shame Loveit, Dorimant determines to pluck off her "mask" and show "the passion that lies panting under." Feeling has become ridiculous, the mask important; the real has given place to the trivial.

The energy of love and of living is expressed in the communication between human beings; but the Restoration reaction against the repression of the Puritan conscience produced a repression as, if not more, disastrous; for license of action was accompanied by restriction of feeling. Throughout *The Man of Mode* one is kept constantly aware that the brilliance is suppressing and vitiating the reality of life and passion. What is serious and important is being destroyed by what is brittle and frivolous. Manners no longer express but contradict reality The secret of the form and the drama of Etherege's last play lies in the tension he creates between the lightness and elegance of fashion on the surface and the underlying reality of passion it conceals. The energy and wit of the former creates in the audience a sympathy, which is questioned by the intimacy and humanity with which the characters are drawn. All the devices of comedy, charm, cleverness and wit, encourage one to laugh with Dorimant at his victims, but the sympathy with which those victims are themselves described make us aware that the approval we have been giving through our laughter is of what we hate. We are given a double view of the situation, a view of the pretense, and of the truth, and before it we are helpless, aware that our intellectual and emotional responses form a devastating contradiction. The laughter and the experience attack each other with the ambiguity of life.

This ambiguity explains the curious contradictions that have arisen in comments upon the play. St. Evremont said that in Dorimant Etherege gave us Rochester with his vices "burnished to shine like perfections."[1] Sir Richard Steele said:

> To speak plainly of this whole work, I think nothing but being lost to a sense of innocence and virtue, can make any one see this comedy, without observing more frequent occasion to move sorrow and indignation than mirth and laughter.
>
> (*Spectator*, No. 65)

Each has taken one aspect of the play and made it into the whole. Dorimant's charm does "burnish" his vices, but only for a moment, the next our sympathy with one of his fellows is showing us more matter for sorrow in what we laughed at before. This ambivalence, this floating between laughter and indignation, is the essence of Etherege's comedy. He knew these emotions did not exclude but reinforce each other, and that the sense of this was one of the most common experiences of life. It is this experience his plays explore. As Congreve put it: "The two Famous Philosophers of *Ephesus* and *Abdera* have their different Sects at this day. Some Weep and others Laugh at one and the same thing."[2] This ambiguity of response is the essence of the comedy of experience.

ROSE A. ZIMBARDO

[*The Country Wife* as Satire]†

* * * *The Country Wife* opens, as satire must, with a declaration of the thesis to be argued. The vice in question is lust, but not lust simply. Rather, it is lust that disguises itself, assuming one or

1. *A Memoir of the Life of John Wilmot, Earl of Rochester . . .* in *The Works of the Right Honorable Earls of Rochester & Roscannon* (1707).
2. *Concerning Humour in Comedy*: Letter to John Dennis (1695) * * *

† From Rose A. Zimbardo, *Wycherley's Drama: A Link in the Development of English Satire* (New Haven, Conn.: Yale University Press, 1965), pp. 154–164. Copyright © 1965 by Yale University. Reprinted by permission of the publisher.

another mask, not out of deference to morality, nor out of shame,
but that it may under the protection of a disguise enjoy greater freedom to operate. The thesis is not declared directly, because there is
no satiric persona in the play to speak it. It is, rather, presented
graphically. As the play opens, Horner and Quack are discovered
discussing Horner's plan. Horner inquires whether Quack has been
diligent in spreading the rumor of his impotence. Quack assures
Horner that he has, but questions the wisdom of the plan.

> HORNER: Dear Mr. Doctor, let vain rogues be contented only to
> be thought abler men than they are, generally 'tis all the pleas-
> ure they have; but mine lies another way.
> QUACK: You take, methinks, a very preposterous way to it, and as
> ridiculous as if we operators in physic should put forth bills to
> disparage our medicaments, with hopes to gain customers.
> HORNER: Doctor, there are quacks in love as well as physic, who
> get but the fewer and worse patients for their boasting; a good
> name is seldom got by giving it one's self . . . Come, come,
> Doctor, the wisest lawyer never discovers the merits of his
> cause till the trial; the wealthiest man conceals his riches, and
> the cunning gamester his play. Shy husbands and keepers, like
> old rooks, are not to be cheated but by a new unpractised
> trick; false friendship will pass now no more than false dice
> upon 'em.
>
> [I, i]

In this dialogue Horner is not expressing, as Underwood and others
have suggested, the duality of art and nature; his subject is lust and
hypocrisy. The "natural" Horner is a satyr, his only art the art of
deception. He is a hypocrite, not a natural man, and certainly not a
hero. He discards the ruse of false friendship not because it is dishonorable but because it does not work We should not dream of
suggesting that Lady Fidget is the heroine of Wycherley's play. We
are quite certain of the author's attitude toward such a lady of
honor; she is a target of satire. Why, then, should we mistake his
attitude toward Horner? Horner spreads the rumor that he is sexually harmless, so that he may more freely indulge his lust. Lady
Fidget spreads the rumor that she is virtuous to the same end. The
only difference between them is that Horner pretends a negative
quality (to be harmless where he is most harmful), while Lady
Fidget pretends a positive quality (to be in possession of the most
grace where she is graceless). True, Horner's is the less usual disguise. It is used to attract our attention, by its very outrageousness,
to the incongruity between what human beings pretend to be and
what they are. In the opening scene Horner is presented as an

emblem, a grotesque exaggeration of the vice we are to watch for in the play. He is, in graphic terms, the declaration of thesis.

The thesis declared, the argument of it begins. Because there are separate actions, of equal importance, that attract our attention by turn to the various aspects of the vice, the scenes maintain a degree of independence from one another. This enables the satirist to turn the vice under consideration around on all sides, to attack it from as many angles as possible. Scene after scene is presented in which some new face of the vice is presented or some aspect already presented is more deeply probed. The movement is circular and continues until all of what Dryden calls the "members" of the central vice have been presented and developed to their fullest extent.

The four faces of disguised lust that the design examines are presented by the end of the second act. First, Horner is introduced to present lust in the mask of impotence, which secures it full freedom. Then Sir Jasper enters with the "ladies of honor," who flaunt their masks of modesty and virtue. Horner, having assumed the role of malcontent-satirist, sounds the depths of their virtue and suspects it to be shallow. When the ladies have gone, he announces his suspicion to Quack, rejoicing in their disguise as well as in the efficacy of his own.

> Your women of honour, as you call 'em, are only chary of their reputations, not their persons; and 'tis scandal they would avoid, not men. Now may I have by the reputation of an eunuch the privileges of one, and be seen in a lady's chamber in a morning as early as her husband.
>
> [I, i]

The scene that presents vice disguised as virtue is followed by a brief interlude of commentary upon the satiric background. Horner, in the company of the wits, observes and comments upon the immorality of the world. Into this commentary a new aspect of disguised lust is introduced in the person of Pinchwife. Pinchwife hides and indulges his gross carnality under the socially respectable façade of marriage.

> HORNER: But, prithee, was not the way you were in better? is not keeping better than marriage?
> PINCH: A pox on't! The jades would jilt me. I could never keep a whore to myself.
> HORNER: So, then you only married to keep a whore to yourself.
>
> [I, i]

Pinchwife's jealousy arises from the desire to maintain intact the socially sanctioned contract, supposedly based upon mutual regard, which provides him his mask for the indulgence of lust. He neither loves nor trusts his wife, and surely he does not esteem her. He chose her not for any virtue he admired in her but for her prime fault, ignorance, which he hoped would protect his own façade. His sole interest, throughout the play, is in forcing her to preserve his "honor" as a husband, which honor is as false as Lady Fidget's virtue or Horner's impotence. In reality, Pinchwife is not a husband but the keeper of a whore, a piece of property that he is anxious to preserve to his exclusive enjoyment. Like Horner and Fidget, he desires freely to indulge his lust under cover of a carefully sustained respectability.

The last aspect of the vice presented is lust disguised as innocence. Perhaps lust is too strong a word to describe Margery's emotion, as innocence is too imprecise to define her ignorance. Her innocence at first is genuine However, once she has fallen in love with Horner, she develops guile, and she feigns innocence to disguise her passion from Pinchwife in the hope that she will thereby find the freedom to satisfy it.

In their first appearance the four aspects of the vice are almost purely comic—Horner's knavery, Fidget's affectation, Pinchwife's jealousy, Margery's rusticity are at first follies. However, at each successive appearance they assume more serious proportions, and by gradual stages the comic tone fades, to be replaced by the satiric. It is highly illuminating of Wycherley's method to trace the course of one aspect of the vice in its development. For example, let us consider lust disguised as virtue. Fidget and her company are wholly comic in their first appearance. They are objects of satire only in their folly of exaggeration—theirs is the "humour" of virtue which is threatened by Horner's wit. In Act II, a new dimension of their viciousness is revealed; their hidden lust, until now only suspected, is uncovered, and with it their whole perverted system of morality.

L.F.: But, poor gentleman, could you be so generous, so truly a man of honour, as for the sakes of us women of honor to cause yourself to be reported no man? No man! And to suffer yourself the greatest shame that could fall upon a man, that none might fall upon us women by your conversation? but, indeed, sir, as perfectly, perfectly that same man as before your going in to France, sir? As perfectly, perfectly, sir?

HORN: As perfectly, perfectly, madam. Nay, I scorn you should take my word; I desire to be tried only, madam.

[II, i]

In the system of values that prevails in the world attacked by the satiric thesis, the greatest honor accrues from building the most complete disguise of one's real motives. Horner is a man of honor because by means of his deception he has ensured free sexual indulgence not only for himself, but for "the sakes of us women of honor." His generosity is in permitting for them the same license he permits himself. Moreover, within this moral system, the "greatest shame that could fall upon a man," is to be sexually incapacitated while perfection rests upon sexual prowess. Here, as in *Love in a Wood*, Wycherley makes his satiric point in the incongruity between the heroic diction of the speakers ("I desire to be tried only, madam") and the base matter of their speech. Their style captures perfectly the duplicity of their characters While the incongruity between vehicle and tenor produces a largely comic effect, the perverted morality of the speakers—measured as it is against the ideal of the satiric antithesis—introduces a strong satiric undertone.

The next appearance of the women of honor is in the famous "china" scene of Act IV. So farcical is the scene, and so perfectly sustained its double entendre, that we are sometimes distracted from its satiric intent by our admiration of Wycherley's technique. If we consider the scene in relation to the others in this line of action, however, we realize that the women who at first affected grotesquely exaggerated virtue, and who at their second appearances could still discuss sexuality only in heroic periphrasis, here become ardent pursuers of Horner. We must not allow the comedy of the scene to blind us to the realization that it is but a hair's breadth short of presenting the sexual act on stage. Yet, as the predatory sexuality of the women more fully reveals itself, so the mask with which they disguise it becomes more pronounced. One minute after their hot pursuit of Horner they are gasping in horror to their gulled guardians,

> L.F.: O Lord, here's a man! Sir Jasper, my mask, my mask! I would not be seen here for the world.
> s.J.: What, not when I am with you?
> L.F.: No, no, my honor—let's be gone.
> SQUEAM: Ah grandmother, let's be gone; make haste, make haste, I know not how he may censure us.
> [IV, iii]

The last appearance of the women, in act V, is the scene described above, which Wycherley models so closely upon Juvenal's rite of the *Bona Dea*. Here the comic tone vanishes completely, for the women, literally and figuratively, drop their masks and do not bother to affect virtue. The stylistic tension between diction and character no longer claims our attention. Instead, satire darkens and damns more directly. Wine has robbed the women of their disguises. They abandon elevated diction and manner. Their tone coarsens and becomes sluttish. As drink loosens their tongues, they damn their husbands and compare them to "old keepers." Their talk, that of prostitutes, indicates that they think of themselves in imagery of commerce ("Women of quality, like the richest stuffs, lie untumbled and unasked for"). And finally, in the passage quoted above, each of them acknowledges that she has enjoyed Horner.

The same progress from comic to satiric is described in the successive appearance of each of the three other aspects of the central vice. Pinchwife's jealousy is ridiculous when he is the butt of the wits' teasing. It becomes a more serious defect when we observe him abusing his wife. In its next appearance, when he threatens "write as I tell you or I will write whore with this pen-knife in your face," it has darkened into cruel sadism. Until, at last, it is distorted into frenzy that drives him to attempt the murder of Margery—a disaster that is averted only when his reputation as husband is rescued by the public assurance of Horner's eunuchry. Following exactly the same pattern, Margery's disguise, at first so charmingly funny, leads at last to her willingness to sacrifice Alithea's reputation in order that, saving her own, she may indulge her passion for Horner. And Horner's knavery, at first so devilishly clever that it escapes our censure, degenerates into mean knavery when at last he sacrifices Alithea's true honor to the preservation of his false disguise.

The satiric thesis is complete when we see that in this world of knaves and gulls the gulls are not a jot the more sympathetic company. Wycherley preserves the unity of his design by using the gulls to "transiently lash" (as Dryden puts it) vices related but subordinate to the main vice. Sir Jasper as a husband bears some resemblance to Pinchwife; he, too, values the reputation of husband alone. It is one part of the public image of which he is so careful and so proud. Sparkish is the male counterpart of Lady Fidget; as she is a would-be lady, he is a would-be man. Her disguise is false modesty, his is false wit. He values Alithea only as an ornament to his reputation and an addition to his wealth. Sir Jasper and Sparkish, the gulls, are then hypocrites. Their hypocrisy differs from that of the other characters only in that it does not disguise strong, animal vice. But they are as contemptible for being hollow men, masking emptiness with a bright façade, as the other characters are for being goats.

The satiric thesis, then, is presented in successively reappearing scenes of vice and folly. With each turn of the spiral, new depths of the vice under consideration are disclosed. But we do not fully gauge the depravity of this world of inverted moral values until we contrast it with the standard presented by the satiric antithesis. The opposing virtue in this play is embodied in Alithea and Harcourt. The argument of the antithesis is stronger here than in most satires. Virtue is presented as a human possibility, not a quaint reminder of the past. Alithea and Harcourt are the twin virtues that oppose the double vice of the thesis. Alithea, as her name suggests, is the truth

that opposes hypocrisy; Harcourt is the romantic love that stands
against lust. For every aspect of vice presented, the opposing virtue
is held up for comparison in Alithea and Harcourt. For Margery's
dishonesty clothed in ignorance is Alithea's sophisticated honesty.
For Sparkish's foppery is Harcourt's manliness. For Pinchwife's jealousy is Harcourt's absolute faith. The scenes of vice are underscored
by corresponding scenes of virtue. For example, Lady Fidget's and
Horner's "perfectly, perfectly" exchange is immediately followed by
a scene in which Harcourt tries to express in the disguise of double-
faced diction his honorable passion for Alithea. Even though Harcourt's romantic love is the exact opposite of Horner's and Fidget's
animal sexuality, Alithea will not allow even honorable love to go
masked. She exposes Harcourt again and again to Sparkish. Again,
the scene in which Margery disguises herself, at the risk of Alithea's
reputation, to satisfy her passion for Horner is balanced by the
scene in which Alithea tries to unmask Harcourt, who has come, disguised as a parson, to prevent her marriage to Sparkish. She insists
upon exposing him even at the cost of injuring herself as well as
Harcourt whom she has come to love. Horner, Fidget, or Margery
will do harm to others by their lies in order to protect themselves.
Alithea, on the contrary, sacrifices her own feeling, her love of Harcourt, to keep the contract she has made with Sparkish. Hers is the
true honor which holds abstract principle above passion—the honor
of the romantic heroine of pastoral that has dwindled in breadth, if
not intensity, to fit the satiric design. It is against Alithea's true
honor that we must measure the empty reputation of the gulls and
the masked vice of the knaves.

Harcourt brings the ideal of romantic love into the design of the
play. The scorn of marriage that is supposed to typify "Restoration
comedy" has no place in this play. It is not marriage but false marriage that we must despise here, as we had despised it in *The Gentleman Dancing Master*. We are to scorn marriage as a commercial
arrangement (Sparkish's view), marriage as a social accoutrement
(the view of Sir Jasper and Lady Fidget), and marriage as the
outlet of bestiality (the view of Pinchwife). These falsities must be
discarded in the face of the marriage that Harcourt offers—marriage
based upon romantic love. Harcourt assures Alithea that the love he
offers her is "matrimonial love." He describes his passion (III, ii) in
the elevated diction of romance. He loves "with all his soul," priz-
ing her above titles or fortune. He offers himself as the man "who
can only match your faith and constancy in love," "who could no
more suspect your virtue, than his own constancy in his love for
you." When the test of Alithea's virtue comes, Harcourt is willing
to ignore reputation, and thereby proves that his faith matches Alithea's virtue.

AL: O—unfortunate woman! A combination against my honour! which most concerns me now, because you share in my disgrace, sir, and it is your censure, which I must now suffer, that troubles me, not theirs.

HAR: Madam, then have no trouble, you shall now see 'tis possible for me to love too, without being jealous; I will not only believe your innocence myself, but make all the world believe it.

[V, iv]

Harcourt and Alithea, as their discourse here suggests, are the faithful shepherd and shepherdess. Although the transition in the focus of Wycherley's vision from St. George to the dragon has been effected, nevertheless in the satires, as in his first pastoral, his standard of virtue is romantic. As we have seen, even in *The Plain Dealer*, where the satiric vision is perfectly achieved, the ideal, though it is envisaged as a lost ideal, is romance. It is against the ideal standard of romance that we must consider the satiric thesis —Pinchwife's socially sanctioned lust, Sparkish's vanity, the bestiality of the ladies of honor, and Horner, their stud. As in all satire vice is manifested in new-fangled manners—men pose as eunuchs, women have drinking parties—while virtue lies in old-fashioned simplicity.

However, though virtue proves more attractive than vice, the satiric design must be preserved. Though the antithesis is stronger here than in Wycherley's last, most perfect satire, *The Country Wife* is, nevertheless, a well-wrought satire. Consequently, like *The Plain Dealer*, it is open-ended. Alithea and Harcourt will presumably live happily ever after in their virtue, but so will Horner, the Fidgets, the Pinchwifes live on as happily in their vice. Horner and the ladies come dangerously close to exposure, but by Quack's intervention their deception is maintained. The life of lust and hypocrisy is therefore assured both for Horner and the ladies. He has learned no more than never to trust his secret to a fool. Dorilant and Sparkish are so wrongly impressed by the example of the happy lovers that they vow never to marry. Sparkish is completely untouched by his experience: "Because I will not disparage my parts, I'll ne'er be [a husband]." His interest, as it has been from the beginning, is the façade he presents. Pinchwife learns only that the cover he had chosen to indulge his lust proves to be only an irksome burden. The example of Harcourt and Alithea is lost upon him. He has not learned what a true husband is but only that his husband disguise is uncomfortable. He hates his wife more heartily than ever, but now he must keep her to serve the ends of reputation rather than lust. "I must be a husband against my will to a country wife, with a country murrain to me." *The Country Wife* presents the alternatives, ugly vice and beautiful virtue, but, in accordance with the demands of the satiric form, leaves the choice to the audience. * * *

NORMAN N. HOLLAND

[*The Way of the World*]†

* * * *The Way of the World* deals with a typical family situation—a fight for the control of an estate. Presiding over the family at the beginning of the play is the absurd Lady Wishfort who holds in a "Cabal," a gossip club, her daughter Mrs. Fainall and her niece Millamant. She controls all of Mrs. Fainall's estate and part of Millamant's as well. As the plot thickens a contest develops as to who shall get these estates from Lady Wishfort: Mr. Fainall or Millamant's lover, Mirabell.

So far, so simple. But Congreve seems to complicate these fairly straightforward family relations by such statements as this by Fainall, "[Sir Wilfull Witwoud] is half Brother to this *Witwoud* by a former wife, who was Sister to my Lady *Wishfort*, my Wife's Mother. If you [Mirabell] marry *Millamant*, you must call Cousins too." Congreve has added (and one wonders why) the confusing brothers Witwoud. Anthony, a town fop, is one of Lady Wishfort's cabal; his half-brother and Lady Wishfort's nephew, Sir Wilfull, comes to town from the country (where he has been a bumpkin these many years) on his way abroad. Lady Wishfort forces him into a half-hearted courtship of Millamant. This terribly complicated family tree can be diagramed (as in the accompanying figure, where the characters in the play are italicized). To an audience, however, only two facts emerge: that Mrs. Fainall is Lady Wish-

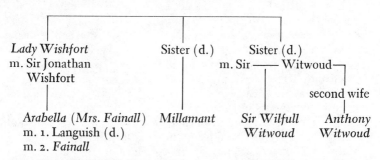

† From Norman N. Holland, *The First Modern Comedies* (Cambridge, Mass.: Harvard University Press, 1959), pp. 176–182, 185–193. Copyright © 1959 by the President and Fellows of Harvard College. Reprinted by permission of the publisher. The footnotes have been slightly edited.

fort's daughter and that Lady Wishfort has control over Millamant's estate. The other relationships, particularly the confusion of
Witwouds, serve only to create the impression of a welter of con-
sanguinity. Congreve is confusing his audience gratuitously, and we
must infer he has some reason for doing so.

He does the same thing with the emotional relations that he does
with the family structure. Behind the already complicated dynastic
relations lie even more complicated emotional affairs. In Act I we
learn that Mirabell has made advances to Lady Wishfort to cover
his wooing of Millamant. Mrs. Marwood, another member of the
cabal, betrayed him to the old lady, who, naturally enough, depises
him now. Act II tells us that Mirabell had been Mrs. Fainall's lover
when she was a widow, and, when she seemed pregnant, he married her off to Fainall. We learn, too, that Mrs. Marwood is now
Fainall's mistress, but yearns for Mirabell.

The discrepancy between the family structure and the emotional
structure plays into the Restoration convention about intrigue: a
discrepancy between appearances (the overt family relations) and
"nature" (the hidden emotional facts) gives power to the man who
knows the discrepancy. At the beginning of the play, Mirabell is
trying to set up such a situation. He has married his servant Waitwell to Lady Wishfort's maid Foible and plans to have Waitwell
disguise himself as a nobleman, court, *and marry* Lady Wishfort.
Then Mirabell plans to reveal the disguise, show Lady Wishfort
that she has married a servant, and offer to release her if she will let
him marry Millamant *cum* estate. Unfortunately, Mrs. Marwood
(who for at least two reasons wants to spike Mirabell's courtship of
Millamant) discovers the plan and tells Lady Wishfort. Mrs. Marwood also tells Fainall of his wife's former affair with Mirabell; he
threatens to publish it to the world unless Lady Wishfort signs over
to him not only his wife's but also Millamant's estate and even the
reversion after her life of Lady Wishfort's own estate. Mrs. Fainall
then ineffectually reveals that she knows Mrs. Marwood is having
an affair with her husband. Finally, however, Mirabell wins the contest by knowing the ultimate discrepancy between appearance and
nature. He produces a deed by Mrs. Fainall conveying all her estate
to him as her trustee; she made it when she was a widow (and could
execute a valid conveyance of her property), and it therefore pre-
dates any deed Fainall could now obtain. These various deeds at
the end of the play combine and fuse the two kinds of reality,
dynastic and emotional, from which the play is built.

Congreve, even though the plot is complicated enough, makes it
seem even more complicated. There are certain hidden facts—we
could call them quanta of knowledge—and a large part of the so-
called complexity simply involves revealing these facts, slowly unrav-

eling the appearances which cover them over. There are only four such quanta in the play: Marwood's desire for Mirabell, Marwood's relationship with Fainall, Mirabell's past affair with Mrs. Fainall, and Mirabell's plot with his disguised servant. But Congreve gives the impression of far greater complexity by measuring out each secret slowly, person by person, until the final complete revelation. He adds even more complexity by having each of these underlying motives and relationships refer back into the group instead of expanding to include outsiders; he makes it seem as though these five people knew only these five people.

An example of the way Congreve uses these quanta of knowledge is his treatment of Mrs. Marwood's and Fainall's liaison. In the first act, there are only a few hints: Fainall reveals he doesn't know his wife's doings; Mirabell describes Marwood ironically to Fainall as "your Friend, or your Wife's Friend"; he remarks to Fainall, who is suggesting Marwood is overfond of Mirabell, "You are conscious of a Concern for which the Lady is more indebted to you, than is your Wife." Act II, scene iii, fully reveals the affair to the audience in the dialogue between Fainall and Marwood. Act III contains only a hint by Mrs. Marwood that Foible, the maid, knows the secret: "Why this Wench is the *Pass-par-toute*, a very master-Key to every Body's strong box." Nothing further is done with this knowledge until Act V, when Foible tells Mrs. Fainall, who tells Mirabell, who tells all. At the last, the revelation, the complete knowledge, contributes virtually nothing to the denouement, because Fainall plays his trump—the threat of scandal—immediately after it.

It is in revealing these hidden facts that Congreve deals with the basic Restoration theme of the contrast between appearance and nature. The first act serves to define the outer, obvious social framework of family relationships, admitted loves, and professed friendships. It is, however, riddled with hints of the underlying currents of emotion, unrevealed until the second act, which is primarily devoted to unmasking—to the audience only—the emotional involvements of Mirabell, the Fainalls, and Mrs. Marwood. In Act III, the characters gain partial awareness of the undercurrents: Marwood and Fainall learn of Mirabell's plan and of his past affair with Mrs. Fainall. The fourth act does not appreciably change the quanta of knowledge the several characters have, but contrasts the decorous, moderated honesty of Mirabell and Millamant with the indecorous openness of Sir Wilfull and the deceptions and pretenses of Lady Wishfort and the other characters. In Act V, all pretenses are destroyed with Fainall's and Mirabell's revelations and the bringing out from a black box of the deed that renders Fainall powerless. The pattern is that the difference between visible and invisible factors gives power to him who knows it; breaking down the difference, i.e., revealing the hidden facts, destroys that power.

Congreve has unduly complicated both kinds of relationship, dynastic and emotional, and in both cases some of the complications are not essential to the plot. We must look for the reason. The confusion which is the prevailing atmosphere of the play becomes almost a kind of symbol for one of the points Congreve wants to make. That is, the confusion asks the question that underlies almost every facet of the play: What is the true interaction between these two kinds of relationships? To some extent, I think, we are meant to be aware simply of the idea "family" and the idea "emotion," without necessarily following through the involved details. The technique is much the same as that in T.S. Eliot's *The Confidential Clerk*, where emotional and dynastic relations proliferate in the same way to define two kinds of reality and test their relative "realness." As it develops, *The Way of the World* does just exactly that; act after act tests the relative realness of dynastic and emotional relations. In Act I, only the family relations and Mirabell's love for Millamant are particularly evident, and they artificially overshadow the implicitly more "real" relations developed in Act II. As the play develops, however, the undercurrents of emotion assume greater and greater force. In Act III, Marwood's role becomes increasingly important. She has no family connection to the central group, but is related instead by her affair with Fainall and resentment of Mirabell, emotional connections. Her overhearing Mirabell's plan and learning of his past affair with Mrs. Fainall are crucial to the plot development. The entrance at this point of Sir Wilfull Witwoud as a country bumpkin ridiculed by the fops reveals the ultimate irrelevance of the dynastic tie that brings him there, compared to the importance of Marwood's emotional tie. Linguistically, there is the contrast between the superficial banter on Sir Wilfull's entrance and the urgent plotting by Marwood and Fainall immediately after. Act IV continues to set off Sir Wilfull's blunt openness against the duplicity of the social situation. His entrance, which was like a breath of fresh air from the country, becomes, when he is drunk, a "Breath like a Bagpipe." His stillborn courtship of Millamant, with only the family tie for a basis, contrasts with Mirabell's supremely urban wooing, derived from an emotional attachment. Mirabell, in turn, establishes a mean between the knight's willfulness and the social pretenders. In the last scene, the emotional undercurrents seem to have established final dominance over the family relations. Marwood and Fainall have complete control, and are manipulating the family relations as a lever to gain their ends. Lady Wishfort's plaintive remark, "Ah! her first Husband, my Son *Languish*, wou'd not have carry'd it thus," seems to mark the nadir of dynastic strength. Sir Wilfull's sword, though on the side of family and good-nature, is powerless; it is Mirabell's deed that saves the day.

The unraveling with its final clue, the deed, suggests the relation between the two complex realities of family and emotional ties: that the "real" reality is the inward, emotional nature; this reality is a changing flux that gives birth to a more stable framework of overt social facts (dynastic relations); when, for whatever reason, these social facts are not true reflections of the underlying emotional relations (Mrs. Fainall's marriage, the projected "marriage" of Lady Wishfort to Mirabell's servant, and the like) a situation of power results in favor of one who knows the inconsistency; the antidote to such situations is to create an overt, social situation which will truly reflect the underlying realities. This interplay between two kinds of reality leads naturally enough, to two kinds of action in the play. The first—I will call it the *unraveling*—peels off bit by bit the surface appearances to get at the real facts of emotion underneath. The second, which I will call the *emancipating*, sets up a new social structure based on those underlying emotional realities.

In the unraveling action, the final end is the final fact, the heart of the whole situation hidden in a mysterious black box. Just as Mirabell's contract with Millamant suggests an ideal of balance between the social and personal aspects of marriage, so this deed represents a fusion of the social and personal aspects of the entire dramatic situation. The deed is effective in law as a result of Mrs. Fainall's social and dynastic status: only as a widow could she make a valid conveyance of her property. Yet the deed formalized a hidden emotional situation. The deed is effective because it destroys the very *res* of Fainall's actions; his motive is brought out into the open and dealt with directly as motive. In all these respects, this deed contrasts with the deed Fainall attempts to get from Lady Wishfort, which is based on an opposition of social and emotional situations. "Ironically," Paul and Miriam Mueschke point out, "the double-dealer whose life has been a sham meets shattering defeat through overconfidence in a spurious document."[1] Fainall's deed is an abortive attempt to make social pressure permanently dislocate emotions, to create a retrograde movement in which the fear of scandal separates Mirabell and Millamant. In the nature of things it fails. There is a third deed to which both the others are contrasted, the one Mirabell's disguised servant Waitwell promises to bring to "prove" his identity to Lady Wishfort. Its connection with the others is established by Waitwell's remark, when he brings the real deed, "I have brought the Black-Box at last, Madam," referring to his earlier promise when he pretended to have a deed. The illusory deed symbolizes the weakness of Mirabell's scheme. It would have created a focus of power by the disparity between the appearances

1. Paul and Miriam Mueschke, *A New View of Congreve's Way of the World,* University of Michigan Contributions in Modern Philology, no. 23 (Ann Arbor: University of Michigan Press, 1958), p. 37.

of the situation, Lady Wishfort's marriage to a gentleman, and Waitwell's nature as a servant, but the scheme is defeated by the breakdown of the difference in knowledge when Marwood discovers the plan. Sir Wilfull's sword-play contrasts with all the deeds. "S'heart an you talk of an Instrument, Sir," says the redoubtable country knight. "I have an old Fox by my Thigh shall hack your Instrument of *Ram Vellam* to Shreds, Sir." His attempt to maintain the social *status quo* is inadequate because it does not take into account either the concealed motives or the outward realities of the situation. It is subsocial, even subhuman ("an old Fox," "a *Beargarden* Flourish"). The final deed is more powerful than either Wilfull's coercive sword or Fainall's or Mirabell's attempts to use disparities between appearances and nature, because this deed harmonizes the social and emotional situations. Because it is a crystallization of an earlier emotional situation into a valid social form, because it moves with the emotional realities rather than against them, the deed can even create a new social order. "It may be a Means, well manag'd, to make you live easily together," says Mirabell to Mrs. Fainall.

The deed is thus not only the most hidden secret in the unraveling action; it is also one of the foundation posts for the new social structure evolved in the emancipating action. In that slow emancipation, by the end of the play, all of the characters who are dependent on Lady Wishfort are freed. The most important, of course, is Millamant. She is won away from her aunt's cabal where she is emotionally imprisoned like a sleeping beauty under the control of witchlike Lady Wishfort; she is drawn into a marriage in which she is at least an equal partner. Mrs. Fainall, Lady Wishfort's daughter, establishes control over her own marriage, and Sir Wilfull is free of Lady Wishfort's matchmaking to "prosecute his Travels." He even plans to take Witwoud and Petulant, members of her cabal, away with him. The last remaining member of the cabal, Mrs. Marwood, has on her own passed beyond the pale. Even Lady Wishfort's maid, Foible, will after the closing curtain retire to the farm she and her new husband, Waitwell, are to receive from Mirabell.

Appropriately enough for the action dealing with the breakdown and build-up of social structures, a dance symbolizes the emancipation. It is held at the end of the play, "that we who are not Lovers," says Sir Wilfull, "may have some other Employment, besides looking on." This particular dance should be an exception to the general rule of omitting the numerous dances and masques with which Restoration comedies are larded. Neither should this dance be the motions Martha Graham-like of improbable young ladies in leotards who so often turn up in productions of old plays calling for dances. Nor do I mean a quick hop-skip-and-jump that suggests only the general embarrassment of actors and director at the whole idea. This dance is worth some time, for it is an important part of the symbolism. For example, some seven speeches before it, the dim-witted Witwoud says, "I'm in a Maze yet, like a Dog in a Dancing-School," and, of course, that is just what Witwoud is when compared to the clever Mirabell and Fainall. The dance suggests the pattern of building up and breaking down social structures that is the stuff of the play. It raises a visible image of rules evolved by people, then imposed restrictively on themselves— Yeats's phrase, "How can we know the dancer from the dance," applies. Though it has become fashionable these days to cry down ritual interpretations, nevertheless this dance quite obviously resembles the *komos* or wedding procession which closed the archetypal fertility drama. Indeed, this very sophisticated play is quite close to the archetypal, primeval pattern of comedy: one can easily think of Lady Wishfort as the "Old King" or winter or death imprisoning the maiden Millamant and of Mirabell as the spring or "New King" who wishes to release her.

* * *

The contract scene, like proviso scenes in earlier plays, shows how social forms can balance and preserve an emotional reality, but this contract scene goes farther: it shows the enchanting Millamant brought from girlhood to maturity. Before the contract scene, Millamant insists on treating love lightly and distantly. She uses her love letters to pin up her hair and, with elaborate casualness, informs her admirers of the fact. She loves to give suitors pain, and looks down on Marwood who has let herself become emotionally involved. It is only after the contract scene that Millamant can make a mature statement about love: "Well, if *Mirabell* shou'd not make a good Husband, I am a lost Thing;—for I find I love him violently." The locked door that forces the showdown not only constrains Sir Wilfull to a social courtship for which he is neither suited nor willing; it suggests also, as Mirabell points out, "That here the Chace must end, and my Pursuit be crown'd." The lovers have found a social edge to what we have called in Congreve's earlier plays the "cult of chase." Millamant, however, insists that she will never be deprived of "the agreeable Fatigues of Solicitation," a girlish reaction belied by her own words in the finale: "Why does not the Man take me? Wou'd you have me give my self to you over again?"

None of her charming but almost feminist provisos deals with the personal aspects of marriage. They all, the Mueschkes point out, "are the result of her desire to prolong and increase the prenuptial glamour."[2] They are developed, with the one exception of her

2. Mueschke, *A New View*, p. 30.

exclamation, "My dear Liberty," in a typically feminine way: by the enumeration of a number of specific things from which one could evolve a general principle, though, of course, Millamant doesn't. Her first proviso in a general sense is that she be able to keep the integrity of her individuality; specifically, it is: "I'll lye a-bed in a Morning as long as I please," in her case, a particularly significant expression of her narcissistic girlishness. Her second is that they will continue to present a decorous appearance in public; the third is that she have free communication with others—both these ideas being represented only by specific instances.

Mirabell's conditions are quite different; they are frankly sexual in content, directed to his not being cuckolded or to her bedroom manners. Just as Millamant's are developed femininely Mirabell's are developed in a typically masculine way. "The wit of Mirabell," the Mueschkes note, "is predominantly judicial, that of Millamant is fanciful."[3] Each of Mirabell's provisos begins with its *inprimus* or *item*: first, the general principle ("that your Acquaintance be general"), then specific instructions ("no she Friend") and an illustration of the forbidden behavior ("to wheadle you a *fop-scrambling* to the Play in a Mask"). One specific instance leads him to the next general principle: the mask to leaving her face alone, beauticians to bawds, bawds to breeding, the foetus' sugar-loaf head to the tea-table. (The way in which each party in this scene presents conditions is certainly the most brilliant of all of Congreve's dramaturgic strokes.) Whereas Mirabell receives Millamant's asexual requirements with equanimity ("Your Demands are pretty reasonable"), she meets his sexual ones with at least pretended disgust: "Detestable *Inprimis*!" "Ah! name it not," "Odious Endeavours!" or "O horrid *Proviso's*!" Mirabell has drawn her out of herself toward maturity.

Just as the contract scene serves both to unravel and to emancipate, so these two actions are fused in the one person who towers over the play. Although she is technically only a supporting character and does not appear until Act III, Lady Wishfort is talked about all through the first two acts, and in the finale she becomes a kind of tribunal before whom the opposed forces in the play plead their causes. She says of herself, "I look like an old peel'd Wall," a metaphor that operates in a number of ways. She is a wall in that she tries to enforce a separation between appearance and nature, not only for herself but for those under her influence. She is a wall, too, in that she stands as an obstacle to the natural progress of passions. The peeling suggests not just the failure of her cosmetics, but that such a wall is bound to decay and crumble. Thus, Lady Wishfort acts as a wall with respect to both the major actions of the

3. *Ibid.*, p. 32.

play, the unraveling of appearances from nature and the emancipating of the younger group.

With respect to the first action, Lady Wishfort tries to maintain a grandly absurd bundle of pretenses. She is preoccupied with cosmetics to cover her age. Her library features Collier's moralistic *Short View*, while she herself is familiar with D'Urfey's ribald *Don Quixote*. Sometimes she uses an affected sesquipedelian speech and sometimes her justly famous "boudoir Billingsgate." Congreve gives her his most magnificent invective, and, revealingly enough, most of her images are taken from lower-class occupations. Her "way of the world," in short, is symbolized by her coachmen perfumed to serve as footmen.

Specifically, Lady Wishfort pretends by substituting art for nature. As Foible, her maid, says: "A little Art once made your Picture like you; and now a little of the same Art must make you like your Picture. Your Picture must sit for you, Madam." When she meets Sir Rowland, her posture is artistically contrived, just as her fifth-act *Weltschmertz* is expressed in the absurdities of literary pastoral: "I would retire to Desarts and Solitudes; and feed harmless Sheep by Groves and purling Streams. Dear *Marwood*, let us leave the World, and retire by our selves and be Shepherdesses." Part of her substitution of art for nature is suggested by her speechtag, "As I am a person," which is, in turn, belied by her continually calling others by subhuman epithets: "Puppet, thou wooden thing upon wires," "Borachio," "Caterpillar," "viper," "serpent," and the like. In a sense, the whole question is whether she really has any personality left at all.

With respect to the first action, Lady Wishfort reverses appearance and nature; she tries to prevent the unraveling. With respect to the second action, emancipation, she stands as a block to the natural growth and development of emotions. She boasts, for example, of her daughter's repressive education: "To impress upon her tender Years a young Odium and Aversion to the very sight of Men,—ay Friend, she would have shriek'd if she had but seen a Man, 'till she was in her Teens." This education, of course, is the real cause of Mrs. Fainall's adult maladjustments. Lady Wishfort, despite her age, blocks the affairs of the younger generation by intruding herself as one of them, and assuming that Mirabell should really be attached to her rather than to Millamant. Her description of Mirabell, like the image of the wall, suggests her age: "He is as terrible to me as a *Gorgon*; if I see him I fear I shall turn to Stone, petrifie incessantly." In the play it is Lady Wishfort who creates most the impression of time's flow.

Not just Lady Wishfort, though, but all the characters are involved in these two actions of unraveling and emancipation. It is these two factors which form, for example, the elusive distinction between the characters of Fainall and Mirabell. Superficially, one seems to be good and the other bad, like Maskwell and Mellefont in *The Double-Dealer*; but in this play, the hero and villain behave very much alike: Mirabell has treated both Mr. and Mrs. Fainall very shoddily indeed, and his scheme for humiliating Lady Wishfort into consent is hardly what one would expect from a virtuous young man like Mellefont. At the opening of this chapter I said that Fainall's language could not be distinguished from Mirabell's. That is not strictly true. There are differences in their speech, but they are far more subtle than the distinguishing marks of the other characters, because Fainall and Mirabell, being the most intelligent characters in the play, tend to react to the external stimuli they share in the same way. We can, however, see differences:

Fainall. But cou'd you think, because the nodding Husband wou'd not wake, that e'er the watchful Lover slept?

Mirabell. Well, have I Liberty to offer Conditions—That when you are dwindled into a Wife, I may not be beyond Measure enlarg'd into a Husband.

Fainall describes himself as divided into two separate roles, lover and husband. He is a man who sees the outer framework of appearances and formalities as perpetually divorced from the inner, "real" nature of emotions and desires. Mirabell sees himself as a self growing into a husband. In general, he seeks a harmony between appearance and nature; though he recognizes the need for keeping a distance between them, he resists outright inconsistency.

Mirabell characterizes Fainall (whose name, of course, is significant) as "a Man lavish of his Morals, an interested and professing Friend, a false and a designing Lover; yet one whose Wit and outward fair Behaviour, have gain'd a Reputation with the Town." Marwood says to him: "Truth and you are inconsistent." To Fainall, dissimulation is an ordinary condition of being. "Had you dissembl'd better," he says to Mirabell, "Things might have continu'd in the State of Nature." The difference between him and Mirabell is summed up neatly in their dialogue about Millamant:

Fainall. For a passionate Lover, methinks you are a Man somewhat too discerning in the Failings of your Mistress.

Mirabell. And for a discerning man, somewhat too passionate a Lover; for I like her with all her Faults; nay like her for her Faults. Follies are so natural, or so artful, that they become her; and those Affectations which in another Woman wou'd be odious, serve but to make her more agreeable.

To Fainall, faults are something to be hidden from outward appearance; to Mirabell, they are natural or derived from an art harmonizing with nature, and to be accepted as part of the total per-

sonality. The play as a whole criticizes, with Mirabell, appearances
and forms which are not the natural outgrowths of inward, private
emotions. His provisos in the contract scene are uniformly against
outward forms that repress or conceal: she-confidantes (he does not
provide against males), masks, cosmetics, house-to-house sales-
women who are really bawds, corseting of unborn children, and tea-
tables that hide carousing. Mirabell seeks the reconciliation of
appearances with the passions that give rise to them. What is frus-
trating him in his love for Millamant is that he cannot help loving
her. He can neither disguise his love nor express it. Reason and passion are at war within him: "Motion not Method is [woman's]
Occupation. To know this, and yet continue to be in Love, is to be
made wise from the Dictates of Reason, and yet persevere to play
the Fool by the force of Instinct." Her insistence on motion, her
failure to stabilize her emotions and give them permanent form
keeps Mirabell in a state of flux, too.

Millamant relishes her own changeability: as Mirabell says of her,
"Think of you! To think of a Whirlwind, tho 'twere in a Whirlwind, were a Case of more steady Contemplation." Over and over
again, she delightedly contradicts herself. She is reluctant to formal-
ize her feelings for fear their social form would stifle her real self.
"Ah!" she cries, "I'll never marry, unless I am first made sure of my
Will and Pleasure." Millamant's love of change is revealed in the
style of her speech as well as the matter. She talks in short sentences tumbling over one another in quick succession. Millamant
keeps herself uninvolved and loves to twit others who fail to do so:
she reduces Marwood to impotent rage by poking fun at her desire
for Mirabell, and she cuts Mirabell to a gasp when she shows she
knows his plan to humiliate Lady Wishfort. She herself avoids the
discrepancy between appearance and nature by having nothing to
conceal.

Mrs. Marwood, on the other hand, thrives on concealment. In
the conventions of the play, a disparity between known appearances
and concealed nature gives power to the one who knows the secret.
Marwood craves this power. Thus, she expresses her pretended aversion to men: "I am thinking sometimes to carry my Aversion
further. . . . by marrying; if I cou'd but find one that lov'd me very
well, and would be thoroughly sensible of ill Usage, I think I should
do myself the Violence of undergoing the Ceremony."

> Mrs. *Fainall.* You wou'd not make him a Cuckold?
> Mrs. *Marwood.* No; but I'd make him believe I did, and that's
> as bad.
> Mrs. *Fain.* Why had you not as good do it?
> Mrs. *Mar.* O if he shou'd ever discover it, he wou'd then know

the worst, and be out of his Pain; but I wou'd have him ever to continue upon the Rack of Fear and Jealousie.

It is she who devises Fainall's plan to blackmail Lady Wishfort, who "will come to any Composition to save her [daughter's] Reputation." She shows the same sense of roles defining personality that Fainall has, when she says, " 'Tis an unhappy Circumstance of Life, that Love shou'd ever die before us; and that the Man so often shou'd out-live the Lover." Her action throughout, like Fainall's, is an attempt to give expression to her passions by the use of intrigue rather than by ordinary social expression; she turns out to be as wrong-headed as her lover.

Between Mrs. Marwood and Mrs. Fainall, there is the same kind of elusive distinction as between Fainall and Mirabell. Both are guilty of illicit affairs, but one seems innately bad, the other innately good—"a pattern of Generosity." (Mrs. Fainall's affair, it should be remembered, is venial by Restoration standards; the least of female lapses was that of a widow, contrasted with the worst, Marwood's, that of an unmarried woman. The worst thing Mrs. Fainall did was to marry Fainall under false pretenses, but he married her under false pretenses, too.) Like Marwood, Mrs. Fainall is (or was) given to extremes of passion. She has, she says, "lov'd without Bounds," and now wants to hate without limits. Like Marwood, she tends to be indifferent to reputation, but therein lies the distinction; while Marwood's indecorum lies in giving too much freedom to her passions and hence undervaluing reputation which stands as a block to their free expression, Mrs. Fainall has learned the folly of giving too much importance to outward appearances, of committing "disagreeable and dangerous Actions" "to save that Idol Reputation." She can say snidely to Marwood, "Madam, you seem to stifle your Resentment: You had better give it vent." "Fy, fy," she says, brushing aside Millamant's coyness, "have him, have him, and tell him so in plain Terms: For I am sure you have a Mind to him." She has learned from her own mistakes the tragedy of allowing an outward convention, her marriage, which did not grow organically from emotion, to impose itself upon and stifle her inner nature.

Lady Wishfort and the two "unnaturals," Witwoud and Petulant, are humor characters who have virtually replaced themselves by their affectations. Witwoud's wit amounts only to extravagant similes that connect things superficially, that is, his similes establish connections (his own wit to a fire, for example), but the connections are not particularly meaningful. Like Witwoud's wit, Petulant's professed animosity comes to nothing. Together these two form an absurd plane of complete and empty sociality against which

the main actions are reflected. They enter the final resolution, "rubbing their Eyes, — just risen from Sleep." Petulant sees the whole
thing as a game: "How now? what's the matter? who's Hand's
out?" Both are guilty of continual oversimplification, Witwoud in
his "similitudes" and Petulant with his "All's one, let it pass." Real
emotions are lost on them. They are ridiculous, all manner and no
substance, as empty as balloons, and blown by whatever random
stimuli come their way.

Sir Wilfull Witwoud, though equally absurd, is their opposite, all
substance and no manner. He is an alien figure like Ben or Manly,
who comes from elsewhere and passes through "the Town" only to
go away again. Like the other alien figures, he serves to suggest an
alternative way of life to that of London, in his case, a mode in
which "great lubberly Brothers slabber and kiss one another when
they meet, like a Call of Serjeants." Lady Wishfort suggests his role
as an alien by telling him, "Thou art not fit to live in a Christian
Commonwealth, thou beastly Pagan." His presence, by suggesting
another way of life, puts the main action into a perspective that
raises the play as a whole beyond the mere description of manners
into a generalized statement about man in and out of society.

Miss Elinor Fuchs in a very astute treatment of the play suggests
that Witwoud and Petulant and Sir Wilfull are "half-men."[4] She
points out that Witwoud and Petulant are described as a pair of
"Battledores" and as "Treble and Base." Witwoud and Sir Wilfull
constitute one tree, "a Medlar grafted on a Crab," or one ass. Their
relationship as half-brothers is significant. Petulant and Sir Wilfull
make "a Pair of Castanets." There is an arithmetical suggestion
that Witwoud and Petulant are each worth one half of Mirabell or
Sir Wilfull. As Fainall had said earlier, describing the "Cabal-
Nights": "Some body mov'd that to avoid Scandal there might be
one Man of the Community; upon which *Witwoud* and *Petulant*
were enroll'd Members." In connection with this concept of "half-
men" we should remember that Mirabell establishes his final relationship with Millamant by supplying her with the second half of a
couplet from Waller. It is as though all *four* of these men were
seeking halves to complete themselves, as in Aristophanes' myth in
the *Symposium*. Man, this half-man metaphor suggests, needs the
completion represented by conventional forms. He needs forms not
only to shield his private life, but also to give his fleeting emotions
a stability and durability.

Professors Brooks and Heilman say the play represents "almost a
symphonic pattern in which the theme of love receives a variety of
treatments, ranging from the somber . . . to the burlesque." Mira-

4. Elinor C. Fuchs, "The Moral and
Aesthetic Achievement of William Congreve" (Cambridge, Mass., 1955, unpub.),
p. 71.

bell and Millamant must come between extremes, an absolute social standard or none, by finding an inner standard. The irony that pervades the play suggests the deviousness of the "way of the world."[5] Miss Fuchs resorts to an even wider concept, concluding that *The Way of the World* is about different kinds of decorum. The "great decorum" achieved by Mirabell and Millamant represents a way of idealizing human potentialities by creating a civilized sensibility that is focused back on the wash of activity out of which it grew. Congreve, she says, seems to demand that life must have form, precise and elegant social forms which can fuse beauty and truth, distilling the positive qualities from a world which mixes indiscriminately wisdom and folly, honesty and falsehood, love and hate, beauty and ugliness.[6] These two interpretations set the play in the tradition of British ceremonial, the Burkean belief in forms that evolve and solidify, embodying a standard to later times. "The King," writes Pepys in 1666, "hath yesterday in Council declared his resolution of setting a fashion for clothes, which we will never alter. It will be a vest, I know not well how; but it is to teach the nobility thrift, and will do good."[7] To Congreve, as to Pepys, Charles II, and Englishmen generally, external forms can be a means of training up the self like a vine on a trellis.

Paul and Miriam Mueschke, by their careful and exact explication of lines and scenes, suggest still another aspect of the play. Very acutely, they point out that *The Way of the World* deals at its most obvious level with the fight between two pairs of adulterers for three legacies. "Congreve," they say, "is not an apologist for, but a satirist of the way of the world." The play attacks (as did *The Double-Dealer*) *both* folly and vice. The folly appears in the persons of Witwoud and Petulant. The vice shows in the contrast between a pair of adulterers (Mirabell and Mrs. Fainall) on the way to reformation and a pair of adulterers (Fainall and Mrs. Marwood) on the way to further degradation. The four standard Restoration types in the play, the rake (Mirabell), the cast mistress (Marwood), the adulteress (Mrs. Fainall), and the cuckold (Fainall), are not treated, as even in Congreve's earlier plays, with amused tolerance. They are all shown as highly intelligent; they are all made to fear and finally to suffer scandal and exposure. "Throughout *The Way of the World* every character who has indulged in illicit relations finds that his present or past adultery hampers his ability to plan for the future—that immorality cannot be quibbled out of existence."[8]

5. Cleanth Brooks and Robert Heilman, *Understanding Drama* (New York: Holt, 1948), p. 446.
6. Fuchs, "Moral and Aesthetic Achievement," pp. 49–50.
7. *The Diary of Samuel Pepys,* ed. Henry B. Wheatley, 8 vols. (London: Bell, 1904), VI, 11 (October 8, 1966).
8. Mueschke, *A New View,* pp. 13–14, 25.

Whether one takes this moral view of the play or the more formal one suggested by Miss Fuchs and Professors Brooks and Heilman, clearly *The Way of the World* deals with much more than "manners." Even so, while these descriptions are the most complete so far suggested, I think they neglect Congreve's sense of co-ordinates that we saw in *The Old Batchelor*. In particular, they neglect the idea of emancipation in the play.

Mirabell and Millament do not simply achieve a form—they first free themselves from an old form that no longer reflects a true state of affairs. The play comprises two actions moving, as it were, at right angles to each other. The first, which I have called an unraveling, evens out the disparities in knowledge that existed at the opening of the play so that at the end everybody knows everything. The second action, which I have called emancipation, creates from the breakdown of the old social order dominated by Lady Wishfort a new social order that grows out of the underlying emotional realities of the situation.

These two actions coalesce in the "way" of the title. "Way," in the sense of habitual manner or style, suggests that discrepancy between appearance and nature which is the ubiquitous "way" of the Restoration world; it is this "way" on which the unraveling action is based. "Way," in the sense of path or direction of motion, suggests that moving force of passions which makes existing forms change in the emancipating action of the play. The three references within the play to its title bear out the pattern. The first occurs when Fainall discovers his wife has played him false, that she married him only to cover up her affair with Mirabell. "I it seems am a Husband, a Rank-Husband," he snarls, "and my Wife a very Errant, Rank-Wife,—all in the Way of the *World*"; by which, I take it, he means not only marital infidelity, but the discrepancy between appearances and the true facts which he sees as a condition of existence. The second time the title is mentioned is when Fainall reassures Marwood as their relationship is revealed: "If it must all come out, why let 'em know it, 'tis but the *Way of the World*." The third reference to the title occurs when Mirabell produces the crucial deed:

> *Fainall.* Confusion!
> *Mirabell.* Even so, Sir, 'tis *the Way of the World*, Sir.

Both these latter "ways of the world" refer to a breakdown of the normal discrepancy between appearance and nature. These, then, are the "ways of the world": the passage of time and the discrepancy between "natural" emotions and social appearances. From these two fundamental characteristics of this world (as opposed to some Paradise), social conventions build up and break down as one generation passes on control to the next. * * *

MARTIN PRICE

[Form and Wit in *The Way of the World*]†

* * * Flexibility, the power to accept and adapt to the world without yielding to it, marks the central figures of Congreve's *The Way of the World*. Here once more the lovers are confronted with a tangle of intrigue, but it is their skill in extricating themselves from it that we admire. They show the same skill in extricating themselves from the patterns of conduct the world imposes; their integrity is preserved by a tact that resists both the shallowness of affectation and the cruelty of blind passion. Mirabell and Millamant exist only within the framework of the play; their characters, like those of the lovers in *All for Love*,[1] are defined by the symmetrical disposition of the other figures around them.

The most obvious foils are Witwoud and Petulant, who, like Fielding's Square and Thwackum, represent contrasting patterns of a common false wit. Petulant is the would-be man of candor, who masks no sentiment, however displeasing. He is, in fact, a bad actor even in that undemanding role, and he is soon exposed in all his vanity and hypocrisy as a man pretending to a more wholesome humor than he possesses. Witwoud is more obvious and yet more interesting. Congreve has presented him in greater depth, and he supplies the most brilliant epitome of wit without judgment. To that extent he is a fine embodiment of the way of the world in which he is a prominent parasite: his every gesture is designed to impress, and the bustling energy of the effort consumes all his powers. He is wholly dedicated to erasing his past and winning acceptance in the world of fashion on whatever terms it sets. Witwoud has his ugly traits, but he is so desperately affable, so fatuously self-congratulatory, and so transparently foolish, that he is at once somewhat shabby and altogether disarming. His harmlessness gives him a privileged status in the reader's eyes as it does in the ladies' cabals. He may remind us of the fictitious author of Swift's *Tale of a Tub*, again a desperate hanger-on, too dense to be guileful, too voluble to be subtle, a fool who gives away the game of the knaves he aspires to imitate. The cynicism of other men's epigrams, as Witwoud repeats them with an air of worldliness, becomes curiously abstract and unmotivated. When he says with a smirk, "a wit should be no more sincere, than a woman constant; one argues a decay of parts, as t'other of beauty," the effect is far different from

† From Martin Price, *To the Palace of Wisdom* (New York: Doubleday & Company, 1964), pp. 241–245. Reprinted by permission of the author.
1. Dryden's tragedy, which Price has discussed earlier in this chapter [Editor].

that created by Fainall's more cruel and urgent remarks. The comparative ingenuousness of Witwoud's stylish malice underlines the strength and depth of Fainall's. Witwoud is a kind of industrious but incompetent apprentice in an inverted world. What Witwoud and Petulant dramatize so well is summed up in Mirabell's couplet at the close of the first act:

> Where modesty's ill-manners, 'tis but fit
> That impudence and malice pass for wit.

Lady Wishfort is, of course, the center of the plot. She is a tyrant, a hypocrite, and a lecherous old fool, but she exists more to be manipulated and hoodwinked than to control the situation. She, too, gives away the game by her overplaying; and there is at least a touch of pathos in the savagery with which she contests the ravage of age:

FOIBLE: Your ladyship has frowned a little too rashly, indeed madam. There are some cracks discernible in the white varnish.

LADY WISHFORT: Let me see the glass.—Cracks, sayest thou?—why I am errantly flayed—I look like an old peeled wall. Thou must repair me, Foible, before Sir Rowland comes, or I shall never keep up to my picture (III, i).

Like Witwoud, Lady Wishfort serves as a bathetic reduction of all the stratagems of this world. Foible remarks, "a little art once made your picture like you; and now a little of the same art must make you like your picture." Art rules nature in this world ("tenderness becomes me best—a sort of dyingness—you see that picture has a sort of a—ha, Foible! a swimmingness in the eye"). And Lady Wishfort is the kind of artist who so crushingly overwhelms nature that she somehow reveals it anew in unexpected ways. Her fondness for ratafia, her closet full of Puritan tracts, her avowed esteem for "decorums"—all these make her a torrential force of humor: her affectations and habits are borne on its surface like the debris that attests to the power of the current. In this way, Congreve frames a world in which the malice and polish are, after all, less universal than they seem. The situation anticipates that of the London of *Tom Jones*, where, beside such consummate scoundrels as Lady Bellaston, the would-be rogues like Lord Fellamar and Jack Nightingale seem backward pupils in an exacting school. The full range of human warmth is suggested too, in the nuptials of Waitwell and Foible, the cheerful stolidity of Sir Willful Witwoud, and the generous lack of jealousy in Mrs. Fainall.

The figures who seem the masters of this world are Fainall and Marwood. It is they who have used the world with a hard and joyless egoism. Fainall, at the opening of the play, sets himself off from Mirabell by the quality of his temperament:

FAINALL: . . . I'd no more play with a man that slighted his ill fortune than I'd make love to a woman who undervalued the loss of her reputation.

MIRABELL: You have a taste extremely delicate, and are for refining on your pleasures.

The note of corruption that Fainall sounds allows us a glance ahead to such cold and perverse sensualists as Blifil; it establishes a character which is consistently presented. He can recall to his mistress the lies she has used in their behalf: "I meant but to remind you of the slight account you once could make of strictest ties, when set in competition with your love to me." And it is with reason that Marwood replies, " 'Tis false, you urged it with deliberate malice! 'twas spoken in scorn, and I never will forgive it" (II, iii). The disdain in which Fainall holds the world is best seen when he confronts Lady Wishfort with his demands, sparing her no humiliation, and finally —as he is defeated—turning upon his wife with all the malice of an outwitted Machiavel.

The case of Marwood is not much different; she wins more sympathy because the passions that possess her are less coldly egocentric. Her resentment of Mirabell's indifference has become a goad that makes her put up with a lover she seems half to hate. But, like Fainall, she flourishes in those moments when she can relieve her bitterness in the promise of pain to others; like Fainall, she needs to be revenged, and her need colors her plotting with a note of extravagant malice. She turns to an easy victim like Lady Wishfort with strong relish: "Here comes the good Lady, panting ripe; with a heart full of hope, and a head full of care, like any chemist upon the day of projection" (III, vii).

Millamant seems to sense this excess of Marwood's temper: in their scene together, she plays upon Marwood's jealousy with a cruel lightness that appears to be the only way to meet the other's rage, and the song she calls for sounds the note of Marwood's and Fainall's ambition:

> Then I alone the conquest prize,
> When I insult a rival's eyes:
> If there's delight in love, 'tis when I see
> That heart, which others bleed for, bleed for me.

I think that we can set Millamant's powers in this scene; she is constantly unsettled herself by the intensity of Marwood's attitude, and she improvises until she finds the right level of malice herself to hold Marwood off and keep their relations on a basis of ingenious insult. Even so, Marwood can scarcely contain herself: "Your merry note may be changed sooner than you think."

What gives the play its form is the way in which Mirabell and Millamant can, through their own peculiar balance of wit and generosity of spirit, reduce the bumbling Witwoud and the mordant Fainall to the same level of false wit. Just as the fools lack any depth of awareness and power of judgment, so eventually the villains overplay their hands. Fainall and Marwood turn out, after all, to be victims of their own passions. Their cynical manipulation of social convention is too assured; they cannot believe in the wit of others or in the capacity of others to elude their control. The way of the world in which Fainall takes taunting pride is more complex than he can understand, and his frustration, like Marwood's, exposes the savage compulsions driving him. If at one point in the play, Fainall's seems the most knowing view of the world, it is finally revealed in its shallowness, a shallowness arising from his disbelief in the reality of any being other than himself.

Mirabell and Millamant dramatize the true wit that is so carefully and symmetrically defined through opposition. An adequate performance of the play must present their strong hold upon each other throughout and their resistance to the claim that each has on the other's integrity. Unlike Dryden's Antony and Cleopatra they do not glory in their oneness, nor celebrate the world they have in each other. They are wary and difficult, resenting the loss of judgment that love imposes even as they accept it. "As for a discerning man, somewhat too passionate a love," Mirabell describes himself; "for I like her with all her faults: nay, like her for her faults. . . . They are now grown as familiar to me as my own frailties; and in all probability, in a little time longer, I shall like 'em as well." And Millamant's charming declaration: "Well, if Mirabell should not make a good husband, I am a lost thing,—for I find I love him violently." These confidences do not prevent their careful and rational testing of each other and of their own chances for honesty in marriage. Millamant's affectations do not reveal her as artificial. They are clearly defensive maneuvers. She seems at every point to be inviting Mirabell to separate himself from this world and to free her from it.

In the famous proviso scene, they are fighting, humorously and banteringly but still generously, for a vision of marriage free from the cant and hypocrisy that surround them. These speeches, like the characters themselves, cannot exist except within the play that contains the Fainalls, Lady Wishfort, and Witwoud. They represent, like Mirabell's successful counterplot, a rational intelligence playing upon the energies it cannot command but can at least direct. The lovers must find their proper order; it is hardly one of saintly abandon of the world—as in *All for Love*—nor is it simply the old order of the flesh of Fainall and Marwood given more shrewdness and lightened to rococo frivolity.

The triumph of the play is in the emergence of lovers who, through a balance of intense affection and cool self-knowledge, achieve an equilibrium that frees them of the world's power. They can use the world and reject its demands. They have assimilated the rational lucidity of the skeptical rake; they are awake to the world's ways and their own, but they are beyond any pained horror or need to wound those who have betrayed honesty. They accept what, through exploration, they have found in themselves; and they need only be sure that they can be both themselves and each other's. The quality that marks them is a critical acuteness—true wit—that is ready to submit to what, by all the rational tests they can manage, promises to be sincere and is, in any case, irresistible love. * * *

PAUL E. PARNELL

The Sentimental Mask†

Fifty years after the modern study of sentimentalism was inaugurated by Ernest Bernbaum, the problem remains whether the term has ever been satisfactorily defined or described. Two recent developments reveal some of the difficulties: Arthur Sherbo in *The English Sentimental Drama* takes five basic criteria considered by most authorities as typical, and shows that they may all apply to plays demonstrably not sentimental.[1] John Harrington Smith, in the preface to *The Gay Couple in Restoration Comedy* (1948), announces that he has completely avoided the term "sentimental" as too vague to be of much value.[2] Yet Ronald Crane, writing fourteen years before, assumed the essential traits of sentimentalism to be fairly clear,[3] and Norman Holland has implied that two criteria borrowed from Bernbaum and Krutch still supply an adequate definition.[4] There is not even agreement whether sentimentality is a positive or negative quality. Krutch and Sherbo feel that it is false and dishonest, therefore bad.[5] Crane concedes that it is somewhat limited intellectually, but emphasizes its humanitarianism and emotional warmth, especially the "self-approving joy" that makes virtue

† From Paul E. Parnell, "The Sentimental Mask," *PMLA*, LXXVIII (1963), 529–532, 534–535. Reprinted by permission of the Modern Language Association. The footnotes have been slightly edited.
1. East Lansing, Mich., 1957, pp. 22–30.
2. Cambridge, Mass., 1948, p. vii.
3. R. S. Crane, "Suggestions toward a Genealogy of the 'Man of Feeling,'"

ELH, I (1934), 206.
4. Holland, *The First Modern Comedies* (Cambridge, Mass., 1959), p. 113. For Krutch and Bernbaum, see notes 5 and 7 below.
5. Joseph Wood Krutch, *Comedy and Conscience after the Restoration* (New York, 1949), p. 252; Sherbo, p. 166.

548 · *Paul E. Parnell*

satisfying.[6] Bernbaum vacillates between sympathy and contempt.[7]

If sentimentalism is hard to define, the word nevertheless means something vivid and unmistakable to its users. Who can read Cumberland's *The West Indian* (1771), or Lillo's *The London Merchant* (1731) and forget that mawkish sweetness, that unctuous virtue, those interminable repentances? Surely there is something unique here that can be distinguished from other literary experiences. And yet the definitions offered by critics have lacked an essential clarity. Sentimentality has something to do with the enjoyment of tears, with the insistence on material rewards for virtue, with an everyday kindliness that may possibly be "spontaneous" (Crane) or "calculated" (Sherbo), with a middle-class emphasis that often features, inconsistently, a titled cast.[8] Criticism so far has simply not defined the basic relationship between sentimentalism and virtue or morality; nor has it explained why the term, if occupied with man's noblest ideals, carries a generally unfavorable connotation. A further investigation is clearly required.

A few passages from Richard Steele and Samuel Richardson suggest a new approach. First, from the Epilogue to Steele's play *The Lying Lover* (1703):

> . . . Laughter's a distorted passion, born
> Of sudden self-esteem and sudden scorn;
> Which, when 'tis o'er, the men in pleasure wise,
> Both him that moved it and themselves despise;
> While generous pity of a painted woe
> Makes us ourselves both more approve and know.[9]

Ordinarily comedy, in Steele's view, raises the self-esteem of the spectator by provoking scorn of other people's faults. But then there is a delayed reaction: after he has thought about the comedy a little, he sees that the criticism applies to him too, and so he feels less important and less worthy. Since Steele is interested in feeling as virtuous as possible, he resents such a presentation and despises the person who perpetrated it. On the other hand, pity for dramatically presented woe has no uncomfortable aftermath. It gives the spectator the feeling that he is of sterling character, that the more he knows himself the more he will find to admire. The personal emphasis is illuminating, since the sentimentalist usually alleges himself to be altruistically concerned with others. Steele asserts in *The Christian Hero*, "How unwilling are we to Eradicate the . . . Satisfaction of Self-Admiration . . . the most senseless and stupid of all our Infirmities."[1] But it is clear that altruism of the sentimental

6. Crane, I, 205–230.
7. Ernest Bernbaum, *The Drama of Sensibility* (Boston, 1915), pp. 101, 103, 267, 268–79.
8. Sherbo, p. 6.

9. *Richard Steele*, ed. G. A. Aitken (London, 1894), p. 187.
1. *Tracts and Pamphlets by Richard Steele*, ed. Rae Blanchard (Baltimore, Md., 1944), p. 28.

sort is a means of further promoting self-admiration. Steele says elsewhere in the same tract, "Christianity has that in it, which makes Men pity, not scorn the Wicked, and by a beautiful kind of Ignorance of themselves, think those Wretches their Equals."[2] Here the assumption of one's own virtue is absolute; the Christian belief that all men are sinners in the eye of God becomes a generous self-delusion, for the purpose of lifting up the morally inferior, who might otherwise be too disgusting. One sees that Bernbaum's principle of "perfectibility of human nature" needs qualification. It is not human nature in general that is perfectible: it is one's own nature, and that is very nearly perfect now. Steele never considers the possibility that he himself might be one of the wicked. One easily infers that if "those Wretches" thought themselves in any way the equals of their condescending betters, the sentimental-Christian mask would quickly fall off. One such scene shows up in Steele's own correspondence. He is writing to Mrs. Charlotte Clayton: "I Sincerely assure you, that I do not Seek this Station upon any other View but to do good to others, and if I do not gett it, you will See my Opposers repent that they would not let me be Humble, For I shall then think myself obliged to show them what place among mankind I am really in."[3]

Here we see beneath the altruism his snobbishness, both moral and social, his conviction that there are limits beyond which Christian virtue cannot be carried, his opportunism, his effectual confession that the humility was just a pose he assumed out of decency, but a pose that ought not to be maintained for a moment if his interests are threatened. But it is important to see that Steele does not think of himself as a hypocrite; on the contary, he shows a certain moral fervor all through the passage. He is a sincere and dedicated altruist, his "opposers" are enemies of the light. It is just that Steele, like most sentimentalists, is playing a double game: he wants to think of himself as continuously virtuous, and he wants to get the job too. And these inconsistent desires require a continuous reinterpretation of every circumstance so as to emphasize the virtue and ignore the unscrupulousness. This reinterpretation is a conscious process, and as logical as the sentimentalist can make it; but, by a necessary inconsistency, the sentimentalist can never admit to himself that his argument is rationalization, or else it would fail of its designed effect: a clearing of his conscience and a conviction of his own sinlessness and altruism. Thus sentimental thinking is balanced delicately between hypocrisy and sincerity, simplicity and duplicity, self-consciousness and spontaneity. Unquestionably, the sentimentalist sees himself as sincerely, simply, and spontaneously

2. *Tracts*, p. 47.
3. *The Correspondence of Richard Steele*, ed. Rae Blanchard (London, 1941), p. 108.

virtuous, but only achieves this belief at the cost of a constant demonstration to himself that his mask of virtue and his face are one.

What is the nature of this mask? It can take many forms, but all
are clearly related to the assumption of moral perfection. The Epilogue to *The Lying Lover* gives one hint:

> What is that touch within which nature gave[?]
> . . . .
> 'Tis that pure joy which guardian angels know,
> . . . .
> When they the good protect, the ill oppose.

Thus the sentimentalist may feel that when he intervenes on the
side of virtue against debauchery and evil, he is directly inspired by
Heaven, and is a kind of guardian angel. Richardson, describing his
heroine in the preface to *Clarissa*, is even more explicit: "As far as
is consistent with human frailty, and as far as she could be perfect,
considering the people she had to deal with, and those with whom
she was inseparably connected, she *is* perfect. To have been impecc-
able, must have . . . carried our idea of her from woman to angel"
[italics Richardson's].[4] Plainly, though, she falls short of an angel
by very little; he is careful to put most of the blame on the "people
she had to deal with," and no more blame can be put on her than
the bare minimum consistent with "human frailty." In fact, as a
virtuous "exemplar to her sex," she is somehow raised above the
human race. And at the same time she is envied and hated for it,
just as Pamela is for her celebrated "virtue." Sentimental heroines
may be abused, scorned, or even violated; but whatever happens,
they die or live triumphant, and work to reclaim the errant. It must
be evident that the sentimentalist in many respects aspires to the
attributes of Christ—sinlessness, while ostensibly taking the blame
on himself for the sins of others, humility that suffers in silence,
altruism, lack of ambition—and at the same time the power to save
such as repent, and the will to damn the others. Of course the
assumption of the Christlike mask gives him considerable leeway,
since he can be either humble or almighty, as the Steele quotation
indicates. The choice of means depends largely on the possibly
opportunistic end in view.

The validity of such assumptions cannot finally be demonstrated
within the space of an article. But examination of a few key scenes
from plays usually regarded as sentimental (ranging in date from
1696 to 1731) provides a test for these criteria. Even so limited a
study may possibly discover evidence applicable on a wider scale.

First, Steele's *Conscious Lovers* (1722) offers a splendid example
of almost pure reinterpretation of motives. In this play Bevil Junior,

in obedience to his father's wishes, has become engaged to Lucinda, who is loved by his friend Myrtle. Bevil Junior really loves the beautiful and penniless Indiana whom he secretly maintains, after rescuing her from a compromising situation. Evil-minded persons might infer that he is keeping her, but Bevil is so noble that such imputations are of course unfair. On the morning of the wedding-day Bevil, still engaged to Lucinda, and already dressed in his wedding-clothes, decides he wants to visit Indiana. One might suppose that such an impulse would be hard to justify. He is in danger of being followed and detected, and his being dressed so elegantly ought to arouse her suspicion. But he wants to see her, and so he lectures himself as follows:

> We must often . . . go on in our good offices, even under the displeasure of those to whom we do them, in compassion to their weaknesses and mistakes.—But all this while poor Indiana is tortured with the doubt of me. She has no support or comfort but in my fidelity, yet sees me daily pressed to marriage with another . . . [If she does, it is not his fault. He has told her nothing, and she has no other direct means of finding out.] The religious vow to my father restrains me from ever marrying without his approbation, yet that confines me not from seeing a virtuous woman . . . the pure delight of my eyes and the guiltless joy of my heart.

This is a true *locus classicus* of sentimental thinking. He cites only those aspects of his action that will be favorable to himself: his generosity, his fidelity to obligation, his love of virtue in others, his tender regard for her ambiguous status. On the other hand, he refuses to recognize the imprudence and irresponsibility of his action. He may be correct in stressing his superiority of position, which is primarily practical—she cannot help herself, and he *can* help her (and furthermore he has not taken any steps to make her independent of him)—but he uses this independence to build up an assumption of his own moral superiority. His moral dominance becomes so overwhelming that he finds an obligation to persevere, whether his actions are appreciated or even welcome. He must go on managing his friends with the same loving pity a parent feels for a child; or to put it more honestly, he feels a right to manipulate his friends as he pleases, provided that he can state his objectives to himself in sufficiently noble terms. But he is not a hypocrite, nor does his rationalizing proceed from an uneasy conscience. He is a sentimentalist, for whom a spontaneous reinterpretation of motives has become a conviction, a way of life.

A few scenes later his complacency is rudely shattered when his friend Myrtle, convinced Bevil intends to marry Lucinda after all, challenges him to a duel. At first fighting seems the only solution.

But this tactic is so crude, and so destructive to Bevil's whole opportunistic fabric, that he can accept it only under the strain of an extreme emotion. At the first slight respite, the emotion that is supposed to dominate in sentimental plays is brought to heel by his "reason." He decides to show Myrtle Lucinda's letter, which he had felt obliged hitherto to keep secret, "except I could . . . serve him, and her, by disobeying her . . . more than I should by complying with her directions." Opportunism could be no franker. He manages to defend his action, however, by an apology to Myrtle for "perhaps too much regard to a false point of honour." A disillusioned commentator might observe that Bevil has got himself out of a nasty predicament by committing an impropriety, when a little frankness earlier would have forestalled the whole crisis. He might appropriately take some of the blame on himself, instead of abusing "honor"; but guilt is precisely what his whole intellectual orientation is designed to avoid. He therefore justifies himself by virtuous considerations: if Myrtle had found the letter about a man he had killed, it would have been worse than death to him. Myrtle, fortunately, is taken aback by this unexpected revelation, and shame at his own hastiness keeps him from resenting the violation of a confidence. Bevil now easily recovers control of the situation: "[*Aside.*] When . . . he has seen himself thoroughly, he will deserve to be assisted towards obtaining Lucinda." Bevil's basically false estimation of his own qualities does not keep him from applying a very shrewd mind throughout to the attainment of his goals. Even in the scene just quoted, Bevil's mind is already moving ahead to the match between Myrtle and Lucinda, because they love and deserve each other, and also because Bevil will not be free to marry Indiana until his fiancée Lucinda is taken off his hands.

* * *

One thing more remains to be said about the sentimentalist. Ostensibly there is no more loyal supporter of religion. After all, if he patterns his life on Christ, what more can we ask? But if this emulation of Christ is only a self-deception for primarily egoistic reasons, then his attitude is presumptuous rather than admirable. And in that case, sentimentalism might be said to make a distinct step away from traditional Christianity. The substitution of oneself for Christ is to a certain degree the substitution of a god one finds irresistibly attractive (oneself) for a god one is no longer willing to worship (Christ). If we must be "insensibly betrayed into morality, by bribing the fancy with beautiful and agreeable images" of virtue,[5] as Steele said, we have probably abandoned the morality and embraced the merely agreeable. There is no doubt that we want

5. *Tatler*, No. 98.

the bribe; it is not so certain that we want the morality or the religion. Actually there is no room in sentimentalism for the awareness of sin and the real sense of humility that Christianity is ordinarily thought to demand. Neither has sentimentalism room for theology, dogma, or ethical speculation. All that has been swept away and replaced with the sentimentalist's own virtue.

And it must not be thought that the sentimentalist is all-forgiving and overflowing with human kindness. That is merely how he thinks of himself. On the contrary, he can be malicious toward those who oppose his ideas of labor to defeat his ends. A common type in sentimental comedy is the hateful character whom everyone wants destroyed. At the end of the play, he is cornered (in *The West Indian*, the Fulmers and Lady Rusport; in *The Conscious Lovers*, Cimberton; in *The London Merchant*, Millwood). Should he be forgiven? His faults seem too gross, but sentimentalists grudgingly give him that chance. To everyone's relief, he refuses; and then the punishment everyone has hoped for may be administered with a clear conscience.

In conclusion, sentimentality seems, from the evidence collected, to have an actual but ambiguous connection with morality. Sentimentality is a state of mind based on the assumption that one's own character is perfect, or as near perfection as necessary, or if certain grave faults seem to emerge, they must not be regarded as inherent. The sentimentalist believes it is the part of Christian morality to see himself as a moral paragon whose behavior is in many respects Christlike; and he consents to indulge in mutual admiration with every person who will reciprocate. The sentimentalist will venture to "forgive" and "save" every erring mortal who will abase himself, theoretically before God, but mainly before him, the sentimentalist; and he will venture to damn every erring mortal who will not so abase himself. The first trait of sentimentality, then, is self-esteem raised to the presumptuous level of self-adoration, self-worship; and since love is a basic Christian attribute, the sentimentalist drenches all his relationships with professions of charity and altruism. Since no one is in fact perfect, and faults and limitations occur, even in sentimental behavior, they have to be explained away by a constant process of reinterpretation. The sentimentalist spends half his time justifying his morally ambiguous actions and the other half exclaiming over the beauties of Christian virtue, including his own. But, although the process of rationalization is more or less conscious, the sentimentalist is so determined to convince himself, and so successful, that he cannot be called a hypocrite. He may share with the hypocrite a determination to keep his opportunism intact; but, unlike the person of conscious duplicity, he feels obliged to wear at all times his sentimental mask.

RAYMOND WILLIAMS

[Sentimentalism and Social History] †

* * * When an art-form changes, as the direct result of changes in society, we meet a very difficult problem in criticism, for it quite often happens that a local judgment will show a form that has been brought to a high level of skill and maturity being replaced by forms that are relatively crude and unsuccessful. With the ending of a Restoration drama based on an aristocratic and fashionable audience, and its replacement by a very mixed middle-class drama based on a wider social group, we see one of the clearest and most famous of these cases. Most critics have been natural Cavaliers, and have represented the change as a disaster for the drama. Yet it is surely necessary to take a longer view. The limited character of Restoration drama, and the disintegration of a general audience which had preceded it, were also damaging. Again, while the early products of eighteenth-century middle-class culture were regarded (often with justice) as vulgar, we must, to tell the whole story, follow the development down, to the points where the "vulgar" novel became a major literary form, and where the despised forms of "bourgeois tragedy" and "sentimental comedy" served, in their maturity, a wide area of our modern drama. The development of middle-class drama is in fact one of the most interesting cases we have of a changing society leading directly to radical innovations in form.

Opposition to the theater, by the commercial middle class, can be traced back to the sixteenth century, and the renewed wave of criticism, from the 1690s, which effectively broke the Restoration dramatic spirit, in one way contains little that is new. Behind the criticism of Collier (*A Short View of the Immorality and Profaneness of the English Stage*, 1698), with its itemized complaint against the licentiousness of current comedies, the old hostility to the theater as such can be detected. But now, with the court changed in character, and no longer actively protecting the theater, middle-class opposition had to be taken more seriously, and while a Vanbrugh replied in kind, Farquhar and a new school of dramatists consciously reformed the drama to meet the immediate objections. The complexity of any adequate judgment of eighteenth-century drama follows from the fact that in some cases forms were changed reluctantly or superficially in response to the new moral tone; in

† From Raymond Williams, *The Long Revolution* (London: Chatto & Win-dus, 1961), pp. 256–260. Reprinted by permission of the publisher.

other cases, new forms were made, by extension or discovery, as a positive expression of the new spirit. This mixed result is understandable in terms of the actual change in audiences. From the 1680s, merchants and their wives had begun to attend the theaters, and in the eighteenth century this element in the audience grew steadily. Yet there was no sudden changeover from a dissolute court audience to a respectable middle-class audience; indeed it was not until Victorian times that the audiences of ordinary theaters became "respectable" in this way. The real situation, in the eighteenth century, is that of elements of the rising middle class joining a still fashionable theater public, at a time when the public tone of the court and aristocracy had itself been modified. Many authors began to be drawn from the commercial middle-class public; this is a period in which the "one-play author" is a characteristic figure. It is fair to say that an important part of eighteenth-century drama offered a conscious image of the middle class and its virtues, but the creative possibilities of this new consciousness were very uneven, and in the drama, particularly, they were further limited. The uncertainty in dramatic forms combined with the strong fashionable element in the audience to produce a concentration of interest on actors as such. Whenever this happens, and plays, in consequence, are valued primarily as vehicles for particular acting talents, the drama tends to become mixed and eclectic. Thus one finds, in eighteenth-century drama, a characteristic interest in theatrical effect for its own sake, and it is in this context that the new forms had to make their limited way.

Sentimental comedy is the least attractive of the new forms, though it has continued to hold the stage, as a majority form of English drama, to our own day. We can trace its conscious development from Cibber's *Love's Last Shift* (1696) and *The Careless Husband* (1705), and Steele's *The Lying Lover* (1704). Elements of its particular consciousness can indeed be traced from much earlier in the century, but the direct application to contemporary behavior is now much more obvious. A passage from Steele's preface to *The Lying Lover* clearly shows the new emphasis:

> He makes false love, gets drunk, and kills his man, but in the fifth act awakens from his debauch with the compunction and remorse which is suitable to a man's finding himself in a gaol]. . . . The anguish he there expresses, and the mutual sorrow between an only child and a tender father in that distress are, perhaps, an injury to the rules of comedy, but I am sure they are a justice to those of morality: and passages of such a nature being so frequently applauded on the stage, it is high time we should no longer draw occasions of mirth from those images which the religion of our country tells us we ought to tremble at with horror.

The essential point here, as a description of the new form, is the mixture of comedy and pathos, with an explicit moral reference, that led to the alternative descriptions of "weeping comedy" or the "comedy of sentiments" (moral opinions)—the two elements uniting in the complicated history of the word "sentimental." Yet we must note also the curious way in which the "compunction and remorse" are approached, for this element of "fifth-act reform," after all the excitements of customary dramatic intrigue, became the basis of continued charges of hypocrisy and sentimentality: "enjoy it while it lasts, then say you're sorry." Goldsmith had this in mind, when in attacking sentimental comedy he wrote:

> If they happen to have faults or foibles, the spectator is taught, not only to pardon, but to applaud them, in consideration of the goodness of their hearts.

This criticism reaches home, in many such plays, and this aspect of sentimental comedy has been so persistent that Goldsmith's words could be transferred, as they stand, to a considerable part of modern drama. He continues:

> But there is one argument in favour of sentimental comedy, which will keep it on the stage, in spite of all that can be said against it. It is, of all others, the most easily written. Those abilities that can hammer out a novel are fully sufficient for the production of a sentimental comedy. It is only sufficient to raise the characters a little; to deck out the hero with a riband, or give the heroine a title; then to put an insipid dialogue, without character or humour, into their mouths, give them mighty good hearts, very fine clothes, furnish a new set of scenes, make a pathetic scene or two with a sprinkling of tender melancholy conversation through the whole, and there is no doubt but all the ladies will cry, and all the gentlemen applaud.

This again is just, but the casual dismissal of the novel should make us pause. Both novels and sentimental comedies were often, certainly, confections of this kind, and Goldsmith despised them by reference to older standards (his attack on mixing comedy and pathos was in classicist terms, as a confusion of the old distinct kinds). Yet, while the bad examples multiplied, the feelings which they exhibited were part of the new consciousness, and could not in fact be summarily dismissed. The ability to take a judgment right through, as in traditional tragedy and comedy, showing sin leading to disintegration and disaster, vice and error to thorough ridicule, rested on a more absolute morality, based either on religious sanctions or the strict standards of an established society, than the new middle class actually had. Already in Elizabethan drama, and cer-

tainly in some seventeenth-century developments, we see the traditional kinds, and their basic attitudes, often confused, and their
modes of judgement muted, for similar reasons. Romantic comedy
had pioneered the way of sentimental comedy, and "fifth-act
reform," where in spite of everything a happy ending must be contrived, is evident from Shakespeare. Restoration comedy contains
these elements, but gains a measure of unity of feeling by confident
judgments with reference to a very limited social scale: to offend
against polite society was to be driven out of it, and that was that;
but equally to offend against God and man, while respecting the
polite code, was forgivable. At different levels, and for some good
reasons, the new middle-class drama tried to go beyond this, to a
new kind of judgment. Certainly, like its predecessors, it contrived
happy endings, and padded the lash of the old comedy, often on
sentimental grounds. But also, in dealing with contemporary life, it
necessarily challenged the temporary certainties of the Restoration
comedy of manners, offering as absolute virtues the sanctity of marriage, the life of the family, and the care of the weak. These had
been neglected, or made ridiculous, in Restoration comedy, simply
because the class which it served was parasitic: the true consequences
of behavior had never to be fully lived out. Narrow as the new bourgeois morality was, it at least referred to a society in which consequence was actual, and in which there was more to do than keep up
with the modes of an artificially protected class. When we speak of
the "sentimentality" of appeals to these values, and of the "smug-
ness" of what we think we can dismiss as merely "domestic virtues," we should be quite sure where we stand ourselves. The iden-
tification which some critics seem to make, in fantasy, between
themselves and the insouciance of Cavalier rakes and whores, is
usually ridiculous, if one goes on to ask to what moral tradition they
themselves practically belong. Nor is this the only respect in which,
if we are honest, we shall confess ourselves the heirs of the eighteenth-century bourgeois. The wider basis of sentimental comedy,
and of a main tradition in the novel, was that particular kind of
humanitarian feeling, the strong if inarticulate appeal to a fundamental "goodness of heart"; the sense of every individual's closeness
to vice and folly, so that pity for their exemplars is the most relevant emotion, and recovery and rehabilitation must be believed in;
the sense, finally, that there are few absolute values, and that tolerance and kindness are major virtues. In rebuking the sentimental
comedy, as in both its early examples and its subsequent history it
seems necessary to do, we should be prepared to recognize that in
the point of moral assumptions, and of a whole consequent feeling
about life, most of us are its blood relations. * * *

LOUIS KRONENBERGER

[*The School for Scandal*] †

* * * *The School for Scandal* remains the most famous comedy
of manners in the language. As a work for the theater, in which
plot, characterization, social background, and a kind of characterizing theme are mingled and blended, it can hardly be held unworthy of its fame. As a work, moreover, that constantly flashes with
witty thought and polished diction, that has a true drawing-room air
and eighteenth-century London lustre, it deserves its fame no less.

The play's characterizing theme is set forth in its title: we are
allowed to watch, as it were, the preparation and distribution of
scandal all the way from manufacturer to consumer. We are shown
scandalmongers who make great oaks from exceedingly little acorns,
who make scandal from what they hear, from what they overhear,
from what they hear wrong. We are offered scandal for scandal's
sake—where the motive is artistic and virtually disinterested; we are
shown it equally for the scandalmonger's sake, where the object is
to draw suspicion to the wrong person. And such scandalmongers as
Lady Sneerwell and Mr. Snake are, we must allow, true artists in
their line. It is part of the fun that when they and Mrs. Candour
get together, they indulge in the same sort of shop talk and trade
secrets that so many booksellers or pastrycooks might go in for. The
tone is set right at the start, and scenes like the opening one recur
all through the play. They constitute its thematic whalebone;
equally they are an illustration of manners and a commentary on
society. They give the play spice; they also give it glitter. And it is
worth noting that the scandalmongers are Sheridan's only way of
providing the play with that sense of naughtiness which is the very
atmosphere of Restoration comedy. The play is concerned with the
imputation of sinning; of sin itself there is absolutely nothing. The
famous screen scene is one of circumstantial evidence only, not at
all of guilt. Not only is Joseph Surface a villain without being
demonstrably a rake, but Sir Peter Teazle is an aging knight without being a cuckold. Even Charles Surface, though the most imprudent of spendthrifts, is nowhere shown to be even the mildest of
libertines.

There is perhaps good reason why, whenever we find much sin or
much scandal, we should find little of the other. In communities
that are habitually sinful, there cannot be anything very newsworthy

† From Louis Kronenberger, *The Thread
of Laughter* (New York: Alfred A.
Knopf, 1952), pp. 195–202. Copyright
1952 by Louis Kronenberger. Reprinted
by permission of the publisher.

about sin; moreover, in a community of glass houses every one thinks twice about throwing stones. Scandal is a kind of amusement tax that virtue exacts of indecorum. For it really to thrive, there must, in other words, be people who behave no less than people who misbehave. Gossip has a certain fellow-feeling about it, an equalitarian basis of talking about others but realizing that one is also talked about oneself. But scandal constitutes a sort of revenue in self-esteem: scandal concerns people who are not just (like oneself) humanly fallible, but who are socially culpable as well. And scandal, I think, is always predicated of people who have a certain amount of relative position, who are the equals or the superiors of those whom the scandal delights. When a society woman's housemaid gets herself into trouble, it may seem to her employer an outrage or a misfortune or both, but it is not a scandal. I mention all this, not from wishing to elevate scandal to the level of philosophy or impose upon it the rules and laws of science, but because it *is*, on the other hand, a permanent and important social phenomenon that, like snobbery, is often slurred over as not worth serious thought. But it *is* worth serious thought, certainly in any study of the comedy of manners; and here, as the very theme of the most famous social comedy in the English language it is worth a good deal of serious thought, the more so as, in English comedy, a devout interest in scandal has by Sheridan's time superseded the old Restoration absorption in sin.

Sheridan is writing for a straiter-laced, a more squeamishly refined audience than Etherege or Congreve did; he is writing in an age when "taste" is not a matter of how you deal with things, but of what things you may deal with. In *The School for Scandal*, quite as in *The Rivals*, no one sexually sins. But as a result, sin now seems far more wicked and important than it used to. Restoration comedy is an almost tedious succession of ladies and gentlemen thrust behind screens, pushed into closets, hidden under beds, flung down back stairways; nothing, after a while, could seem more routine. And now here we have Lady Teazle hiding behind a screen—in what is certainly the most famous scene in all English social comedy, just as the moment when that screen is knocked over represents the most climactic moment in all English social comedy. Some of this is doubtless due to Sheridan's great gifts as a playwright, to his building up the scene to get the utmost from it. But some of it is surely due to its being, as similar scenes a century earlier never were, so zestfully scandalous. We are back in an age when sex has become glamorous through being illicit.

Scandal also, at least superficially, harmonizes with the study of manners: for it is not only something that people talk about in drawing-rooms, it is something that taxes all their ability to be clever and insinuating in talk. Scandal is, indeed, most an art in that it seeks to suggest far more than it actually can say. And scandal concocted by artists for the enjoyment of audiences, scandal that not only causes loss of reputation but is leveled at people who have reputation to lose, is one of the worldliest of recreations. Though nothing improper happens in the whole course of *The School for Scandal*, impropriety is yet the very essence of what goes on.

All this bright scurrility and malice is the framework for a story that of itself is almost obstreperously fictional and by no means at the highest level of comedy. It is a good story, to the extent that we regard it as nothing more than one, and it is worked out by somebody who has clearly mastered his medium. The key point about Sheridan—or at least Sheridan's great success—is not his comic but his dramatic sense, the way he can give, even to his scandalmongers, not just the sheen of wit, but the deviousness of spiders; the way he can raise a colloquy into a scene; the general way that he can plot; the specific way that he can unravel or expose. *The School for Scandal* tells, just so, of a well-knit *group*: of Sir Peter and Lady Teazle, and Joseph, Charles, and Sir Oliver Surface; while even Lady Sneerwell and Mr. Snake have their places in the plot, and perhaps only Maria takes less of the limelight than we should expect. The whole thing has the conciseness of good artificial comedy: Maria is Sir Peter's ward; Sir Peter and Sir Oliver are old friends; Maria wants Charles for a husband; Lady Sneerwell wants Charles for a lover; Joseph wants Maria for a wife; Joseph wants Lady Teazle for a mistress. Thus the story is both concentrated and complicated. The plot thickens, as a good plot should. The hero's future darkens, as a proper hero's must. With but two acts to go, Sheridan leaves himself an enormous lot to work out and clear up.

Sheridan solved everything in the fourth act—including the perennial success of the play. And he solved it not just with the ingenuity of some one with a knack for plot, but with the visual magic of some one who has a sense of the footlights. First, Charles Surface's fortune is made in the picture scene, when he refuses to put his uncle's portrait up for auction. Then Joseph's goose is cooked in the screen scene, when Lady Teazle exposes and denounces him. One such scene immediately following and, as it were, capping the other, the two constitute between them a triumph of stagecraft. They also provide an exhilarating contrast, one scene showing how essentially good is the bad boy, the other, how essentially bad is the good one.

They are not quite the same *kind* of scene, however. The screen scene, descending straightforwardly from the Restoration, belongs wholly to the comedy of manners. In altogether classic style, it involves the husband, imperils the heroine, and unmasks the villain; in equally classic style, it maintains the tone of artificial comedy. The picture scene—at least on Sheridan's terms—would be very unusual, would be hardly possible, in Restoration comedy. Its appeal, to the audience quite as much as to Charles's uncle, is unabashedly sentimental; and though audiences in Sheridan's age and forever since have found the appeal irresistible, one may doubt whether audiences would have done so in the age of Charles II. The theme of the good and bad brother is literally the oldest in the world, for it turns up first—and perhaps most forcefully—with Cain and Abel. But the Restoration, which much modified conventional ideas of virtue and vice, rather transformed good and bad brother into better and worse one, and preferred to contrast the two, less in terms of good and bad than of naïveté and sophistication, of gaucherie and grace. Perhaps what I am now going to say argues a Restoration cynicism on my part; but I suspect that had any Restoration playwright thought up the picture scene, *his* Charles would have refused to part with the portrait through being shrewd rather than warmhearted. The effect would have been the same on the story, but not on the audience, who instead of dabbing at their eyes would have knowingly nodded their heads, and—it may be—would less have condemned Charles for his wiliness than Uncle Oliver for his vanity. But more to the point, any young man who would have behaved in an Etherege comedy as Charles Surface does in Sheridan's, would have seemed a very singular fellow. A hundred years later—as well as two hundred years later—and he is simply a conventional hero. In other words, it is the Restoration, not Sheridan, that is anomalous; the Restoration, not Sheridan, that runs counter to popular taste and "normal" sentiment. And though the Restoration stage is as extreme in offering such scanty virtue and decency, as other ages are suspect for offering such an abundance, it is just because the Restoration provides such an offset that we feel a certain gratitude toward it. Lack of feeling is at least superior to fraudulent feeling.

Charles and Joseph Surface are not, indeed, really in descent from characters like Shadwell's Belfond senior and junior; they descend much more plainly and immediately from Tom and Blifil in *Tom Jones*. Fielding, a really humane and not really a sentimental man, with his deep hate of hypocrisy and warm sympathy for heedless youth, felt a strong compulsion to contrast a Tom with a Blifil, to insist that goodness was a thing of the heart, that decorum was not virtue, nor animality vice. But for all that, his contrast is too pat, and his dénouement a little too pleasant. Yet though Fielding may be voted over-generous, he was not, like Sheridan, too genteel. Tom's heart might be made of gold, but his will power was made of tinfoil and his moral scruples were scarcely sawdust. For almost two centuries, and in certain quarters perhaps even now, the character and the book alike were attacked because Tom allowed himself to be kept by Lady Bellaston. Charles Surface, so far as we know, isn't even the lover of any fine lady. There is only enough wrong with him to make him endearing. He drinks—but presumably like a gentleman. He is careless of money and always in debt—but as much from being goodhearted as extravagant. Although he needs money, he won't sell his uncle's picture; though he needs money, he gives much of what he obtains to a struggling kinsman.

One tends to make fun of Charles not because he is particularly implausible, but because he is so exceedingly calculated—and for the light he throws on Sheridan, who begot him, and on the theater, that boasts of him. The theater *may* boast, but art, in the finest sense, must blush. And blush the more for having also something to be proud of. The neatness of the plotting in *The School for Scandal*, the vividness of the scene-writing, the brightness of the dialogue, the brilliance of the scandalmongers, above all the perfect understanding of the tone of artificial comedy—all this is admirable. Call it adroit and scintillating theater, and—with due allowance for the ravages of time—it would be hard to find anything better on the English stage. But that is the most that you *can* call it: it offers neither a genuine point of view, as does all the best Restoration comedy, nor a serious criticism of life, as does all important literature. The trouble is not that it is artificial, but that it is superficial, and not, again, that it snaps its fingers at realistic truth, but that it clicks its heels before conventional morality. A man who acquiesces in the common morality of his age may just escape with his life—by rejecting the usual trickery of his profession. He may escape rather better if, while using the tricks of technique, he preserves his independence of mind. But a man who succumbs to both temptations, who gives in to a stage effect and audience-effect alike, cannot get off scotfree. What Sheridan wrote here was, I think, the most brilliant box-office comedy in the English language.

His sense of the theater wins out, in the end, over his knowledge of the world. *The School for Scandal* has more motion than Restoration comedy, which is to the good, but it posits more characters whose fortunes are at stake and fewer who express a point of view; it offers more situations that interest us for their story value than that interest us in themselves. And Sheridan, far more than the Restoration playwrights, deals at the end in outright rewards and punishments. And all this is to be sharp and emphatic in the way the theater loves to be and life does not; which, because it harmonizes with the genius of the theater, isn't necessarily a fault. What *does* seem a fault is to combine such sharp and emphatic dramaturgy with such mild and sanctified subject-matter; to indulge only in what is generally acceptable, to inveigh only against what is demonstrably safe. Sheridan satirizes scarcely anything that the world does not condemn; nowhere does he challenge fashionable opinion or shock fashionable complacence. Wycherley may not have shocked his own generation, but he still shocks us. Shaw may not shock us, but he did shock his own generation. So effervescent a writer as Etherege at least touches on much that is true and even tragic about human nature; so ambiguous a dramatist as Oscar Wilde will time and again, if only in an epigram, explode against his trashy plots social criticism that is challenging and even subversive. But Sheridan, though sometimes delightfully impudent, is *never* challenging or subversive. His scandalmongers are a kind of Greek chorus in a play that Sheridan never got round to writing. Their air of iniquity is a false-front for the play's intrinsic innocence. The most brilliant thing about it, perhaps—in terms of Sheridan's mastery of his trade—is not the actual brilliance of its dialogue, but the seeming wickedness of its plot.

Selected Bibliography

(Items included in the Criticism section are not repeated here.)

RESTORATION COMEDY: GENERAL STUDIES

Bateson, F. W. "Second Thoughts: L. C. Knights and Restoration Comedy," *Essays in Criticism*, 7 (1957), 56–67.

Berkeley, David S. "Preciosité and the Restoration Comedy of Manners," *Huntington Library Quarterly*, 18 (1955), 109–128.

Birdsall, Virginia Ogden. *Wild Civility: The English Comic Spirit on the Restoration Stage.* Bloomington, Ind.: Indiana University Press, 1970.

Cecil, C. D. "Libertine and Précieux Elements in Restoration Comedy," *Essays in Criticism*, 9 (1959), 239–253.

Lynch, Kathleen M. *The Social Mode of Restoration Comedy.* University of Michigan Publications in Language and Literature, Vol. III. New York: Macmillan, 1926.

McDonald, Charles O. "Restoration Comedy as Drama of Satire: An Investigation into Seventeenth-Century Aesthetics," *Studies in Philology*, 61 (1964), 522–544.

Mignon, Elisabeth. *Crabbed Age and Youth: The Old Men and Women in the Restoration Comedy of Manners.* Durham, N.C.: Duke University Press, 1947.

Scouten, Arthur H. "Notes Toward a History of Restoration Comedy," *Philological Quarterly*, 45 (1966), 62–70.

Smith, John Harrington. *The Gay Couple in Restoration Comedy.* Cambridge, Mass.: Harvard Univ. Press, 1948.

Sutherland, James. *English Literature of the Late Seventeenth Century.* Oxford: Oxford University Press, 1969. (Chapters II and III.)

Vernon, P. F. "Marriage of Convenience and the Mode of Restoration Comedy," *Essays in Criticism*, 12 (1962), 370–387.

Wain, John. "Restoration Comedy and Its Modern Critics," *Essays in Criticism*, 6 (1956), 367–385.

Wilson, John Harold. *A Preface to Restoration Drama.* Boston: Houghton Mifflin, 1965.

EIGHTEENTH-CENTURY COMEDY: GENERAL STUDIES

Bateson, F. W. *English Comic Drama: 1700–1750.* Oxford: The Clarendon Press, 1929.

Dobree, Bonamy. *English Literature in the Early Eighteenth Century: 1700–1740.* Oxford: The Clarendon Press, 1959. (Chapter VII.)

Krutch, Joseph Wood. *Comedy and Conscience after the Restoration.* New York: Columbia University Press, 1924.

Loftis, John. *Comedy and Society from Congreve to Fielding.* Stanford, Calif.: Stanford University Press, 1959.

Loftis, John. *The Politics of Drama in Augustan England.* Oxford: The Clarendon Press, 1963.

Sherbo, Arthur. *English Sentimental Comedy.* East Lansing, Mich.: Michigan State University Press, 1957.

THE COUNTRY WIFE

Berman, Ronald. "The Ethic of *The Country Wife*," *Texas Studies in Literature and Language*, 9 (1967), 47–55.

Craik, T. W. "Some Aspects of Satire in Wycherley's Plays," *English Studies*, 41 (1960), 168–179.

Righter, Anne. "William Wycherley," in *Restoration Theatre*, edited by John Russell Brown and Bernard Harris. London: Edward Arnold, 1965.

Vieth, David M. "Wycherley's *The Country Wife*: An Anatomy of Masculinity," *Papers on Language and Literature*, 2 (1966), 335–350.

THE MAN OF MODE

Davies, Paul C. "The State of Nature and the State of War: A Reconsideration of *The Man of Mode*," *University of Toronto Quarterly*, 39 (1969), 53–62.
Hayman, John G. "Dorimant and the Comedy of a Man of Mode," *Modern Language Quarterly*, 30 (1969), 183–197.
Underwood, Dale. *Etherege and the Seventeenth-Century Comedy of Manners*. New Haven, Conn. Yale University Press, 1957.

THE WAY OF THE WORLD

Leech, Clifford. "Congreve and the Century's End," *Philological Quarterly*, 41 (1962), 275–293.
Muir, Kenneth. "The Comedies of William Congreve," in *Restoration Theatre*, edited by John Russell Brown and Bernard Harris. London: Edward Arnold, 1965.
Mueschke, Paul, and Miriam Mueschke. *A New View of Congreve's Way of the World*. University of Michigan Contributions to Modern Philology, No. 23. Ann Arbor, Mich.: University of Michigan Press, 1958.
Taylor, D. Crane. *William Congreve*. Oxford: Oxford University Press, 1931.
Van Voris, W. H. *The Cultivated Stance: The Designs of Congreve's Plays*. Dublin: Dolmen, 1965.

THE CONSCIOUS LOVERS

Loftis, John. *Steele at Drury Lane*. Berkeley, Calif. University of California Press, 1952. (*See also* Eighteenth-Century Comedy: General Studies *above*.)

THE SCHOOL FOR SCANDAL

Gibbs, Lewis. *Sheridan*. London: Dent, 1947.
Rodway, Allan. "Goldsmith and Sheridan: Satirists of Sentiment," in *Renaissance and Modern Essays Presented to Vivian de Sola Pinto*, edited by G. R. Hibbard. London: Routledge and Kegan Paul, 1966.
Schiller, Andrew. "*The School for Scandal*: The Restoration Unrestored," *PMLA*, 71 (1956), 694–704.
Sprague, Arthur C. "In Defence of a Masterpiece: *The School for Scandal* Re-examined," in *English Studies Today*, 3rd Series, edited by G. I. Duthie. Edinburgh: Edinburgh University Press, 1964.